Tactical Small Arms
of the 21st Century

D1552399

Charles Cutshaw

©2006 Charles Cutshaw
Published by

Gun Digest Books
An imprint of F+W Publications
700 East State Street • Iola, WI 54990-0001
715-445-2214 • 888-457-2873

Our toll-free number to place an order or obtain
a free catalog is (800) 258-0929.

Library of Congress Catalog Number: 2004098425

ISBN 10-digit: 0-87349-914-X
ISBN 13-digit: 978-0-87349-914-9

Designed by Paul Birling
Edited by Kevin Michalowski

Printed in United States of America

Dedication

This book is dedicated to my loving wife Dianne, my guide, mentor and taskmaster who kept me focused throughout writing and editing process and without whose tireless work this book would have never have been. Without my wife, who is truly the "wind beneath my wings," I would be nothing. A book like this also is the result of the work of many people too numerous to list individually. To all those who helped me, and you know who you are: My heartfelt THANKS!

Charlie Cutshaw
December 2005

TABLE OF CONTENTS
Tactical Small Arms of the 21st Century

PREFACE

As indicated by the title, this volume is intended as a comprehensive and authoritative reference on tactical small arms of the 21st Century. The reader will not find any historic small arms herein, as was the case with Krause's Military Small Arms of the 20th Century, other than those still in active use by military, police or paramilitary forces. This volume reflects the best information available to the authors at the time of its publication, although as with any imperfect human effort, there are bound to be errors both of commission and omission. We hope to provide the reader with an affordable reference that includes not only operational small arms, but developmental ones, as well. This is a time of transition for small arms and we hope that we have captured that in the pages that follow. With the continuing War on Terror, small arms have undergone a renaissance. In both Afghanistan and Iraq, the primary means of carrying the war to the enemy is small arms. In this new milieu, some small arms have fallen aside and others have seen a resurrection. In this preface, a brief examination of each type of small arms is covered along with its role in the new and evolving type of warfare.

The War on Terror is not characterized by the types of military operations as with previous wars. There are, of course, conventional military operations involving large numbers of massed troops in division and even corps levels, attacking the enemy in formations and using tactics that would be recognizable to soldiers from World War II. Only the weapons and equipment have changed. These types of operations, however, have been brief and once ended the conduct of the war was transformed into what once was characterized as "small war." Conventional operations are conducted at the battalion, company and platoon levels, generally in urban environments, as in Iraq or in mountainous terrain such as that in Afghanistan, where the brunt of fighting is borne by special operations forces operating in small teams. Indeed, special operations forces have become more

and more critical to the conduct of this new kind of war and the primary weapons they employ are small arms and a few light support weapons, such as grenade launchers, mortars and other light infantry support weapons and equipment that are beyond the scope of this book. In the crucible of war, some weapons have proven themselves, while others have disappointed the troops at "the pointed end of the spear."

The war has resulted not only in resurrection of some weapons that if time in service were the only measure, should have long ago been retired. One such weapon is the venerable M-1911A1 .45 ACP pistol, now being procured in limited numbers for US Special Operations Forces and the US Marine Corps from Kimber and Springfield Armory. This old warhorse will assuredly be in military service well beyond the centennial of its introduction into military service. Another such pistol is the Browning M-1935 in 9x19mm. Both pistols soldier on, while every other small arm that was in service or introduced at the time these handguns entered service long ago was retired. Pistols, though, are generally a self defense weapon, although in special operations, they are occasionally used offensively, i.e. to carry the fight to the enemy. The M-1911A1 pistol aside, virtually all handguns in military service today are in 9x19mm NATO caliber. Also, virtually all are semiautomatic based on the Browning system that originated in its basic form in 1905. There are some pistols in military service that use other operating systems, notably the Beretta 92, but the vast majority are modified versions of the tried and true Browning design. Revolvers are included herein, not because they are widely used by any military force, but because they are in use by many police forces worldwide.

Submachine guns as a class of small arm are generally in decline for a number of reasons. First, by definition, they fire a pistol caliber cartridge which is far less lethal than the "intermediate" cartridges fired by assault rifles and carbines. (Intermediate cartridges are those that ballistically fall between pistol cartridges and full power rifle cartridges, such as the 7.62x51mm NATO [.308 Winchester] round.) Pistol caliber cartridges as a class are easily defeated by body armor and it is a well-documented fact that many enemy soldiers have been shot repeatedly with pistols, particularly the NATO standard 9x19mm, and continue to fight, even though their wounds might ultimately prove fatal. This is one reason that many US Special Operations Forces have returned to .45 ACP pistols. Another reason for the decline of the submachine gun is the fact that many intermediate caliber 5.56x45mm (.223 Remington) carbines are as compact in size as most submachine guns, but far more lethal. Although submachine guns will continue in limited use, their military role is generally being fulfilled by intermediate caliber carbines, such as the 5.56x45mm US M-4/M-4A1 and 5.45x39mm Russian AKS-74U.

Assault rifles are by definition select fire weapons capable of both semiautomatic and fully automatic fire. The term is rumored to have been coined by no less than Adolph Hitler to describe the Maschinenpistole 43/44, which was chambered for the first intermediate class cartridge, the 7.92x43mm. More probable, however, is that the nomenclature was changed to reflect the true nature of the weapon, which for the first time placed a powerful select fire weapon that could be controlled in full automatic fire in the hands of infantry troops. The Sturmgewehr 44 or StG44 set the pattern for all such weapons that have followed, from the AK-47 to the recently adopted US SCAR-L. Regardless of the operating system, the general features of every assault rifle (there is no such thing as an "assault weapon" other than in the minds of those who know little or nothing about small arms) are the same:

- "Straight line" design that directs the recoil forces in such a way as to minimize muzzle rise.
- Pistol grip.
- Large capacity detachable box magazine
- Intermediate class cartridge

Developments in assault rifles have been driven by the War on Terror. The US M-16 is well-established and has the distinction of having served as the standard military rifle longer than any other rifle in American history. The M-4/M-4A1 carbines, however, have not fared so well and are in the process of being replaced by a new carbine. The carbine is primarily the weapon of special operations and the US special operations community has long been dissatisfied with the M-4 carbine family. A 2001 USSOCOM study stated, "All earlier M-16-based carbines and the M-4A1 Carbine are fundamentally

flawed." The problems of the M-4 family do not arise until the weapon is fired in full automatic, so semiautomatic versions are unaffected by the problems defined in the SOCOM study. Nonetheless, USSOCOM set out to design a new family of modular small arms, called the Special Forces Combat Assault Rifle (SCAR). There are two versions, the SCAR-Light and SCAR-Heavy. These are discussed in detail in the main portion of this book, but the adoption of the SCAR by the US Special Forces has dramatic implications for the entire American small arms program. Since the Special Forces are the primary users of the M-4 Carbine family, the M-4 will eventually be withdrawn from special operations service as it is replaced by the SCAR. Further, the adoption of the SCAR calls to question the viability of the Army's XM-8 program, which largely duplicates the capabilities of the SCAR. Although the SCAR is intended for special operations use, two distinct small arms families in the US military do not pass the "sanity test" from an operational and logistical viewpoint. Only time will tell the outcome, but the M-4 Carbine's days are clearly numbered as a special operations small arm in US service.

The layman does not often think of the shotgun as a military weapon, but the fact is that the US military has used the shotgun in every war since the Indian Wars of the 19ᵗʰ Century. The tactical shotgun today is one of the premier small arms in the War on Terror because it is highly versatile, being capable of firing an amazing array of ammunition, from less-lethal to high explosive grenades. The tactical shotgun is also arguably the most devastating close quarters battle (CQB) small arm in existence. For those reasons, the tactical shotgun is in widespread use by military forces worldwide and continues to be a particularly effective weapon for use at ranges of less than 100 meters. Photographs and news footage from both Afghanistan and Iraq show troops with shotguns, ranging from traditional pump operated guns to the latest semiautomatics. The tactical shotgun will be in use by military and law enforcement for the foreseeable future. Tactical shotguns are dominated by 12-gauge weapons, although some forces use 20 gauge guns and in some Russian units, .410-bore guns have found applications. The 12-gauge dominates for the simple reason that there is such a huge variety of ammunition available for it. The smaller calibers do not have the interior shell volume to accommodate the specialized ammunition available in 12-gauge.

Precision tactical rifles, or sniper rifles, have also seen a renaissance, and there are many manufacturers of these highly accurate long range small arms. Most are bolt-action rifles with five- to 10-round magazine capacities. There is no reason for these rifles to have large capacity magazines because if the sniper gets into a firefight requiring a large volume of fire, he has probably failed in his mission. Military snipers are primarily an intelligence asset with lethal capability. This is reflected in the US Marine Corps organization for snipers, which operationally places them under the S-2 (intelligence) officer. Law enforcement snipers have a different role, but are still intelligence assets in addition to their use as the last resort to resolve certain situations. Most precision tactical rifles are currently chambered for 7.62x51mm, although some are in .300 Winchester Magnum and smaller calibers, primarily 5.56x45mm. There is a growing trend towards military .338 Lapua caliber precision tactical rifles. The .338 Lapua round is inherently accurate and the rifles can be made light enough to be comfortably carried by one individual, unlike .50 BMG antimaterial rifles that weigh upwards of 25 pounds. Moreover, the .338 Lapua extends the effective range of the sniper to well over 1,000 meters, as opposed to the 800- to 1000-meter effective range of 7.62x51mm rifles.

Antimaterial rifles actually began as antitank rifles early in the 20ᵗʰ Century, but as tank armor became too thick for them to defeat, these large heavy rifles fell into disuse. The antimaterial rifle renaissance began with a young Tennessee man named Ronnie Barrett, who today manufacturers most of the world's antimaterial rifles. Barrett's semiautomatic .50 Browning Machine Gun (BMG) caliber M-82 and bolt-action M-95 rifles dominate the antimaterial rifle world, with service in the military forces of nearly 40 nations. The US Army recently (2004) ordered 5,000 M-82A3 (M-107) rifles and production continues. The M-82 shows no signs of being supplanted by any other antimaterial rifle as of the time of this writing. Although there are some other manufacturers, Barrett Firearms continues to dominate this military "niche" market.

Machine guns are still in widespread use, but like other small arms, the machine gun is transitioning. The 5.56x45mm squad automatic weapon (SAW) category is dominated by FN Herstal's Minimi, in service with most of the world's major military forces. FN Herstal also dominates the general purpose machine gun (GPMG) market with its MAG-58, again, the premiere such weapon. It is ironic that the US military replaced its M-60 GPMG with the MAG-58, which was turned down as inferior to the M-60 in 1959. The M-60 continued on in its M-60E4 guise as the Mark 43, Mod 0 with US Special Operations until 2004, when it began being replaced by the FN Herstal Mark 48, Mod 0. Although most Western countries use one version or another of the MAG-58, former Soviet Bloc nations continue to use the PK family of machine guns.

In sum, although small arms technology can be described as "mature," i.e. the technology does not lend itself to any breakthroughs such as smokeless powder or self contained cartridges that revolutionized small arms, materials and technology is moving small arms in new directions that make these basic soldier weapons more effective, more reliable and as warfare itself transitions, so will small arms transition to accommodate the changes in tactics and operations.

Charles Q. Cutshaw
Dianne M. Cutshaw
February 2005

LIST OF ABBREVIATIONS

ABM	Air Burst(ing) Munition
ABMS	Air Bursting Munition System
ABS	Air-Bursting System
ACOG	Advanced Combat Optical Gun sight
ACP	Automatic Colt Pistol
ACR	Advanced Combat Rifle
AE	Action Express
AGL	Automatic Grenade Launcher
AICW	Advanced Individual Combat Weapon
AMR	Anti-Materiel Rifle
AMU	Army Marksmanship Unit (Ft Benning, Georgia)
AP	Anti-Personnel
AP	Armor Piercing
APDS	Armor Piercing Discarding Sabot
APERS	Anti-personnel
APFSDS	Armor Piercing Fin-Stabilized Discarding Sabot
API	Armor Piercing Incendiary
AR	Assault Rifle, Armalite Rifle
ARDEC	Armament Research, Development and Engineering Command
AT	Anti-Tank
ATD	Advanced Technology Demonstrator
ATF	Alcohol, Tobacco and Firearms (Also BATF)
ATK	Alliant Techsystems
AUG	Armee Universal Gewehr
BATF	Bureau of Alcohol, Tobacco and Firearms (Also ATF)
BBSP	Blow Back Shifted Pulse
BDA	Browning Double Action
BFA	Blank Firing Attachment
BT	Bullet Trap
CCD	Charge Coupled Device
CCO	Close Combat Optic
CEP	Circular Error Probability
CENTCOM	Central Command
cd	candela; candlepower
CIS	Chartered Industries of Singapore
CQBW	Close Quarters Battle Weapon
CRISAT (NATO)	Collaborative Research Into Small Arms Technology
CRT	Cathode Ray Tube
CTA	Cased Telescoped Ammunition
CW	Chemical Warfare
DA	Double Action
DAO	Double Action Only
DARPA	Defense Advanced Research Projects Agency
DA/SA	Double Action/Single Action
DC	Direct Current
DMR	Dedicated Marksman Rifle
DoD	Department of Defense
DP	Dual Purpose
EOD	Explosive Ordnance Disposal
ER	Extended Range
FAL	Fusil Automatique Leger
FBI	Federal Bureau of Investigation
FCS	Fire-Control System/Subsystem
FIRM	Floating Integrated Rail Mount
FLEA	Frangible Low Energy Ammunition
FLIR	Forward-Looking Infra-Red
FMJ	Full Metal Jacket

FMJBT	Full Metal Jacket Boat Tail
FMJLF	Full Metal Jacket Lead Free
FNH	FN HERSTAL
FRAG	Fragmentation
FRANG	Frangible
FUE	First Unit Equipped
FY	Fiscal Year
GL	Grenade Launcher
GPMG	General Purpose Machine Gun
GPS	Global Position System
H&K, HK	Heckler and Koch
HB	Heavy Barrel
HBAR	Heavy Barrel Assault Rifle
HDS	Holographic Diffraction Sight
HE	High Explosive
HEAT	High Explosive Anti-Tank
HEDP	High Explosive Dual Purpose
HE-FRAG	High Explosive Fragmentation
HEI	High Explosive Incendiary
HEI-T	High Explosive Incendiary, Tracer
HEMP	High Explosive Multi-Purpose
HEP	High Explosive Plastic
HESH	High Explosive Squash Head
HMG	Heavy Machine Gun
HMMWV	High Mobility Multi-purpose Wheeled Vehicle
HP	High Power; Hollow Point
HPT	High Pressure Test
HWS	Holographic Weapon Sight
I	Incendiary
IDW	Individual Defense Weapon
II	Image Intensifier
IM	Insensitive Munition(s)
INSAS	Indian Small Arms System
IOC	Initial Operational Capability
IOF	Ordnance Factory
IR	Infra-Red
IS	Internal Security
ISGU	Integrated Sight and Guidance Unit
IW	Individual Weapon
JHP	Jacketed Hollow Point
JSCS	Joint Service Combat Shotgun
JSP	Jacketed Soft Point
JSSAMP	Joint Services Small Arms Master Plan
JSSAP	Joint Services Small Arms Program
KAC	Knight's Armament Company
KE	Kinetic Energy
LAM	Laser Aiming Module
LAR	Light Automatic Rifle
LC	Laser Collimator
LCD	Liquid crystal display
LD	Low drag
LE	Law Enforcement
LED	Light Emitting Diode
LF	Linked Feed
LMG	Light Machine Gun
LP	Liquid Propellant
LPG	Liquid Propellant Gun
LR	Long-Range, Long Rifle

LRIP	Low-Rate Initial Production
LRN	Lead Round Nose
LRSA	Long Range Sniper Ammunition
LSW	Light Support Weapon
LWC	Lead Wad Cutter
LWSS	Lightweight Shotgun System
MAR	Micro Assault Rifle
MARS	Multi-purpose Aiming Reflex Sight, Mini Assault Rifle System
MEU(SOC)	Marine Corps Expeditionary Unit (Special Operations Capable)
MG	Machine Gun
MILSPEC	Military Specification
MIL-STD-xxxx	Military Standard (followed by a number that designates the specific standard)
mm	millimeters(s)
MMG	Medium Machine Gun
MOA	Minute Of Angle
MoD	Ministry of Defense
MOUT	Military Operations in Urban Terrain
MP	Machine Pistol
MPI	Mean Point of Impact
MTBF	Mean Time Between Failure
MV	Muzzle Velocity
MWS	Modular Weapon System
NATO	North Atlantic Treaty Organization
NBC	Nuclear, Biological and Chemical
NDI	Non-Developmental Item
Ni/Cd	Nickel Cadmium
NV	Night Vision
NVD	Night Vision Device
NVG	Night Vision Goggle
NVS	Night Vision System
OCSW	Objective Crew-Served Weapon
OFSA	Objective Family of Small Arms
OFW	Objective Force Warrior
OHWS	Offensive Hand Weapon System
OICW	Objective Individual Combat Weapon
OOTW	Operations Other Than War
OPDW	Objective Personal Defense Weapon
OSW	Objective Sniper Weapon
PC	Personal Computer
PCC	Police Compact Carbine
PD	Point Detonating
PDRR	Program Definition Risk-Reduction
PDW	Personal Defense Weapon
PH	Probability of Hit
PIBD	Point Initiating Base Detonated
PIP	Product Improvement Program
PK	Probability of Kill
PM	Product Manager
POF	Pakistan Ordnance Factory
PWP	Plasticized White Phosphorus
QCB	Quick Change Barrel
RAAM	Rifle-launched Anti-Armor Munition
RARDE	Royal Armaments Research and Development Establishment
RAS	Rail Adapter System
RAW	Rifleman's Assault Weapon
RF	Rimfire
RHA	Rolled Homogenous Armor
RIS	Rail Interface System
RLEM	Rifle-Launched Entry Munition
RO	Royal Ordnance (no longer in use)
RP	Red Phosphorus
RPG	Rocket Propelled Grenade
RRTR	Reduced Range Training Round
RSAF	Royal Small Arms Factory, UK (closed)
RSAUM	Remington Short Action Ultra Magnum
RTE Shop	Rifle Team Equipment Shop (US Marine Corps facility where sniper and match firearms are manufactured. (Marine Corps Base, Quantico, Virginia)
S&W	Smith & Wesson
SABR	Selectable Assault Battle Rifle (See OICW)
SAC	Small Arms Collimator
SANDF	South African National Defence Force
SAP	Semi-Armor-Piercing
SAPHEI	Semi-Armor-Piercing High Explosive Incendiary
SASR	Special Application Sniper Rifle
SAW	Squad Automatic Weapon
SEAL	Sea/Air/Land
SEP	Soldier Enhancement Program
SJFN	Semi-Jacketed Flat Nose
SJHP	Semi-Jacketed Hollow Point
SLAP	Saboted Light Armor Penetrator
SLR	Self-Loading Rifle
SMG	Submachine Gun
SOCOM	Special Operations Command
SOF	Special-Operations Force(s)
SOPMOD	Special Operations Peculiar Modification (M4)
SP	Soft Point
SPAS	Special Purpose Automatic Shotgun
SPC	Special Purpose Cartridge
SPP	Special Purpose Pistol
SPR	Special Purpose Rifle
SPW	Special Purpose Weapon
SRAW	Short Range Assault Weapon
SRT	Special Response Team
SSW	Squad Support Weapon
STANAG	Standardization Agreement (NATO)
STK	Singapore Technologies Kinetics
SUIT	Sight Unit Infantry Trilux
SUSAT	Sight Unit Small Arms Trilux
SWAT	Special Weapons And Tactics
SWC	Semi Wadcutter
SWS	Sniper Weapon System
T	Tracer
TDD	Target Detection Device
TI	Thermal Imager
TIM	Thermal Imaging Module
TNT	Trinitrotoluene
TP	Target Practice or training practice
TWS	Thermal Weapon Sight
UMP	Universal Machine Pistol
USP	Universal Self-loading Pistol
UTL	Universal Tactical Light
UTM	Universal Transverse Mercator
UV	Ultraviolet
UW	Urban Warfare
VLI	Visible Light Illuminator
WP	White Phosphorus
WSM	Winchester Short Magnum
WSSM	Winchester Super Short Magnum

Operating Systems

THE OPERATING CYCLE or CYCLE OF OPERATION

All firearms, whether manual, semiautomatic or full automatic in operation follow the same steps in their operation and this operating cycle forms the basis by which all small arms are evaluated. The operating cycle consists of the following steps:

- **Feeding:** The act of transferring a cartridge from the magazine or other feeding device into the chamber.
- **Chambering:** The round is fully seated into the chamber by the bolt.
- **Cocking:** A firing mechanism is made ready to strike the primer to initiate firing a cartridge.
- **Locking:** The breech is locked, whether physically locked by mechanical means, such as locking lugs or other methods, or by inertia in the case of blowback operated firearms.
- **Firing:** The cartridge is fired by the physical impact of a firing pin or in rare cases, by electrical impulse.
- **Unlocking:** The breech is unlocked.
- **Extracting:** The fired case is extracted from the chamber.
- **Ejecting:** The fired case is ejected from the firearm. At this point, the cycle of operations starts over.

The vast majority of military and law enforcement tactical small arms operate in either semiautomatic or select fire, i.e. semi- or fully automatic. Virtually none are manually operated, except for precision tactical rifles and some antimaterial rifles. For that reason, we will discuss only self-loading principles herein, as manual operation is so simple as to require no detailed explanation. The basic operating principles consist of blowback, recoil and gas operation. Within each category of operation are subcategories that we will discuss in detail in the pages that follow.

Basic Operating Principles

BLOWBACK OPERATION

Blowback operation of a small arm is defined as a method of operation in which the energy required to carry out the cycle of operation is supplied to the bolt by the backward movement of the cartridge case, caused by gas pressure. Blowback operation can be sub-divided into four categories:

- Straight or simple blowback.
- Blowback with advanced primer ignition.
- Delayed Blowback.
- Blowback with locked breech.

Before these methods can be discussed in detail it is necessary to look at the conditions in the chamber when a round is fired. These conditions largely apply regardless of the method of operation employed, but they have special significance in the case of blowback-operated firearms.

When a round is fired inside the chamber the propellant burns and produces some 14,000 times its own volume of gas. The pressure caused by the rapid burning of the propellant builds up quickly and reaches its peak value in approximately three quarters of a millisecond – i.e. 0.00075 second after ignition of the primer. The rate of burning is proportional to the pressure and shortly after peak pressure all the propellant is consumed. This point of "all burned" is shown on Figure 1.

The pressure produced by the rapid expansion of the gas drives the bullet out of the case and into the leade, which is the interface between the chamber and the rifling. The leade aligns the bullet to engage the rifling and the bullet is held in contact with the developing rifling until sufficient pressure has built up to engrave the bullet jacket. This buildup in shot start pressure can be seen as a slight irregularity of the pressure curve at about 0.4 milliseconds. As the projectile moves out of the leade the chamber volume increases. Shortly before 'all burned,' the rate of increase of chamber volume is greater than the increase in the rate of gas production and so the pressure starts to drop.

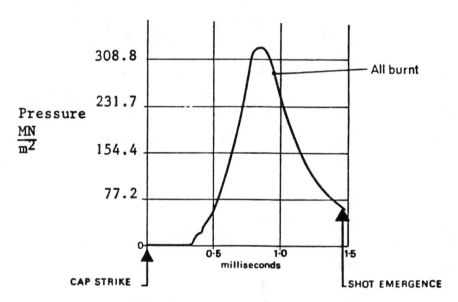

FIG 1: PRESSURE-TIME CURVE FOR 7.62x51MM (308 Winchester) ROUND

When the bullet leaves the muzzle, the propellant gases follow it out and the gases accelerate and expand very quickly degrading to atmospheric pressure giving a backward impulse to the whole weapon. The bullet emerges about 1.5 milliseconds after the firing pin strikes the primer and the muzzle gases have fully expanded down to atmospheric pressure some 4-5 milliseconds after primer ignition.

Having seen how the pressure has developed, its effects can be studied. The pressure produced inside the case acts in every direction.

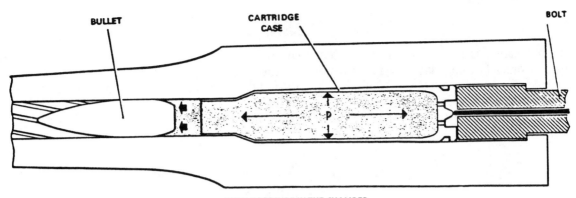

FIG 2: PRESSURE IN THE CHAMBER

The pressure exerted on the base of the bullet produces a force of magnitude pressure times the cross section area of the base of the bullet, which drives the bullet up the bore. The case is forced outwards sealing off the chamber to provide obturation and so prevents the backward escape of the gas through the breech closing mechanism. When considering case expansion, it should be noted that with the high pressures developed in modern rounds a dry cartridge case will grip the chamber walls with great force and this force will resist any backward movement of the case while it is maintained by the pressure.

In addition to expanding the case radially, there will be a forward force on the case if the neck is tapered and a large backward force equal in magnitude to the pressure times the cross sectional area of the interior of the base of the case. This latter force will drive the case rearwards against the face of the bolt. When the case movement rearwards is resisted by a locked bolt the forward movement of the front part of the case expands the tapered or bottlenecked portion to fill the gap between the case and the small cone of the chamber and so the walls of the cartridge case are placed in longitudinal tension. But if the bolt allows the case to move rearwards it will be driven back by a force equal to the difference between the backward and forward components of the actual force developed within the case. The net effect of this difference is to produce a force that drives the bolt back, equal to the pressure multiplied by the cross section area of the bore. This can be seen by looking at Figure 3.

PRESSURE PRODUCING TENSION IN CASE

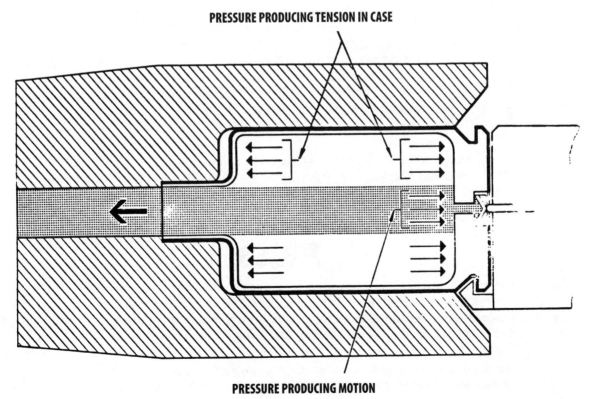

PRESSURE PRODUCING MOTION

FIG 3: THE EFFECT OF AXIAL PRESSURE ON CARTRIDGE CASE MOVEMENT

The net backward force described above causes the case to move backwards. This backwards movement within the chamber is in 3 phases.

PHASE 1

Modern propellants, particularly ball powders, tend to burn more slowly than the earlier nitrocellulose that replaced the very quick burning black powder. Depending on the design of the primer, the propellant starts to burn and build up pressure in one to 3 tenths of a millisecond. During this period, the very thin brass in the mouth of the case is expanded against the chamber wall to create a seal, called obturation. The pressure is not high at this point, and there is little friction developed between the cartridge case and the wall of the chamber and the case slides back to contract the bolt face and take up any excess cartridge head space.

PHASE 2

This phase covers the development and decrement of chamber pressure from its peak value.

First we will consider an unlubricated case. The case expands radially, producing a very high-pressure metal to metal contact between the brass case and the steel chamber wall. At the same time, if there is any spare space behind the base of the case it will be filled by the pressure acting on the interior cross section area of the base that drives the case back. If this space is excessive the cartridge case will stretch until the base is in firm contact with the breech face and the taper of the case is against the small cone of the chamber. If the space is too large or the resistance of the breechblock is inadequate to prevent the stretching of the case from exceeding the allowable elongation, the case will separate.

The tendency of the case to move backwards to take up excessive headspace also has an effect on the design of the cartridge case employed in blowback operated guns. If a bottlenecked or heavily tapered case is used the forward component of the pressure will force the shoulders forward and so deform them to fill the space left when the case is moved back. This can result in a ruptured case if the deforming force produces a stress exceeding the ultimate tensile strength of the brass. It will be found that parallel sided and slightly tapered cases are generally used for this type of operation. This shape is very suitable because as the case moves back through the operation the obturation of the gases is maintained. When it is required to have one round that must be used in a number of weapons with different operating systems such as the 7.62x51mm round then a parallel sided case cannot be used.

When the case is lubricated with a coat of oil or grease, this provides a continuous film which will prevent metal to metal contact between the cartridge case and the wall of the chamber. The case can now slide easily in the chamber because the frictional resistance is virtually absent and excess cartridge head space can easily be taken up without fear of rupturing the case. Lubricated cases have been popular in Europe in the past and have been used in numerous machine guns and automatic cannon, including the Schwarloze machine gun and the Breda light machine gun in rifle caliber and the 20 mm Oerlikon and Polsten automatic cannons. The practical difficulties in using lubricated cases for service weapons are numerous, however. The presence of sand, dust or any foreign matter in the lubricant acts as a grinding paste and causes considerable wear of the gun mechanism and the chamber and can even cause stoppages.

Phase 2 ends when the gases emerging from the muzzle as the bullet exits degrade to atmospheric pressure. In a rifle caliber weapon the pressure will remain above atmospheric for some 3 to 4 milliseconds after the bullet has gone. This pressure alone is sufficient to operate the blowback system.

PHASE 3

This phase begins as soon as the pressure drops sufficiently to allow the case to contract enough to free itself from the chamber wall. When this occurs, what pressure remains will drive the cartridge case to the rear, pushing the unlocked breech back and imparting enough energy for it to carry out the functions of ejecting, storing energy in the recoil or return spring, feeding, chambering and firing the following round.

Phase three ends when the gases emerging from the muzzle as the bullet exits expand into the atmosphere. In a rifle caliber firearm, pressure will remain above ambient atmospheric pressure for three to four milliseconds after the bullet has exited, and this alone is usually sufficient to operate a blowback system.

If the case moves back while the bullet is in the bore and the pressure is still above a certain level, the case and bolt will accelerate very rapidly backwards. This can easily result in the rear end of the case emerging from the chamber totally unsupported. The brass case wall is thicker at the rear and there is a hardness gradient along the case increasing from neck to rim. This is illustrated for the 7.62x51mm round at Figure 5.

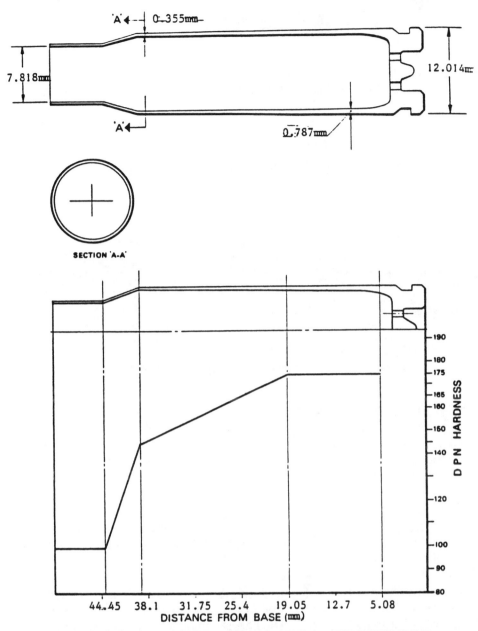

FIG 5: THICKNESS AND HARDNESS GRADIENT OF THE 7.62x51MM CARTRIDGE CASE

In spite of the increased thickness and hardness of the brass case at the rear end it can withstand only very limited pressure if unsupported. As a general rule, rifle caliber cases must not protrude more than 3 mm. This places limits on the design of the weapon.

BASIC PROBLEMS OF BLOWBACK DESIGN

There are two basic requirements for a blowback-operated weapon. The case must be free to move in the chamber to:

- Take up excess cartridge head space.
- Provide the force against the breechblock on which the entire system depends.

The case must be restrained in the chamber when the pressure is high or cases will separate across the weakest section of the neck of the case while the case is still fully in the chamber or there will be an unsupported portion of the rear of the case emerging from the chamber and this will rupture.

It can be seen that these requirements are mutually contradictory and the necessity to comply with them both has resulted in comparatively sophisticated systems such as blowback with delaying devices and even blowback with a fully locked breech. These will be discussed in detail below.

STRAIGHT OR SIMPLE BLOWBACK

In this system, blowback provides all the operating energy and the movement of the cartridge case is restrained and controlled solely by the mass, and inertia dependent upon that mass, of the breechblock and the strength of the spring.

BREECH CASING   BOLT   RETURN SPRING

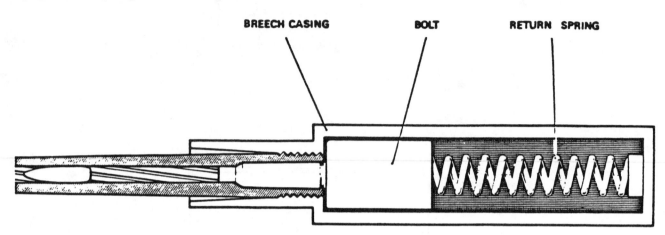

FIG 6: A TYPICAL STRAIGHT BLOWBACK SYSTEM

The straight blowback mechanism consists of a chamber, with a parallel sided cartridge case and a stationary breechblock that supports the rear end of the case in the chamber. The bolt is unrestrained except for the return spring and is free to move back. Behind the bolt is a fairly heavy spring which stores the kinetic energy imparted to the bolt and returns the bolt to its forward position after each round is fired. Within the bolt is a firing pin or striker. The latter contains its own spring to drive the pin forward when released or a separate firing pin can be driven forward by a hammer.

When the cartridge is fired the pressure of the gas generated drives the bullet up the bore and at the same time an exactly equal force drives the cartridge case rearward against the resistance of the bolt and return spring. The pressure generated is not high and the parallel sided case provides complete obturation as it slides back. The elastic limit of the brass is not exceeded and so the case rapidly returns to its original dimensions when the pressure has passed its peak and the case does not adhere to the chamber.

The weight of the breechblock is so calculated that it does not permit a movement of more than 3mm during the period of about 5 milliseconds that the pressure is above 5.2 MN/m^2 This gives a mean velocity in the 5 millisecond of slightly over 0.66 mls. The bolt is subjected to an accelerating force for about 6 milliseconds in a rifle length barrel and of somewhat less in a pistol. After this, the gas pressure is zero as is the force available to accelerate the bolt, but the case and bolt have now acquired sufficient momentum to continue to move back. As the cartridge case pushes the bolt back it extracts itself from the chamber and is ejected. The bolt slows down as the resistance of the return spring and the buffer, if one is fitted, and the friction forces establish an equilibrium with the force imparted by the propellant.

When the bolt velocity reaches zero all the kinetic energy imparted to it (less extraction, ejection and possibly cocking losses) has been converted to potential energy stored in the return spring. The return spring drives the bolt forward to pick up a fresh round from the magazine, feed it to the chamber, chamber it and come to rest behind it.

Just before the bolt reaches its fully forward position the potential energy of the spring (less losses due to the feeding and chambering processes and friction) has been fully converted into the kinetic energy of the bolt and cartridge. The bolt is moving at a high velocity and the kinetic energy it possesses must be absorbed, in part by compression against the cartridge case and the remainder by impact.

When the trigger is pulled again the cycle is repeated.

This system is rarely used on fully-automatic weapons other than pistol caliber submachine guns due to the lack of accuracy caused by the vibrations set up by the heavy breechblock and the changes of the center of gravity during firing.

General Characteristics of Straight or Simple Blowback Operated Weapons are as follows:

- **Unlocked breech.**
- **Heavy "inertia type" breech block.**
- **Simplicity.**
- **Strong return spring.**
- **Parallel sided cartridge case.**
- **Generally poor accuracy in hand-held automatic fire due to cyclic movement of heavy block and consequent vibrations during firing.**

WEAPON	MAKAROV	WALTHER	VZOR 61
Origin	Russia	Germany	Czech
Popular Name	PM	PPK/S	Skorpion
Caliber (mm)	9x18mm	9x17mm	.32 ACP
Length (mm)	160	150	269.25[1]
Weight Empty (Kg)	0.663	0.9	1.544[2]
Barrel Length (mm)	92.2	80	111.75
Magazine Capacity	8	8	10 or 20
Types of Fire	SA	SA	Selective
Practical Range (m)	50	50	50[3]
ROF Semi-auto	35	35	35
ROF Auto	N/A	N/A	835

Table 1: Typical Straight Blowback Firearms

Notes:
1. 513mm with wire stock extended.
2. With empty 20-round magazine
3. With stock 200 meters

BLOWBACK WITH ADVANCED PRIMER IGNITION

In the simple blowback system described, the bolt or breechblock is heavy and although it travels forward fairly slowly it has quite a lot of kinetic energy, which is lost by crushing the cartridge case at impact. The bolt is stationary when the next round is fired and the entire rearward impulse is available to give the bolt a rearward momentum. This leads to a heavy bolt to keep the velocity down to a level where no undue amount of cartridge case is allowed to project unsupported while the pressure is high. The kinetic energy possessed by the bolt as it chambers the round can be used effectively if it is possible to time the ignition so that a round is fired just before the bolt reaches the limit of its forward travel. The impulse of the propellant explosion now has two functions:

- To slow and stop the forward moving bolt.
- To propel the bolt to the rear.

In practice the final forward velocity of the bolt induced by the return spring is very nearly the same as the initial velocity backwards produced by the propellant impulse. Thus, if the bolt velocity is unchanged, the mass of the bolt can be reduced to half its previous value because only half of the firing impulse is being used to drive the bolt backwards.

There are other advantages of advanced primer ignition. The cartridge case is placed in compression due to friction forces resulting from the high gas pressure as the forward movement of the bolt is slowed. Compressive stresses do not cause case separation and therefore have no ill effects. When the case is driven back, the time where it is subjected to longitudinal tensile stress is halved. Since the distance the case can project without support remains constant, bolt velocity can be twice as high as in the simple blowback systems. This increase in permissible velocity allows a further reduction in bolt weight and also can increase the rate of fire. The net effect of advanced primer ignition alone is to reduce the bolt weight by a factor slightly greater than two. This means that the weight of a rifle bolt operated on this system could be reduced to about 18 pounds. This is still completely impractical, however, and no rifle working on advanced primer ignition has been adopted for military service by any country but there have been some heavy machine guns and a considerable number of submachine guns that use this principle. xxxx

A typical example of an advanced primer ignition submachine gun is the British L2A3 (Sterling) submachine gun (SMG).

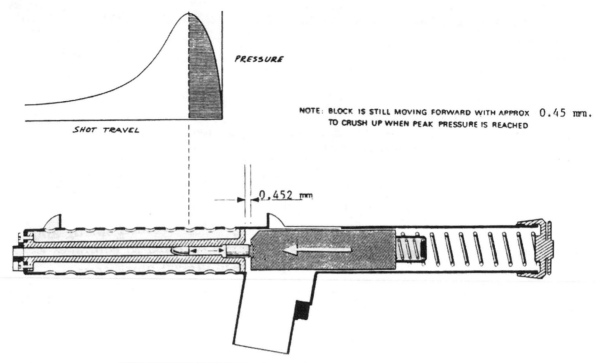

FIG 7: ADVANCED PRIMER IGNITION – BRITISH 9x19MM L2A3 (STERLING) SMG

When the weapon is cocked ready for firing the breechblock is to the rear held by the sear. The recoil (return) spring is compressed. When the trigger is pulled, the sear disengages the breechblock which is driven forward by the spring. The face of the block strips a cartridge from the magazine, drives it forward and the nose enters the chamber. As the cartridge enters the chamber, the continued forward movement of the block forces the round to align itself with the axis of the bore and the primer is lined up with the fixed striker on the front face of the breechblock. As soon as the friction force between round and chamber is sufficient, the primer is fired. The primer is thus fired while both the cartridge and breechblock are moving forward. The precise moment when the cap is detonated depends on a number of factors including:

Dimensions of the chamber and round. A chamber of minimum diameter and a cartridge case of the largest diameter will produce early firing, whereas a chamber at the outer limits of toleranced diameter and a cartridge case at the lower end of permitted diameter would fire later.

Friction in the chamber. The better, or smoother, the finish of the chamber, the more firing will be delayed due to reduced friction, all other actors being equal.

The accumulation of carbon, primer residue, etc. will increase friction and cause premature firing. Grit, dirt, sand, etc. in the chamber and on the ammunition will produce the same effect. As a general approximation, the Sterling bolt has some three inches to go before it encounters the breech face. The impulse given by the burning of the propellant causes a rapid slowing up of the forward movement of the breechblock so that when the maximum chamber pressure has developed as shown in Figure 7, the breechblock is still 0.4572 mm clear of the rear face of the chamber and still moving forward. Thus while the bullet is still in the bore the breechblock is either moving forward, momentarily at rest, or being driven slowly backwards. Since the cartridge case is parallel sided, the breech will be fully obturated until the cartridge case mouth leaves the chamber. The further rearward movement of the block stores energy in the return spring and the block is then either held up on the sear or continues forward to complete the cycle of operations. This reciprocating movement of the breechblock causes considerable changes in the center of gravity of the weapon and also sets up vibrations when the case is being crushed up. The small submachine gun as a class will not provide accurate fire.

DISADVANTAGES OF ADVANCED PRIMER IGNITION

The entire advanced primer ignition system depends on the primer being detonated at the right moment while the breechblock is moving forward. If detonation is significantly early or late the system will not work. The hazards to which the system is subject are:

Premature ignition. Buildup of carbon in the chamber can cause premature firing. Another cause of premature ignition is the entry of grit or dirt into the mechanism. Premature ignition leads to peak pressure developing before the case is fully inside the chamber, leading to a ruptured case.

Late firing- hangfire. The bolt may have bounced back from a crushed case and actually be moving backwards when firing takes place. In such an event, the bolt will be driven back at a velocity of nearly 3 times its normal rate, meaning that its kinetic energy is nearly nine times normal. The return spring may well fail to accommodate such a high level of energy, resulting in serious damage to the weapon.

Obstruction in the chamber. A separated case will leave its forward portion in the chamber, preventing the next round from fully entering the chamber and thus fired prematurely.

Hand chambering. If a round was manually chambered and the bolt released, the case will be stationary, fully seated and the bolt velocity will be terminated by impact long before the peak pressure is reached. This will result in a rearward bolt velocity of two to three times normal, which could lead to a damaged gun.

SAFETY DEVICES

Although none of the dangers mentioned above are of great importance in a 9x19mm pistol or submachine gun, they can be extremely hazardous in larger caliber weapons, but these are beyond the scope of this book, as most such guns are of 20mm caliber and above.

SUMMARY: CHARACTERISTICS OF BLOWBACK WITH ADVANCED PRIMER IGNITION

* Breechblock is still moving forward when the primer is fired.

* Breech unlocked (Inertia lock)

* Heavy breechblock

* Powerful recoil/return springs

* Simple design

* Special safety devices to prevent damage from double feed, early ignition, or hang fire

* Parallel sided (straight taper) cartridge cases best

* Lubricated cases sometimes necessary

* Poor accuracy in hand held weapons due to the movement of heavy breechblock during firing

* Susceptibility to variation in ammunition.

DELAYED OR RETARDED BLOWBACK

Although the advanced primer ignition represents more than a 50% saving of weight in the reciprocating parts compared to straight blowback operation, it can only be used in small caliber submachine guns and in large heavy machine guns carried on a massive mounting. It is not suitable for a firearm requiring an accurate first round shot because not only are the reciprocating parts heavy, but the system depends on firing from an open breech (open bolt) which leads to inaccuracy from two sources:

* The change in the center of gravity as the heavy bolt reciprocates.
* The long lock time that is found in any open-breech system.

Both of these disadvantages are overcome in what is known as "delayed blowback". In the delayed blowback system the rearward movement of the bolt face after the round is fired, is retarded until the pressure has dropped to a level where it can safely be allowed to drive the bolt face back and so permit the cartridge case to become unsupported, without fear of danger.

This system almost invariably depends upon some mechanical arrangement using light components which insures that the bolt must act through a very considerable mechanical disadvantage to overcome inertia before the bolt face can readily move rearwards.

Whatever the detailed arrangements used to produce the delay the essential part of the design must be to ensure that the delay is NOT uniform in its action. It must impose maximum restraint on the movement of the bolt face immediately as firing takes place and pressure is high, yet as soon as the pressure drops off it must allow progressively increasing freedom to the bolt to accelerate rearwards to reach a relatively high velocity without which a reasonable rate of fire is impossible. This is illustrated at Figure 8.

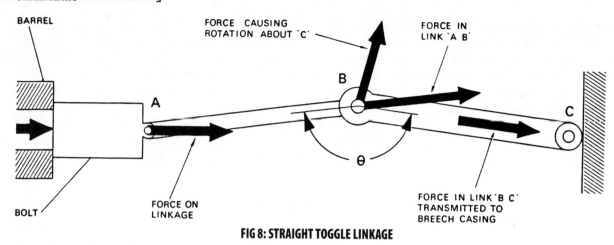

FIG 8: STRAIGHT TOGGLE LINKAGE

MECHANICAL DELAY

This mechanism is so arranged that when the bolt is closed the angle made between the two struts is nearly 180 degrees. Most of the force exerted on the linkage at A is not effective in opening the bolt but is taken directly through the links to the rear receiver casing at C. Only a very small force acts at the junction of the struts B in the direction required to overcome the inertial resistance to movement about
point C. The result of this is that the relatively small inertial resistance of the mass of the linkage is multiplied so that it is equivalent to a heavier mass at A. It should be noted that the retardation offered by the system is not constant but decreases as the bolt opens. This means that as the pressure in the chamber drops the resistance offered by the mechanism is reduced and the bolt movement rearward is reasonably smooth. This type of toggle linkage takes up a lot of room in a gun's receiver and has not been used in small arms for many years.

Modern practice is not to employ toggle-joints with their large moments of inertia but to use two-part breechblocks. Relative motion between the two parts is obtained by means of a simple internal lever or a pair of rollers. Figure 9 shows the system used in the French AA52 general purpose machine gun.

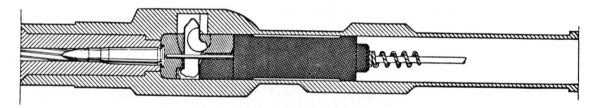

1. Position at Firing

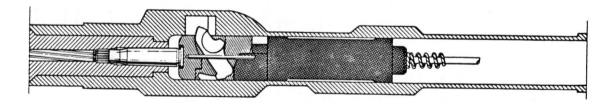

2. Lever rotating. Bolt receiver moving back.

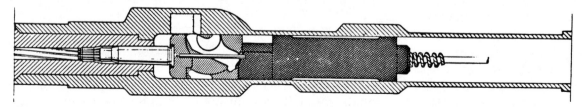

3. Lever disengaged from receiver. Entire bolt assembly moving to the rear.

FIG 9: THE FRENCH AA52 GPMG

When the weapon fires, the lever carried in the bolt head is forced back into the recess in the gun's receiver. The lever is thus forced to rotate. The fulcrum of the lever is not at the center point so that there is a velocity ratio obtained as the lever rotates and this causes the bolt receiver to be accelerated relative to the bolt head. When the pressure has dropped to an acceptably low level the lever rotates out of the receiver and residual blowback action forces the entire breechblock to the rear with no further change in the displacement of the two parts. Energy is stored in the return spring which drives the block forward again. The lever cannot rotate until it comes opposite the recess in the receiver and so the bolt receiver is held back. When the round is fully chambered, the lever rotates and the bolt receiver comes forward, strikes the firing pin held in the bolt head, and completely closes up the gap between the two sections of the block.

The essential element of the design is that while the pressure is high a slight rearward movement of the breech face produces a movement of three times the displacement, and therefore the velocity, of the bolt receiver, which thus acquires momentum. When the lever is out of the receiver, the bolt head is accelerated back at a velocity that is increased by residual gas pressure.

The diagrams at Figure 10 show the German G3 (HK91) rifle. This rifle was designed in Spain shortly after World War II by displaced German engineers, was derived from the wartime German StG45 and designated the CETME when it entered Spanish military service. The G3 is a modified version of the basic CETME design. The top diagram shows the rifle ready to fire with a cartridge in the chamber, fully supported by the bolt head of the two-piece breechblock.

When firing occurs, gas pressure forces the cartridge case back against the breech face, which is moved rearwards. The bolt head carries two rollers that are engaged in recesses in the barrel extension.

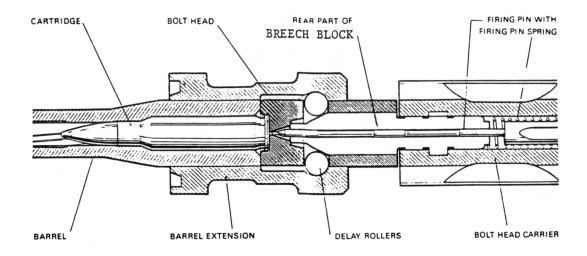

RIFLE LOADED, READY TO FIRE

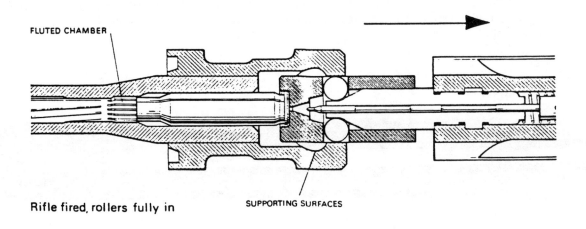

Rifle fired, rollers fully in

FIG 10: THE G3/HK91 RIFLE - METHOD OF OPERATION

Before the breechblock can move back these two rollers must be forced in to clear the recesses in the barrel extension: This is done by the reaction of the recesses to the firing force. The inward movement of the rollers is resisted by the inertia of the bolt receiver as it is driven backwards, by the action of the rollers over the inclined plane at the front of the bolt receiver. This slows down the rate at which the bolt head comes back. By the time the rollers are free from the barrel extension, the bullet has left the muzzle and the components of the breechblock are forced to the rear by the residual gas pressure.

The relative position of the breechblock parts remains unchanged until the next round is chambered. The front part of the block is then halted and the rear part is able to force the rollers out into the recesses in the barrel extension in preparation for firing the next round. The Swiss SIG 710-3 machine gun and SIG 510-4 rifle work on similar principles.

The differential action whether it is obtained via a roller system or directly from a lever, in addition to initially limiting the bolt head of the breechblock to a shorter movement than the bolt receiver, assists a relatively light return spring to resist the rearward thrust of the case, since for a small rearward movement of the case and bolt head the bolt receiver is required to move a greater distance until the lever is disengaged or the rollers are freed from their recesses and the working load of the spring is thereby increased during this differential action.

The striker is also operated by the differential action between the two portions of the breechblock and this ensures that the round cannot be fired until the lever is rotated in front of the shoulder in the receiver or the rollers are fully engaged in the recesses of the barrel extension. The position of firing is thereby controlled.

Mechanical delay is achieved by:

- Differential action between two portions of the breechblock.
- Engagement of a lever or rollers in the gun receiver or barrel extension.
- Increase in return spring effect caused by initial differential action of the breechblock.

GAS PRESSURE DELAY DEVICES

As an alternative to mechanical delay devices, during World War II the Germans evolved two distinct systems of gas pressure delay devices, one for use in a self-loading carbine and the other in an assault rifle. The S Carbine was known as the Volksturm Gewehr which was produced in 1944 as a weapon to be issued to the Home Guard for the last-ditch defense of Germany. It fired the 7.92x33mm round used in the StG 44 rifle. The weapon fired from a closed breech with the breechblock stationary. No attempt was made to lock the breech and so on firing the breech could be accelerated backwards at high speed as the bullet traveled up the bore and the cartridge case could emerge and be totally unsupported causing:

- Ruptured cartridge cases.
- Back blast of propellant gases.
- Heavy impact of the breechblock on the rear of the receiver.
- Damage to the return spring.
- Lower gas pressure on the base of the bullet reducing the muzzle velocity.

To prevent these effects the breechblock was made heavy and was carried forward on a tubular extension that surrounded the barrel. The barrel was shaped to leave an annular space between the barrel itself and the surrounding sleeve at the forward end of the sleeve. A number of holes were drilled through the barrel wall into the forward part of the annular chamber.

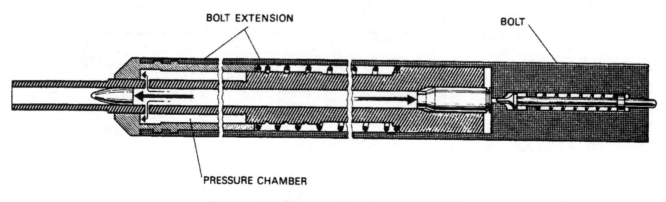

FIG 11: GAS PRESSURE DELAY DEVICE - VOLKSTURM GEWEHR

When the carbine was fired, the bolt was blown back like a simple blowback design but as soon as the bullet passed the radial holes in the barrel, gas escaped to fill the annular chamber. The buildup of pressure immediately slowed down the sleeve and the breechblock. It can be seen from Figure 11 that once the sealing ring at the front of the sleeve passed over the holes in the barrel the gas was trapped, and further rearward movement of the bolt increased the gas pressure in the annular cavity, which then acted as a gas spring.

After the gas pressure arrested the bolt, the combined forces of the gas spring and the mechanical spring drove the sleeve and bolt forward. The gas was exhausted into the barrel and out of the muzzle and the carbine was ready to fire another round.

The other gas delay device was used in an early experimental model of the German assault rifle the MP43. This rifle used the 7.92x33mm round. There is no record of this method being employed in Service. It is generally called the Grossfuss system from the firm of that name. This was a simple gas delay system with a gas channel taken backwards from the leade and the gas pressure used to drive a piston upwards to engage the breechblock and reduce its speed of rearward movement. (See Figure 12).

The angle between the piston and the block was critical. When the gas pressure diminished, the angle of the breechblock surface and the relative areas of the interior of cartridge case and the piston, allowed the breechblock to be driven rearwards. Modified versions of this system have occasionally been used in handgun designs in recent years, but without notable success.

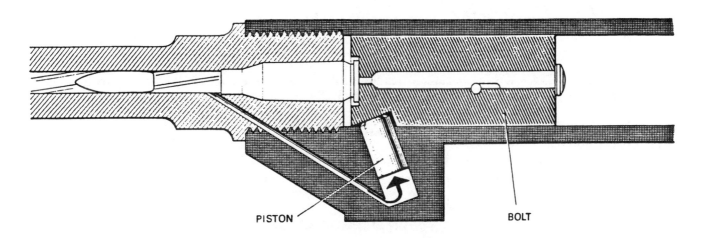

PISTON   BOLT

FIG 12: GAS PRESSURE DELAY DEVICE - MP43 (EXPERIMENTAL)

BLOWBACK WITH LOCKED BREECH

In this system the weight of the breechblock is reduced to the minimum compatible with the required strength. The block is locked while the pressure is high and after the point of maximum pressure has passed, the breechblock is unlocked and the residual gas pressure forces the block back as in the simple blowback system.

The force chosen for unlocking the block may be produced from gas pressure or recoil of the barrel but the energy required to operate the cycle is given to the bolt entirely from blowback and so it is not logical to describe these weapons as operated by a "combination of principles" as had been done in the past.

An example of a hand-held weapon firing from a locked breech and using recoil force to unlock the breech when the pressure has dropped to a safe level, is the Johnson .30-06 caliber light machine gun (LMG). (See Figure 13). This was developed in 1941 and used by the United States Marines in some Pacific campaigns.

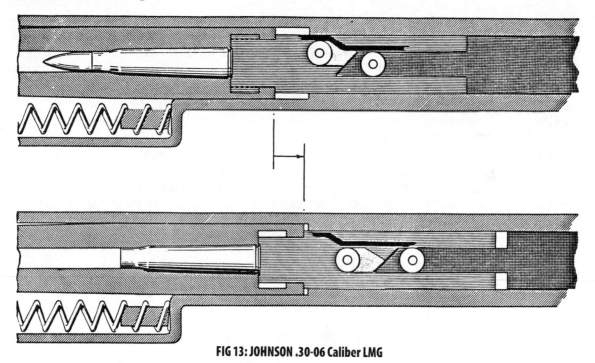

FIG 13: JOHNSON .30-06 Caliber LMG

The bolt rotates to lock and is in two parts. When firing takes place the breechblock and barrel recoil together. The front part of the bolt or breechblock carries a roller which after 3rnm free travel contacts a cam path in the receiver of the gun. This causes the bolt head to rotate and unlock. In so doing the rear part of the block is forced back. As soon as unlocking is completed the residual pressure forces the entire breechblock rearwards to carry out the cycle of operations.

The system is expensive, complicated and was not generally popular although it should be noted that the Johnson LMG weighed only 5.6 kg as compared to the 8.6 kg of the Bren gun.

PRIMER PROJECTION

In the past the idea of using the backward projection of a primer to supply the energy to unlock the bolt and then to use blowback to carry out the cycle has appealed to designers of such weapons as the Roth rifle, the prototype Garand rifle and the early Pedersen rifle. It requires the use of special ammunition and therefore when a new round is being considered the idea of the primer projection occasionally arises. During the development of the US Special Purpose Individual Weapon (SPIW) project, one version of this flechette firing weapon was produced in which the breechblock was unlocked by primer projection and then blowback was used for the operating cycle.

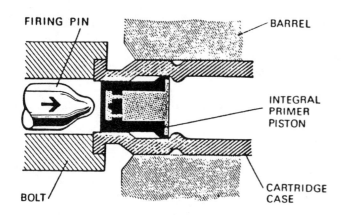

A. Weapon ready to fire

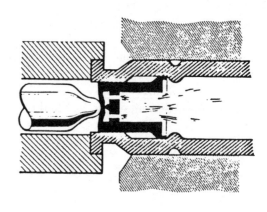

B. Firing pin fires primer

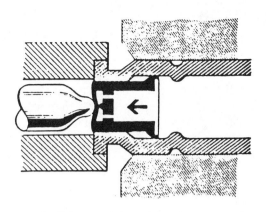 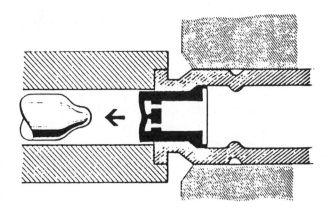

C. Primer piston driven rearwards   D. Pin, driven back, unlocks breech

FIG 14: BLOWBACK WITH PRIMER PROJECTED UNLOCKING

It should be noted that in all blowback operated weapons the breech opens early and as soon as movement has broken down the case obturation, fumes will be blown back through the breech. This is not important in an infantry weapon but where firing takes place in an enclosed space e.g., inside a tank turret, arrangements must be made to ventilate the confined volume or the toxic fumes can be dangerous.

The muzzle velocity given from a given round will be less when a blowback weapon is employed because the rapid increase in chamber volume as the case moves back leads to some reduction in working pressure.

The blowback system has no provision for adjustment of power to allow for the increased friction in the working parts caused by fouling, dirt, sand, dust etc. It will be found that the action tends to be harsh when the system is clean and the accumulation of fouling gradually slows down the action with a consequent reduction of cyclic rate and a slowing up of the speed of case ejection.

SUMMARY

A summary of the characteristics and normal uses of the four types of blowback operation is given below.

CATEGORY	STRAIGHT BLOWBACK	ADVANCED PRIMER IGNITION	BLOWBACK WITH DELAY	BLOWBACK WITH LOCKED BREECH
Complexity	Simple	Simple	Less Simple Timing sensitive	Fairly complicated
Cost	Cheap	Cheap	Fairly Cheap	Fairly expensive
Block	Heavy	Lighter	Generally 2-part	Light
Case	Parallel sided, low power	Parallel sided, open breech	Any form, fluted chamber	Any form
Type of Weapon	Very low power, usually pistol or SMG	SMG, few HMGs	All, usually rifles, LMGs	HMGs

All blowback weapons tend to suffer from the following defects:

    1. Toxic fumes.

    2. Fouling on bolt head and receiver

    3. Reduced muzzle velocity

RECOIL OPERATION

GENERAL

Recoil operation is defined as: "The method of operation in which the energy required to carry out the cycle of operations is supplied to the bolt by the reaction of the bolt and barrel, locked together and free to move, to the force produced by the propellant gases". The elementary gun shown at Figure 15 can be used to illustrate the principle.

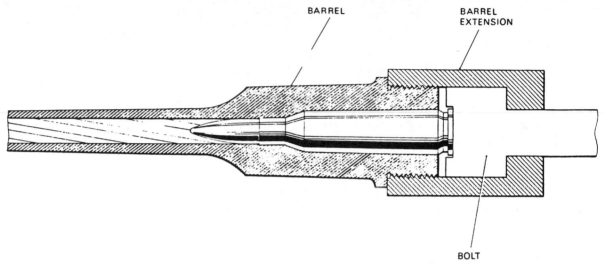

FIG 15: AN ELEMENTARY GUN

The force produced by the expanding gases drives the bullet up the barrel. An exactly equal force acts against the bolt head and tries to drive the bolt to the rear. Since the bolt is securely locked to the barrel - NOT to the receiver of the gun - and the barrel is free to move to the rear within the receiver, the breechblock will recoil relative to the receiver, pulling the barrel with it. This movement of breechblock and barrel is the source of energy for recoil operation.

The recoil of breechblock and barrel is relative to the gun's receiver. All guns in which the breechblock is locked to the receiver will recoil but since the entire weapon recoils there is no relative movement between barrel and the receiver, therefore the gun cannot employ the recoil system of operation.

RECOIL-OPERATED SYSTEMS

There have been many examples of recoil-operated guns in the past and there have been a very large number of detailed mechanical arrangements by which the system has been applied. These have varied widely, but in spite of these differences all recoil-operated weapons can be regarded as falling into one of two basic categories – long recoil and short recoil.

Long recoil is a system in which the breechblock and barrel are locked together and move to the rear over a distance which exceeds the length of an unfired round. This movement is the source of energy to operate the system. When the rearward movement is completed the bolt is unlocked from the barrel and continues to the rear while the barrel moves back forward, leaving the empty case on the breechblock face for ejection. When the barrel has moved forward sufficiently to allow sufficient space for feeding, the bolt is released. The bolt is then driven forward by the return spring to carry out feeding and chambering and it is then locked to the barrel prior to the next round being fired.

In a short recoil-operated weapon the barrel and breechblock are detached after a very short travel. This distance is much less than that required to allow feeding. After unlocking occurs the barrel will only move back a very short distance and then it is either stopped or returned to its fully forward position. The bolt continues to the rear under its own momentum, which is occasionally increased mechanically by the use of an accelerator. As the bolt or breechblock moves to the rear, the spent casing is ejected. The bolt movement must be sufficiently prolonged to produce an opening large enough for feeding an unfired cartridge and then the bolt will be driven forward to carry out the functions of feeding, chambering and locking. Where the barrel has previously been stopped at the end of its rearward movement, the bolt energy will suffice to drive it forward to the firing position.

LONG RECOIL

The general principles of the operation of a long recoil system are as follows. The round is in the chamber with the bolt locked to the barrel. This situation is shown in the top diagram (A) of Figure 16. When the round is fired the breechblock is driven back pulling the barrel with it. The influence of the uncompressed return spring is small and the recoil acceleration is decided by the magnitude of the recoiling mass.

Pressure is sustained for a short while after the bullet has left the muzzle but it soon drops to zero and the bolt and barrel move to the rear. They are slowed down by the increasing resistance offered by the barrel spring and return spring until they come to rest fully recoiled. This is shown in Figure 16 (B). The bolt is still locked to the barrel and the only part of the cycle of operations completed - except firing - is the storage of energy in the springs.

The bolt is held to the rear and the barrel is released (Figure 16 (C)) moving forward to produce extraction and ejection. When the barrel has gone forward sufficiently, the next round is fed forward. The barrel will have a lot of kinetic energy as it runs out and this must be absorbed by a buffer in larger calibers or by impact in smaller weapons.

When the barrel completes its run out it operates a bolt release mechanism and the bolt is driven forward to feed and chamber the next round and then lock on to the barrel. The kinetic energy of the bolt is absorbed by crushing up the cartridge case and by impact.

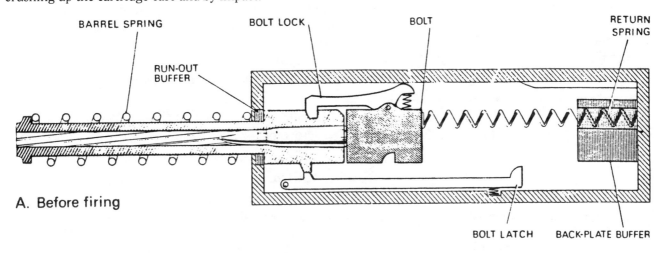

A. Before firing

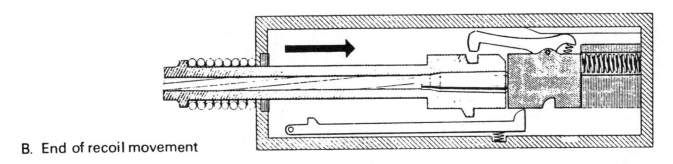

B. End of recoil movement

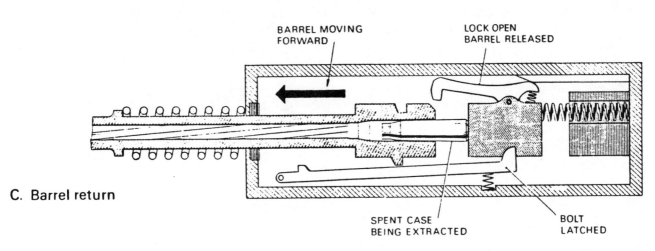

C. Barrel return

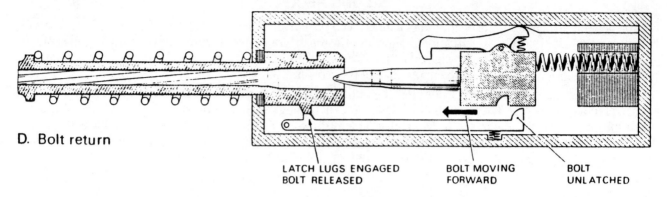

D. Bolt return

LATCH LUGS ENGAGED
BOLT RELEASED

BOLT MOVING
FORWARD

BOLT
UNLATCHED

FIG 16: DIAGRAM OF A LONG RECOIL SYSTEM

Since the breechblock does not become unlocked until full recoil has been accomplished, half the reciprocating cycle elapses before the normal functions of extraction, ejection and feeding can begin. This leads to an extremely low rate of fire in automatic weapons - probably about 1/5 to 1/4 of the rate achieved in the same caliber using a different method of operation.

Thus the main characteristics of a long recoil operated system are:
- Reduced stress in the system - particularly in the recoil-recuperator mechanisms.
- A slow rate of fire in automatic weapons.
- Increased complexity and more expensive mechanisms in comparison to other systems.
- A change in the center of gravity as the barrel reciprocates.

SHORT RECOIL

In the short recoil system of operation the barrel and bolt remain locked together and recoil together only until the chamber pressure has dropped to a safe level. The recoil movement is then utilized to unlock the bolt and after unlocking, the barrel is stopped while the bolt continues to the rear until the opening between barrel and bolt is sufficient to permit ejection and feeding the next round. The essential elements of a gun working on the short recoil system are shown schematically at Figure 17.

The essential components of a short recoil operated system are the bolt, the locking system, occasionally an accelerator, a barrel stop and the springs required to return the barrel and breechblock to the forward position. In the diagrammatic representation shown at Fig 22 the barrel returns to the fully run out position as soon as separation occurs and in modern weapons this is the usual arrangement but in some older weapons such as the Browning machine gun designed in 1905 - the barrel is held to the rear until the breechblock comes forward to it on the feed stroke.

THE CYCLE OF OPERATIONS

The short recoil cycle starts with a round in the chamber and with the bolt locked to the barrel. (Figure 17(A)). When firing occurs, the gas pressure that drives the projectile up the bore forces the breechblock to the rear. The breechblock recoils within the gun's receiver pulling the barrel back with it. As in long recoil, acceleration is controlled by the mass of the recoiling parts. After about (lost fraction) inch of free travel in a rifle-caliber gun, the breechblock can be unlocked because the pressure has dropped to a safe level (Figure 17 (B)).

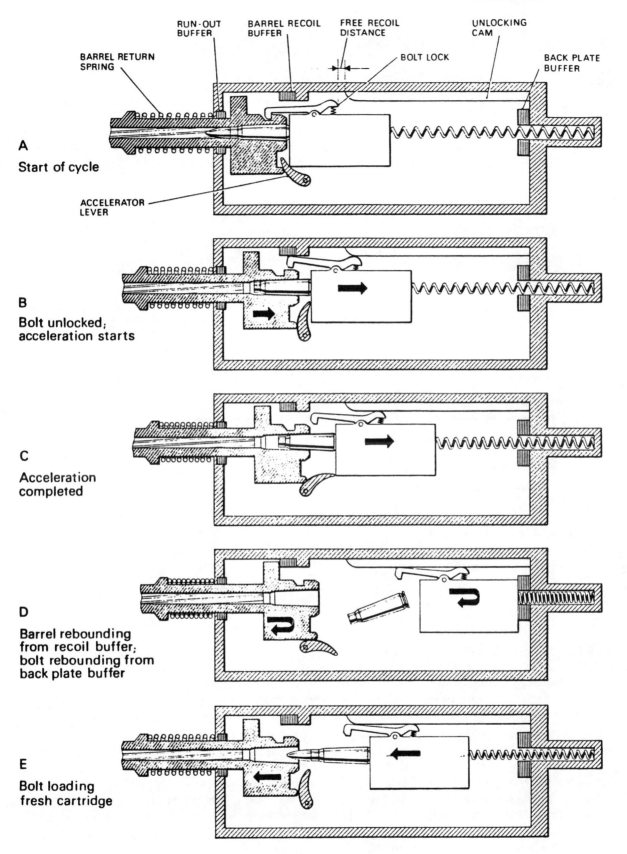

FIG 17: DIAGRAM OF A SHORT RECOIL SYSTEM

Shortly after the breechblock has been unlocked from the barrel, the latter contacts the accelerator (Figure 17(B)). There are several different forms of accelerator but the lever type shown in Figure 17 is the most common. This is illustrated in more detail at Figures 18 and 19.

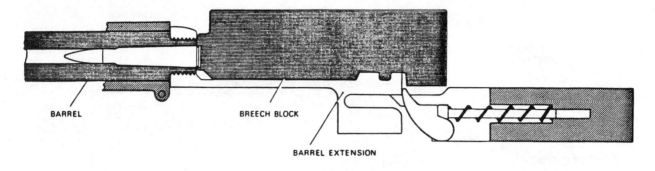

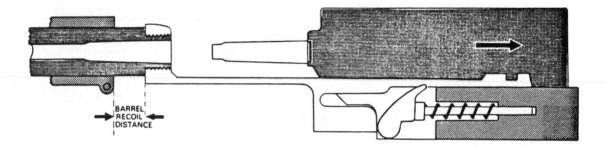

BARREL

BREECH BLOCK

BARREL EXTENSION

BARREL RECOIL DISTANCE

FIG 18: SHORT RECOIL OPERATION - BROWNING M1919 MACHINE GUN

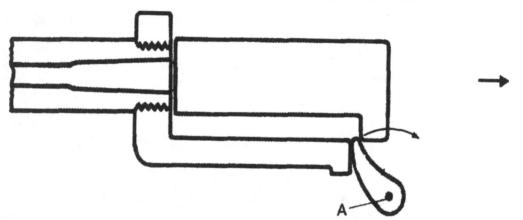

A

FIG 19: ACCELERATOR SYSTEM - BROWNING MACHINE GUN

The barrel extension first contacts the lever at its extremity and as the barrel recoils further to the rear the level rotates and the point of contact between the barrel extension and the lever moves progressively closer to the lever pivot thus increasing the velocity ratio.

After the bolt has been accelerated, the barrel is brought to a halt. According to the design the barrel may be latched in this position or - as is more usual in modern design - driven forward again by its own spring.

If the bolt has opened early enough, its rearward velocity will be increased by blowback action and this plus the accelerator will give it enough energy to travel back far enough to allow sufficient space to feed the next round. The empty case is extracted from the chamber and then ejected from the gun. The backward motion of the bolt compresses the return spring. This spring has to store only enough energy to drive the bolt forward when it is held to the rear by the sear prior to firing the first round. It is therefore a light spring and allows the bolt to travel throughout its recoil motion at a high velocity. The bolt then strikes the back plate buffer and this gives the forward velocity needed for feeding and chambering the next round. The coefficient of restitution of this buffer is less than unity and so some bolt velocity is lost at rebound.

During the feed stroke the bolt is assisted by the return spring as it supplies energy to overcome the friction losses caused by the feeding a round from the belt and chamberingit. This allows the bolt to maintain a high forward velocity. The round is chambered while the barrel still has a forward movement and in some designs the round is fired before the barrel comes to rest. In heavier guns this is extremely valuable because the shock of contact as the barrel runs out is cushioned by the backward impulse imparted by the burning propellant.

FEATURES OF DESIGN IN SHORT RECOIL

The short recoil system when well designed can produce a very high cyclic rate of fire. The German General Purpose Machine Gun designed in World War II and known as the MG 42 - now called the MG 3 - is a good example of this. Using the higher rate of fire its cyclic rate is 1,200 rounds a minute. This high rate of fire comes from three factors:

- The high recoil velocity of the barrel and bolt at the time of unlocking.
- Blowback assistance.
- Accelerator effect.

The high recoil velocity at unlocking comes from the impulse produced by the chamber pressure. From the conservation of momentum, the rearward momentum of barrel and bolt equals that of the bullet and gases. The lighter the combined weight of the barrel and block, the faster they will cycle.

To produce sustained fire in a machine gun, for example, the barrel must be massive to cope with the heat and will therefore be heavy. The barrel, barrel extension, bolt head and locking device are all subjected to forces resulting from high gas pressures and must therefore also be strong. This also means they will be heavy. These heavy parts cannot be accelerated at the rate required to produce a high rate of fire and it is necessary to incorporate an additional source of energy to accelerate the barrel and bolt. This takes the form of a recoil intensifier or as it is often called a muzzle booster. A typical muzzle booster is shown at Figure 20.

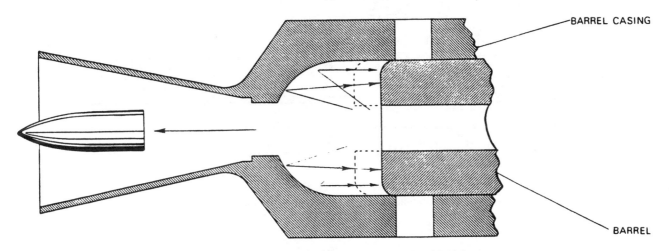

BARREL CASING

BARREL

FIG 20: RECOIL BOOSTER – 7.62x51mm GERMAN MG3, GPMG

In the MG3, a non-recoiling casing surrounds the barrel. This casing forms an expansion chamber beyond the muzzle. When the bullet passes through this expansion chamber, the gases following it build up pressure at the muzzle, which drives the barrel back. This increases the recoil velocity of the barrel and breechblock just before unlocking occurs and thus the energy available to be transferred by the accelerator to the bolt is increased.

The next point to consider is the additional velocity given to the bolt by blowback action after the bolt is unlocked from the barrel. In a short recoil operated gun, the effect is very similar to the action in a delayed-blowback system. The principal factor affecting the selection of the time of opening the breech is the allowable movement of the cartridge case in the chamber during the action of the residual gas pressure. Effective blowback action depends on the free movement of the cartridge case in the chamber and this cannot take place if the case binds to the chamber wall. If breech opening is delayed until the reduced gas pressure allows the cartridge case to return to its original dimensions, there will be no effective blowback action. However, since the breech is opened by the recoil action the design can incorporate a device to produce "initial extraction" to free the case from the chamber. When this feature is incorporated in the unlocking mechanism, the bolt is not completely unlocked at first but a slow powerful leverage is applied which slightly withdraws the bolt face causing the taper of the cartridge case to break free of the chamber wall. There is no way in which this initial extraction can be supplied in a blowback operated gun as the case is pushing the bolt back whereas in a recoil operated gun the bolt can initially move away from the barrel and unseat the case. Thereafter, the freed case can push the bolt back and accelerate it.

Blowback action has been considered previously, so it is sufficient to say that the weight of the breechblock and the time of unlocking must be selected so that the amount of case emerging unsupported from the chamber does not exceed that which can withstand the internal pressure without rupturing. The third factor controlling the bolt velocity is the accelerator, if present. The accelerator should only come into action after the full benefit has been gained from the bolt velocity at unlocking (including the bonus from any recoil intensifier) and from the blowback action.

Accelerator design is fairly complex. It must act smoothly and transfer energy from the barrel to the bolt without shock or friction. The action of the accelerator can only last a few milliseconds and if the transfer is not smooth, there will be hammering of the mating parts, deformation and frequent breakages. The fundamental requirements for accelerators are therefore simplicity, reliability, strength and smoothness of operation. The velocity ratio achieved between barrel and bolt depends on the relative masses of these two parts as well as the dimensions of the accelerator. It is not possible to use the accelerator to bring the barrel to a complete halt and thus the system can never be 100 percent efficient. In a well-designed accelerator the velocity ratio will be about 1.5:1.

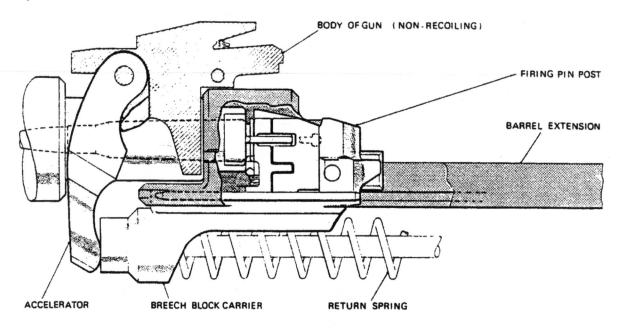

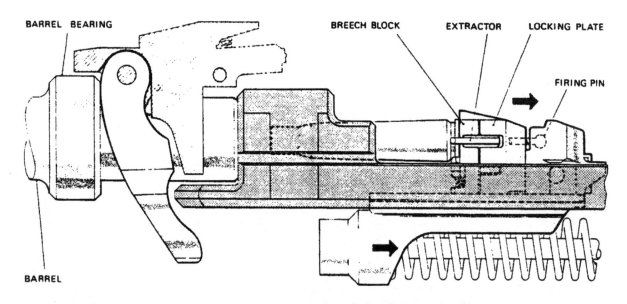

FIG 21: TYPICAL ACCELERATOR (US .50 BMG M85 MACHINE GUN)

The M 85 tank heavy machine gun shows an example of how the requirements of bolt velocity at unlocking, blowback assistance and accelerator action can be met. The bolt is very small and light and thus to some extent offsets the massive barrel required. The breech opens early for blowback action. The accelerator is well designed and virtually brings the barrel to rest thus producing maximum energy transfer.

EXAMPLES OF RECOIL OPERATION

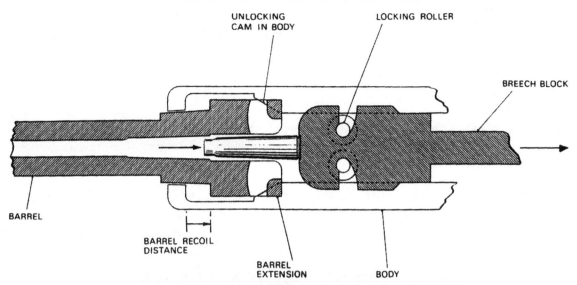

FIG 22: SHORT RECOIL OPERATION (ROLLER LOCK) - GERMAN MG3, GPMG

The German General Purpose Machine Gun MG 3 (Fig 22) is one of the most efficient sustained fire machine guns produced, despite having been designed over 60 years ago. When the cartridge is fired the breechblock and barrel recoil together for approximately (lost fraction) inch. During this short period of free travel the recoil booster accelerates their movement. The locking rollers (see Figure 22) are then forced inwards and the differential action caused by the variation in angle between the slots cut in the barrel extension and those in the head of the bolt, cause the bolt to be accelerated relative to the barrel. The bolt is given blowback assistance as it moves through the open portion of the barrel extension and is accelerated rapidly back. There is a substantial steel coil buffer which drives it forward with "the minimum of loss" and feeding and chambering occur. The anvil (Figure 23) holds the locking rollers into the undercut portion of their slot until the bolt head enters the barrel extension, when they are forced outwards to lock the bolt head in the extensions. The anvil can then pass through, driving the firing pin into the cartridge primer and thus firing the chambered round.

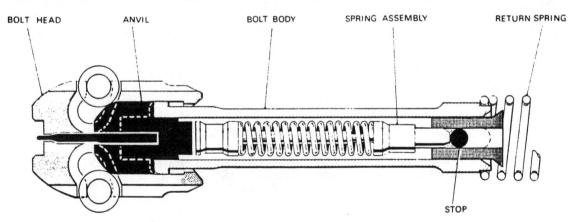

Rollers held out by force of return spring only

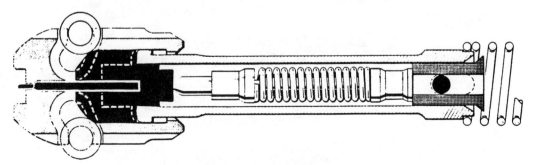

Rollers held out by combined force of return spring and internal spring assembly

FIG 23: ALTERNATE RATE OF FIRE DEVICE – MG 3 BOLT

This weapon also features an interesting method of producing alternative rates of fire. There are 3 ways in which the rate of fire can be controlled:

- By varying the volume of the expansion chamber of the recoil booster and thus varying the rearward velocity of the unlocked barrel and bolt.

- By slowing down the action of the accelerator.

- By changing the buffer spring.

The normal rate of fire of 1200 rounds/minute is achieved as shown in the top diagram of Figure 23. The return spring forces the anvil forward to hold the rollers out in the locked position and resist their inward motion.

When the slower rate of fire of 600 rounds per minute is chosen, the bolt is removed from the gun and a spring assembly reversed as shown in the lower drawing at Figure 23. This adds considerably to the spring force on the anvil and greatly increases the resistance to unlocking. The unlocking action takes longer and the effect of the accelerator is reduced. The lowered rearward velocity of the bolt produces a reduced rate of fire.

Different rates of fire can be achieved by changing the weight of the reciprocating parts, in conjunction with the return spring rates.

APPLICATION OF SHORT RECOIL TO SEMIAUTOMATIC PISTOLS

The recoil principle is widely used in semiautomatic pistols, which are normally semiautomatic only, but do complete an automatic cycle using the energy of the propellant charge, a mechanism being inserted to ensure that only single shots are fired.

The reason for the application of the recoil principle to semiautomatic pistols, would at first appear to be contradictory to the inherent characteristics of the recoil principle. There are, however, fundamental differences in a pistol as opposed to a machine gun, which make it practical.

- The mass of the bullet and barrel are closer to each other and therefore plenty of energy is available.

- Because of the short barrel, mechanical delay to ensure bullet exits before the opening of the breech is not so important.

- Owing to the barrel's short length, it can easily be encased, usually by the slide. The barrel casing can then be made integral with the breechblock and the barrel can be designed to lock into the barrel casing. This system eliminates many separate working and recoiling parts, simplifying the mechanism and making for a lightweight weapon. It would not be possible if sustained or automatic fire were required and neither would it be compatible with accuracy, although some select-fire pistols such as the Russian Stechkin and Glock 18 are manufactured.

Most of the current heavy military semiautomatic pistols follow a similar pattern in the application of the recoil principle. An example is shown at Figure 24.

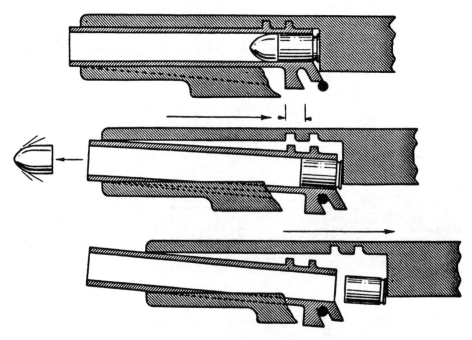

FIG 24 RECOIL OPERATION – 9x19mm BROWNING HIGH POWER

When the pistol is ready for firing the round is chambered and locking lugs on the top surface of the barrel are engaged in recesses cut into the slide. When the trigger is pulled, the hammer drives the firing pin into the primer and the bullet starts to move up the bore. The block, which is integral with the slide, moves back in recoil and a lug attached to the barrel rides over a fixed stud in the receiver. After a short period of free recoil, during which the bullet leaves the barrel and the pressure drops, the stud is engaged by a second lug and the breech end of the barrel is forced down. This unlocks the barrel from the slide and brings it to rest. The slide continues to the rear under its own momentum, extracting the spent case from the chamber and ejecting it. The slide moves forward under pressure of the recoil spring, feeding a new cartridge from the magazine, chambering it and lifting the barrel into the locked position.

This system is simple, safe and produces a rugged and reliable weapon. Due to the pivoting motion of the barrel it is necessary to have some clearance on the front barrel bushing and as a result wear takes place at the muzzle, eventually resulting in degraded accuracy.

The classic .45 ACP M1911 is illustrated at Figure 25 and functions on exactly the same principles as the Browning High Power, but uses a swinging link to carry out the tilting and unlocking of the barrel.

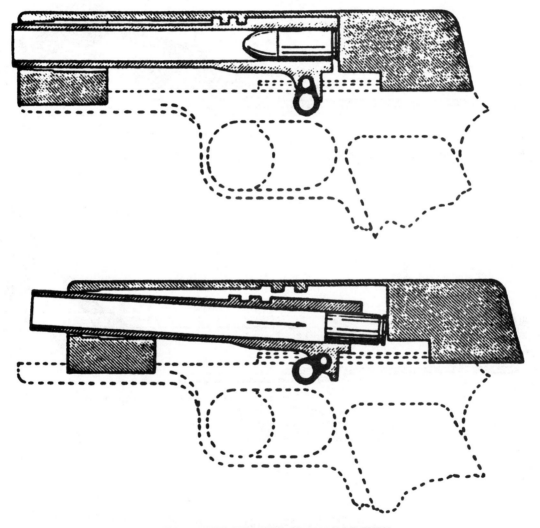

FIG 25: RECOIL OPERATION - M1911 .45 ACP PISTOL

The German Luger pistol (see Figure 26) is also recoil-operated but the application of the principle is somewhat different. Here the barrel recoils back along its axis and no tilting occurs. The breechblock reciprocates along the same axis and there is no slide.

When the firing pin strikes the primer, the bullet moves down the barrel and there is a period of free travel with the barrel locked to the breechblock until the toggle joint is broken and the breechblock unlocked. This method of breech locking is discussed in some detail below, so it will suffice here to say that although this system is somewhat more complicated and expensive to produce, it does have an advantage in that the barrel motion is purely linear, there is no tilting of the barrel and accuracy life is longer. This is offset, however, by reduced reliability as opposed to Browning-derived designs.

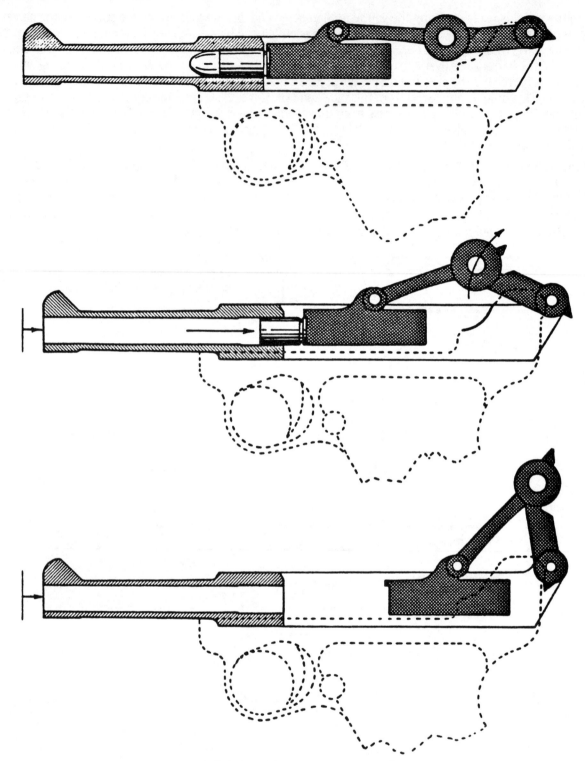

FIG 26: RECOIL OPERATION – P.08 LUGER PISTOL

FACTORS AFFECTING RECOIL OPERATIONS

Lack of Energy. In rifle caliber short recoil-operated machine guns there is a lack of energy available to carry out the cycle of operations. The total energy available for recoil is only about 0.1 percent of the energy in the propellant whereas muzzle blast which can be used to produce gas operation is about 40 percent i.e. 400 times as great. This means that recoil intensifiers, accelerators, and a very efficient buffer must be used to make the most of what energy is available. From this it follows that there is a very small reserve of energy to allow the gun to function under adverse conditions, or in elevation or depression. Similarly there is little energy available to lift a long length of belt up to the gun. Because of this, recoil operation is currently limited as a rule to shotguns and pistols.

Weight Distribution. In short recoil-operated weapons, the energy to carry out the cycle of operations is imparted to the block by:

- Its initial velocity when separation from the barrel occurs.

- Blowback action.

- The accelerator transferring energy from the barrel to the bolt.

Design Limitations. From this it follows that:

- .Both barrel and breechblock must be as light as possible to achieve a sufficient velocity before separation.

- The breechblock must be as light as possible to get maximum acceleration from blowback action.

- The breechblock-to-barrel weight ratio must be as small as possible to get the maximum benefit from the accelerator.

In general, both bolt and barrel should be light, but practical considerations of strength, heating and wear impose restrictions to the amount by which the barrel can be reduced. Designers therefore tend to concentrate on reducing the bolt or breechblock weight to a minimum compatible with the strength required to carry out the required tactical role.

Accuracy. A barrel moving back and forth must be accurately controlled. This leads to heavy, costly bearings which demand close manufacturing tolerances and produce problems of differential expansion as the barrel heats up. Since the barrel reciprocates the muzzle end is generally attached to the pistol slide or receiver. In the instance of rifles or machine guns, the sights are generally attached to the barrel jacket. Because for a weapon with more than one barrel it should be possible to carry out zeroing so that the replacement of a new barrel by a worn one will not radically affect the mean point of impact.

Cooling. Cooling in automatic weapons can be achieved by having a heavy barrel that acts as a heat sink. It can also be obtained from changing the barrel. Both methods are in use with short recoil operated guns. The control of the barrel position is important when it recoils but once that problem is mastered, recoil operated guns lend themselves particularly well to rapid barrel changing. Once the bolt has been withdrawn to the rear to unlock it from the barrel, the barrel can readily be withdrawn.

Fouling. Recoil-operated guns – unlike either blowback or gas-operated weapons – are generally not prone to stoppages due to fouling.

GAS OPERATION

GENERAL

In all semiautomatic or select-fire small arms, excepting those powered by external sources like Gatling Guns, the fundamental operating energy is the pressure created by the expanding propellant gases, regardless of whether the gun is blowback, recoil- or gas-operated, although the term "gas operation" is reserved for the type of operation in which the gases themselves directly provide the force to operate the system.

The barrel of the gun acts as an expansion chamber and the pressure varies along the barrel as the projectile passes. Thus gas at any pressure varying from that at the chamber to that at the muzzle can be drawn off and used to operate the action.

It was previously noted that some 40 percent of the energy contained within the propellant is ejected at the muzzle in the form of muzzle blast. This energy provides a useful source of power to operate a either semiautomatic or fully automatic system and weapons using this are known as "gas-operated".

It should be noted that the energy required for the efficient functioning of the cycle of operations is largely obtained from that which would otherwise be wasted at the muzzle and therefore there is little effect on the velocity imparted to the bullet.

Gas that is tapped off at the muzzle after the bullet has left the barrel has little effect on the bullet. A muzzle trap system was therefore used in early gas operation systems. A schematic diagram of a muzzle trap gas operated system is at Figure 27. A practical application as used in an early gas operating system is shown at Figure 28.

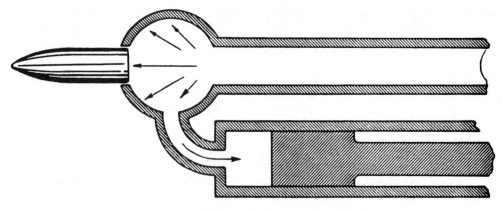

FIG 27: MUZZLE TRAP AND GAS CYLINDER PRINCIPLE

The 7.92x57mm G-41 rifle was used by the German Army in 1941-42 but was not successful. The gases tapped off at the muzzle cooled rapidly and the piston quickly became fouled. There was also differential expansion between the barrel and the piston.

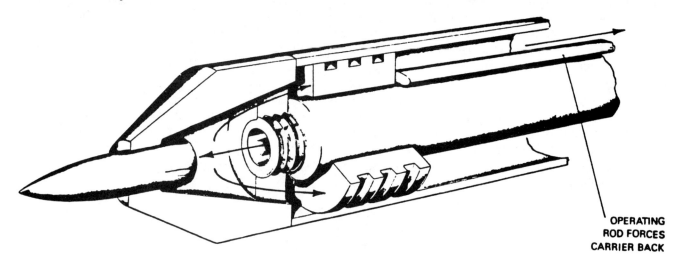

OPERATING
ROD FORCES
CARRIER BACK

FIG 28: MUZZLE TRAP PISTON OPERATION - GERMAN 7.92x57MM Gew 41 RIFLE

Gas that is tapped off in the barrel to operate a piston is contained between the piston and cylinder and even if the cylinder is vented the gas will not escape until the bullet has left the muzzle.

The factors involved in tapping the gas off near the muzzle are:
- Minimum effect on the ballistics.
- Low-pressure gas requires large volume to carry out required task.
- Muzzle gases contain a lot of solid carbon, which has been re-sublimated.

The factors involved in tapping the gas off near the breech are:
- High-pressure gas - therefore parts involved must be robust.
- Short delay before gas is available - this is an advantage where a high rate of fire is required.
- Hot gases will erode the gas hole in the barrel.

These factors generally lead to a compromise in which the gas is tapped off some 7 to 12 inches from the muzzle in a rifle or LMG. This gives the power required without unacceptable erosion or fouling.

As already stated the gas system of operation can employ many types of gas actuation devices. Although the functional characteristics of a firearm will largely depend on the particular type of device used, all gas-operated guns are basically similar in their operation. Since some form of gas piston is by far the most common actuating device it will be used here to illustrate the principle involved.

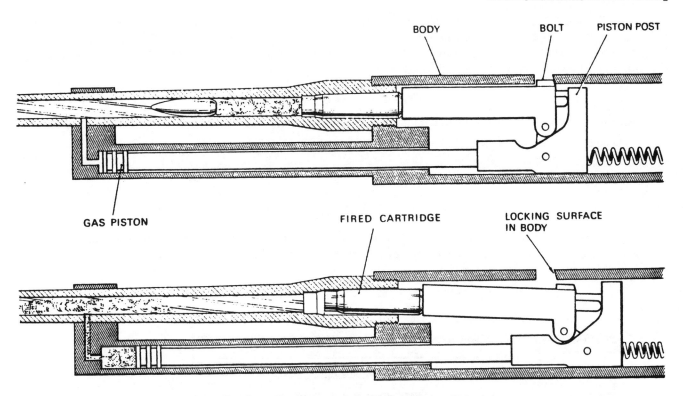

FIG 29: TYPICAL GAS OPERATED GUN

Figure 29 shows the essential elements of a gas operated system. These elements consist of a piston, a bolt, an arrangement for locking the bolt and later unlocking it, a return spring for returning the piston and bolt to the forward position and behind the return spring a back plate (not shown) which often carries a buffer.

CYCLE OF OPERATION

The operating cycle of a typical gas-operated gun is straightforward and occurs as follows:

The cycle begins with a round chambered and the bolt locked either to the barrel extension or to the receiver of the gun. When the cartridge is fired, gas pressure drives the projectile forward and at the same time those parts of the weapon designed to recoil will move back. In the great majority of cases there will be no barrel movement within the receiver and so the entire weapon recoils.

The time at which the projectile passes the port in the barrel will depend on the location of the port and will generally be about 0.75 to 1.5 milliseconds after primer initiation for a rifle or light machine gun. As soon as the bullet passes the gas port, the gas will enter the cylinder and pressure will build. Due to throttling effect, the cylinder pressure will be approximately one-third that of the barrel pressure during the period that the impulse is applied to the piston. There will always be a period of free travel of the piston before the unlocking of the bolt commences, to allow the bore pressure to drop to a safe operating limit and in most cases the bullet will be well clear of the muzzle when unlocking occurs.

After unlocking occurs, residual bore pressure continues to exert a force on the piston and also provide some blowback action on the cartridge case. After the unlocking of the bolt the piston accelerates the bolt, and the piston and bolt move rearward together. The normal cycle of operations is carried out.

In those cases where the recoiling mass of barrel and bolt have independent cycles, the barrel return spring will restore the recoiling masses to the battery position.

In those cases where the bolt and barrel recoil within the receiver, the bolt will have acquired a rearward velocity before unlocking takes place and so the bolt velocity will be high. If there is no recoil movement of the barrel and bolt which is the usual case in rifles, LMGs and GPMGs, then immediately after unlocking there will be an acceleration of the bolt as the piston drives it rearwards and any blowback action is felt. Unless care is taken in the design this acceleration can be violent and result ultimately in undue wear of the piston and/or bolt and possibly failure. It is common modern practice to use a roller on the piston post to reduce wear on this component when the piston post is used to rotate the bolt into and out of the locked position.

The bolt extracts the fired case, which is ejected from the gun and throughout the backward movement of the bolt the return spring stores energy. When the breechblock/bolt ceases its rearward travel, its kinetic energy has been transferred to potential energy stored in the return spring and is available to drive the bolt forward to complete the functions of feeding, chambering and locking.

TYPES OF GAS OPERATION

Over the years the design of gas-operated infantry firearms has developed into three distinct categories. These are:

- Long-stroke pistons.
- Short-stroke pistons.
- Direct gas impingement.

LONG-STROKE PISTONS

The long-stroke piston is permanently attached to the breech block and controls its position and velocity throughout the cycle. There are many examples of this type of gas operation. The illustration at Figure 30 is that of the FN Herstal MAG 58 GPMG (US M240).

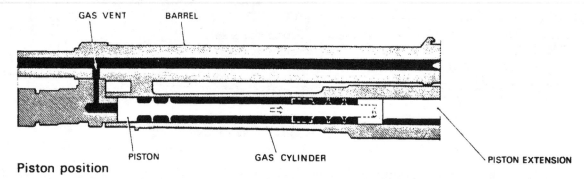

Piston position

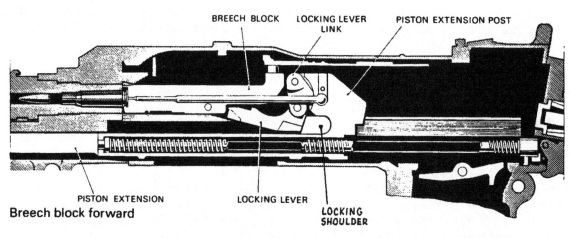

Breech block forward

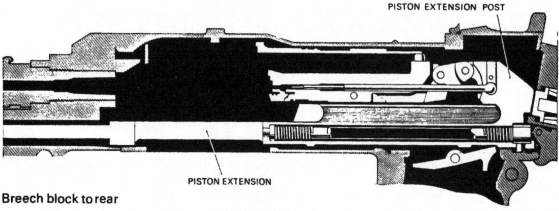

Breech block to rear

FIG 30: LONG-STROKE PISTON – MAG58 GPMG

When the bullet passes the gas port, gas enters the cylinder and the piston is driven back. There is a period during which the piston motion has no effect on the bolt, which remains fully locked. The locking lever link during this period of mechanical safety is approaching the vertical position and until this is achieved there is no force exerted on the locking lever, which remains firmly in contact with the locking shoulder in the receiver. Thereafter the locking lever is progressively lifted out of engagement with the locking shoulder until unlocking is completed. The bolt is then carried to the rear by the piston, extracting and ejecting the spent case. The return spring is aligned with the piston and assists the piston forward on rebound from the back plate buffer. The piston thus controls the position and velocity of the bolt throughout the operating cycle.

By careful design, i.e. choosing the correct position and size of the gas port, the correct area of the piston head and the appropriate mass of the piston, the correct piston velocity and energy can be obtained to provide a chosen rate of fire for any given gas pressure.

In early designs the gas port was located at the bottom of one of the rifling grooves to ensure that material was not stripped from the bullet's cupro-nickel or gilding metal jacket which would block off the gas hole. In many modern designs, the positioning of the gas hole relative to the rifling is entirely at random. For example in the FN FAL rifle or MAG 58 machine gun, the hole will be drilled at a fixed distance from the breech face. It is usual to locate the gas cylinder above or below the barrel but there are exceptions.

The long-stroke piston is the type of design most commonly employed in gas-operated LMGs and GPMGs. The bolt is always correctly positioned relative to the position of the piston and the piston always controls the method of locking.

TYPES OF CYLINDER FOR LONG STROKE PISTONS

The piston may move inside a closed, vented or open cylinder. With vented or open cylinders, gas pressure can only be sustained until the piston reaches the vents or the open end of the cylinder. Thereafter, kinetic energy of the piston and bolt carries out the cycle of operation. The reason for a vented cylinder is to allow the gases and the carbon particles contained in the gases to be blown clear of the gun. An example of a vented cylinder is the British Bren gun. The open cylinder allows the entire piston to emerge and so the cylinder is then completely open to the atmosphere and the fumes and carbon particles are completely dissipated.

The closed cylinder is rarely encountered in modern weapons. There are some adaptations of the Garand rifle still in service and these have a closed cylinder. The Lewis gun of the 1910s and 1920s was another example.

The piston head is not always a male member moving in a female cylinder. Sometimes the gas is passed through a spigot into a hollow cupped head on the piston which envelopes the spigot. The piston may have a sufficiently deeply cupped head to remain over the spigot throughout the full movement of the bolt as in the German Gew 43 semiautomatic rifle or, more usually, the piston head will leave the spigot after a short rearwards travel, to allow the gases to vent. The best example of this is shown in Figure 31 where the Russian RPD LMG is illustrated.

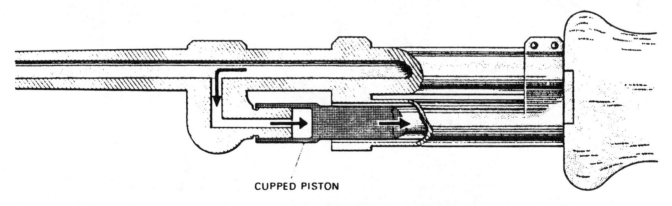

CUPPED PISTON

FIG 31: LONG-STROKE CUPPED PISTON - RUSSIAN RPD LMG

SHORT-STROKE PISTONS

In the short-stroke piston system of gas operation gas is tapped off at some point along the bore and led into a cylinder. A piston is given an impulse blow, which drives it rearwards. The piston either (a) comes into direct contact with the breech block carrier or (b) drives back an operating rod which is permanently attached to the bolt. The piston imparts energy to the breech mechanism and is then returned by its own spring to the forward position. Thus the piston is not attached to the breech block, does not serve the breech block throughout its cycle and once having delivered energy to the breech block it follows an independent cycle.

An example of the first type – i.e. the piston delivering an impulse to the bolt carrier is shown in Figure 32. This is the Belgian FN-FAL Rifle. The gas pressure drives back the piston, which, after a brief travel, contacts the bolt carrier or slide. The bolt carrier is driven back and then picks up the bolt, unlocks it from the receiver of the gun and carries it rearward. The process of extraction takes place as the case is pulled out of the chamber. As soon as the piston has transferred its energy to the bolt assembly the greater momentum of the latter carries it rearwards and the piston spring drives the piston forward again. Thus the piston is in contact with the bolt carrier for only about 1/3 of the bolt travel.

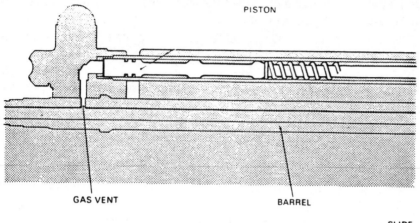

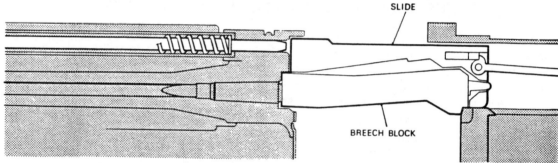

Breech block and slide forward and locked

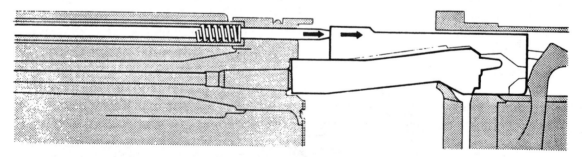

Piston pushing slide to rear (breech block unlocked)

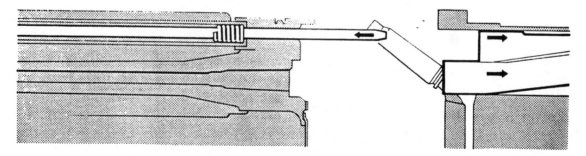

Piston moving forward while
breech block and slide continue to rear

FIG 32: SHORT-STROKE PISTON - FN FAL RIFLE

An example of the use of an actuating rod to operate the bolt assembly is shown in Figure 33, which illustrates the piston/tappet system used in the US M1/M2 Carbine. Here the piston travel is only a fraction of an inch and the piston itself is a short-stroke tappet which delivers a blow to the operating rod that has sufficient energy to control the bolt throughout its cycle. The completion of this short movement by the piston seals off the gas, which eventually returns into the bore and disappears with the rest of the residual fumes. The actuating rod returns to the forward position ready for the next round and repositions the piston.

In general, short-stroke pistons save weight, but to obtain the necessary energy the gas must be tapped off from the correct location. The general rule for such a location is the shorter the stroke, the nearer the breech.

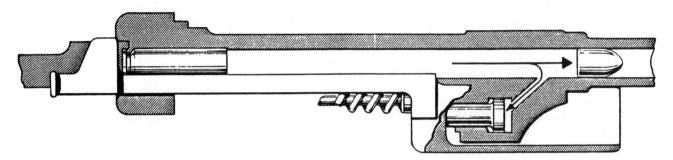

FIG 33: SHORT-STROKE PISTON/TAPPET – MI/M2 CARBINE

The short-stroke piston system has been used in the past with a piston wrapped round the barrel instead of being located in the usual position above or below. This results in a symmetrical thrust around the barrel axis, which, it is claimed, helps to reduce the turning moment on firing. The illustration of this at Figure 34 is taken from the Czech VZ 52 rifle.

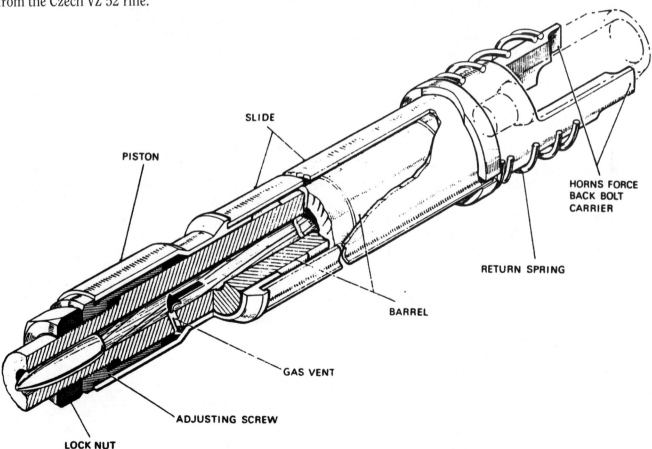

FIG 34: WRAP-AROUND PISTON - CZECH RIFLE, 7.62 MM VZ 52

The gas is tapped off in the normal way and builds up pressure in a chamber formed between the barrel and the piston which is in the form of a sleeve. The sleeve is forced back and the rear end applies an impulse blow to the bolt carrier which after a short free travel unlocks the bolt and carries it backwards. The chamber volume can be varied as required to produce a higher or lower pressure, but this necessitates stripping the forend, undoing the lock nut and varying the position of the adjusting screw which is not a quick process in the field.

Neither the German Gew 41 nor the Czech rifle, both of which used this type of piston arrangement, was successful. The barrel was bulky resulting in a relatively heavy weapon. When the barrel was hot there was differential expansion between it and the piston sleeve which led to a slowing down of the working parts and eventually to stoppages.

DIRECT GAS IMPINGEMENT

In this system, gas is tapped from the barrel and taken through a tube to act directly on the breech-closing device to unlock it. This system was first used on the Madsen – Ljungman and some time later on the French MAS 44 and Egyptian Hakim rifles. This system is most notable for its use on the AR-10, AR-15/M16 and their derivatives, illustrated at Figure 35 by the original M16 system. Direct impingement gas operation is often referred to as the Ljungman system, after the original rifle on which it was used.

The gas is tapped off from the barrel and led back via a stainless steel tube into a chamber between the bolt head and the bolt carrier. The gas expands in this chamber and drives back the bolt carrier. The bolt head is locked into the barrel extension and cannot move. As the carrier moves back a curved cam slot cut in its upper surface rotates the bolt head via a pin riding in the cam slot and the bolt head is unlocked. The carrier has already picked up considerable momentum and this, plus the blowback action on the breech face causes the bolt to move rearwards, extracting the empty case. No gas regulator is necessary.

This system is light, simple and cheap. The main drawback is that carbon fouling and powder particles are blown back into the breech and bolt carrier. These become hard on cooling and can build up over time. If clean-burning powders are not used, the gun is liable to frequent stoppages due to excess fouling, as was the case during the early days of the M16, when ball powder was specified by the US Army. This powder fouled the breech and bolt carrier so badly that many soldiers were killed or wounded because their rifles failed during firefights. The problem was largely overcome by changing to a different powder, but the AR-15/M16 and all other firearms derived from the basic weapon remain maintenance-intensive guns. A weapon that is not frequently cleaned is liable to incur stoppages with this system. To reduce stoppages the M16 has a chrome-plated chamber and barrel.

CONTROL OF OPERATING ENERGY

There is a great deal of energy available to drive a gas operated gun. It is desirable to control the amount of energy supplied and to vary it according to the operational requirements. A clean gun firing under ideal conditions requires a much smaller energy supply than a hot dirty gun operating in a desert environment where sand may add sufficiently to the friction forces to produce stoppages. Similarly, a gun firing continuously downhill will require more operating energy than one firing on level ground.

There are several ways of controlling the flow rate of gas to the operating system. These are:

- A variable size gas track.
- A control varying the amount of gas exhausted to atmosphere.
- A constant volume valve which shuts off the gas supply after a pre-determined movement of the piston.
- A variable expansion volume at the head of the piston.

These are described in more detail below.

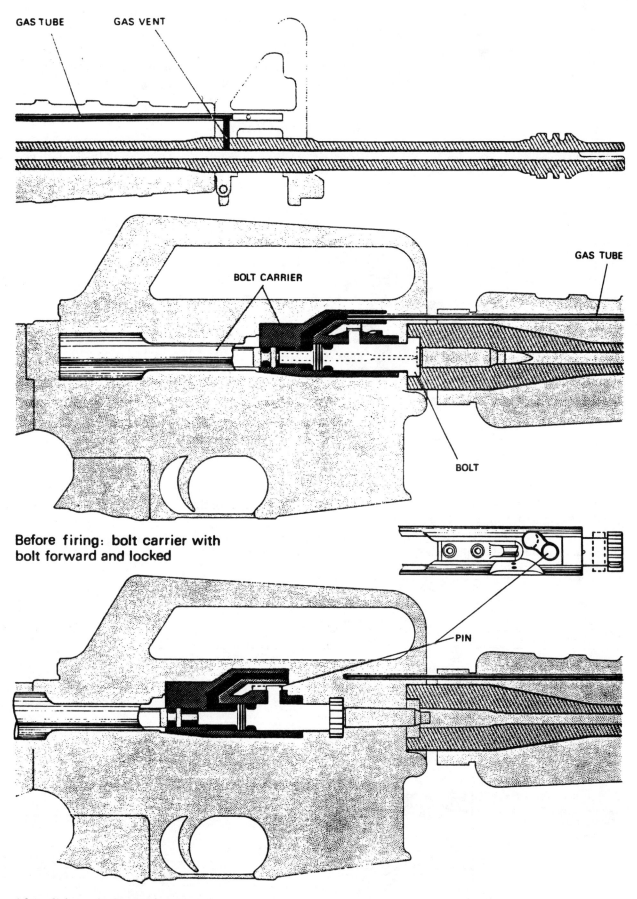

GAS TUBE

GAS VENT

GAS TUBE

BOLT CARRIER

BOLT

Before firing: bolt carrier with
bolt forward and locked

PIN

After firing: bolt carrier to rear;
bolt rotated and unlocked

FIG 35: DIRECT GAS IMPINGEMENT – M16 RIFLE

Variation of gas force also allows a variation in the rate of fire. The more gas to the piston head the greater the rate at which it will accelerate backwards and the shorter the time of the cycle of operations.

It should also be noted that insufficient gas will frequently drive the piston back sufficiently to allow extraction, ejection and feed, but will not give sufficient backward movement to enable the piston stop to ride past the sear. Thus when the trigger is released and the sear rises the gun will not stop firing and a runaway gun results.

VARIABLE GAS TRACK

This system is one of the oldest and simplest to operate. A gas regulator carries a number of tracks each of different size. Figure 36 shows the British Bren LMG, derived from the Czech Zb 30.

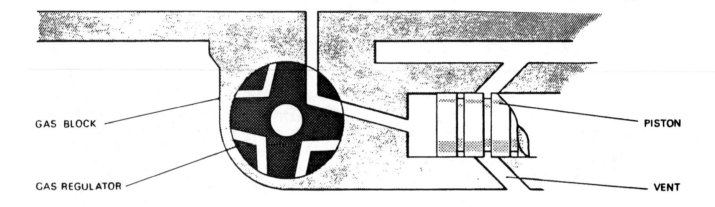

FIG. 36: VARIABLE GAS TRACK - BREN LMG

A similar system is used in the Russian Goryunov M43 medium machine gun (see Figure 37). Here there are only three tracks which are not drilled through the gas block as in the case of the Bren, but are grooved on the outside of the regulator which fits into a sleeve in the block.

In both of these examples the gunner varies the energy supply to the piston head by rotating the regulator within the gas block to align a different sized track with the barrel vent.

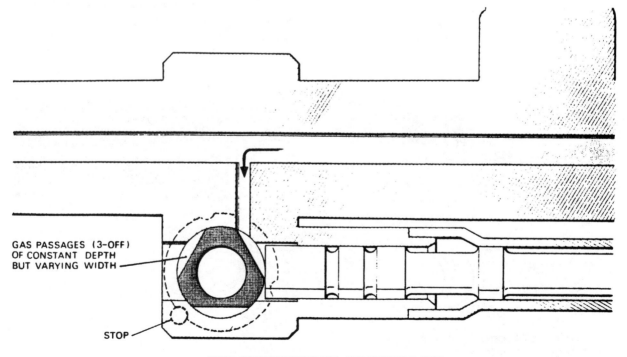

FIG 37: VARIABLE GAS TRACK - GORYUNOV M43 MMG

VARIABLE EXHAUST TO ATMOSPHERE

This system utilizes the basic principle that more energy is available than will generally be required. A fairly large hole drilled in the barrel allows gas to pass through the gas block and into an expansion chamber. Some of the gas then escapes through a series of radial holes around the chamber, to atmosphere. The remainder of the gas is used to drive back the piston.

When the gun requires more power as it gets hotter and dirtier the gas regulator is rotated to close off the radial holes and so less gas is exhausted to atmosphere and more is available to operate the cycle. This method is employed very successfully in the FN rifles, the FAL, CAL and in their MAG-58 machine gun. (See Figure 38).

This system also allows the rate of fire to be varied from about 700 to 1,100 rounds per minute.

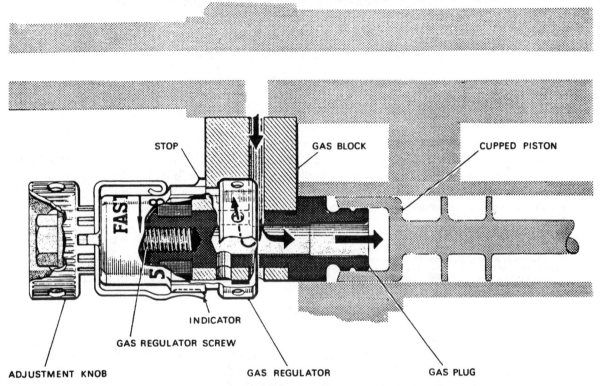

FIG 38: EXHAUST TO ATMOSPHERE SYSTEM – MAG 58 GPMG

CONSTANT VOLUME SYSTEM

In this system the gas passes through the barrel wall and then through the wall of the piston head. It expands inside the cup of the piston and drives the piston rearwards. When the piston has moved back a little way the hole in the piston wall is no longer aligned with the vent in the barrel and so no further gas enters. This is a self regulating system and so no control by the firer is required. A variation of this system is employed in the US M60 GPMG (see Figure 39). A hollow piston has a number of holes with a groove connecting them. The gas can enter any of these holes so that the piston does not have to be indexed relative to the barrel vent. The hollow piston moves back a short way and transmits its energy to an operating rod,which is permanently attached to the bolt. Thus although the piston has a short stroke action the bolt is controlled by the operating rod.

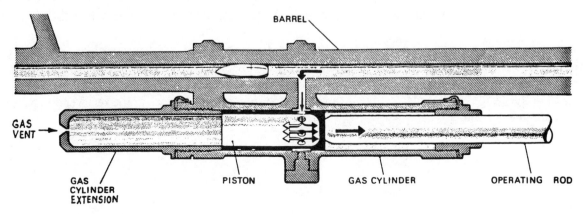

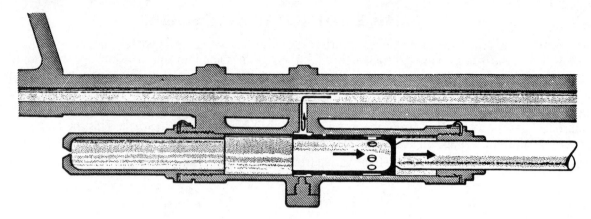

FIG 39: CONSTANT-VOLUME REGULATOR - M60 GPMG

The primary object of this system of gas control is to enable a weapon to fire various types of ammunition, which have different pressures at the barrel gas port. This means that both ball rounds with lead cores and armor-piercing rounds with steel or tungsten carbide cores and higher-velocity ammunition can be digested by the gun. The valve shuts off the gas supply when a certain amount of energy has been taken in and the system is sometimes referred to as a "constant energy system". This is really a misnomer because the amount of energy the gun requires to operate is itself not constant but varies with the increased frictional forces produced by dirt, heat, lifting an ammunition belt of differing length and when firing in elevation or depression. Thus if the resistance to piston motion is high, the gun tends to slow down, although more energy will be tapped off due to the sluggish piston motion.

ADVANTAGES AND DISADVANTAGES OF GAS OPERATION

ADVANTAGES

Flexibility. The principle advantage of gas operation, which is not available to blowback and recoil-operated weapons, is its flexibility. When the weapon is clean and firing under ideal conditions the impulse required to operate the firearm is small. With a dirty gun more power is required. A gas regulator accommodates this requirement and gas-operated guns have proven themselves in deserts, swamps, arctic and under all conditions where frictional forces can become excessive.

Light weight. The selection of the correct gas pressure enables the working parts to be lightly constructed and so as a rule a typical gas-operated gun will be lighter than recoil- or blowback-operated firearms.

Rate of Fire. A gas-operated gun can be designed to produce a very high rate of fire. By tapping off gas close to the chamber and unlocking the breech while the pressure is still relatively high, thus obtaining block back assistance, the timing of the operating cycle can be kept to a minimum.

Accuracy. The working parts are light, there is little change in the position of the center of gravity and the vibrations caused by locking are minimized. The barrel is fixed relative to the receiver, so a gas operated gun can be extremely accurate.

DISADVANTAGES

Fumes. All gas operated guns emit fumes and are therefore not basically suitable for use in enclosed spaces over an extended period

Erosion. Hot gases erode the gas port. In time this leads to an increased gas flow as well as an irregularity in the bore.

Carbon. Propellant gas contains carbon which will eventually foul the system unless special arrangements are incorporated in the design – e.g. vented cylinders, an exhaust system or extra spaces in the receiver and working parts to accommodate fouling.

Pistols

Handguns were devised very early in the history of firearms and have been in use by both military and law enforcement throughout history, usually as a backup to more lethal and effective "long guns," although in the case of police in many parts of the world, the handgun has become essentially the symbol of police authority. In military circles, the handgun also has become a symbol of sorts in that it usually is issued to personnel whose hands are otherwise occupied with other tasks, such as machine gunners, communications personnel and some officers. Most officers in combat, however, prefer to be armed with the rifle for a number of reasons. First, because the pistol identifies them as a target of some importance to snipers and enemy soldiers and second, because a rifle is a much more effective weapon than a handgun. Thus, handguns are essentially a defensive weapon, although some handguns are considered offensive weapons by the military.

An offensive weapon is one that is used to carry the fight to the enemy and thus some handguns are used offensively. A typical "offensive" handgun is the special operations' Mark 23 Mod 0, manufactured by Heckler & Koch. M1911A1 pistols have also been converted for offensive use by some elements of the US military, most of whom consider the Mark 23 too large. Regardless of one's opinion as to one firearm versus another, special operations units tend to have large budgets and can usually purchase any item of equipment they desire within bounds of reason and fiscal policy.

In today's American military and law enforcement organizations, the pistol has largely replaced the revolver. The US military bought its first pistol in 1911 – the classic M1911 that is still in widespread use by military and police units to this day and shows no signs of demise. Until the 1980s, most law enforcement organizations used revolvers, but that is no longer the case and revolvers have been largely replaced by Glock pistols of one version or another. There are advantages and disadvantages to both types of handgun and we will explore these in some detail below.

The military pistol is almost universally chambered in 9x19mm, or 9mm Parabellum, introduced by Germany in 1902. The same is generally true for law enforcement, except in the United States, where the .40 Smith & Wesson cartridge predominates. In the US military, the 9mm is the cartridge of choice for the "big" military, but many special operations organizations continue to use handguns in .45 ACP, either the Mark 23, Mod 0 or modified versions of the M1911A1, mentioned above. In general, 9x19mm is almost universally the pistol cartridge of choice, primarily because it has reasonable stopping power and mild recoil. It is also the official pistol cartridge of NATO, whose treaty terms call for standardization of ammunition, among other things. Despite this, the United States announced that its next military handgun will be in .45 caliber, probably due to many wartime reports of the relative ineffectiveness of the 9mm against enemy personnel.

Although the pistol predominates in the handgun world of the early 21st Century, there is still room for the traditional revolver, which has many attributes. First, the revolver is simple to operate. With any modern double action revolver, i.e. one in which pulling the trigger cocks the hammer, rotates the cylinder and releases the hammer to fire the revolver, all that is necessary is to pull the trigger through one full cycle. If better accuracy is desired, the hammer can be manually cocked and the revolver fired single action.

A modern revolver is inherently safe. The hammer is prevented from contact with the firing pin via a transfer bar on most modern revolvers unless it is cocked and the trigger pulled. A limitation of the revolver is that no revolver can hold as many cartridges as some high capacity pistols. The greatest number of rounds that can be carried in a .38 Special/.357 Magnum revolver is eight, whereas many pistols have magazine capacities of 15 rounds or more. For those who are not willing to undergo the specialized training that is necessary to operate a semiautomatic pistol, the revolver remains the best choice. For example, if a pistol misfires, there is a set procedure that must be followed to clear the stoppage and this procedure must be ingrained and instinctive. With a revolver, all that is necessary in case of a misfire is to pull the trigger, bringing a fresh cartridge in line with the barrel. For this reason, many police organizations continue to issue revolvers to their officers who generally are not sufficiently trained in the use of firearms to use a pistol. This is the case with Singapore, whose government recently ordered 10,000 Taurus .38 Special revolvers for issue to its police officers.

Although the handgun, whether pistol or revolver is generally a secondary military weapon, it remains the primary weapon of most law enforcement agencies and will continue to do for the foreseeable future. Although there have been efforts by some firearms manufacturers in Europe to introduce "personal defense weapons" in calibers whose ballistics are closer to those of a .22 Magnum than a 9mm, these have yet to seriously challenge the traditional handgun.

With respect to handgun ammunition, there have been few revolutionary developments. Two companies in the United States, LeMas Ammunition and Extreme Shock USA have recently introduced ammunition that purports to deliver revolutionary terminal ballistics. The author has personally witnessed tests of this ammunition against anesthetized pigs and indications are that it does, indeed, deliver levels of performance far beyond conventional handgun ammunition, although it is too early to make definitive statements regarding this new ammunition's effectiveness. Both types of ammunition make use of new technologies in their bullet construction, which apparently causes enhanced terminal ballistics.

Austria

Glock 17, 17L, 17C, 22, 24/24C and 31
9x19mm/.40 S&W and .357 SIG pistols

The basic Glock system that originated with the Glock 17 is used in all Glock pistols is a locked-breech polymer-framed handgun. Rather than traditional locking lugs, the Browning system has been modified so that a squared portion of the breech interfaces with the ejection port to lock the slide and barrel together. The slide rides on steel rails molded into the polymer frame. The pistol is striker fired, with overall function controlled by the trigger. Initial pressure on the trigger disengages the trigger safety, a small tab that blocks the trigger's movement when not depressed. Five millimeters further trigger movement causes the trigger bar to cock the striker, which is essentially in a half-cock and secure position at all times when the pistol is ready to fire. Continued movement releases the integral striker lock. The striker is then released to fire the pistol. Trigger pull can be adjusted by fitting trigger bars and springs of different configurations. There is no external safety, since the trigger safety, firing-pin safety and drop safety will not permit the pistol to fire unless the trigger is correctly pulled. All three safeties work automatically and independently of each other. They disengage in sequence when the trigger is pulled and re-engage automatically after each round has been fired and the trigger has been released.

Since its introduction in the early 1980s, the Glock 17 and Glock pistols in other calibers have been adopted by thousands of military and police forces worldwide. The Glock 17, in particular, is noted for its longevity, reliability and ruggedness. The record number of rounds fired through a Glock 17 is some 300,000-rounds and the pistol was still functioning afterwards. Glocks have been frozen, immersed in mud, sand and about any material known to exist on planet earth and they continue to function with almost total reliability.

Glock 17L/24

This model is of the same design as the Glock 17 except for a longer barrel and slide. Most components are interchangeable with the Glock 17. The Glock 24 is identical except for being chambered for .40 S&W caliber.

Glock 17C and 24C (Compensated)

The Glock 17C and 24C pistols have integral compensators that reduce muzzle jump by some 25 to 30 percent, improving control for quick follow-up shots. Other than the compensator, the Glock 17C and 24C is identical to the Glock 17 and 22, respectively.

Glock 22

The Glock 22 is virtually identical to the standard Glock 17 except being chambered for the more powerful .40 S&W cartridge. The Glock 22 has gained widespread acceptance by US Law enforcement and is the standard-issue pistol of many agencies, including the FBI.

Glock 31/31C

The Glock 31/31C is identical to the basic Glock 17/17C, except for its .357 SIG caliber and small weight differences.

Glock 17

SPECIFICATIONS:
Caliber: 9x19mm; G22/24: .40 S&W; G31, .357 SIG
Operation: Short-recoil, semiautomatic
Locking: Modified Browning system
Feed: 17-round detachable box magazine.
G22/24: 15-round detachable box magazine.
Empty weight: G17, 22.07 ounces; G17/24L 23.63 ounces;
G17/24C 21.87 ounces; G31/31C, 23.28/23.10 ounces.
Overall Length: 7.32 inches (G17L/24 8.85 inches)
Barrel length: 4.49 inches (G17L/24 6.02 inches)
Rifling: hexagonal rh, 1 turn in 9.84 inches
Sights: Fixed or click-adjustable, depending on model.
Front, blade; rear: notch

Glock 18 select-fire pistol

The Glock 18 selective-fire automatic pistol was developed from the Glock 17 by adding a fire-selector assembly allowing semiautomatic or automatic fire and offering a larger magazine capacity. The Glock Model 18C has a built-in compensator with four ports in the barrel to assist the shooter in maintaining control when the pistol is fired in the automatic mode.

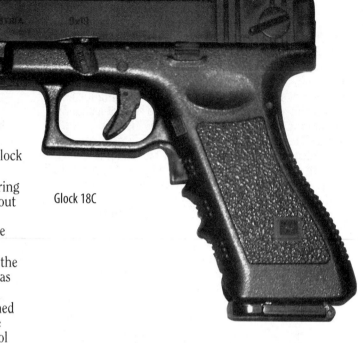

Glock 18C

For security reasons, the main components of the Glock 18 are not interchangeable with the Glock 17.

The Glock 18 provides the user with the option of firing trigger-controlled bursts from a lightweight pistol without the need for a shoulder stock. The optional 31-round box magazine provides a sufficient amount of immediate firepower.

By simply changing the position of the fire selector, the Glock 18 can be used in the same semiautomatic mode as the other Glock models.

Glock strongly recommends that only specially trained personnel should as a general rule be allowed to use the Glock 18, since the effective and safe operation of a pistol when fired in the automatic mode requires special training and high personal discipline.

SPECIFICATIONS:

Caliber: 9x19mm
Operation: short-recoil, select-fire
Locking: Modified Browning system
Feed: detachable box magazine, 17, 19 or 31-rounds
Empty weight, 21.9 ounces
Overall length: 7.32 inches
Barrel length: 4.49 inches
Rifling: hexagonal, rh, 1 turn 9.84 inches
Cyclic rate: approx 1,200 rounds per minute

Glock 19

GLOCK 19/19C, 23/23C, 25 and 32/32C, 9x19mm, .40 S&W, /9x17mm(.380 ACP) and .357 SIG pistols

The Glock 19 9x19mm pistol is a compact version of the Glock 17 intended for concealed carry. Except for different dimensions, The Glock 19 is the same basic design as the Glock 17 and most components will interchange. The Glock 19 magazine holds only 15-rounds, although Glock 17 magazines can be inserted into a Glock 19, they will protrude well below the Glock 19's magazine well. The Glock 23 is identical to the Glock 19, except for chambering in .40 S&W. The Glock 25 is identical to the Glock 19, save for being chambered in 9x17mm/.380 ACP. The Glock 25 is intended primarily for civilian ownership in areas where pistols chambered in 9x19mm are prohibited. The Glock 25 is not available in the United States. The Glock 32 is dimensionally identical to the Glock 19 except that it is chambered for .357 SIG.

GLOCK 19C, 23C and 32C

The Glock 19C, 23C and 32C have integral compensators that reduce muzzle jump some 25 to 30 percent, improving control for fast follow-up shots. The Glock 19C, 23C and 32C are dimensionally identical to the standard Glock 19, 23 and 32.

Glock 26

SPECIFICATIONS: Data for Glock 19, 23, 25 and 32

Caliber: Glock 19, 9x19mm; Glock 23, .40 S&W, Glock 25, 9x17mm/.380 ACP; Glock 32, .357 SIG
Operation: short-recoil, semiautomatic
Locking: Modified Browning system
Feed: 15-round detachable box magazine
Empty weight: Glock 19, 1.3 lb. 19C, 1.29 lb. G23, 1.32 lb. 23C, 1.31 lb.; G32, 1.34 lb. oz; 32C, 1.33 lb.
Overall length: 6.85 inches
Barrel length: 4.02 inches
Rifling: hexagonal, rh, G19/23/25 1 turn in 9.84 in.; G32, 1 turn in 15.9 in
Sights: Front, blade; rear: notch

GLOCK 26, 27, 28 and 33 9x19mm/.40 S&W/ 9x17mm (.380 ACP)/.357 SIG subcompact pistols

The 9x19mm Glock 26 was introduced in the mid 1990s, followed shortly by the .40 S&W Glock 27, the Glock 28 in 9x17mm (.380 ACP) and the Glock 33 in .357 SIG caliber. All four pistols are virtually identical, except for caliber. In the United States, the Glock 28 is available only to law enforcement agencies. These are among the most compact Glock pistols available and are widely used by law

enforcement officers for backup or off-duty carry, having generally replaced the traditional small-framed revolvers for similar purposes. The subcompact Glocks offer twice the number of cartridges in a package that is smaller than five- or six-shot compact revolvers.

SPECIFICATIONS:

Caliber: G26,9x19mm; G27, .40 S&W ; G28, 9x17mm (.380 ACP); G33, .357 SIG
Operation: short-recoil, semiautomatic
Locking: Modified Browning system
Feed: G26/G28, 12-round detachable box magazine; G27, detachable 10-round box magazine, G33, 11-round detachable box magazine.
Empty weight: 1.23 lb.
Overall length: 6.29 inches
Barrel length: 4.46 inches
Rifling: hexagonal, rh, 1 turn in 9.84 inches (G33, 1 turn in 15.98 inches)
Sights: Front, blade; rear: notch

Glock 29 and 30 10mm and .45 ACP subcompact pistols

The Glock 29 10mm and 30 subcompact pistols were developed to meet a market requirement for compact pistols combining maximum major-caliber firepower with standard Glock features. These models differ in only a few details as noted below.

SPECIFICATIONS:

Caliber: G29, 10mm Auto; G30, .45 ACP
Operation: short-recoil, semiautomatic
Locking: Modified Browning system
Feed: 10-round detachable box magazine
Empty weight: G29, 1.54 lb.; G30 1.49 lb.
Overall length: 6.77 inches
Barrel length: 3.78 inches
Rifling: G29, hexagonal, rh, 1 turn in 9.84 inches; G30, octagonal, rh, 1 turn in 15.75 inches
Sights: Front, blade; rear: notch

Glock 33

Glock 29

Austria
Glock

Glock 34

Glock 34 and 35 pistols

The Glock 34 and 35 pistols were developed to meet the requirements of competitive shooters who have to meet requirements for a competition pistol that essentially matches the dimensions of an M1911 Government Model pistol. The Glock 34 is chambered in 9x19mm, while the Glock 35 fires .40 S&W ammunition. Although designed for competition use, both pistols, especially the Glock 35, have gained widespread use in American law enforcement as duty weapons.

SPECIFICATIONS:		
Model	GLOCK 34	GLOCK 35
Caliber:	9x19mm	.40 S&W
Operation: short-recoil, semiautomatic		
Locking: Modified Browning system		
Feed: Detachable box magazine		
Magazine Capacity:	17-rounds	15-rounds
Empty Weight:	1.43 lb.	1.53 lb.
Overall Length:	8.15 inches	8.15 inches
Barrel Length:	5.32 inches	5.32 inches
Sights: Front, blade; rear: notch		

Glock 36 .45 ACP slim-line subcompact pistol

The Glock 36 .45 ACP subcompact pistol was introduced in early 1999. The G36 uses a single-stack magazine as opposed to the double-stack magazines of all other Glock pistols in order to reduce the overall size of the grip, while still maintaining the .45 ACP cartridge. Because of this, magazine capacity is reduced to six rounds. The G36 retains all the normal features associated with Glock pistols.

SPECIFICATIONS:
Caliber: .45 ACP
Operation: short-recoil, semiautomatic
Locking: Modified Browning System
Feed: six-round detachable box magazine
Empty weight: 1.25 lb.
Overall length: 6.77 inches
Width: 1.13 inches
Barrel length: 3.78 inches
Rifling: hexagonal, rh, 1 turn in 15.75 inches
Sights: fixed or click-adjustable; front, blade; rear: notch

Glock 37 .45 GAP Pistol

The Glock 37 .45 GAP (Glock Automatic Pistol) pistol was introduced in 2003. The Glock 37 is a 'full-size' Glock pistol similar in size to the Glock 17, rather than to the larger Glock 21. The Glock 37 was developed with its new cartridge to provide a pistol with ballistics comparable to those of the larger Glock 21, but with grips small enough to accommodate the hands of smaller shooters, many of whom have problems with the Glock 21's relatively large grip area.

The .45 GAP cartridge is slightly shorter than the standard .45 ACP to allow a smaller magazine well and grip. The case head is slightly rebated to accommodate the slide originally designed for 9mm pistols. The cartridge was a joint development between CCI/Speer and Glock. .45 GAP ballistics are comparable to the longer .45 ACP.

SPECIFICATIONS:
Caliber: .45 Glock Automatic Pistol (GAP)
Operation: short-recoil, semiautomatic
Locking: Modified Browning system
Feed: 10-round detachable box magazine
Empty weight: 1.43 lb.
Overall length: 7.8 inches
Barrel length: 4.6 inches
Width: 1.13 inches
Rifling: octagonal, rh, 1 turn in 15.75 inches
Sights: Front, blade; rear: notch

Glock 36

Belgium

FNH Browning High Power M1935 pistol

The initial design work for the Browning High Power pistol was begun in 1925 by John M. Browning and he was granted a US Patent for it in February 1927, some three months after his death. At the time of Browning's death, the pistol design was little more than a few preliminary drawings. It was left to Dieudonne Saive, Browning's assistant and protégé at FN, to finalize the design and get it into production. Although less well known than Browning, Saive was a genius whose talents were nearly equal to those of his mentor. Saive was also responsible for several other firearm designs, not the least of which was the FN Fusil Automatique Leger, or FAL (See separate entry.)

The High Power entered production in 1935 and is still often referred to as the Model 1935. When initially introduced, two versions were available: the 'standard model' with fixed sights, and a model with a tangent rear sight graduated to 500 meters with a dovetail slot in the backstrap to accept a shoulder stock attached to a leather holster, was known as the 'adjustable rear sight model'. The pistol was designated Grande Puissance or GP by FN. This translates into "High Power" in English, and the name has been associated with the pistol ever since.

The High Power was notable for several "firsts," the most significant of which was the 13-round high-capacity "double-stack" magazine that enabled the pistol to carry nearly twice the number of cartridges of the "single-stack" designs. The High Power also incorporated a magazine safety that prevented the pistol from firing with the magazine withdrawn, although many Special Forces users of the pistol remove this feature, a task that is simple and quick to accomplish.

The High Power was originally manufactured in Belgium by FN Herstal SA (now FN HERSTAL), Liege. At the outbreak of World War II, it was in service not only in Belgium, but in Denmark, Lithuania, The Netherlands and Romania. During World War II the pistol was made by FN for the German military, which captured the plant. Dieudonne Saive escaped to Britain and although he had no drawings for the High Power, he developed an entire technical data package from memory and took it to Canada where the High Power was produced by the John Inglis Company for use by Australian, British, Canadian and Chinese troops. It remains in production in several countries and continues in active military and law enforcement service worldwide. An example of the longevity of this classic handgun is the 2001 UK Ministry of Defense order for 2,000 High Power pistols (known to the British Army as the 9mm L9A1) from FNH.

FNH states that the number of High Power pistols produced, including the later versions, is well over 10 million. It has seen service in over 100 countries. The only major modification to the pistol's overall design since its introduction has been an improved extractor, incorporated in the 1960s. Minor changes include ambidextrous safety switches and the availability of match-type adjustable sights.

In the 1990s the High Power was also produced in .40 S&W caliber. Since the cartridge dimensions of the .40 S&W are close to those of the original 9x19mm, the redesign was not an overly difficult one and the High Power continues to be manufactured in both calibers.

SPECIFICATIONS:
Caliber: 9x19mm and .40 S&W
Operation: recoil, semiautomatic
Locking: Browning system
Feed: 13-round detachable box magazine (10-round detachable box magazine)
Empty weight: 1.9 pounds
Overall length: 7.8 inches
Barrel length: 4.6 inches
Rifling: 6 grooves, rh, 1 turn in 9.8 inches
Sights: Front, blade or barleycorn, depending on model; rear: square notch or other types, depending on model.

FN Herstal's Five-seveN Pistol

FN Herstal's (FNH) Five-seveN pistol's genesis dates to the mid-1980s when FNH began design work on what would eventually become the 5.7x28mm P90 submachine gun (SMG). The P90 was originally envisioned as a weapon for troops who needed both hands for other tasks, such as officers, NCOs and technical troops who also needed more "punch" than a 9x19mm pistol could offer. The 5.7x28mm cartridge was designed to defeat NATO CRISAT body armor that replicated Soviet body armor of the time. The main defeat mechanism is the SS190 bullet that contains a steel and aluminum core. Other bullets in the 5.7x28mm family do not have the same capabilities as the SS190. With the demise of the Soviet Union and changing threats, the vision of the P90 also changed and FNH's focus for the weapon shifted to special operations and law enforcement. As time progressed, it became clear that a pistol was needed as an adjunct to the P90 SMG, so in the mid-1990s FNH set out to design a handgun to accompany the "high-tech" P90 SMG. Early Five-seveN pistols had a different appearance than current ones and also were functionally somewhat

WW II INGLIS M1935

FNH M1935

different. The "Five-seveN" name with emphasis on the "F" and "N" reminds everyone of the pistol's origin. We'll go into the various permutations of the Five-seveN pistol below, but first we need to examine the ammunition, which is the most controversial aspect of the handgun.

Some have claimed that the 5.7x28mm bullet "tumbles" when it encounters tissue, suggesting that the bullet actually tumbles end over end, acting like a small buzz saw as it passes through. This is patently false. No bullet "tumbles" in such a way when it strikes tissue. What some high-velocity bullets do is rotate a half turn or 180 degrees until they are base-forward. This is because the naturally stable condition of any pointed bullet is base-forward. Bullets are stabilized nose-forward by the spin imparted to them by the barrel's rifling. If a bullet is traveling with sufficient velocity, when it strikes a target and begins to slow down both in velocity and spin rate, it loses its stability and tries to return to its naturally stable state – base-forward. This creates a larger wound path over a short length as the bullet takes a half turn, but it does not "tumble." The 5.7mm bullet is no different in this regard.

The original Five-seveN was aimed at the military market, which was and remains limited – primarily due to logistics that simply cannot accommodate yet another cartridge and firearm in an already stressed system. Thus FN began exploring other markets, primarily law enforcement. The original Five-seveNs were available in two versions – a double action only (DAO) and a single

action (SA) "Tactical" version. These versions also had a proprietary mounting rail on the dust cover for lights and lasers and a rounded trigger guard specifically designed to accommodate gloved fingers. Approximately two years ago, FNH USA began importing the Individual Officer's Model (IOM) Five-seveN, with target type sights, magazine disconnector and MIL-STD-1913 rail mount on the dust cover for sale to authorized police officers. The current Five-seveN being offered by FNH USA is the USG (US Government) Model that incorporates quite a number of improvements over earlier models.

Generally, all Five-seveN models follow the same design with a steel slide enclosed by a polymer cover that, except for the ejection port and a small section at the muzzle end, completely surrounds the slide. The slide itself is unusual in that it cycles on an innovative "three-rail" system. There are two short rails at the rear of the frame and a long single "T" shaped rail inside the dust cover that mates to a similar shaped interface at the slide front. The rear slots in the slide are conventional in appearance and function. Although the slide is relatively heavy and all steel beneath the polymer cover, the only metal in the frame is the fire-control mechanism and guide rails. All Five-seveN pistols are delayed blowback operated with a strong spring that surrounds the barrel and is retained by a collar at the muzzle end. The collar is fixed in place by a small spring-steel ring just behind the muzzle. An unusual loaded chamber indicator is located on the left side of the slide

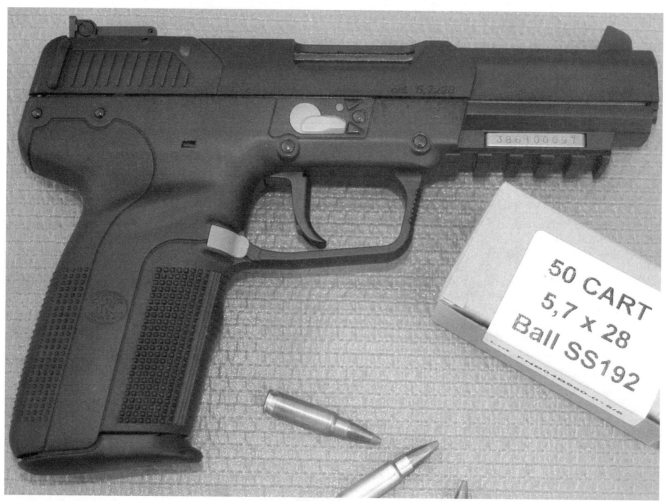

FNH Five Seven

just behind and opposite the ejection port. The indicator is a small stainless steel pin whose lower end protrudes into the breech face. When a cartridge is chambered, it rises above the slide surface providing both a visible and tactile indicator of the load status of the pistol. A magazine safety prevents the pistol from firing with the magazine removed. The barrel is cold hammer forged, hard-chrome plated, and is claimed to have a service life of 20,000 rounds.

As mentioned, the current USG Model has some significant modifications and improvements over earlier pistols. Although the USG Model appears to be striker-fired from external appearances, it is actually a single-action handgun that can be carried in Condition One or "cocked and locked." Thus, the manual of arms is essentially similar to the classic M1911, although the ambidextrous safety is in a different location forward on the frame just above the trigger. The location is ideal for manipulation with the index finger on the right side or, if one is using a two-handed grip, by the supporting hand's thumb. The complaint about the safety is that it is a bit narrow for positive manipulation, especially when moving it to the "on" position, although this is less critical than sweeping it off. An added benefit of this location for the safety is that it helps shooters keep their fingers off the trigger until they are ready to shoot. The magazine release is excellent and can be reversed by the user if he or she happens to be left-handed. The slide release is a right-hand-only proposition and given the internals of the Five-seveN, there isn't much FNH could do about it – the fire-control components are in the way of an ambidextrous slide release. All controls are well-placed and it is clear that FNH took some care in getting the ergonomics right.

Besides serrations at the rear of the slide, there are two raised "bumps" at the very rear of the slide. These make pulling the slide really easy with the thumb and index finger. Sights are excellent with a fully adjustable rear notch and large square blade front sight.

The frame of the USG Model Five-seveN has been significantly improved over previous versions. The grip has nicely embossed checkering everywhere it counts and nobody should have problems gripping this pistol. There are thumb rests on both sides and the trigger guard has been squared off as opposed to the rather odd rounded one of previous models. Moreover, FNH kept the grip angle of the M1911 and M1935 that makes those pistols and this one point naturally.

We've noted that the USG Five-seveN is a single-action pistol. The hammer is internal and connected to the trigger by a transfer bar. The trigger mechanism is a two-stage type with short take up, some creep and a crisp break with no discernable backlash. As the trigger reaches the end of its travel to release the sear and drop the hammer, a small finger rotates into position to press and release the firing pin safety. It is an excellent design that does not affect trigger pull.

SPEFICICATIONS: FNH USG Five-seveN Pistol

Caliber: 5.7x28mm
Operation: delayed blowback, semiautomatic
Overall length: 8.2 inches
Empty weight: 1.7 lbs.*
Barrel length: 4.75 inches
Width: 1.25 in. (measured at safety)
Height: 5.75 in.
Magazine capacity: 20 rounds

Belgian equipment display

Brazil

Taurus PT92, PT99, PT100 and PT101 series 9x19mm and .40 S&W Pistols

The original Taurus PT92 was developed when Forjas Taurus took over a manufacturing facility established by Beretta to produce Model 92 pistols. Taurus undertook several modifications to the original design by changing over to complete use of forgings for all major components and by making significant modifications to the fire control system. The Beretta system with the safety switch and de-cocker on the slide was moved to the frame and made more easily accessible to the shooter's thumb. Controls are fully ambidextrous. The Taurus pistols can safely be carried "cocked and locked" or can be used with double-action for the first shot and single-action thereafter (DA/SA). The topmost position of the safety is "safe," the intermediate position "fire" and pressing the switch fully down de-cocks the pistol. Latest versions have a firing pin safety and Taurus' proprietary locking system that allows the pistol to be locked and rendered inoperable with a small key. The lock rises above the surface of the backstrap when

9mm Imbel

Brazil special operations forces

Taurus PT92

engaged, giving a visible and tactile indication that it is engaged. Taurus pistols have a loaded-chamber indicator that provides a visible and tactile indication of whether or not a cartridge is chambered.

Locking is by falling block similar to that introduced by Walther and the pistols operate by the short-recoil principle.

These pistols are available in a variety of finishes, including standard blue and stainless steel. The PT 92 and PT100 have fixed sights, while the PT99 and PT101 have sights that are adjustable for windage and elevation. Trijicon tritium sights are optional on the latter pistols. A variety of grips are also available, including standard rubber, rosewood and mother of pearl.

Taurus PT99

SPECIFICATIONS: PT92/99 *(PT100/101 in parentheses where different)*
Caliber: 9x19mm (.40 S&W)
Operation: Semiautomatic, short-recoil
Locking: Falling block
Feed: 17-round detachable box magazine (11-round detachable box magazine)
Empty weight: 2.1 lb.
Overall length: 8.5 inches
Barrel length: 5 inches
Sights: PT92/100:Front, blade, rear fixed notch. PT99/101:Front, blade; rear: notch adjustable for windage and elevation. Tritium optional.

Taurus 24/7 9x19mm and .40 Smith & Wesson Pistol

The Taurus 24/7 was the result of over four years of research into the requirements of law enforcement and tactical users and the result is the first Taurus handgun designed from the outset for law enforcement and tactical users. The 24/7 has a polymer frame with the rails on which the slide rides separate from the frame itself and pinned into place so that if the polymer frame is damaged, it can be replaced. Unlike many polymer-framed pistols, the 24/7 system provides full length rails for support and consistency.

The 24/7 grip angle mimics that of the classic M1911 pistol, which most authorities consider to be the best natural pointing handgun ever developed. The 24/7 grip is a rubber "overmold" design with ribs called "RIbber Grips ®" that adapt to the contour of any shooter's hand. Recessed "memory pads" on either side of the frame help achieve a consistent grip, aiding accuracy.

Taurus .40S&W PT24-7

Despite being a double-action only striker fired pistol with several passive safeties including a firing pin safety that blocks the pin until the trigger is fully squeezed, the 24/7 incorporates a manual safety, since it has been proven that officers who have their pistols taken by a suspect may well survive, since most street criminals do not know how to release a manual safety. Once the use of the safety is learned, it becomes instinctive and is as fast into action as any system.

The 24/7 also features a bushingless barrel and a MIL-STD-1913 rail on the dust cover for mounting lights and lasers. Sights are of the combat type with tritium night sights optional. Like all recent Taurus pistols, the 24/7 has a locking system and loaded-chamber indicator. Both provide visible and tactile indicators of status. Blue or stainless slides are available.

SPECIFICATIONS: (SPECIFICATIONS: are for 24/7 9x19mm; .40 S&W in parentheses where different)

Caliber: 9x19mm (.40 S&W)
Operation: Short-recoil, semiautomatic
Locking: Modified Browning system
Feed: Detachable box magazine 17-round capacity (15-round capacity)
Empty weight: 1.7 lb.
Overall length: 7.125 inches
Barrel length: 4 inches
Sights: Front, blade; rear: combat type, fixed

Taurus PT911, PT938 and PT940 9x19mm, .380 ACP and .40 S&W Pistols

The 9x19mm PT911, .380 ACP PT938 and .40 S&W PT940 medium framed pistols are essentially scaled down versions of the PT92 and PT100 series above with the addition of .380 ACP (9x17mm) caliber and modifying the larger pistols to use a modified Browning locking system rather than the falling block system of the larger handguns. Other features are virtually identical to the larger pistols, except for overall size and magazine capacity. Controls are virtually identical to the larger pistols.

Like the larger Taurus pistols, these medium framed handguns are available in a variety of finishes and with rubber, rosewood and mother of pearl grips.

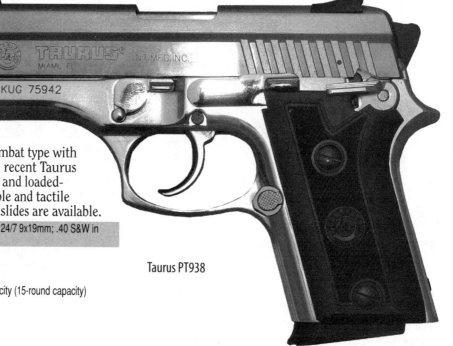

Taurus PT938

SPECIFICATIONS: PT1911
(Data for PT938 and PT940 in parentheses where different.)
Caliber: PT911, 9x19mm; PT138, .380 ACP; PT940, .40 S&W.
Operation: Short-recoil, semiautomatic.
Locking: Modified Browning system.
Feed: Detachable box magazine, 15-round capacity (PT940, 11-round capacity)
Empty weight: 1.76 lb. (PT138, 1.64 lb.)
Overall length: 7 inches
Barrel length: 4 inches
Sights: Front, blade; rear notch, combat type. (Tritium night sights available)

Taurus PT938 and PT945 .38 Super and .45 ACP pistols

The large framed Taurus PT38 and PT945 pistols are derived from the PT92 and PT100, but with a Browning type locking system and grip angle modified to that of the M1911. In .45 ACP caliber, the PT945 actually feels and shoots like a M1911 in "Commander" configuration.

Controls are identical to those of the PT92 and PT100, with three position safety that allows the pistol to be carried safely "cocked and locked" for speed into getting the pistol into action. The frame of these pistols is of hammer forged aircraft aluminum for strength and reliability as are slides and barrels. Controls are fully ambidextrous and these pistols also have Taurus' usual loaded-chamber indicator and unique security system. Both provide a visible and tactile indication of their status.

A variety of finishes and grips are available, including blue or stainless. Grip options include rubber, rosewood or mother of pearl. Sights are combat type with tritium night sights optional. The .38 Super PT938 is available only in stainless steel with mother of pearl grips and gold-plated controls as of the time of this writing. (Late 2004)

SPECIFICATIONS: PT945 (PT938 in parentheses where different)
Caliber: .45 ACP (.38 Super)
Operation: Short-recoil, semiautomatic.
Locking: Modified Browning system.
Feed: Detachable box magazine, 8 rounds capacity (10 rounds capacity)
Empty weight: 1.84 lb.
Overall length: 7.5 inches
Barrel length: 4.25 inches
Sights: Front, blade; rear: notch, combat type (Tritium night sights available)

Bulgaria

Arcus-98DA and Arcus-98DAC 9mm pistols

The Arcus-98DA pistol is chambered for the 9x19mm cartridge and is similar to the earlier 9mm Arcus-94 (see separate entry). The differences are that the Arcus-98 incorporates a double-action feature for the first shot and that the magazine holds 15-rounds. The Arcus-98DA is a conventional design with many similarities to Browning pistols and it somewhat resembles the Browning M1935, although numerous cosmetic alterations have been made to the pistol's exterior. The Arcus-98DA is available in several varieties with optional grips, finishes and magazine capacities of either 10 or 15-rounds.

There is also an Arcus-98DAC (Compact) model. The DAC's barrel is shorter and the pistol's weight somewhat reduced. Magazine capacity of the compact version is 13-

Arcus 98DA

rounds, but other features are the same as the full size Arcus-98DA.

The Arcus-98DA can be converted to fire .22LR cartridges for training purposes. The kit (Arcus-98M) is installed by simply exchanging the slide and barrel for the components in the kit, and replacing the standard magazine with a .22LR unit of eight rounds capacity.

SPECIFICATIONS: Arcus-98DA (Arcus-98DAC in parentheses)
Caliber: 9x19mm
Operation: Recoil, semiautomatic, double-action/single-action
Locking: Modified Browning system
Feed: 10- or 15-round box magazine (10- or 13-round box magazine)
Empty weight: 2.1 pounds (2.0 pounds)
Overall length: 8 inches (7.3 inches)
Height: 5.5 inches (5.1 inches)
Barrel length: 4.7 inches (4.0 inches)
Rifling: 6 grooves, RH twist
Sights: Three Dot. Front: blade; rear: notch, adjustable for windage

China

NORINCO 7.62x17mm Type 77 Pistol

The NORINCO 7.62x17mm Type 77 is a light pistol intended for use by senior officers, military attaches, diplomatic security, undercover police and other personnel who do not require a rifle or service-type pistol. It fires the rimless 7.62x17mm Type 64 cartridge, which is also used with the Type 64 silenced pistol.

The Type 77's design is somewhat unusual, reviving a one hand cocking operating system that originated with the German Lignose/Bergmann pistols in the early 20th Century. The pistol operated by delayed blowback and usually is carried with a loaded magazine and an empty chamber. To fire the pistol, the trigger finger is hooked around the front edge of the trigger guard, which is then pulled to the rear. This retracts the slide and when the finger is released, the slide returns to battery, stripping a cartridge from the magazine and chambering it. By simply moving the finger to the trigger, the weapon is ready to fire. The trigger guard is not fixed to the slide and thus does reciprocate when the pistol is fired. This method of operation also allows the slide to quickly be retracted single handedly in case of a misfire, ejecting the faulty round and chambering a fresh one.

The chamber is fluted to reduce gas pressure on the cartridge case base, thus reducing slide velocity.

The NORINCO 9x19mm Type 77B pistol uses a similar operating system.

SPECIFICATIONS:
Caliber: 7.62 x 17mm (Type 64)
Operation: Delayed blowback
Feed: 7-round detachable box magazine
Empty weight: 1.1 pounds
Overall length: 5.8 inches

NORINCO 7.62x25mm Type 54 and 9x19mm Series 213 Pistols

The NORINCO Type 54 7.62x25mm pistol is a copy of the Soviet 7.62x25mm Tokarev TT-33 and for many years was the standard People's Liberation Army handgun. The Chinese version is distinguished from Soviet or Polish versions by the slide serrations. The Soviet and Polish pistols have a series of alternate wide and narrow vertical cuts while Chinese manufactured pistols have uniform

Norinco Type 213

Norinco Type77

Norinco Type 54

narrow vertical serrations. The
Hungarian Model 48 and Serbian Model
M57 also have uniform narrow slots, but
the Type 54 has Chinese markings on the receiver or top of
the slide. The Serbian pistol is marked "7.62mm M57" on
the left side of the slide, while the Hungarian Model 48 has
a Communist emblem consisting of a star, sheaf of wheat
and hammer surrounded by a wreath on the grip.

The Series 213 pistols are commercial models
chambered in 9x19mm caliber. There are three models.

The basic Model 213 is essentially a Type 54 modified to
fire 9x19mm cartridges.

The Model 213A is a Model 213 with a 14-round capacity
box magazine.

The Model 213B is a Model 213 with contoured grips to
enhance comfort while shooting.

SPECIFICATIONS: Type 54

Caliber: 7.62 x 25mm
Operation: recoil, semiautomatic
Locking: Modified Browning System
Feed: 8-round detachable box magazine
Empty weight: .9 pounds
Overall length: 7.7 inches
Barrel length: 4.5 inches
Rifling: 4 grooves, rh twist
Sights: front, blade; rear: notch
Max effective range: 50 m

Series 213 Model 213A Pistol

Caliber: 9x19mm
Operation: recoil, semiautomatic
Locking: Modified Browning System
Feed: 14-round box magazine
Front: 2.0 pounds
Overall length: 7.7 inches
Barrel length: 4.6 inches
Rifling: 4 grooves, rh twist
Sights: Front, blade; rear: notch

Norinco Type 84

NORINCO 7.62x17mm Type 84 pistol

The NORINCO 7.62mm Type 84 pistol is described in
Chinese literature as a 'special purpose anti-riot weapon'.
This miniature pistol is intended for use by security
personnel aboard aircraft, ships and trains. It was designed
for undercover use and is intended to subdue criminals
attempting to commit crimes where the penetration of
higher-velocity, larger caliber weapons would damage the
aircraft or vehicle on which the weapon is used.

The Type 84 pistol fires a 7.62 x 17mm cartridge,
produced only in China. It is blowback operated and striker
fired. While the Type 84-round will not penetrate the
passenger compartment walls of an airplane at 2 yards, it is
claimed to be lethal against human targets at 15 yards.

The standard Type 84 cartridge has a velocity of
approximately 1200 feet per second. The pistol also is
intended to be used with the 7.62x17mm Type 64 subsonic
cartridge with a velocity of only 525 feet per second.

Service life of the Type 84 Pistol is stated to be only
500-rounds, an astonishingly low expectancy.

SPECIFICATIONS:

Caliber: 7.62 x 17mm Type 84
Operation: blowback, semiautomatic
Feed: 6-round detachable box magazine
Empty weight: 3.4 ounces
Length: 4.7 inches
Barrel length: 2.2 inches
Sights: Front, blade; rear: notch, adjustable for windage

NORINCO 7.65x17mm Type 64 and Type 67 silenced pistols

The NORINCO Type 64 is a pistol produced only in
suppressed configuration. It may be used either as a
manually operated single-shot arm or as a self-loader.

When the maximum suppression is desired, the
selector is pushed to the left, the lugs of the rotating bolt
in the slide engage in recesses in the receiver and the
weapon fires from a locked-breech. The slide does not
cycle in this mode. After the round has been fired the slide
is hand-operated to unlock the bolt, retract the slide and
extract the fired case. When the selector is pushed to the
right, the locking lugs do not engage in the recesses in the
receiver and the pistol functions as a blowback-operated
semiautomatic. This is noisier, since the slide reciprocates
and the empty case is ejected. The cartridge is 7.65 x
17mm, made only in China. It is rimless and unique to this
pistol; no other round can be used.

Norinco Type 67

The suppressor is a large device on the front of the receiver extending well forward of the muzzle. The gases leave the muzzle and expand into a wire mesh cylinder surrounded by a metal sleeve. The bullet passes through a series of rubber baffles that trap the gases. When used as single-shot manually operated pistols the Type 64 and 67 are very quiet, but reduced muzzle velocities have a negative effect on terminal ballistics.

The Type 67 is an improved version of the Type 64; it is essentially the same as the Type 64, but the suppressor has been redesigned, making the weapon easier to carry in a holster. There are a few minor changes in the assembly of the suppressor, but the principle of operation remains the same. The Type 67 is chambered for the 7.62x17mm Type 67 cartridge, a subsonic rimless, necked round.

SPECIFICATIONS: Data for Type 64; where Type 67 differs, shown in parentheses

Caliber: 7.65 x 17mm rimless (7.62 Type 67 rimless)
Operation: Manual, single-shot or blowback, semiautomatic
Locking: Rotating bolt or inertia
Feed: 9-round box magazine
Empty weight: 2.1 lb. (2.3 lb.)
 Overall length: 8.7 inches (8.9 inches)
Barrel length: 3.7 inches (3.5 inches)
Rifling: 4 grooves, rh
Sights: Front, blade; rear: notch
Max effective range: 30 yards

NORINCO 9x19mm pistol Model 77B

The NORINCO 9x19mm Model 77B pistol is marketed for commercial and military sales and is similar in design to the 7.62mm Type 77 described in a separate entry. Not only does Type 77B fire the 9x19mm Parabellum cartridge but it apparently has a Browning-type locking system. The Model 77B carries over the single-handed cocking principle used with the Type 77, which operates by retracting the front of the trigger guard with one finger. The external appearance of the Model 77B is substantially different from the Type 77 and overall dimensions are much larger than those of the Type 77.

Once cocked, the Model 77B fires double-action only, and is provided with manual and magazine safeties.

The NORINCO 9x19mm NP 20 is similar to the Type 77B, but has a fixed trigger guard and conventional cocking. The weight is increased to 1.1 kg. The otherwise similar NP 24 has a 15-round magazine.

SPECIFICATIONS:

Caliber: 9x19mm Parabellum
Operation: short-recoil, semiautomatic
Feed: 9-round box magazine
Empty weight: 2.2 pounds
Overall length: 7.4 inches
Barrel length: 5 inches
Sights: Front: blade; rear: adjustable notch

NORINCO 9x18mm Type 59 pistol

The NORINCO 9x18mm Type 59 pistol is a copy of the Russian Federation Makarov pistol, so it is a blowback weapon with a double-action trigger. Further information can be found at the Makarov entry.

There is also a commercial version of the pistol, designated Type 59A or NP19, in .380 ACP (9x17mm) caliber. A third version, the NP39 is chambered for .32 ACP (7.65x17mm).

SPECIFICATIONS:

Caliber: 9x18mm Soviet (Type 59 in China)
Operation: blowback, semiautomatic double-action/single-action
Feed: 8-round detachable box magazine
Empty weight: 1.6 lb.
Overall length: 6.3 inches
Barrel length: 3.7 inches
Rifling: 4 grooves, rh
Sights: Front: blade, rear: U-notch

Norinco Type 59A

Norinco Type77B

Croatia

9x19mm/.40 S&W/.357 SIG HS 2000 (XD) pistol

The 9x19mm HS2000 pistol was first shown in 1999 and is basically an updated version of the earlier HS95 pistol The pistol has a metal frame bedded in a molded polymer grip to reduce both manufacturing costs and weight. The slide is steel. The polymer receiver is available not only in black, but green.

Several types of sights are available. Apart from the usual fixed rear and front sights, adjustable sights are also available, while the Trijicon or Heinie tritium sights are optional. The trigger mechanism is double-action-only. When a round is loaded in the chamber, the extractor rises above the slide surface to provide a visual and tactile indication that the pistol is loaded. A grip safety is provided. The grip safety not only blocks the striker, but also prevents the slide from being pulled to the rear unless it is depressed. A trigger safety similar to that of Glock, prevents the trigger from being pulled unless it is depressed. When the pistol is ready to fire, the striker protrudes from the rear of the slide, providing a visual and tactile indication of the pistol's status. All versions are equipped for mounting a tactical light on the dust cover. The basic service model is chambered in 9x19mm Parabellum, but is also available in .40 S&W and .357 SIG.

Field stripping is accomplished by withdrawing the slide, locking it back, removing the magazine, rotating a takedown lever and pulling the trigger to allow the slide to be removed to the front. These actions must be accomplished in the sequence indicated or the pistol cannot be disassembled. Because of its method of disassembly, the HS2000/XD cannot inadvertently be fired while being field stripped.

The HS2000 is manufactured by IM-METAL and is intended for military, police and civilian self-defense service. It has been marketed outside Croatia and has achieved notable success in both civilian sales and law enforcement agencies in the United States, where it is marketed by Springfield Armory as the XD. The basic service model has a 4-inch barrel, while a "tactical" version has a 5-inch barrel and the concealed carry sub compact has a 3-inch barrel and grip that is reduced in size for concealment.

SPECIFICATIONS:

Caliber: 9x19mm, .40 S&W or .357 SIG
Operation: Short-recoil, modified Browning system, semiautomatic.
Feed: 15-round box magazine (12-rounds in .40 S&W and .357 SIG) Subcompact Model has a 10-round capacity.
Empty weight: 1.56 lb.
Overall Length: Service Model, 7 inches; Tactical Model, 8 inches; Subcompact Model, 6 inches.
Barrel length: Service Model, 4.05 inches; tactical Model, 5 inches; Subcompact Model, 3 inches.
Rifling: 6 grooves, rh,
Sights: Front, blade; rear notch.

HS 2000

HS-2000 XD

Czech Republic

CZ Model 75 pistol

The CZ Model 75 pistol (CZ 75) was a new design that incorporated the best features of several other pistols. The designers were Josef and Frantisek Koucky. The CZ 75 is available in both 9x19mm Parabellum and .40 S&W.

CZ 75

The slide and frame are cast steel, while the barrel is forged. Grips can be either walnut or plastic. The angle and size of the grip is notable for its comfort and proper angle for excellent pointing characteristics. The slide stop, safety lever and magazine release are all on the left side of the frame. The CZ 75 was the first pistol to incorporate the "slide in frame" design with the slide operating on rails inside the frame rather than outside, a feature that resulted in enhanced reliability and better control because the barrel could be lowered significantly in the frame.

The CZ 75 was one of the first pistols with a large double-stack magazine of 16 rounds capacity in 9x19mm. The inertial firing pin is out of contact with the cartridge primer until struck by the hammer. Drop tests have shown that repeated muzzle down falls from 2 meters onto concrete will not cause the pistol to fire. The double-action first round capability does not require the slide to be retracted or the hammer cocked, so the pistol can be carried safely with a round in the chamber so that upon drawing the pistol to shoot, the only action necessary is to pull the trigger.

The CZ 75 has been adopted by numerous military and police forces worldwide and is extremely popular in the United States.

Variants

CZ Model 75B

This model is the current standard CZ 75 and incorporates a firing pin safety block.

CZ Model 75B/SD Tarantule

This is a suppressed version of the CZ 75B with a 15-round magazine and a 4.5 inch barrel threaded for a 11-inch-long, 1.3-inch-diameter suppressor. The suppressor is of steel and aluminum construction. With the suppressor fitted the pistol weighs 53.6 ounces empty and is 19.1 inches in overall length. The CZ75B/SD version is marketed in Europe by Caliber Prague Limited.

CZ Model 75BD

The CZ 75BD eliminates the safety lever, replacing it with a de-cocking lever that allows the hammer to be lowered with a round in the chamber. Otherwise the CZ75BD is identical to the CZ 75B.

CZ Model 75 SA

This is a single-action model with a drop free magazine that can safely be carried "cocked and locked."

CZ Model 75 Champion

This model, chambered in either 9x19mm or .40 S&W, is intended for IPSC shooting, with a three-port compensator at the muzzle, a single-action trigger mechanism, a match trigger, 12-round magazine, an extended magazine release and competition sights. The 9x19mm Parabellum version has a two port compensator and a 16-round magazine.

Kadet .22 LR Adapter

This is an accessory that converts a CZ 75 pistol to fire .22 LR ammunition. There is also a Kadet pistol dedicated in .22 LR. Some versions have a suppressor interface the CZ 75 Kadet SD Blecha. In this configuration the magazine holds 15-rounds and the weight is 1.06 kg. The suppressor is 130mm long and has a diameter of 30mm. The suppressor is constructed of steel and aluminum. With the suppressor fitted the pistol is 336mm long. This version is marketed by Caliber Prague Limited.

SPECIFICATIONS: CZ75B

Caliber: 9x19mm Parabellum; .40 S&W
Operation: short-recoil, modified Browning system, semiautomatic
Feed: 9x19mm: 6-round detachable box magazine; .40 S&W: 12-round detachable box magazine
Empty weight: 2.2 pounds
Length: 8.1 inches
Height: 5.4 inches
Width: approx 1.4 inches
Barrel length: 4.7 inches
Rifling: 6 grooves, rh,
Sights: Front, Blade; rear: square notch

9x19mm CZ Model 75 Compact

The CZ 9x19mm Model 75 compact is manufactured in 9x19mm Parabellum. The CZ 75 Compact retains all the features of the CZ75 B in a smaller overall size for concealed carry. The barrel and slide are shortened by .78 inch, while the grip is attenuated by .393 inch, reducing the magazine capacity to 13-rounds.

SPECIFICATIONS:

CZ 75 Compact
Caliber: 9x19mm
Operation: short-recoil, modified Browning system, semiautomatic
Feed: 13-round detachable box magazine
Empty weight: 2.0 lb.
Overall length: 7.3 inches
Barrel length: 3.9 inches
Height: 5.0 inches
Width: 1.4 inches
Rifling: 6 grooves, rh,

CZ 75 Compact

CZ Model 75 9x19mm Automatic Pistol

The CZ 9mm Model 75 select-fire pistol retains all the functions of the Model 75, but can be fired in either semiautomatic mode or fully automatic at a cyclic rate of about 1,000 rounds per minute. An adapter in front of the trigger guard provides for the installation of a laser pointer or an inverted spare magazine which is used as a forward handgrip.

On early versions of this model, the barrel was lengthened, with three slots in the upper surface close to the muzzle, to counter muzzle rise. On later models, this feature was eliminated.

SPECIFICATIONS:

Caliber: 9x19mm Parabellum
Operation: short-recoil, modified Browning system, select-fire
Feed: 15 or 25-round detachable box magazine
Overall length: Standard: 8.11 inches; Long barrel, 9.8 inches
Empty weight: 2.25 lb.
Height: without front grip: 5.4 inches; with front grip: 6.3 inches
Width: 1.4 inches
Rifling: 6 grooves, rh,
Cyclic rate, 1,000 rounds per minute

CZ 75 FA

CZ 85

CZ Model 83 Pistol

The CZ Model 83 is a conventional blowback operated pistol chambered for the .380 ACP (9x17mm) cartridge. In Europe it is also available in 9x18mm. It is similar in design to the Russian Makarov and Walther PP/PPK.

The CZ83 is of all-steel construction, has an ambidextrous safety and an ambidextrous magazine release behind the trigger guard. The double-action clockwork incorporates an automatic safety which positively blocks the hammer until the trigger has been fully pulled. The trigger guard controls dismantling. A detent holds the guard either open or closed and is linked so that the weapon cannot be stripped if the magazine is in place, and the magazine cannot be inserted unless the trigger guard is closed.

The pistol may be finished in either blue or satin nickel.

SPECIFICATIONS:

Caliber: .380 ACP (9x17mm) or 9x18mm (Europe)
Operation: blowback
Feed: 12-round detachable box magazine
Empty weight: 1.5 lb.
Overall length: 6.8 inches
Barrel length: 3.8 inches
Rifling: 6 grooves, rh,
Sights: Front: fixed blade with white insert; rear: adjustable square notch with 2 white dots

9x19mm CZ Model 85B pistol

The 9x19mm Model 85B is essentially an improved version of the CZ75B pistol. Major modifications include fully ambidextrous controls. Minor internal mechanical changes have been introduced to improve the action and reliability. A fully automatic version of the Model 85 was developed but did not enter production.

The Model 85B Combat has adjustable sights, adjustable trigger overtravel and a drop-free magazine.

Available finishes include polymer, bright blue, satin nickel or two-tone steel.

SPECIFICATIONS:

Caliber: 9x19mm Parabellum
Operation: short-recoil, modified Browning system, semiautomatic, double-action/single-action
Feed: 16-round box magazine
Weight: 2.2 pounds
Overall length: 8.1 inches
Barrel length: 4.7 inches
Height: 5.4 inches
Rifling: 6 grooves, rh
Sights: Front: fixed blade; Rear: notch

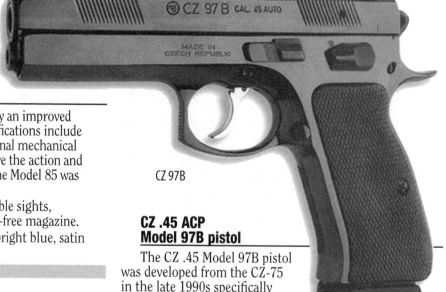

CZ 97B

CZ .45 ACP Model 97B pistol

The CZ .45 Model 97B pistol was developed from the CZ-75 in the late 1990s specifically for the American market. The CZ97 is mechanically identical to the earlier CZ75, but it larger to accommodate the .45 ACP cartridge. The CZ 97B comes with a manual safety, a firing pin safety block and a loaded-chamber indicator. The 10-round magazine is of the double-column type, with the slide remaining open when the last cartridge has been fired. A 12-round magazine is also available.

CZ 100

SPECIFICATIONS:

Caliber: .45 ACP
Operation: Modified Browning system, short-recoil, semiautomatic
Feed: 10-round detachable box magazine
Empty weight: 2.5 pounds
Overall length: 8.3 inches
Height: 5.9 inches
Width: 1.4 inches
Barrel length: 4.8 inches
Sights: Front, blade; rear adjustable notch.

CZ Model 100

The CZ Model 100 represents a move into the latest generation of pistols, complete with the introduction of ergonomic controls, polymer materials, advanced safeties and striker firing.

The frame is high-impact polymer plastic, and the slide is steel. There is no tension on the firing system until the trigger is squeezed. An automatic striker safety prevents the striker from operating unless the trigger is fully pulled. There is also a loaded-chamber indicator. A protrusion behind the ejection port facilitates one hand cocking by pressing it against a table top or other hard surface and pressing down to retract the slide. Laser pointers or lights can be fitted to the rail mount beneath the dust cover.

SPECIFICATIONS:

Caliber: 9x19mm Parabellum; 9 x 21mm (Europe only); .40 S&W
Operation: short-recoil, modified Browning system, semiautomatic
Feed: 9x19mm 13-round box magazine;
.40 S & W: 10-round box magazine
Empty weight: 1.5 pounds
Overall length: 7.1 inches
Barrel length: 3.9 inches
Height: 5.1 inches
Width: 1.2 inches
Rifling: 6 grooves, rh
Sights: Front: fixed blade with white insert;
Rear: fixed square notch with white outline. Adjustable sights available

France

MAB PA15 9x19mm pistol

When the French military required pistols in the early 1970s, there were no military manufacturers available. Manufacture d'Armes Automatiques Bayonne (MAB) manufactured a variety of commercial and target pistols. Among these was the "unique" Modele R Para. This was modified and adopted as the MAB PA15 by the French Army.

The MAB PA15 operates via the delayed-blowback principle, via a rotating barrel. The barrel has two lugs above and below the chamber. The lower lug engages in a slot cut in the recoil spring guide, which is pinned to the frame, allowing the lug to rotate but preventing its movement either backward or forward. The top lug engages a groove machined into the top inside surface of the slide. This groove is shaped so that the initial opening of the slide rotates the barrel through about 35 degrees, after which the track is straight so that the slide can recoil while the barrel remains fixed. Barrel rotation initially is resisted by combined inertia and the torque effect of the bullet passing through the rifling. By the time the barrel has rotated and the slide begins moving to the rear: the chamber pressure has reached a safe level and the slide moves back, compressing the recoil spring and cocking the hammer. The empty case is ejected to the right of the gun. The slide runs forward into battery and the pistol is set to fire another round. A magazine safety prevents the hammer from falling when the magazine is removed.

The MAB 15 has also been manufactured in limited numbers by Zastava Arms in the former Yugoslavia.

SPECIFICATIONS:
Caliber: 9x19mm Parabellum
Operation: delayed blowback, semiautomatic
Feed: 15-round detachable box magazine
Empty weight: 2.37 lb.
Length: 8 inches
Barrel length: 4.6 inches
Rifling: 6 grooves, rh
Sights: Front: blade; rear: notch

PAMAS G1 9x19mm Pistol

The PAMAS G1 9x19mm pistol is essentially a copy of the Beretta Model 92G manufactured under license by the Manufacture Nationale d'Armes de Saint Etienne, now part of Giat Industries. It was adopted first by the French Gendarmerie Nationale (National Police), later by the French Air Force and finally by the French Army .

The PAMAS G1 resembles the Beretta Model 92F but has only a de-cocking lever, instead of the combined safety/de-cocking lever of the Model 92F. Once the hammer has been lowered and the de-cocking lever released, it returns to the ready-to-fire position. There is no manual safety catch, per se.

SPECIFICATIONS:
Caliber: 9x19mm Parabellum
Operation: short-recoil, falling block, semiautomatic, double-action/single-action
Feed: 15-round detachable box magazine
Weight: 2.12 lb.
Overall length: 8.54 inches
Barrel length: 4.92 inches
Height: 5.4 inches
Rifling: 6 grooves, rh, 1 turn in 9.8 inches
Sights: Front: blade integral with slide; Rear: notch, adjustable for windage

French troops on pistol target range with PAMAS G1 and MABPA15

Germany

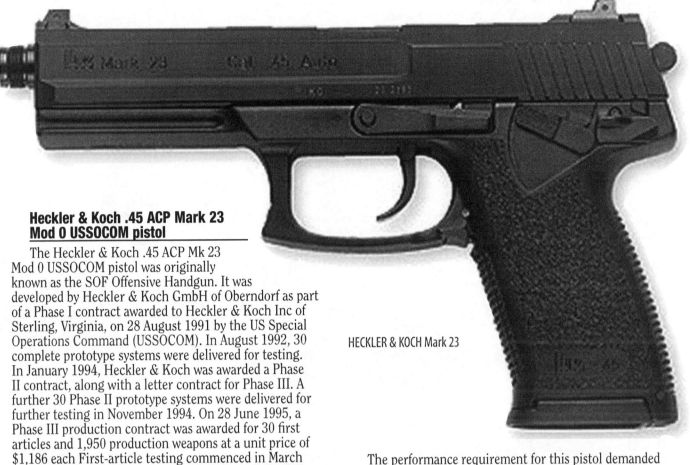

Heckler & Koch .45 ACP Mark 23 Mod 0 USSOCOM pistol

The Heckler & Koch .45 ACP Mk 23 Mod 0 USSOCOM pistol was originally known as the SOF Offensive Handgun. It was developed by Heckler & Koch GmbH of Oberndorf as part of a Phase I contract awarded to Heckler & Koch Inc of Sterling, Virginia, on 28 August 1991 by the US Special Operations Command (USSOCOM). In August 1992, 30 complete prototype systems were delivered for testing. In January 1994, Heckler & Koch was awarded a Phase II contract, along with a letter contract for Phase III. A further 30 Phase II prototype systems were delivered for further testing in November 1994. On 28 June 1995, a Phase III production contract was awarded for 30 first articles and 1,950 production weapons at a unit price of $1,186 each First-article testing commenced in March 1996, with first deliveries in May 1996. A total of 1,350 production suppressors and 30 first articles were purchased from Knight's Armament Company of Vero Beach, Florida, for delivery beginning in September 1996. A total of 650 Laser Aiming Modules (LAMs) were procured from Insight Technology Inc.

A limited number of these pistols - virtually identical to the military version, but with a 10-round magazine - were offered for commercial sales as the SOCOM pistol beginning in August 1996. These pistols are marketed as the Heckler & Koch Mark 23. As of September 2004, 12-round magazines were generally available for the American market.

The Heckler & Koch .45 ACP Mark 23 Mod 0 USSOCOM pistol is a .45 ACP caliber semiautomatic double-action/single-action weapon based on technology developed for the Heckler & Koch USP pistol. A Knight's Armament Company flash and noise suppressor and an Insight Technology AN/PEQ-6 Laser Aiming Module can be attached. The suppressor is screwed onto the threaded muzzle while the AN/PEQ-6 clamps onto grooves on the dust cover.

A mechanical recoil-reduction system that reduces felt recoil by approximately 30 percent is standard. The design incorporates both springs and a polymer buffer. The frame is made from reinforced polymer plastic. The slide is machined from a steel billet and the barrel employs Heckler & Koch's polygonal rifling. The polymer box magazine has a capacity of 12 rounds and the pistol is rated to fire standard M1911 military .45 ACP ball or Olin/Winchester 185-grain Jacketed Hollow Point (JHP) +P ammunition.

HECKLER & KOCH Mark 23

The performance requirement for this pistol demanded a service life of 30,000-rounds, with minimal parts breakage and 6,000 mean rounds between failures. Accuracy was required to meet a standard of an extreme spread of 14 inches for each five-shot group at 25 meters, with a total of 272 groups fired.

The suppressor is required to have a 15,000-round service life with a noise reduction of 24 dB dry and 33 dB wet using M1911 ball ammunition, which is subsonic. The flash reduction requirement was 75 percent using M1911 ball ammunition. The point of impact change after attaching the suppressor is less than 2 inches.

The pistol is double-action on the first shot and single-action thereafter, or single-action only. In the latter configuration, the Mark 23 can be carried "cocked and locked." The manual safety is fully ambidextrous. The de-cocking lever, designed to be operated by gloved hands, is separate and is used to silently lower the hammer. The slide release is extended for easy reach without changing grip on the pistol as is the ambidextrous magazine release.

SPECIFICATIONS:
Caliber: .45 ACP; M1911 Ball or Olin +P 185-gr JHP
Operation: short-recoil; modified Browning system, semiautomatic
Feed: 12-round box magazine
Empty weight: 2.42 pounds
Overall length: 9.65 inches
Barrel length: 5.87 inches
Width: 1.53 inches
Height: 5.9 inches
Rifling: polygonal, rh
Sights: Front adjustable blade; rear adjustable notch

Heckler & Koch 4.6x30mm MP7A1

The HK MP7 and the 4.6 x 30mm family of ammunition were developed to provide penetration and lethality approaching that of an assault rifle in a package small and portable enough to be carried like a handgun. Adopted by the German special operations unit KSK or Kommando Spezialkräfte in 2002, the MP7 is now available to US military and law enforcement organizations. The small, lightweight MP7 (less than 4 pounds loaded) is capable of penetrating modern body armor, including that of the former Soviet Bloc special forces, now the standard NATO test target. (CRISAT) Vests like these are now commonly found in the hands of terrorists and criminals and make conventional pistol caliber weapons ineffective. The MP7 is the size of a pistol, while providing performance on a par with intermediate caliber carbines.

The MP7 can be fired with one or two hands or from the shoulder using a retractable stock. The MP7A1 handles like a pistol, yet allows targets to be engaged like a rifle.

SPECIFICATIONS:
Caliber: 4.6x30mm
Operation: Gas, select-fire
Feed: Detachable box magazine, 20- or 40-round capacity
Overall length: Stock collapsed, 14.96 inches; Stock extended, 23.2 inches
Barrel length: 7.03 inches
Width: 1.65 inches
Height: 6.7 inches
Weight: 3.5 pounds.
Cyclic rate: 950 rd/min

HECKLER & KOCH MP7A1

A folding vertical foregrip allows the weapon to be fired with excellent controllability to increase hit probability at all ranges. At 50 yards distance, the HK MP7 is capable of firing 10-shot semiautomatic groups at of less than 2 inches. The MP7A1 is fully ambidextrous.

The MP7 is gas-operated and fires from the closed bolt using a rotary multi-locking lug bolt similar to that of HK's G36 assault rifle.

The MP7A1 is generally constructed of carbon fiber-reinforced polymer with metal components embedded where needed. The weapon can be field stripped without tools and requires minimum cleaning and maintenance due to its unique gas system. Some key features of the MP7A1 are as follows:

- Patented HK recoil reduction system
- Corrosion-resistant finish
- Corrosion-proof fiber-reinforced polymer frame
- Universal mounting grooves for installing accessories
- Ambidextrous magazine release lever
- Extended slide release
- Extractor is used as a loaded-chamber indicator

Heckler & Koch USP pistols

The Heckler & Koch USP (Universal Semiautomatic Pistol) was the first H&K pistol designed to incorporate features demanded by American civilian, law-enforcement and military users. It was introduced in 1993. The USP can be safely carried 'cocked and locked' as with an M1911. The frame-mounted control lever has a positive stop and returns to the 'fire' position after de-cocking.

The USP was initially designed for the .40 Smith & Wesson (S&W) cartridge but has also been produced in 9x19mm and .45 ACP. The latter was introduced in 1995.

The USP Expert is produced specifically for match shooting and has a longer barrel (132mm) and fully adjustable sights. The Expert is available in 9x19mm, .40 S&W and .45 ACP.

A 9x19mm version designated P8 has been adopted by the German and Spanish armed forces.

The USP was used as the basis for the Heckler & Koch .45 ACP Mk 23 Mod 0 USSOCOM pistol.

wear. All USP pistols have polygonal rifling as standard for their chromium/steel barrels.

The USP control lever can be switched from the left to the right side for left-handed shooters. The pistol can also be converted from double-action/single-action (DA/SA) to a double-action-only (DAO) configuration. There are nine USP variants, with differing control-lever configurations, as follows:

Variants

Variant 1. Double-action/single-action with 'safe' position and control lever (manual safety/de-cocking lever) on the left side of the frame.

Variant 2. Double-action/single-action with 'safe' position and control lever (manual safety/de-cocking lever) on the right side of the frame.

Variant 3. Double-action/single-action without 'safe' position and control lever (manual safety/de-cocking lever) on the left side of the frame.

HECKLER & KOCH USP

The USP uses a modified Browning dropping barrel system with a patented Heckler & Koch recoil reduction system. The polymer frame was designed with experience derived from earlier designs such as the VP70 and P9S pistols. All metal components are corrosion-resistant. Exterior surfaces are protected by an extremely hard nitro-gas carburized black oxide finish. Stainless steel slides are also available. Internal metal parts, including springs, are coated with a Dow Corning process that reduces friction and

Variant 4. Double-action/single-action without 'safe' position and control lever (manual safety/de-cocking lever) on the right side of the frame.

Variant 5. Double-action only, with 'safe' position and control lever (manual safety) on the left side of the frame.

Variant 6. Double-action only, with 'safe' position and control lever (manual safety) on the right side of the frame.

Variant 7. Double-action only, without control lever (no safety/de-cocking lever).

Variant 8. Not officially assigned. Later developed into the law enforcement module (LEM), an innovative DAO system that provides the long pull of a DAO with a break of only 7.5 to 8 pounds.

Variant 9. Double-action/single-action with 'safe' position and control lever (manual safety/no de-cocking lever) on the left side of the frame.

Variant 10. Double-action/single-action with 'safe' position and control lever (manual safety/no de-cocking lever) on the left side of the frame.

HECKLER & KOCH
USP Tactical Pistol

The recoil-reduction mechanism is integral with the recoil/buffer-spring assembly below the barrel. The system buffers the slide and prevents battering the frame, plus reducing felt recoil somewhat, thus improving accuracy.

The dust cover is grooved for fitting a Heckler & Koch Universal Tactical Light (UTL) laser pointer or white lights such as Surefire or Laser Devices.

SPECIFICATIONS:

Data for .40 S&W; data for 9x19mm in parentheses where different
Caliber: .40 S&W (9x19mm)
Operation: short-recoil, modified Browning system, semiautomatic
Feed: 13- (15-) round detachable box magazine
Empty weight: 1.66 pounds (1.65 pounds)
Overall length: 7.64 inches
Barrel length: 4.25 inches
Height: 5.35 inches
Width: 1.26 inches
Rifling: polygonal,
Sights: Front: blade; rear: square notch, adjustable for windage (tritium sights optional)

Caliber: .45 ACP

Operation: short-recoil, modified Browning system, semiautomatic
Feed: 12-round box magazine
Empty weight: 1.74 pounds
Overall length: 7.87 inches
Barrel length: 4.41 inches
Height: 5.55 inches
Width: 1.26 inches
Rifling: polygonal,
Sights: Front: blade; rear: square notch, adjustable for windage (tritium sights optional)

Heckler & Koch USP Tactical Pistol

Heckler & Koch developed the Tactical Pistol originally in .45 ACP to provide a special-operations handgun that was nearly the equal of the Mark 23 Mod 0 USSOCOM pistol but at a reduced cost. The Mark 23 was not universally adopted by the US Special Operations community and several organizations continue to use modified M1911A1 pistols that are reaching the end of their service lives. The Tactical was a response to US special-operations requirements for a pistol to replace the aging M1911A1 pistols with a newer, more modern and more reliable pistol yet in a smaller package and at lower cost than the Mark 23.

The Tactical pistol combines the best features of the Mark 23 USSOCOM pistol and the USP45. It has a polymer frame and steel slide. US Special Operations forces have never been completely satisfied with the terminal ballistics of the 9x19mm cartridge and some continued to specify .45 ACP for their handguns. Many American police SWAT

teams use .40 S&W pistols, so H&K subsequently developed a tactical pistol in .40 S&W.

The H&K Tactical employs the O-ring barrel design of the Mk 23, but somewhat shorter and with suppressor threads reversed so that the Mk 23 suppressor cannot be fitted because the H&K Tactical will not function with the Mk 23 suppressor. The H&K Tactical suppressor is externally identical to that of the Mark 23 and is also made by Knight's Armament Company. The O-ring achieves consistent 'lock-up' of the barrel and slide, resulting in excellent accuracy without hand-fitting components. The O-ring has a service life of 20,000-rounds and can be replaced by the user in seconds without tools.

The H&K Tactical incorporates the adjustable trigger mechanism of the USP "Expert" Match pistol. The service life of the H&K Tactical is claimed to be approximately 25,000-rounds of high-velocity '+P' ammunition before maintenance is required.

Like all USP pistols, the H&K Tactical can be set to any one of nine variants by unit armorers. The finish of the H&K Tactical is the standard Heckler & Koch 'Hostile-Environment' finish, rather than the Mark 23's special marine coating.

SPECIFICATIONS:

Caliber: .40 S&W or .45 ACP, rated for +P ammo (.40 S&W in parentheses, where data is different)
Operation: Short-recoil, modified Browning system, semiautomatic
Feed: detachable box magazine, 12 rounds capacity
Empty weight: 1.9 pounds
Height: 5.9 inches (5.7 inches)
Width: 1.26 inches
Overall length: 8.64 inches
Barrel length: 5.09 inches (5.7 inches)
Rifling: polygonal,
Sights: Front: adjustable blade; rear: adjustable notch (Tritium optional)

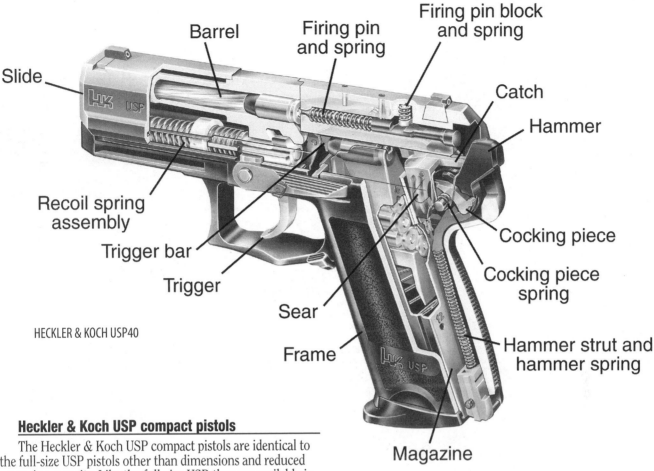

Slide

Barrel

Firing pin and spring

Firing pin block and spring

Catch

Hammer

Cocking piece

Cocking piece spring

Hammer strut and hammer spring

Recoil spring assembly

Trigger bar

Trigger

Sear

Frame

Magazine

HECKLER & KOCH USP40

Heckler & Koch USP compact pistols

The Heckler & Koch USP compact pistols are identical to the full-size USP pistols other than dimensions and reduced magazine capacity. Like the full-size USP, they are available in .40 Smith & Wesson (S&W), 9x19mm and .45 ACP..

A 9x19mm version of the USP compact has been certified for fielding by all German police forces, where it is known as the P10.

Accessory grooves on the dust cover allow mounting of accessories such as laser pointers and tactical lights. Stainless-steel slides are available in lieu of the matte black finish.

SPECIFICATIONS:

Data for .40; data for 9x19mm and .357 Sig in parentheses where different
Caliber: .40 S&W, 9x19mm or .357 Sig
Operation: Short-recoil, modified Browning system, semiautomatic
Feed: 12- (13-) round box magazine
Empty weight: 1.47 pounds
Overall length: 6.81 inches
Barrel length: 3.58 inches
Height: 5.0 inches
Width: 1.14 inches
Rifling: polygonal,
Sights: Front: blade; rear: square notch, adjustable for windage (tritium sights optional)

Caliber: .45 ACP

Operation: Short-recoil, modified Browning system, semiautomatic
Feed: 8-round detachable box magazine
Empty weight: .6 pounds
Overall length: 7.09 inches
Barrel length: 3.8 inches
Height: 5.06 inches
Width: 1.14 inches
Rifling: polygonal, 1 turn in 406mm
Sights: Front: blade; rear: square notch, adjustable for windage (tritium sights optional)

HECKLER & KOCH USP Compact

Heckler and Koch P2000 pistol

The Heckler and Koch P2000 was announced during late 2001 in 9x19mm caliber and is intended primarily for the police and civilian self-defense markets. It derived from the technology of the Heckler and Koch USP Compact LEM pistol. The pistol was designed to enhance handling and shooting comfort. Like most recent Heckler and Koch pistol designs, the P2000 can be modified to suit individual needs. The grip is modular with replaceable back straps to adjust to individual hand sizes. There are no external safeties.

The law enforcement module (LEM) is a patented system that pre-cocks the hammer and provides a very smooth and relatively light DAO trigger. Standard pull is 7.3 to 8.5 pounds, but a lighter trigger of 5.5 pounds pull weight can be installed by H&K armorers.

The P2000 SK is a more compact version for concealed carry.

HECKLER & KOCH P2000

SPECIFICATIONS:

Caliber: 9x19mm or .40 S&W (.40 S&W in parentheses where data is different)
Operation: Short-recoil, modified Browning System, semiautomatic
Feed: 13-round detachable box magazine
Empty weight: 1.37 pounds
Overall length: 7.0 inches
Barrel length: 3.62 inches
Height: 5.04 inches
Width: 1.34 inches
Rifling: polygonal
Sights: Front: blade; rear: square notch

P2000SK

Caliber: 9x19mm or .40 S&W (.40 S&W in parentheses where different)
Operation: Short-recoil, modified Browning system, semiautomatic
Feed: Detachable box magazine, 10-rounds (9-rounds)
Empty weight: 1.3 pounds (1.4 pounds)
Overall length: 6.42 inches
Barrel length: 2.48 inches
Height: 4.61 inches
Width: 1.28 inches
Rifling: Polygonal
Sights: Front, blade; rear notch, adjustable for windage.

Heckler and Koch 9x19mm P7M8 pistol

The 9x19mm P7M8 pistol was developed by Heckler and Koch primarily for police use. The pistol is delayed blowback operated, with a gas braking system that delays breech opening until after gas pressure in the barrel has dropped to a safe level. There were originally two versions available, the P7M8 and P7M13, with the 8 and 13 denoting the magazine capacity. There were also .40 S&W and .380 ACP (9x17mm) versions, but the only version currently in production is the P7M8. The action of the P7 pistol is delayed by gas pressure developed when a round is fired.

HECKLER & KOCH P2000

HECKLER & KOCH P7M8

When the pistol is fired, part of the propellant gas is drawn into a cylinder beneath the barrel. A piston attached to the front end of the slide, enters the front of the cylinder, and when the slide begins to move to the rear under the recoil, the piston's movement in the cylinder is resisted by gas pressure. This delays movement of the slide, which delays opening of the breech.

When the user grips the pistol, his fingers automatically depress the "squeeze-cocking" grip that forms the front strap of the pistol. This cocks the firing pin and it remains engaged in the cocked position as long as pressure is maintained on the cocking lever. As soon as the grip is released, the cocking lever moves forward, automatically de-cocking the striker. If the pistol is dropped, it will be de-cocked and safe before it hits the ground. The cocking lever also releases the slide stop after a new magazine has been inserted. Since there is no slide release, nor any safety catch to be manipulated, the P7 can be used by either right- or left-handed individuals. The pistol can be silently de-cocked by pulling back the slide approximately .5 inch, releasing the cocking lever and then allowing the slide to go forward.

SPECIFICATIONS:

Caliber: 9x19mm
Operation: Delayed blowback
Feed: 8-round detachable box magazine
Empty weight: 1.72 pounds
Overall length 6.73 inches
Width: 1.14 inches
Height: 5.1 inches
Barrel length: 4.13 inches
Rifling: Polygonal
Sights: Front: blade; rear: notch

P11 7.62x36mm Underwater Pistol

Although the P11 7.62x36mm underwater pistol is manufactured by Heckler & Koch, if the few company sales brochures the author has seen are an indication, the company has never officially acknowledged its existence. Based on the best available information, the development of the P11 began in the 1970s as an underwater weapon for use by special operations personnel. Since then, it has been produced in significant, but unknown, numbers. Among nations reported to have used the P11 are Denmark, France, Germany, Israel, Italy, the Netherlands, Norway, the UK's SAS and SBS and the United States.

The P11 fires 7.62mm darts from a sealed five-barrel unit. The ammunition is ignited electrically from a battery pack when the trigger is pulled. The user cannot reload the P11's barrels. Once all five barrels have been fired; the entire barrel unit is replaced with a loaded one. Loading must be carried out at a specially equipped facility, probably the original manufacturer's.

The P11 consists of two main components – the five-barrel firing unit with sealed and waterproofed barrels

HECKLER & KOCH P11

arranged around a central axis and the frame with pistol grip containing the batteries and fire controls. The waterproof battery pack contains two 12-volt cells connected in series, providing the power to ignite the dart propellant in individual sequence. Controls consist of an on/off battery switch and a safety lever.

SPECIFICATIONS:

Caliber: 7.62 x 36mm darts
Operation: electric priming, single shot
Feed: 5 unitary barrels
Empty weight with barrels in place; 42.3 ounces
Length: 7.87 inches
Width: 2.36 inches
Rifling: rh twist
Sights: Front: fixed blade; rear: notch
Max effective range: underwater, 15 m; open air, 25 m

Walther .32 ACP and .380 ACP PP and PPK pistols

The Walther .380 ACP (9x17mm) and .32 ACP (7.65mm) Model Polizei Pistole (PP) was introduced in 1929 for carrying on the uniform belt and was widely adopted by German and European police forces. The pistol was originally made in .32 ACP caliber, but was later manufactured in .22

Long Rifle (LR) and .380 ACP. A few .25ACP models were also made. .22LR and .25 ACP pistols have not been made by Walther for many years.

In 1931, a smaller Walther pistol called the PPK was introduced in the same calibers. This was intended for police use as a concealed weapon, and the initials stood for 'Polizei Pistole Kriminal'. The PPK differed in size and in construction of the handgrip. The PP grip was forged as part of the frame and had plastic grip panels, but the PPK grip was rectangular, covered by a plastic grip that provided the rear contour. Both the PP and PPK were blowback-operated and were well constructed and finished. Center fire versions used a pin in the slide above the hammer to indicate a loaded chamber.

After the Second World War, the French company Manurhin produced the pistols under license in .22 LR (PP), .32 ACP (PPK) and .380 ACP (both). The pistols were also copied and manufactured in Turkey and Hungary.

Production of the Walther PP and PPK ceased in Germany in December 1999, the PPK is still in production by Walther USA of Springfield, Massachusetts via an arrangement with Smith & Wesson

Walther PP

Walther PPKS

The Walther PP and PPK are straight blowback pistols with external hammers, double-action/single-action triggers and good safety features. The hammer is prevented from reaching the firing pin when the trigger is pulled until the sear moves the block clear. The disconnector works into a recess in the slide, and until the slide is fully in battery allowing the disconnector to rise, the sear cannot rotate.

The PPK/S, designed to meet the US Gun Control Act of 1968 has been manufactured by Walther both in Germany and under license in the US. The PPK/S has the frame of the PP model mated to the barrel and slide of the PPK. Both blue and stainless versions have been available.

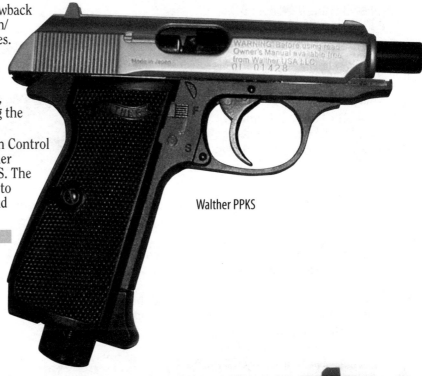

Walther PPKS

SPECIFICATIONS:
Caliber: .32 ACP or .380 ACP (7.65mm or 9x17mm)
Operation: blowback
Feed: Detachable box magazine 8-round (PP) or 7-round (PPK) capacity
Empty weight: PP: 1.53 lb.; PPK: 1.28 lb.
Overall length: PP: 6.8 inches; PPK: 6.1 inches
Barrel length: PP: 3.9 inches; PPK: 3.4 inches
Rifling: 6 grooves, rh twist,
Sights: Front: blade; rear: notch

Walther 9x19mm Model P38 and P1 pistol

The Walther P38 and its derivative P1 began development in the late 1930s as an offshoot of the concealed hammer Armee Pistole, which did not achieve any significant commercial success. The German military evaluated the pistol and dictated that an exposed hammer be incorporated into the design. Walther complied and the pistol was formally adopted in 1940 as the Pistole 38 or simply "P38." Thousands were made by a variety of manufacturers such as Mauser and Spreewerk during World War II, but production ceased at war's end. Walther put the pistol back into production in 1957 with an alloy frame and it was adopted by the Bundeswehr as the P1.

The P1 version of the P38 was used until the mid 1990s when it began being replaced by the Heckler & Koch P8 version of the USP. Thousands of P1s were declared surplus by the German government and sold on the international arms market. Although no longer in front line service, both P38s and P1s can be expected to be encountered worldwide.

The primary components of the P38/P1 pistol are the barrel, the frame, the slide and the locking lug. The P38/P1 incorporates double-action/single-action (DA/SA) trigger mechanism that fires the first shot double-action and subsequent shots single-action. The hammer can also be manually cocked to produce a single-action shortened trigger pull distance and weight. If the pistol is set to 'safe' with the hammer cocked, the hammer is dropped, but the selector switch locks the firing pin so that it cannot go forward. Some late World War II production P38s were made of inferior materials and are unsafe to drop the hammer

Walther P38

onto a loaded chamber as the safety may fail allowing the firing pin to move. It should be noted that the P38/P1 can also be assembled without the locking block in place, which will cause a catastrophic failure.

A training version in .22 LR was also manufactured in small quantities.

SPECIFICATIONS:
Caliber: 9x19mm Parabellum
Operation: short-recoil semiautomatic double-action
Locking: Falling block
Feed: Detachable box magazine, 8 rounds capacity
Empty weight: P38, 2.0 lb.; P1, 1.7 lb.
Overall length: 8.4 inches
Barrel length: 5 inches
Rifling: 6 grooves, rh twist,
Sights: Front: blade, drift adjustable for windage; rear: U-notch

Walther 9x19mm Model P5 and P5 Compact pistol

The Walther 9x19mm Model P5 is derived from the earlier P38/P1 pistols, and was developed to provide a reliable and safe pistol for police and military use. The basic requirement was initiated by the German police forces, which demanded a high standard of safety in handling, together with the ability to fire double-action without having to release safety devices before pulling the trigger.

The Walther P5 is a locked-breech short-recoil operated pistol of conventional appearance, but with several unusual features. There are four built in passive safeties:

- The firing pin is held out of line with the hammer nose until the hammer is released by the trigger.

-The firing pin is held opposite a recess in the face of the hammer until the moment of firing. Should the hammer be released by any means other than the trigger, it will not move the firing pin.

- The hammer has a safety notch

- The trigger bar is disconnected unless the slide is fully locked in battery.

There is no conventional safety, but a de-cocking lever on the left side of the frame, just behind the trigger. This lever takes spring tension off the hammer and moving parts after the pistol is loaded. Once the pistol is loaded, the de-cocking lever is pressed down and allowed to come up. This engages all the safeties and releases the hammer which moves forward to rest against the rear of the slide with its recess enclosing the projecting end of the firing pin. The firing pin is completely protected from any external blows and is held in place by a notch in the pin engaging a lug in the slide. The hammer is held by the safety sear.

The P5 is also available in 7.65 x 21mm (.30 Luger) and 9 x 21mm calibers. The 9 x 21mm chambering is primarily for sale in those countries which do not permit civilian ownership of firearms in military calibers.

The P5 Compact is identical to the standard P5 except that it is shorter and lighter with a different magazine release.

Walther P5

SPECIFICATIONS: P5

Caliber: 9x19mm, .30 Luger (7.65x21mm), 9 x 21mm
Operation: Short-recoil, locked-breech
Locking: Falling block
Feed: Detachable box magazine, 8 rounds capacity
Empty weight: 1.75 lb.
Overall length: 7.1 inches
Barrel length: 3.54 inches
Rifling: 6 grooves, rh twist
Sights: Front: blade; rear: square notch

SPECIFICATIONS: P5 Compact:

Caliber: 9x19mm Parabellum
Operation: short-recoil, semiautomatic
Locking: Falling block
Feed: 8-round detachable box magazine
Empty weight: 1.71 lb.
Overall length: 6.65 inches
Barrel length: 3.11 inches
Rifling: 6 grooves, rh twist
Sights: Front: blade; rear: square notch with white contrast markings; adjustable for elevation and windage

Walther 9x19mm Model P88 Compact Pistol

The Walther 9mm Model P88 Compact pistol is derived from the Model P88, which ceased production in 1996. It employs a modified Browning method of locking in which the squared-off chamber section of the barrel locks into the ejection port. Unlocking is accomplished by a cam beneath the barrel acting on a lug in the frame. Standard caliber is 9x19mm, but the P88 is also available chambered for the 9x21mm cartridge for those markets where military calibers are prohibited.

The Walther 9mm Model P88 Compact is a double-action/single-action (DA/SA), hammer-fired semiautomatic pistol with an ambidextrous manual safety. An automatic firing pin safety prevents the firing pin from moving unless the trigger is fully squeezed. An ambidextrous magazine release is located in the front edge of the grip below the trigger guard.

SPECIFICATIONS:

Caliber: 9x19mm or 9x21mm
Operation: short-recoil, semiautomatic
Locking: Modified Browning system
Feed: Detachable box magazine, 14 rounds capacity
Empty weight: 1.81 lb.
Overall length: 7.13 inches
Barrel length: 3.82 inches
Rifling: 6 grooves, rh twist
Sights: Front: blade; rear: adjustable square notch

Walther 9x19mm Model P99 pistol

The Walther 9mm Model P99 pistol entered production late in 1996 and was developed to meet German police pistol specifications. It is a DA/SA pistol with an internal striker. There is also an alternative double-action only (DAO) model. There are four independent safety mechanisms: a passive trigger and internal striker safeties, along with active de-cocking and drop lever safeties. When the pistol is loaded with a round in the chamber, the first round to be fired requires 0.6 inches of rearward trigger movement and a 8 lb. trigger pull; the following shots then require only 0.2 inches of trigger travel and a 4.4 lb. trigger pull.

Three other variants are available: the P990 is a DAO model; the P99 QA has a pre-cocked firing pin and the P99 QPQ has a stainless steel slide.

The backstrap in the pistol grip is replaceable, so that the grip contour can accommodate virtually any size of hand. Each pistol is supplied with three different sized backstraps. The finish is corrosion resistant Tenifer.

A loaded-chamber indicator gives visual and tactile indication when the chamber is loaded. There is also a tactile and visual indicator showing when the striker is cocked. The magazine release is recessed and cannot be unintentionally operated, but is easily released when desired.

The P99 can accommodate a small tactical light or a laser aiming device via rails on the dust cover.

Variants

P22

The Walther P22 is a .22 LR version of the P99 for low-cost training or sport shooting. It is virtually identical to the P99 except for caliber. Two barrel lengths are available. Standard barrel length is 4 inches, while the competition length barrel is 5 inches. The barrels are interchangeable. Magazine capacity is 10 rounds.

Smith & Wesson SW99

See separate entry under United States.

SPECIFICATIONS:

Caliber: 9x19mm, 9x21mm or .40 S&W
Operation: recoil, semiautomatic, double-action and single-action
Locking: Modified Browning system
Feed: Detachable box magazine: 16 rounds (9x19mm); 12 rounds (.40 S&W)
Empty weight: 1.56 lb.
Overall length: 7.11 inches
Barrel length: 4 inches
Rifling: 6 grooves, rh twist
Sights: Front: interchangeable blade; rear: 2-dot square notch, adjustable for windage

Walther P99

Hungary

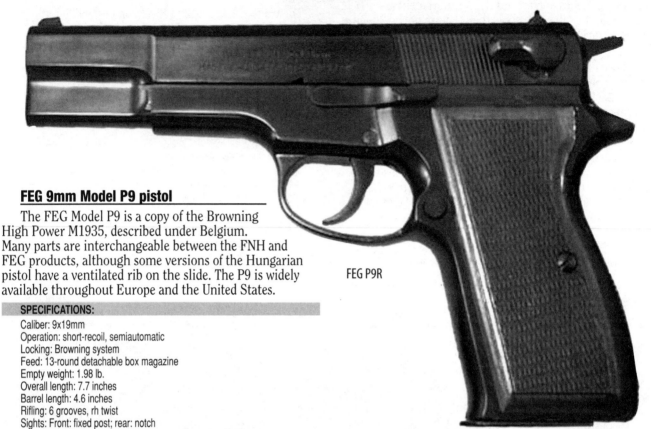

FEG P9R

FEG 9mm Model P9 pistol

The FEG Model P9 is a copy of the Browning High Power M1935, described under Belgium. Many parts are interchangeable between the FNH and FEG products, although some versions of the Hungarian pistol have a ventilated rib on the slide. The P9 is widely available throughout Europe and the United States.

SPECIFICATIONS:

Caliber: 9x19mm
Operation: short-recoil, semiautomatic
Locking: Browning system
Feed: 13-round detachable box magazine
Empty weight: 1.98 lb.
Overall length: 7.7 inches
Barrel length: 4.6 inches
Rifling: 6 grooves, rh twist
Sights: Front: fixed post; rear: notch

FEG 9x19mm Model P9R and P9RA pistols

These pistols are derived from the FEG 9x19mm Model P9, but with modifications to make them competitive with more modern pistols. The principal change is the adoption of double-action trigger mechanism with a slide-mounted safety/de-cocker that lowers the hammer when engaged. Engaging the safety blocks the firing pin and interposes a stop between it and the hammer. The mechanism is otherwise identical to the Browning High Power M1935 pistol.

The Model P9R differs from the P9RA in that it has a steel frame, while the P9RA has an aluminum alloy frame. A left-handed version of this pistol is available with the safety catch, slide release and magazine release on the right side of the frame. There is also a short-barreled version designated P9RK for concealed carry.

SPECIFICATIONS:

Caliber: 9x19mm Parabellum
Operation: short-recoil, semiautomatic
Locking: Browning system
Feed: 14-round detachable box magazine
Empty weight: P9R, 2.1 lb.; P9RA, 1.8 lb.
Overall length: 8 inches
Barrel length: 4.6 inches

FEG .380 ACP (9x17mm) and .32 ACP (7.65x17mmSR) AP and 9x18mm PA-63 Pistols

These pistols are virtual copies of the German Walther PP pistol, The only difference being that the PA-63 is made in 9x18mm Makarov, and was until recently the official

sidearm of Hungarian military and police forces. The AP is produced both in .380 ACP (9x17mm) and .32 ACP (7.65x17mmSR) calibers for commercial sale. Both pistols have an aluminum frame and a steel slide. With the entry of Hungary into NATO, many of the PA63 pistols have been declared surplus and have been sold on the international small arms market. They may thus still be encountered almost anywhere that 9x18mm ammunition is available.

SPECIFICATIONS

Caliber: .32 ACP (7.65x17mmSR), .380 ACP (9x17mm)
or 9x18mm Makarov
Operation: blowback, double-action/single-action (DA/SA)
Feed: detachable box magazine, 7 rounds capacity
(8 rounds in .32 ACP)
Empty weight: 1.31 lb.
Overall length: 6.89 inches
Barrel length: 3.94 inches
Rifling: 6 grooves, rh twist
Sights: Front: blade; rear: notch

India

OFB .32 Mark 1 revolver

The OFB .32 Mark 1 Revolver is a true anomaly in the modern small arms market, being derived from a design that dates to the 19th Century. This antiquated revolver design was standardized by the Indian Ordnance Factory Board (OFB) in 1995 and offered on the international defense market. It is based on the British Enfield revolver, which was itself an enhanced version of the 19th Century Webley revolver series.

SPECIFICATIONS
Caliber: 9x19mm Parabellum
Operation: short-recoil, semiautomatic, DA/SA
Locking: Modified Browning system
Feed: 15-round detachable box magazine
Empty weight: 1.87 lb.
Overall length: 7.7 inches
Height: 5.5 inches
Barrel length: 4.4 inches
Rifling: 6 grooves, rh twist
Sights: Front: blade; rear: square notch adjustable for windage

OFB Mark1 Revolver

The anachronistic Enfield break-open reloading and automatic spent-case ejection mechanism have all been retained in the OFB Mark 1. The grip shape has been modified from that of Enfield designs, but the general appearance and design are identical. The Webley/Enfield design is noted for ruggedness and reliability, so this may have been a factor in standardizing this revolver, but in modern small arms, a revolver of any type for military or serious law enforcement use is unusual, to say the least. The OFB Mark 1 can be fired single or double-action.

Even more unusual is the choice of cartridge for the OFB Mark 1, namely the .32 S&W Long, a low-pressure cartridge long considered obsolete for police use and never officially used by any military force to the author's knowledge. It would thus appear that the OFB Mark 1 revolver is probably intended for police and security markets, but with so many more modern revolvers and pistols available, one must wonder why the Indians standardized such an anachronistic revolver and cartridge.

SPECIFICATIONS
Caliber: .32 S&W Long (7.65x32mm)
Operation: revolver, single or double-action
Feed: 6-round cylinder
Empty weight: 1.53 lb.
Overall length: 7.0 inches
Barrel length: 3 inches
Rifling: 6 grooves, rh twist
Sights: Front: fixed blade; rear: fixed notch

Iran

PC9 9x19mm pistol

There is little information available regarding the Iranian PC9 9x19mm pistol, once known as the ZOAF. It appears to be an unlicensed copy of the Swiss SIG-Sauer (now SAN Swiss Arms) P226, although there are slight differences in the grip shape. The PC9 fires 9x19mm ammunition, the only type manufactured in Iran.

At least two models are produced, one with a stainless steel finish for commercial sales and the other with a military standard matte finish.

Iraq

Tariq pistols

Two Beretta-type semiautomatic pistols have been manufactured in Iraq and are included herein because they may still be encountered in the Middle East. Both pistols are designated Tariq, but are different in both type and in caliber.

- The smaller Tariq is a copy of the blowback operated Beretta Model 70 in .32 ACP (7.65x17SRmm) caliber.

- The larger pistol is a copy of the recoil operated 9x19mm Beretta Model 51, formerly the standard pistol of the Italian armed forces and adopted by Egypt as the Helwan and also by Israel. Although considered obsolescent, the Tariq and similar pistols may still be encountered.

Both pistols can be recognized by their markings to have been manufactured in Iraq. The right side of the slide is marked in English, while the left side of the slide has a prominent Arabic script. On both models, the grips have circular medallions containing the head and shoulders of an Iraqi historical figure.

SPECIFICATIONS:		
Model:	**Tariq (copy of Model 70)**	**Tariq (copy of Model 1951)**
Caliber:	.32 ACP (7.65x17SRmm)	9x19mm
Operation:	Blowback,	Short-recoil, single-action, dropping block
Feed:	Detachable box magazine, 8 rounds	Detachable box magazine, 8 rounds
Empty weight:	1.46 lb	2.05 lb
Overall length:	6.2 inches	8 inches
Barrel length:	3.54 inches	4.5 inches
Rifling:	6 grooves, rh twist	6 grooves, rh twist
Height:	4.8 inches	5.4 inches
Sights:	Front: square blade	square blade
Rear:	notch	notch

Tariq Pistol

Israel

IMI 9x19mm Uzi Pistol

The Israel Military Industries (IMI) 9mm Uzi pistol is a simplified, shortened and lightened modification of the Micro Uzi submachine gun, modified to permit only semiautomatic fire. Although cumbersome in appearance compared to pistols of conventional design, the Uzi Pistol has the advantage of a magazine capacity of 20, 25 or 30-rounds and a shape that allows a very steady two-handed grip. The Uzi's bulk helps to absorb felt recoil so that it is easy to control for quick follow up shots during rapid fire situations. Although heavy, the Uzi is well balanced, with the center of balance over the shooter's hand. Because the bolt telescopes over the breech end of the barrel, the UZI Pistol is very compact, despite its relatively heavy weight.

Although the Uzi pistol was designed for commercial sale, it has also seen some use military and security forces.

SPECIFICATIONS

Caliber: 9x19mm Parabellum
Operation: blowback, semiautomatic
Feed: Detachable box magazine, 20, 25 or 30 rounds
Empty weight: 3 pounds, 12 ounces
Overall length: 9.45 inches
Barrel length: 4.35 inches
Rifling: 4 grooves, rh twist
Sights: Front: post; rear: notch

IMI UZI Pistol

IMI Jericho semiautomatic pistol

Although resembling the Desert Eagle (see separate entry), the Israel Military Industries (IMI) Jericho pistol is a more conventional type of locked-breech recoil-operated pistol, relying on the Browning system of operation to unlock the breech. The slide moves on internal rails. One feature of this weapon is its ability to change calibers; it is simply a matter of field-stripping the pistol and reassembling it with the appropriate components to make the conversion. Two calibers are available: 9x19mm Parabellum and .40 S&W (Smith & Wesson). At one time, a .41 Action Express model was marketed, but it is no longer available. The chromed barrels on all models have six-polygonal-groove rifling. There are five basic models, all of all-steel construction:

- the 941, with a slide-mounted safety
- the 941F, with a frame-mounted safety (F)
- the 941S, with a shortened barrel (S)
- the 941B `Baby', an ultracompactmodel with shorter grip and a reduced magazine capacity

IMI Jericho Full Size and Compact

- the 941PS Police Special, a short model with a frame-mounted safety and a muzzle compensator.

Various combinations are available involving these model states, such as FB or FS. Single-Action Only (SAO) and Double-Action Only (DAO) options are available. 941F models can have ambidextrous safeties. Further options include matte-black or stainless-steel finishes.

Optional accessories include a butt-located safety lock operable by a key, and a silencer kit consisting of a special barrel and a suppressor assembly.

The Jericho FL has the same operating characteristics and external profile of the steel-framed versions but has a polymer frame, referred to as 'polimeric'. There is also a rail for fitting various accessories on the lower frame in front of the trigger guard. The only difference between the steel and polymer versions is the lower weight of the polymer version, at 1.8 lb.

BERETTA Model 1951

SPECIFICATIONS:
Calibers: 9x19mm; .40 S&W
Operation: short-recoil, semiautomatic, DA/SA
Locking: Modified Browning system
Feed: detachable box magazine, 16 rounds capacity (9x19mm); 12 rounds capacity (.40 S&W) 941FB: 9x19mm: 13 rounds; .40 S&W: 9 rounds
Empty weight: 941 and 941F: 2,4 lb; 941FS: 2.1 lb; 941FB: 2.08 lb
Overall length: 941 and 941F: 8.4 inches; 941FS and 941FB: 7.2 inches
Barrel length: 941 and 941F: 4.4 inches; 941FS and 941FB: 3.54 inches
Rifling: 9x19mm: 6 polygonal grooves, rh twist, 1 turn in 10 inches; .40 S&W: 1 turn in 16 inches
Sights: Front: blade with luminous dot; rear: square notch with 2 dots, both sights adjustable for windage.

KSN 9x19mm/.40 S&W Golan semiautomatic pistol

The Golan pistol was originally manufactured by the Yugoslav firm Zavodi Crvena Zastava and were designated CZ-99 and the CZ-40, respectively. The outbreak of hostilities between the former Yugoslav states ended commercial manufacture of the pistols until the Israeli firm KSN Industries Ltd. of Kfar Saba, acquired manufacturing rights and began production of the pistols.

The Golan is a double-action/single-action (DA/SA) pistol with a magazine capacity of 15 9x19mm rounds or 11 .40 S&W rounds. There is no manual safety; the hammer can be de-cocked via an ambidextrous combined slide stop lever and de-cocking lever. The firing pin has a drop-proof block that prevents the pin from moving except during final trigger movement. The magazine release is also ambidextrous.

The Golan's frame is aluminum alloy and the slide is forged steel. The barrel is chrome-lined. The grips are plastic with an ergonomic design for a firm non-slip grip. Various finishes are available.

SPECIFICATIONS:
Caliber: 9x19mm or .40 S&W
Operation: short-recoil, semiautomatic, DA/SA
Locking: Modified Browning system
Feed: Detachable box magazine, 15 rounds capacity (9mm); 11 rounds capacity (.40 S&W)
Empty weight: 1.83 lb
Overall length: 6.7 inches
Barrel length: 3.8 inches
Sights: fixed, three-dot

Italy

Beretta 9x19mm Model 1951 Semiautomatic Pistol

The Beretta Model 1951 was for many years the standard pistol of the Italian armed forces, and was adopted by several other countries as well. It has now been replaced in Italian service by Beretta Model 92 series pistols and is included herein because it may still be encountered in many areas of the world and because it formed the basis for the widely popular 92 and 96 series Beretta pistols. As of 2003, the Model 1951 may still be found in limited service with the Israel Defense Force and the Egyptian Army; and has been manufactured under license both in Egypt (Helwan) and in Nigeria. The Iraqi Tariq was a virtual clone of the M1951.

The M1951 is a locked-breech, short-recoil operated single-action pistol that uses a dropping block locking system similar to that of the Walther P38. Although design work on the pistol began in 1950, the M1951 did not appear commercially until 1957.

The Beretta Model 1951 has three major components: the frame, barrel and slide. The frame contains the magazine and fire control mechanism and has full-length rails. The barrel carries a "drop down" locking piece with lugs that lock into the slide. It pivots from a lug on the bottom of the barrel and is disengaged by a floating pin that impacts the frame as the barrel and locking piece move to the rear under recoil. Locking is automatic as the slide moves forward under pressure of the recoil spring and forces the lugs into recesses in the slide.

SPECIFICATIONS:
Caliber: 9x19mm
Operation: short-recoil, semiautomatic, single-action
Locking: Dropping block
Feed: Detachable box magazine, 8 rounds capacity
Empty weight: 1.87 lb
Overall length: 8 inches
Barrel length: 4.5 inches
Rifling: 6 grooves, rh twist
Sights: Front: blade; rear: square notch, drift adjustable for windage

BERETTA Model 92

Beretta 9x19mm Model 92 Semiautomatic Pistol

The Beretta Model 92 entered production in 1976 and forms the basis of virtually all Beretta large-frame pistols. The Model 92 is essentially an updated and improved Model 1951, with a high-capacity magazine and double-action/single-action fire controls.

In general, the Model 92 resembles the other pistols in the series. It has a double-action trigger system working on the same principles, a similar firing pin assembly and a similar procedure for stripping. The short-recoil system employs a falling locking block that is driven down to disengage the slide from the barrel and halt the rearward motion of the barrel. Otherwise the extraction, cocking and loading operations are similar to those of the smaller weapons; the extractor provides the same loaded chamber indication and the slide is locked to the rear when the magazine is empty.

SPECIFICATIONS

Caliber: 9x19mm
Operation: short-recoil, semiautomatic, DA/SA
Locking: Falling block
Feed: Detachable box magazine, 15 rounds capacity
Empty weight: 2.12 lb
Overall length: 8.54 inches
Barrel length: 4.92 inches
Sights: Front: blade integral with slide; rear: notch, drift adjustable for windage

Beretta 9x19mm Model 92G Pistol

The "G" designation of the Beretta Model 92G indicates 'Gendarmerie', as the Gendarmerie Nationale de France adopted this Model 92 variant in 1989. The 92G was later adopted by the French Army, as well. It is produced under license in France by Giat Industries as the PA-MAS-G1. The Model 92G generally resembles the Model 92FS but is fitted with a de-cocking lever only, rather than with the combined safety/de-cocking lever of the Model 92FS. Once the hammer is lowered and the de-cocking lever is released, it returns to the "fire" position. There is no manual safety.

This pistol is also available chambered for the .40 S&W cartridge as the Model 96G. The magazine capacity for this version is 11 rounds. Otherwise, specifications are the same as the Model 92

Beretta 9x19mm Model 92S Pistol

The Beretta 9x19mm Model 92S is identical to the Model 92 but has a modified and improved safety mechanism. Whereas the Model 92's safety is mounted on

BERETTA Model 92S

the frame the Model 92S safety is moved to the slide where it adds a de-cocking option. When applied, the de-cocker deflects the firing pin out of the path of the hammer, drops the hammer and disconnects the link between the trigger bar and the sear.

If the pistol is cocked, application of the safety allows the hammer to fall safely to the uncocked position. If the pistol is not cocked, pulling the trigger will not operate the hammer. If the hammer is inadvertently operated, the weapon will not fire even if there is a round in the chamber.

SPECIFICATIONS:

Same as the Model 92 except that empty weight is 34.5 ounces

Beretta 9x19mm Model 92SB semiautomatic pistol

The Beretta 9x19mm Model 92SB is a direct development of the Model 92S, and is the pistol which Berretta submitted to the US Army pistol trials. The Model 92SB differs from the 92S in the following features:

- The safety lever is ambidextrous, so left-handed shooters can easily use the pistol.
- The magazine release was moved behind the trigger guard, where it can be pressed without taking the hand from the grip. The magazine release can be switched from the left side to the right side.
- A new combination of safeties was added as follows:
- The manual safety disengages the trigger from the sear.
- The firing pin is blocked until the final movement of the trigger on firing.
- The firing pin is inertia operated.
- A half-cock position was added to the hammer.
- The front and back straps are grooved to improve the grip.

SPECIFICATIONS:
Other than the features stated above, the 92SB is identical to the 92S

Beretta 9x19mm Model 92SB Compact Pistol

The Beretta 9x19mm Model 92SB compact is a smaller and handier version of the Model 92SB. The main differences are in the size and the magazine capacity. All other features are the same as for the Model 92SB.

SPECIFICATIONS:
Feed: Detachable box magazine, 13 rounds capacity
Overall length: 7.7 inches
Barrel length: 4.3 inches

Beretta 9x19mm Model 92FS Pistol

The Beretta Model 92FS is one of the most widely used military and law enforcement pistols in the world. It gained this distinction partly as a result of being adopted by the US Army in the early 1980s. After successful testing, the US Army required several modifications prior to formally adopting the pistol as the M9. These modifications were:

- Reshaping the trigger guard to facilitate a two-handed grip
- Extending the magazine base
- Toe of the front strap slightly curved
- Different grip panels
- Lanyard loop

BERETTA Model 92FS

Beretta 9x19mm Model 92FS Brigadier Pistol

The Beretta 9x19mm Model 92 Brigadier FS was developed from the Beretta Model 92FS series and is intended for combat competition shooting and other applications where large numbers of rounds are fired over extended periods. Because of this, Brigadier models feature a reinforced slide. Otherwise the Model 92 Brigadier is similar to other models in the Model 92FS series.

Two double-action-only (DAO) models, the Model 92 and 96 Brigadier D, are also available. In addition to the 9x19mm Parabellum and .40 S&W models, a 9x21mm version (Model 98 Brigadier FS) is available for those locales where ownership of military-caliber handguns is prohibited.

Beretta 9x19mm Model 92D and Model 92DS Pistols

The Beretta 9mm Model 92D and 92DS pistols are similar in that they are both double-action only pistols. The Model 92D differs from the 92DS in that there is no manual safety. This feature is termed by Beretta as a 'slick slide'.

The Model 96D and 96DS are identical pistols chambered for the .40 S&W cartridge. The magazine capacity of these pistols is 11 rounds.

Beretta 9x19mm Model 92FS Compact and Model 92 Compact L Pistols

The 9x19mm Beretta Model 92FS Compact is identical to the 92SB Compact modified in the same manner as the Model 92FS, with improvements designed to facilitate handling and shooting comfort. The Model 92 Compact L is identical.

BERETTA Model 92SB Compact

BERETTA Model 92FS Brigadier

BERETTA Model 93R

BERETTA Model 96

Beretta 9x19mm Model 93R Select-fire Pistol

The Beretta 9x19mm Model 93R select-fire pistol is a modified semiautomatic pistol which fires either semiautomatic or in three-round bursts. When firing in burst mode, Beretta recommends that both hands be used and if possible the shooter attach the folding carbine stock and fire the pistol from the shoulder. To assist in controlling the 93R when firing bursts, a muzzle brake with six vertical slots helps reduce muzzle climb.

The frame of the Beretta Model 93R is similar to that of the Model 92. The selector lever is positioned above the left grip, and the dust cover is deepened to accommodate the hinges of the forward grip. The selector lever can be moved with the thumb to select either single shots or three-round bursts without disturbing the aim, and the safety can be similarly applied or released.

The metal folding stock quickly clips on to the bottom of the grip without interfering with the magazine.

SPECIFICATIONS:
Caliber: 9x19mm
Operation: Short-recoil, select-fire, semiautomatic or three-round burst
Locking: Falling block
Feed: detachable box magazine, 15 or 20 rounds capacity
Empty weight: 2.46 lb
Overall length: 9.45 inches
Barrel length: 6.14 inches
Sights: Front: blade, integral with slide; rear: notch, drift adjustable for windage
Cyclic rate: Approx 1,100 rounds per minute

Beretta Centurion Series Pistols

Beretta Centurion pistols have the frame and magazine capacity of the 92FS or 96 models combined with the reduced barrel and slide length of the Compact versions. Special D and G D Centurion models are available in some markets. These pistols incorporate features of the D and G versions.

SPECIFICATIONS:
Caliber: Model 92FS: 9x19mm; Model 96: .40 S&W
Operation: Short-recoil, semiautomatic, double-action/single-action
Feed: Detachable box magazine, 15 rounds capacity (9mm); 11 rounds capacity (.40 S&W)
Empty weight: 2.06 lb
Overall length: 7.75 inches
Barrel length: 4.2 inches

Beretta Model 81BB, 84BB and 84FS semiautomatic pistols

These Beretta models are among the Beretta medium-frame pistols marketed under the name Cheetah. Although of greater magazine capacity than the Models 82 and 85 (see separate entry), Models 81BB and 84BB are derivatives of Models 81 and 84 and resemble them in most essential features. Model 81BB is in 7.65mm, and the Model 84BB is in 9mm short. For the general method of operation, reference should be made to the entry for the Model 81. Models 81BB and 84BB are double-action pistols, incorporating double-column detachable box magazines (12-round capacity in the Model 81BB; 13-round capacity in the Model 84BB); loaded-chamber indicator; reversible magazine release button; stripping catch arrangement (as described for Model 81) and a manual safety operable from either side of the weapon. The safety system is as described for the Models 82BB and 85BB. A magazine safety, acting on the trigger mechanism when the magazine is removed, is optional.

The Model 84FS, now known as the Model 84FS Cheetah, is similar to the BB series but has the additional feature of a hammer de-cocking facility, operated by the safety catch. Pressing the safety catch will allow the hammer to fall safely on to an interceptor bar, lock the slide and disconnect trigger and sear.

The front and back straps of the grips are longitudinally grooved to ensure a firm hold in wet conditions or during rapid firing. Plastic grips are optional. It is also available in a limited deluxe series featuring gold-plated hammer and trigger, walnut grips and blued or gold-plated finish.

SPECIFICATIONS:
Model 81BB as for Model 81, except:
Operation: blowback, semiautomatic, double-action
Model 84 BB as for Model 84

Beretta Model 82BB, 83FS, 85BB, 85F, 87BB and 87BB/LB semiautomatic pistols

These Beretta pistols are derivatives of the Models 81 and 84, and in most of the essential features, they are the same. The Model 82BB is in 7.65 x 17mm SR, while the 83FS, the 85BB and the 85FS are in 9x17mm and the 87BB and the 87BB/LB are in .22 LR caliber. For a general description, reference should be made to the entry for the Beretta 7.65 x 17mm Model 81 pistol.

These Beretta models are among the Beretta medium-frame pistols marketed under the name Cheetah. The differences between these models and the Model 81 are as follows:

BB models

The main differences are the loaded-chamber indicator, the magazine capacity and the safety system.

Loaded-chamber indicator: a pin projects laterally from the slide to indicate when a round is in the chamber. This pin is colored red and it gives both a visual and a tactile indication. Magazine capacity: the magazine is single-column only, so allowing a lighter and thinner grip. This favors the smaller hand and also makes the pistols easier to conceal.

- New safety system: this is really divided into four sections: the manual safety breaks the connection between the trigger and the sear, the firing pin is permanently locked until the last stage of the trigger pull when it is released, the firing pin is operated by inertia and so there is no direct contact with the primer, there is a half-cock position. It is worth noting that these pistols can be fired from the half-cock position by simply pulling the trigger to raise and drop the hammer.

FS models

These have all the features of the BB models described above, with the addition of a hammer de-cocking facility built into the applied safety system. To lower the hammer safely, the manual safety catch is applied; this drops the hammer against an interceptor, locks the slide in the closed position and interrupts the connection between trigger and sear.

The half-cock hammer position is not available in these models. The FS models also have the barrel and chamber chrome-plated. The 83FS differs from the 85FS in having a 101mm barrel and a seven-round magazine.

87BB/LB model

This model differs from the remainder of the group in being single-action-only. The notation '/LB' indicates the use of a long (150mm) barrel.

SPECIFICATIONS: As for Models 81 and 84 except:
Caliber: Model 82BB: 7.65 x 17mm SR (0.32 ACP)
        Models 83FS, 85BB, 85FS: 9x17mm (0.380 ACP)
        Models 87BB, 87BB/LB: .22 Long Rifle Rim Fire
Feed: box magazine
Magazine capacity: 7.65 x17mm SR: 9 rounds;
                    9x17mm: 8 rounds
                    .22 LR: 7 rounds
Weight: Model 82BB: 1.4 lb
       Models 85BB, 85FS: 1.4 lb
       Model 87BB: 1.3 lb
       Model 87BB/LB: 1.5 lb

BERETTA Model 86

BERETTA Model 87 Target

Bernardelli P.ONE Pistols

Bernardelli P.ONE semiautomatic double-action/single-action (DA/SA) pistols are available in a variety of calibers including 7.65x21mm Parabellum (.30 Luger), 9x19mm, 9x21mm and .40 S&W. All models have a forged steel frame, slide and barrel and are available in a variety of finishes. Blue with checkered plastic grips are standard and checkered walnut grips are optional.

The P.ONE has a manual thumb safety/de-cocking lever that can be used to lower the hammer or to lock the slide back for disassembly. Half-cock, magazine and firing pin block safeties are also included. An ambidextrous safety is optional and the magazine release can be configured for operation by either hand. The extractor also acts as a chamber-loaded indicator.

TANFOGLIO 99

Compact versions of the P.ONE are also available, with the additional availability of .380 ACP (9x17mm) caliber in this version. The magazine capacity of compact models is reduced to 14-rounds (10-rounds for .40 S&W), and the weight is also slightly reduced.

SPECIFICATIONS:

Caliber: 7.65x21mm Parabellum (.30 Luger); 9x19mm; 9x21mm; .40 S&W
Operation: Short-recoil, semiautomatic, double-action/single-action (DA/SA)
Locking: Falling block locking breech
Feed: detachable box magazine; 16 rounds capacity (9mm);
12 rounds (.40 S&W)
Empty weight: 2.13 lb
Overall length: 8.3 inches
Barrel length: 4.8 inches
Rifling: 6 grooves, rh
Sights: Front: blade with one white dot; rear: notch with two white dots;
optional: micro adjustable for windage

Bernardelli P6 and P8 semiautomatic pistols

The Bernardelli P6 and P8 pistols are virtually identical single-action external hammer semiautomatic compact pistols similar in design to the Walther PP, but differ in their safety arrangements. The P8 has a manual thumb half-cock magazine and autolocking firing pin safeties to accommodate the United States market. Other features of the P8 include a loaded-chamber indicator and click adjustable rear sights. Both pistols have lightweight alloy frames.

Both the P6 and the P8 are available in .22 LR, .32 ACP (7.65x17mmSR) and .380 ACP (9x17mm). Plastic and walnut grips are available.

SPECIFICATIONS:

Caliber: .22 LR, .32 ACP (7.65x17mmSR), .380 ACP (9x17mm)
Operation: Blowback, semiautomatic
Feed: detachable box magazine, 8 rounds capacity (.22LR); 8 rounds capacity
(.32 ACP & .380 ACP)
Empty weight: 1.2 lb
Overall length: 6.6 inches
Barrel length: 3.5 inches
Sights: Front: blade; rear: notch (adjustable for windage on P8)

Tanfoglio double-action semiautomatic pistols

All Tanfoglio double-action pistols are locked-breech weapons with a dropping barrel on the Colt/Browning system using a double-column magazine. The pistols are available in the following calibers: 9x19mm Parabellum (P19), .40 Smith & Wesson (P40), .41 Action Express (AE), .45 ACP (P45) and 10mm auto, as well as in the so-called 'Italian' calibers, 9 x 21mm IMI and .45 HP.

The frame is of forged steel, as are the slide and the barrel; all steels are chrome-molybdenum alloy. All pistols are supplied in black finish or hard-chromed and are also available with the frame and the slide in stainless steel. Numerous accessories and conversion kits to change between models and calibers are available.

On the standard models, there is a manual safety catch on the slide which operates to lock the firing pin and releases the hammer and the trigger, ensuring safety at all times.

On the combat models, there is a manual cocked-and-locked safety mounted on the frame, with automatic firing-pin safety that operates to lock the firing pin until the trigger is pulled.

The Tanfoglio compact standard models are similar to the standard models but with smaller overall dimensions.

The Tanfoglio combat models comprise the P19, the P40 and the P45 combat models, which differ from the standard models solely in their safety arrangements. The dimensions are the same in all respects.

The Tanfoglio compact combat models are similar to the combat models but with smaller overall dimensions.

The Tanfoglio L is a sport version of the combat models, with a longer barrel (121mm) and slide.

The Tanfoglio Model S is a compensated version of the combat models that is fitted with a muzzle compensator to reduce both recoil and muzzle rise on firing. All data is as for the standard models, other than that the weight is 2.6 pounds, the length is 9.8 inches and the barrel length is 5.2 inches.

Tanfoglio Force

Tanfoglio Force Compact

Combat model, while the Force Compact is similar to the Tanfoglio Compact model.

SPECIFICATIONS: Force model

Caliber: 9x19mm Parabellum; 9 x 21mm; .38 super; .40 S&W;
10mm auto; .45 ACP; .45 HP
Operation: recoil, semiautomatic, double-action
Locking: Modified Browning System
Feed: Detachable box magazines: 9mm, 16 rounds; .40, 12 rounds; 10mm, 12 rounds; .45, 10 rounds; .38 Super, 16 rounds
Empty weight: approx. 1.9 pounds
Length: 8.3 inches
Barrel length: 4.4 inches
Sights: Front: fixed blade; rear: adjustable U-notch

Force Compact model

Caliber: 9x19mm Parabellum; 9 x 21mm; .38 Super; .40 S&W; 10mm Auto; .45 ACP; .45 HP
Operation: recoil, semiautomatic, double-action
Locking: Modified Browning System
Feed: Detachable box magazines: 9mm, 14 rounds; .40, 10 rounds; 10mm, 9 rounds; .45, 8 rounds; .38 Super, 14 rounds
Empty weight: approx. 1.8 pounds
Length: 7.4 inches
Barrel length: 3.5 inches
Sights: Front: fixed blade; rear: adjustable U-notch

Japan

Model 60 New Nambu .38 special Revolver

This Smith & Wesson-type revolver chambered in .38 special has been the official Japanese police revolver since 1961, and apparently was adopted due to American influence of the time. Although semiautomatic pistols have been proposed, the Model 60 remains in Japanese police service. Oddly for a service revolver, the Model 60 cylinder holds only five rounds. The revolver is also issued to the Japanese Maritime Safety Guard. With its small grip and limited cartridge capacity, the Model 60 is an anachronism in the 21st Century.

SPECIFICATIONS:

Caliber: .38 Special
Operation: manual; revolver, single- or double-action
Feed: five chamber cylinder
Empty weight: 1.5 lb
Overall length: 7.75 inches
Barrel length: 3.03 inches
Sights: Front: serrated ramp; rear: square notch

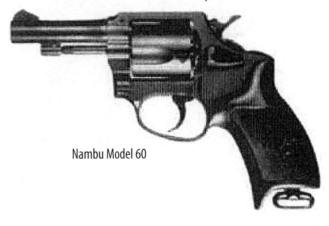

Nambu Model 60

SPECIFICATIONS: Standard models

Caliber: 9x19mm Parabellum; 9 x 21mm; .38 super; .40 S&W;
.41 AE; 10mm auto; .45 ACP; .45 HP
Operation: recoil, semiautomatic, double-action
Locking: dropping barrel
Feed: detachable box magazine
Magazine capacity: 9mm: 16 rounds; .38 super: 16 rounds;
.40 S&W: 12 rounds; .41 AE: 11 rounds; .45 calibers: 10 rounds
Empty weight: approx 2.5 lb
Length: overall: 8.3 inches
Barrel length: 4.4 inches
Sights: Front: fixed blade; Rear: adjustable U-notch

Compact models

Caliber: 9x19mm Parabellum; 9 x 21mm; .38 super;
.40 S&W; .41 AE; 10mm auto; .45 ACP; .45 HP
Operation: recoil, semiautomatic, double-action
Locking: dropping barrel
Feed: detachable box magazine
Magazine capacity: 9mm: 14 rounds; .38 super: 14 rounds; .40 S&W: 10 rounds; .41 AE: 9 rounds; 10mm: 9 rounds; .45 HR: 8 rounds
Length: overall: 7.5 inches
Barrel length: 3.7 in
Sights: Front: fixed blade; Rear: adjustable U-notch

Tanfoglio Force and Force Compact pistols

With the Force and Force Compact pistols, Tanfoglio has introduced a plastic/polymer frame to offer lighter models of pistol. Apart from their plastic/polymer frames, the pistols are virtually identical to the Tanfoglio steel-frame double-action pistols, and many of the components are identical. The Force model equates to the Tanfoglio

Korea, North

Type 64 .32 ACP semiautomatic pistol

The North Korean Type 64 pistol is virtually identical to the Browning Model 1900. The North Korean Type 64 has the stamping '1964 7.62' on the left side but is chambered for the .32 ACP (7.65x17mmSR) cartridge. There is also a silenced version of the Type 64 with a shortened slide and threaded barrel.

Why the North Koreans would manufacture what is essentially is a 19th Century pistol design chambered for a cartridge that is hardly suited for military service is a mystery.

The essential characteristics of the pistol are identical to those of the Browning Model 1900.

SPECIFICATIONS:

Caliber: .32 ACP (7.65x17mmSR)
Operation: Blowback, semiautomatic
Feed: detachable box magazine, 7 rounds capacity
Empty weight: 1.37 lb
Overall length: 6.75 inches
Barrel length: 4.0 inches
Rifling: 6 grooves, rh
Sights: Front: blade; rear: notch

Korea, South

Daewoo .380 ACP DH380 Semiautomatic Pistol

The design of the Daewoo .380 DH380 appears to have been influenced by the German Walther PP series and is a blowback operated semiautomatic pistol chambered in .380 ACP (9x17mm) caliber. The pistol operates in double-action for the initial shot and single-action thereafter (DA/SA).

SPECIFICATIONS:

Caliber: .380 ACP (9x17mm)
Operation: Blowback, semiautomatic,
Double-action/single-action (DA/SA)
Feed: 8-round detachable box magazine
Empty weight: 1.6 pounds
Overall length: 7.0 inches
Barrel length: 3.8 inches
Sights: Front: blade with white dot; rear: square notch, 2 white dots

Daewoo .40 S&W DH40 and .45 ACP DH45 Mk II Semiautomatic pistols

The Daewoo DH40/45 Mk II is generally similar to the DP51 Mk II (see separate entry), except that it is chambered for the .40 S&W cartridge. The DH40/45 is intended primarily for military or police use and has a double-action/single-action operating mechanism that functions using the delayed blowback principle of operation. Delay is achieved by a radially grooved chamber that prevents the cartridge case from moving until pressure has dropped to a safe level.

This operating mechanism is described as the 'fast-shooting mechanism', with 3H, an acronym standing for High-accuracy first shot, High-speed shot, High reliability, also known as Fastfire™ Tri-Action™. To select this function, the pistol is cocked and the hammer lowered to activate the fast-shooting mechanism. When selected, the mechanism operates in the same manner as double-action, but with lighter and smoother trigger function. Using the patented action, trigger pull weight is reduced to approximately five pounds as compared to some 12 pounds for conventional double-action pull weight. Conventional double-action/single-action firing remains possible.

SPECIFICATIONS:

Caliber: .40 S&W/.45 ACP
Operation: delayed-blowback semiautomatic, single or double-action, plus fast-shooting
Feed: detachable box magazine, 10- or 12-round capacity (.40 S&W); 8 rounds (.45 ACP)
Empty weight: 1.75 lb
Overall length: 7.48 inches
Barrel length: 4.13 inches
Sights: Front: blade with white dot; rear: square notch, 2 white dots

Daewoo 9x19mm DP51 Mk II Semiautomatic Pistol

The Daewoo 9mm DP51 Mk II is a semiautomatic pistol in 9x19mm Parabellum caliber operating on the delayed blowback system. Designed for military and police use, it

DAEWOO DH380

DAEWOO DH40

has a patented double-action trigger mechanism called Fast-Shooting Mechanism that has been described under previous entries

The sights are fitted with luminous dots for operation in poor light conditions. The frame is high-tensile aluminum alloy.

The Daewoo 9mm DP51 Mk II is in service with the South Korean armed forces where is carries the designation 9mm Pistol K5.

A 9mm DP51C MKII Compact version is also available. This version weighs 24 ounces, is 6.9 inches in length, and has a 3.5 inch barrel, with a 10-round magazine capacity.

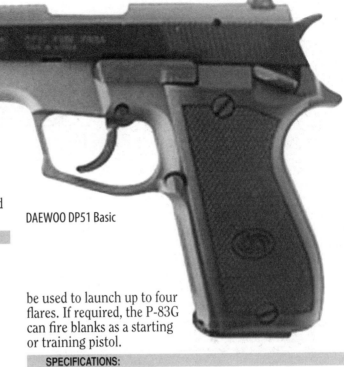

DAEWOO DP51 Basic

SPECIFICATIONS:

Caliber: 9x19mm Parabellum
Operation: delayed blowback, semiautomatic, single or double-action, plus Fast-Shooting
Feed: 10- or 12-round detachable box magazine
Empty weight: 1.76 lb
Overall length: 7.5 inches
Barrel length: 4.13 inches
Sights: Front: blade with white dot; rear: square notch, 2 white dots

Poland

VANAD P-83 semiautomatic pistol

Development of the VANAD P-83 pistol began in the late 1970s, the object being to replace the earlier P-64 with a similar pistol but one which would be less expensive and easier to manufacture. The resulting weapon was introduced as the VANAD P-83, a simple fixed-barrel blowback-operated pistol chambered either for the 9x18mm Makarov or for the 9x17mm cartridges and generally similar to the P-64 in its principles. The difference lies in manufacture, much use being made of pressings, forgings and welding, with reductions both in cost and in the consumption of production raw materials.

The trigger is double-action, and an external safety lever drops the cocked hammer when applied; at the same time, the rear of the firing pin is lowered so that it is opposite a hammer arm and thus cannot strike a cartridge in the chamber. There is also a chamber-loaded indicator. The standard finish is a black-oxide coating, although the whole pistol or some of its components can be delivered with a bright or dull chrome finish. Other options include high-contrast sights and adjustable rear sights.

P-83G gas pistol

The P-83G gas pistol is basically a blank-firing VANAD P-83 pistol with a muzzle attachment capable of projecting disabling gas pellets. An alternative muzzle attachment can

be used to launch up to four flares. If required, the P-83G can fire blanks as a starting or training pistol.

SPECIFICATIONS:

Caliber: 9x18mm Makarov; 9x17mm
Operation: blowback, semiautomatic, single-action or double-action
Feed: detachable box magazine
Magazine capacity: 8 rounds
Empty weight: 1.7 lb
Length: overall: 6.5 inches
Barrel length: 3.5 inches
Sights: Front: blade: rear: notch
Sight radius: 4.7 inches
Muzzle velocity: 9x18mm Makarov: 312 m/s; 9x17mm: 284 m/s

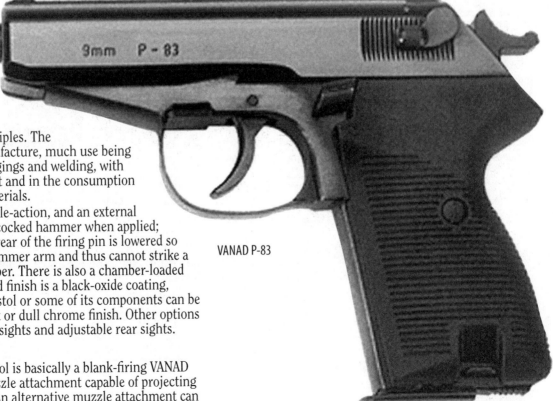

VANAD P-83

9x18mm P-93 pistol

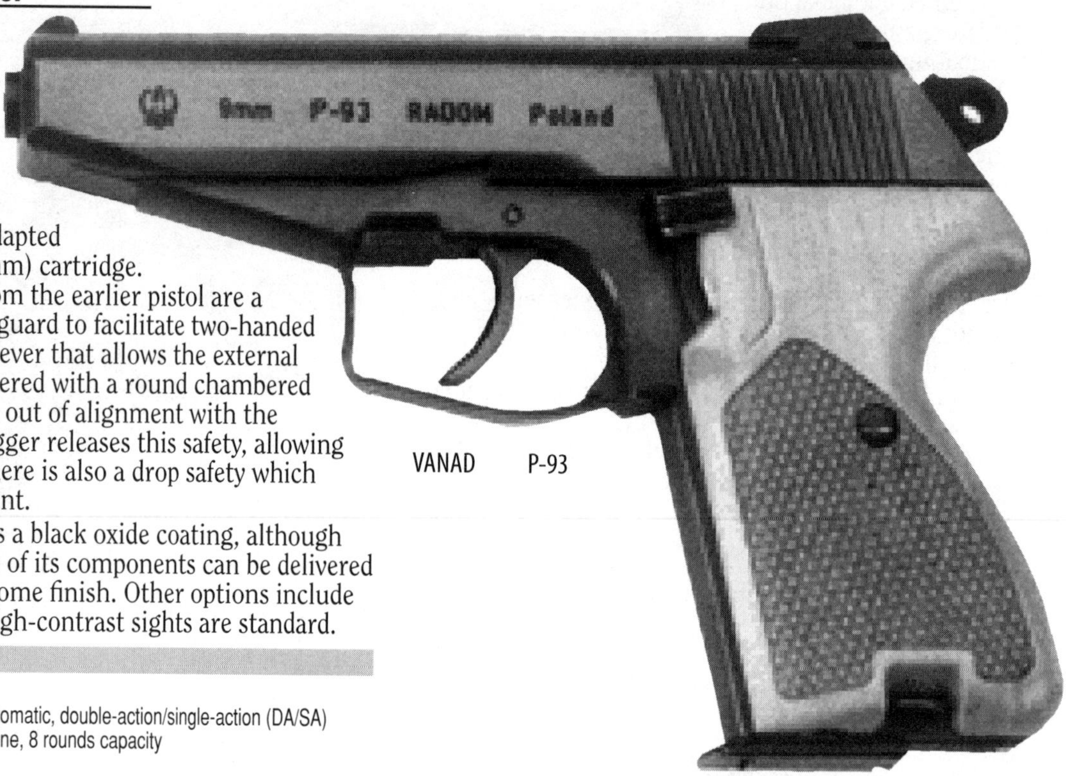

The 9x18mm P-93 pistol was developed from the earlier Vanad P-83 pistol chambered for the 9x18mm Makarov cartridge, although the design could be easily adapted for the .380 ACP (9x17mm) cartridge. The primary changes from the earlier pistol are a revised grip and trigger guard to facilitate two-handed firing and a de-cocking lever that allows the external hammer to be safely lowered with a round chambered by moving the firing pin out of alignment with the hammer. Pulling the trigger releases this safety, allowing the round to be fired. There is also a drop safety which blocks hammer movement.

The standard finish is a black oxide coating, although the whole pistol or some of its components can be delivered with a bright or dull chrome finish. Other options include adjustable rear sights; high-contrast sights are standard.

VANAD   P-93

SPECIFICATIONS:

Caliber: 9x18mm Makarov
Operation: Blowback, semiautomatic, double-action/single-action (DA/SA)
Feed: Detachable box magazine, 8 rounds capacity
Empty weight: 1.65 lb
Overall length: 7.0 inches
Barrel length: 2.5 inches
Sights: Front: blade; rear: notch adjusted to 25 m

MAGAZINE 95, MAGAZINE 98 and MAGAZINE 98c semiautomatic pistols

The MAGAZINE 95, MAGAZINE 98 and MAGAZINE 98c are conventional DA/SA pistols that incorporate design features from both Browning and SIG designs into one pistol. The short-recoil operating system uses the widely employed modified Browning system in which the barrel locks into the ejection port. A double-action/single-action (DA/SA) trigger mechanism works in combination with a SIG-type de-cocking lever that allows the external hammer to be safely lowered with a round chambered. The barrel is chrome-plated to prolong its life and to permit easier cleaning.

The MAGAZINE 95, MAGAZINE 98 and MAGAZINE 98c are designed to be used by both right-handed and left-handed shooters and are configured to facilitate two-handed firing. A laser pointer can be mounted in front of the trigger guard. Standard finish is a matte black, but a bright or matte chrome finish is optional.

SPECIFICATIONS:

Caliber: 9x19mm Parabellum
Operation: short-recoil, double-action with external hammer
Locking: Modified Browning system
Feed: Detachable box magazine, 15 rounds capacity.
20-round extended magazine optional
Empty weight: MAGAZINE 95: 2.3 pounds; MAGAZINE 98: 2.0 pounds; MAGAZINE 98c: 2.0 pounds
Height: 5.5 inches
Width: 1.4 inches
Overall length: 7.9 inches
Barrel length: 4.5 inches
Sights: Front: fixed blade; rear: notch high-contrast with illumination; rear sight adjustable on MAGAZINE 98c

WIFAMA Gward .38 Revolver

The WIFAMA Gward (Guard) .38 revolver is a conventional handgun based on the DA/SA Smith & Wesson design and is intended primarily for police applications. It is chambered for .38 Special ammunition with a six-round swing-out cylinder. There are mounting points for optics or laser pointers. Two barrel lengths are available, 2.5 or 4 inches.

SPECIFICATIONS:

Caliber: .38 Special
Operation: Manual, revolver, DA/SA
Feed: six-chamber cylinder
Empty weight: 1.6 lb
Overall length: 7.7 or 9.25 inches
Barrel length: 2.5 or 4 inches
Sights: Front: fixed blade; rear: notch calibrated for 25 m, adjustable for windage.

Romania

ROMARM .32 ACP (7.65x17SRmm) Model 74 pistol

The ROMARM .32 ACP (7.65x17SRmm) Model 74 pistol is a conventional blowback operated pistol based on the proven Walther PPK. It is made entirely from steel, with plastic grip panels. Versions chambered for .380 ACP (9x17mm) and .22LR are also available, as is a tear gas model.

SPECIFICATIONS:

Caliber: .32 ACP (7.65x17SRmm), .380 ACP (9x17mm), .22LR
Operation: blowback, semiautomatic
Feed: .32 ACP, 8-round detachable box magazine; .380 ACP, 7-round detachable box magazine; .22LR, 10-round detachable box magazine.
Empty weight: .32 ACP, 1.1 pounds; .380 ACP, 1.5 pounds; .22 LR, 1.1 pounds
Overall length: 6.6 inches
Barrel length: 3.5 inches
Sights: Front: blade; rear: fixed notch

ROMARM 9x19mm Model 92 pistol

The ROMARM 9x19mm Model 92 pistol was originally intended for the export market. It is a conventional design based on Browning principles, with magazine capacity of 15 cartridges. Construction is all steel, with plastic grip panels. The Model 92 can be equipped with a tactical light or a laser pointer.

SPECIFICATIONS:

Caliber: 9x19mm
Operation: recoil, semiautomatic, double-action only
Locking: Modified Browning system
Feed: 15-round box magazine
Empty weight: 2.3 pounds
Overall length: 8.1 inches
Barrel length: 4.4 inches
Sights: Front: blade; rear: fixed notch

Russia

Russian KGB pistol range

12.3mm Udar revolver

The 12.3mm Udar ('Blow') revolver is an unusual weapon both in terms of appearance and caliber. Factory sales literature describes the Udar as a multipurpose revolver for use by security personnel, with the multipurpose function provided by an array of cartridges produced for a variety of operational uses, all based on brass 32-gauge shotgun cartridges. These include a lethal ball, armor piercing projectile with a subcaliber steel projectile for defeat of soft body armor, a shot cartridge, plastic or rubber baton rounds, a "pyroliquid" cartridge which is an irritant similar to CS or pepper spray and blank.

Three models of the Udar have been identified. The basic model is the Udar which is intended to be carried either concealed or in an open holster. This version has a shrouded hammer to prevent snagging on clothing and a sharply raked grip.

The Udar-S (S stands for 'service') has an exposed hammer and a more conventional grip angle. Noticeable variations in frame dimensions and shapes have been observed even between these two models. The Udar-S fires a special 12.3x22mm PM32 cartridge. The third model is the Udar-TS, a training version limited to firing paint, rubber bullets and blanks. The cylinder used in the Udar-TS cannot accommodate operational cartridges which are 1.96 inches long. Standard Udar and Udar-S revolvers can be converted to the Udar-TS standard simply by inserting the training cylinder.

12.3mm UDAR Revolver

Cartridges are loaded into the removable five-round cylinder either singly or via a "full moon" clip. Drums can be changed rapidly using a release catch on the left-hand side of the frame. Operation is either single or double-action with provision of a prominent shaped trigger guard for two-handed aiming and firing.

The 12.3x50mm ball cartridge has an effective range of up to 164 feet and is claimed to have more lethal power than the 9x18mm Makarov or 9x19mm Parabellum cartridges. Accuracy is such that most bullets will fall within a 1.6 inches radius at 82 feet. Steel bullets weighing 138 grains and with a muzzle velocity of 935 f/s have been reported, along with a 108 grains armor-piercing, subcaliber projectile with a muzzle velocity of 1148 feet per second.

The latter is stated to be capable of penetrating a .2 inches steel plate at operational ranges. The 12.3 x 46mm SP-9N non-lethal plastic baton round containing three balls can strike and partially disable a target without causing serious physical injury at ranges up to .6 inches. At one inch most baton projectiles will maintain sufficient accuracy to fall within a 7.9 inches radius.

The 12.3 x 50mm SP-9G 'pyroliquid' cartridge will discharge an irritant fluid within a 5.9 inches radius cone at .2 inches. Mention has also been made of a cartridge containing a .02 ounces load of pellets which are discharged with a muzzle velocity of 984 f/s. The SP-9H blank cartridge is apparently intended to disorientate as well as simulate firing and signaling sounds as the cartridge will create a sound pressure level of not less than 150 dB at 4.9 feet. For training, a 12.3 x 46mm paint cartridge is available. It weighs .007 ounces and has a muzzle velocity of 508.5 feet per second. Also available is a rubber bullet weighing .007 ounces in a 12.3 x 46mm case, also with a muzzle velocity of 508.5 feet per second.

SPECIFICATIONS: Udar-S

Caliber: 12.3mm, various cartridge lengths
Operation: double- or single-action revolver
Feed: 5-round cylinder clip
Empty weight: 2.09 lb
Overall length: 8.2 inches
Barrel length: Approximately 2.5 inches
Width: 1.7 inches
Sights: Front: fixed blade; rear: notch

12.5mm DOG-1 revolver

The 12.5mm DOG-1 revolver was developed to meet internal security requirements and for use by bodyguards or security personnel.
It was developed by the Vyatskie Polyany Mechanical Engineering Factory MOLOT (Hammer) and fires converted shotgun cartridges with a caliber given as 12.5x35mm. The exact nature of these cartridges is not known but it is probably that they follow the same general characteristics as those fired from the UDAR revolvers described elsewhere. Other than the caliber, the DOG-1's overall design is conventional. Cylinder capacity is five rounds.

SPECIFICATIONS:

Caliber: 12.5x35mm
Operation: Double or single-action (DA/SA) revolver
Feed: 5-round cylinder
Empty weight: 2.2 pounds
Overall length: 8.3 inches
Barrel length: 3.5 inches
Sights: Front: fixed blade; rear: notch

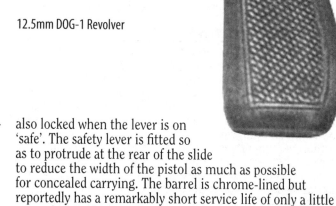

12.5mm DOG-1 Revolver

5.45x18mm Pistolet Samozaryadiny Malogabaritniy (PSM) Pistol

The 5.45x18mm PSM pistol was introduced into service in 1975 and was developed by a consortium including Tikhon Lashnev, Anatoliy Simarin and Lev Kulikov. It is the standard sidearm of many police and internal security forces and also with security elements of the armed forces. PSM stands for Pistolet Samozaryadiny Malogabaritniy ('pistol, semiautomatic, small'). It fires the 5.45x18mm 7N7 bottlenecked cartridge designed by A D Denisova. The features of the pistol and cartridge would indicate low performance, but tests have shown that it has a remarkable ability to defeat soft body armor, penetrating up to 55 layers of Kevlar at typical CQB distances.

The PSM resembles a miniature Walther PP and was clearly derived from the Makarov PM, being a double-action/single-action (DA/SA) blowback-operated pistol with a fixed barrel. If the safety lever is rotated forward to the 'safe' position, the hammer will drop onto a block, preventing it from striking the firing pin; the slide is

also locked when the lever is on 'safe'. The safety lever is fitted so as to protrude at the rear of the slide to reduce the width of the pistol as much as possible for concealed carrying. The barrel is chrome-lined but reportedly has a remarkably short service life of only a little more than 3,000 rounds.

Examples produced for commercial rather than military sales have molded plastic grips with a more comfortable outline than the standard flat alloy castings. Several commercial versions are also manufactured for civilian sales, including models chambered in .25ACP, .22LR and for tear gas cartridges.

SPECIFICATIONS:

Caliber: 5.45 x 18mm MPTs (7N7)
Operation: blowback, double-action
Feed: 8-shot detachable box magazine
Empty weight: 1.05 pounds
Overall length: 6.01 inches
Width: .69 inches
Barrel length: 3.3 inches
Sights: front, fixed blade; rear: fixed notch

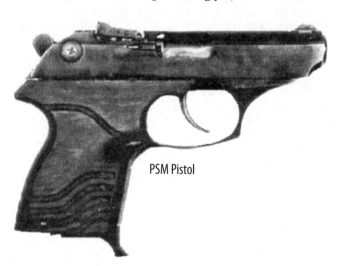

PSM Pistol

5.45x18mm OTs-23 Drotik (Javelin) Pistol

The 5.45x18mm SBZ Drotik (Javelin) was developed to meet a requirement of the Scientific Research Institute for Special Equipment for the MVD (Ministry of Internal Affairs). The Drotik was developed at Tula and is employed only by MVD personnel. The SBZ designation is derived from the Stechkin, Balster and Zinchenko design team that developed the pistol.

The Drotik is a blowback-operated, select-fire double-action/single-action (DA/SA) machine pistol. The slide-mounted selector switch has three positions. Topmost is Safe, next down is semiautomatic and lowest position gives a three-round burst at a cyclic rate of approximately 1,800 rounds per minute each time the trigger is pulled.

To compensate for muzzle rise, a muzzle brake in the form of a slot in the top of the receiver coinciding with a hole drilled in the top of the barrel is situated just behind the muzzle. The selector lever allows the hammer to be locked in the released or cocked position.

The Drotik pistol also features an external indicator by means of which the shooter can determine by touch how many rounds remain in the magazine. Grooves for mounting tactical accessories are provided on the dust cover.

SPECIFICATIONS:

Caliber: 5.45 x 18mm
Operation: blowback, select-fire with fixed three-round bursts, double-action
Feed: 24-round detachable box magazine
Empty weight: 2.1 lb
Overall length: 7.6 inches
Barrrel length: Approximately 5 inches
Sights: Front: blade; rear: fixed notch
Cyclic rate: three-round burst, approximately 1,800 rounds per minute

7.62x35mm MSP "Groza" Silent Pistol

The MSP Groza (Thunderstorm) was designed by TSNIITOCHMASH and produced by the Tula Arms Plant in the 1970s and 1980s for use by SPETsNAZ, KGB and other special operations forces for what the Russians refer to as "wet work", a euphemism for assassinations. The pistol itself is a conventional appearing double-barreled over/under derringer-type two-shot weapon that fires what appear to be 7.62x39mm cartridges held in a special clip. These are, however, special silent cartridges that make no sound whatsoever.

The pistol has no firing pins; these are in the base of the silent cartridges. When the cartridge is fired, an internal piston is driven forward by the expanding powder gases, propelling the bullet out of the barrel. The gases are retained inside the thick walled case by a piston against the shoulder of the cartridge case and protrudes some distance beyond the case mouth. This precludes automatic extraction, but results in absolute silence when the pistol is fired, as opposed to an exterior suppressor. When the barrels are tipped upwards, an extracting rod moves back and pushes the spent cartridges out of the breech for manual ejection. Cocking is via a separate lever beneath the trigger guard. Eliminating a large external suppressor also results in a very compact pistol that can be unobtrusively carried concealed.

Rifling on fired bullets appears to be the same as that in 7.62x39mm Kalashnikov rifles. The bullets themselves also appear to be standard 7.62x39mm types. The MSP is known to have been used operationally in Central America during the Cold War and by SPETsNAZ units in Afghanistan. Although obsolescent in Russian service, the MSP is included herein because it is virtually unknown in the West, despite having been in Soviet/Russian service for over 30 years.

SPECIFICATIONS:

Caliber: 7.62 x 35mm silent
Operation: manual
Locking: projecting lug
Feed: two-round clip
Empty weight: 0.75 lb
Length: 115mm
Barrel length: 2 x 66mm
Sights: Front: blade; rear: notch

MSP "Groza" Silent Pistol

S4M Silent Pistol

7.62x62.6mm S4M Silent Pistol

Little is known of the development of the 7.62x62.8mm S4M Silent Pistol. It appears to have been developed as a follow-on and improvement to the MSP Groza, as it shares the same basic concept but with improvements in both ammunition and general operation of the pistol.

Like the MSP, the S4M is a two-barreled over/under derringer intended for the same type of missions as the MSP. It is slightly larger than the MSP to accommodate the longer cartridges. Ammunition is similar in concept but is different from that of the MSP. The 7.62x62.8mm cartridge used with the S4M, bears no resemblance to any other cartridge and has much thicker case walls than the 7.62x38mm MSP cartridge, indicating that there may have been case failures with the earlier ammunition. The 7.62x62.8mm cartridge employs a piston system similar to that of the 7.62x38mm cartridge to propel the bullet. Like the MSP, the S4M has no firing pins, which are integral to the cartridge. The bullets are identical to those fired from an AK-47 or AKM rifle, and again like the MSP, rifling on fired bullets appears similar to that of bullets fired from the rifles.

The overall design of the S4M is an improvement on that of the MSP in that opening the barrel of the S4M automatically cocks the pistol. The MSP was manually cocked via a separate lever beneath the trigger guard. The protruding piston of the spent cartridge precludes conventional extraction and ejection, but this system results in almost absolute silence when the pistol is fired.

NRS Scouting Knife

PSS Silent Pistol

Moreover, on missions for which the S4M or MSP pistols would be used, leaving spent cartridge casings on the ground is not desirable.

SPECIFICATIONS:

Caliber: 7.62x62.8mm
Operation: manual
Feed: Two-round clip
Overall length: 5.5 inches
Height: 4.1 inches
Barrel length: 2 barrels, approx 3.14 inches
Sights: Front: blade; rear: notch, adjustable for windage

NRS Scouting Knife

The NRS scouting knife, also known as the NRS-2, incorporates a silent firearm in a utility knife. The handle of the knife incorporates a chamber and short barrel, into which is loaded one 7.62x42mm SP-4 captive piston silent cartridge of the type described below under the PSS Silent Pistol. This cartridge, like other captive piston cartridges, is virtually silent in use.

The muzzle of the pistol is at the butt end of the knife handle. To fire, the knife is reversed in the hand and is fired by pressure in a trigger bar set into the handle. A notch in the knife's handguard acts as a rudimentary sight. There is a sliding safety catch to prevent accidental discharges.

The knife appears to be a substantial field tool capable of cutting steel rods up to 10mm diameter. The scabbard is insulated to permit cutting electrical cables. It also incorporates a screwdriver.

SPECIFICATIONS:

Caliber: 7.62 x 42mm SP-4
Operation: Manual, single shot
Empty weight: .8 pounds (Knife alone); 1.4 pounds (knife with scabbard)
Overall length: 11.2 inches
Blade length: 162 x 28 x 3.5mm

7.62x42mm PSS Silent Pistol

Designed by Viktor Levchenko and developed by Tsniitochmash, the PSS, also known as the Vul ('volcano'), is a medium-sized blowback-operated pistol that fires the SP-4 7.62x42mm captive-piston cartridge, which is totally silent in operation. The author has fired this pistol and

PSS Silent Pistol

the only sound is that of the slide cycling back and forth. The trigger mechanism is single-action or double-action with an external hammer, and there is a slide-mounted safety lever that lowers the hammer safely on to a loaded chamber.

There is no external suppressor. Instead, the SP-4 cartridge contains a piston between the propelling charge and the cylindrical steel projectile, which has a brass driving band at the front end. On firing, the propelling charge drives the piston forward, which in turn propels the bullet forward down the barrel. The piston is arrested internally by the cartridge shoulder, where it also obturates, sealing the peopelling gases inside the case. Gases are slowly bled off to the atmosphere so that eventually interior pressure drops to nil. The bullet has an effective range of 164 feet and the fixed sights are calibrated for that range. The SP-4 bullet can penetrate .08 inches of vertical steel plate or a standard US Kevlar helmet at 8 feet range and still have sufficient energy to inflict a lethal wound. The author has verified this in testing

The PSS can be employed over a temperature range of -50 to +50°C.

MR-446 Viking

SPECIFICATIONS:

Caliber: 7.62 x 42mm SP-4
Operation: recoil-operated semiautomatic, single-action or double-action
Feed: detachable box magazine
Magazine capacity: six rounds
Empty weight: 1.5 lb
Overall length: 6.5 inches
Barrel length: 3 inches
Sights: Front: fixed blade; rear: notch, drift adjustable for windage

9x19mm 6P35 Grach Semiautomatic Pistol
9x19mm MR-446 Viking Semiautomatic Pistol

The search for a replacement for the PM Makarov pistol began during the early 1980s although it was not until late in the decade that final operational requirements were agreed upon. The project was given the cover name of Grach (Rook), with three alternative designs under consideration. The Grach-1 combined blowback with gas delay but was not considered worthy of continued development. The Grach-3 eventually entered service as the PMM a modified Makarov with higher capacity magazine and a more powerful cartridge. The PMM, however, was an interim pistol until the Grach-2 could be developed and selected for the Russian armed forces as the 6P35 Grach, or PYa (Pistolet Yarygin after the head designer, Vladimir Yarygin). The Russian military decided to adopt an indigenously designed 9x19mm designated 7N21 cartridge with an armor-penetrating bullet. Although the 7N21 is almost exactly the same dimensionally as standard 9x19mm NATO rounds, it has a higher muzzle velocity. The version of the 6P35 specifically designed to fire standard 9x19mm ammunition is designated the 9mm MR-446 Viking semiautomatic pistol. It is almost identical to the 6P35 but has a polymer frame.

Both pistols were developed at the Precision Mechanical Engineering Central Research Institute at Klimovsk.

The 9mm 6P35 semiautomatic pistol utilizes a Browning type, short-recoil, operating mechanism. Cartridges are fed from a 17-round magazine. The extractor serves as a loaded-chamber indicator, protruding above the slide's surface when a round is chambered. The frame is steel, with the grooved grip manufactured of polymer. The pistol is double-action/single-action (DA/SA) in operation. The safety is ambidextrous and blocks the hammer mechanism in the cocked or released position. When the safety is engaged, the sear, trigger and hammer are all locked.

The 9x19mm MR-446 Viking chambered in standard 9x19mm is very similar to the 6P35 Grach pistol in design and execution, other than the MR-446's polymer frame which makes it approximately 4 ounces lighter than the 6P35. The MR-446 has steel components molded in at stress points in the frame.

SPECIFICATIONS: 6P35

Caliber: 9x19mm 7N21
Operation: short-recoil, modified Browning system
Feed: 17-round detachable box magazine
Empty weight: 2.2 pounds
Overall length: 7.7 inches
Barrel length: 4.4 inches
Sights: Front: blade; rear: low-profile notch adjustable for windage

9x18mm Makarov pistol (PM)

The 9mm Makarov (PM) pistol dates from the early 1950s and has for many years been the standard pistol for Soviet and Russian forces and most members of the former Warsaw Pact. It has been manufactured in many countries other than Russia and is now widely available in the United

Makarov Pistol (PM)

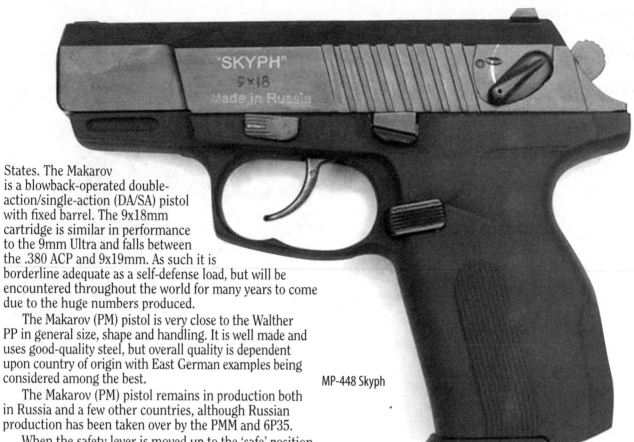

MP-448 Skyph

States. The Makarov is a blowback-operated double-action/single-action (DA/SA) pistol with fixed barrel. The 9x18mm cartridge is similar in performance to the 9mm Ultra and falls between the .380 ACP and 9x19mm. As such it is borderline adequate as a self-defense load, but will be encountered throughout the world for many years to come due to the huge numbers produced.

The Makarov (PM) pistol is very close to the Walther PP in general size, shape and handling. It is well made and uses good-quality steel, but overall quality is dependent upon country of origin with East German examples being considered among the best.

The Makarov (PM) pistol remains in production both in Russia and a few other countries, although Russian production has been taken over by the PMM and 6P35.

When the safety lever is moved up to the 'safe' position, it interposes a block between the hammer and firing pin; shortly afterwards, a projection meets a tooth on the sear and lifts the sear away from the hammer. The hammer falls and is locked in its forward position by the safety. When the safety is applied, the slide is locked.

Because the ballistic performance of the 9x18mm cartridge is close to that of the .380 ACP, many Makarovs have been converted to .380 ACP by having their barrels replaced. Shooters should verify caliber prior to firing.

Variants

PMM: See following entry.

OTs-35: See separate entry.

Baikal-422

Described as a sporting pistol, the Baikal-442 is available chambered either for the 9x18mm Makarov cartridge, with eight-, 10- or 12-round magazine capacities, or for the 9x19mm Parabellum. For the latter, the magazine capacity is eight rounds, and the empty weight is 1.8 ounces. The Baikal has a revised trigger-guard outline and is provided with adjustable rear sights for windage and elevation. A laser target indicator is an option. On this model, the safety de-cocks the hammer and blocks the firing pin and slide. The grip plates have also been ergonomically revised. This model is produced under the Baikal label by Izhevsky Mekhanichesky Zavod of Izhevsk.

IZH-71

This commercial sales model is chambered for the 9x17mm short (.380 ACP) cartridge, and the magazine holds eight rounds. A model with an increased magazine capacity (10 rounds) is also available. The empty weight of the eight-round model is 1.7 pounds, and that of the 10-round model is 1.8 pounds.

IZH-71H

The IZH-71H pistol is a private security services variant of the PM, produced under the Baikal label by Izhevsky Mekhanichesky Zavod of Izhevsk. Chambered for the 9x17mm (.380 ACP) cartridge, it features a fixed or removable laser target pointer mounted on the pistol frame and activated by the trigger travel. Magazines for eight, 10 or 12 rounds are available. The empty weight of the 12-round model is 1.9 pounds with the laser target pointer or 1.7 pounds without.

MP-448 Skyph

The MP-448 Skyph is an updated version of the basic Makarov design, incorporating a molded polymer frame, with the controls more ergonomically shaped. This pistol is chambered in .380 ACP (9x17mm), with a 10-round box magazine. The barrel is 3.6 inches long, with an overall length of 6.5 inches. The weight, unloaded, is 22.5 ounces. A Skyph Mini compact pistol exists, with a barrel length reduced to 2.9 inches. Its overall length is 5.7 inches and the unloaded weight is 20.8 ounces. Magazine capacity is eight rounds.

SPECIFICATIONS:

Caliber: 9x18mm Makarov (57-N-181S)
Operation: blowback, semiautomatic, double-action
Feed: 8-round detachable box magazine
Empty weight: 1.7 lb
Length: 6.3 inches
Height: 5.0 inches
Barrel length: 3.7 inches
Sights: Front: blade; rear: fixed notch

9x18mm PMM Semiautomatic Pistol

The 9x18mm PMM semiautomatic pistol is an updated version of the PM Makarov pistol chambered for a "high performance" 9x18mm 57-N-181SM cartridge, which has the same overall dimensions as the standard 9x18mm Makarov (57-N-181S) cartridge but has greater muzzle velocity, penetration and operates at much higher chamber pressures. At one time known under the project name of Grach-3, the PMM was always intended as an interim design pending the final selection of a new Russian armed forces service pistol. The 9x19mm 6P35 Grach ('rook') semiautomatic pistol was ultimately selected.

The conversion of the Makarov PM pistol to accommodate the new cartridge was undertaken at the Izhevsk Mechanical Plant, by designers B Pletsky and R Shogapov. Mass production of the PMM commenced in January 1994.

A polymer-framed version of this pistol with a 12-round magazine capacity also exists.

The 9x18mm PMM semiautomatic pistol is similar to the Makarov PM, although the grip has been reconfigured to improve the shooter's control of the pistol. The grip is slightly wider to accommodate a 12-round magazine. With the 12-round magazine, the pistol is known as the PMM-12, a variant that retains the original eight-round magazine carries the designation PMM-8. The PM has been changed to delayed blowback operation to accommodate the higher-pressure cartridges, via three spiral grooves in the chamber surface. The spiral grooves retard the extraction of the spent cases to allow the chamber pressure to drop before the slide starts to move to the rear. The PMM pistol will function with standard 9x18mm Makarov (57-N-181S) cartridges, but not vice versa. The 57-N-181SM cartridge can be chambered in a standard PM, but firing it usually causes the PM to catastrophically fail because it was not designed to function with such high-pressure cartridges. There have been reports of severe injuries when individuals mistakenly fired 57-N-181SM cartridges in a standard PM.

The 57-N-181SM bullet is conical in shape with a flat nose, partly to differentiate it from standard cartridges. It can penetrate .3 inches of steel at 32.8 feet and .3 inches at 65.6 feet. (Same penetration at different distances????)

Variant

OTs-35: See following entry.

OTs-35

SPECIFICATIONS:
Caliber: 9x18mm 57-N-181SM; 9x18mm 57-N-181S
Operation: delayed blowback, semiautomatic, double-action/single-action (DA/SA)
Feed: PMM-12, 12-round box magazine; PMM-8, 8-round box magazine
Empty weight: 1.62 lb
Overall length: 6.6 inches
Barrel length: 3.6 inches
Sights: Front: blade; rear: notch, drift adjustable for windage

9x18mm OTs-35 semiautomatic pistol

The OTs-35 pistol was developed by the KBP Instrument Design Bureau at Tula and is a variant of the PMM, differing only in that it has a muzzle brake/compensator that reduces the felt recoil and muzzle rise to the levels produced by the standard 57-N-151S cartridge when the increased power 57-N-151SM cartridge is fired. Control is thereby improved, especially during rapid fire.

Other than the muzzle brake, the OTs-35 is identical to the PMM pistol.

SPECIFICATIONS:
Caliber: 9x18mm 57-N-181SM
Operation: delayed blowback, semiautomatic, double-action/single-action (DA/SA)
Feed: Eight-round detachable box magazine
Empty weight: 1.7 pounds
Length: 7.3 inches
Barrel length: 93.5 inches
Sights: Front: blade; rear: fixed notch
Max effective range: 82 feet

9x19mm MR-443 Grach Semiautomatic Pistol

The 9mm MR-443 Grach (Rook) pistol was developed by Izhmash in response to a military requirement for a replacement for the Makarov PM. The MR-443 and the other pistols developed in response to the new requirement, represent a new direction in Russian military handguns in that they are chambered in 9x19mm caliber rather than Russian-developed cartridges.

The MR-443 is a conventional "full size" double-action/single-action (DA/SA) semiautomatic pistol with a steel frame and slide, ambidextrous safety, wraparound non-slip contoured rubber grips and a detachable 17-round box magazine. Locking is via the modified Browning system with a barrel lug locking into the ejection port. Stripping can be accomplished without tools by simply locking the slide to the rear: pressing out the slide stop and removing the slide and barrel assembly to the front.

PMM

MR-443 Grach

The first shot can be fired double-action with subsequent shots in single-action or the pistol can safely be carried "cocked and locked" with the hammer back and the safety on. The double-column magazine is stainless steel, with holes on the right side to show the number of rounds remaining. The extractor serves as a loaded-chamber indicator. The safety lever and magazine release positions can be reversed to accommodate both right- or left-handed shooters.

SPECIFICATIONS:

Caliber: 9x19mm
Operation: Short-recoil, modified Browning system
Feed: 17-round double-column detachable box magazine
Empty weight: 2.12 lb
Overall length: 7.8 inches
Barrel length: 4.4 inches
Sights: Front: blade; rear: low-profile notch adjustable for windage

9x19mm MR-444 Baghira and MR-445/446 Varyag Semiautomatic Pistols

The Russian press has reported the MR-444 as a replacement for the Makarov PM. The 9mm MR-444 Baghira is a compact semiautomatic pistol of modern design and has reported to be chambered not only in 9x19mm but also in .380 ACP (9x17mm) and 9x18mm Makarov as well, although these reports are unconfirmed as of this writing. The frame is reinforced polymer with steel components at stress points. The steel guide rails are retained mechanically rather than molded in place. The front rails are held in place by the slide pin stop, while a screw retains the rear guide rail unit. There are grooves in the dust cover for the attachment of laser aiming devices or tactical lights. The MR-445 is identical except that it is chambered in .40 S&W. The MR-445S is a compact model, while the MR-446 is an MR-445 chambered in 9x19mm.

Operation is by the modified Browning system. The barrel is unlocked by the interaction of two inclines, one on the bottom of the barrel and the other integral with the recoil/buffer mechanism. Locking is accomplished by the interaction of a barrel lug with the ejection port. As the slide and barrel move to the rear under recoil, the inclines force the rear of the barrel down, unlocking the pistol and allowing the spent case to be extracted and ejected. An integral buffer reduces felt recoil, enhances control and

reduces wear. While the MR-444 appears to be hammer fired, what appears to be a hammer is actually a cocking lever that resembles a hammer. This allows the shooter to manually cock the striker for an improved trigger pull. The first shot can also have a longer, heavier double-action type trigger pull that cocks the striker prior to firing. The ejector also serves as a loaded-chamber indicator.

SPECIFICATIONS:

Caliber: 9x19mm; .380 ACP (9x17mm), 9x18mm or .40 S&W (MR-445)
Operation: short-recoil, modified Browning system
Feed: 15-round double column box magazine
Empty weight: 1.7 lb
Overall length: 7.3 inches
Barrel length: 4.0 inches
Sights: Front: blade; rear: low-profile notch adjustable for windage

9x21mm P-9 Gurza/SR-1 Vektor pistol

The 9x21mm P-9 Gurza (Viper) pistol was developed to meet a Russian military and police requirement for a pistol that offered a significant increase in terminal ballistics over any 9x18mm or 9x19mm pistol in the inventory at the time. The pistol had to defeat soft body armor and

P-9 Gurza/SR-1 Vektor

P-9 Gurza/SR-1 Vektor

light vehicle bodies.
According to the
manufacturer,
the Gurza is in
use by both the
Russian Police
(Militsiya) and
Military Intelligence
Directorate (GRU).
The bullet from the
Gurza's 9x21mm SP-10 cartridge is claimed to penetrate
30 layers of Kevlar, which has been confirmed by testing
in the West. The SR-1 Vektor was developed from the
P-9 Gurza and has apparently replaced it in production
although the name Gurza continues to be used for
marketing purposes.

The P-9 Gurza is an unconventional and innovative design.
The operating system is similar to that of the Beretta 92 in
that locking is by a falling block rather than the modified
Browning systems that the appearance would suggest. The
frame is part polymer and part steel. There are no manually
operated safeties. An automatic grip safety completely
disengages the trigger mechanism from the sear unless it is
depressed. Pulling the trigger with the hammer down has no
effect; the hammer must first be placed in an intermediate
half-cock position, which engages the sear, enabling a double-
action first shot. Subsequent shots are single-action. There
is also a trigger safety that prevents the pistol from firing
unless it is depressed. The grip and trigger safeties are linked
and both must be depressed before the pistol will fire. The
magazine release is ambidextrous and operates with a forward
push of the thumb or index finger.

There are two 9x21mm rounds used in this pistol: the
SP-10 and SP-11. The SP-10 is an armor-piercing bullet
with a hardened steel insert to defeat body armor. The
cartridge is 1.3 inches in overall length and weighs .38
ounces. The bullet weighs 88 grains and has a muzzle
velocity of 1,378 fps. The SP-11 is a ball round, also 1.3
inches in overall length and weighs 185 grains. The bullet
weighs 123 grains and has a muzzle velocity of 1,280 fps.
The SP-11 bullet may be frangible.

SPECIFICATIONS:
Caliber: 9 x 21mm Russian SP-10 and SP-11
Operation: Short-recoil, semiautomatic, double or single-action (DA/SA)
Locking: Falling block
Feed: 18-round detachable box magazine
Empty weight: approx. 2.1 lb
Overall length: 7.9 inches
Sights: Front: fixed blade; rear: fixed rectangular notch

9x19mm PMS-1 Semiautomatic Pistol

In early 1999, Molot JSC announced an updated
version of the Stechkin APS chambered in 9x19mm and
in semiautomatic only. The new model is designated
the Pistolet Modernizirovanniy Stechkina (Stechkin
Modernized Pistol) or PMS-1. According to Molot, the
PMS-1 has been in production since 1997.

Molot states that the PMS-1 is blowback-operated,
although this mode of operation in a 9x19mm pistol is
unlikely. A more probable system would be delayed blowback,
perhaps using the rate reducer of the APS. The quality of the
PMS-1 appears to be high but, as with the APS, the PMS-1 is
a large, complex and relatively heavy pistol.

OTs-27 Berdysh

SPECIFICATIONS:
Caliber: 9x19mm
Operation: Blowback (see text), semiautomatic only
Feed: 20-round double column detachable box magazine
Empty weight: 1.4 lb
Overall length: 230mm
Barrel length: 138mm
Sights: Front: blade; rear: notch, adjustable for windage and elevation

9x18/9x19mm OTs-27 (PSA) Berdysh pistol

The 9mm OTs-27 pistol was originally developed as a
replacement for the PM Makarov but was not adopted. The
Russian Interior Ministry subsequently adopted a modified
version of the pistol, which is described in herein. PSA is
an acronym indicating Pistol, Stechkin, Avramov, after the
designers.

The 9mm PSA (OTs-27) Berdysh (Poleax) pistol is
primarily designed for the standard 9x18mm 57-N-151S
and the more powerful 57-N-151SM cartridge but by simply
replacing the barrel and magazine, it can be converted to
fire 9x19mm ammunition. In 9x19mm, the designation is
changed to OTs-27-2.

The OTs-27 Berdysh is a stated to be a blowback operated,
double-action pistol with a box magazine containing 18
rounds, although it is more likely to be delayed blowback
given that it is chambered for two cartridges that are not
suitable for straight blowback operation. A loaded-chamber
indicator is provided. An ambidextrous safety lever is provided
on each side of the slide just forward of the hammer.

The OTs-27 Berdysh pistol can be equipped with a laser
target indicator and a sound suppressor.

SPECIFICATIONS:
Caliber: 9x18mm Makarov 57-N-181S and 57-N-181SM; 9x19mm
Operation: Delayed blowback, semiautomatic, double-action/single-action (DA/SA)
Feed: 18-round detachable box magazine
Empty weight: 2.12 lb
Overall length: 7.8 inches
Barrel length: Approximately 5 inches
Sights: Front: blade; rear: notch

9x18mm R-92/R-92KS Revolvers

The unusual-appearing 9x18mm R-92 revolvers are produced by the Tula KBP Instrument Design Bureau, and were developed for the Scientific Research Institute for Special Equipment for the MVD (NIIST). They are intended to provide a conceal-carry, instant readiness revolver for Russia's internal security forces. The overall design is light and compact, with the swing-out cylinder holding five 9x18mm Makarov (57-N-151S) cartridges in a "full moon" clip. Cartridges can be fired without the clip, but must be individually ejected. The R-92KS is chambered in .380 ACP (9x17mm).

The R-92 is normally fired in double-action, although it can be fired single-action by manually cocking the partially shrouded hammer. The front sight is rudimentary and the rear sight is limited to a groove along the top of the frame in keeping with a concealment weapon for close quarters combat.

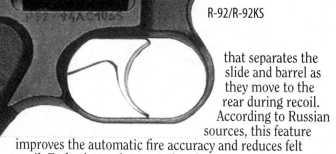

R-92/R-92KS

that separates the slide and barrel as they move to the rear during recoil. According to Russian sources, this feature improves the automatic fire accuracy and reduces felt recoil. To further reduce recoil and compensate for muzzle rise, some propellant gases are diverted into a slide cavity that acts as a muzzle brake and compensator, deflecting the gases upward to stabilize the barrel.

The safety/fire selection lever is fully ambidextrous. The usual issues of recoil forces reducing accuracy and wasting ammunition are at least partially overcome by attaching a folding metal stock at the base of the grip.

SPECIFICATIONS:

Caliber: 9x18mm or .380 ACP (9x17mm)
Operation: double- or single-action revolver
Feed: Five-round cylinder
Empty weight: 1.2 lb
Overall length: 6.1 inches
Sights: Front: small fixed blade; rear: groove along frame

SPECIFICATIONS:

Caliber: 9x18mm Makarov 57-N-181S and 57-N-181SM
Operation: Delayed blowback, double-action/single-action (DA/SA), select-fire
Feed: 18- or 27-round box magazine
Empty weight: without stock, 2.5 lb; with stock, 3.1 lb
Overall length: 8.7 inches; with stock attached, 21.2 inches
Sights: Front: blade; rear: notch, adjustable

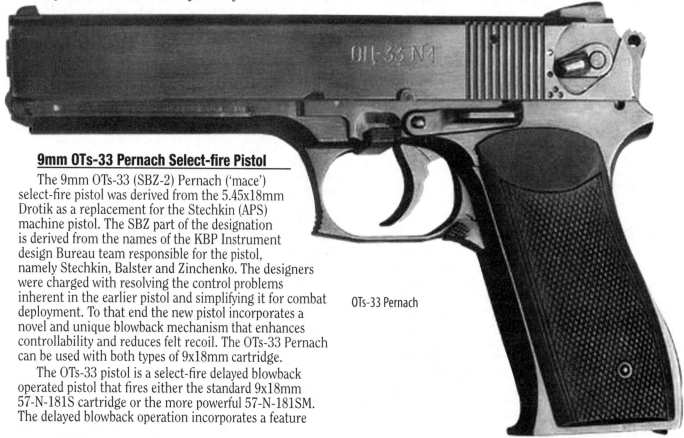

9mm OTs-33 Pernach Select-fire Pistol

The 9mm OTs-33 (SBZ-2) Pernach ('mace') select-fire pistol was derived from the 5.45x18mm Drotik as a replacement for the Stechkin (APS) machine pistol. The SBZ part of the designation is derived from the names of the KBP Instrument design Bureau team responsible for the pistol, namely Stechkin, Balster and Zinchenko. The designers were charged with resolving the control problems inherent in the earlier pistol and simplifying it for combat deployment. To that end the new pistol incorporates a novel and unique blowback mechanism that enhances controllability and reduces felt recoil. The OTs-33 Pernach can be used with both types of 9x18mm cartridge.

The OTs-33 pistol is a select-fire delayed blowback operated pistol that fires either the standard 9x18mm 57-N-181S cartridge or the more powerful 57-N-181SM. The delayed blowback operation incorporates a feature

OTs-33 Pernach

9x18mm Stechkin automatic pistol (APS)

The Stechkin (APS) pistol is no longer in service with regular Russian forces, but it continues to turn up in many parts of the world as it is still available for production and is marketed for export sales. The APS is unusual in that is a select-fire pistol. Firing a pistol like the APS on full automatic is generally considered a waste of ammunition since the weapon is too light and not properly configured to be controllable, even with its optional carbine-style stock. It appears that the Soviet armed forces came to this conclusion and withdrew the weapon from regular use. Despite this, the OTs-33 Pernach pistol was developed as a replacement. An export version designated PMS-1 chambered for 9x19mm is available.

Mechanically the Stechkin is similar to the Makarov in that it is a blowback operated pistol that fires the standard 9x18mm 57-N-181S cartridge. The main difference is that the APS has a selector lever that permits single shots or automatic fire, and it is larger and heavier. The design is very complex and expensive to manufacture.

A variant, the Stechkin APS-B with a sound suppressor was also produced. When not in use the suppressor could be clipped to a skeleton wire shoulder stock which could be bolted to the grip.

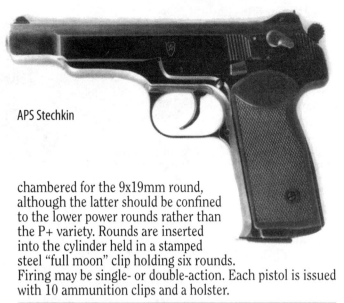
APS Stechkin

SPECIFICATIONS:
Caliber: 9x18mm (57-N-181S)
Operation: blowback, single or double-action, selective fire
Feed: 20-round box magazine
Empty weight: 2.3 pounds; with holster stock, 3.5 pounds
Length: 8.6 inches; with stock attached, 21.3 inches
Barrel length: 5.5 inches
Sights: Front: blade; rear: notch, adjustable by rotating drum to 1, 2, 4 or 6 inches
Cyclic rate: 750 rounds per minute ; practical, 40 to 80 rounds per minute

9mm AEK 906 Nosorog (Rhinoceros) Revolver

The Nosorog 9mm AEK 906 revolver is unusual in that the barrel is aligned with the bottom chamber in the cylinder, rather than the usual top. This arrangement has been selected to improve the balance of the revolver by moving the approximate center of gravity towards the bore axis and dropping the line of fire relative to the shooter's hand. This is claimed to reduce the recoil reactions produced on firing and thus enabling the sights to be placed back onto a target more quickly. It would also appear to result in a very robust construction for the pistol.

The standard Nosorog AEK 906 revolver is chambered for the 9x18mm cartridge, while the AEK 906-1 is

chambered for the 9x19mm round, although the latter should be confined to the lower power rounds rather than the P+ variety. Rounds are inserted into the cylinder held in a stamped steel "full moon" clip holding six rounds. Firing may be single- or double-action. Each pistol is issued with 10 ammunition clips and a holster.

SPECIFICATIONS:
Caliber: 9x18mm (AEK 906-1, 9x19mm Parabellum)
Operation: Double- or single-action revolver
Feed: 6-round cylinder
Empty weight: 1.8 pounds
Overall length: 8.5 inches
Sights: Front: fixed blade; rear: notch

12.5x40mm OTs-20 "Gnom" revolver

The 12.5x40mm OTs-20 "Gnom" (gnome) revolver is designed for use by internal security and paramilitary units. It fires 12.5x40mm cartridges based on brass-cased 32-gauge shotgun shells. These include the STs110 armor-piercing cartridge with a steel projectile, the STs110-04 containing a solid lead projectile and the STs110-02 shot cartridge.

The steel-framed OTs-20 Gnom is a conventional single-action or double-action revolver with a five-round cylinder. The cylinder swings to the left for reloading. A laser pointer is available as an option. The armor-piercing projectile fired from the STs110 cartridge can penetrate .18 inch of armor plate at a range of 25 meters.

SPECIFICATIONS:
Caliber: 12.5 x 40mm
Operation: double- or single-action revolver
Feed: 5-round cylinder
Empty weight: 2.43 lb
Overall length: 9.8 inches
Barrel length: approximately 5.5 inches
Sights: Front: fixed blade; rear: notch

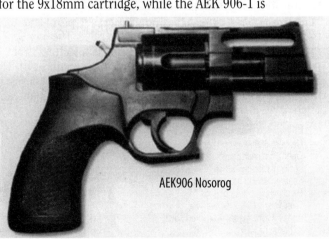
AEK906 Nosorog

OTs-20 "Gnom"

9x19mm GSh-18 Semiautomatic Pistol

The 9mm GSh-18 was developed by Tula KBP and was based on the earlier P-96 pistol. The GSh-18 is intended primarily for close-quarter employment and fires a powerful Russian-designed armor-piercing 9x19mm cartridge known as the 7N31 or PBP with a 63-grain bullet. This bullet contains a hardened steel core that penetrates up to .32 inches of steel plate or Level 3A body armor at 20 meters. The pistol can also fire standard 9x19mm ammunition.

The GSh-18 is described by KBP as being a "new-generation personal defense weapon." It resembles Glock pistols both in concept and in execution, although the external appearance of the two designs is quite different. It also exhibits features of recent Beretta designs.

The GSh-18 is probably intended for concealed carry, as indicated by its rounded contours, narrow profile (only 34mm) and its stainless or electroless nickel-plated slide. Both these materials are corrosion resistant. The GSh-18 has an ergonomically molded polymer frame and steel slide, and a striker firing mechanism.

The GSh-18 has no external safeties. The trigger safety that prevents the trigger from engaging the sear is considered sufficient. The GSh-18 striker firing system appears similar to that of Glock in that it is not fully cocked when the trigger is at rest. Unlike Glock pistols, the GSh-18 uses a rotating barrel-locking system similar to that of the Beretta 8000 series. A laser pointer can be installed.

GSH-18

SPECIFICATIONS:

Caliber: 9x19mm Parabellum 7N31 (PBP)
Operation: short-recoil
Locking: rotating barrel
Feed: 18-round box magazine
Empty weight: 1.3 pounds
Overall length: 7.2 ounces
Sights: Front: blade; rear: fixed notch

9x18mm/.380 ACP OTs-01 and OTs-01S Kobalt (RSA) revolvers

The 9mm OTs-01 and OTs-01S Kobalt revolvers are developments of the RSA revolver. The design of the OTs-01 9mm revolver has been credited to Igor Stechkin and Boris Avramov; hence it is also called the Revolver Stechkina-Aramova (RSA). Development of the RSA commenced in 1991 to meet a requirement for a standard service revolver for the Russian Federation Interior Ministry and was completed in 1992.

The OTs-01 is chambered for the 9x18mm (57-N-181S) cartridge, while the OTs-01S is chambered in .380 ACP (9x17mm). Rounds are fed into the swing-out cylinder in two "half moon" clips, each holding three rounds. The rounds are located in the clips so that they load into alternate chambers. The two clips are thus located with one clip placed over the previously loaded clip.

An unusual feature is a safety catch on the left of the frame. Actuating the safety catch locks the external hammer and blocks cylinder rotation.

The service life is given at some 3,000-rounds, which is surprisingly low. Various grip configurations are available.

SPECIFICATIONS:

Caliber: 9x18mm (57-N-181S) or .380 ACP (9x17mm)
Operation: double- or single-action revolver
Feed: 6-round cylinder
Empty weight: 1.76 lb
Overall length: 7.8 inches
Barrel length: Approximately 4 inches
Sights: Front: fixed-blade; rear: notch

9x19mm P-96 /P-96S Semiautomatic Pistol

The P-96 is one of the first Russian "new generation" pistols chambered in 9x19mm and with a polymer frame and striker firing mechanism similar to that of Glock. The short-recoil mechanism is similar to that of the Beretta 8000. The P96 formed the basis for the later and very similar GSh-18. Full details of the operating system and specifications can be found under that entry.

The P-96S is a compact version of the P-96 pistol and is chambered in .380 ACP (9x17mm) cartridge. The box magazine holds 10 rounds. The frame is manufactured from polymers, with a steel slide and steel reinforcements in the frame at points of stress. An automatic trigger safety allows the pistol to safely be carried with a cartridge in the chamber. There is no manual safety lever.

SPECIFICATIONS:

Caliber: .380 ACP (9x17mm)
Operation: short-recoil
Locking: rotating barrel
Feed: 10-round box magazine
Empty weight: 1.02 pounds
Overall length: 5.9 inches
Sights: Front: blade; rear: fixed notch

SPP-1/SPP-1M Underwater Pistol

4.5x39mm SPP-1/ SPP-1M Underwater Pistol

The 4.5X39mm SPP-1 underwater pistol entered service in 1971 and is a four-barreled pistol that fires a drag-stabilized dart with sufficient power be lethal up to a range of 55.8 feet underwater, depending on the depth at which the pistol is fired; at a depth of 131 feet, the lethal range is reduced to 19.7 feet. The lethal range is based on the ability of the dart to penetrate a padded underwater diving suit or a .2 inch-thick glass face piece.

The dart comprises the 4.5mm (.177 caliber) bullet fired from the SPS rounds, which are held in a four-round clip that is loaded into the barrels of the pistol from the rear and secured by the firing chamber and the breechblock. A double-action mechanism with a rotating firing pin fires one cartridge sequentially with each pull of the trigger. When all cartridges have been expended, the clip with the spent cartridge cases is manually ejected. Fresh rounds can be pressed into the clip using a special tool carried in a waterproofed carrying case together with the pistol. If required, loaded clips can be carried on a belt or on a sling inside waterproofed containers, each holding one loaded clip. The lid of the waterproof carrying case contains three holders, along with a cleaning kit. A complete SPP-1 system includes the pistol, 10 cartridge clips, a holster, a device for loading SPS cartridges into the clips, and a sling to carry the pistol and three containers with loaded clips.

The SPP-1M pistol is essentially the same as the SPP-1 but with an additional spring above the sear to improve the trigger pull. In addition, the trigger guard is enlarged to accommodate diving gloves.

The 4.5mm dart is 4.5 inches long and weighs 197 grains. The complete SPS round is 5.7 inches in overall length.

SPECIFICATIONS:
Caliber: 4.5 x 39mm SPS
Operation: breech-loading four-shot repeater, tip-down barrels
Feed: 4-round clip (see text)
Empty weight: 2.09 pounds
Overall length: 9.6 inches
Barrel length: Approximately 7 inches
Effective range: in air: 20 m; in water: 5 m depth: 17 m;
20 m depth: 11 m; 40 m depth: 6 m

South Africa

Vektor Z-88 semiautomatic pistol

In 1985, the South African Defense Force expressed a requirement for a new pistol. Because of the arms embargo at the time, South African acquisition of foreign pistols was very difficult, so it was decided to investigate the possibility of local manufacture. Discussions between the police and Armscor led to requirements specification in April 1986. Lyttelton Engineering Works (LIW), now a division of Denel (Pty) Ltd., was instructed to proceed with the project, with the goal of beginning production within two years. The project proceeded according to schedule and by August 1988, 200 pistols had been manufactured, confirming the production capability and allowing the pistols to be to field-tested. Full production got underway in early 1989.

The Z-88 pistol takes its name from the late Mr. T D Zeederberg (former general manager of LIW, who was instrumental in the successful handling of the project by the company) and from its year of introduction.

The Vektor Z-88 is based on the Beretta 9x19mm Model 92, although there are a few minor differences between the Beretta and the Vektor product. The pistols are for all intents and purposes identical.

SPECIFICATIONS:
Caliber: 9x19mm Parabellum
Operation: short-recoil, semiautomatic, double-action/single-action (DA/SA)
Locking: falling block
Feed: detachable box magazine, 15 rounds capacity
Empty weight: 2.3 lb
Overall length: 217mm
Barrel length: 125mm
Sights: Front: blade integral with slide; rear: notched bar dovetailed into slide with tritium luminous sights provided front and rear.

Vektor SP1 and SP2 pistols

The Vektor SP1 was developed by LIW, a division of Denel (Pty) Ltd., from the earlier Z-88 and was adopted by the South African National Defense Force. It is a recoil-operated semiautomatic pistol with double-action/single-action (DA/SA) trigger mechanism and a 15-shot magazine for 9x19mm ammunition. The manual safety is fully ambidextrous and the magazine release can be reversed for left-handed shooters.

The Vektor SP2 was developed to fire the .40 Smith & Wesson (S&W) cartridge. On the SP2, magazine capacity is 11 rounds and the rifling is six polygonal grooves, right-hand twist. An optional conversion kit permits the firing of 9x19mm cartridges. This kit consists of a barrel, a recoil spring and a magazine, the only components affected by the caliber change. The conversion is simply a matter of field-stripping the pistol and substituting these parts for the corresponding .40 S&W parts.

The Vektor SP1 slide is machined from solid bar steel and the frame is made from aircraft-quality aluminum alloy. The principal components of the pistol are manufactured on modern CNC machinery.

An automatic firing-pin-blocking safety ensures that the pistol will not fire unless the trigger is pressed. The ambidextrous safety locks the slide and sear. The barrel is cold hammer-forged.

Variants

SP1 and SP2 General's Models pistols: See following entry.

SPECIFICATIONS:
Data for SP1; where SP 2 differs, shown in parentheses

Caliber: 9x19mm (.40 S&W)
Operation: recoil, semiautomatic
Locking: Falling block
Feed: 15-round detachable box magazine (11-round detachable box magazine)
Empty weight: 2.3 lb
Overall length: 210mm
Barrel length: 118mm
Sights: Front: blade; rear: square notch. Tritium inserts optional

Vektor SP1 and SP2 General's Model pistols

The Vektor SP1 and SP2 General's Model pistols are basically identical to the standard Vektor SP1 and SP2 pistols except for their shorter barrels and their reduced overall dimensions. The 9x19mm SP1 and .40 S&W SP2 General's Model retains the full 15- and 11-round ammunition capacity. The SP2 General's Model can incorporate a recoil buffer that reduces firing stresses by 20 percent. Other specifications are as for the standard Vektor SP1 and SP2.

SPECIFICATIONS: Data for SP 1 General's Model; where SP 2 General's Model differs, shown in parentheses

Caliber: 9x19mm Parabellum (.40 S&W)
Operation: recoil, semiautomatic
Locking: Falling block
Feed: 15-round detachable box magazine (11-round detachable box magazine)
Empty weight: 2.0 lb
Overall length: 190mm
Barrel length: 103mm
Sights: Front: blade; rear: square notch

Vektor SP1 Pistol

ADP Mk II pistol

The ADP Mk II lightweight pistol takes its name from the designer, Alex Du Plessis, who also developed the LDP submachine gun. The original ADP design was replaced by the ADP Mk II in 1994, which included several enhancements, primarily a more ergonomic design to enable the relatively small-dimensioned pistol to fit the hand with greater user ease and comfort. The safety lever is fully ambidextrous and the magazine release can be reversed for left-handed users. Another change is a magazine extension for grip comfort and the sights have been raised for easier aiming. An optional 15-round box magazine was also introduced. The pistol was originally chambered in 9x19mm, .380 ACP (9x17mm), .40 S&W and .45 ACP. Currently, the only calibers produced are 9x19mm and .40 S&W.

The ADP Mk II was originally manufactured by Reutech Defense Industries, but the South African manufacturer is presently Truvelo Manufacturers (Pty) Ltd. Tanfoglio of Italy has produced the ADP pistol under license since 1994.

The pistol frame is high-impact molded polymer with embedded steel slide rails. The slide is of cast and machined steel and the entire pistol is covered with a black oxide surface finish. Operation is by delayed blowback; a gas port in the barrel vents into a cylinder in the frame where the high-pressure gas acts against a piston attached to the front end of the slide. So long as the pressure in the barrel and cylinder remains high, the slide is prevented from moving rearward. As soon as the bullet has left the barrel the gas is able to exhaust from the cylinder and the slide can then move back to perform the reloading cycle. The firing mechanism is a self-cocking striker. Pulling the trigger causes a sear to engage in the striker and force it back, further compressing the striker spring. As the spring becomes fully compressed so the operating arm is disengaged and the striker moves forward to fire the round in the chamber. A manual safety catch interposes a block behind the trigger, preventing it from engaging the striker. There is also an open breech disconnector. The magazine catch can be reversed to suit left-handed shooters.

The front sight is a fixed blade with a rear sight adjustable for windage. Beta night sights with tritium inserts are optional. An extended barrel is available for the attachment of a sound suppressor.

SPECIFICATIONS:
Caliber: 9x19mm ; .40 S&W
Operation: Gas delayed blowback
Feed: Detachable box magazine: 10 rounds capacity (9x19mm);
8 rounds capacity (.40 S&W)
Empty weight: 1.3 lb
Overall length: 160mm

Spain

(NOTE: Astra (Unceta y Compania, Guernica) and Star (Star Bonifacio Echeverria SA, Eibar) closed their doors in 1997 and while there have been some attempts to resume production of pistols under the name ASTAR, neither Astra nor Star pistols are being manufactured as of the time this is written, late 2004. Recent Astra and Star pistols are included herein because they were widely exported and may still be encountered.)

Astra 9x19mm Model A-70 pistol

The Astra 9mm Model A-70 is a locked-breech, recoil-operated, single-action semiautomatic pistol. The effective cartridges and its relatively small size make it suitable for self-defense, police or military use.

The pistol employs three independent safeties: an automatic firing pin safety that ensures that the firing pin cannot move unless the trigger is fully pressed; a manual safety applied with the thumb which, with the hammer cocked, blocks the trigger and slide and a half-cock notch on the hammer which prevents the hammer striking the firing pin should the hammer be allowed to slip during cocking or de-cocking the weapon.

SPECIFICATIONS:
Caliber: 9x19mm
Parabellum; .40 S&W
Operation: short-recoil,
semiautomatic
Locking: barrel/slide
insert
Feed: 8-round (9mm)
or 7-round (.40 S&W)
detachable box magazine
Empty weight: 1.82 lb
Overall length: 6.5 inches
Barrel length: 3.5 inches

Astra 9x19mm/.40 S&W A-75 pistol

The Astra A-75 is a compact pistol designed to meet the needs of police and military forces. A recoil-operated weapon, it uses the usual cam-dropped barrel system, the squared-off chamber area locking into the ejection port of the slide. There are three independent safety systems: an automatic firing pin safety, which keeps the firing pin securely locked except during the last movement of the trigger when deliberately pulled; a hammer safety which, should the hammer slip during thumb-cocking, arrests the hammer in the rebounded position and prevents it striking the firing pin (which is, in any case, locked); and a de-cocking lever, whereby the hammer can be lowered safely onto a loaded chamber. The firing mechanism is double-action, and the pistol can be fired from the de-cocked condition by simply pulling through the trigger, which releases both the firing pin and hammer safeties.

In 1994 it was announced that the A-75 was available with an aluminum frame. A variant in .45 ACP was introduced during October 1994.

SPECIFICATIONS:
Caliber: 9x19mm Parabellum; .40 S&W
Operation: short-recoil, semiautomatic, double-action/single-action (DA/SA)
Locking: barrel/slide insert
Feed: 8-round (9mm) or 7-round (.40 S&W) detachable box magazine
Empty weight: 1.93 lb
Overall length: 6.5 inches
Barrel length: 3.5 inches

Astra 9x19mm Model A-80 pistol

The Astra Model A-80 is reminiscent of the SIG-Sauer (now SAN Swiss Arms) P220 in its general appearance and function, such as its de-cocking lever. When the pistol has been loaded, the de-cocking lever is pressed, releasing the hammer, which falls to a step on the de-cocking lever and travels down until it is arrested by a notch on the sear, preventing the hammer from contacting the firing pin. The firing pin itself is restrained from movement by a spring-loaded plunger, which is engaged at all times except when the trigger is pulled. When the trigger is pulled, the action of the sear in releasing the cocked hammer forces the plunger out of engagement and permits the pin to move when struck by the hammer. Unless the trigger is pulled, even an accidental fall of the hammer cannot drive the firing pin forward. There is thus no manual safety on the Model A-80.

The de-cocking lever is on the left side of the frame where it can be operated conveniently by a right-handed shooter's thumb. For left-handed shooters the lever can be removed and a replacement installed on the right side of the frame.

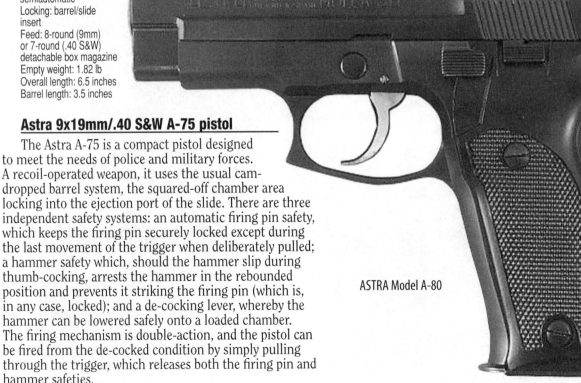

ASTRA Model A-80

The magazine holds 15 rounds and has holes that show when there are 5, 10 or 15 rounds in the magazine.

SPECIFICATIONS:

Caliber: 9x19mm
Operation: short-recoil, semiautomatic
Locking: Browning system
Feed: 15-round detachable box magazine
Empty weight: 2.16 lb
Overall length: 7.0 inches
Barrel length: 3.8 inches
Sights: Front: blade; rear: notch, adjustable for windage

Astra 9mm Model A-90 pistol

The Astra 9mm Model A-90, which ceased production prior to Astra's demise, was introduced in 1985 as an updated version of the A-80. It has an improved double-action mechanism, adjustable sights, a large magazine capacity and compact external dimensions.

Operational safety is emphasized, and the facilities on the A-90 permit the user several safety options. First, pressing a hammer-de-cocking lever releases the sear, allowing the hammer to drop, but the de-cocking lever arrests the hammer stroke so that the hammer does not contact the firing pin. There is also a manual safety on the slide, which operates to rotate a portion of the two-piece

firing pin out of the hammer's path; this safety can be applied regardless of the hammer's position. Finally, the front portion of the firing pin is locked by an automatic block that is released only when the trigger is fully pulled. At all other times, the forward part of the firing pin cannot move, regardless of the status of any other safety.

SPECIFICATIONS:

Caliber: 9x19mm
Operation: recoil, semiautomatic, double-action
Locking: barrel/slide insert
Feed: 17-round detachable box magazine
Empty weight: 2.16 lb
Overall length: 7.0 inches
Barrel length: 3.8 inches

Astra Model A-100 pistol

The Model A-100 is a further development in the Astra A-70/80/90 series. It is basically the same pistol as the A-90 but without the manual safety. Operation relies entirely upon passive safeties and the de-cocking lever. After loading the pistol, the de-cocking lever can be pressed. This lowers the hammer under control until it engages a safety notch in the sear that holds it out of contact with the firing pin. A spring-loaded block also locks the firing pin so that it cannot move forward far enough to contact the primer

ASTRA Model A-90

ASTRA Model A-100

Fabrinor Minimax

unless the trigger is pulled. To fire, all that is required is either to pull the trigger or cock the hammer. In either case, pressure on the trigger will rotate the sear and allow the hammer to fall. The sear also has an upper arm that presses against the firing pin lock and at the instant the hammer is about to be released, lifts it to free the firing pin. As soon as the shot has been fired and the trigger released, the firing pin lock automatically moves back into place.

SPECIFICATIONS:
Caliber: 9x19mm Parabellum; .40 S&W; .45 ACP
Operation: short-recoil, semiautomatic
Locking: barrel/slide insert
Feed: 17-round (9mm), 13-round (.40 S&W), or 9-round (.45 ACP) detachable box magazine
Empty weight: 2.16 lb
Overall length: 7.0 inches
Barrel length: 3.8 inches
Sights: Front: blade; rear: notch, adjustable for windage

Fabrinor .357 Modelo Comanche revolver

The Fabrinor (formerly Llama) .357 Modelo Comanche revolver is a near copy of Smith & Wesson revolvers chambered for the .357 Magnum cartridge. It is a conventional solid-frame revolver with a six-round chamber that swings out to the left. The main difference from similar revolvers is that the .357 Modelo Comanche incorporates a feature of Llama revolvers whereby the hammer only moves to a central position to strike the firing pin when the trigger is deliberately pulled. At all other times the hammer rests against the frame, out of alignment with the firing pin. The hammer moves to this position every time the trigger is released.

SPECIFICATIONS:
Caliber: .357 Magnum
Operation: double-action revolver
Cylinder capacity: 6 rounds
Empty weight: (4-inch barrel) 2.28 lb; (6-inch barrel) 2.49 lb
Overall length: (4-inch barrel) 9.25 inches; (6-inch barrel) 11.2 inches
Barrel length: 4 or 6 inches
Sights: Front: blade; rear: square notch, micrometer adjustable

Fabrinor Minimax Semiautomatic Pistols

Fabrinor (formerly Llama) Minimax pistols are compact and intended to combine small size with maximum firepower, hence the designation "Minimax". The overall 'no-frills' design is simple and rugged. Locking is of the falling-block type. The pistols have an extended beavertail grip safety and an automatic firing pin safety. Construction is all steel, with a matte-satin chrome blued finish and neoprene grips standard. An overall satin chrome steel finish and a 'duotone' finish with a satin chrome frame and a matte-satin chrome blued slide is also available

Minimax pistols are available in three calibers: .45 ACP, .40 S&W and 9x19mm. There is also a Minimax II, available only in .45 ACP.

Variant

Minimax Subcompact Pistol. The .45 Minimax subcompact pistol is a subcompact version of the Minimax pistols, but is available chambered only for .45 ACP. All the features of the Minimax pistols are retained, and the magazine holds 10 rounds and has an extension for easier handling. An extended beavertail grip safety is provided, along with an automatic firing-pin safety. Construction is all steel, with a matte-satin stainless, blued, or chrome and blue "duotone" finish. Neoprene grips are standard.

SPECIFICATIONS:
Caliber: 9x19mm; .40 S&W; .45 ACP
Operation: recoil, semiautomatic, double-action/single-action (DA/SA)
Locking: Falling block
Feed: Detachable box magazine. Capacities: 9x19mm: 8 rounds; .40 S&W: 7 rounds; .45 ACP: 6 rounds
Minimax II and Minimax Subcompact: 10 rounds
Empty weight: kg (Minimax Subcompact, 1.95 lb)
Overall length: 7.3 inches (Minimax Subcompact, 6.7 inches)
Barrel length: 3.5 inches
Sights: 3-dot combat: Front: fixed blade; rear: fixed notch

Fabrinor 9x19mm M-82 Semiautomatic Pistol

The Fabrinor M-82 was previously known as the Llama M-82. It is a locked-breech 9x19mm pistol using double-action/single-action mechanism in which the first shot is fired double-action and subsequent shots in single-action. Locking is accomplished by a falling block, similar to that of the Walther P38 pistol. There is a slide-mounted safety that locks the firing pin and disconnects the trigger bar when engaged. A visible and tactile button serves as a loaded-chamber indicator.

SPECIFICATIONS:
Caliber: 9x19mm
Operation: Short-recoil, semiautomatic
Locking: falling block
Feed: detachable box magazine, 15 rounds capacity
Empty weight: 2.43 lb
Overall length: 8.23 inches
Barrel length: 4.48 inches
Sights: Front: blade; rear: laterally adjustable notch

Fabrinor 9x19mm M-87 Pistol

The Fabrinor 9x19mm M-87 pistol, previously known as the Llama M-87, is basically an enlarged and improved version of the M-82. The basic operating mechanism is unchanged, with the same falling-block locking system. The barrel is lengthened with the slide extended via an attachment that acts as a balance weight and as a muzzle brake with ports at the upper sides. The frame and magazine are treated with a corrosion resistant nickel finish. The magazine release is enlarged and the magazine well beveled to ease magazine insertion. The trigger is adjustable for length and pull weight.

SPECIFICATIONS:
Caliber: 9x19mm
Operation: recoil, semiautomatic, double-action single/action (DA/SA)
Locking: falling block
Feed: 15-round detachable box magazine
Empty weight: 2.71 lb
Overall length: 9.6 inches
Barrel length: 5.2 inches
Sights: Front: blade; rear: square notch

Fabrinor MAX-II pistols

The Fabrinor (formerly Llama) MAX-II pistols are the latest versions of the Llama Models IX-C and IX-D, both essentially Colt M1911A1 pistols dating back to 1936. Two sub-models, both very similar to the Llama originals, are available. They are the MAX-II L/F and the MAX-II C/F, with the L/F indicating large frame and the C/F indicating compact frame. The two variants differ only in overall and barrel lengths and weight. Both variants are available in 9x19mm, .40 S&W, or .45 ACP.

SPECIFICATIONS: (.45 ACP version only):
Caliber: .45 ACP (.40 S&W and 9x19mm also available)
Operation: Short-recoil, semiautomatic
Locking: Browning system
Feed: 10- or 13-round detachable box magazine
Empty weight: C/F, 2.42 lb; L/F, 2.6 lb
Overall length: C/F, 7.8 inches; L/F, 8.5 inches
Sights: Front: blade; rear: square notch; both fixed

Llama Model IX-C semiautomatic pistol

The Llama Model IX-C pistol is a development of a design that first appeared in 1936. It is a conventional semiautomatic pistol derived from the Colt M1911A1 and

STAR .45 ACP Megastar

except for some minor differences in the shape of the slide, it is almost identical to the Colt. It uses the same components, disassembles and reassembles in the same way, and is chambered for the .45 ACP cartridge. The major difference is the magazine, which holds 13-rounds in a double stack. This led to some changes in the grip and frame around the magazine well. Though fractionally shorter than the M1911A1, it is slightly heavier.

STAR Model 31P

SPECIFICATIONS:

Caliber: .45 ACP
Operation: Short-recoil, semiautomatic
Locking: Browning System
Feed: 13-round detachable box magazine,
Empty weight: 2.6 lb
Overall length: 8.5 inches
Sights:Front: blade; rear: square notch, adjustable for windage

Star 10mm/.45 ACP Megastar Pistols

The Megastar is a large pistol chambered either in 10mm Auto or .45 ACP caliber. It is a recoil-operated, double-action/single-action (DA/SA) design with de-cocking lever and high-capacity magazines.

The Megastar locks via the tried and true Browning system with a barrel lug and cam slot beneath the chamber that controls locking and unlocking. The manual safety catch on the slide is ambidextrous. When the safety is engaged, the firing pin is retracted into the slide and locked. If the safety lever is pressed beyond the "safe" position, it functions as a de-cocking lever. When the de-cocking lever is released, it immediately springs back to the 'safe' position. There is also a magazine safety; when the magazine is withdrawn, the trigger is disconnected from the firing mechanism.

Dimensions and data are identical for the two calibers except for weight and ballistic performance.

SPECIFICATIONS:

Caliber: 10mm Auto; .45 ACP
Operation: Short-recoil, semiautomatic, double-action
Locking: Browning system
Feed: Detachable box magazine: 10mm, 14 rounds capacity;
.45 ACP, 12 rounds capacity
Empty weight: 10mm, 3.08 lb; .45 ACP, 2.99 lb
Overall length: 8.3 inches
Barrel length: 4.5 inches
Sights: Front: blade; rear: square notch, white dots

Star Model 31P and Model 31PK pistols

These two pistols, that went out of production prior to the demise of Star, are updated versions of the earlier Star Models 30M and 30PK. The same general features of the previous models were retained, but were updated from the original Star Model 28 series.

Both models have been revised to incorporate various features for ease of handling. The mechanical strength of all components has been improved. The Model 31PK differs from the Model 31P in having an aluminum alloy frame. Four different safeties are incorporated: an ambidextrous safety that blocks the firing pin, a half-cock, a magazine

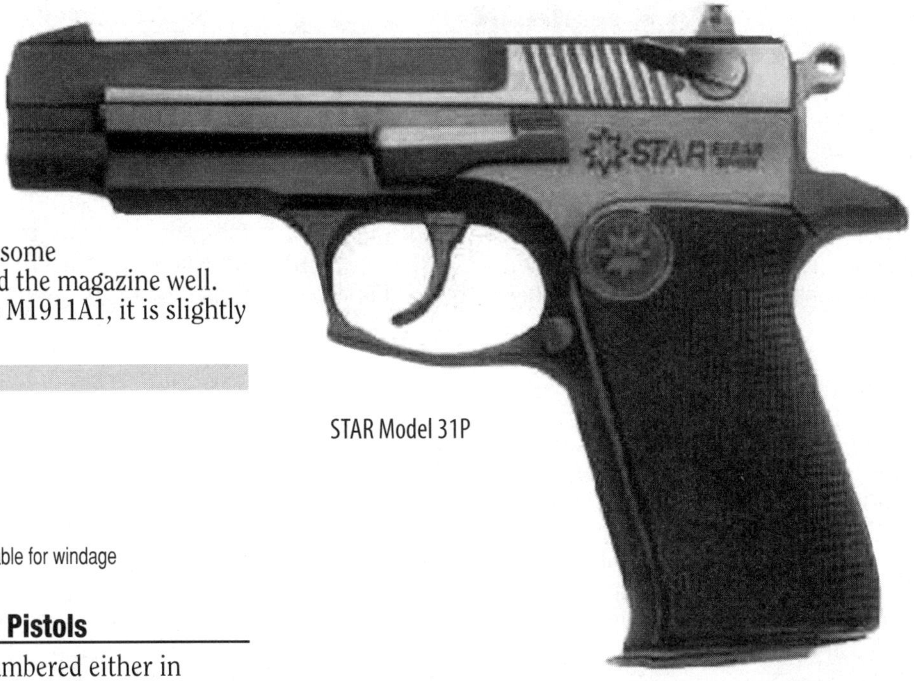

safety and a lockup safety that prevents the pistol from firing until it is fully locked into battery. A loaded-chamber indicator is provided. This consists of a red dot on the surface of the extractor that appears when a round is chambered.

A .40 S&W variant was also available.

SPECIFICATIONS:

Caliber: 9 x19mm
Operation: Short-recoil, semiautomatic
Locking: Browning system
Feed: 15-round detachable box magazine
Empty weight: 31P, 2.47 lb; 31PK, 1.89 lb
Overall length: 7.6 inches
Barrel length: 4.5 inches
Sights: Front: blade; rear: notch, adjustable for windage

Star Ultrastar M-205 Semiautomatic Pistol

The Ultrastar M-205 pistol marked Star Bonifacio Echeverria SA's transition to polymer-frame construction. Full-length steel guide rails are molded into the frame and all metal parts are treated for corrosion resistance. The barrel no longer employs the Star conical muzzle but relies on close tolerances in the locking areas.

The Ultrastar M-205 can be fired either in single-action or double-action mode and has an external hammer. An ambidextrous thumb safety on the slide retracts and immobilizes the firing pin and doubles as a de-cocking lever. There is no magazine safety, but an automatic firing pin block is engaged until pressure is applied to the trigger. The magazine release can easily be configured for right-handed or left-handed shooters.

SPECIFICATIONS:

Caliber: 9x19mm
Operation: Short-recoil semiautomatic
Locking: Browning system
Feed: 9-round detachable box magazine,
Empty weight: 1.7 lb
Overall length: 6.8 inches
Barrel length: 3.3 inches
Sights: Front: blade, white dot; rear: notch, adjustable for windage, 2 white dots

Switzerland

MTE9 and MTE 45 9x19mm and .45 ACP Pistols

The MTE pistols were designed by Martin Tuma who developed the Sphinx series of pistols. This pistol is licensed, manufactured and marketed in the Czech Republic by Caliber Prague Limited as the MTE9 and MTE.45. They have also been marketed under the Advanced Small Arms Industries AG (ASAI) label as the ASAI onePRO 9 and onePRO.45.

All key components of the MTE pistols are manufactured using chrome-nickel-molybdenum steel or special aircraft aluminum alloy in the case of the frame. The finish employs techniques taken from space technology to ensure durability. A polymer-frame model is available. MTE9 locking is via a rotating barrel, while MTE.45 locks via the Browning system. MTE pistols have a patented de-cocking lever mechanism that lowers the hammer into a safety intercept notch. In conjunction with an automatic firing pin lock, this allows the pistol to safely be carried loaded and de-cocked.

The barrel can quickly be changed using a conversion kit. Ambidextrous controls are optional. A double-action only (DAO) model is available.

SPECIFICATIONS: MTE.45

Caliber: .45 ACP
Operation: Short-recoil, semiautomatic
Locking: Browning system
Feed: 10- or 15-round detachable box magazine
Empty weight: light alloy frame, 1.83 lb; polymer frame, 1.80 lb
Overall length: 7.0 inches
Barrel length: 3.8 inches;
4.5 inches optional

SPECIFICATIONS: MTE9

Caliber: 9x19mm Parabellum (9 x 21
Operation: Short-recoil, semiautoma
Locking: rotating barrel
Feed: 10- or 11-round box magazin
(16-round box magazine optional)
Empty weight: 1.58 lb
Overall length: 6.4 inches
Barrel length: 3.1 inches

SIG 9x19mm P210

In 1937, Schweizerische Industrie-Gesellschaft (SIG - now within SAN Swiss Arms AG), took up Charles Petter's patents from Societe Alsacienne de Constructions Mecaniques (SACM). Development continued over the years 1938-46 and a series of weapons was produced, culminating with the SIG P210. The SIG P210 pistol was produced in several versions: the P210-1, with polished finish and wooden grips; the P210-2, with sandblast finish and plastic grips; the P210-4, a special production model for the German Border Police; the P210-5, a target version with 150mm barrel; and the P210-6, also a target model but with a 120mm barrel.

The P210-1, -2 and -6 were produced in either 9x19mm or 7.65x19mm. The caliber can be changed by substituting one barrel for the other, along with its own recoil spring. The pistols can also be converted to .22 LR by changing the barrel, recoil spring, slide and magazine.

Although military production is complete, the 9x19mm P210 remains available from SIGARMS Inc. for commercial sales as a target pistol in the USA.

SPECIFICATIONS: (Data is common to 9mm, 7.65mm or .22 versions unless otherwise specified.)

Caliber: 9x19mm Parabellum (or 7.65mm Parabellum or .22 LR)
Operation: Short-recoil, semiautomatic
Locking: projecting lug
Feed: 8-round detachable box magazine
Empty weight: 2.3 lb
Overall length: 8.5 inches
Barrel length: 4.75 inches
Sights: Front: blade; rear: notch

SAN Swiss ARms P220

SIG P210

SAN Swiss ARms P225

SAN Swiss Arms P220 (SIGARMS)

pistols

The SAN Swiss Arms (formerly SIG-Sauer) P220 is a short-recoil-operated, semiautomatic, double-action/single-action (DA/SA) pistol with an aluminum alloy frame. The magazine release is below the heel of the grip (except for the P220-1 .45 ACP model, where it is a button in the front edge of the front grip strap).

The slide is pulled to the rear and released to feed a round into the chamber. If the shooter does not intend to fire the weapon immediately, the cocked hammer is lowered by pressing down on a de-cocking lever above and slightly behind the trigger on the left side of the frame. Depressing this lever lifts the sear out of engagement with the hammer which is rotated by its spring until the safety notch is caught by the sear and it comes to rest held clear of the firing pin. Raising the de-cocking lever safely lowers the hammer. The firing pin is locked by a pin forced through it by a spring and cannot move even if the pistol is dropped.

The pistol can be fired double-action on the first shot by a long pull on the trigger with subsequent shots in single-action, or it can be used single-action by cocking the hammer by hand.

In addition to the standard Stavenhagen high-contrast sights, tritium front and rear luminous night sights are available as an option, as is a hard rubber floorplate pad for the magazine.

The design of the Iranian ZOAF pistol appears to have been heavily influenced by the 220.

SPECIFICATIONS: (Data for 9x19mm version. Others are identical except as specified.)

Caliber: 9x19mm Parabellum; .45 ACP; .38 Super
Operation: short-recoil, semiautomatic, double-action/single-action (DA/SA)
Locking: Modified Browning system
Feed: 9-round (9mm, and .38 Super) or 7-round (.45 APC) detachable box magazine
Empty Weights: 9mm, 1.71 lb; .45 ACP, 1.7 lb; .38 Super, 1.71 lb
Overall length: 7.8 inches
Barrel length: 4.4 inches
Sights: Front: blade; rear: square notch

SAN Swiss Arms 9x19mm P225 pistol (SIGARMS)

The SAN Swiss Arms (formerly SIG-Sauer) 9mm P225 pistol is slightly smaller and lighter than the P220 and carries one less round in the magazine. It is similar in operation in that it is a mechanically locked short-recoil operated pistol with an automatic firing pin lock, double-action/single-action (DA/SA) trigger, de-cocking lever and external slide release. An additional safety has been built in which provides an absolute firing pin block even if the pistol is accidentally dropped muzzle down with the hammer cocked, de-cocked, or half cocked.

The P225 was designed specifically for police forces, and much design emphasis went into ensuring that a shot can be fired only by actually pulling the trigger. The design of the grips and the positioning of the center of balance ensure good handling characteristics and positive control of the pistol.

The sights are adjustable. Adjustment for windage is possible on either the front or rear sights. Elevation is adjusted by changing sights, either front or rear. Six rear sights and five front sights are available.

The P225PT is a training version that fires 9x19mm PT (Plastic Training) ammunition.

In Germany the P225 is known as the P6. Tritium front and rear luminous sights are available as an option, as are wooden grip panels.

SPECIFICATIONS:

Caliber: 9x19mm Parabellum
Operation: Short-recoil, double-action/single-action (DA/SA)
Locking: Modified Browning system
Feed: 8-round detachable box magazine
Empty weight: 1.7 lb
Overall length: 7.1 inches
Barrel length: 3.6 inches
Sights: see text

SAN Swiss Arms 9mm P226 pistol (SIGARMS)

The SAN Swiss Arms (formerly SIG-Sauer) 9mm P226 pistol was conceived in the 1980s as a candidate in the United States competition for a new military automatic pistol in 9x19mm, where it finished as a "technically acceptable finalist." Like all P220 series pistols, the P226 is a locked-breech short-recoil pistol with an automatic firing pin lock, double-action/single-action (DA/SA) trigger, de-cocking lever and external slide release.

Despite losing the US Army pistol contest to the Beretta M9, numbers of P226 pistols have been acquired by the US Coast Guard, US Navy and FBI. It has also been procured by the UK Ministry of Defense as the L105A1, and other armed forces around the world, including the New Zealand Army and Navy, have either acquired the P226 for standard issue or for special forces use. The P226 is also available chambered in .357 SIG.

In addition to the standard sights, tritium front and rear luminous sights are available as an option, as is rubber bumper pad for the magazine floorplate.

SAN Swiss ARms   P226

SPECIFICATIONS: Data for 9x19mm; .357 SIG in parentheses

Caliber: 9x19mm (.357 SIG)
Operation: short-recoil, semiautomatic, double-action/single-action (DA/SA)
Locking: Modified Browning system
Feed: 15-round detachable box magazine
Empty weight: 1.8 pounds
Overall length: 7.7 inches
Barrel length: 4.4 inches
Sights: Front: blade; rear: square notch

SAN Swiss Arms 9mm P228 pistol (SIGARMS)

The SAN Swiss Arms (formerly SIG-Sauer) 9x19mm P228 pistol is a compact pistol with large magazine capacity. It is a locked-breech, short-recoil operated semiautomatic pistol in 9 x19mm caliber and is particularly suitable for concealed carrying and for individuals with smaller hands.

SAN Swiss ARms P228

The P228 was selected by the US Army as its 9mm Compact Pistol M11 issued to Military Police and is also in US service with the Federal Bureau of Investigation, the Drug Enforcement Administration, the Bureau of Alcohol, Tobacco and Firearms, the Internal Revenue Service, the Federal Aviation Administration, and numerous other federal, state and law enforcement departments. The P228 has also been procured by the UK Ministry of Defense as the L107A1.

Functionally, the P228 is identical to other pistols in the P220 series.

SPECIFICATIONS:

Caliber: 9x19mm
Operation: Short-recoil, semiautomatic, double-action/single-action (DA/SA)
Locking: Modified Browning system
Feed: 13-round detachable box magazine
Empty weight: 1.9 pounds
Overall length: 7.1 inches
Barrel length: 3.9 inches
Sights: Front: blade; rear: square notch (tritium aiming dots available)

SAN Swiss Arms P229 pistols (SIGARMS)

Other than minor changes in the slide contours, the SAN Swiss Arms (formerly SIG-Sauer) P229 pistol is virtually the same as the P228. It was developed primarily for law-enforcement officers, using high-contrast sights and having the usual SIG double-action/single-action (DA/SA) operation, automatic firing-pin safety and de-cocking lever.

The P229 is available in 9x19mm, .40 S&W and .357 SIG calibers. P229 pistols have steel slide and aluminum alloy frame. All that is required to change a .40 S&W version to .357 SIG is a barrel change.

The P229 was the first SIG pistol to be partially manufactured and assembled in the United States.

The SAN Swiss Arms P239 is a variant of the P229 and is identical except for reduced magazine capacity and a slightly smaller grip for persons with smaller hands.

SAN Swiss ARms P229

SAN Swiss ARms P232

SPECIFICATIONS:

Caliber: .40 S&W; 9x19mm; .357 SIG
Operation: short-recoil, semiautomatic, double-action/single-action (DA/SA)
Locking: Modified Browning system
Feed: 12-round box magazine (9mm, 13-rounds)
Empty weight: 2 pounds
Overall length: 7.1 inches
Barrel length: 3.9 inches
Sights: Front: blade; rear: square notch; both adjustable for windage by lateral movement and adjustable for elevation by changing sights.

SAN Swiss Arms P232 pistol (SIGARMS)

The SAN Swiss Arms (formerly SIG-Sauer) P232 pistol replaced the earlier P230. First deliveries were made during 1997. The P232 is primarily intended for covert police work or as backup weapon.

The P232 has many features carried over from the P230 and shares the same general operating and handling features. The P232 is available in either .32 ACP (7.65x17SRmm or .380 ACP (9 x17mm). A double-action only (DAO) model is also available (P232 DAO).

P232 pistols are available in all blue finish with a light-alloy frame (P232), with a stainless slide and blue frame (P232 B&W), or in all stainless steel (P232 SL). Other options include wooden or rubber grips and tritium night sights.

SPECIFICATIONS:

Caliber: .380 ACP (9 x17mm);
.32 ACP (7.65x17SRmm)
Operation: blowback, semiautomatic, double-action/single-action (DA/SA)
Feed: .380 ACP, 7-round detachable box magazine; .32 ACP, 8-round detachable box magazine
Empty weight: .380 ACP P232 & P232 B&W, 1.1 pounds; .32 ACP P232 & P232 B&W, 1.1 pounds; .32 ACP P232 SL, 1.4 pounds; .32 ACP SL, 1.5 pounds
Overall length: 6.6 inches
Barrel length: 3.6 inches
Sights: Front: blade; rear: notch; Stavenhagen pattern

SAN Swiss Arms .45 ACP P245 Compact pistol (SIGARMS)

The SAN Swiss Arms (formerly SIG-Sauer) .45 ACP P245 Compact pistol was introduced in December 1998. It

is intended primarily for North American law enforcement and commercial markets. The P245 Compact follows traditional SIG-Sauer design features, including the various safeties. The main difference from other models, is the single-stack magazine that holds six rounds.

The P245 Compact is available in both double-action only or single-action/double-action (DA/SA) versions. Various finishes are available. Accessories include night sights, rubber or wooden grip panels and spare magazines.

 The P245 Compact is distributed in the USA by SIGARMS Inc. of Exeter, New Hampshire.

SPECIFICATIONS:

Caliber: .45 ACP
Operation: short-recoil, semiautomatic, DA/SA or DAO
Locking: Modified Browning system
Feed: Detachable box magazine, 6 rounds capacity
Empty weight: 1.9 pounds; magazine, empty, .6 pounds
Overall length: 7.2 inches
Barrel length: 3.9 inches
Sights: Front: blade; rear: square notch

SAN Swiss ARms P245

SAN Swiss Arms Sig Pro™ SP 2009 and SP2340 pistols (SIGARMS)

The SAN Swiss Arms (formerly SIG) Sig Pro™ SP 2340 pistol was the first SIG pistol with a polymer frame. Although the pistol is generally similar to earlier designs, several new features have been incorporated.

The SP 2340 was introduced to the market in June 1998 and was initially available chambered in .40 S&W and .357 SIG. The SP 2009 chambered for 9x19mm was introduced in March 1999.

The SP2009/2340 pistols carry over most of the features of earlier SAN Swiss Arms/SIG pistols, including the functional safeties of earlier models.

The fire control mechanism the SP2009/2340 pistol is modular and can be converted from double-action/single-action (DA/SA) operation to double-action only (DAO) in a matter of minutes. Rails are provided on the dust cover accessories such as a laser pointer or white light.

SPECIFICATIONS:
Caliber: .40 S&W, .357 SIG or 9x19mm (P2009)
Operation: short-recoil, semiautomatic, single or double-action or double action only
Locking: Modified Browning system
Feed: 12-round detachable box magazine (SP 2009, 15-round box magazine)
Empty weight: SP 2009, 1.56 lb; 2340, 1.68 lb
Overall length: 7.4 inches
Barrel length: 3.9 inches
Sights: Front: blade; rear: square notch

Taiwan

T75K1 9mm pistols

The T75K1 9x19mm pistol is a local development of the original T75 pistol, which was derived from Beretta Model 92 series. Few T75s were produced before the modified and shorter T75K1 entered limited production for the Republic of China armed forces. One of the main changes introduced on the T75K1 is a revised locking mechanism.

There is a slightly shorter "Commando" version of the T75K1 for issue to special forces. The 15-rounds magazine capacity is maintained.

The number of T75K1 pistols in service with Taiwan is not large as the American .45 ACP M1911A1, which continues to be favored.

SPECIFICATIONS:
Caliber: 9x19mm Parabellum
Operation: short-recoil, semiautomatic
Locking: Falling block
Feed: 15-round detachable box magazine
Empty weight: 2.0 lb; Commando variant, 1.95 lb
Overall length: 8.7 inches; Commando variant, 7.6 inches
Barrel length: 4.5 inches, Commando, 4.17 inches
Sights: Front: blade; rear: notch

SAN Swiss ARms SP2340

T75K1

Turkey

MKE .380 ACP and .32 ACP pistols

These pistols are produced by Makina ve Kimya Endustrisi Kurumu (MKEK) at Kirikkale, Ankara. They are derived from the Walther PP. The pistols are marked "MKE" on the grip and MKEK and the caliber on the slide. A further distinguishing feature is the 'bobble' surface finish on the plastic grip plates.

The method of operation is identical to the Walther PP. There are only minor external changes such as the shape of the magazine finger rest.

SPECIFICATIONS:

Caliber: .380 ACP (9x17mm) or .32 ACP (7.65x17SRmm)
Operation: blowback, double-action/single-action (DA/SA)
Feed: 7-round detachable box magazine
Empty weight: .380 ACP, 1.68 lb; .32 ACP, 1.60 lb
Overall length: 6.69 inches
Barrel length: 3.8 inches
Sights: Front: blade; rear: notch

United States

Colt .45 ACP Model 1911A1 automatic pistol

Development of this pistol by John Browning began in 1896 and culminated in a comprehensive trial by the US Army in 1910. There the Colt/Browning design was approved, but required a few modifications and the perfected design was approved as the M1911, entering US service early in that year.

The pistol was used during the First World War, during which some minor defects were noted. These were corrected after the war and the following modifications were made: the mainspring housing was contoured with a curved shape and either checkered or serrated, depending upon manufacturer, a shorter grooved trigger was fitted and the frame chamfered behind the trigger. The grip safety was slightly lengthened to prevent "hammer bite" on the web of the shooter's hand between the thumb and forefinger, and the hammer spur was shortened for the same reason. These changes took effect in 1926 and the pistol was designated the M1911A1, remaining virtually unchanged ever since.

M1911A1 pistols have been generally replaced by the 9mm Pistol M9 in US Army service but large numbers remain in use, especially in special operations. Despite the introduction of more modern pistols, the M1911 and M1911A1 remain favorites and show no sign of falling from favor, especially with special forces troopers who have developed their own modified versions to suit their requirements. Typical of these is the US Marine Corps MEU(SOC) .45 ACP pistol (see entry below). Many of the World War II-era pistols have been rebuilt several times[1].

The M1911A1 is still available from Colt's Manufacturing Company and Springfield Armory as copies of military M1911A1 pistols that were used in World War II, Korea and Vietnam.

Variants of the M1911 continue in US military and law enforcement service. Large orders for specialized versions have been placed by the FBI, US Marshals, Texas Rangers and many other law enforcement agencies, especially SWAT units. Virtually all of these pistols are Kimber or Springfield Armory products. The US military has recently begun purchasing limited quantities of both Kimber

COLT 1911

WWII M1911A1

United States
M9 pistol

and Springfield Armory M1911A1 type pistols for special operations' use.

The M1911 introduced the locking system known as the Browning "swinging link" in which the barrel has raised lugs on its upper surface, which mate with recesses on the inner surface of the slide. Beneath the chamber of the barrel is a hinged link, pinned to the barrel at its upper end and secured to the frame by the slide stop lever pin at its bottom end. With the slide forward and locked in battery, held in place by the recoil spring pressing against the front of the slide, the link is vertical and holds the barrel up so that the lugs engage the slide. When the pistol is fired, the slide recoils and carries the barrel with it, and the breech remaining closed, for a very short distance. As the barrel moves back, the link pivots on the slide lock pin and top end of the link is pulled down, drawing the rear end of the barrel downwards until the locking lugs are free of the slide and the bottom of the chamber contacts the frame and stops further movement. The slide continues rearward, extracting and ejecting the spent case, cocking the hammer and compressing the recoil spring.

As the slide moves forward, it strips a fresh round from the magazine and chambers it. Pressure against the base of the cartridge forces the barrel forward and because of the link, the barrel rear is raised until the lugs reengage the slide. The pistol is now ready for the next shot. A manual safety lever is fitted to the left rear of the frame, although almost all modern versions have ambidextrous safeties, and there is a grip safety in the rear of the grip that locks the firing mechanism except when pressed in when the pistol is grasped. A disconnector prevents the pistol from firing unless the slide is fully forward and in battery. Many modern versions of the M1911A1, such as Colt and Smith and Wesson versions, also have firing pin safeties. Most new production pistols also are fitted with a "beavertail" grip safety that not only improves "hammer bite" protection, but lowers the pistol in the hand, increasing control and reducing felt recoil.

As the 21st Century progresses, the venerable M1911A1 shows no sign of obsolescence. It is now made not only in the United States, but in many other nations, as well. It is still the pistol of choice for many military and law enforcement officers who consider it the finest achievement in handgun design ever.

1. As World WarII pistols wear out, new pistols that duplicate the MEU(SOC) are being purchased from Springfield Armory.

SPECIFICATIONS:
Caliber: .45 ACP
Operation: short-recoil, semiautomatic
Locking: Browning system
Feed: detachable 7- or 8-round box magazine
Empty weight: 39.5 ounces
Length: 8.5 inches
Barrel length: 5 inches
Sights: Front: blade; rear: U-notch, adjustable for windage (Many versions are equipped with fully adjustable sights.)

US Marine Corps MEU(SOC) .45 ACP pistol

The US Marine Corps Marine Expeditionary Unit (Special Operations Capable) (MEU(SOC)) pistol was designed by the Marine Corps Weapons Training Battalion at Quantico, Virginia, to be a backup weapon for Marines armed with the M4 carbine. The MEU(SOC) pistol is a modified M1911A1 .45 ACP pistol, chosen because of its inherent reliability and lethality at close ranges. Modifications were made to the basic M1911A1 to enhance reliability, accuracy and ergonomics.

The MEU(SOC) .45 pistol is converted by armorers at the Marine Corps Weapons Training Battalion's Rifle Team Equipment (RTE) Shop at Quantico, Virginia. The pistol is based on the proven M1911A1 design, using frames from World War II pistols, but with new slides and other components. The MEU(SOC) .45 incorporates an ambidextrous safety, a match-grade barrel and trigger. The hammer spur is rounded to prevent snagging on clothing and equipment. For greater comfort and control the MEU(SOC) pistol has textured rubber grips and an extra wide "beavertail" grip safety. The standard sights are replaced by commercial high-profile combat sights. All components are hand-fitted. The magazine well is beveled to ease reloading under combat conditions and standard "issue" magazines are replaced by stainless steel commercial models with rounded polymer followers and extended floor plates for reliability and quick, positive reloads.

SPECIFICATIONS:
Caliber: .45 ACP
Operation: short-recoil, semiautomatic
Locking: Browning system
Feed: detachable 7-round box magazine
Empty weight: 39.5 ounces
Length: 8.5 inches
Barrel length: 5 inches
Sights: Front: high profile blade; rear: high-profile notch, adjustable for Windage and elevation.

U.S. Marine

U.S. Marine Corps M1911A1

The 1911 pistol has served since world war1 and is again being returned to active military service.

Kel-Tec 9x19mm P-11 pistol

The Kel-Tec 9mm P-11 pistol entered production in early 1995 and is one of the smallest and lightest production pistols ever made in 9x19mm. It is intended to be a backup weapon for police and military personnel.

The P-11 is a double-action only (DAO) pistol with the breech locked by the Browning system. SAE 4140 steel is used for the barrel and slide, while the frame is machined from solid aircraft-grade aluminum. The grip is high-impact polymer and forms the magazine well and trigger guard. The hammer is driven by an unusual free-floating extension spring and connects via a floating transfer bar to the hammer, which impacts a lightweight firing pin to fire the primer.

Kel-Tec P-11

SPECIFICATIONS:

Caliber: 9x19mm Parabellum
Operation: Short-recoil, semiautomatic, double-action only (DAO)
Locking: Modified Browning system
Feed: 12-round detachable box magazine
Empty weight: 0.88 lb
Overall length: 5.6 inches
Barrel length: 3.07 inches
Sights: Front: fixed blade; rear: fixed notch; both high contrast

United States
M1911A1

M9

Pistol, 9mm M9

This pistol is Beretta's Model 92F or FS, initially manufactured in Italy and subsequently by Beretta USA, the American subsidiary. For details, refer to the entry under Beretta in Italy.

The initial US Army order was for 315,930 pistols at a cost of $53 million. Since 1985 the US Army has procured approximately 180,332 pistols, of which 158,711 are currently issued, the remainder being held in reserve.

American made M92FS pistols have gained widespread acceptance and use by American law enforcement.

Ruger .357 Magnum GP100 revolver

The Ruger GP100 is a six-shot revolver in .357 Magnum caliber. The frame width has been increased in critical areas to support the barrel and both frame sidewalls are solid and integral providing strength and rigidity.

The lock mechanism is contained within the trigger guard, which is inserted into the frame as a single subassembly. The locking notches are offset and are located in the thickest part of the cylinder walls between the centers of the chambers. When the cylinder is in the firing position it is securely locked into the frame by a unique Ruger mechanism.

The heavy barrel with full-length ejector shroud is made from ordnance-grade 4140 chrome molybdenum alloy steel. The long shroud helps achieve a slightly muzzle heavy balance. The patented Ruger Cushioned Grips are of live rubber, with polished wood inserts.

The design incorporates a number of original Ruger innovations, which have been in use for many years. These include the frame-mounted floating firing pin, the transfer bar safety system that prevents the hammer from striking the firing pin unless the trigger is pulled and the exclusive use of coil springs throughout. The revolver is available in either blued or stainless steel finish.

Variant:

GP100 Fixed Sight Model

The 76mm and 102mm barrel models are available with full or short ejector shroud in .357 Magnum and .38 Special, with fixed sights, in blued or stainless steel. An optional red insert front sight is available. The Fixed Sight Model also uses a patented smaller round grip with one-piece cushioned grip pad.

SPECIFICATIONS:

Caliber: .357 Magnum or .38 Special
Operation: double-action revolver
Feed: 6-round cylinder
Empty weight: 2.7 lb
Length: 9.4 inches
Barrel length: 4.0 inches
Rifling: 5 grooves, rh, 1 turn in 18 inches
Sights: Front: interchangeable blade;
rear: adjustable square notch with white outline

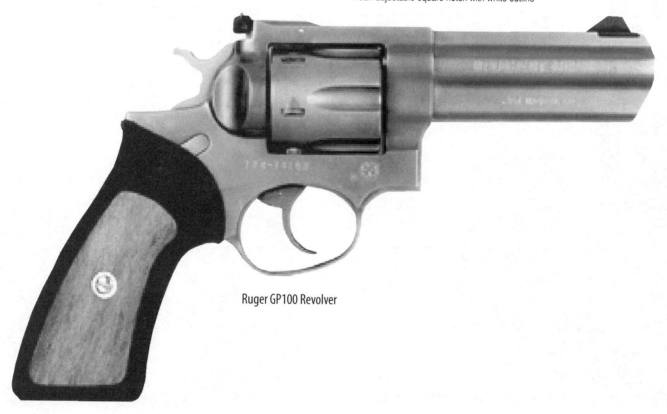

Ruger GP100 Revolver

Ruger KP90DC De-Cocker

Ruger KP97 Revolver

Ruger .45 ACP KP90DC De-Cocker pistol

The Ruger .45 ACP KP90DC De-Cocker pistol is essentially the same as the Ruger 9x19mm De-Cocker pistol P89DC but in .45 ACP. The pistol is approximately the same size (200mm long) and weight (964 g) as many 9mm pistols and is made entirely from stainless steel except for the frame, which is of investment cast aluminum alloy. An oversized trigger guard permits use with a gloved hand, and a lanyard loop is standard. High-visibility sights have white-dot inserts, and the rear sight is drift adjustable for windage.

Ruger .45 ACP KP97 pistols

With the .45 ACP KP97, Sturm Ruger made an improvement in their P-series pistols to produce a design that is lighter, slimmer and shorter than any previous Ruger .45 ACP pistols. Many features from the previous pistols have been retained, but all components are produced specifically for the KP97.

The KP97 features a frame constructed using a custom compounded high-strength Fiberglas-reinforced polymer. The frame is corrosion and solvent resistant, lightweight and compatible with most oils and lubricants. The grip area is shaped and sized to allow the average hand to assume a comfortable grip, and is wide and rounded enough at the rear to allow recoil forces to spread into the hand.

While the KP97 continues to use a modified Browning system to lock and unlock, a patented cam lock system is incorporated. During the firing cycle the barrel is accelerated as it moves back and down to unlock from the slide. Once it is free of the slide, the barrel is brought to a stop without impact damage to the polymer frame. The barrel itself is manufactured using 400 series stainless steel.

The KP97 is available in De-cock-Only (KP97D) and Double-Action-Only (KP97DAO) configurations and in semi-gloss black or stainless steel finishes.

SPECIFICATIONS:
Caliber: .45 ACP
Operation: short-recoil, semiautomatic
Locking: Modified Browning system
Feed: 8-round detachable box magazine
Empty weight: 2.0 pounds
Overall length: 7.6 inches
Barrel length: 4.2 inches
Sights: Front: blade with white dot;
rear: notch with 2 white dots, Drift adjustable for windage.

Ruger 9x19mm KP93 Compact pistol

The Ruger 9x19mm KP93 Compact pistol is slightly shorter and approximately 14 percent lighter than the KP89 pistol, and slight changes in the contours result in a sleeker appearance. The frame is of aluminum alloy with a matte silver hard finish. The center of gravity and center of mass are nearly identical, resulting in excellent handling.

The barrel, slide, trigger, hammer and most internal metal parts are of stainless steel. The magazine holds 15 rounds in a double column and is interchangeable with the magazine of the KP89.

Two models are available: a double-action-only and a de-cocker version. Sights are provided with white dots for aiming in poor light and the rear sight is drift adjustable for windage.

SPECIFICATIONS:
Caliber: 9x19mm
Operation: Short-recoil, semiautomatic, double-action/single-action (DA/SA) or double-action only (DAO)
Locking: Modified Browning system
Feed: 15-round detachable box magazine
Empty weight: 2.0 pounds
Overall length: 7.3 inches
Barrel length: 3.9 inches
Sights: Front: blade; rear: square notch, adjustable for windage. White dots

Ruger 9x19mm P89 pistol

The P89 was announced early in 1987 and was the first military-type pistol developed by Sturm, Ruger & Company. The pistol was originally designated P85, but was slightly redesigned and designated the P89. The P89 is a conventional double-action/single-action (DA/SA) pistol, using the familiar modified Browning system to unlock the breech during recoil. The chamber section is squared off and locks into the ejection opening in the slide. The barrel is stainless steel, as are the hammer, trigger and most internal components. The frame is of lightweight aluminum alloy, is hardened to resist wear and is finished in matte black. The slide is of chrome-molybdenum steel and is also matte black or stainless. There is an external hammer and the ambidextrous safety lever is at the rear of the slide. The safety locks the firing pin, blocks the hammer and disconnects the trigger when engaged.

The trigger guard is proportioned so that the pistol can be fired with gloved hands, and the forward edge of the trigger guard is shaped to allow a grip for the non-firing hand. The magazine release is just behind the trigger guard and is ambidextrous.

The P89DC is the same as the basic P89 but with ambidextrous de-cocking levers slide in place of the normal safety lever. The de-cocking lever simultaneously blocks the firing pin as it is engaged. Once the hammer is down the lever can be released, whereupon returns to its original position. The pistol can be fired by a double-action pull or by thumb-cocking the hammer and a single-action pull.

The Double-Action-Only P89 (P89DAO) is yet another variant of the P89 in DAO. The hammer follows the slide home after each shot and cannot be manually cocked.

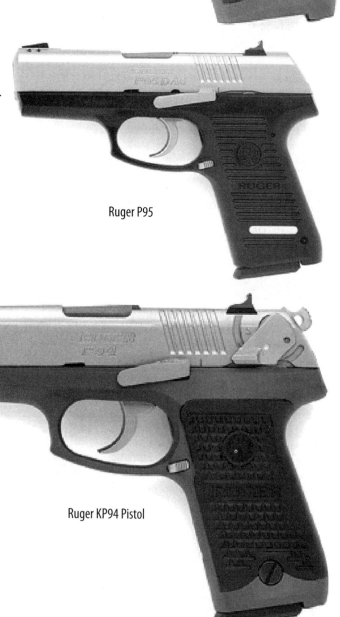

Ruger KP89

SPECIFICATIONS:
Caliber: 9x19mm Parabellum
Operation: short-recoil, semiautomatic, double-action/single-action (DA/SA) or DAO
Locking: Modified Browning system
Feed: 15-round detachable box magazine
Empty weight: 2.1 pounds
Overall length: 7.9 inches
Barrel length: 4.5 inches
Sights: Front: blade; rear: square notch, adjustable for windage

Ruger 9mm P95 pistols

The Ruger 9mm P95 continues the development of the earlier Ruger 9mm semiautomatic pistols and is suitable for firing the 9x19mm +P cartridges. The final design of the P95 was the outcome of a program that involved successfully firing over 20,000-rounds of +P ammunition without any significant wear or loss of performance.

The P95 features a frame constructed using a Fiberglas-reinforced high-strength polymer that is resistant to solvents and compatible with most oils and lubricants. The grip area is shaped and sized to allow the average hand to assume a comfortable grip and is wide and rounded enough at the rear to distribute recoil forces into the hand for comfortable shooting over extended periods with full power loads.

The P95 uses the same modified Browning system fully described under the KP97 entry. The P95 is available in De-cock-Only (P95DC) and Double-Action-Only (P95DAO) configurations and in blue or stainless steel finishes.

Ruger P95

SPECIFICATIONS:
Caliber: 9x19mm +P
Operation: short-recoil, semiautomatic
Locking: Modified Browning system
Feed: 15-round detachable box magazine
Empty weight: 765 g
Overall length: 7.3 inches
Barrel length: 3.9 inches
Sights: Front: blade with white dot; rear: notch with 2 white dots, Drift adjustable for windage.

Ruger KP94 pistol

The KP94 is midway between the full-size P series and the compact KP93, and uses the link-actuated short-recoil action. The frame is of hard-anodized aircraft aluminum

Ruger KP94 Pistol

and the slide is stainless steel. The pistol is available in manual safety (KP94), de-cocker (KP94D) or double-action-only (KP94DAO) configurations.

Three-dot Patridge sights assist rapid and accurate alignment. The windage-adjustable rear sight locks into place with a setscrew and the front sight blade is replaceable. Ergonomically designed unbreakable Xenoy grip panels are suitable for users with smaller hands.

Index marks on the slide and frame identify the position whereby the slide stop pin can be withdrawn or inserted.

All models have a fully ambidextrous magazine release. Ambidextrous slide-mounted de-cocking or safety levers on respective models feature reduced rotation to safely drop a cocked hammer. The patented Ruger 'push-forward' safety system positively engages and restrains the firing pin, moving it forward and away from contact with the hammer when the de-cocking lever or safety lever is engaged. This independent, redundant safety feature functions in addition to the passive firing pin block, which blocks the firing pin until the trigger is pulled fully rearward.

Double-action-only models cannot be thumb-cocked; their bobbed hammers transferring no energy to the firing pin even if dropped on the rear of the slide. The double-action pistol's hammer is positioned away from contact with the firing pin.

SPECIFICATIONS:
Caliber: 9x19mm or .40 S&W
Operation: short-recoil, semiautomatic
Locking: Modified Browning system
Feed: 15-round (9mm) or 11-round (.40 S&W) box magazine
Empty weight: 2.1 lb
Overall length: 7.6 inches
Barrel length: 4.2 inches
Sights: Front: blade with white dot; rear: notch with 2 white dots. Rear sight drift adjustable for windage.

Smith & Wesson .38 Special Model 10 and Model 64 Military and Police Revolvers

The Smith & Wesson Model 10 Military and Police revolver was introduced in 1899 and is still in production. It has been used in every conflict of the 20th Century and continues in service as a secondary weapon in the 21st Century. The Model 64 is the stainless steel version that is more durable under arduous conditions. The metal is satin finished and the grips, formerly of walnut, are now supplied with synthetic combat grips. The standard 4-inch barrel is designated as a "heavy" barrel. A 2-inch or 3-inch barrel is also available.

SPECIFICATIONS:
Caliber: .38 Special +P
Operation: double-action revolver
Feed: 6-round cylinder
Empty weight: 2.5 lb
Overall length: 9.0 inches
Barrel length: 4.0 inches
Sights: Front: serrated ramp; rear: square notch

Smith & Wesson .38 Special /.357 Magnum Model 686 Series Revolvers

The Smith & Wesson Model 686 Series revolvers are included herein as typical of the many Smith & Wesson revolvers likely to be encountered in the hands of numerous military and paramilitary forces worldwide. It is a model from Smith & Wesson's Medium Frame range of revolvers and is chambered in .357 Magnum, enabling it to also fire any type of .38 Special cartridge. The frame is stainless steel. Molded synthetic grips are standard. Barrel lengths include 2.5 inches, 4 inches and 6 inches. The fluted cylinder accommodates six rounds, while the 686 Plus chambers seven rounds.

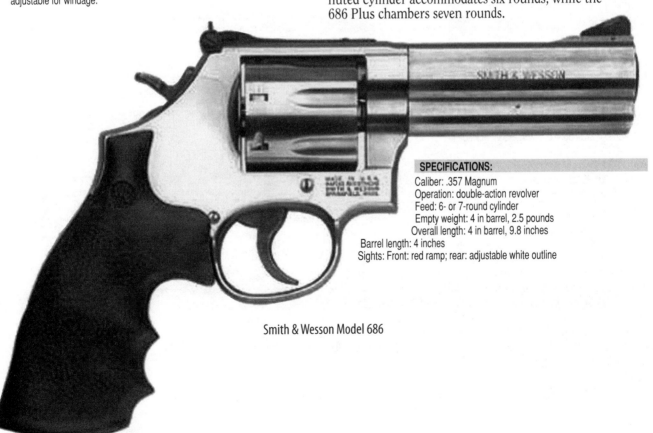

SPECIFICATIONS:
Caliber: .357 Magnum
Operation: double-action revolver
Feed: 6- or 7-round cylinder
Empty weight: 4 in barrel, 2.5 pounds
Overall length: 4 in barrel, 9.8 inches
Barrel length: 4 inches
Sights: Front: red ramp; rear: adjustable white outline

Smith & Wesson Model 686

Smith & Wesson Model 4003

Smith & Wesson Model 5906

Smith & Wesson Model 4000 Series Pistols

The Smith & Wesson Model 4000 series of pistols introduced the .40 S&W cartridge, making it possible to adapt a 9x19mm frame without having to make serious changes to the magazine well dimensions. Apart from the change in caliber and magazine capacity, the 4003 is generally the same as the other standard models in this group, having an ambidextrous safety. On the Model 4003 the frame is aluminum alloy and stainless steel. The Model 4006 has an all-stainless steel frame. The Model 4043 is double-action-only with alloy frame and stainless steel slide, while the Model 4046 is also double-action-only but entirely of stainless steel.

The Model 4013 and Model 4053 are 'compact' models with aluminum alloy and stainless steel or stainless steel frames respectively. Similar pistols are available in .45 ACP caliber as the Model 4513 and 4563 series

SPECIFICATIONS: Model 4003 (Model 4006)

Caliber: .40 S&W
Operation: recoil, semiautomatic, double-action/single-action (DA/SA)
Locking: Modified Browning system
Feed: 11-round detachable box magazine
Empty weight: 1.8 pounds
Overall length: 7.5 inches
Barrel length: 4 inches
Sights: Front: post with white dot; rear: U-notch fixed with two white dots, or adjustable for windage and elevation

Smith & Wesson .40 Model 410 pistol

The Smith & Wesson .40 Model 410 double-action/single-action (DA/SA) pistol is chambered for the .40 S&W cartridge and features a single-column 10+1-round capacity magazine (10-rounds in the magazine, plus one in the chamber) and a one-piece Xenoy grip. The frame is aluminum alloy with a steel slide, with a matte blue external finish. The Model 410 also has a slide-mounted manual safety/de-cocking lever on the left-hand side, enabling the pistol to be carried in safety with a round chambered but ready for immediate firing. This pistol is available with a 'light-gathering' HIVIZ green-dot front sight.

SPECIFICATIONS:

Caliber: .40 S&W
Operation: Short-recoil, semiautomatic, double-action/single-action (DA/SA)
Locking: Modified Browning system
Feed: 10-round detachable box magazine
Empty weight: 1.8 pounds
Overall length: 7.5 inches
Barrel length: 4 inches
Sights: 3-dot; fixed

Smith & Wesson 9x19mm 5900 series pistols

The Smith & Wesson 9x19mm 5900 series consists of two models, the 5903 and 5906. The 5903 has a stainless steel slide, fixed sights and an aluminum alloy frame. The 5906 has a steel frame and is available with adjustable sights.

SPECIFICATIONS:

Caliber: 9x19mm Parabellum
Operation: recoil, semiautomatic
Locking: Modified Browning system
Feed: 15-round magazine
Empty weight: 5903 1.8 lb; 5906, 2.4 lb
Overall length: 7.5 inches
Barrel length: 4 inches
Sights: Front: post with white dot; rear: notch fixed with 2 white dots; adjustable sights optional on 5906

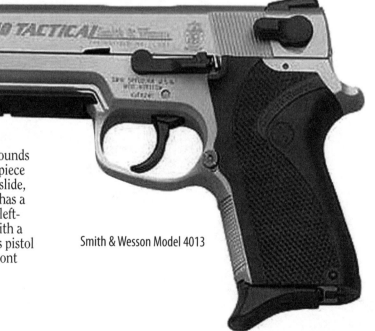

Smith & Wesson Model 4013

Smith & Wesson Model 410

Smith & Wesson Model 910

Smith & Wesson Model 910 and 410 Pistols

The Smith & Wesson Model 910 and 410 pistols are chambered for the 9x19mm and .40 S&W cartridges, respectively. The pistols have an aluminum alloy frame with a carbon steel slide and a matte bead-blasted blue external finish. The grips are lightweight and durable Xenoy. There is a slide-mounted manual safety/de-cocking lever on the left side, enabling the pistol to be carried safely with a round chambered but ready for immediate firing.

SPECIFICATIONS:

Caliber: 9x19mm or .40 S&W
Operation: Short-recoil, semiautomatic, double-action/single-action (DA/SA)
Locking: Modified Browning system
Feed: 15-round box magazine
Empty weight: 1.75 lb (910); 1.78 lb (410)
Overall length: 7.6 inches (910); 7.5 inches (410)
Barrel length: 4 inches
Sights: 3-dot; fixed

Smith & Wesson Sigma series pistols

The Sigma series was introduced in 1994 after being developed over some 10 years. The frame is of high-strength polymer and incorporates a self-cocking "double-action only" striker firing system. The pistol is robust,

Smith & Wesson Sigma

simple to maintain and operate, with a smooth and consistent trigger pull. The original Model SW40F was chambered for the .40 S&W cartridge, and the Model SW9F was provided for those who prefer the 9x19mm cartridge.

As of late 2004, there are four versions of the Sigma available. They are as follows:

Model SW9VE - 9 x19mm Parabellum with white dot front sight and fixed two-dot rear sight

Model SW40VE - .40 S&W with white dot front sight and fixed two-dot rear sight

Model SW40P - .40 S&W with Tritium night front sight and fixed two-dot rear sight

Model SW40G - .40 S&W with Tritium night front sight fixed two-dot rear sight and NATO green finish grip

The Sigma series pistols employ a "double-action-only" action with modified Browning system locking. A high degree of safety has been engineered into the series, including a trigger safety that prevents the pistol from firing if it is dropped. Only when the trigger is fully depressed and an internal striker safety plunger is lifted, can the pistol be fired.

The frame was designed incorporating human factor analysis to produce an optimum fit of web angle, grip girth, grasp angle and trigger reach to accommodate a very wide range of users, including those with small hands.

All models can accommodate tactical accessories on a dust cover rail. The maximum cartridge capacity of the magazines is 16 rounds for 9 x19mm and 14 rounds for .40 S&W.

SPECIFICATIONS:

Caliber: .40 S&W (9x19mm)
Operation: Short-recoil, semiautomatic, double-action-only
Locking: Modified Browning system
Feed: 14-round magazine (16-round magazine)
Empty weight: 1.5 lb
Overall length: 7.25 inches
Barrel length: 4 inches
Sights: 3-dot, Tritium optional (see text)

Smith & Wesson SW99 pistols

The Smith & Wesson SW99 is the result of an alliance with Walther of Germany which supplies P99 pistol frames to Smith & Wesson for them to introduce features more suitable to the US market. Essentially, the SW99 is mechanically and operationally identical to the Walther P99 although there are some differences. The top of the SW99 slide is curved while that of the P99 is square. The original Walther P99 trigger guard profile has been replaced by a more curved shape on the SW99. On the SW99 the accessory rail on the dust cover can accept a Weaver ring, and the slide stop is surrounded by a molded guard to prevent accidental engagement. Like the P99, the grip backstraps of the SW99 can be changed to accommodate a wide variety of hand sizes.

Smith & Wesson SW99

The SW99 can be chambered for .45 ACP (nine rounds), .40 S&W (12 rounds) or 9x19mm (16 rounds). Tritium night sights are optional. The SW99 can also be supplied with the Smith & Wesson Saf-T-Trigger™, a mechanical trigger block that raises a post into position behind the trigger using a special key.

For full details of the Walther P99, with which most aspects of the SW99 are identical, refer to the entry under Germany. The following data is from Smith & Wesson.

SPECIFICATIONS:

Caliber: 9x19mm ; .40 S&W; .45 ACP
Operation: recoil, semiautomatic, double-action and single-action
Locking: linkless, modified Browning system
Feed: 9mm, 16-round box magazine; .40, 12-round box magazine; .45 ACP, nine-round box magazine
Empty weight: 9mm, 1.6 pounds
Overall length: 9mm, 7.125 inches; .40 S&W, 7.25 inches; .45 ACP, 7.5 inches
Barrel length: 9mm, 4 inches; .40 S&W, 4.125 inches; .45 ACP, 4.25 inches
Sights: Front: interchangeable blade; rear: laterally adjustable square notch; three dot; Tritium optional

Smith & Wesson SW1911 M1911-type Pistol

The SW1911 Pistol is an improved and modified version of the classic M1911 design that adds several improvements to the basic design. The SW1911 incorporates a firing pin safety that has no effect on trigger pull and has a vastly improved extractor that should prove much more reliable than the original design. The SW1911 also uses Wolff springs throughout, a Texas Armament match trigger, a Briley barrel bushing, Wilson magazines, Chip McCormack hammer and safety and Novak Low-Mount Combat sights. The SW1911 is available with black or matte stainless finishes. A Scandium alloy version is also available. A small amount of scandium, when introduced into an aluminum alloy, makes the alloy nearly as durable as steel by changing its molecular structure. Thus, a pistol can have the weight of aluminum with the strength of steel. For specifications, see M1911 entry above.

Springfield .45 ACP Professional Model FBI Special Weapons and Tactics (SWAT) Pistol

The Springfield Armory Professional Model, originally designated Bureau Model, was the winner in a competition for a new pistol for the US Federal Bureau of Investigations (FBI) regional Special Weapons And Tactics (SWAT) teams.

The pistol was specified in an FBI requirement to be a highly modified M1911A1 type pistol and several major US handgun manufacturers of this type of firearm entered the competition. The ultimate winner was Springfield Armory. The requirement was a 50,000-round service life before gunsmith maintenance was necessary.

The Springfield Armory Bureau Model is a highly modified M1911A1-type pistol of conventional design. It is quite different from standard M1911A1 pistols in that it has many custom features, including a custom-fitted slide and frame, barrel, polished feed ramp and throated barrel, a specially fitted trigger mechanism tuned to 4 pounds pull, a lowered and flared ejection port and tuned extractor, a custom-fitted beavertail grip safety and ambidextrous thumb safety, Novak tritium sights, a special magazine well beveled to fit for positive reloading, and special checkering on the frame. All components are individually serial numbered to the pistol. The pistol is finished in proprietary Black T, which is highly wear-resistant, virtually impervious to oxidation and is self-lubricating to a certain extent. Each pistol is issued with six Metalform magazines.

Springfield Professional Model (FBI)

Springfield Armory 1911A1

Soldiers of all ranks train and qualify with the M-9 pistol.

SPECIFICATIONS:

Caliber: .45 ACP
Operation: short-recoil, semiautomatic
Locking: Browning system
Feed: 7- or 8-round detachable box magazine
Empty weight: 2.4 pounds
Overall length: 8.7 inches
Barrel length: 5 inches
Sights: Novak Combat: Front: blade; rear: low-profile adjustable notch;
both with tritium inserts

Springfield Armory .45 ACP 1911A1 Service Model pistols

These pistols are for the most part standard configuration M1911A1 type pistols, although built to a very high standard. Although of standard 1911A1 design, the Springfield Armory versions are made entirely of hardened and heat-treated steel machined forgings. All parts have been surface treated for long life and wearing qualities. Numerous variants are available, with detail differences such as a stainless steel or Parkerized finish and including a "Loaded" model with numerous value-added features. A key-operated integral locking system is available as an option, including as a retrofit kit. While Springfield Armory manufactures a wide variety of 1911-type pistols, those that follow are most applicable to military and police use.

-GI .45 MIL SPEC: A close replica of the basic M1911A1. Parkerized finish. Original type sights and ejection port.

-Tactical Response Operator: This version is being purchased in limited quantities by the US Military for special operations use. It features a match-grade barrel, tuned and polished extractor, Pachmayr grips, Novak

tritium sights, lowered and flared ejection port, beveled magazine well, Delta lightweight hammer, ambidextrous safety, MIL-STD-1913 rail on the dust cover and green and black two tone Armory Kote™ finish.

-Service Model: a standard M1911A1 built to a high standard of fit and finish with lowered and flared ejection port, Pearce grips, Delta lightweight hammer, beveled magazine well, ambidextrous safety and other custom features. Finish is green Armory Kote.™ This model is also available in matte stainless steel and Parkerized finishes.

SPECIFICATIONS:

TRP Operator
Caliber: .45 ACP
Operation: Short-recoil, semiautomatic
Locking: Browning system
Feed: 7 or 8-round box magazine
Empty weight: 2.4 pounds
Overall length: 8.7 inches
Barrel length: 5 inches
Sights: Novak Combat tritium Front: blade; rear: square notch,
three aiming dots with tritium inserts

Sub machine Guns

Submachine guns, sometimes called machine pistols, as a class of small arm are in decline and it is likely that few, if any will see military service as the 21st Century progresses. Submachine guns continue to be used by law enforcement special teams, but as with the military, submachine guns are gradually being replaced by carbines chambered in intermediate calibers, such as 5.56x45mm.

There are a number of reasons for the decline of the submachine gun. By definition, submachine guns fire pistol cartridges, which have terminal ballistics far inferior to those of carbines in intermediate calibers that are only marginally larger than a submachine gun. Both military and law enforcement operations have been characterized by the increased presence of body armor, not only by "friendlies," but by enemy forces and criminals. Since body armor is designed to protect against almost all pistol calibers, especially 9x19mm that prevails in military and in many law enforcement organizations, submachine guns are ineffective against individuals wearing body armor unless the submachine gun shooter is able to achieve a head shot.

The US military began replacing submachine guns in the 1990s and today virtually all units that might once have used submachine guns now are equipped with either M-4 or M-4A1 carbine versions of the M-16, although these are in turn being replaced as this goes to press. Most foreign special tactical teams have also gone over to a carbine of some sort. Although some refer to their

carbines as "submachine guns," the latter by definition fires a pistol cartridge, so short barreled versions of assault rifles, exemplified by the M-4/M-4A1 and AKS-74U, are actually carbines, not submachine guns.

The most recent submachine gun designs are the Heckler & Koch UMP (Universal Machine Pistol), MP-7 4.6x30mm PDW (personal defense weapon) and FN Herstal's 5.7x28mm P-90. Neither the MP-7 nor the P-90 have been sold in significant numbers, although a few special tactical teams have purchased them. It is probable that the submachine gun as a significant class of small arm will continue to decline and will be replaced in both military and police organizations by compact carbines.

Argentina

FMK-3

9x19mm FMK-3 Mod 2 submachine gun

The 9mm FMK-3 Mod 2 submachine gun is a blowback-operated weapon of modern design. It was formerly produced in two models, one with a fixed plastic stock and the other with a collapsible stock similar to that of the US M3 SMG. The 'Modification 2' model is produced only with a sliding stock. The receiver is a metal stamping and there is a screw-threaded cap at the front end to facilitate barrel removal. A plastic forearm is under the receiver. The 25- or 40-round box magazine fits into the pistol grip, which has a grip safety at the back. There is also a safety position on the selector.

The cocking handle is forward on the left side of the receiver with a slide that covers the cocking slot to keep out dirt. The FMK-3 is designed with a telescoping bolt that encloses 7.1 inches of the barrel that is 11.4 inches in overall length.

A semiautomatic variant designated FMK-5 carbine is the same basic weapon as the FMK-3 Mod 2 without the select-fire feature.

SPECIFICATIONS:

Caliber: 9x19mm
Operation: blowback, select-fire
Feed: 25- or 40-round box magazine
Empty weight: 7.9 pounds
Overall length: stock retracted, 20.5 inches; stock extended, 27.2 inches
Barrel Overall length: 11.4 inches
Sights: Front, post; rear: flip aperture, 50 and 100 m
Cyclic rate: 600 rounds per minute

Austria

Steyr AUG-A1

Steyr AUG-A1 9mm Para Submachine gun

The Steyr AUG-A1 9mm Para is a submachine gun version of the standard AUG-A1 assault rifle. It uses the existing stock and receiver but is fitted with a barrel chambered in 9x19mm, a special bolt group, a magazine adaptor and a 25-round box magazine. The chamber is chrome-plated. An optional muzzle device is available for launching riot control grenades and the barrel is threaded to accept various sound suppressors. A bayonet attachment point is also available.

SPECIFICATIONS:

Caliber: 9x19mm
Operation: blowback, select-fire
Feed: 25-round detachable box magazine
Empty weight: 8.2 pounds
Overall length: 26 inches
Barrel length: 16.5 inches
Rifling: 6 grooves, rh, 1 turn in 9.8 inches
Sights: integral 1.5x optic
Muzzle velocity: ca 400 m/s
Cyclic rate: 670-770 rounds per minute

Steyr TMP

Steyr SMG Kit

Steyr 9x19mm
Tactical Machine Pistol (TMP)

The TMP is a locked-breech weapon in 9x19mm caliber. There are only 41 component parts, and the frame and top cover are made from a plastic material. An integrated mounting rail is provided over the receiver for optical and electro-optic sighting devices.

Locking is via a rotary barrel, controlled by a single lug that engages in a groove in the frame to turn the barrel and thus unlock it from the bolt. The cocking handle is at the rear of the weapon, beneath the rear sight. Selection of single-shot or semiautomatic fire is performed by a three-position safety bar. Magazines hold 15 or 30-rounds.

The TMP has facilities for attaching a sound suppressor or a laser aiming device. Another combat accessory is a detachable shoulder stock made from plastic-based materials.

The TMP is also available in semiautomatic-only, designated "Special-Purpose Pistol" (SPP).

SPECIFICATIONS:

Caliber: 9x19mm
Operation: closed locked bolt, delayed blowback, semiautomatic (TMP select-fire)
Locking: rotating barrel
Feed: 15-round or 30-round box magazine
Empty weight: 2.9 pounds
Overall length: 11.1 inches
Barrel length: 5.1 inches
Sights: front, blade; rear: notch
Cyclic rate: Approx. 900 rounds per minute

Austrian Steyr AUG-A1

Belgium

FN P90

FN 5.7 x 28mm P90 submachine gun

This weapon was originally developed by FN Herstal to equip military personnel whose prime activity was not that of operating small arms, such as artillery, signals, transport and troops whose duties require that they be effectively armed for self-defense but who do not need to be burdened by a heavy weapon while performing their normal tasks. The SMG has since been marketed as a special operations and law enforcement weapon.

The ball projectile is claimed to penetrate more than 48 layers of Kevlar at 200 meters. Recoil forces are stated to be one-third of those produced by a 5.56x45mm cartridge.

Tracer, subsonic and blank rounds are available, in addition to the SS190 ball round. Winchester-Olin license-produces 5.7x28mm ammunition in the United States. A pistol in 5.7 x 28mm caliber is known as the Five-seveN.

Sales of the P90-series of weapons are limited to government agencies only.

The P90 is a blowback weapon firing from a closed bolt. The overall design places great reliance on ergonomics, for example, the pistol grip, with a thumb-hole stock, is well forward on the receiver so that when gripped, the bulk of the receiver lies along the firer's front arm. The controls are fully ambidextrous; a cocking handle is provided on each side, and the rotary selector switch is located under the trigger. Even the forward sling swivel can be located on either side of the weapon.

The magazine lies along the top of the receiver above the barrel, and the cartridges are aligned at 90 degrees to the weapon long axis. The 50-rounds lie in double-row configuration, and as they reach the mouth of the magazine, they are directed into a single row by a fixed ramp. A spiral ramp then turns the round through 90 degrees as it is being guided down into the feedway so that it arrives in front of the bolt correctly oriented for chambering. The magazine is translucent plastic so that its contents can be visually checked at any time.

The integral sight unit is a reflex collimating sight produced by Ring Sights. The reticle is a circle and dot; in low light, a tritium-illuminated crosshair appears. The sight can be used with both eyes open and allows rapid

target acquisition and accurate fire. Should the sight be damaged, two sets of iron sights are machined into the sight base, one on each side, another aspect of the overall ambidextrous design.

The weapon strips easily into three basic groups for field maintenance. Much of the receiver and internal mechanism is of high-impact polymer, only the bolt and barrel are of steel. Moving parts require little lubrication. Empty cartridge cases are ejected downwards through the pistol grip, which is shaped to offer a grip for the "weak" hand when firing from the shoulder.

Externally mounted tactical lights and laser aiming devices can be located either side of the sight assembly on an accessory rail. Also available are a combat sling, a blank firing attachment, a cleaning kit and a magazine pouch and filler. A sound suppressor that screw-clamps over the muzzle attachment is available.

The P90 TR variant has been dubbed the 'Flat Top', since the usual sight is replaced by a section of MIL-STD-1913 rail, together with two shorter lengths of rail on each side. This arrangement allows the user to select an optical sighting system. The side rails can be used to attach combat accessories such as tactical lights or laser pointers. All other aspects of the basic P90 remain as before, although the loaded weight decreases to 5.5 pounds.

Two special operations variants of the P90 are available, each with a laser target designator. The P90 LV uses an 8 mW visible laser for use in low-light conditions and in indoor situations. The P90 Laser Intercept Receiver (LIR) has a 4.5 mW infra-red laser which can be detected with night-vision devices.

SPECIFICATIONS: Basic P90

Caliber: 5.7 x 28mm
Operation: blowback; select-fire, closed-bolt firing
Feed: 50-round magazine located horizontally above barrel
Empty weight: 5.6 pounds
Overall length: 19.7 inches
Barrel length: 10.1 inches
Sights: optical reflex, 1x, plus emergency iron sights
Rate of fire: 900 rounds per minute
Range: max combat: 200 m

The FN P90 has been adopted by a few defense and police agencies.

Brazil

Taurus 9x19mm MT-12 Series Submachine guns

After the Brazilian Army in the mid-1960s adopted the weapon the Beretta Model 12 was manufactured under license by Industria e Comercio Beretta SA of Sao Paulo. In June 1980, Forjas Taurus SA acquired the company and some minor modifications were added to the gun.

The MT-12 was a direct copy of the original Beretta Model 12. The later MT-12A was based on the Beretta Model 12S but featured a spring-loaded cover on the ejection port, a new spring-loaded, stock-folding system to permit single-handed operation, and an enlarged grip safety. The MT-12AD was provided with a disconnector in the trigger mechanism to avoid a problem with earlier models, involving unwanted two- or three-round bursts when the selector was set for semiautomatic.

Production ceased during the early 1990s. All basic specifications are similar to those of the Beretta equivalents.

Bulgaria

Arsenal 9mm Shipka submachine gun

The Arsenal Shipka submachine gun is a conventional blowback design chambered either in 9x18mm or 9x19mm cartridges fed from 32-round or 25-round box magazines, respectively. Two barrel lengths (5.9 inches or 7.9 inches) are available for the 9x19mm version. The barrel life is stated to be more than 5,000-rounds. Firing is fully automatic only. A simple upwards-folding wire stock is provided, while the forend and the pistol grip are manufactured using high-impact plastic-based materials. A web sling is optional.

A chamber-type suppressor, providing an effective noise-dampening level of 20 dB is also optional. Made from light alloy, it is 1.8 inches in diameter and is 8.6 inches in length. The suppressor may be used in conjunction with a laser pointer located under the front handguard, but it is not offered for the 9x19mm model.

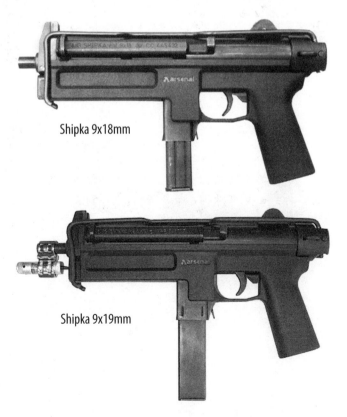

Shipka 9x18mm

Shipka 9x19mm

SPECIFICATIONS: Data for 9x18mm (9x19mm in parentheses)
Caliber: 9x18mm (9x19mm)
Operation: blowback, automatic only
Feed: 32-round box magazine (25-round box magazine)
Empty weight: 4.9 pounds (5.3 pounds)
Overall length: stock folded: 13.3 inches (14.2 or 16.1 inches) stock extended:
Barrel length: 5.9 inches (5.9 or 7.9 inches)
Sights: front: post; rear: flip notch, set for 150 m
Cyclic rate: >700 rounds per minute
Max effective range: 60 m

Chile

FAMAE Mini-S.A.F. 9mm submachine gun

The FAMAE Mini-S.A.F. 9mm submachine gun uses the same basic mechanism as the standard S.A.F. but has a much shorter barrel, no shoulder stock, and a forward handgrip which also has a guard to prevent hands from slipping in front of the muzzle. The standard 30-round magazine can be used, although a special 20-round short magazine is made for this weapon to provide maximum compactness.

SPECIFICATIONS:

Caliber: 9x19mm
Operation: blowback, select-fire, with three-round burst limiter
Feed: 20- or 30-round box magazine
Empty weight: without magazine, 5.1 pounds
Overall length: 12.2 inches
Barrel length: 4.5 inches
Sights: front, post, adjustable for elevation; rear: aperture, adjustable for windage
Cyclic rate: 1,200 rounds per minute

FAMAE SAF

FAMAE SAF

FAMAE S.A.F. 9x19mm submachine gun

The FAMAE S.A.F. 9mm submachine gun fires from a closed bolt and the design is based upon the SIG 540 rifle, also manufactured in Chile under license by FAMAE. Certain modifications to the SIG mechanism were made, notably in a cocking-handle release catch, in the firing mechanism and in a new three-round burst limiter, but the basic hammer and floating firing pin system of operation is retained. Operation is by blowback. The barrel and bore are chrome plated.

Three types are manufactured: the standard model with fixed stock, standard with side-folding skeleton stock, and a silenced model, also with side-folding stock. 20- or 30-round magazines are available, although the 30-round magazine is standard. The 30-round magazines are of translucent polymer which permits visual checking at any time. These magazines also have studs and slots in their sides which permit two or more magazines to be clipped together; in this configuration one magazine can be inserted into the gun's magazine housing and fired, and when empty it can be quickly slipped out and a connected, loaded, magazine slipped into the housing.

FAMAE SAF Mini

SPECIFICATIONS:

Caliber: 9x19mm
Operation: blowback, select-fire with three-round burst limiter
Feed: 20- or 30-round plastic box magazine
Empty weight: fixed stock standard, 5.9 pounds without magazine; folding stock standard, 6.4 pounds without magazine; silenced model, 6.6 pounds without magazine Overall length: standard, stock folded 16.1 inches; standard, stock extended, 25.2 inches; silenced, stock folded, 22.4 inches; silenced, stock extended, 31.9 inches;
Barrel length: standard, 7.8 inches; silenced, 8.7 inches
Rifling: 6 grooves, rh, 1 turn in 9.8 inches
Sights: front, post, adjustable for elevation; rear: aperture, adjustable for windage
Cyclic rate of fire: standard, 1,120-1,280 rounds per minute; cyclic, silenced, 980 rounds per minute

Chinese troops in a training exercise.

China

NORINCO 7.62X25mm Type 79 Light Submachine gun

The NORINCO Type 79 is a lightweight weapon, chambered for the 7.62 x 25mm (Type 51) pistol cartridge, which has excellent performance against soft body armor. The receiver is made from steel stampings, and it has a safety and selector lever over the pistol grip on the right side, similar to that of AK-series rifles.

The Type 79 is gas-operated with a short-stroke tappet above the barrel. This drives a short piston attached to a bolt carrier, operating a rotating bolt. This design eliminates the heavy bolt and long bolt travel of blowback operated weapons, making the weapon lighter and more controllable.

SPECIFICATIONS:
Caliber: 7.62 x 25mm (Type 51)
Operation: gas, select-fire
Locking: rotating bolt
Feed: 20-round box magazine
Empty weight: 4.2 pounds
Overall length: stock folded, 18.5 inches; stock extended, 29.1 inches
Cyclic rate: 650 rounds per minute

NORINCO 7.62x25mm Type 85 Light Submachine gun

The NORINCO Type 85 Light Submachine gun is a modified and simplified version of the Type 79. It is a blowback-operated weapon, with a cylindrical receiver into which the barrel is fitted along with the bolt and recoil spring. There is a folding stock, and the weapon uses the same magazine as the Type 79. The manufacturers claim the weapon can fire reduced-velocity Type 64 pistol ammunition as well as the standard Type 51 cartridge.

SPECIFICATIONS:
Caliber: 7.62 x 25mm pistol (Type 51)
Operation: blowback, select-fire
Feed: 30-round box magazine
Empty weight: 4.2 pounds
Overall length: stock folded, 17.5; stock extended, 26.9 inches
Sights: front, blade; rear: flip aperture; sighted to 200 m
Cyclic rate: 780 rounds per minute
Max effective range: 200 m

NORINCO 7.62x25mm Type 85 Silenced Submachine gun

The NORINCO 7.62mm Type 85 is a simplified and lightened version of the silenced 7.62mm Type 64 submachine gun, produced principally for export. It appears to be based on the simple mechanism of the Type 85 Light Submachine gun, but is of about the same size as the Type 64 and uses similar silencing arrangements.

The Type 85 is intended to be used primarily with the 7.62x25mm Type 64 silenced cartridge but it is also possible to fire the standard Type 51 pistol cartridge, although the silencing effect is greatly reduced. With the Type 64 cartridge, the sound of discharge is reduced to less than 80 dB.

SPECIFICATIONS:
Caliber: 7.62 x 25mm Type 64; 7.62 x 25mm Type 51
Operation: blowback, select-fire
Feed: 30-round box magazine
Empty weight: 5.5 pounds
Overall length: stock folded, 24.8 inches; stock extended, 34.2 inches
Sights: Front, blade; rear: flip aperture; sighted to 200 m
Cyclic rate: 800 rounds per minute ; practical, 200 rounds per minute
Max effective range: 200 m

Norinco Type 85

Croatia

Agram 2000 and 2002 9z19mm Submachine guns

With the breakup of the former Yugoslavia, several states were left with significantly reduced arms production capability. In order to be able to provide small arms to their police and military forces in the civil war, a number of weapons were designed to be produced in local machine shops. The Agram 2000 and 2002 submachine guns are such weapons and were produced in Croatia. They may be regarded as typical of several other models of Croatian submachine gun produced on a limited scale during the early days of the Croatian conflict with Serbia.

The Agram 2000 and 2002 submachine guns are in essence variations on the same design, the primary difference being the sights and the lack of a front grip on the Agram 2002. The weapons are constructed of simple metal tubes, stampings and molded plastic. Magazines are of the Uzi type. A wing-type safety on the left side of the weapon has three positions, S for safe, R for fully automatic and 1 for semiautomatic fire. The reciprocating cocking handle is on the left and ejection port on the right. Rear sights on the Agram 2000 are simple flip-type, with settings for 50 and 150 m, while the front sight is adjustable for windage. Rear sights on the Agram 2002 are tangent leaf type with settings for 50, 100 and 150m.

A sleeve covers the barrel when the standard suppressor is not in use. The suppressor is a simple screw-on device and the barrel is pre-drilled to optimize suppressor effectiveness. There is no provision for a shoulder stock on either weapon.

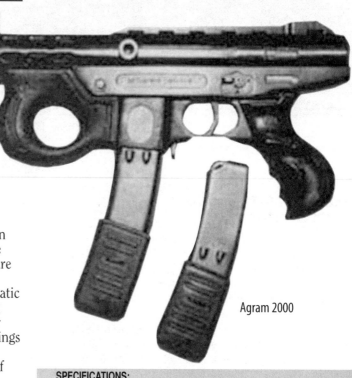

Agram 2000

SPECIFICATIONS:
Caliber: 9x19mm
Operation: blowback
Feed: 20- or 32-round detachable box magazine
Empty weight: 4.2 pounds
Overall length: without suppressor, 13.8 inches; with suppressor, 19 inches
Barrel length: ca 6 inches
Sights: Agram 2000: front, adjustable for height and deflection; rear: settings for 50 and 150 m Agram 2002: front, fixed; rear: tangent leaf with settings for 50, 100 and 150 m

ERO 9x19mm submachine gun

The design of the ERO 9mm submachine gun was derived from the Israeli IMI 9x19mm Uzi submachine gun, so the principle of operation and the general mechanical details are similar to those of the Uzi. The location of the cocking handle over the receiver makes operation simple for both right-handed and left-handed users, while the ERO has a double safety system. An automatic safety located in the rear of the pistol grip prevents either cocking or firing until the shooter tightens the hand pressure on the grip and releases the safety. The ordinary safety acts directly on the trigger and is operated by the changeover lever on the left-hand side above the pistol grip. The sights consist of an adjustable blade front sight and a flip rear sight that can be tilted for ranges of 100 and 200 m.

SPECIFICATIONS:
Caliber: 9 x19mm
Operation: blowback, open bolt, select-fire
Feed: 32-round box magazine
Empty weight: 7.8 pounds
Overall length: stock, retracted, 18.5 inches; stock, extended, 25.6 inches
Barrel length: 10.2 inches
Sights: Front, post; rear: flip aperture 100 and 200m
Cyclic rate: 650 rounds per minute

Mini-ERO 9x19mm Submachine gun

In 1995, the Republic of Croatia began to manufacture a smaller version of the ERO submachine gun known as the Mini-ERO. The Mini-ERO is visually virtually identical to the larger model and differs only in size, weight and firing characteristics. In addition, a 20-round magazine is available for this weapon.

The Mini-ERO incorporates design aspects from both the Israeli IMI Mini-Uzi and Micro-Uzi submachine guns, along with a telescopic wire stock apparently based on that for the US Ingram M10. Combining features from both weapons produces a compact submachine gun that can be easily concealed or carried in vehicles. The Mini-ERO is thus intended for use by security and law-enforcement personnel as well as for special-forces operations.

SPECIFICATIONS:
Caliber: 9 x19mm
Operation: blowback, select-fire
Feed: 20-round or 30-round box magazine
Empty weight: 4.9 pounds
Overall length: stock, retracted, 12.6 inches; stock, extended, 21.5 inches mm
Barrel length: 5.9 inches
Sights: Front, post; rear: flip aperture 75 and 150 m
Cyclic rate: 1,100 rounds per minute

Czech Republic

Sa 58/98 Bulldog 9mm submachine gun

With the reduction in numbers of the Czech and Slovak armies, the Czech military had a surplus of Model 58 7.62x39mm assault rifles. In an attempt to make use of some parts of these rifles, the Czech Military Institute for Weapon and Ammunition Technology (VTUVM) has used many Model 58 rifle components to produce the Sa 58/98 Bulldog 9mm submachine gun, a relatively low-cost firearm intended to attract export orders. The Sa 58/98 Bulldog (Sa stands for Samopal - 'submachine gun') is chambered for the 9x19mm cartridge.

It appears that the only original components used in the conversion are the trigger and the grip assembly, complete with the select-fire mechanism and parts of the receiver. The original operating mechanism has been replaced by a blowback system, and the original magazine housing has been modified to accommodate a straight box magazine

holding 30 9x19mm rounds. The stock is replaced by a simple single-strut design that folds to the left. The top of the Sa 58/98 Bulldog receiver can be used to mount an optical or night sight and a laser aiming device can be installed.

The Sa 58/98 S is a silenced version of the Sa 58/98 Bulldog with a shortened barrel (7.1 inches) and a permanently fitted sound suppressor, which increases the overall length of the firearm to 31.9 inches with the stock extended. The suppressor reduces the muzzle velocity to 984 feet per second when firing conventional ammunition.

SPECIFICATIONS:

Caliber: 9x19mm
Operation: blowback, select-fire
Feed: 30-round box magazine
Empty weight: 7.5 pounds, (Sa 58/98 S, 7.7 pounds)
Overall length: Sa 58/98 stock retracted 445mm, stock extended 660mm; Sa 58/98 S

Georgia

SCH-21 Gorda 9x19mm Submachine gun

The SCH-21 Gorda 9mm select-fire submachine gun is an indigenous Georgian design chambered in 9x19mm. It was designed primarily for use by 'Internal Ministry' units and special operations units.

The Gorda is based on the receiver of the AKM assault rifle with modification made to the magazine well. Operation is by a conventional blowback and ammunition is fed into the weapon from a straight 30-round box magazine inserted from the bottom of the receiver. The fire selector switch is exactly the same as the AKM assault rifle. A Romanian pattern right-folding stock is provided.

Two models are known to exist. The standard model is provided with a fixed front grip. A second model does not have a front grip and is provided with an oversize integral suppressor for clandestine operations. The suppressed model appears to lack a front sight.

Accessories include a collimator 'red dot' sight, a laser target indicator, a tactical light and various optics.

SPECIFICATIONS:

Caliber: 9x19mm
Operation: blowback, select-fire
Feed: 30-round box magazine
Empty weight: 6.8 pounds
Overall length: stock folded, 15 inches; stock extended, 22.8 inches
Sights: Front, blade; rear: notch; red dot or optical sights optional
Cyclic rate: 700 rounds per minute

Georgian Light Infantry

Germany

Heckler & Koch MP7

Heckler & Koch 4.6x30mm MP7 Personal Defense Weapon (PDW)

Following experimental and development work that commenced during the early 1990s at Oberndorf, Germany, in August 1999 Heckler & Koch released preliminary details regarding its 4.6x30mm Personal Defense Weapon (PDW), later known as the MP7. The MP7 is intended to arm a number of military personnel who by the very nature of their duties cannot carry a full-size weapon such as an assault rifle. This category is further defined as 'personnel whose primary task does not involve an assault against the enemy but who require a close-range self-defense capability'. The concept is thus very similar to that of FN Herstal's 5.7x28mm P90.

One of the most novel features of the MP7 is the ammunition, developed by Royal Ordnance, now part of BAE Systems, RO Defense, at Radway Green. The main combat round, a ball round with a steel bullet, consists of a 4.6 x 30mm rimless center-fire cartridge. The copper-plated solid hardened steel bullet weighs some 26 grains. Seven types of 4.6x30mm ammunition are available: ball (steel bullet), tracer, ball training (a low-cost, copper-clad bullet), blank, ball frangible, ball spoon nose (increased lethality deforming round) and drill. Future ammunition types could include ball tracer, a ROTA training round with reduced range, and a spoon-nosed copper training round.

The MP7 has been used operationally in the Balkans by German troops.

The MP7 is a gas-operated weapon firing from a locked bolt with a rotating bolt head. It can be fired using only one hand, although a two-handed grip is preferred, with a forward handgrip folding up in front of the trigger. For firing at ranges up to 200 meters, a telescopic shoulder stock is provided. The construction makes extensive use of synthetic polymer materials to reduce weight. The barrel is hard chrome plated.

Ammunition is fed from double-row 20- or 40-round box magazines inserted through the pistol grip. Primary sights are a Helsoldt reflex red-dot optical unit, along with backup iron sights, both calibrated for use up to

200 meters. A length of MIL-STD-1913 rail allows the installation of other sighting systems. Shoulder or thigh holsters can be provided. A sound suppressor, combined with special subsonic rounds, is available.

SPECIFICATIONS:

Caliber: 4.6 x 30mm
Operation: gas, select-fire
Locking: rotating bolt head, 6 lugs
Feed: 20- or 40-round box magazine
Empty weight: without magazine, 3.3 pounds
Overall length: stock folded, 15 inches; stock extended, 23.2 inches
Barrel length: 7.1 inches
Sights: optical and adjustable iron, calibrated up to 200 m
Cyclic rate of fire: 950 rounds per minute
Max effective range: 200 m

Heckler & Koch 9x19mm MP5 submachine gun

The Heckler & Koch MP5 submachine gun was developed from the G3 rifle and has the same delayed blowback roller lock method of operation. The submachine gun was adopted in late 1966 by the West German police forces and border police. It has since been purchased by many military and police forces worldwide. The MP5 remains one of the most widely deployed of all current submachine guns and has been developed into a family with numerous variants.

The Heckler & Koch MP5 submachine gun usually offers only a choice of semi- or full automatic, but a burst-fire device, allowing two-round or three-round bursts each time the trigger is operated, is available for those requiring this capability. This fire control unit can be fitted to all automatic weapons in the Heckler & Koch series. With the selector lever placed on 'safe', the selector spindle lies over the trigger lug and prevents sufficient movement of the trigger to disengage the sear from the hammer notch. The position of the safety can vary from model to model.

The breech mechanism is of the same design as that used in the G3 rifle. It essentially is a two-part bolt with rollers projecting from the bolt head. The heavier bolt carrier lies forward against the bolt head when the weapon is ready to fire where inclined planes force the rollers out into recesses in the barrel extension. Upon firing, gas

Heckler & Koch MP5/40

pressure places backward force on the bolt head, which is unable to go back, since the rollers are in the recesses in the barrel extension and must move in against the inclined planes of the heavy bolt carrier. The selected angles of the recesses and the incline on the bolt body produce a velocity ratio of about 4:1 between the bolt carrier and the bolt head. Thus, the bolt head moves back only about .04 inch, while the bolt carrier moves some .15 inch. As soon as the rollers are fully retracted, the two breech components are driven back together. The empty case is held to the bolt face by the extractor until it strikes the ejector and is thrown out of the ejection port. The recoil spring is compressed during the backward movement of the bolt and drives the bolt forward. A round is fed into the chamber, and the bolt face comes to rest. The bolt carrier continues to move forward, and the inclined planes again drive the rollers out into the barrel extension recesses. The bolt carrier closes against the bolt head, and the weapon is ready to fire another round. The MP5 fires from a closed bolt, making it more accurate than the conventional blowback submachine gun.

If the selector is set to full automatic, the trigger has moved up sufficiently for the nose of the sear to be depressed so far that it does not re-engage the hammer. The next round is fired as soon as the bolt is fully closed, and the safety sear is moved out of engagement with the hammer. If the selector is for a single shot, the trigger is unable to rise fully, and the spring-loaded sear holds the hammer until the trigger is released and pressed again. Provided the bolt is fully closed, the hammer will be released.

If a burst-fire control is fitted, a ratchet counting device in the trigger mechanism holds the sear off the hammer until the allotted number of rounds has been fired. This device ensures that the correct number of cartridges (two or three) are discharged in a single burst and that any interruption, for example an empty magazine, starts a fresh count. After the burst, the trigger must be released to set the counter back to zero, and another sustained pressure on the trigger fires another burst of two or three rounds.

Fire control groups vary from model to model; on some models, pictograms depict the rates of fire. Most trigger groups are interchangeable. The following types are available:

- SEF: S, safe; E, semiautomatic; F, fully automatic
- Numerical: S, safe; 1, semiautomatic; 20/25, fully automatic
- SF (single-fire) Pictogram: safe; semiautomatic

- 0-1-2 Pictogram: safe; semiautomatic; 2-round burst
- 0-1-3 Pictogram: safe; semiautomatic; three-round burst
- Navy Pictogram: safe; semiautomatic; fully automatic (extended pictogram)
- 2-round burst Pictogram: safe; semiautomatic; 2-round burst; fully automatic
- three-round burst Pictogram: safe; semiautomatic; three-round burst; fully automatic.

The Navy trigger group was originally developed for use on the MP5-N model for US Navy SEAL teams. The MP5-N trigger group is ambidextrous, and the muzzles are threaded for the installation of various suppressors.

The first MP5 models were fitted with a straight box magazine, but in 1978 this was changed to a magazine with a slight curve. It was found that the curved shape improved the feeding characteristics with the many different types of bullet and nose shapes likely to be encountered with 9x19mm ammunition.

The MP5 is manufactured under license in Greece, Iran, Mexico, Turkey and Pakistan.

Variants

10mm MP5/10 submachine gun

The MP5 chambered for the 10mm auto cartridge

.40 S&W MP5/40 submachine gun

The MP5 chambered for the .40 Smith & Wesson (S&W) cartridge.

C-Magazine MP5

The Beta Company of the USA produces a version of its C-Magazine high-capacity magazine specifically for MP5-type submachine guns. Known as the C-Magazine MP5, the unit can hold up to 100-rounds. Empty weight is 2 pounds.

SPECIFICATIONS: MP5A2

Caliber: 9x19mm
Operation: delayed-blowback; select-fire
Locking: rollers
Feed: 15- or 30-round curved box magazine
Empty weight: without magazine, 5.6 pounds
Overall length: 26.8 inches
Barrel length: 8.6 inches
Sights: Front, fixed post; rear: apertures for different eye relief, adjustable for windage and elevation
Cyclic rate: 800 rounds per minute

German HK-MP7

Heckler & Koch MP5KA4

Heckler & Koch 9x19mm MP5K-series submachine guns

Heckler & Koch introduced its 9mm MP5K-series submachine guns for use by special operations units. They are extra-short versions of the standard MP5 and are meant for concealed carry or carry in other limited space. They offer all the fire options of the MP5. The MP5K is fitted either with adjustable open sights or with an optical sight. The MP5KA1 has a smooth top surface with small front and rear sights, so that there is little to catch in clothing or on a holster as the gun is drawn. The MP5KA4 is similar to the MP5K but has a three-round burst capability along with semiautomatic and automatic fire. The prominent forearm grip gives the shooter the optimum control under all firing conditions. A shoulder stock is not fitted and is replaced by a receiver cap, as the weapon is meant to normally be fired from the hands, although a folding stock identical to that of the MP5-PDW is available. Variants are produced under license in Iran, Pakistan and Turkey.

SPECIFICATIONS:
Caliber: 9x19mm
Operation: Roller delayed blowback, select-fire
Feed: 15- or 30-round detachable box magazine
Empty weight: without magazine, 2.03 kg
Overall length: 12.8 inches
Barrel length: 4.5 inches
Sights: Front, post; rear: open rotary adjustable for windage and elevation, or x4 telescopic
Cyclic rate: 900 rounds per minute

Heckler & Koch 9x19mm MP5SD submachine gun

The Heckler & Koch MP5SD is a suppressed version of the MP5 submachine gun. Its mechanism is the same as that of the MP5, but the weapon differs in having a barrel into which 30 holes have been drilled. The suppressor on the barrel features two chambers, one of which is over the holes in the barrel, serving as an expansion chamber for the propellant gases, thereby reducing gas pressure to slow the acceleration of the projectile. The second chamber

diverts the gases as they exit the muzzle, so muffling the exit report. The bullet leaves the muzzle at subsonic velocity, so it does not generate a sonic shockwave. The suppressor requires minimal maintenance; rinsing in an oil-free cleaning solvent is all that is prescribed.

There are six versions of the MP5SD.

- The MP5SD1 has a receiver end cap and no stock.
- The MP5SD2 has a fixed stock; its components are identical to those of the MP5A2.
- The MP5SD3 has a retractable stock; its components are identical to those of the MP5A3.
- The MP5SD4 has a three-round burst capability in addition to semiautomatic and automatic fire.
- The MP5SD5 is the MP5SD2 with a three-round burst option.
- The MP5SD6 is the MP5SD3 with a three-round burst option.

It should be noted that the three latest models have a slightly changed pistol grip contour. Each may be used with open sights, an optical sight, a Hensoldt aiming point sight, or an image intensifier sight. Similar models are produced under license in Greece.

SPECIFICATIONS:
Caliber: 9x19mm
Operation: Roller delayed blowback, select-fire
Feed: 15- or 30-round box magazine
Empty weight: MP5SD1, 7.5 pounds; MP5SD2, 6.8 pounds; MP5SD3, 7.6 pounds
Overall length: MP5SD1, 21.7 inches; MP5SD2, 30.7 inches; MP5SD3, 25.7 inches or 31.7 inches
Barrel length: 5.7 inches
Rifling: 6 grooves, rh
Sights: Front, fixed post; rear: apertures for different eye relief, adjustable for windage and elevation; Various optics may be fitted
Cyclic rate: 800 rounds per minute

Heckler & Koch MP5 SD

Heckler and Koch 10mm MP5/10 Submachine gun

The Heckler and Koch MP5/10 is an improved version of the Heckler and Koch MP5 submachine gun that was designed especially for use by US law enforcement agencies. The operation and functioning of the MP5/10 is exactly the same as that of the standard MP5, except that this weapon is chambered for the 10mm Auto cartridge. The MP5/10 was subsequently produced in .40 S&W due to the popularity of that cartridge in US law enforcement, virtually eclipsing the 9x19mm and 10mm cartridges.

A newly designed carbon fiber reinforced magazine was developed with a straight shape in place of the usual curve. A metal clamp allows two magazines to be held together on the weapon, facilitating rapid magazine changes.

The standard MP5/10 has a HK select-fire trigger assembly with a three-round burst limiter, but trigger mechanisms allowing any combination of firing modes can be supplied. This model also marked the introduction of a two-round burst feature, which is also available on all recent MP5 models. This allows firing two rounds with a single trigger pull, producing an automatic "double-tap."

SPECIFICATIONS:
Caliber: 10mm Auto/ .40 S&W
Operation: Roller delayed blowback, select-fire with 2- or three-round burst limiter
Feed: 30-round detachable box magazine
Empty weight: fixed stock, 5.9 pounds; retractable stock, 6.3 pounds
Overall length: stock retracted, 19.3 inches; stock extended, 26 inches; with fixed stock, 26.8 inches
Barrel length: 8.6 inches
Sights: Front, hooded post; rear: rotary aperture, fully adjustable

Heckler and Koch 9x19mm MP5K-PDW (Personal Defense Weapon)

The MP5K-PDW Personal Defense Weapon was developed by Heckler and Koch Inc. in the USA as a compact weapon for executive protection, vehicle or aircraft crews, or for other roles in which a rifle or full-sized submachine gun is inappropriate. It can be easily carried in a holster or concealed under a coat or inside a brief case or laptop computer bag.

The MP5K-PDW is identical to the Heckler and Koch MP5K with the addition of a side-folding stock and three lugs on the barrel to permit the fitting of either a flash or sound suppressor. When the stock is not required it can be quickly removed and replaced with a receiver cap. All controls are ambidextrous; the standard firing mechanism permits select-fire, and a two- or three-round burst fire control unit is optional.

SPECIFICATIONS:
Caliber: 9x19mm; +P rated
Operation: Roller delayed blowback, select-fire
Feed: 15- or 30-round detachable box magazines
Empty weight: 6.2 pounds
Overall length: stock folded, 14.5 inches; stock extended 23.7 inches
Barrel length: 5.5 inches
Sights: Front, hooded post; rear: rotary aperture, fully adjustable

Heckler & Koch MP5K-PDW

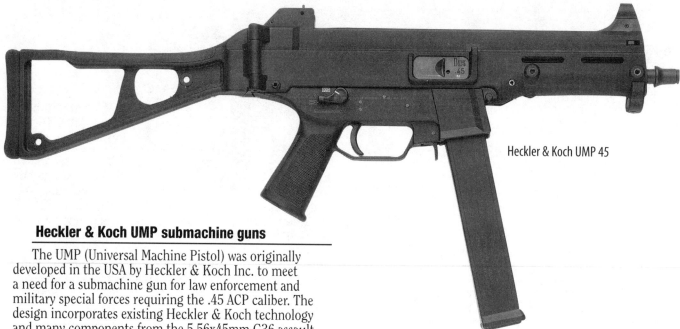

Heckler & Koch UMP 45

Heckler & Koch UMP submachine guns

The UMP (Universal Machine Pistol) was originally developed in the USA by Heckler & Koch Inc. to meet a need for a submachine gun for law enforcement and military special forces requiring the .45 ACP caliber. The design incorporates existing Heckler & Koch technology and many components from the 5.56x45mm G36 assault rifle. Design work, began in 1996 with the first production models available during 1999. The UMP is also marketed chambered for the 9x19mm and .40 S&W cartridges.

The UMP operates using the straight blowback principle and makes extensive use of glass fiber reinforced polymers throughout. Metal inserts are provided in stressed areas. The barrel is cold hammer forged, hard chrome lined and rifled in Heckler & Koch polygonal rifling. Select-fire controls can include pre-selected combinations of safe, semiautomatic, fully automatic and two-round burst, using an ambidextrous selecting lever. Ammunition is fed from high impact polymer box magazines holding 30-rounds. Magazines have a transparent strip through which the magazine contents can be observed. All types of .45 ACP, 9x19mm or .40 S&W ammunition can be fired, including enhanced velocity +P rounds. To facilitate magazine changes, the magazine well is flared.

The UMP fires from a closed bolt and has a forward assist notch accessible through the oversize ejection port on the right of the receiver. A passive internal firing pin block inside the bolt prevents the weapon from firing if dropped. The UMP can be field-stripped into three basic groups by removing a single locking pin. To reduce the overall length, the stock, which has a rubber butt pad and cheekpiece, can be folded along the right side of the receiver.

A MIL-STD-1913 rail with eight locating points is molded into the top of the receiver for mounting optics and accessories. More rails can be added to the receiver sides or under the forearm. The standard flip-up rear sights are adjustable for windage and elevation using an Allen wrench. The front sight post is protected by a detachable hood. Tritium sights are optional.

The muzzle is provided with a quick-connect interface to permit the attachment of a suppressor. Other options include a multipurpose sling, forward mounting rails, tactical white light and a vertical foregrip.

SPECIFICATIONS:

Caliber:	9x19mm/.40	SW .45 ACP
Operation:	blowback, select-fire	blowback, select-fire
Feed:	30-round box magazine	30-round box magazine
Empty weight:	4.6 pounds	4.9 pounds
Overall length:	17.7 inches	17.7 inches (stock retracted)
Overall length:	23.6 inches	23.6 inches (stock extended)
Barrel length:	7.9 inches	7.9 inches
Sights	Front, hooded post; rear: flip	Front, hooded post; rear: flip

Aperture adjustable for windage and elevation windage and elevation
Cyclic rate: 600 rounds per minute 700 rounds per minute

Hungary

KGP-9 9x19mm Submachine gun

The KGP-9 submachine gun is a blowback operated weapon with a side-folding steel stock. The receiver is stamped steel reinforced by precision castings. The bolt is fitted with a floating firing pin and the firing mechanism is of the hammer type. The safety and fire selector are in front of the trigger. The sheet steel magazine is the double

KGP-9

stack type. The rear sight is a two-range flip aperture. The weapon is easily dismantled. One feature is that the barrel can be removed and replaced by a 9.8 inch barrel to increase velocity and effective range.

The magazine housing is ahead of the trigger and the substantial synthetic forearm provides a firm grip. The nonreciprocating charging handle is on top of the receiver, offset from the line of sight.

SPECIFICATIONS:

Caliber: 9x19mm
Operation: blowback, select-fire
Feed: 25-round detachable box magazine
Empty weight: 6.1 pounds
Overall length: stock folded, 14 inches; stock extended, 24.2 inches
Barrel length: submachine gun, 7.5 or 9.8 inches
Sights: Front, post; rear: two-position flip aperture
Cyclic rate: 900 rounds per minute

India

Indian troops carry a variety of weapons.

OFB 1A1 and 2A1 9x19mm Submachine gun Carbine

The 1A1 Submachine gun Carbine is virtually identical to the out of production British L2A3 9x19mm Sterling submachine gun. However, some of the data provided by Indian sources differs somewhat from the data for the British original. Unlike the Sterling, the 1A1 remains available for production and is offered for export sale, hence its inclusion herein.

The 2A1 9mm submachine gun carbine is a suppressed version of the 1A1. The long suppressor was locally developed, but closely follows the Sterling-Patchett L34A1 suppressor, now no longer in production. On the 2A1, the suppressor is covered by a canvas insulating sleeve. The weight of the 2A1, loaded and with a sling, is 10.4 pounds.

SPECIFICATIONS:

Caliber: 9 x19mm
Operation: blowback, select-fire
Feed: 34-round curved box magazine
Empty weight: 6.3 pounds
Overall length: stock retracted, 19 inches; stock extended, 27.5 inches
Barrel length: 7.8 inches
Sights: Front, blade; rear: flip aperture
Cyclic rate: 550 rounds per minute

IMI Micro Tavor

Israel

Mini-UZI

IMI 9x19mm Micro-Tavor Submachine gun

The IMI 9mm Micro-Tavor submachine gun was derived from the 5.56x45mm Micro-Tavor assault rifle. It has the same bullpup configuration as the rifle but is altered in several respects. First, the operating system was changed from gas to blowback. Another feature of this submachine gun is that it can be altered to accommodate .40 S&W or .45 ACP ammunition in addition to the standard 9x19mm.

The magazine well was also altered to accommodate pistol cartridge magazines. The 9x19mm version uses existing Uzi submachine gun magazines. Like the Tavor rifle, the fire control selector is ambidextrous, as is the position of the cocking handle. A short length MIL-STD-1913 rail is provided above the receiver for mounting optics.

SPECIFICATIONS:

Caliber: 9 x19mm; also .40 S&W or .45 ACP
Operation: blowback, select-fire
Feed: 20-, 25- and 32-round box magazines
Empty weight: 7.3 pounds
Overall length: 20.5 inches
Barrel length: 9.8 inches
Sights: reflex or other

IMI 9x19mm Uzi submachine gun

The IMI Uzi submachine gun is a blowback-operated submachine gun using advanced primer ignition in which the round is fired while the bolt is still moving forward before the round is fully chambered. This produces a reduced impulse to the bolt and as a result the weight of this component can be reduced to approximately half that of a weapon using standard primer ignition.

The IMI Uzi submachine gun is approximately 17 inches long from the muzzle to the rear of the receiver and in its short length it contains a 10.2 inch barrel. This is accomplished by telescoping the bolt over the breech end of the barrel and recessing the breech face some 3.7 inches back from the bolt face. At the moment of firing the bolt completely surrounds the breech end of the barrel except for a cutout section on the right side that allows the fired case to be ejected.

The magazine is inserted into the pistol grip; 20-, 25- and 32-round vertical box magazines are available. This makes magazine changes easy in the dark. When the gun stops firing, the bolt locks to the rear. When the trigger is pulled the bolt is released to move forward, strip a round from the magazine and feed it into the chamber. The cartridge is held in the magazine at an angle with the nose slightly raised so that it does not align with the fixed firing pin on the breech face until the cartridge case enters the chamber.

The selector lever has three positions: Automatic (A), semiautomatic (R) and Safe (S). A grip safety must be fully depressed before the gun can be either cocked or fired. An extra safety is provided via a ratchet in the cocking handle slide to prevent accidental discharge if the hand cocking the gun should slip off the charging handle, after the bolt has come back behind the magazine. After the cocking handle has come this far, it is blocked from forward movement until it has been withdrawn fully to the rear.

Italy

Caliber: 9 x19mm
Operation: blowback, open bolt, select-fire
Feed: 20-, 25- and 32-round box magazines
Empty weight: metal stock, 7.7 pounds; wood stock, 8.4 pounds
Overall length: metal stock, retracted, 18.5 inches; metal stock, extended, or wood, 25.6 inches
Barrel length: 10.2 inches
Sights: Front, post; rear: L type flip aperture, 100 and 200 m
Cyclic rate: 600 rounds per minute

IMI 9x19mm Micro-Uzi submachine gun

The IMI Micro-Uzi submachine gun is essentially the Uzi submachine gun reduced to its least practical size. The Micro Uzi's operation is the same as that of the larger weapons, but the bolt has a tungsten insert which increases the mass and thus keeps the cyclic rate of fire down to a reasonable figure. Firing is from the closed bolt position only. The stock lies alongside the left of the receiver when folded.

The Micro-Uzi has been produced in .45 ACP caliber, using a 16-round magazine.

SPECIFICATIONS:

Caliber: 9x19mm
Operation: blowback, closed bolt, select-fire
Feed: 20-, 25- or 30-round box magazine
Empty weight: 4.4 pounds; with loaded 25-round magazine, 5.5 pounds
Overall length: stock retracted, 11.1 inches; stock extended, 19.1 inches
Barrel length: 5.3 inches
Sights: Front, post; rear, aperture
Cyclic rate: ca 1,700 rounds per minute

Beretta 9x19mm Models 12S and PM12S2 Submachine guns

The Model 12S is generally similar to the earlier Model 12 and was supplanted by the PM12S2. The principle differences from the earlier model are a new manual safety and fire selector and sight modifications. The rear cap catch has also been modified, and new buttplate has been added. A corrosion and wear resistant epoxy resin finish was also introduced. The safety and fire selector have been incorporated into a single lever that can be operated by the right thumb without removing the hand from the grip. The three positions are marked 'S' (safe), 'I' (semiautomatic) and 'R' (automatic). When the safety is applied in the 'S' position, both the trigger mechanism and the grip safety are blocked. On the PM12S2, there is also a cocking handle safety to prevent accidental firings.

The rear cap catch has been moved to the top of the receiver, to facilitate fastening and unfastening and to enable the user to see at a glance whether the catch is secured. The metal stock's buttplate has been modified by adding a catch that gives positive locking in the open and closed position. As with the Model 12, a detachable wooden stock is available.

Accessories include a sling and magazine loaders. Other combat accessories include a high-intensity white light located under the muzzle incorporated into forward grip. A rechargeable battery within the grip powers the lamp, and an infrared filter is available. It is possible to fit a night vision scope or a laser aiming device over the receiver. With a modified barrel, a suppressor can be attached. A tear gas grenade launcher can be fitted to the muzzle, although this requires a special cartridge, recoil spring and receiver end cap.

SPECIFICATIONS:

Caliber: 9x19mm
Operation: blowback, select-fire
Feed: 32-round detachable box magazine with options of 20- or 40-round box magazines
Empty weight: Model 12S: folding metal stock, 7.1 pounds without magazine; wooden stock, 7.9 pounds without magazine; PM12S2: empty, 7.5 pounds
Overall length: metal stock folded, 16.5 inches; metal stock extended, 26 inches; wooden stock, 26 inches
Barrel length: 7.9 inches
Sights: Front, post, adjustable for elevation and windage; rear: flip aperture for 100 and 200 m
Cyclic rate: 550 rounds per minute

IMI Micro-UZI

BERETTA Model 12S

Italian soldiers on the range

Korea, South

Daewoo K7 9x19mm Silenced Submachine gun

The Daewoo K7 silenced submachine is derived from the Daewoo K1A1 5.56x45mm assault rifle, modified to fire 9x19mm ammunition through a suppressor permanently secured over a short perforated barrel. The receiver is basically the same as that for the K1A1 rifle, although the internal mechanism is altered to blowback and the magazine well is modified to accept a 30-round 9mm box magazine. Firing modes are carried over from the assault rifle: safe, semiautomatic, three-round burst and fully automatic. The fully automatic fire rate is 1,150 rounds per minute.

For firing at night or under low light conditions, the front sight incorporates a luminous tritium insert. The K7 can also be provided with a PAQ-91K infra-red target illuminator that can be used in conjunction with night-vision equipment.

SPECIFICATIONS:

Caliber: 9x19mm
Operation: blowback, select-fire, three-round burst
Feed: 30-round detachable box magazine
Empty weight: 7.5 pounds
Overall length: stock retracted, 23.9 inches; stock extended, 31.0 inches
Barrel length: 5.3 inches
Sights: Front, tritium tube; rear: aperture
Cyclic rate: 1,150 rounds per minute

Pakistan

Pakistan Ordnance Factories 9x19mm SMG-PK submachine gun

The Pakistan Ordnance Factories (POF) SMG-PK submachine gun was first displayed in 1999 and apparently is derived from the Heckler and Koch MP5K submachine gun series although POF claims it to be an "in-house" design. The SMG-PK appears to be virtually identical to the MP5K but there are some slight differences, although many components clearly originated with Heckler and Koch.

The SMG-PK is produced in two versions. The SMG-PK1 has a retractable stock and a three-position fire control switch with Safe, Semiautomatic and Automatic. The SMG-PK-2 has no stock as the receiver is provided with an end cap. The four-position fire selector consists of Safe, Semiautomatic, three-round burst, and automatic.

Each SMG-PK is provided with a sling and spare magazines. Optional accessories include a double magazine clip to clamp two magazines together for rapid changing.

SPECIFICATIONS:

Caliber: 9x19mm
Operation: Roller delayed blowback, select-fire
Feed: 15-round detachable box magazine
Empty weight: 4.4 pounds
Overall length: 13.4 inches
Barrel length: 4.5 inches
Sights: Front, post; rear: open rotary adjustable for windage and elevation
Cyclic rate: 900 rounds per minute

Philippine Marines train to deploy from a helicopter.

Peru

MGP-84 9x19mm Submachine gun

The MGP-84 was once designated the MGP-15 and is a compact submachine gun designed for use by special forces and security guards who require compact firepower. It is blowback operated, the operating system being the same as the earlier MGP-79A and MGP-87 submachine guns, neither of which is currently in production. The barrel is not exposed and the magazine housing is incorporated into the pistol grip. The folding stock is hinged at the rear of the receiver and folds to the right so that when folded the shoulder piece can be used as a front grip. The safety and fire selector are incorporated into a single switch, located at the front of the trigger in a position to be operated by the non-firing hand. The bolt is of the telescope type, similar to the Uzi, and the magazines are compatible with Uzi magazines, which can be used.

A suppressor is available and can be fitted by simply unscrewing the barrel-retaining cap and screwing the suppressor onto the receiver in its place.

Servicio Industrial de la Marino-Electronica (SIMA-ELECTRONICA) manufactures the 9mm MGP-84, and its variants.

The MGP-14 "pistol carbine" is based on the MGP-84, except that it is semiautomatic only. External dimensions are identical, but the empty weight of the MGP-14 is 5.4 pounds due to a heavier bolt.

The MGP-14 Micro "assault pistol" is based on the MGP-84 but lacks the folding stock. The MGP-14 Micro has a folding front grip and an additional safety on the forward left side of the weapon. The MGP-14 Micro can use either 20- or 32-round magazines. Weight with a loaded 20-round magazine is 6.3 pounds.

SPECIFICATIONS:
Caliber: 9x19mm
Operation: blowback, select-fire
Feed: 20- or 32-round box magazines
Empty weight: 5.1 pounds; with loaded 32-round magazine, 6.4 pounds
Overall length: stock folded, 11.2 inches; stock extended, 19.8 inches
Barrel length: 6.5 inches
Sights: Front, adjustable blade; rear: two-position notch, 100 m and 200 m
Cyclic rate: 650-750 rounds per minute

Philippines

Floro International 9x19mm Mk 9 submachine gun

The Floro International Mk 9 submachine gun's receiver is of simple tubular construction. The standard model has a 13-inch heavy barrel to withstand sustained fire and improve accuracy; the specifications below apply to this model. A short barrel model with a barrel length of approximately 10 inches also exists. Both models have part of the barrel protected by a perforated steel collar. Ammunition is from 25- or 32-round detachable box magazines, with the cocking handle on the left of the tubular receiver.

Construction is all steel with a black or gray phosphate, non-reflective finish. The pistol grip is molded black matte polymer. The barrel, bolt and trigger guard assemblies can all be quickly removed for maintenance. The standard model has a simple tubular stock that folds and locks into position to the right of the receiver. The Mk 9 used Uzi magazines. A small optical sight mounted over the rear sight is optional.

SPECIFICATIONS:
Caliber: 9x19mm
Operation: blowback, select-fire
Feed: 25- or 32-round detachable box magazines
Empty weight: 8 pounds
Overall length: stock folded, 25 inches; stock extended, 33.9 inches
Barrel length: 13 inches
Sights: Front, hooded post; rear: notch adjustable for windage and elevation

Poland

GLAUBERYT PM-84 and PM-84P Submachine guns

The GLAUBERYT submachine guns are available in two models, the PM-84 chambered for the 9x18mm cartridge and the PM-84P chambered for the 9x19mm cartridge for potential export sales. The maximum effective range for both models is claimed to be 150 meters. The design is very similar to the Uzi, with a telescoped bolt that surrounds the breech end of the barrel. The GLAUBERYT fires from the closed bolt. A rate reducer in the pistol grip controls the cyclic rate of fire at approximately 600 rounds per minute.

The nonreciprocating charging handle is ambidextrous. The safety catch, when engaged, locks the hammer, breech and trigger.

It is possible to fire either version of the GLAUBERYT using only one hand. For accurate fire and when firing fully automatic it is recommended to fire from the shoulder using the stock and the front grip.

Each GLAUBERYT is issued with one 15-round and three 25-round box magazines. A semiautomatic version is also available.

SPECIFICATIONS:
Caliber: PM-84, 9x18mm; PM-84P, 9x19mm
Operation: blowback, select-fire
Feed: 25-round or 15-round detachable box magazine
Empty weight: PM-84, 4.6 pounds; PM 84P, 4.8 pounds; (loaded) PM-84, 5.4 pounds
PM-84P, 5.7 pounds
Overall length: stock folded, 14.8 inches; stock extended, 22.6 inches
Barrel length: 7.3 inches
Sights: Front, blade; rear: 75 and 150 m aperture settings
Cyclic rate: PM-84, 600 rounds per minute ; PM-84P, 640 rounds per minute

GLAUBERYT PM-84

Portugal

INDEP 9x19mm Lusa A2 submachine gun

The INDEP Lusa A2 submachine gun replaced the earlier Lusa A1 and is a blowback-operated automatic weapon with a detachable barrel and retractable stock. The Lusa is very similar to Heckler & Koch MP5 designs, but is apparently not a direct copy. The magazine housing doubles as a front grip and there is an extending steel rod stock which slides into a recess on the receiver. Firing modes include semiautomatic, three-round burst and fully automatic. Rounds are fed vertically from a detachable 30-round steel box magazine. Options include a laser aiming device and a suppressor. The Lusa has reportedly never been sold outside Portugal, although it is the standard submachine gun of the Portuguese military

SPECIFICATIONS:

Caliber: 9x19mm
Operation: blowback, select-fire with three-round burst
Feed: 30-round detachable box magazine
Empty weight: 6.3 pounds
Overall length: stock folded, 18 inches; stock extended, 23 inches
Barrel length: 6.3 inches
Sights: Front, protected post; rear: flip aperture
Cyclic rate: 900 rounds per minute

Russia

OTs-02 Kiparis 9x18mm submachine gun

The OTs-02 Kiparis ('Cypress') submachine gun was designed in 1972 but did not enter service until 1991. It fires the standard 9x18mm 57-N-181S cartridge and can accommodate the more potent 9x18mm 57-N-181SM round. The weapon operates on straight blowback design and is of conventional appearance. Construction is stamped steel with a polymer pistol grip. Stamped steel is also used for the magazines of 10, 20 or 30 rounds capacity. A simple steel folding stock folds over the receiver so that the simple skeleton butt plate extends downwards on either side of the muzzle forming a forward hand grip.

The Kiparis is supplied with a suppressor with a claimed service life of 6,000-rounds, the same as the weapon's barrel. With the suppressor fitted, the Kiparis is known as the OTs-02-1. The OTs-02 Kiparis can also be fitted with a laser aiming device that attaches forward of the magazine housing so that the bottom of the laser aiming device can be used as a forward grip.

SPECIFICATIONS:

Caliber: 9x18mm 57-N-181S; 9x18mm 57-N-181SM
Operation: blowback, select-fire
Feed: 10, 20- or 30-round detachable box magazine
Empty weight: without suppressor or laser target designator, 3.5 pounds
Overall length: stock folded, 17.8 inches; stock extended, 28.7 inches
Barrel length: 6.1 inches
Sights: Front, fixed post; rear: notch graduated for 25 and 75 m
Cyclic rate: 600-800 rounds per minute
Max effective range: 75 m

PP-90 and PP-90M 9mm submachine guns

The PP-90 submachine gun appears to be derived from the American Ares design dating from the 1980s. It is a folding submachine gun intended to be used as a concealed self-defense weapon.

The PP-90M is basically similar to the PP-90 but differs slightly visually, especially in the shoulder stock, as well as some dimensional differences. The PP-90M1 version is chambered in 9x19mm. A second completely different submachine gun also carries the designation PP-90M1 and is covered elsewhere in this volume.

Unconfirmed sources in Russia indicate that the PP-90 proved unsatisfactory and has been withdrawn from service.

When carried folded the PP-90 and PP-90M submachine guns could be mistaken for a rifle magazine or small container, as only a protruding hook at one end gives any indication otherwise. To prepare the weapon for firing, the two halves are simply pulled apart. The weapon opens and the loaded magazine snaps down into place as one half becomes a rudimentary stock. The entire sequence takes only 1.5 to 2 seconds.

The PP-90 is blowback operated. Overall construction is of stamped steel, and the weapon's ergonomics are poor, although since it is apparently a weapon for emergencies, this probably is of little consequence.

OTs-02

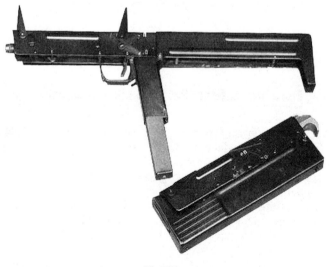

PP-90M

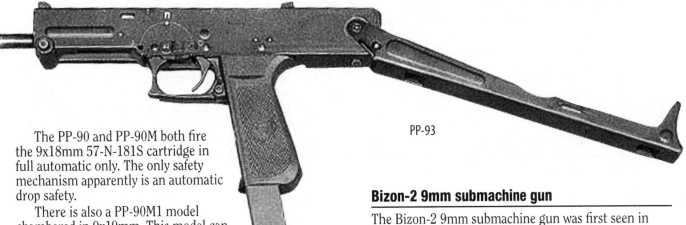

PP-93

The PP-90 and PP-90M both fire the 9x18mm 57-N-181S cartridge in full automatic only. The only safety mechanism apparently is an automatic drop safety.

There is also a PP-90M1 model chambered in 9x19mm. This model can be identified by raised ribs on the back end of the receiver. Suppressors and laser pointers are optional accessories.

SPECIFICATIONS:

Caliber: 9x18mm 57-N-181S (PP-90M1, 9x19mm)
Operation: blowback, automatic only
Feed: 30-round folding box magazine
Empty weight: PP-90, empty, 4 pounds
Overall length: unfolded, 19.3 inches
Dimensions: PP-90, folded, 10.7x3.5x1.3 inches;
PP-90M, folded, 11x3.5x1.3 inches
Sights: Front, folding frame; rear: folding slot
Cyclic rate: 600-700 rounds per minute

PP-93 9x18mm Machine Pistol

The PP-93 is described as a light machine pistol. It can fire the standard 9x18mm or the more powerful 57-N-181SM cartridge. It can also fire a 9x19mm armor piercing cartridge, with the bullet claimed to be capable of piercing a .375 inch (10mm) steel plate at a range of 10 meters. The PP-93 is blowback operated and is constructed from stamped steel. It features a simple folding stock that hinges up and over the receiver when folded. The weapon can accommodate 20- or 30-round box magazines which are inserted through the pistol grip. A suppressor and a laser pointer are available and can be supplied, together with the weapon and a cleaning kit, in a specially fitted carry case. A belt holster is also available.

SPECIFICATIONS:

Caliber: 9x18mm 57-N-181S; 9x18mm 57-N- 181SM
Operation: blowback, select-fire
Feed: 20- or 30-round box magazine
Empty weight: 3.2 pounds
Overall length: stock folded, 12.8 inches; stock extended, 21.5 inches
Sights: Front, fixed post; rear: notch sighted to 100 m
Cyclic rate: 600-800 rounds per minute
Maximum effective range: 100 m

Bizon-2 9mm submachine gun

The Bizon-2 9mm submachine gun was first seen in 1993 and is manufactured by the Kalashnikov JSC factory at Izhevsk. The Bizon-2 makes use of many components from existing Kalashnikov designs but is notable for its 64-round helical-feed magazine located under the forend.

At least eight models have been produced thus far, as follows.

Bizon-2. Chambered for standard 9x18mm and 9x18mm 'Special' 57-N-181SM (high-velocity) cartridges.

Bizon-2-01. Chambered in 9x19mm.

Bizon-2-02. Chambered in 9x17mm.

Bizon-2-03. Chambered in standard 9x18mm, with integral suppressor.

Bizon-2-04. Chambered in standard 9x18mm, semiautomatic only.

Bizon-2-05. Chambered in 9x19mm, semiautomatic only.

Bizon-2-06. Chambered in 9x17mm, semiautomatic only.

Bizon-2-07. Chambered in 7.62x25mm. This version replaces the Bizon's helical-feed magazine with a 35-round box magazine.

The Bizon-2 9mm submachine gun is a compact, blowback-operated select-fire weapon. The action is buffered to provide stability during firing. About 60 percent of the parts used in the Bizon are taken from other Kalashnikov models, primarily the AK-74 series, including the left-folding stock, the fire control mechanism and the receiver cover.

To fit the magazine, two lugs at the forward end protrude over two pins under the muzzle attachment. The feed end of the magazine is then lifted to engage with a

Bizon-2

standard Kalashnikov magazine catch. The magazine can be used as a front grip. The latest type of helical magazine is made of polymer.

The Bizon-2 can fire both the standard 9x18mm or the newer 9x18mm 57-N-181SM high-velocity cartridges. The effective range of the Bizon-2 with the latter ammunition is claimed to be 200 meters, compared to 100 meters for standard 9x18mm ammunition.

All models of the Bizon-2 are issued with a single magazine, a sling, cleaning kit, an oil bottle and a magazine pouch. Various collimator, optical or night vision sights are available. All versions can be fitted with a suppressor.

SPECIFICATIONS:

Model	Bizon-2	Bizon-2-01	Bizon-2-02	Bizon-2-03
Caliber:	9x18mm	9x19mm	9x17mm	9x19mm
Operation:	blowback, select-fire	blowback, select-fire	blowback, select-fire	blowback, select-fire
Feed:	64-round helical magazine	53-round helical magazine	64-round helical magazine	64-round helical magazine
Empty wt:	5.9 pounds	6.6 pounds	5.9 pounds	7.1 pounds
Length, stock folded:	17.8 in	17.8 in	17.8 in	22.4 inches
Length stock extended:	27.2 in	27.2 in	27.2 in	31.1 inches
Cyclic rate:	680 rounds per minute	700 rounds per minute	680 rounds per minute	680 rounds per minute
Max effective range:	100 or 200m	200m	100m	100m
Model	**Bizon-2-04**	**Bizon-2-05**	**Bizon-2-06**	**Bizon-2-07**
Caliber:	9x18mm	9x19mm	9x17mm	7.62 x 25mm
Operation:	blowback semiautomatic	blowback semiautomatic	blowback semiautomatic	blowback select-fire
Feed	64-round helical magazine	53-round helical magazine	64-round helical magazine	35-round box magazine
Empty wt:	5.9 pounds	6.6 pounds	5.9 pounds	6.6 pounds
Length, stock folded:	17.8 in	17.8 in	17.8 in	20.9 in
Length, stock extended:	27.2 in	27.2 in	27.2 in	27.2 in
Cyclic rate:	N/A	N/A	N/A	750 rounds per minute
Max effective range:	100m	200m	100m	200m

KEDR and Klin 9mm machine pistols

During the early 1970s the Soviet Army issued a requirement for a machine pistol to replace the 9x18mm Stechkin automatic pistol. Two competing designs were considered at the time, one by Dragunov and the other by Afanasyev, but the contest was terminated because ammunition performance at distances over 50 meters was limited. During the early 1990s, the Dragunov design was resurrected and modified for mass production as the KEDR (Konstruktsiya Evgeniya Dragunova - designed by Evgeni Dragunov). The KEDR fires the standard 9x18mm cartridge (57- N-181S). Further development at the Izhevsk facility resulted in a number of variants including the KEDR model PP-91-01 with a flash-hiding silencer, a semiautomatic pistol without a folding stock, and the Klin machine pistol firing the more powerful 9x18mm 57-N-181SM high velocity cartridge. The Klin is also available in 9x19mm.

A second version of the KEDR, designated KEDR-B, was developed to meet Russian Internal Ministry requirements. The KEDR-B has an integral suppressor and the weapon is not intended to be fired without the suppressor in place. The KEDR-B barrel has a series of holes that bleed off expanding propellant gases into the suppressor where they are cooled and slowly escape through internal baffles and stainless steel mesh. 20 dB noise level reduction is claimed as compared to the standard KEDR. The KEDR-B is chambered only in standard 9x18mm, as this round is subsonic.

The KEDR and Klin 9mm machine pistols are identical in overall construction and operation, the main difference being that the Klin can fire the 9x18mm 57-N-181SM high velocity cartridge that has a 25 percent higher chamber pressure than the standard round. The Klin can also fire the standard cartridge, although the reverse is not the case.

Both machine pistols are blowback operated. Safeties include a manual lock that engages both the trigger and the bolt. The stamped steel stock folds over the receiver with the rudimentary buttplate acting as a vertical handgrip. Ammunition feed is from 20 or 30-round box magazines inserted through a housing in front of the trigger assembly.

SPECIFICATIONS: Data for KEDR; Klin in parentheses

Caliber: 9x18mm 57-N-181S; 9x18mm 57-N-181SM; (Klin, 9x19mm optional)
Operation: blowback, select-fire
Feed: 20- or 30-round box magazine
Empty weight: 30-round magazine, 3.5 pounds (3.4 pounds) KEDR-B, 4.6 pounds
Overall length: stock folded, 12 inches; stock extended, 20.9 inches (21.2 inches); KEDR-B, 26.4 inches
Barrel length: 4.7 inches
Sights: Front, blade; rear: notch; sighted for 25m; laser target designator optional
Cyclic rate: 1,000 rounds per minute (975-1,060 rounds per minute)
Max effective range: 50 m (>150 m)

KEDR

Klin

Kovrov AeK-919 and AyeK-919 Kashtan 9x18mm Submachine guns

The AeK-919 Kashtan (Chesnut) was designed to meet a Russian Interior Ministry requirement. It is similar to the Uzi, with a bolt that telescopes over the breech end of the barrel to reduce overall length. The AeK-919 is manufactured from steel stampings and polymers. The removable barrel is retained by a threaded cap and has polygonal rifling. The cocking handle is located on the left side of the receiver and is non-reciprocating. The notch rear sight is graduated at 50 or 100 meters. The AeK-919 fires from the open bolt and has a safety mechanism to prevent the weapon from firing if dropped. A suppressor is provided as standard equipment. Optical sights are optional.

The AeK-919 has been used operationally in Chechnya. Based on user feedback, an improved version with enhanced reliability has been developed.

The Kovrov Mechanical Plant is reportedly developing a 9x19mm version of the Kashtan.

OTs-22 9x19mm submachine gun

The OTs-22 submachine gun is a development from the KBP Instrument Design Bureau at Tula and is unusual among Russian submachine guns in that it was designed from the outset to fire 9x19mm ammunition. Designed to be compact and light, the select-fire OTs-22 , like some other designs, is similar in concept to the Uzi, with the magazine inserted through the pistol grip and a bolt that telescopes over the breech end of the barrel to reduce overall length. Twenty- or 30-round magazines are available.

The square cross section receiver and the upwards-folding stock are made of steel stampings. A selection/safety lever is ambidextrous and a grip safety is on the forward side of the pistol grip.

SPECIFICATIONS:

Caliber: 9x19mm
Operation: blowback, select-fire, semi or fully automatic
Feed: 20- or 30-round detachable box magazine
Empty weight: without magazine, 2.6 pounds
Overall length: stock folded, 9.8 inches; stock extended, 18.1
Sights: Front, post; rear: flip type protected notch
Cyclic rate: 800 to 900 rounds per minute
Max effective range: 100m

AeK-919

SPECIFICATIONS:

Caliber: 9x18mm (58-N-181S)
Operation: blowback, select-fire, semi or fully automatic
Feed: 20- or 30-round detachable box magazine
Empty weight: 3.7 pounds
Overall length: stock folded, 12.8 inches; stock extended, 19.1 inches
Barrel length: 6.6 inches
Sights: Front, protected post; rear: flip type protected notch
Cyclic rate: 900 rounds per minute
Max effective range: 100 m

Russia

PP-90M1

PP-90M1 9x19mm submachine gun

The PP-90M1 submachine gun was first shown publicly in 2001. Although another submachine gun from the same manufacturer has an identical designation, these are not the same firearm. See the separate PP-90/PP-90M entry for details of the other submachine gun.

The compact PP-90M1 is marketed as a special forces weapon, fires 9x19mm ammunition and makes extensive use of high-strength polymers, including for the frame. Operation is straight blowback, with a recoil buffer and a relatively heavy bolt for added stability. These features limit the cyclic rate of fire to between 450 and 540 rounds per minute.

There are two types of interchangeable magazines. The standard magazine is a conventional 32-round box magazine. The second is a 64-round helical-type magazine that fits under the barrel and receiver. Changing from one magazine type to the other involves changing only the magazine and the plastic front grip, and takes under a minute. Once the helical magazine is in position, it acts as the forearm.

SPECIFICATIONS:

Caliber: 9x19mm
Operation: blowback; select-fire
Feed: 32-round box magazine or 64-round helical magazine
Empty weight: with box magazine, 4.4 pounds; helical magazine, 4.9 pounds
Overall length: stock extended, 25 inches; stock folded, 16.7 inches
Sights: Front, post; rear: notch
Cyclic rate: 450-540 rounds per minute
Effective range: ~100m

Rex Firearms 9mm Gepard submachine gun

The Gepard (Leopard) was developed as a modular weapon for use by military and police forces. The weapon is derived from the AKS-74U compact assault rifle and has 65 percent parts commonality with the AKS-74U.

The Gepard submachine gun is a modular design capable of firing several 9mm cartridges. The Gepard is claimed to fire 9x17mm (.380 ACP), 9x18mm, 9x19mm, and 9x21mm Russian ammunition by simply changing recoil springs and bolt groups. Firing the recently developed Russian 9x30mm Grom (Thunder) cartridge requires changing chambers, as the standard chamber is limited to 21mm case length. The chamber section of the barrel extension is removable, but it is difficult to imagine why the designers simply did not provide two barrels for

SR-1 / SR-2

Serbia and Montenegro

Gepard

the gun. Barrels are hard chrome lined. The 9x30mm cartridge was developed by the Rex Firearms Company and has a muzzle velocity of approximately 1970 feet per second when fired from this weapon.

Depending on the ammunition, the Gepard functions via blowback, delayed blowback, or gas operation with a rotary locking bolt. Magazines hold either 22 or 40-rounds and reportedly accept any of the rounds for which the Gepard is chambered.

A variety of modular muzzle devices, including muzzle brakes, flash hiders and suppressors are available.

SPECIFICATIONS:

Caliber: 9x17mm (.380 ACP); 9x18mm; 9x19mm; 9x21mm Russian; 9 x 30mm Grom)
Operation: select-fire, blowback; delayed blowback or gas
Locking: none or rotating bolt, depending on method of operation
Feed: 22- or 40-round detachable box magazine
Empty weight: 4.4 pounds
Overall length: stock folded, 16.5 inches; stock extended, 25.2 inches
Barrel length: 9.3 inches
Sights: Front, adjustable post; rear: adjustable notch with 100 and 200m settings
Cyclic rate: 600 to 750 rounds per minute

SR-2 9x21mm Russian Submachine gun

The SR-2 is a product of the Central Scientific-Research Institute of Precise Mechanical Engineering (TSNIITOCHMASH) and was first shown in 1999. It is intended to defeat body armor and light equipment such as communications vans and motor vehicles at ranges up to 100 meters. The layout is the Uzi type with 20- or 30-round box magazines inserted through the pistol grip. A detachable front grip is optional. Other options include optical sights.

Four types of 9x21mm ammunition are available for the SR-2:

SP-10 - armor-piercing
SP-11 - ball
SP-12 - expanding bullet
SP-13 - armor-piercing tracer.

The most common cartridges are the SP-10 and SP-11. The SP-10 is an armor-piercing bullet with a hardened steel insert in the nose to defeat body armor, while the SP-11 has a gliding metal jacket.

SPECIFICATIONS:

Caliber: 9x21mm Russian
Operation: gas operated, select-fire
Locking: rotary bolt
Feed: 20- or 30-round detachable box magazine
Empty weight: 3.4 pounds
Overall length: stock folded, 14.4 inches; stock extended, 23.7 inches
Maximum effective range: 200 meters

Zastava 9x19mm M97 Submachine gun

The Zastava 9mm M97 submachine gun is a copy of the Israeli IMI Mini-Uzi submachine gun and appears to differ from the original only in slight detail. The M97 is available in two forms:

- The standard M97 has an 8-inch barrel.
- The shorter M97K has a 6.5-inch barrel lacks a folding stock

Both models use either a 20- or 32-round box magazine. A laser target indicator and a screw-on sound suppressor are optional on both models.

SPECIFICATIONS: (M97K in parentheses)

Caliber: 9x19mm
Operation: blowback; select-fire
Feed: 20- or 30-round curved box magazine
Empty weight: 7.5 pounds (5.8 pounds)
Overall length: stock folded, 14.4 inches; stock extended, 22.8 inches (11.8 inches, no stock)
Barrel length: 8 inches (6.5 inches)
Sights: Front, post; rear: flip aperture calibrated from 75 and 150 m
Cyclic rate: 950 rounds per minute (1,050 rounds per minute)

Russian

Sweden

Saab Bofors Dynamics 6.5x25mm CBJ MS Personal Defense Weapon

The Saab Bofors CBJ MS Personal-Defense Weapon (PDW) was first shown in 2000. It is an unusual weapon in several respects, not the least that it is claimed to combine the functions of PDW, assault weapon and Light Support Weapon (LSW). It is also capable of being converted to fire two types of ammunition. The CBJ MS fires a new 6.5x25mm CBJ cartridge; but by simply changing the barrel, it can fire 9x19mm ammunition.

The 6.5x25mm CBJ cartridge has the same overall dimensions as the 9x19mm cartridge and generates the same level of firing impulse. The projectile is a tungsten insert held in a plastic sabot, fired at a muzzle velocity of approximately 1,675 feet per second with the claimed ability to defeat current body armor. The cartridge case is aluminum. Each 6.5 x 25mm CBJ cartridge has an overall length of 1.17 inches. The projectile weighs 30 grains. The combat range of the cartridge is claimed to be up to 400 meters, although this claim is not in consonance with the ballistics of such a light bullet.

The Saab Bofors CBJ MS PDW is an extremely compact weapon, only 14.3 inches in length with the telescopic wire stock retracted. With the stock extended, the length is 22.2 inches. In general appearance, the weapon resembles a Mini-Uzi, with a forward grip that can accommodate a spare magazine.

The weapon operates on straight blowback and fires from the open bolt with a fixed firing pin. Closed-breech firing and a floating firing pin are optional. Manual and grip safeties are provided. Fire control is via the trigger, similar to the Steyr AUG. Initial pressure delivers semiautomatic fire, while continued pressure results in automatic fire. The cyclic rate is approximately 575 rounds per minute.

Ammunition is fed from 20- or 30-round box magazines, the length of the 20-round magazine coinciding with that of the pistol grip. A 100-round drum magazine is also available. Ammunition is provided in 30- or 36-round clips, along with a magazine loading device. A spent casing bag attaches to the receiver.

Changing from 6.5 x 25mm CBJ to 9x19mm caliber is accomplished simply by changing the barrel. Barrels are changed by unscrewing the barrel locking nut, removing one barrel, replacing it with another and retightening the lock nut. The 9mm barrel accepts a titanium suppressor.

A length of MIL-STD-1913 rail is attached to the top of the receiver to accommodate optics.

SPECIFICATIONS:
Caliber: 6.5 x 25mm CBJ or 9x19mm
Operation: blowback from open or (optional) closed bolt; select-fire
Feed: detachable box or drum magazine
Magazine capacity: box: 20 or 30 rounds; drum: 100 rounds
Empty weight: 5.8 pounds
Overall length: Stock retracted: 14.3 inches; stock extended: 22.2 inches
Sights: Front: post, adjustable for elevation with tritium insert; rear: 3-position aperture, adjustable for windage
Claimed effective range: 6.5mm CBJ, 400 meters

Taiwan

9x19mm T77 Submachine gun

The T77 submachine gun was developed in Taiwan by the Combined Services Force Arsenal. The design was derived from the Ingram M10 and M11, although with some changes. Development began in 1985 and the T77 was type classified in 1988. The T77 submachine gun is blowback operated. Feed is via a 30-round box magazine inserted into the pistol grip. The cyclic rate is from 1,200 to 1,500 rounds per minute. A two-slot muzzle brake helps reduce muzzle climb. The T77 barrel can be quickly removed for cleaning or change via a release lever. The tubular stock folds to the right of the receiver. A suppressor and a laser pointer are optional.

SPECIFICATIONS:
Caliber: 9 x19mm
Operation: blowback, automatic
Feed: 30-round box magazine
Empty weight: 6.2 pounds
Overall length: stock folded, 14 inches; stock extended, 24.1 in
Barrel length: 8.5 inches
Sights: Front, post; rear: flip
Cyclic rate: 1,200 -1,500 rounds per minute
Max effective range: 150 meters

United States

Colt 9x19mm Submachine gun

The Colt submachine gun is a light and compact weapon that embodies the same straight-line construction and design as the Colt 5.56mm M16A2 rifle. This straight-line construction, coupled with the lower recoil impulse of the 9x19mm cartridge, provides highly accurate fire with reduced muzzle climb.

Like the M16 rifle, the Colt 9mm submachine gun fires from a closed bolt, with the bolt remaining open after the last round has been fired, allowing the user to replace magazines and rapidly reopen fire. The Colt SMG is equipped with a collapsible stock and can be disassembled without tools. The manual of arms is virtually identical to M16 rifles and M4 carbines, thus MINIMIzing training for individuals familiar with the other weapons. The Colt SMG fires all standard 9x19mm ammunition using 32-round box magazines.

COLT SMG

RUGER MP-9

An optional hydraulic buffer reduces the cyclic rate by 100 to 200 rounds per minute, improving accuracy, enhancing control and reducing recovery time.

There are two variants of the Colt SMG:

RO635: Safe, semiautomatic, full automatic
RO639: Safe, semiautomatic, three-round burst

SPECIFICATIONS: Colt Model RO635

Caliber: 9x19mm
Operation: Blowback, select-fire
Locking: Inertia
Feed: 32-round box magazine
Empty weight: without magazine, 5.75 pounds
Overall length: stock retracted, 25.6 inches; stock extended, 28.9 inches
Barrel length: 10.5 inches
Sights: Front, post adjustable for elevation; rear: flip aperture (50 m and 100 m), adjustable for windage.
Cyclic rate: 700 to 1,000 rounds per minute
Max effective range: 100m

Ruger 9x19mm MP-9 submachine gun

The Ruger MP-9 submachine gun was the result of a joint venture between Bill Ruger and Uzi Gal based on an Uzi Gal design with final design work by Jim Sullivan. The MP-9 first entered production in 1994. A few minor changes were incorporated in 1995.

The Ruger MP-9 submachine gun is essentially an Uzi submachine gun modified fire from a closed bolt. The barrel utilizes Bellville spring washers to cushion the impact of the bolt as it goes into battery. A major change from the Uzi is a new telescopic stock design that can be folded downwards when fully collapsed to form a close fit under the receiver and behind the grip. The entire lower receiver is glass fiber reinforced Zytel, a hard-wearing polymer material. The upper receiver is blued steel alloy while the barrel is heat-treated chrome molybdenum steel. The barrel can be easily removed by unscrewing a locking nut.

The 32-round double-stack box magazine is inserted upwards through the pistol grip. A sliding control switch on the left of the grip has three positions: safe (rear), semiautomatic, and full automatic. There is a trigger-actuated disconnector and a firing pin block. Standard accessories include a sling and two 32-round magazines.

SPECIFICATIONS:

Caliber: 9x19mm
Operation: blowback, closed bolt, select-fire
Feed: 32-round box magazine
Empty weight: 6.6 pounds
Overall length: stock folded, 14.8 in; stock extended, 21.9 in
Barrel length: 6.8 in
Sights: Front, protected post, adjustable for elevation; rear: dual aperture, adjustable for windage; optical sights optional
Cyclic rate: 550 to 650 rounds per minute

United States

Assault Rifles

The rifle is the basic weapon of the infantry and other combat units and as such even is used to symbolize infantry in many countries, including the United States. In the early 21st Century, the rifle is in transition.

During the 1950s, what have come to be called "battle rifles" predominated the world's military forces, except the Communist Bloc, whose forces were largely equipped with AK-47 assault rifles, which will be discussed below. These battle rifles were full size military rifles, differing in their bolt action predecessors only in terms of semiautomatic or in some cases select fire function. All weighed about 10 pounds and were about 40 inches or more in overall length. The most widely employed of these rifles and the one that is most typical is the FN Herstal Fusil Automatique Leger, better known simply as the FAL. The FAL was used by nearly 100 countries worldwide and still is in widespread use. Another such rifle was the Heckler & Koch G3, which was employed by over 40 countries. The American M-14 never saw such widespread use being essentially no more than a modified M-1 Garand. Although the M-14 was a select fire rifle, the selector switch was removed, as the M-14 was impossible to control on full auto. The M-14, however, continued in use by the US Navy long after it had been replaced in ground forces service by the M-16 assault rifle. Recently, the M-14 has been resurrected for US Special Forces use as the Mark 14, Mod 0 Enhanced Battle Rifle. This newest version of the M-14 arguably transforms the rifle into what it should have been in the first place. That said, the Mark 14, Mod 0 is only a transitional rifle, adopted as an interim measure until the Special Operations Combat Assault Rifle – Heavy (SCAR-H) is developed in 7.62x51mm. Although the battle

rifle is no longer in general military service in most nations, enhanced versions of it will continue in special operations use for the foreseeable future. The FAL, for example, is still in production and the American firm DSA manufactures many versions of the FAL for special operations use.

The first assault rifles were developed during World War II, by the Germans. The MP-43/Sturmgewehr 44 set the pattern for all such rifles that followed, from the Avtomat Kalashnikova-47 (AK-47) to the M-16 and beyond. These rifles are characterized by being chambered for a cartridge that is intermediate between pistol and full size rifle in terms of overall ballistics, by being capable of fully automatic fire and by being relatively light weight. Although some have come to call any rifle that looks like an assault rifle an "assault weapon," there is in reality no such thing. Any weapon that is used in an assault, whether it is a knife, pistol, rifle or ball bat is an "assault weapon." The Russian AK-47 and its successors, the AKM of 1959, AK-74 of the 1970s and the current AK-100 series assault rifles are the most widely manufactured infantry weapons in history, with some 50+ million of them having been manufactured worldwide. The AK is simple to operate, rugged, rock solid in reliability and sufficiently accurate at typical military combat ranges. It remains in widespread service around the world.

Although the United States adopted the M-14 battle rifle in 1957, it was only a few years before it was replaced by the M-16, designed by Eugene Stoner, Jim Sullivan and Robert Fremont. The M-16 brought the US military its first and thus far, only true assault rifle. The M-16 is second only to the AK in terms of worldwide distribution and although it has its shortcomings, they are nothing that cannot be overcome by simple modifications, such as replacing the direct impingement Ljungmann type system with a piston and operating rod to eliminate the fouling that is blown directly back into the receiver when the rifle is fired. Although the US Army is currently exploring replacements for the M-16, none improve upon it in any meaningful way. The M-16 has been developed into a true modular rifle that can be changed to fire a variety of different cartridges simply by replacing the upper receiver, as with the special operations 6.8x43mm Special Purpose Cartridge (SPC).

The 6.8x43mm SPC was developed as a result of lack of stopping power of the 5.56x45mm M855 cartridge used in the special operations M-4 and M-4A1 carbines. The standard military 5.56mm simply did not reliably disable enemy troops in Afghanistan and Iraq and an immediate resolution was desired. The problem was noted as early as 1993 and was mentioned in Blackhawk Down." The reasons for this problem are beyond the scope of this introduction, but the standard M855 round does not perform well in Special Forces carbines. The problem was partially offset by the introduction of the Black Hills Ammunition manufactured 77-grain Mark 262, Mod 0 and Mod 1 5.56mm rounds, but these are still 5.56mm, so development of the new round proceeded.

The M-4 Carbine itself has been plagued with problems since its introduction. Again, these are beyond the scope of this introduction, but the problems were related to full automatic fire, which causes stresses that do not exist in semiautomatic-only firearms. The inability to correct these problems led Special Operations Command (SOCOM) to set about developing a replacement family of small arms under the aegis of the SCAR Program alluded to above. The SCAR-Light (SCAR-L) contract was recently awarded to FN Herstal and the weapon will probably be manufactured at the company's US facility in South Carolina. The SCAR-L is capable of conversion to several calibers and is covered in detail in this section.

As mentioned, rifles are in transition, at least in the United States. Whether the US adopts the Heckler & Koch XM-8 is still open to question, but military sources

have informally told the author that the XM-8 does not have significantly improved performance over the present family of small arms. Moreover, the wisdom of having one family of small arms for special operations units and an entirely different one for conventional units is highly questionable, particularly since the contract for the special operations weapon has already been awarded. Whatever the outcome, it is probable that the M-16 family will be replaced in the not too distant future, although many of the weapons will remain in service for years to come. The M-16 has the honor of being the longest serving military rifle in United States history.

As to the rest of the world, rifles have changed but little. The Heckler & Koch G-36 has been adopted by several nations, but the M16 still predominates. The XM-8 is no more than a G-36 with different polymer furniture. The 5.56x45mm cartridge is the most widely used rifle caliber cartridge in the world. Even former Communist countries have gone over to it, although Russia retains the similar 5.45x39mm. Many manufacturers now offer AK variants in 5.56x45mm, so that former Warsaw Pact countries can change over to NATO specification weapons by simply rechambering their existing rifles. Even Izhmash, the manufacturer of Kalashnikov rifles, offers AKs in 5.56x45mm.

There have been several bullpup design rifles introduced since the Steyr AUG of the late 1970s, notably the French FAMAS of the early 1990s, Singapore's SAR-21 and Israel Military Industries' Tavor (TAR-21). Although the Steyr has seen some success, bullpups as a class of rifle have not been notably successful, although they offer the advantages of very compact size coupled with a standard length barrel.

For the foreseeable future, the military forces of the world will probably continue with proven designs such as the M-16 and AK families. Both have proven themselves in battle and with the exception of the United States developments, there will very likely not be many truly new designs, as small arms technology is mature. Other than caseless ammunition or truly new materials technologies, small arms development has gone about as far as possible.

That said, there are developments in finishes that hold great promise. The details of this technology is beyond the scope of this introduction, but coatings presently exist that are self-lubricating, turn into a extremely hard ceramic when cured at room temperature, and can be applied in colors. Best of all, fouling cannot adhere to ceramics, so cleaning consists of simply wiping what little fouling there is away with a rag. The ceramic coating can even be applied inside the barrel. Since there is no heat involved in the application and curing process, the gun's metal parts are unaffected. We predict that ceramic finishes will be the next major step in small arms technology.

Albania

Albanian 7.62x39mm AK-Type Assault Rifles

When Albania isolated itself from the western world the only nation with whom regular relations continued was the Peoples' Republic of China. When weapons were required to replace an aging inventory, the Chinese came to Albania's assistance, supplying designs, tools, machines, supervisory personnel and expertise to the extent that some Chinese designs, such as the AKM-type 7.62x39mm Type 56 assault rifle, were direct copies. The Albanians gradually introduced their own modifications, thus creating another set of Kalashnikov variants. Production of these rifles continued until approximately 1997.

The exact designations of these Albanian Kalashnikovs is unknown, so for identification are named here as the Type I, Type II and Type III. Apparently all variants were known colloquially as AK-47s.

The Type I is a direct copy of the Chinese 7.62x39mm Type 56 rifle, complete with folding bayonet, and was the first weapon of this type to be manufactured in Albania. The rear sights are graduated to 800 meters.

The Type II is derived from the Type 56 with the barrel extended forward of the muzzle. A grenade launcher spigot is fitted over the barrel extension with a gas cut-off lever on the right side of the gas port. The rear sight is repositioned to a new central location on a revised dust cover. This dust cover is hinged at the forward end similar to the 5.45mm AKS-74U. There is no provision for a bayonet. The rear sights are calibrated to 1,000 meters.

The Type III is a further modification of the Type 56 but with a longer barrel. A grenade launcher spigot is fitted over the barrel extension like the Type II but there is no provision for gas cutoff when firing grenades. This variant may have been intended to be deployed as a squad support weapon as the front sight block has a rear-facing extension with a partial collar allowing a bipod to be clamped under the muzzle. The rear sights are graduated to 1,000 meters.

SPECIFICATIONS:

Type:	Type I	Type II	Type III
Caliber:	7.62x39mm	7.62x39mm	7.62x39mm
Operation:	gas, select-fire	gas, select-fire	gas, select-fire
Locking:	rotating bolt	rotating bolt	rotating bolt
Feed:	30-round box	30-round box	30-round box
Empty weight:	9.3 pounds	9.1 pounds	9.7 pounds
Overall length:	34.7 inches	40.7 inches	43.2 inches
Barrel length:	16.3 inches	22.2 inches	26.4 inches

Armenia

5.45x39mm K-3 assault rifle

First revealed in October 1996, the K-3 assault rifle is essentially a Kalashnikov action modified into a bullpup configuration. As of October 1996, only about 40 K-3s had been manufactured. The K-3 was designed by the Military Industrial Department of the Armenian Ministry of Defense, the K-3 has been produced in a basic open sight version with the ability to remove the open sights and replace them with a standard PSO-1 4x telescopic sight, also produced in Armenia.

The K-3 can be fired only by right-handed shooters. The muzzle has an attachment that allows the firing of small rifle grenades. Most of the furniture is polymer, as is the 30-round curved box magazine, derived from that of the AK-74 rifle.

Little has been heard of the K-3 since its 1996 debut, and its status remains uncertain.

SPECIFICATIONS:

Caliber: 5.45x39mm
Operation: gas, select-fire
Locking: rotating bolt
Feed: 30-round detachable box magazine
Empty weight: 8.8 pounds
Overall length: 27.6 inches
Barrel length: 16.3 inches
Sights: Front: raised hooded blade; Rear: aperture, PSO-1 optic available
Cyclic rate: 600 rounds/min
Effective range: 500 m

Australia

F88 Austeyr 5.56mm assault rifle

The F88 Austeyr is the Australian-manufactured version of the Steyr AUG 5.56x45mm assault rifle. For particulars, see the following entry.

Austria

Steyr 5.56x45mm AUG rifle

The Armee Universal Gewehr (AUG) assault rifle was developed by Steyr in conjunction with the Austrian Army, with the first production models appearing in 1978.

Austeyr F88

Australian F88 Austeyr

Austrian Alpine Steyr AUG

The AUG was designed to be easily converted to different configurations: a parachutist's short assault rifle with a 350mm barrel, a carbine with a 407mm barrel; and a standard assault rifle with a 508mm barrel. The AUG can also be configured as a squad automatic rifle with a 621mm barrel. The rifle versions all use a 30-round box magazine except the squad automatic variant, which uses a 42-round magazine and has a bipod. All versions have an optical sight integral with the carrying handle, but customers may specify a sight-mounting bracket instead for mounting a variety of optics.

A modified AUG-A2 model was introduced in 1997. The primary difference is that the standard optical sight housing can be retained or replaced by either a short or extended-overall length MIL-STD-1913 rail for optics. Barrel options for the AUG-A2 are 407mm and 508mm.

The AUG is a bullpup design, intended to be a light, handy gun with particular emphasis on use in and from vehicles. The AUG can be altered for use by a left-handed person by changing the bolt and moving a cover from the left ejection opening to the right.

The barrel is cold hammer forged. Both chamber and barrel are chromed to reduce wear and fouling. An external sleeve is a press fit onto the barrel and carries the gas cylinder, gas regulator and the forward handgrip hinge clamp. There is a short cylinder that contains a piston and its associated recoil spring. The gas regulator has two positions. The large position is to be used if the rifle's operation is affected by fouling or dirt. A flash suppressor is screwed to the muzzle, and it is internally threaded to take a blank-firing attachment. The barrel length locks into the receiver by a system of eight lugs arranged around the breech end that engage with a locking sleeve in the receiver. The bolt locks into the rear half of this sleeve.

The receiver is made from an aluminum casting which holds the bearings for the barrel lugs and the guide rods. The carrying handle and the sight are integral with the receiver casting, and the receiver does not carry or guide the bolt and is thus unstressed. The charging handle works in a slot on the left side of the receiver and is operated by the shooter's left hand.

The hammer mechanism is contained in the rear of the stock, covered by the synthetic rubber buttplate. Other than springs and pins, it is entirely made of plastics and is contained in an open-topped plastic box that lies between the magazine and the stock-plate, and the bolt group recoils over the top of it. Since the trigger is some distance away, it transmits its pressure through a sear lever that passes by the side of the magazine. There is no selector lever for different modes of fire; single shots are fired by pulling the trigger a short distance to the first semiautomatic position. Further pressure on the trigger places the sear in the automatic mode.

The mode of operation of the AUG can be changed by replacing the hammer mechanism unit. For police use, a mechanism that permits only semiautomatic fire is available. For military use, the standard mechanism offers the usual options of semiautomatic or full automatic fire. A third mechanism has a selector switch that permits the user to withdraw it and select either full automatic fire or three-round burst fire as the alternative to single shots. The option can be changed only by withdrawing the fire control mechanism to make the choice.

The multiple bolt is contained in a carrier and operated by a cam path in the carrier. The carrier has two guide rods brazed to it, and these rods run in steel bearings in the receiver. All movement is thus isolated from the receiver. The guide rods are hollow and contain the recoil springs. The left-hand rod takes the pressure from the cocking handle, and it can be locked to the handle by a catch so that the firer can push the bolt home, though in normal firing the cocking handle is free of the rod and does not reciprocate. The right-hand rod is the piston which operates the bolt. The left-hand rod can also be used as a cleaning rod if the gas cylinder becomes fouled. The bolt locks by seven lugs into the locking sleeve in the receiver and has an extractor in place of an eighth lug.

The magazine is entirely plastic, other than the spring. The magazine body is translucent, so that the cartridges can be seen. The stock group is almost entirely plastic. The pistol grip has a large forward guard that completely encloses the firing hand.

The AUG is a conventional gas-operated rifle and is unusual only in that the gas cylinders are offset to the right and work on one of the two guide rods.

The 1.5-magnification optical sight has been optimized for battle ranges, and the reticle is a black ring in the field of view. This can be placed quickly and easily around a man-sized target at ranges up to 300 meters, though after that it may take some care to get the target in the center. However, for all normal infantry engagements, it offers an easily taught and rapidly used sight with very good accuracy and performance in poor light.

An alternative reticle with a fine dot in the center of the aiming circle is also available, allowing a more precise aim. This reticle is supplied as standard on police models.

A special receiver group, with a flat mounting platform in place of the optical sight, permits the use of all types of optical sights.

A revised AUG-A2 model was introduced in 1997. The main change is that the standard optical sight housing can be retained or replaced by either a short or extended-length MIL-STD-1913 picatinny rail for various types of optical or night sight. Barrel length Overall length options for the AUG-A2 are 407mm and 508mm.

A 9x19mm submachine gun variant using the AUG receiver is also produced; see the entry under Austria.

The AUG has been adopted by the Austrian Army as the StG 77. and by the armed forces of Australia, Ireland, Malaysia, New Zealand, Oman, Saudi Arabia, Taiwan and other countries.

SPECIFICATIONS:
Cartridge: 5.56x45mm
Operation: gas, select-fire
Locking: rotating bolt
Feed: 30 or 42-round detachable box magazine
Sights: Optical sight set in carrying handle, x1.5 power
Dimensions:

	Short assault rilfe	Carbine	Standard assault rifle	Heavy-Barrel
Overall length:	24.6 ins.	28.1 ins.	31.7 ins.	36.0 ins.
Barrel length:	13.8 ins.	16.0 ins.	20 ins.	24.4 ins.
Empty weight:		7.3 pds.	7.9 pds.	11.0 pds.

Belgium

FN HERSTAL 5.56x45mm F2000 Modular Assault Weapon System

The FN HERSTAL (FNH) 5.56mm F2000 Modular Assault Weapon System was announced in March 2001, following a development period dating back to 1995. Because of potential for a multitude of military roles and missions, ranging from peacekeeping to all-out warfare, FNH decided to adopt a modular approach to what became the F2000, the intention being that not only could the base rifle be configured to meet a specific mission requirement, it also would be adaptable to incorporate whatever technical small arms innovations might arise for the foreseeable future.

The FNH F2000 Modular Assault Weapon System is based around a compact 5.56x45mm bullpup rifle with polymer furniture and smooth lines. The F2000 action uses the well-established rotary lock system operated via a gas port and piston rod. This system combines strength and reliability and MINIMIzes gases or fouling

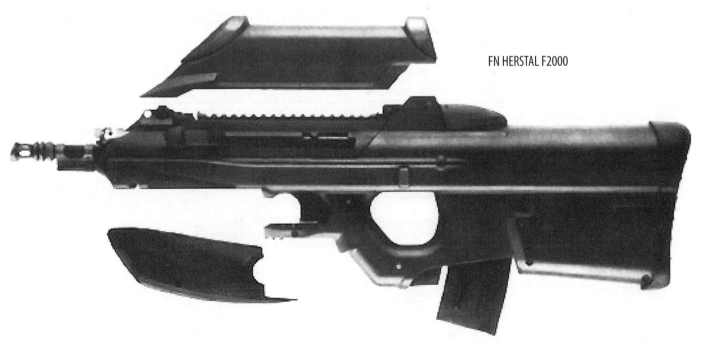

FN HERSTAL F2000

entering the receiver area. There are no external apertures for the possible ingress of dirt and debris. The cocking slot is sealed and ejection is forward through a small sealed circular ejection port. Standard M16 type NATO specification 30-round magazines are used.

A 1.6-magnification optical sight is mounted on a MIL-STD-1913 rail in a molded housing over the receiver. The housing incorporates molded notch and post backup sights. The cocking handle is on the left of the receiver and can be operated by either hand.

Several design features from the 5.7x28mm P90™ submachine gun are carried over to the F2000, including the ambidextrous selector switch under the trigger. The ambidextrous feature is also carried over to the method of ejection for on the F2000; spent cases are ejected forward through a port just behind and to the right of the muzzle. The bolt head has an unusual feature to facilitate this. To be ejected forward, the spent cases must be extracted and moved into an ejection tube above the barrel. This is accomplished using a rocker assembly over the bolt head. As the case is extracted it is held while the rocker assembly tilts to lift it above and clear of the feed path as the next round is taken from the magazine. As the fresh round is chambered, the spent case enters the ejection tube. This results in the first few rounds apparently failing to eject. Only when the ejection tube contains more than three or four cases is the first of them ejected forwards from the rifle.

Should the situation require it, the F2000 forward hand grip molding can be easily removed and replaced by a 40x46mm grenade launcher, designed and manufactured by FNH. The FNH launcher maintains the normal point of balance around the trigger area when a loaded magazine is in position. The grenade launcher trigger is positioned below the rifle's trigger guard for tactile location and operation. The grenade launcher barrel is 230mm.

Although the F2000 can be provided with standard 40mm open sights, studies demonstrated that this sighting technique usually lowers the effectiveness of the grenadier by introducing incorrect range estimations. FNH therefore initiated the use of a simple, soldier-proof Fire Control System (FCS) for the F2000.

The F2000 FCS replaces the existing optical sight and housing on the MIL-STD-1913 rail. The FCS can still be used to aim the rifle component, but its primary function is to accurately determine and indicate the range of a grenade target. Placing the point of aim on a target and depressing a button below the trigger actuates a low power laser rangefinder. The range, accurate to plus or minus one meter, is then shown in the sight display along with a red light. Tilting the rifle to the correct elevation results in the light changing to green once the correct angle is achieved.

If the user wishes to fire the grenade from the hip, three further red/green lights are located in a well on top of the FCS housing. Also on top of the housing are add/subtract range correction buttons to account for head or tail winds that could affect point of impact. The F2000 FCS contains the software to deal with up to six types of 40x46mm grenade and the system can be reprogrammed to take advantage of future ammunition improvements, including any change to 20mm, 30mm or some other grenade caliber.

The FCS is powered by a battery pack housed in the stock. This pack is intended to power not just the FCS but any other combat accessories or systems that could be introduced. One future feature of the F2000 is an optional programmable electronic cyclic rate controller, still under development . Since it has been demonstrated that single shot or slow rates of fire greatly improve hit probability at longer ranges, the optimum maximum rate being determined in testing is from 300 to 400 rounds per minute; controlled bursts can also be preset. However, it is intended that the full cyclic rate of 850-rounds per minute in automatic fire will be retained so the user has the assurance that high rates of fire can be delivered when necessary.

Other options under development for the F2000 include a three-round grenade launcher, a shotgun attachment and a less-lethal attachment such as the FN 303.

There is no "definitive" version of the F2000 as it was designed to be readily adapted to accommodate any changes, upgrades and innovations that future tactical situations and technical innovations might require. The F2000 is ready for production

SPECIFICATIONS:

Caliber: 5.56x45mm NATO (SS109)
Operation: gas, select-fire
Locking: rotating bolt
Feed: 30-round detachable box magazine
Empty weight: 7.95 pounds; grenade launcher, 2.2 pounds
Overall length: 28.6 inches
Barrel length: 15.75 inches
Sights: Optical, 1.6x.
Cyclic rate: 850-rounds per minute (see also text)

FN Herstal Fusil Automatique Leger (FAL) 7.62x51mm rifle

The FN Herstal FAL 7.62mm rifle has been adopted by more than 90 countries all over the world. It is, or has been, manufactured under license in several countries, and some of these have incorporated their own minor modifications to suit their own particular needs. In some instances, these modifications have resulted in deviations from the original specification to the extent that some licensed weapons are not interchangeable with others. The

FN Herstal FN FAL

different types are known as "inch-pattern" or "metric-pattern" FALs. The inch-pattern were made in Britain and the nations of the British Commonwealth, while the metric pattern rifles were manufactured almost everywhere else.

The FAL has been widely manufactured over the years and remains in production in the United States in several configurations, the primary manufacturer being DSA, Inc., which produces FALs on original FNH machinery and tooling. FALs are available from DSA in a large number of configurations and the company has developed a number of improvements to the FAL to modernize the rifle and make it much more versatile.

The FAL has served with, among others, the military forces of Argentina, Australia, Austria, Barbados, Belgium, Brazil, Burundi, Canada, Chile, Cuba, Dominican Republic, Ecuador, Gambia, Germany, Ghana, Guyana, India, Indonesia, Ireland, Israel, Kuwait, Liberia, Libya, Luxembourg, Malawi, Malaysia, Mexico, Morocco, Mozambique, New Zealand, Nigeria, Norway, Oman, Paraguay, Peru, Portugal, Sierra Leone, Singapore, South Africa, United Arab Emirates and Venezuela and may still be encountered throughout the world.

SPECIFICATIONS: (Standard FAL):

Caliber: 7.62x51mm NATO (.308 Winchester)
Operation: gas, select-fire or semiautomatic only
Locking: dropping bolt
Feed: 20-round steel detachable box magazine
Empty weight: 9.5 pounds
Overall length: 41.5 inches
Barrel length: 21 inches
Sights: Front, cylindrical post; rear: sliding aperture
Cyclic rate: 600-700 rounds/min
Max effective range: 600 m

FN Herstal FNC 5.56x45mm Assault Rifle

The FNH FNC is a 5.56x45mm assault rifle. Construction is from steel, aluminum alloy and, for non-stressed parts, plastics.

There are two versions of the rifle. The first, known as the standard, has a standard length barrel, along with a folding tubular light-alloy stock encased in a plastic coating and braced by a plastic strut. The second model, the Para, is similar but has a shorter barrel. Optional on the standard is a fixed polyamide stock. A special bracket to accept the US M7 bayonet is provided on the standard barrel.

The layout of both models follows the general pattern of FNH rifles, and the receiver opens on a front pivot pin that allows the working components to be removed in much the same way as the Fusil Automatique Leger (FAL).

The FNC is license produced in Indonesia and in Sweden, although in a much modified form.

The FNC is gas-operated, using a conventional piston and cylinder mounted above the barrel. A rotating bolt locks the breech with a two-lug head locking into the barrel extension. The bolt and carrier are among the very few items that require precision machining. The gas regulator acts directly on the gas passage at the port opening, and the vent is opened or shut by the gas cylinder. The open hole is the standard setting and is used for all normal firing. The closed hole allows full gas to flow and is meant for use only in adverse conditions when the rifle is fouled or extremely dirty.

The receiver is made from pressed steel with separate inserts for bolt carrier. The trigger frame is of light alloy. The top and bottom of the receiver are held together at the front by a pin, and are locked at the rear by a pin that pushes in from the right side just above the pistol grip. When this pin is pushed out, the lower receiver can be pivoted away, the working parts are exposed and can then be removed. No tools are needed, and in the field no further stripping is necessary.

The movement of the cocking handle opens the cover by a simple cam action, but it closes as soon as the handle reaches the forward position.

The sights are conventional with an adjustable post for the front sight and an aperture for the rear sight, which is adjustable for windage and elevation. For grenade firing, a gas-tap is folded up beside the front sight, and this cuts off the flow of gas to the cylinder, thereby allowing the maximum pressure behind the grenade. The skeleton tubular stock folds to the right, below the cocking handle. This reduces the overall length of the standard version to 756mm and the overall length of the Para version to 680mm. There is also a fixed-stock version of the standard model.

The magazine is interchangeable with the M16 series rifle, and both types of magazines can be used for the FNC, the MINIMI light machine gun and the M16.

There are two rifling twist rates; one for the NATO standard FN Herstal SS109/M855 cartridge with a twist of 1:7 inches. The second twist rate, available on special order, is the same as the M16A1 1:12 inches for the M193 or FNH SS92 cartridge.

The FNC was adopted by Belgium, Indonesia, Latvia, Nigeria, Sweden and others.

SPECIFICATIONS:

Caliber: 5.56x45mm (M193 or SS109)
Operation: gas, select-fire with three-round burst controller
Locking: rotating bolt
Feed: 30-round detachable box magazine
Empty weight: 8.3 pounds
Overall length: Stock extended 39.25 inches, stock folded 30.15 inches
Barrel length: 7.7 inches
Sights: Front, cylindrical post; rear: flip aperture 250 and 400 m
Cyclic rate: 650-750 rounds/min
Max effective range: 450 m; with optical sight, 600 m

FN HERSTAL FNC

Brazil

IMBEL 5.56x45mm MD2 and MD3 rifles

Using the 7.62x51mm FAL (Brazilian LAR) as a starting point, IMBEL developed two 5.56x45mm assault rifles for use by the Brazilian Army and for export. Prototypes, known as the MD1 first appeared in 1983, with proprietary box magazines while later models have M16 type magazines.

The gas operated MD2 rifle has a folding stock, is select-fire and fires either M193 or SS109 ammunition. The MD3 is similar, but uses a fixed polymer stock. Both rifles are normally supplied in select-fire form but if required, can be supplied in semiautomatic-only operation, indicated by the suffix A1. In this form the MD2A1 has a folding stock while the MD3A1 has a fixed stock.

The rifles have been designed and developed in conformity with various international and NATO standards and have the advantage of a high proportion of parts interchangeability with the 7.62mm Light Automatic Rifle (LAR).

Optical sights are optional and a light bipod is available.

SPECIFICATIONS:
Caliber: 5.56x45mm M193 or SS109
Operation: gas, select-fire
Locking: rotating bolt
Feed: 20- or 30-round M16 type magazine
Empty weight: MD2, 9.6 pounds; MD3, 10.0 pounds
Overall length: MD3 and MD2 with stock extended, 39.76 inches; MD2 with stock folded,
30.07 inches.
Barrel length: 7.83 inches
Sights: Front, post; rear: flip aperture 150 m and 250 m (Paratroop version) or 200 m and 600 m (Standard version); adjustable for windage
Cyclic rate: 700-750 rounds/min

IMBEL Model L and LC 5.56mm rifles

Using its MD2 and MD3 rifles as a basis, IMBEL is developing an updated 5.56x45mm rifle in both standard (Model L) and carbine (Model LC) configurations. The Model L and LC are under development to meet requirements established by the Brazilian Army and are intended for use in jungle and mountain terrain as well as for issue to police forces. The Model L is appreciably lighter than previous models although many dimensions are the same.

The Model L continues to employ a gas-operated multilug rotating bolt and carries over the M16 type magazine interface of the MD2 and MD3. A folding stock is standard on both the Model L and Model LC. The Model L can accommodate a 40mm grenade launcher.

IMBEL is concentrating on the Model LC (Leve Curto - Light Short), also known as the Intermediate model. The translucent magazines have an M16 interface and hold 30-rounds.

SPECIFICATIONS:
Caliber: 5.56x45mm M193 or SS109
Operation: gas, select-fire
Locking: multi-lug rotating bolt
Feed: 20- or 30-round M16 type magazine
Empty weight: Model L, 8.2 pounds; Model LC, 6.4 pounds
Overall length: Model L, stock extended, 39.8 inches, stock folded, 29.5 inches; Model LC, stock extended, 31.9 inches, stock folded, 21.7 inches
Barrel length: Model L, 17.8 inches; Model LC, 10 inches
Cyclic rate: Model LC, 700 to 750 rounds/min
Max effective range: Model L, 600m; Model LC, 400m

IMBEL 7.62x51mm semiautomatic rifle SAR

IMBEL produces the standard FN FAL rifle in semiautomatic-only, standard and paratroop configuration, for supply to the armed forces of Brazil and other countries. The dimensions and data are the same as for the Belgian original. IMBEL FAL components have been widely exported throughout the world, especially to North America, where they have been used in conjunction with surplus "parts kits" to assemble semiautomatic-only metric-pattern FAL rifles.

Bulgaria

Arsenal 5.56x45mm AK-74U short assault rifle

The Arsenal 5.56x45mm AK-74U short assault rifle is a variant of the Kalashnikov 5.45x39mm AKS-74U. It is frequently referred to as a submachine gun because of its compact size, although it is actually a compact carbine. The main change from the original is the change of caliber to 5.56x45mm NATO to attract possible export sales from outside the former Warsaw Pact bloc.

IMBEL MD2

ARSENAL AK74U

Arsenal also supplies a standard 5.45x39.5mm version of its AK-74U for issue to the Bulgarian armed forces. This variant is also offered for export sale.

The Arsenal 5.56mm AK-74U short assault rifle is virtually identical to the standard AKS-74U, other than the changes made necessary to accommodate the 5.56x45mm cartridge. The magazine holds 30-rounds, and the maximum sighting range is 500 m. It is claimed that skilled shooters can engage targets using single shots at ranges up to 350 m. When firing in the burst mode, the maximum effective aiming range against multiple targets is 250 m.

Each 5.56mm AK-74U is issued with four magazines, a carrying pouch, a sling, a cleaning rod, an oiler and various other accessories.

SPECIFICATIONS:

Caliber: 5.56x45mm
Operation: gas, select-fire
Feed: 30-round box magazine
Empty weight: 5.6 pounds
Overall length: Stock folded: 19.3 inches; stock extended: 28.7 inches
Barrel length: 8.1 inches
Cyclic rate: 700-750 rounds/min

Arsenal 7.62x39mm AK-47M1 assault rifles

Despite being out of production elsewhere, Bulgarian former state factories, now transformed into Arsenal Joint-Stock Company (JSC), continue to manufacture the 7.62x39mm AK-47 assault rifle and offer it for export sale. For some reason, the Bulgarian weapons-procurement authorities chose to skip the AKM generation and proceeded directly from AK-47 to 5.45x39mm AK-74 series while retaining the capability to continue manufacturing AK-47s.

Two standard-length AK-47M1 models are offered by Arsenal, plus a .22 LR training rifle, all of high quality and including some features also seen on the AKM series.

The Arsenal AK-47M1s are identical in operation to the original Soviet/Russian AK-47.

The AK-47M1s make considerable use of polymer furniture but are otherwise similar to other AK-47s. The basic AK-47M1 is virtually identical to late-production Soviet/Russian models, as is the AKS-47M1 with a folding stock.

The AK-47M1 has black all-plastic furniture and can be fitted with a 40mm GP-25 grenade launcher under the forend. It can also be fitted with a night sight. Magazines may be polymer or metal. Each rifle is shipped with a bayonet, four magazines in a pouch, a sling, spares, an oiler and other accessories.

SPECIFICATIONS: AK-47M1

Caliber: 7.62x39mm
Operation: gas, select-fire
Locking: rotating bolt
Feed: 30-round detachable box magazine
Empty weight: 7.3 pounds
Overall length: 34.8 inches
Barrel length: 16.3 inches
Sights: Front: post, adjustable; rear: U-notch tangent, adjustable to 800m with battle sight for 200m
Cyclic rate: 600 rounds/min

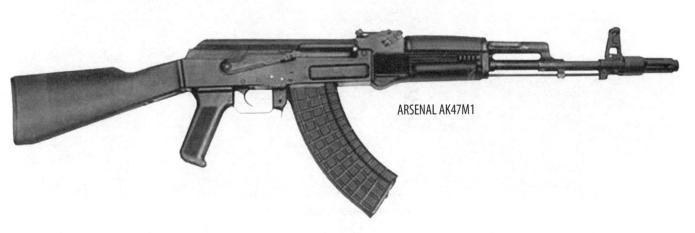

ARSENAL AK47M1

Arsenal AK-74 assault rifles

Arsenal AK-74 assault rifles are manufactured in three basic models, chambered either in 5.45x39mm or in 5.56x45mm ammunition, both versions intended for export sale.

The Arsenal AK-74s use plastic furniture and are generally built to late- production AK-74 standards. The basic Arsenal AK-74, as with the other Bulgarian AK-74 models, can be fitted with a 40mm GP-25 grenade launcher under the forend. The AKS-74 has a side-folding stock. The AKN-74 is an AK-74 fitted with a NSPU night sight. All three models are shipped with a bayonet, four magazines in a pouch, a sling, spares, an oiler and other accessories.

It has been reported that the United States has purchased a large number of these rifles in 5.56x45mm to replace 7.62x39mm AK-type rifles in Iraqi military and police service.

SPECIFICATIONS:

Caliber: 5.45x39mm or 5.56x45mm NATO
Operation: gas, select-fire
Locking: rotating bolt
Feed: 30-round detachable box magazine
Empty weight (AKS-74): 7 pounds
Overall length: AK-74: 19.3 inches; AKS-74: stock folded: 27.6 inches; stock extended: 37.1 inches
Barrel length: 16.3 inches
Sights: Front: post, adjustable; rear: U-notch
Cyclic rate: 5.45mm: 600 rounds/min; 5.56mm: 650 rounds/min

Bulgarian Kalashnikovs

The Bulgarian Defense marketing agency Kintex has offered so many models of Kalashnikov assault rifles that a summary follows so that the reader can get an appreciation for the variety of models offered on the international arms market. All rifles are manufactured by the Arsenal Joint Stock Company (JSC).

Over time the marketing designations of some of the current production models have been changed. Where possible, the revised designations are provided, but the following list should not be considered definitive.

AK-74

Chambered in 5.45x39mm, this AK-74 is produced to the latest standards with black plastic furniture. It may be fitted with a GP-25 40mm grenade launcher and a night sight.

AKS-74

The same as the AK-74, except that this model has a skeleton side-folding stock.

AKS-74U

This is the short carbine version of the AKS-74.

AK-N

Chambered in 5.56x45mm, this AK-74 variant can be supplied fitted with a GP-25 40mm grenade launcher and a night sight.

AKS-N

This is the 5.56x45mm equivalent of the AKS-74 with a folding stock.

AKS-NU

This 5.56x45mm short carbine is the equivalent of the AKS-74U.

Bulgarian troops in training.

ARSENAL AK74 AR-SF

AKS 74U

AKS-NUF

This 5.56x45mm short carbine is almost identical to the AKS-NU but has a slightly longer barrel.

AK-47M1

An updated version of the AK-47 complete with black plastic furniture and chambered in 7.62x39mm. May be fitted with a GP-25 40mm grenade launcher and a night sight. This model is also designated AR -M1.

AK-47M1A1

This is an AK-47M1 chambered for 5.56x45mm NATO ammunition. This model is also known as the 5.56mm AR-M1.

AKS-47M1

Produced to the same standard as the AK-47M1, this model has a under folding steel stock.

AKS-47M1A1

This is the AKS-47M1 chambered in 5.56x45mm.

AKS-47S

The 7.62mm short assault rifle version of the AK-47, this has a side-folding or an under-folding stock. Late production models have a revised one-piece muzzle attachment.

AKS-47UF

This 7.62x39mm short assault rifle is almost identical to the AKS-47S. It has an under folding stock. This rifle is also designated 7.62mm AR-SF. It is available equipped with a laser pointer under the muzzle brake.

AR-SF

Although it has the same designation as the 7.62mm AR-SF and is visually identical to the AKS-47UF/7.62mm AR-SF, this rifle is chambered in 5.56x45mm. Like the other rifle, it is available with a laser pointer under the muzzle device.

AKS-93SM6

This is a late-production 7.62x39mm AK-47 variant with under folding stock and a modified, locally developed, muzzle device. There is no provision for fitting a grenade launcher.

RKKS

A 7.62mm heavy-barrel version of the AK-47 with a 590mm barrel and a bipod near the muzzle. This variant can use a standard 30-round magazine, a 40-round box magazine or a 75-round drum.

AKT-47

This is a training version of the AK-47 chambered in .22 LR.

Canada

Diemaco 5.56x45mm C7 Assault Rifle

The Canadian forces adopted a new generation of 5.56x45mm caliber weapons for all services in 1984. The rifles, designated C7, were based on an M16A2 model license-produced by Diemaco; Colt Model Number 715.

The Netherlands armed forces adopted the C7 family of weapons in 1994. The order included 50,680 C7 rifles, some being the C7A1 with 3.4 optical sights and 1,400 C8 carbines, for the gendarmerie.

The Danish armed forces also adopted the C7A1 along with a number of C8 carbines. Several European special forces have also adopted the C7, C7A1 and C8.

The Diemaco 5.56x45m mm C7 rifles are true select-fire; there is no three-round burst feature. The C7 is generally the same as the M16A2 except for the full automatic capability. The barrel is cold hammer forged with chrome lining rifled to accept both SS109 (M855) and M193-type ammunition.

The C7 A1 is identical to the C7 except that it has a MIL-STD-1913 rail on top of the receiver and a removable carrying handle. The MIL-STD-1913 rail accommodates a variety of optics.

SPECIFICATIONS:

Caliber: 5.56x45mm
Operation: direct gas impingement, select-fire
Locking: rotating bolt
Feed: 30-round detachable box magazine
Empty weight: 7.4 pounds
Overall length: 40.16 inches
Barrel length: 20 inches
Sights: Front: post , adjustable for elevation; rear: 2-position aperture, adjustable for windage and elevation
Cyclic rate: 800 rounds/min

Diemaco C7A1 5.56x45mm Assault Rifle

The Diemaco C7A1 5.56mm assault rifle is an improved version of the basic

C7 rifle, incorporating a low-mounted ELCAN optical sight mounted on the MIL-STD-1913 rail on the upper receiver. The C7A1 has a removable carrying handle which is usually removed and replaced by the aforementioned ELCAN optical sight. A fully capable back up iron sight fits into the stock trap of the C7A1 for use should the optic not be fitted or fail.

SPECIFICATIONS:

are the same as the basic C7, except as noted above.

Diemaco C8 5.56x45mm Carbine

The Diemaco C8 carbine is a compact version of the Canadian forces standard C7 rifle. The C8 features a collapsible stock and a shortened barrel, while retaining most other components in common with the C7 rifle. The carbine is issued to armored vehicle crews, special forces and other users requiring a more compact personal weapon than the C7. This model is in service with the Netherlands special forces and with the Danish armed forces, where it is known as the C8A1 or C8A2. C8 carbines in service with British special forces are reportedly fitted with a Heckler & Koch AG36 40x46mm underbarrel grenade launcher.

Variants:

C8A1: C8 with MIL-STD-1913 flat top upper receiver.
C8A2: C8A1 with heavy barrel for sustained fire and short MIL-STD-1913 rails at the front of the handguard.

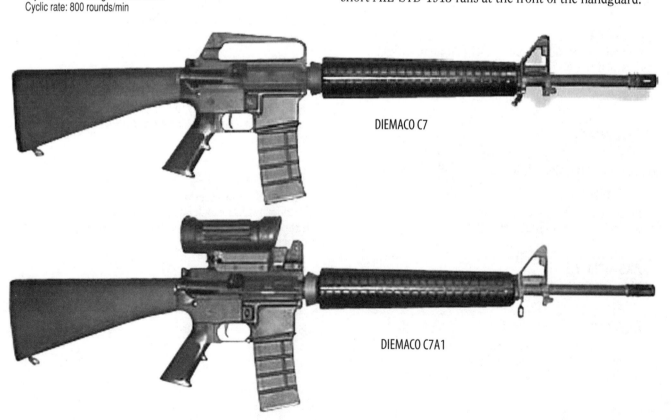

DIEMACO C7

DIEMACO C7A1

DIEMACO C8

FAMAE SG540-1

Chile

Three-round burst is also available. Weight: 5.9 pounds. 14.5-inch barrel.

C8CQB (Close Quarters Battle): C8A2 with 10-inch barrel. Weight: 5.8 pounds.

C8SFW (Special Forces Weapon): C8A2 with modifications similar to the US SOPMOD that include Knight Armament Rail Adapter Handguard, Otis Technologies pistol grip cleaning kit, Buffer Technologies "Magazine-Cinch" dual magazine clamp and Ambi-Catch ambidextrous magazine release. Weight: 7.5 pounds. 16-inch barrel.

C8CT (Custom Tactical): This is a semiautomatic only version of the C8 designed for target interdiction and counter sniper work to a range of 600 meters. It incorporates a Harris bipod, free floated, fluted heavy bull barrel, titanium firing pin for reduced lock time, adjustable target pistol grip and buttplate, Ambi-Catch ambidextrous magazine release and a variety of day- and night-vision optics. Weight: 5.9 pounds. 16-inch barrel.

SPECIFICATIONS: (C8/C8A1)
Caliber: 5.56x45mm
Operation: direct gas impingement, select-fire
Locking: rotating bolt
Feed: 30-round detachable box magazine
Empty weight: 5.9 pounds
Overall length: stock collapsed, 29.2 inches; stock extended, 33.07 inches
Barrel length: 14.5 inches
Sights: Front, adjustable post; rear: aperture adjustable for windage and elevation.
Cyclic rate: ~ 900 rounds/min

FAMAE 5.56mm SG540-1 assault rifle FAMAE 7.62mm SG542-1 assault rifles

These rifles are variants of the SIG SG540 and SG542, fully described under Switzerland. The Chilean versions are built by FAMAE in accordance with a license from SIG and form part of a 'weapons family', with a high percentage of common components.

Both rifles are manufactured with weight-saving design concepts, including a heavy cold hammer-forged barrel that forms the chamber and bore in one operation.

Other features include a three-round burst capability; adjustable gas regulator; two-stage trigger; a bipod attached to the forend; adjustable sights for both windage and elevation; and a hard-chromed chamber in the SG542-1 version. Both rifles are produced with fixed or folding stocks.

SPECIFICATIONS:
Model:	540-1	542-1
Cartridge	5.56x45mm	7.62x51mm
Operation gas, select-fire		
Locking rotating bolt		
Feed: 20- or 30-round box magazines		
Empty weight:		
fixed stock	7.8 pounds	8.4 pounds
folding stock	7.9 pounds	8.4 pounds
Overall length:		
fixed stock	37.4 inches	40.1 inches
stock folded	28.4 inches	29.7 inches
Barrel length:	18.1 inches	18.3 inches
Length:	16.2 inches	16.2 inches
Sights: rear aperture, front blade		
Cyclic rate: 650-800 rounds/min		

China

Type 81

NORINCO 5.56x45mm Type CQ Assault Rifle

The NORINCO Type CQ rifle is a virtual copy of M16A1, from which it differs only in minor details. It is rifled for the Chinese Type CJ 5.56x45mm rifle cartridge, the equivalent of the M193. The construction of the rifle differs only slightly from that of the M16A1, in that the stock and pistol grip group are removed entirely for field stripping, rather than hinged at the front of the receiver.

In March 2001, the Iranian Defense Industries Organization (DIO) announced a rifle that appears identical to the CQ, called the S-5.56 Rifle. See entry under Iran.

SPECIFICATIONS:
Caliber: 5.56x45mm Type CJ (M193)
Operation: direct impingement gas, select-fire
Locking: rotating bolt
Feed: 20-round box magazine
Empty weight: 7.1 pounds
Overall length: 38.9 inches
Barrel length: 20 inches
Maximum effective range: 460 m

Type 81 7.62x39mm Assault Rifle

The Type 81 is the second-generation assault rifle to enter service with the PLA. It replaced the Type 56 (Chinese copy of the AK-47) to serve as the standard individual assault weapon for PLA infantry and other services. Initially deployed in the 1980s in the Sino-Vietnam border conflicts, the Type 81 rifle is known in China for its reliability and accuracy. The Type 81 assault rifle and Type 81 squad machine gun is likely to remain in service with the PLA until replaced by the recently introduced Type 95.

The PLA began studies on a new generation 7.62x39mm squad weapon family in the 1970s to develop a family of small arms to replace the Type 56 semiautomatic

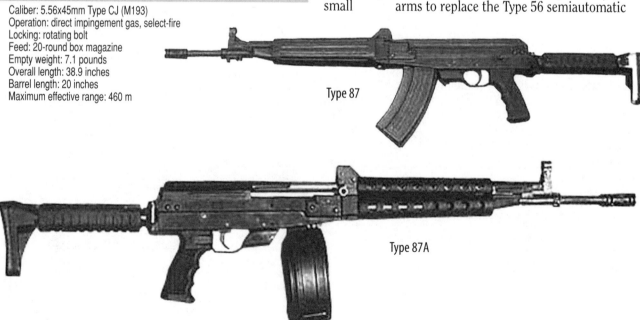

Type 87

Type 87A

Chinese troops train to reload the Type 81 rifle

rifle (SKS), the Type 56 (AK-47) rifle, and the Type 56-I squad machine gun. The new weapon family was expected to combine features of the semiautomatic rifle (accuracy), the automatic rifle (firepower), use same ammunition, and have many parts in common. This led to the introduction of the Type 81 squad weapon family in 1981.

The Type 81 is the PLA's first true small arms family, which includes the 7.62mm Type 81 and Type 81-1 assault rifles, and the Type 81 Squad Automatic Weapon. By the end of the 1980s, the Type 81 family had replaced the Type 56 semiautomatic rifle, Type 56 automatic rifle, and the Type 56-I squad machine gun.

The PLA is currently replacing the Type 81 with the 5.8x42mm Type 95 squad weapon family, but it will be at least another decade until all Type 81s are completely retired from service.

The Type 81 rifle is an air-cooled, gas-operated, magazine-fed, select-fire weapon. The Type 81 has a fixed stock, while the Type 81-1 has a collapsible stock. The Type 81 is a conventional design, similar to the Type 56/AK-47. The Type 81 is capable of firing a variety of muzzle launched 60mm grenades grenade cartridges.

SPECIFICATIONS: (Type 81 Assault Rifle):

Caliber: 7.62x39mm
Feed: 20 or 30-round detachable box magazine
Overall Length: 37.6 inches (Type 81); 29.5 inches (Type 81-1)
Empty weight: 37.7 pounds (Type 81); 7.5 pounds (Type 81-1)
Maximum Effective Range: 400m

5.8x42mm Type 87 Assault Rifle

The PLA's studies on small-caliber infantry weapons can be traced back to the early 1970s, when both the United States and the Soviet Union began to equip their armies

with the M-16A1 and the AK-74. The PLA, however, was unconvinced as to the military effectiveness of these small-caliber rounds and after comprehensive studies and tests, chose 5.8x42mm as the caliber for its next generation small arms family.

The first 5.8mm rifle and squad machine gun were introduced in 1987 with the designation Type 87. The Type 87 was a 5.8x42mm variant of the 7.62x39mm Type 81 rifle with some minor modifications. The Type 87 fires DBP87 bullets, which are claimed to have better performance than the Russian 5.45x39mm and NATO 5.56x45mm SS109/M855-rounds.

In the late 1980s, the improved Type 87A rifle was introduced with a redesigned stock, barrel assembly, hand guard and magazine using plastic and aluminum alloy materials. The Type 87A was the full production version of the Type 87 rifle, with a small number delivered to the PLA Airborne Troops for test and evaluation purposes.

Despite its improved performance over earlier designs, the Type 87A was ultimately refused by the PLA because it did not constitute a significant technological advance over the Type 81. The technology involved in the Type 87 was later used in developing the Type 95 rifle/SAW family.

The Type 87 is very similar to the Type 81 rifle. It is a lightweight, air-cooled, gas-operated, magazine-fed, select-fire rifle. The stock is collapsible.

SPECIFICATIONS:

Caliber 5.8x42mm, Model DPB87 cartridges
Operation: Gas, select-fire
Feed: 30-round detachable box magazine
Overall length: 37.2 inches (normal) or 28.7 inches(stock collapsed)
Empty weight: 8.7 pounds
Maximum Effective Range: 400 m
Cyclic rate: (maximum) 700 rounds/min

Type 95

5.8x42mm Type 95 Assault Rifle

The Type 95 5.8mm series is the latest service rifle with the PLA. Introduced in 1995, the weapon first entered service with special operations , marine and airborne units. The Type 95 series includes the basic assault rifle, a carbine and the squad automatic weapon (LMG). The Type 95 is a gas operated, air cooled, select-fire magazine or drum fed individual weapon in bullpup configuration. It is chambered in 5.8x42mm, a cartridge indigenous to China, but similar in concept to the recently introduced American 6.8x43mm. Extensive use of polymer materials help reduce the weapon's weight.

General dissatisfaction with the 5.8x42mm Type 87 assault rifle led the PLA to develop an entirely new small arms family, the Type 95 (also known as QBZ-95) assault rifle, carbine and light machine gun. There is also an export version designated Type 97 (QBZ-97), which is virtually identical to the Type 95, but is chambered in 5.56x45mm.

The Type 95 assault rifle was first seen in use by the PLA Hong Kong garrison troops in 1997 at the turnover ceremonies from Britain to China. The rifle subsequently entered service with special operations, airborne and Marine Corps units. However, Chinese sources indicate that the PLA is not entirely satisfied with the weapon's performance. Unspecified technical problems and design flaws have been reported in official Chinese sources, and the Type 95 is unlikely to replace the Type 81 and Type 56 assault rifles in the near future. Although the Type 95 seems to be acceptable for close range work, specific complaints have arisen from troops regarding excessive smoke, noise, heat and ejection pattern of spent cases. Moreover, Chinese sources report that the PLA Air Force and Navy have been given a higher priority than land forces in the short term. Given these facts, the future of the Type 95 is uncertain as of this writing (late 2004).

Accessories include optical and night vision sights, sound suppressor, laser designator, and an underbarrel 35mm grenade launcher.

SPECIFICATIONS: Type 95 Assault Rifle
(Type 95 squad automatic weapon in parentheses)

Caliber: 5.8x42mm
Operation: Gas, select-fire
Feed: Detachable box magazine, 30 rounds capacity or 75-round drum
Overall length: 29.4 inches (31.5 inches)
Empty weight: 7.7 pounds (8.7 pounds)
Maximum Effective Range: 400 meters (600 meters)

China Elite Force Type 95

Czech Republic

CZ 2000 5.56x45mm Small Arms Family

When the CZ 2000 small arms family first appeared in 1993, it was known as the LADA. At that time, it was promoted for either the 5.45x39mm or the NATO 5.56x45mm cartridges. The choice was given added significance by an announcement of intent by the Czech armed forces to switch from Eastern-bloc to NATO standards for all munitions, from small arms to artillery. The changeover has been slowed by funding constraints and production of the CZ 2000 family seems to be on hold for the moment, although it almost certainly will be the next Czech service rifle and is being offered for export.

There are three components in the CZ 2000 family of weapons: the standard assault rifle, a carbine and a light machine gun (LMG). Many components are interchangeable among the three weapons.

CZ 2000 rifles are gas operated and employ a rotating bolt for locking. Three fire modes are possible: semiautomatic, full automatic, and three-round burst. Fire modes are chosen using the selector lever on the right of the receiver. The receiver is constructed from steel pressings, and there are obvious resemblances to Kalashnikov-series rifles. The pistol grip and the handguard are polymer. Feed is from a transparent plastic magazine holding 30-rounds, although the 75-round drum magazine of the CZ 2000 light machine gun can also be used, as can M16-type magazines.

Assault rifle rear sights are graduated from 100 to 800 meters in 100-meter increments. The front and rear sights have luminous dots to facilitate shooting in low light. It is possible to use the optical sight-mounting bar fitted to the CZ 2000 light machine gun on the assault rifle after factory modification. The light machine gun bipod also can

be fitted to the rifle. Neither of these options applies to the carbine, which has a barrel length of 7.3 inches compared to the assault rifle's 15 inches.

The stock is of the side-folding type with tubular steel struts and a single-piece buttplate.

SPECIFICATIONS:
Data refers only to the 5.56mm versions
Caliber: 5.56x45mm NATO
Operation: gas, select-fire
Locking: rotary-bolt
Feed: detachable box magazine, 30 rounds capacity or 75-round drum
Empty weight: Standard: 6.7 pounds; short: 5.8 pounds
Overall length: stock extended: standard: 33.46 inches; short: 26.6 inches
Stock folded: standard: 25.3 inches; short: 18.0 inches
Barrel length: Standard: 15 inches; short: 7.28 inches
Sights: Front: post; rear: aperture,
graduated in 100 m increments from 100 to 800 m
Cyclic rate: 750 to 850 rounds/min

Model 58 7.62x39mm Assault Rifles

The Czech Army is equipped with the Model 58 rifle (Samopal vzor 58), an original Czech design. The earliest versions had wooden stocks, pistol grips and forends, but most production weapons have wood fiber-filled plastic furniture. There are three standard versions:
- the Model 58 P, which has a fixed stock
- the Model 58 V, which has a folding stock
- the Model 58 Pi, which is a P version with a long dovetail bracket on the left side to accept a night sight. This version usually is fitted with a bipod and a conical flash hider.

The Model 58 bears a superficial resemblance to the Soviet AK-47, but there are significant differences. The Model 58 is no longer in series production, although it remains available from Ceska Zbrojovka.

CZ 2000

Model 58

Numerous Model 58 rifles in a new or as-new condition have also been updated by the addition of various combat accessories and are now marketed by Caliber Prague Ltd.

It was once suggested that the Model 58 rifles currently in use by the Czech military would be replaced by the CZ 2000 5.56mm series rifles, but it appears that a lack of funds within the Czech Republic has delayed CZ 2000 production for the immediate future.

The Model 58 is gas operated, with a vent opening into a cylinder above the barrel. There is no gas regulator and the full gas force is exerted on the gas piston, which is chrome plated to prevent fouling.

The short tappet-like stroke of the piston strikes the breech block carrier and drives it rearward. After brief free travel, an inclined plane on the bolt carrier moves under the locking piece and lifts it out of engagement with the locking shoulders in the receiver. The locking piece swings and provides the necessary leverage for primary extraction. The breechblock is then carried rearwards, extracting the empty case from the chamber. A fixed ejector in the receiver passes through a groove in the bolt, and the case is ejected upwards. The continued rearward movement of the carrier and bolt compresses two springs. The larger of these fits into the top hole of three in the bolt carrier, and the smaller rests in a hollow steel tube, which acts as a hammer. The carrier is driven forward, and the feed horns on the underside of the bolt face strip a round out of the magazine and into the chamber. When the round is fully chambered, the carrier is still moving forward. As it advances, a transverse cam face forces the locking piece down, and two lugs enter the locking shoulders in the receiver. A major design flaw is that the weapon can be assembled and fired without the locking piece.

Unlike the majority of self-loading and automatic rifles, the Model 58 does not have a rotating hammer. Instead, the hammer is a steel tube that contains the mainspring . This hammer enters the hollow bolt and drives a fully floating firing pin forward to fire the rifle.

The selector is on the right side of the receiver.

Czech soldiers on the range with model 58 rifles

Semiautomatic is indicated by '1', and full automatic by '30'. In the 'safe' position, with the selector pointing vertically downwards, the trigger bar and the disconnector are lowered, so there is no connection between the trigger and the sear which holds the hammer.

Variants

7.62x39mm Mark 58/98 sniper rifle

The Mk 58/98 sniper rifle was introduced in 1998 as a low-cost sniper rifle based on Model 58. Few details of this rifle have been released, but it appears that most of the original Model 58 assault rifle components have been retained but with a longer barrel with a CZ 2000/M16A2-pattern muzzle brake. The rifle fires semiautomatic only. An optical sight is mounted on a rail over the receiver along with back-up iron sights. Other features include a folding stock, a revised and enlarged forearm that houses a folding bipod, and a five or 10-round box magazine. The Empty weight is 8.4 lbs., and the overall length with stock extended is 433 inches (34.3 inches with stock folded).

7.62x39mm Model 58/96 GR Bison

This is a standard Model 58 with a Romanian 40mm grenade launcher, the AG-40 Model 80, marketed by RomArm. The empty weight of the rifle with the launcher attached is 9.7 pounds.

7.62mm Model 58/98 GL

This is a standard Model 58 with a Singapore Technologies Kinetics 40GL 40mm grenade launcher. The grenade launcher is attached to the rifle using a special bracket. The empty weight of the rifle with the launcher attached is 9.9 pounds.

7.62mm Model 58/96 SD Zmije

The Model 58/96 SD Zmije is provided with a sound suppressor. The empty weight of this variant is 8.6 pounds, and it is 45.1 inches long. A sub-variant of this model is available with a retractable stock; it can accommodate a bipod and night-vision optics.

7.62mm Model 58/96 Vyr

For this model, a standard Model 58 is provided with a Pilkington weapon sight. Options include a bipod and a muzzle flash suppressor.

7.62mm Model 58/96 TR

This variant incorporates a laser-aiming device secured under the barrel with the actuator switch fastened to the front grip. The empty weight of the rifle with the laser

device in place is 7.4 pounds. Options include a bipod and a muzzle flash suppressor.

7.62mm Model 58/96 LS Sova

This is a standard Model 58 with an underbarrel 1.5mW infrared laser aiming device.

SPECIFICATIONS: Basic Model 58
Caliber: 7.62x39mm
Operation: gas, select-fire
Locking: pivoting locking piece
Feed: detachable box magazine, 30 rounds capacity
Empty weight: 6.9 pounds
Overall length: stock extended: 33.2 inches
Barrel length: 15.8 inches
Sights: Front: post; rear: tangent leaf V-notch
Cyclic rate: 750 to 850 rounds/min
Max effective range: 400m

Egypt

Misr 7.62x39mm assault rifle

The Misr 7.62mm assault rifle is a direct copy of the Soviet AKM. It is available for export sales and has reportedly been sold in significant numbers. A semiautomatic version known as indigenously as the ARM was also manufactured and was sold on the sporting arms market in the United States under the name "Maadi." It is included herein because it is still widely distributed throughout the world.

Variant

ARM The ARM is a semiautomatic version of the Misr and is available with fixed or side-folding stocks which render the ARM externally identical to the Misr. The only changes are to the trigger mechanism which allows semiautomatic fire only, although the selector has only two positions, "fire" and "safe." A version is available with a wooden 'sporting' thumbhole stock.

SPECIFICATIONS:
Caliber: 7.62x39mm
Operation: gas, select-fire
Locking: rotating bolt
Feed: 30-round detachable box magazine
Empty weight: 8.5 pounds
Overall length: 34.7 inches
Barrel length: 16.3 inches
Sights: Front, adjustable post; rear: U-notch
Cyclic rate: 600 rounds/min
Max effective range: 300 m

Misr

Finland

Sako M90 assault rifles

The Sako M90 is an improved version of the earlier M62/M76 series of assault rifles and thus is based on the Kalashnikov action, but has been lightened and refined. A new side-folding stock has been added, along with new rear sights with an adjustable tangent aperture and a fixed combat sight and a new flash suppressor, which also functions as a grenade launcher. Tritium night sights are standard.

The M90 is available in two calibers, 7.62x39mm or 5.56x45mm. Optional equipment includes a removable bipod, optical day and night sights, bayonet and a blank-firing attachment.

Sako also developed a new cartridge with a hard-core K413 bullet. Both the bullet and its cartridge case are made from alloy steel.

SPECIFICATIONS: Data for 7.62x39mm version

Caliber: 7.62x39mm
Operation: gas, select-fire
Locking: rotating bolt
Feed: 30-round detachable box magazine
Empty weight: 38.5 pounds
Overall length: stock folded, 26.6 inches; stock extended, 36.6 inches
Barrel length: 16.3 inches
Sights: Front, hooded blade with tritium dot; rear: adjustable aperture, 150-300-400 m, with tritium dots.
Cyclic rate: 600-750 rounds/min

Sako M95 Assault Rifle

Sako's M95 Assault rifle continued the process of refining the Kalashnikov system that previously included the Sako M62, M76 and M90 rifles. The M95 is essentially an enhanced M90 with improvements to make the weapon even more rugged and reliable under a wide range of environmental and temperature extremes.

Although initial reports were that the Finnish Armed Forces were going to replace their M90 rifles with M95s, only one production batch, plus spare parts, was ordered. M95 production has ceased.

The Finnish Defense Force designation for the M95 is 7.62 RK 95 TP (Rynnakkokivaari 95 Taittopera - assault rifle 95 with folding stock).

A semiautomatic sporting model with a folding stock was also produced, as was a 5.56x45mm export model. The M95's skeleton stock folds to the right side of the receiver. With the stock folded, it is still possible to operate the trigger and fire-control selector. A large arctic trigger guard is standard. The cocking handle can be operated by both left-handed and right-handed shooters.

The gas valve has two positions: 'open' for normal firing and 'closed' for launching rifle grenades. It is also possible to mount an M203 40mm grenade launcher under the forearm via a Sako mounting adapter.

The receiver dust cover has an optics mounting rail that can be configured to meet customer requirements. The standard rear sight has an open square notch for close combat that becomes visible when the twin rotating apertures for 200 and 400 m (150 and 300 m for 7.62mm examples) are in the middle position. Tritium night sights are standard. The front sight is adjustable for windage and elevation.

The M95 is available in two calibers, 7.62x39mm or 5.56x45mm. Accessories include a sling, removable bipod, bayonet, cleaning kit and a blank-firing device. 7.62mm M95 rifles can be fitted with a suppressor.

SPECIFICATIONS:

Caliber: 7.62x39mm or 5.56x45mm NATO
Operation: gas, select-fire
Locking: rotating bolt
Feed: 30-round box magazine
Empty weight:, 9.9 pounds
Overall length: stock folded, 26.6 inches; stock extended, 36.8 inches
Barrel length: 16.5 inches
Sights: Front, hooded blade with tritium dot; rear: adjustable tangent aperture, combat, 200 m and 400 m (150 and 300mm for 7.62mm), with tritium dots
Cyclic rate: 600 to 750 rounds/min

SAKO M95

France

FAMAS F1 5.56mm assault rifle

The FAMAS F1 5.56x45mm is a delayed blowback operated bullpup assault rifle that can be fired from either shoulder without the difficulty of spent case ejection associated with most bullpup rifles. This issue has been overcome by providing two extractor positions on the bolt face and reversible ejectors. The rifle is issued with the extractor on the right and ejector to the left and with this arrangement, spent cases are ejected to the right. By reversing the extractor and ejector, ejection is reversed and the cheek rest is removed and positioned on the other side of the stock, where it closes off the ejection port on that side. The cocking handle is centrally placed above the receiver to permit operation by either hand and the sights are also ambidextrous.

The barrel is of plain steel and has a fluted chamber. The muzzle brake/flash suppressor also serves as a grenade launcher. An adjustable collar controls the position of the grenade and so varies the velocity and thus the range. The receiver is of light alloy, and the other assemblies are pinned to it.

The delay lever has two parallel angled arms joined by a crosspiece. The arms connect the breechblock to the carrier and the crosspiece controls the position of the firing pin. The lower ends of the arms bear against a hardened steel pin across the receiver and the upper ends rest against the back face of the breechblock carrier. This is the means of holding up the breech face while the chamber pressure is high and transferring energy to the carrier. It also controls the trigger mechanism by operating the safety sear.

The trigger mechanism is self-contained in a plastic box that is pinned to the receiver. It provides semiautomatic, full automatic and three-round bursts.

The polymer stock contains a buffer in the upper half to cushion the blow of the reciprocating parts as they recoil. A rubber shoulder pad reduces the impact on the shooter's shoulder. The carrying handle is plastic and protects the sights against accidental damage.

The box magazine holds 25-rounds and has holes in the sides to indicate the number of rounds it contains.

Production of the FAMAS F1 has ceased. Approximately 400,000 were produced. The FAMAS was exported to Djibouti, Gabon, Senegal and the United Arab Emirates.

Variants

FAMAS G1 and G2. See entry below

FAMAS Export: This was the standard 5.56mm rifle modified for semiautomatic only operation. The FAMAS Export was intended for the overseas commercial market.

FAMAS Civil: This model was intended for the French commercial market, and in order to comply with French firearms laws, it has had its barrel lengthened to 22.4 inches and the caliber changed to .222 Remington chambering. It is semiautomatic only and has no grenade-launching rings.

FAMAS Commando: The FAMAS Commando was a short version intended for use by special forces. The barrel length was shortened to 16 inches, and there was no grenade-launching capability. It was otherwise the same as the service rifle and offered the full range of select-fire options.

SPECIFICATIONS:
Caliber: 5.56x45mm
Operation: delayed blowback, select-fire
Method of delay: vertical delay lever
Feed: 25-round detachable box magazine
Empty weight: 7.95 pounds
Overall length: 757 inches (This is incorrect)
Barrel length: 19.2 inches
Sights: Front, blade; rear: aperture 0-300m
Cyclic rate: 900 to 1,000 rounds/min
Max effective range: 300m

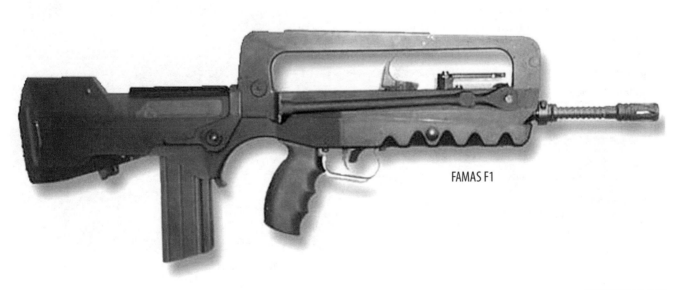

FAMAS F1

FAMAS G2

FAMAS G2 5.56x45mm assault rifle

The FAMAS G2 5.56mm assault rifle was developed by Giat Industries as a private venture and is primarily intended for export. It is an updated version of the FAMAS G1, which could accommodate only the standard FAMAS F1 25-round box magazine and is no longer in production.

The French and several other armies ordered the FAMAS G2. The French Navy ordered 20,000 in December 1995, for delivery in 1997 and 1998.

Mechanically, the FAMAS G2 is the same as the FAMAS F1 and is chambered in 5.56x45mm cartridge. However, the standard rifling is one turn in nine inches, so it can be used with either M193 or SS109/M855 ammunition. The barrel can also be rifled one turn in seven inches or one turn in 12 inches.

The external appearance has changed by the adoption of a full-hand trigger guard, similar to that of the Steyr AUG. The breech-block buffer has been reinforced so as to better withstand firing rifle grenades and the magazine housing now accepts all M16-type magazines.

The selector lever was moved inside the trigger guard and the front of the handguard has alip added to prevent the hand from sliding forwards onto a hot barrel.

SPECIFICATIONS:
Caliber: 5.56x45mm
Operation: delayed blowback, select-fire
Locking: differential leverage
Feed: 30-round M16 type magazines
Empty weight: 8.4 pounds
Overall length: 29.8 inches
Barrel length: 19.2 inches
Sights: Front, blade; rear: aperture graduated to 17.7 inches; provision for optical sights
Cyclic rate: 1,100 rounds/min
Max effective range: open sights, 450m; optical sight, 600m

A french trooper takes position during a training drill.

Germany

Heckler & Koch 7.62x51mm G3 rifle

The Heckler & Koch G3 has been the service rifle of the German Army since

1959, but is now being replaced by the G36. It was derived from the Spanish CETME, which was in turn derived from a German World War II design that never got into production. The G3 remains in production in other countries where licensed production has been negotiated. Many manufacturers also have marketing rights, so G3 rifles may be encountered almost anywhere throughout the world. In semiautomatic-only form, the G3 has been extensively marketed as the HK91.

The G3 receiver is pressed steel, grooved on either side to guide the bolt and accommodate the backplate, and carry the barrel. A tubular extension above the barrel houses the cocking lever and the bolt's forward extension. The cocking lever runs in a slot cut in the left side of the housing and can be locked in the open position by a locking notch. The barrel is threaded at the muzzle with a serrated collar to engage the retaining spring of the flash suppressor. The chamber has 12 longitudinal flutes extending back from the leade to rear of the chamber. These allow gas to leak back along the sides of the cartridge case, providing a film of gas upon which the case floats, preventing the case from adhering to the chamber walls so that extraction is positive and case heads are not ripped off by the lack of primary extraction inherent in the delayed blowback system.

The bolt is shaped with a hollow forward extension that guides the recoil spring and extends into the tube above the barrel. The bolt carrier has grooved bearing surfaces on each side that slide in the grooves in the sides of the receiver. The bolt head carries two rollers that project on either side and are forced out by the inclined front faces of a 'locking piece'. The rollers engage recesses in the barrel extension. The bolt head and locking piece seat in the bolt carrier and are held by a locking lever to prevent bounce on chambering the cartridge.

When the rifle is fired, pressure generated in the chamber forces the cartridge case rearwards and exerts a force on the breechface, which drives the bolt head to the rear. The rollers in the bolt head are pushed back, and the angle of the recesses in the barrel extension forces the rollers inwards against the inclined planes on the front of the locking piece. This inward force drives the locking piece back along with the bolt carrier. The angle of the locking-piece face is such that the velocity ratio between bolt-head carrier and bolt head is 4:1.

As the carrier moves back, the bolt-locking lever is disengaged. After the bolt face has moved back a little over a millimeter, the rollers have cleared the recesses in the barrel extension, and the entire bolt is driven back by residual pressure, with the bolt head and the bolt carrier maintaining their relative displacement of about .25 inch. The bolt carrier cocks the hammer and compresses the recoil spring. The cartridge case hits the ejector and is ejected to the right. As it is driven forward by the recoil spring, the bolt head strips a cartridge from the magazine and chambers it. The locking piece and the bolt carrier then close the .25-inch gap, and the rollers are pushed out into the recesses of the barrel extension. The bolt locking lever engages the bolt shoulder, thus preventing bounce. The weapon is then ready to be fired again.

Commercial production of the G3/HK91 was undertaken in the United States using H&K machinery and tooling by JLD Enterprises. These rifles are identical to H&K products in every way.

Variants

The standard rifle is designated the G3A3 and has a plastic stock and handguard. With a telescopic sight this rifle is called the G3A3ZF. When the fixed stock is replaced by a retractable stock, the rifle is called the G3A4.

The G3K model is a carbine with retractable stock standard. This, combined with a shorter 12.7 inch barrel, reduces the minimum overall length to 28.4 inches, or 35.4

HECKLER & KOCH G3

HECKLER & KOCH G3K

HECKLER & KOCH HK33A2

inches with the stock extended. The empty weight, without magazine, is reduced to 9.7 pounds.

The G3A5 was produced for sale to Denmark.

The G3A6 is the designation given to a version for license production in Iran.

The G3A7 is the designation given to a version for license production in Turkey by MKEK. These are produced in two versions, the G3A3 with a fixed stock and the G3A4 with a collapsible stock.

Besides the German Army, the armed forces of many countries have adopted Heckler & Koch G3 rifles and are completely or partially equipped with them. These include: Cyprus, Denmark (G3A5), France, Germany, Greece, Italy, The Netherlands, Norway, Portugal, Sweden, Turkey. Angola, Burkina Faso, Burundi, Chad, Democratic Republic of the Congo (formerly Zaire), Cote d'Ivoire, Ethiopia, Gabon, Ghana, Kenya, Libya, Malawi, Mauritania, Morocco, Niger, Nigeria, Senegal, Somalia, Sudan, Tanzania, Togo, Uganda, Zambia, Zimbabwe, Bolivia, Brazil, Chile, Colombia, Dominican Republic, El Salvador, Guyana, Haiti, Mexico, Paraguay, Peru, Bahrain, Lebanon, Iran (G3A6), Jordan, Qatar, Saudi Arabia, United Arab Emirates, Yemen (North), Bangladesh, Brunei, Indonesia, Myanmar (Burma), Pakistan and The Philippines.

SPECIFICATIONS:

Caliber: 7.62x51mm
Operation: delayed blowback, select-fire
Delay method: rollers
Feed: 20-round detachable box magazine
Empty weight: fixed stock, 9.7 pounds; retractable stock, 10.4 pounds
Overall length: fixed stock, 1025 mm; retracted stock, 840mm
Barrel length: 17.7 inches
Sights: Front, post; rear: aperture at 100, 200, 300 and 400m
Cyclic rate: 500 to 600 rounds/min
Max effective range: 400m

Heckler & Koch 5.56x45mm HK33 rifle

The Heckler & Koch 5.56mm HK33 rifle is a delayed blowback, air cooled, select-fire rifle, using the Heckler & Koch system roller locking system which employs a two-part bolt, the action of which has been described in the entry for the G3 rifle. The HK33 is for all intents and purposes a scaled-down version of the 7.62x51mm G3 rifle and uses the same trigger and firing mechanism as the larger rifle. The mechanism provides automatic and semiautomatic operation and a 'safe' position. Commercial versions are designated HK93 and are semiautomatic only.

There originally were five HK33 variants: the standard rifle with fixed stock (HK33A2), rifle with retractable stock (HK33A3), rifle with bipod, sniper rifle with telescopic sight (HK33 SG1) and the HK33K carbine version.

The product line was later simplified and the final production models were as follows: HK33E (E - Export) and the short HK33EK, both of which could be ordered with a fixed or retractable stock. Both stocks are interchangeable. In addition, different firing-mode options were available:

- Safe, semiautomatic, full automatic
- Safe, semiautomatic, three-round burst, full automatic
- Safe, semiautomatic, three-round burst

Following production at H&K's Oberndorf-Neckar factory, HK33 production was switched to Heckler & Koch (GB) at Nottingham, UK. It was there that production for Ecuador was completed. Latest license production is in Turkey by MKEK. The HK33 has also been manufactured in Thailand. The HK33 has been widely exported and manufactured under license. Users include the Brazilian Air Force, Chile, Malaysia, Thailand and Turkey. The HK33 has also been sold in Southeast Asia, Africa and South America.

A short-barreled version of the HK33 designated the HK53 was available with a very short (8.3-inch) barrel and was intended to fill the gap between rifle and submachine gun, offering assault rifle cartridges in a pistol-caliber submachine gun sized package.

SPECIFICATIONS: Data for HK33E; where HK33EK differs, shown in parentheses

Caliber: 5.56x45mm
Operation: delayed blowback, select-fire
Method of delay: rollers
Feed: 30-round box magazine
Empty weight: fixed stock, 8.6 pounds;
retracting stock, 8.8 pounds (8.6 pounds)
Overall length: fixed stock, 36.2 inches; extended stock, 29.1 inches (extended stock,34.1 inches; retracted stock, 34.3 inches)
Barrel length: 16.1 inches (12.7 inches)
Sights: Front, post; rear: V battle sight 100m; apertures for 200, 300 and 400m; optical, 4 x 24 telescope, six range increments from 100 to 600m; adjustable for windage and elevation
Cyclic rate: 750 rounds/min (700 rounds/min)
Max effective range: 600m

Heckler & Koch 5.56x45mm G36 and G36K Assault Rifles

With the demise of the Heckler & Koch 4.73mm G11K3 rifle and its caseless ammunition, the Bundeswehr still required a new service rifle. To obtain a rifle with ammunition that would conform to NATO specifications, the Bundeswehr conducted testing using the HK50, a Heckler & Koch private design and the Steyr AUG. The HK50 rifle was selected for service and given

HECKLER & KOCH G36E

the Bundeswehr designation G36. Deliveries to the Bundeswehr's NATO rapid-reaction force began during the third quarter of 1996.

In addition to the standard G36, a short version, the G36K, is issued to German special operations units. A light machinegun version, the LMG36, termed as a light support weapon, is described separately.

In July 1998, the G36 was selected by the Spanish armed forces. The total Spanish requirement is approximately 115,000 rifles. The Spanish version of the G36 is manufactured under license in Spain by Empresa Nacional Santa Barbara.

The G36E is the export version of the G36 series, differing mainly in having a 1.5x optical sight in place of the 3x sight of the indigenous G36.

The Heckler & Koch G36 assault rifle is a gas-operated, air-cooled select-fire rifle of conventional design and was clearly derived from the Armalite AR-18 of the late 1960s/early 1970s. The operating system is virtually identical to the AR-18 with the exception of the recoil spring layout. A skeleton stock folds to the right of the receiver to reduce overall length. Much of the G36 receiver and other components are constructed of high-strength polymer. An integral carrying handle receiver contains a 3x optical sight and a 1x red-dot sight. There are backup iron sights for use if the optical sight is damaged.

The spring-loaded cocking handle is under the carrying handle and can be swung to either side of the receiver for use by left-handed or right-handed shooters. If necessary, the handle may be used as a forward-assist lever. Ejection is to the right.

The locking system is the widely used rotating bolt and multi-lug system and as stated is almost identical to that of the Armalite AR-18. This was incorporated to keep

The G36E in action.

German HK-G36E

HECKLER & KOCH G36 Compact

down the overall weight and to simplify the overall design, as the AR-18 piston and rod system is considered by many authorities to be superior to the direct gas impingement system of the AR15 because it reduces fouling, improves reliability and simplifies maintenance. The gas system consists of a short stroke piston and operating rod that transmits the gas thrust to the bolt. The free-floating, cold hammer forged barrel is chrome plated.

The receiver, carrying handle, grip and stock are all molded from high-strength polymers that are not affected by temperatures. These assemblies are constructed in a modular fashion so that they can be removed and replaced by the user.

Feeding is from 30-round translucent polymer magazines. Each magazine has studs allowing up to five magazines to be joined and carried side-by-side on the rifle ready for rapid magazine changes. A 100-round Beta C-Magazine is available.

A 40x46mm, low-velocity grenade launcher developed specifically for the G36 and G36K is known as the AG36. It cannot be used with the G36C.

G36K

The short G36K differs from the G36 by the shortened barrel length and the slotted flash suppressor and a shorter handguard. The G36Ks in service with German special operations units are issued with 100-round Beta C-Mags.

G36C

The G36C is the G36 Commando. This version is similar to the G36K, but the barrel length is reduced to 9.0 inches, and the overall length with stock extended is 28.4 inches. The short handguard has six attachment points, one of which could be used for a vertical front grip. With the stock folded, the G36C is actually shorter than a MP5 submachine gun.

SPECIFICATIONS:

Model:	G36	G36K	G36C
Cartridge:	5.56 NATO	5.56 NATO	5.56 NATO
Operation:	gas; select-fire	gas; select-fire	gas; select-fire
Locking:	rotating-bolt, 6 lugs	rotating-bolt, 6 lugs	rotating-bolt, 6 lugs
Feed:	30-round box magazine	30-round box magazine	30-round box magazine
Empty weight without magazine:			
	8.00 pounds	7.36 pounds	6.21 pounds
Overall length:			
stock extended	39.3 inches	33.9 inches	28.4 inches
stock folded	29.8 inches	24.2 inches	19.7 inches
Barrel length:	8.9 inches	12.5 inches	9.0 inches
Sights:	3x optical; auxiliary iron sights	3x optical; auxiliary iron sights	3x optical; auxiliary iron sights
Cyclic rate, 750 rounds/min			

Heckler & Koch 7.62x51mm G8 rifle

The Heckler & Koch G8 rifle is a revised model of the HK11E with a magazine feed.

The operating mechanism is the familiar Heckler & Koch roller-locked retarded blowback system with select-fire and three-round burst. Feed is by means of a standard box magazine, but a special 50-round drum magazine is also available. The G8 can be adapted to belt feed by use of a conversion kit. The G8A1 variant will not accept the belt feed mechanism and is magazine fed only. The barrel is heavier than the G3, and can be quickly changed when the weapon is being used in the full automatic mode.

SPECIFICATIONS:

Caliber: 7.62x51mm NATO
Operation: delayed blowback, select-fire and three-round burst facility
Delay Method: rollers
Empty weight: 17.97 inches
Overall length: 40.6 inches
Barrel length: 17.7 inches
Sights: mechanical: adjustable 100 to 1,100m in 100m steps
Cyclic rate: ~800 rounds/min

Hungary

AMD-65M 7.62mm assault rifle

The AMD-65 is a derivative of the earlier AMD-63 rifle, which was a modified AKM. Hungary further modified its AKM-63 assault rifle to facilitate its use inside vehicles and confined spaces, resulting in the AMD-65M assault rifle. The modifications include a shorter barrel and a folding stock. The shorter barrel produces more muzzle blast and flash which is countered by a large flash hider with two holes in either side.

The folding stock of the AMD-65M is a single tubular strut. Grenade launching rifles have an extra shock-absorbing device on the stock to allow some recoil movement. This same rifle has an optical sight specifically for firing grenades and lacks the forward pistol grip.

AMD-65 rifles have been observed in the hands of US Special Forces troops operating in Afghanistan.

SPECIFICATIONS:

Caliber: 7.62x39mm
Operation: gas, select-fire
Locking: rotating bolt
Feed: 30-round detachable box magazine
Empty weight: 7.21 pounds; loaded, 8.27 pounds
Overall length: stock folded, 23.6 inches; stock extended, 33.3 inches
Barrel length: 14.9 inches
Cyclic rate: 600 rounds/min
Max effective range: 350m

India

Since the late 1950s, Indian armed forces were equipped with 7.62x51mm NATO L1A1 self-loading rifles. As 7.62x51mm self-loading rifles started to become obsolete in the 1980s, India began to develop an indigenous design designated INSAS (Indian National Small Arms System), which incorporated features from several foreign designs. The INSAS system was originally intended to consist of three elements- a standard rifle, a carbine, and a squad automatic

rifle (LMG), all chambered in 5.56x45mm. In 1997 the rifle and LMG were ready for mass production and in 1998 the first INSAS rifles were formally shown in an Independence Day parade. The full fielding of INSAS rifles was initially delayed by the lack of the domestically made 5.56x45mm ammunition and India bought large quantities of 5.56x45mm from the Israeli firm IMI. Some 300,000 INSAS rifles are presently in service with the Indian army. INSAS rifles are made by the Ishapore Rifle Factory.

The INSAS rifle has some features of the Kalashnikov design, but with several modifications. The basic gas operated action with long stroke gas piston and a rotating bolt, as well as the stamped sheet steel receiver are generally similar to AKM/AK-74 rifles, but the INSAS has a manual gas regulator, similar in design to that of FAL rifles, as well as a gas cutoff for launching grenades. The charging handle has been moved from the bolt carrier to the left side of the forearm, similar in position and operation to German G3/HK33. The selector switch is located at the left side of the receiver above the pistol grip for easy access by the shooter's thumb and allows semiautomatic and three-round burst fire. The rifle is fitted with a folding carrying handle and either a solid or folding metal buttstock. Furniture can be made from wood or polymer. Standard magazines are made from translucent polymer and accommodate 20 or 30 rounds. The 30-round magazines are primarily for the INSAS LMG but can also be used in the rifle. The sights consist of a hooded front, mounted on top of the gas block, and a diopter rear mounted on the receiver cover. The flash suppressor accepts NATO-specification rifle grenades.

SPECIFICATIONS:

Caliber: 5.56x45mm NATO
Operation: Gas, select-fire
Feed: 20- or 30-round detachable box magazine
Overall length: 37.2 inches with fixed stock ; 37.8 inches / 29.5 inches with folding stock
Barrel length: 464mm
Empty weight 7.01 pounds
Cyclic rate: 650 rounds per minute

AMD-65

NATO L1A1

Indonesia

Pindad SS1 series 5.56x45mm Assault Rifles

The SS1 assault rifles are licensed copies of the Belgian FNH FNC rifle manufactured in Indonesia by PT Pindad. Indonesian ammunition is based on the SS109-round, and all four weapons are rifled with six grooves, right-handed, one turn in seven inches. Firing modes are full automatic, three-round burst or semiautomatic. All models accept optical sights.

- The SS1-V1 is the standard rifle with a 449mm barrel length and a side-folding, tubular metal stock.

- The SS1-V2 is a carbine with a 363mm barrel and a side-folding tubular metal stock.

- The SS1-V3 is the standard model with a fixed solid polymer stock.

- The SS1-V5 is a short carbine intended for special forces; barrel length is 252mm and it has a side-folding, tubular metal stock.

- The SS1-V1 Police is a special police model with a 449mm barrel length and a side-folding, tubular metal stock; the empty weight is 4 kg

The SS1-V1 and SS1-V2 flash suppressor accepts the PGT grenade launcher adapter. This enables the rifles to deliver riot control or smoke grenades to a range of up to 150 m. The SS1-V1 can be fitted with the Pindad SPG-1A 40x46mm grenade launcher.

Variant

Sabhara: In addition to the above models, two special select-fire variants, known as the Sabhara-V1 and the Sabhara-V2, are available chambered in a locally developed cartridge, the 7.62 x 45mm. This cartridge is produced by necking up a 5.56x45mm cartridge case to accommodate a 7.62x51mm ball bullet. The cartridge weight is 231 grains, and the muzzle velocity is 1640 ft/sec. The resultant round is the MU-11 TJ.

There is also an anti-riot round with a rubber projectile known as the MU-11 PHH.

The Sabhara-V1 rifle has a 14.3 inch barrel and a folding tubular metal stock.

The Sabhara-V2 carbine has a 10 inch barrel and is otherwise identical to the Sabhara V1.

SPECIFICATIONS:

Model	SS1-V1	SS1-V2	SS1-V3	SS1-V5
Caliber	5.56x45mm	5.56x45mm	5.56x45mm	5.56x45mm
Operation	gas, select-fire	gas, select-fire	gas, select-fire	gas, select-fire
Locking	rotary bolt	rotary bolt	rotary bolt	rotary bolt
Feed for all: 30-round box magazine				
Empty weight with empty magazine:				
	8.84 pounds	8.62 pounds	8.84 pounds	7.73 pounds
Overall length, stock extended				
	38.5 inches	35.0 inches	38.5 inches	30.3 inches
Overall length, stock folded				
	30.2 inches	26.2 inches	n/a	21.9 inches
Barrel length	17.7 inches	14.3 inches	17.7 inches	9.9 inches

Sights for all: Front, protected post; rear: O type and two positions for 0-300m and 300-450 m
Cyclic rate 720 to 760 rounds per minute

Iran

S-5.56 5.56x45mm Assault Rifle

In March 2001, the Iranian Defense Industries Organization (DIO) announced that it was manufacturing and offering for sale the S-5.56 rifle. Although it has been claimed that the weapon is locally designed, the S-5.56 appears to be a direct copy of the Chinese Type CQ rifle, itself an almost direct copy of the US M16A1. The Iranian S-5.56 is in production and is offered for export sales.

It is probable that the S-5.56 is identical in function and operation to the M16. As with the Type CQ, the only visual change from the original M16 is in the revised pistol-grip outline. However, the S-5.56 is available in two versions:

- The S-5.56A1 has a barrel length 505.5mm long and rifled one turn in 12 inches for the M193 55-grain cartridge.

- The S-5.56A3 has a barrel length 508mm long and rifled one turn in 7 inches for the SS109/M855 62-grain cartridge.

Interestingly, neither the Chinese nor the Iranians seem to be aware that a twist rate between 1:12 and 1:7 will accommodate both bullet weights, eliminating the need to manufacture barrels with specialized twist rates.

SPECIFICATIONS:

Caliber: 5.56x45mm M193 or SS109
Operation: direct impingement gas, select-fire
Locking: rotating bolt
Feed: 20-round box magazine
Empty weight: 7.1 pounds
Overall length: S-5.56A1, 38.9 inches; S-5.56A3, 39 inches
Barrel length: S-5.56A1, 19.9 inches; S-5.56A3, 20 inches
Sights: Front, post; rear: two apertures, for ranges up to 300m and 300 to 500m. Adjustable for windage
Cyclic rate: 700 to 950 rounds/min
Max effective range: 460 m

Iranian Troops

SABHARA

Israel

An Israeli soldier engages the enemy with an M16 equpped with a grenade launcher.

IMI 5.56mm and 7.62mm Galil Assault Rifles

The experience gained by the Israeli Defense Forces (IDF) during the Six-Day war of 1967, showed deficiencies of the FAL rifles, at the time the main armament of the IDF infantry. The FAL rifles were sensitive to fine sand and dust of Arab deserts and too long and bulky to carry and maneuver in vehicles and confined spaces. The same war showed that the Kalashnikov assault rifles used by Arab infantry had attractive features. Subsequently, the IDF decided to develop a new assault rifle to replace the FAL battle rifles and UZI submachine guns. It was also decided that the new assault rifle should be built around the 5.56x45mm cartridge. During the late 1960s the IDF tested two rival designs, one of the Uziel Gal, and the other of the Israel Galil. The latter design, based on the Finnish Valmet assault rifle, won the competition and was selected as a new IDF assault rifle in the 1973, but its adoption was delayed by the Yom Kippur War of 1973. The machinery and documentation package was bought from

Valmet and transferred to the state-owned Israel Military Industries (IMI) company. The basic Galil rifle evolved into several configurations, including the full-size 5.56x45mm AR and ARM assault rifles, compact 5.56x45mm SAR rifle for tank and vehicle crews, 7.62x51mm NATO AR selective-fire and 7.62mm NATO semiautomatic Galatz, 5.56x45mm MAR subcompact carbine, also known as the Micro-Galil, and some other modifications, such as the unsuccessful .30 Carbine Magal police rifle.

Although a successful weapon, the Galil was not widely issued to the IDF during its lifetime, because during the late 1960s and early 1970s Israel received large shipments of the US M16 assault rifles at almost no cost. M16 rifles became the major armament of the IDF, with the Galils mostly issued to the armored and artillery troops and some units of the Israeli Air Force. The Galil rifles were exported to several South American, African and Asian countries. Estonia also received some Galil rifles in the early 2000s. The R4, R5 and R6, slightly modified versions of the Galil rifle are manufactured

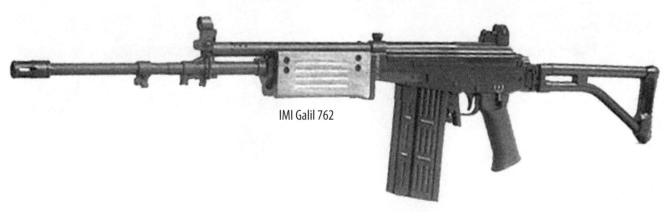

IMI Galil 762

by the Vektor Company, a division of the DENEL in South African and are used by the South African Military. Another derivative of the Galil is the Croatian APS-95 assault rifle. Semiautomatic-only versions of the both 5.56mm and 7.62mm Galil AR rifles were extensively sold in both domestic and foreign markets. Service includes the Israeli Defense Force and other armies including Bolivia, Botswana, Chile, Colombia, Democratic Republic of Congo (Zaire), Costa Rica, Guatemala, Haiti, Honduras, Nicaragua, Philippines, Rwanda, Swaziland, and Trinidad and Tobago.

The Galil assault rifle is essentially a modified Kalashnikov design. The key differences between the Galil and the AK are as follows. The Galil features a machined steel receiver similar to the original AK-47 rifles. The AK-style selector switch on the right side of the gun is supplemented by a smaller switch at the left side of the receiver, above the pistol grip that can easily be reached by the shooter's thumb. The cocking handle is bent upward, so it can be operated with either hand. Galil sights feature a front hooded post on the gas block, with the rear diopter sight mounted on the dust cover. The rear sight has settings for 300 and 500 meters. Additional folding night sights with luminous inserts can be raised into position, which allows aiming up to 100 meters in low-light conditions. The flash suppressor can be used to launch rifle grenades. The folding buttstock is patterned after that of the FN FAL Para and folds to the right. Some of the late production Micro-Galil (MAR) rifles also are fitted with a MIL-STD-1913 rail, which allows mounting of optics. All 5.56mm Galil rifles feed from a proprietary 35- or 50-round box magazine with AK-style locking. M16-type magazines can be used with an adapter. 7.62mm Galil rifles are fed using proprietary 25-round box magazines.

SPECIFICATIONS: Data for 5.56x45mm ARM/AR except as noted

Caliber: 5.56x45mm
Operation: gas, select-fire
Locking: rotating bolt
Feed: 35- or 50-round box magazine
Empty weight: ARM, with bipod and carrying handle, 9.6 pounds; AR, without bipod or
handle, 8.7 pounds; SAR, without bipod or handle, 8.27 pounds
Overall length: ARM/AR overall, 38.5 inches; with stock folded, 29.2 inches; SAR overall,
33.1 inches; with stock folded, 24.2 inches
Barrel length: ARM/AR, 18.1 inches; SAR, 13.1 inches
Sights: Front, post, with protector; rear: flip aperture, 300 and 500 m.
Tritium night sights
Cyclic rate: 650 rounds/min

SPECIFICATIONS: Data for 7.62mm rifles

Caliber: 7.62x51mm
Operation: gas, select-fire
Locking: rotating bolt
Feed: 25-round box magazine
Empty weight: ARM, 8.8 pounds; AR, 8.7 pounds; SAR, 8.3 pounds
Overall length: ARM/AR overall, 41.3 inches; stock folded, 31.9 inches; SAR
overall, 36.0 inches
stock folded, 26.6 inches
Barrel length: ARM/AR, 21.1 inches; SAR, 17.7 inches
Sights: Front, post with protector; rear: aperture, 300 and 500m. Folding tritium
night sights
Cyclic rate: ARM/AR, 650 rounds/min; SAR, 750 rounds/min

IMI 5.56x45mm Galil MAR Micro Assault Rifle

The IMI 5.56mm Galil MAR Micro assault rifle was claimed to be the smallest and lightest assault rifle in the world before the IMI 5.56x45mm Micro Tavor. It is a shortened version of the 5.56mm Galil assault rifle intended for special forces and special applications such as commandoes and tank crews. The basic user controls and mechanism of the Galil rifle are retained virtually unaltered, as are many components. The barrel length has been shortened to 7.7 inches, and only the 35-round curved box magazine is employed. The maximum effective range is claimed to be 300m.

The front grip of the Galil MAR is made from a shatterproof nylon reinforced polymer and is contoured that the forward part acts as a guard to prevent the shooter's hand getting too close to the muzzle. A folding aluminum alloy stock is provided to make the weapon even more compact.

The special operations Galil Micro Special can be fitted with a suppressor, a tactical light, reflex sights and a laser pointer. Another variant of the Galil MAR Micro can be configured as a Personal Defense Weapon (PDW). This model has an full-length MIL-STD-1913 rail over the receiver and a modified stock.

SPECIFICATIONS:

Caliber: 5.56x45mm
Operation: gas, select-fire
Locking: rotating bolt
Feed: 35-round box magazine
Empty weight: rifle only, 6.5 pounds; loaded, 8.1 pounds
Overall length: stock folded, 17.5 inches; stock extended, 27.2 inches
Barrel length: 7.7 inches
Sights: Front, post, with protector; rear: flip aperture, 300 and 500m.
Cyclic rate: 600 to 750 rounds/min

IMI Galil MAR

IMI 5.56x45mm TAR-21 Tavor Assault Rifle

The TAR-21 Tavor assault rifle was developed by Israel Military Industries in cooperation with the Israeli Defense Forces starting in 1993 to provide a successor to the various small arms then in service. During 2001 and 2002, the Tavor underwent operational testing against the US M4 carbine from which the Tavor emerged as the preferred choice. By mid-2003 the first infantry brigades were replacing their existing M16s with the Tavor.

In December 2002 it was announced that India had ordered the Tavor rifle. The agreement was for an initial $20 million, although the exact quantity of rifles involved was not stated. The agreement also included 5.56x45mm ammunition, night sights, laser rangefinders and other equipment. India is also considering the acquisition of "several thousand" Tavor rifles to equip units currently armed with 7.62mm AKM assault rifles.

Despite unclear prospects for the TAR-21 family of weapons, IMI continues the development of the Tavor as the Tavor OICW project that will combine the modified Tavor rifle with the advanced electronic sighting and fire control technology. If successful, this will create a system generally similar to that developed in the USA under the OICW/ Land Warrior project. IMI also is developing a less ambitious modification called the Tavor-2. This rifle is a heavily modified MTAR-21 assault rifle, with a short 10-inch barrel and modified stock layout and controls. The rail is raised above the rifle housing and the standard scope now is a more affordable Meprolight reflex scope. This version, unlike the original TAR-21 family, also will be available in a submachine gun variant, chambered in either 9x19mm or .40 S&W.

The Tavor TAR-21 is a gas-operated, select-fire, magazine-fed bullpup assault rifle. It is available in several configurations that differ in barrel lengths and accessories. The basic configuration is the TAR-21 assault rifle with 18.1-inch barrel. The compact assault rifle, called CTAR-21, has a 15-inch barrel, and finally, the micro assault rifle, with a barrel length of only 10 inches, designated MTAR-21. In general, the TAR-21 represents the mainstream of the present assault rifle development. It shares all the "modern" features, such as bullpup layout, polymer construction, optical sights as primary, modular design

with several different configurations available. The TAR-21 has no conventional receiver. All parts are mounted within an impact-resistant polymer housing, reinforced with steel inserts as necessary. Access to all the internal parts is accomplished by the opening the hinged buttplate, which is swung down for inspection and disassembly. The TAR-21 utilizes a long piston stroke, rotating bolt-action, with the gas piston attached to the bolt carrier. The gas cylinder is located above the barrel and is completely enclosed by the housing. The rotating bolt is similar to that of the M16 and has seven lugs. There are ejection ports on both sides of the rifle and right or left side ejection can be selected by installing the bolt with the ejector mounted on the right or on the left. The bolt carrier rides on a single guide rod, with the recoil spring located above it inside the hollow gas piston rod, similar to the AK system. The charging handle is located at the front left side of the rifle and does not reciprocate. Charging handle slots are cut on the both sides of the housing, so the handle can be installed on either side of the weapon. The ambidextrous selector switch is located above the pistol grip. The TAR-21 utilizes STANAG-compliant, M16 type magazines, with standard capacity of 30 rounds. The TAR-21 can be fitted with a 40x46mm M203 underbarrel grenade launcher

The TAR-21 has no conventional sights. It is fitted with a MIL-STD-1913 rail on the top of the rifle. Presently the standard sight for the TAR-21 series rifles (except for the STAR-21 sniper rifle) is the Israeli-made ITL MARS, a reflex-type sight with the built-in laser aimer.

SPECIFICATIONS:

Model:	TAR-21	CTAR-21	MTAR-21	STAR-21
Role:	Assault rifle	Commando	Special forces	Sharpshooter
Caliber:	5.56x45mm	5.56x45mm NATO	5.56x45mm NATO	5.56x45mm NATO or 9x19mm Parabellum
Operation:	gas, select-fire for all			
Locking:	rotary bolt	rotary bolt	rotary bolt	rotary bolt
Feed:	20- or 30-round box magazine for all			
Empty weight:	7.5 pounds	5.6 pounds	6.4 pounds	7.5 pounds
Combat:	9.8 pounds	7.8 pounds	8.7 pounds	9.8 pounds
Overall length:	28.4 inches	22.5 inches	18.9 inches	28.4 inches
Barrel length:	18.1 inches	15 inches	9.8 inches	18.1 inches
Sights:	integral red-dot and laser designator for all			
Cyclic rate:	750 to 900 rounds per minute			

IMI Tavor TAR-21

Italy

Beretta 5.56mm 70/90 Assault Rifles

Beretta Spa began development of a new assault rifle chambered in 5.56x45mm in 1968. The resulting rifle was shown in 1972 and was adopted by the Italian Special Forces, as well as a few foreign armies. The rifle was designated AR-70/223, and was available in three basic versions. The basic assault rifle AR-70/223, a carbine SC-70/223 with a folding stock, and a special carbine SCS-70/223 with folding stock and a shortened barrel. A light machine gun variation with a heavy quick detachable barrel also was developed, but never produced in quantity.

The basic AR70/223, however had some flaws, and when the Italian army decided to replace its 7.62x51mm BM 59 rifles with a new rifle in 5.56x45mm, Beretta submitted an upgraded version of the 70/223 in 1985. This rifle was adopted in 1990 as the AR-70/90 assault rifle, along with two other versions. The SC-70/90 had the same barrel length, but with a folding buttstock and the SCP-70/90 carbine had a shortened barrel and folding stock. A heavy-barreled squad automatic weapon with heavy barrel and detachable bipod is available as AS-70/90. Besides being general issue with the Italian Army the AR70/90 is offered for export. The 70/90 rifle is also available in semiautomatic only.

The AR-70/223 and AR-70/90 rifles are similar in design, but with some differences. The following description is for the AR-70/90 with differences from the 70/223 noted, where appropriate.

The AR-70/90 is a gas-operated, magazine-fed, select-fire rifle. The receiver is made of stamped sheet steel and consists of upper and lower halves connected by pins at the front and rear. For maintenance and field stripping the rear pin is pushed out and the receiver is separated by rotating it upward on the front pin. If required, the front pin can also be removed, much like the AR15/M16. The AR-70/223 upper receiver is square, but this did not provide sufficient strength and the AR170/90 receiver was changed to a trapezoidal shape.

The gas operation of the AR-70/90 is conventional, with a long-stroke gas piston, located above the barrel. The operating rod is linked to the bolt carrier using the charging handle to lock it in place. The recoil spring surrounds the gas piston/operating rod. The gas block has a two-position regulator and a gas cutoff that is automatically operated by raising the grenade sight. The rotating bolt and locking arrangement is similar to that of AK-type rifles, with two large lugs lock into a trunnion welded into the receiver.

The barrel is attached to the receiver using a barrel nut, so that barrel replacement can be carried out with minimum headspace adjustments. The bore is chrome-plated.

The fire control mechanism allows for semiautomatic and full automatic fire on the AR-70/223 rifles and for semiautomatic, three-round bursts and full automatic fire on AR70/90 rifles. The selector switch is ambidextrous on AR-70/90 series rifles, and is located on the right side of the receiver on AR-70/223 series rifles.

The AR70/90 feeds from an M16-type STANAG compliant magazine, with an ambidextrous release button located at the both sides of the magazine well. On the AR-70/223 rifles, feeding was from a proprietary magazine, with the release located between the magazine and the trigger guard. Both rifle feature a bolt stop, which holds the bolt open when the last round is fired. The bolt release is on the left side of the receiver above the magazine well.

AR-70/90 rifle sights are a hooded front blade on the top of the gas block, and an aperture rear sight, marked for 250 and 400 meters range. The top surface of the receiver is fitted with a MIL-STD 1913 accessory rail. A detachable carrying handle is available for all AR-70/90 series rifles.

SPECIFICATIONS: (Data for AR70/90)

Caliber: 5.56x45mm
Operation: gas, select-fire
Locking: rotating bolt
Feed: 30-round detachable box magazine
Empty weight: AR70/90, SC70/90 and SCP70/90, 8.9 pounds; SCP70/90 with grenade launcher, 9.3 pounds
Overall length: AR70/90, SC70/90 with stock extended, 39.3 inches; SC70/90 with stock folded, 29.8 inches; SCP70/90 stock extended, 35.7 inches; SCP70/90 with stock folded, 26.1 inches
Barrel length: AR70/90, SC70/90, 17.7 inches; SCP70/90, 14.5 inches
Sights: Front, post, adjustable for elevation; rear: two-position aperture, 250 and 400m, adjustable for elevation and windage

BERETTA 70/90

The Italian trooper on the left is armed with a beretta 70/90.

HOWA Type 89

Japan

Howa 5.56x45mm Type 89 Assault Rifle

The Howa Type 89 is a light assault rifle. Howa Machinery Limited cooperated in the development under a contract with the Japan Defense Agency.

The Type 89 rifle comes in two versions: one with a folding tubular light alloy stock with a plastic buttplate and the other with a fixed polymer stock.

The Japanese military purchased 2,948 Type 89 assault rifles during 2002.

The Type 89 rifle is gas-operated and uses a unique piston and cylinder system with a long gas expansion chamber. The piston's diameter at the front is smaller than that of the rear and is positioned in the center of the cylinder some distance from the gas port. The expanding propellant gas is drawn into the cylinder, causing a slight delay and starting bolt carrier movement with a light blow, thus enhancing reliability and component service life.

A seven-lug rotating bolt that locks into a barrel extension locks the breech. The receiver and the trigger housing are pressed and welded steel welding.

A separate and removable three-round burst device is installed in the rear portion of the trigger housing. This device is completely separate from the basic fire control mechanism that controls semiautomatic or fully automatic firing.

A high-efficiency muzzle brake/flash suppressor reduces felt recoil. A bipod is standard but is easily removable.

SPECIFICATIONS:

Caliber: 5.56x45mm
Operation: gas, select-fire with three-round burst limiter
Locking: rotating bolt
Feed: 20- or 30-round detachable box magazine
Empty weight: 7.7 pounds
Overall length: stock folded, 26.4 inches; stock extended, 36.1 inches
Barrel length: 16.5 inches
Sights: front, square post, adjustable for zero; rear: aperture, adjustable for elevation and windage
Cyclic rate: 650-850 rounds/min

Korea, South

Daewoo DAR 21 5.56x45mm Assault Rifle

The Daewoo DAR 21 assault rifle is essentially the Daewoo K2 and K1A1 5.56mm assault rifles converted to bullpup configuration. The bullpup configuration enables a longer barrel to be fitted, while the overall weapon length is compact for use in confined spaces or from vehicles. Another innovation is the introduction of a MIL-STD-1913 on the receiver for optical or night sight installation. Backup iron sights are provided. A short MIL-STD-1913 rail is also located below the handguard for accessory attachment.

The stock and furniture are molded from high-strength polymer. M16/STANAG compliant magazines can be used. The barrel length is rifled to accommodate either M193 or SS109/M855 5.56x45mm cartridges to be fired. The muzzle device reduces both muzzle climb and flash. The selector switch is set into the stock on the left side with safe, semiautomatic, three-round-burst and full automatic selections.

A carbine version of the DAR 21 with a 17.7 inch barrel is under consideration.

SPECIFICATIONS:
Caliber: 5.56x45mm M193 or SS109/M855
Operation: gas, select-fire
Feed: 20-round or 30-round detachable box magazine
Empty weight: 8.4 pounds
Overall length: 30.7 inches
Barrel length: 20 inches
Sights: optical, 3x adjustable in windage and elevation; backup iron sights
Cyclic rate: 800 rounds/min
Max effective range: 800 m

Daewoo K1A1 5.56mm Short Assault Rifle

The Daewoo K1A1 5.56x45mm short assault rifle uses the same lower receiver as the K2 rifle, but the upper receiver is different, combining features of AR15/M16 and AR-18 rifles. The gas system of the K1A1 is the direct-impingement type used in AR15/M16 rifles. The bolt carrier is similar in shape to that of the AR15/M16 but uses the dual rod and recoil spring design of the AR-18. The rods are astride the bolt carrier and engage a lug at the top.

The charging handle is identical to that of the K2 5.56mm assault rifle and is dovetailed into the bolt carrier. Ejection is also identical to the K2, with a fixed ejector in the lower receiver. K1A1 and K2 extractors are identical but differ from those of the Armalite rifles. The Daewoo extractor is longer to provide increased force on the case, in an attempt to resolve a longstanding problem with AR15/M16-type rifles.

The collapsible wire stock of the K1A1 is similar to that of the US M3 .45 ACP submachine gun. The muzzle brake/flash suppressor eliminates flash and also reduces muzzle climb.

SPECIFICATIONS:
Caliber: 5.56x45mm
Operation: gas, select-fire with three-round burst
Feed: 20- or 30-round detachable box magazine
Empty weight: without magazine, 6.3 pounds
Overall length: stock retracted, 25.7 inches; stock extended, 32.9 inches
Barrel length: 14.3 inches
Rifling: 6 grooves, rh, 1 turn in 12 inches
Sights: front, post; rear: aperture
Cyclic rate: 700 to 900 rounds/min
Max effective range: 250m

DAEWOO K1AI

DAEWOO K2

POF G3

Daewoo K2 5.56x45mm Assault Rifle

The Daewoo K2 assault rifle is a gas-operated select-fire rifle with a folding polymer stock. The gas-operated system employs a long-stroke piston and bolt carrier, similar to that of the AK rifles, although the rotating bolt is similar to that of AR15/M16 rifles. The upper and lower receivers are machined from aluminum alloy forgings, and although the lower receiver appears similar to that of the M16, the two are not interchangeable. The selector lever rotates in either direction and has four positions for safe, automatic fire, three-round burst and semiautomatic. The burst control mechanism does not reset when the trigger is released; when the trigger is pulled a second time, the burst picks up from where it stopped in the previous cycle.

The barrel is fitted with a muzzle brake/compensator; without a bottom slot to prevent dust being raised by muzzle blast. The stock folds to the right of the receiver and uses a locking system similar to that of the FN FNC. The rear sight has a two-position aperture with a cam-actuated elevation control. The normal position of the aperture offers a small aperture for precise shooting. The other position of the aperture provides two small dots for night shooting. Front and rear sights are provided with luminous dots for firing in poor light.

SPECIFICATIONS:

Caliber: 5.56x45mm
Operation: gas, select-fire with three-round burst
Locking: rotating bolt
Feed: 30-round detachable box magazine
Empty weight: 7.2 pounds
Overall length: stock folded, 28.7 inches; stock extended, 38.6 inches
Barrel length: without compensator, 18.3 inches
Rifling: 6 grooves, rh, 1 turn in 7.3 inches
Max effective range: 600 m

Pakistan

Pakistan Ordnance Factories 7.62x51mm G3 Rifle

Pakistan Ordnance Factories (POF) manufacture Heckler and Koch G3 assault rifles under license. Both the G3A3 (fixed stock) and G3K (collapsible stock) versions are manufactured for the Pakistan armed forces and for export. These rifles are virtually identical to the German originals but POF data is provided here, as there are minor differences in technical description.

SPECIFICATIONS:

Caliber: 7.62x51mm NATO
Operation: roller-delayed blowback, select-fire
Feed: 20-round detachable box magazine
Empty weight: G3A3, 9.7 pounds; G3P4, 10.4 pounds
Overall length: G3A3, overall, 40.3 inches; G3P4, stock retracted, 33.1 inches; stock extended, 40.2 inches
Barrel length: 17.7 inches
Sights: front, hooded fixed post; rear: rotary with 4 adjustments (100m 'V' notch, 200m, 300m and 400m) and aperture adjustable for windage and elevation
Cyclic rate: 500 to 600 rounds/min

Philippines

Floro International M1 Garand Rifle Conversion

Although the M1 Garand .30-06 rifle has long since passed from operational use with major military forces, large numbers are stockpiled in the Philippines where their use is limited by a lack of .30-06 ammunition and the eight-round clips. Floro International Corporation has proposed that these stocks be modernized to M14 standard, firing standard 7.62x51mm NATO ammunition from 20-round magazines. The conversion procedure includes reducing barrel length, modifying fire control and receivers as well as adding a 20-round magazine. Barrel length is reduced by 1.6 inches.

It has been proposed that a dual track program be initiated. The initial track will involve approximately 50,000 operational M1 rifles while the optional second phase will involve bringing an unspecified number of non-operational rifles up to the standard of the first track rifles.

The converted rifles will be available to the Philippine military to augment its current rifle inventory or for issue to internal security and similar organizations.

If initiated, the program is estimated to take five years to complete.

SPECIFICATIONS:

Caliber: 7.62x51mm NATO
Operation: gas, semiautomatic
Feed: 20-round detachable box magazine
Empty weight: 8.8 pounds
Overall length: 40.9 inches
Barrel length: 22.4 inches
Sights: Front, fixed post; rear: aperture, adjustable for windage and elevation.

STANDARD M1 GARAND RIFLE

M1 CONVERSION RIFLE

FLORO INTERNATIONAL M1 Garand Conversion

Poland

Beryl 5.56x45mm Model 96 Assault Rifle

The Beryl Model 96 assault rifle is derived from the earlier Tantal 5.45x39mm assault rifle, modified to fire 5.56x45mm NATO ammunition. Both the Tantal and Beryl Model 96 assault rifle is based on the Russian AK-74S. The main difference between the original AK-74, apart from the 5.56mm caliber, is that the Polish rifles have three fire modes: semiautomatic, three-round burst and fully automatic. The Beryl has a twin-strut stock with rubber buttplate that folds to the right side of the receiver. All furniture is high-impact polymer.

SPECIFICATIONS:
Caliber: 5.56x45mm NATO
Operation: gas, select-fire, three-round burst
Locking: rotating bolt
Feed: 20- or 30-round detachable box magazine
Empty weight: 7.39 pounds
Overall length: stock folded, 29.2 inches; stock extended, 37.1 inches
Barrel length: 18 inches
Sights: Front: post; rear: U-notch, calibrated from 100 to 1,000m
Cyclic rate: 690 rounds/min
Max effective range: 600m

Mini-Beryl 5.56mm Model 96 Short Assault Rifle

The Mini-Beryl 5.56mm Model 96 short assault rifle is based on the Russian AK-74S and the earlier Polish Onyx rifles. The main difference compared to the original AK-74, other than the 5.56x45mm caliber, is that the Mini-Beryl has three fire modes: semiautomatic, three-round burst and fully automatic.

The rear and front sights are provided with luminescent dots to assist aiming under low light conditions. The rear sight is calibrated in 100, 200 and 400 meter increments. Other sighting systems available include a passive night sight, a telescope, a red dot collimator sight and a telescope with a laser target indicator.

SPECIFICATIONS:
Caliber: 5.56x45mm
Operation: gas, select-fire, three-round burst
Locking: rotating bolt
Feed: 20- or 30-round detachable box magazine
Empty weight: 6.6 pounds
Overall length: stock folded, 20.7 inches; stock extended, 28.7 inches
Barrel length: 9.3 inches
Sights: front, post; rear: U-notch, calibrated in 100, 200 and 400m increments
Cyclic rate: 690 rounds/min
Max effective range: 400m

Portugal

INDEP 7.62mm Heckler and Koch G3A2, A3 and A4 Rifles

INDEP manufactured Heckler and Koch G3 rifles under license. INDEP rifles are identical to the German models. The INDEP tooling was recently sold to an American firm, JLD Enterprises, which has undertaken production of semiautomatic only versions of these rifles in the United States under the designation PTR-91. These rifles are identical in every way to Heckler and Koch HK91 semiautomatic rifles.

SPECIFICATIONS:
Caliber: 7.62x51mm
Operation: delayed blowback, select-fire
Feed: 20-round detachable box magazine
Empty weight: fixed stock, empty, 9.7 pounds; retractable stock, empty, 10.4 pounds
Overall length: retracted stock, 33.1 inches; fixed stock, 40.3 inches
Barrel length: 17.7 inches
Rifling: 4 grooves, rh, one turn in 12 inches
Sights: Front, post; rear: V battle sight at 100m. Apertures for 200, 300 and 400m
Cyclic rate: 500 to 600 rounds/min
Max effective range: 400m

MINI-BERYL Model 96

BERYL Model 96

Romania

RomArm 5.45x39mm Assault Rifles

When the Romanian concern RomArm began production of 5.45x39mm assault rifles, they did not produce a direct copy of the AK-74 but converted the 7.62x39mm AKM to 5.45x39mm. This initial model lacked the muzzle brake of the AK-74 and featured a solid wood stock. This model retained the usual Romanian trademark of a forward pistol grip. Eventually a close copy of the standard AK-74, with the upper handguard extended forward to the gas port replaced the original version.

The latest version is almost identical to the original AK-74. There is also a short-barrel model, described below, and a 5.56x45mm model designated Model 97. The RomArm 5.45mm AK-74 models are identical in operation to their Russian counterparts, where greater detail can be found. All models have a fire selector for semiautomatic, full automatic and three-round burst. In addition, all models can accommodate a 40mm grenade launcher.

RomArm rifles are produced in three versions. The base model is identical to the AK-74 for all intents and purposes. The Model 86 is the same, but with a side folding stock. The third model, intended for special forces, has the same side folding frame stock as the Model 86, but the barrel length is reduced from the standard 16.3 inches to 11.9 inches. This short barreled model has a flash hider at the muzzle, and there is no provision for a bayonet.

A training rifle in .22LR was produced at one time.

SPECIFICATIONS: Short Barrel Version

Caliber: 5.45x39mm and 5.56x45mm
Operation: gas, select-fire, three-round burst
Locking: rotating bolt
Feed: 30-round detachable box magazine
Empty weight: 6.4 pounds
Overall length: stock folded, 23.8 inches; stock extended, 31.7 inches
Barrel length: 11.9 inches
Sights: Front, blade; rear: fixed notch calibrated from 100 to 500m
Cyclic rate: 600 rounds/min
Max effective range: 500m

Standard Versions

Cartridge: 5.45x39mm and 5.56x45mm
Operation: gas, select-fire, three-round burst
Locking: rotating bolt
Feed: 30-round detachable box magazine
Empty weight: fixed stock, 7.6 pounds; Model 86, 6.9 pounds
Overall length: fixed stock, and Model 86, 37 inches; Model 86, stock folded, 28.9 inches
Barrel length: 16.3 inches
Sights: Front, blade; rear: fixed notch calibrated from 100-1,000 m
Cyclic rate: 600 rounds/min
Maximum effective range: 500 meters

RomArm 7.62x39mm AKM Assault Rifles

The standard Romanian armed forces assault rifle until recently was a variant of the Russian AKM manufactured by SN RomArm SA, although other variants of this model have been developed.

In August 1995, it was announced that India had contracted to purchase 100,000 AKM assault rifles from Romania at a cost of approximately $85 to $90 per unit. This purchase resulted from delays in the production schedule for the Indian INSAS small arms system. Israeli 5.56x45mm Tavor rifles will eventually replace these rifles as the result of a 2002 agreement between IMI and India.

For many years, Romanian Kalashnikovs could be readily recognized by the laminated wood forward pistol grip. This feature was discontinued on recent production models by a conventional handguard. In all other respects, RomArm AKM models are nearly identical to those of other nations.

RomArm 7.62mm AKM-based assault rifles are produced in four versions, as follows:

AKM Model 63

This is the base AKM with a fixed stock and a 415mm barrel length.

Model 65

This is basically the same as the Model 63 but with a standard AKM-pattern folding stock.

Model 90

The Model 90 is basically a Model 63 with a side-folding metal frame stock.

Model 90 short barrel

As the name implies, this is a Model 90 with side-folding frame stock, but with a shorter (302mm) barrel.

SPECIFICATIONS: Models 63, 65 and 90

Caliber: 7.62x39mm M1943
Operation: gas, select-fire
Locking: rotating bolt
Feed: 30-round detachable box magazine
Empty weight: Model 63, 7.6 pounds; Model 65, 7.1 pounds; Model 90, 6.9 pounds
Overall length: Models 63, 65 and 90, 34.6 inches; Model 65, stock folded, 25.2 inches; Model 90, stock folded, 26.6 inches
Barrel length: 16.3 inches
Sights: Front, blade; rear: fixed notch, calibrated from 100-1,000 m
Cyclic rate: 600 rounds/min
Max effective range: 1,000m

Model 90 Short Barrel

Caliber: 7.62x39mm M1943
Operation: gas, select-fire
Locking: rotating bolt
Feed: 20- or 30-round detachable box magazine
Empty weight: 7.5 pounds
Overall length: stock folded, 23.8 inches; stock extended, 31.7 inches
Barrel length: 11.9 inches
Sights: front, blade; rear: fixed notch, calibrated from 100-500 m
Cyclic rate: 600 rounds/min
Max effective range: 500m

Romanian AKM Model 63

Romanian AKM

Russia

7.62x39mm AKM Assault Rifle

Although no longer manufactured in Russia, the AKM remains in production elsewhere and is still widely employed throughout the world and is included for that reason.

The AKM assault rifle was first manufactured in 1959 and is a modernized version of the AK-47. A receiver of stamped steel replaced the forged and machined receiver of the AK-47.

There are several features that distinguish the AKM from the AK-47. On the AKM:

- There is a small recess in each side of the receiver that serves as a magazine guide.

- The lower handguard has a finger groove.

- The dust cover has transverse ribs.

- There is an additional bayonet lug under the gas port.

- The four gas escape holes on each side of the gas cylinder are missing

- The sight is graduated to 1,000 meters instead of to 800 meters.

- A small wedge-shaped compensator is fitted to the muzzle on all but the earliest production models.

There is no essential difference between the functioning of the AKM and the AK-47. There is an additional assembly in the trigger mechanism, a device to delay the fall of the hammer during automatic fire until the breech is closed and locked.

SPECIFICATIONS: AKM

Caliber: 7.62x39mm M1943
Operation: gas, select-fire
Locking: rotating bolt
Feed: 30-round detachable box magazine
Empty weight: 8.5 pounds
Overall length: 34.7 inches
Barrel length: 16.3 inches
Sights: front, post; rear: U-notch
Cyclic rate: 600 rounds/min
Maximum effective range: 300 m

5.45x39mm AK-74 and AK-74M assault rifles

The AK-74 assault rifle is a smaller-caliber version of the AKM. It is similar in size, but slightly heavier. The effective range has decreased, but is still within infantry fighting ranges. The magazine has the same capacity (30 rounds) as that of the AKM; and the 40-round RPK-74 light machine gun magazine is interchangeable with that of the AK-74.

The AK-74 remains in production by several nations outside Russia, where it has been replaced by the AK-100 series rifles. Some of these nations, such as Bulgaria, Hungary, Poland and Romania, also manufacture the AK-74 to fire 5.56x45mm NATO ammunition to make their products more attractive to prospective purchasers in the West.

The early plywood furniture resembles that of the AKM, except that the AK-74 has a horizontal groove along each side of the stock. This is probably a caliber rapid-recognition feature rather than an aid to holding, and, together with the muzzle brake, it forms the quickest way of picking out an AK-74 from other AK-series rifles. Late production AK-74s have black polymer furniture.

On early AKS-74s, the folding stock is a tubular skeleton that folds by swinging to the left where it lies alongside the receiver. Recent AK-74M folding stock versions have a solid plastic stock. All versions of the AK-74 can be used in conjunction with underbarrel 40mm GP-15, GP-25 Kastyor or GP-30 grenade launchers.

The AK-74 is notable for its highly efficient muzzle brake that allows the user to fire bursts without the muzzle moving away from the line of sight. The brake works by allowing the emerging gases to strike a flat plate at the front of the assembly. This deflects the gas and produces forward thrust. To counter the upward movement during automatic fire, gases escaping through three small ports on the upper part of the muzzle brake force the muzzle down, compensating for muzzle rise.

AK-74

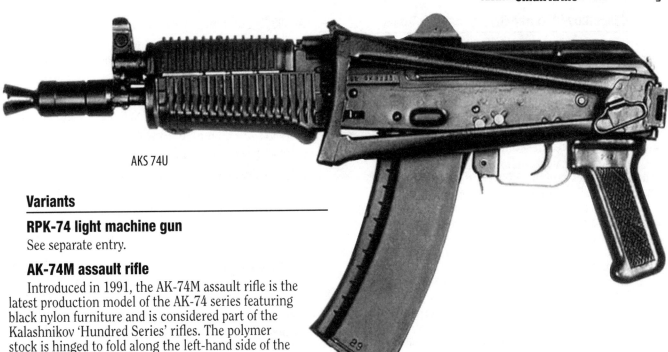

AKS 74U

Variants

RPK-74 light machine gun
See separate entry.

AK-74M assault rifle
Introduced in 1991, the AK-74M assault rifle is the latest production model of the AK-74 series featuring black nylon furniture and is considered part of the Kalashnikov 'Hundred Series' rifles. The polymer stock is hinged to fold along the left-hand side of the receiver.

AK-74MN2 assault rifle
(Note: Russian military practice is to change designations to indicate the type of special equipment installed on a small arm, hence the different designations for otherwise identical rifles fitted with different night vision optics.)

The AK-74M fitted with a 1PN58 night sight on a detachable mounting.

AK-74MN3 assault rifle
The AK-74M fitted with a 1PN51 night sight on a detachable mounting.

AKS-74Y
A version of the AKS-74 with a special barrel surrounded by a suppressor sleeve is known as the AKS-74Y. This model fires subsonic ammunition.

SPECIFICATIONS: AK-74M
Caliber 5.45x39mm
Operation: gas, select-fire
Locking: rotating bolt
Feed: 30-round plastic box magazine
Empty weight: 7.5 pounds
Overall length: 37.1 inches; stock folded, 27.8 inches
Barrel length: 16.3 inches
Sights: front, post; rear: U-notch
Cyclic rate: 650 rounds/min
Maximum combat range: 440m

5.45x39mm AKS-74U Short Carbine

The AKS-74U short carbine, also known as the AKSU-74, is a variant of the AKS-74. Izhmash designed it but all Russian production has been at Tula KBP. The AKS74U differs from previous AK models by having the receiver cover hinged at the trunnion block so it hinges forward on opening rather than lifting off. The AKS-74U is often referred to as a submachine gun and is employed as such, but its 5.45 x 45mm caliber places it in the short carbine category.

The barrel is fitted with a cylindrical muzzle device that incorporates a bell-mouthed flash suppressor. It is understood that the receiver of the attachment forms an expansion chamber that performs two functions. It gives a sudden pressure drop before the bullet exits the muzzle, reducing the high pressure in the gas tube and on the gas piston caused by tapping off propellant gas close to the chamber. Second, it reduces the flash and blast that would be inherent from firing a rifle cartridge from such a short barrel.

The rear sight is a simple flip-over pattern with two U-notches, marked for 200 and 400 meters. The skeleton metal stock folds to the left and locks into a spring-loaded lug on the side of the receiver. Other than the shortness of the gas piston, recoil spring and guide rod, the internal mechanism is virtually identical to that of the AK-74 rifle.

An unusual combat accessory produced for it is the BS-1 silenced underbarrel grenade launcher firing a shaped charge grenade.

Variants

AKS-74U variants chambered in 5.56x45mm NATO have been manufactured in Bulgaria, Poland and the former Yugoslavia. All have been offered for export sales.

AKS-74UN3
This version is equipped to mount various forms of night sights.

SPECIFICATIONS
Caliber: 5.45x39mm
Operation: gas, select-fire
Feed: 30-round detachable box magazine
Empty weight: 5.6 pounds
Overall length: stock folded, 19.3 inches; stock extended, 28.7 inches
Barrel length: 8.1 inches
Cyclic rate: 650 to 735 rounds/min
Max effective range: 300m

Kalashnikov 'Hundred Series' Assault Rifles

There are five basic rifles in the Kalashnikov "Hundred Series." Two of them assault rifles, while the other three fall into the carbine category. All five weapons incorporate the latest improvements to the Kalashnikov rifle family and are manufactured using modern materials and production techniques. In order to make these "export model" firearms attractive to a wide range of potential purchasers the models are produced in several calibers.

The two full-scale assault rifles in the Kalashnikov "Hundred Series" are the AK101 and AK103, the AK101 chambered in 5.56x45mm while the AK103 fires the 7.62x39mm cartridge. Both rifles are based on the AK-74M, are visually identical and are constructed with provision to accommodate a wide range of optical and night sighting equipment. The 5.45x39mm AK-74M is also included as a member of the series.

Carbines include the AK102 in 5.56x45mm, while the AK104 is chambered in 7.62x39mm cartridge. The AK105 fires the 5.45x39mm cartridge and will eventually replace the AKS-74U with RFAS armed forces. All three carbine models are visually identical and can accommodate a wide range of optical and night sighting equipment.

All rifles have cold hammer forged barrels, are provided with black polymer furniture and have a black phosphate finish. The stocks can be folded forward on the left-hand side of the receiver, although this interferes with the optics mount. On both rifles the plastic forend is ribbed to improve the grip. The muzzle brake is identical to that of the AK-74M. On the AK103 the standard AK-74M type muzzle brake can be replaced by a PBS flash suppressor to reduce the firing signature. Both weapons can be fitted with 40mm GP-25 or GP-30 grenade launchers.

Variants

AK101 5.56x45mm: Introduced in 1993.

AK101-1 5.56x45mm: Semiautomatic version intended for use by security forces.

AK101-2 5.56x45mm: Three-shot burst mechanism.

AK101N2 5.56x45mm: With 1PN58 night sight.

AK101N3 5.56x45mm: With 1PN51 night sight.

AK102 5.56x45mm: Carbine with short barrel.

AK103 7.62x39mm: Introduced in 1993.

AK103-1 7.62x39mm: Semiautomatic version intended for use by security forces. A variant of this model is marketed by Kalashnikov USA.

AK103-2 7.62x39mm: Three-shot burst mechanism.

AK103N2 7.62x39mm: With 1PN58 night sight.

AK103N3 7.62x39mm: With 1PN51 night sight.

AK104 7.62x39mm: Short barrel carbine.

AK105 5.45x39mm: Short barrel carbine.

AK105-1 5.45x39mm: Short barrel semiautomatic carbine intended for use by security forces.

AK105-2 5.45x39mm: Short barrel carbine. Three-shot burst mechanism.

AK105N2 5.45x39mm: Short barrel carbine with 1PN58 night sight.

AK105N3 5.45x39mm: Short Barrel carbine with 1PN51 night sight.

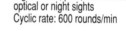

SPECIFICATIONS: Data for AK101, AK103 shown in parentheses

Caliber: 5.56x45mm (7.62x39mm)
Operation: gas, select-fire
Locking: rotating bolt
Feed: 30-round detachable box magazine
Empty weight: 7.5 pounds (7.3 pounds)
Overall length: 37.1 inches; stock folded, 27.6 inches
Barrel length: 16.3 inches
Sights: front, post; rear: U-notch; provision for fitting optical or night sights
Cyclic rate: 600 rounds/min
Max effective range: 500 meters

Short carbine versions

Caliber: AK102, 5.56x45mm; AK104, 7.62x39mm; AK105, 5.45x39mm
Operation: gas, select-fire
Feed: 30-round detachable box magazine
Empty weight: AK102, 6.6 pounds AK104, 6.4 pounds AK105, 6.6 pounds
Empty weight: AK102, 7.1 pounds; AK104, 6.9 pounds; AK105, 7.2 pounds
Overall length: stock folded, 23.1 inches; stock extended, 32.4 inches
Barrel length: 12.4 inches
Sights: front, post; rear: U-notch; provision for fitting optical or night sights
Cyclic rate: 600 rounds/min

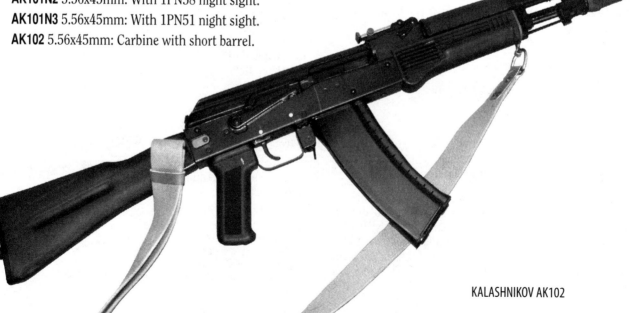

KALASHNIKOV AK102

KALASHNIKOV AK103

AK-107 and AK-108 Assault Rifles

The AK-107 and the AK-108 are 5.45x39mm and 5.56x45mm versions, respectively, of the same rifle. The designation AK does not indicate Avtomat Kalashnikova but Alexandrov/Kalashnikov, indicating the incorporation of a new gas system for AK rifles designed by Yuriy Alexandrov. These new rifles were derived from the AL-7 experimental rifle of the early 1970s. The AL-7 incorporated a new 'balanced' gas operating system developed by Tsniitochmash that essentially eliminated felt recoil and muzzle rise. The system was modified by Alexandrov, then a junior engineer at Izhmash, and prototypes were produced under the designation AL-7. The AL-7 was considered too complex and expensive for production at that time, and no further development occurred until the mid-1990s, when Alexandrov, then a senior engineer, updated his design for production as a less expensive alternative to the AN-94.

The new rifle differs only slightly from the original AL-7. The AK-107/AK-108 receiver is not fluted, and a three-round burst feature has been added. There is otherwise little difference between AL-7 prototypes and current rifles.

The AK-107 and the AK-108 represent a significant change to the original Kalashnikov operating system. The new rifles incorporate a "balanced" system derived from Newton's third law, which mandates that for any action, there is an equal and opposite reaction. Alexandrov's system uses two operating rods that move in opposite directions, thereby providing balance that cancels out the reaction portion of the operating cycle. The upper operating rod has a gas piston facing forward, while the bolt carrier also has a gas piston. The gas tube at the forward end of the rifle is double-ended to accommodate the two rods. The enlarged gas tube cover of the upper handguard guides both rods. When the rifle is fired, gas from the gas port enters the gas

AK-107

tube, driving the bolt carrier to the rear and driving the counter recoil upper rail forward. The critical timing of the reciprocating parts is accomplished by a toothed sprocket wheel that links and synchronizes both components, causing them to reach their maximum extension, or null point where forces are exactly equal, at precisely the same instant. Felt recoil is thus virtually eliminated, enhancing accuracy and assisting control during full automatic fire. The travel distance of the AK-107/AK-108 reciprocating parts is less than that for other Kalashnikov designs, so the cyclic rate is higher, at 850 to 900 rounds per minute However, as the felt recoil is virtually eliminated, the manufacturer claims that accuracy is enhanced by 1.5 to 2 times, especially during burst fire.

In addition to semiautomatic and full automatic a three-round burst capability has been incorporated. The system on the AK-107/AK-108 resets to three-round burst each time the trigger is released, even if only one or two rounds have been fired.

External differences between the AK-107/AK-108 and its predecessors are minor. They include a modified ejection port and thicker operating rod cover. The receiver cover is hinged at the front, much like the AKS-74U. The rear sight is also attached directly to the receiver cover rather than to the receiver itself. Optical and night sights can be installed, along with 40mm GP-25 grenade launchers.

SPECIFICATIONS: Data for AK-107 (AK-108 in parentheses)

Caliber: 5.45x39mm (5.56x45mm)
Operation: gas, select-fire, three-round burst or fully automatic
Locking: rotating bolt
Feed: 30-round detachable box magazine
Empty weight: 7.6 pounds
Overall length: 37.1 inches; stock folded, 27.6 inches
Barrel length: 16.3 inches
Sights: Front, protected post; rear: U-notch; provision for fitting optical or night sights
Cyclic rate: 850 rounds/min (900 rounds/min)
Max effective range: 500-600 meters

9x39mm AS Silent Assault Rifle

The 9mm AS/Val silent assault rifle (also referred to as 6P30) can trace its origins back to the time when Gary Powers was shot down with his U-2 reconnaissance aircraft over the former USSR in May 1960. Among his equipment was a silenced pistol that so impressed Soviet military officials that a requirement for a similar weapon was issued. The Central Scientific Research Institute for Precision Machinery Construction (Tsniitochmash) at Klimovsk, examined the captured pistol leading to the creation of a series of silenced weapons.

Included in this series are two silenced rifles, the AS (or Val - 'rampart' or 'shaft') and the VSS (or Vintorez - thread-cutter). Both these weapons are based on the receiver of the MA submachine gun and differ only in detail. The AS primarily is intended for use with the 9x39mm SP-6 cartridge, while the SP-5 is intended to be used with the VSS, although cartridges can be interchanged.

The designers of the AS regard it not as a single firearm, but as a 'complex', a term encompassing not just the rifle, but the ammunition and accessories as well.

The 9mm AS silenced assault rifle uses a modified Kalashnikov action – a gas-operated rotating bolt with an integral sound suppressor — to provide a very low noise signature along with far greater range and penetrating power than is usual with suppressed weapons. The cartridge is a 9x39mm round, essentially a necked up 7.62x39mm, firing a heavy 250-grain bullet at a muzzle velocity below the speed of sound. Two cartridges are available – the SP5 ball and the SP6 armor piercing. The weapon is capable of semiautomatic or automatic fire without sustaining damage to the sound suppressor.

The suppressor used with both the AS and the VSS relies on a dual-chamber principle. As the propellant gases produced after firing a cartridge pass down the barrel, they can escape through specially designed barrel perforations to enter the first chamber. Inside the chamber, expanding gases lose pressure and heat prior to passing through a series of mesh screens which break up the gas stream still further before passing them into the outer portions of the suppressor. The resulting sound signature is far less than that from an unsuppressed rifle.

The rifle has a short forend and a side-folding tubular-steel skeleton stock. A built-in sight bracket on the left side of the receiver will mount any Russian military optical sight. Backup open sights are also provided.

The 20-round magazine carries a unique series of indentations to provide tactile identification and prevent confusing this magazine with similar Kalashnikov type magazines. The AS can also use the 10-round box magazine of the VSS rifle.

The 9x39mm SP-5 Ball and SP-6 armor-piercing rounds were developed to provide optimum terminal ballistics at the

AS Silent

9A-91

subsonic velocities required to optimize sound suppressor effectiveness. The SP-6 and the less-expensive PAB-9 9x39mm were specifically designed to defeat body armor up to Class III at ranges up to 400 meters.

SPECIFICATIONS:
Caliber: 9x39mm SP-5, SP-6, PAB-9
Operation: gas, select-fire
Locking: rotating bolt
Feed: 10- or 20-round detachable box magazine
Empty weight: 5.5 pounds
Overall length: stock folded, 25.6 inches; stock extended, 34.4 inches
Cyclic rate: 800 to 900 rounds/min
Max effective range: day, 400m; night, 300m

9A-91 Series Compact Assault Rifles

The 9A-91 Series was developed to meet a military and interior ministry requirement for a compact, lightweight weapon for use at ranges up to 400 meters. The original 9A-91 was chambered for the 9x39mm SP-5/SP-6 cartridge developed by Tsniitochmash. The 9A-91 is the basic weapon in the A-91 family. The 9x39mm cartridge fires a heavy 259-grain bullet at subsonic velocity to achieve terminal effectiveness at the required ranges.

Other versions of the 9A-91 have been developed and offered for sale in 5.45x39mm (5.45A91); 5.56x45mm (5.56A91) and 7.62x39mm (7.62A91). A sniper variant, the VSK-94, is identical to the 9A-91, save for the rigid polymer stock, standard suppressor and PSO-1 optical sight.

The 9A-91 is a gas-operated, detachable box magazine fed, select-fire compact assault rifle. It can be equipped with a variety of accessories, including the GP-25 40mm underbarrel grenade launcher, PSO-1 4-power telescopic sight, suppressor, laser sight and night-vision devices. A special PK-01 collimating sight has been developed specifically for the 9A-91.

SPECIFICATIONS 9A-91 (VSK-94 in parentheses)
Caliber: 9x39mm, SP-5 ball or SP-6 armor-piercing, or PAB-9
Operation: gas, select-fire
Locking: rotating bolt
Feed: 20-round detachable box magazine
Empty weight: 4.6 pounds (6.4 pounds)
Overall length: stock folded, 15.1 inches; stock extended, 23.8 inches
Width: 1.7 inches
Sights: Front, fixed post; rear: flip aperture. Optical sights optional
Cyclic rate: 600 to 800 rounds/min (700-900 rounds/min)
Effective Cyclic rate: semiautomatic, 30 rounds/min; automatic, 90 rounds/min
Max effective range: 200m

Russian Federation troops in training.

Russian Federation

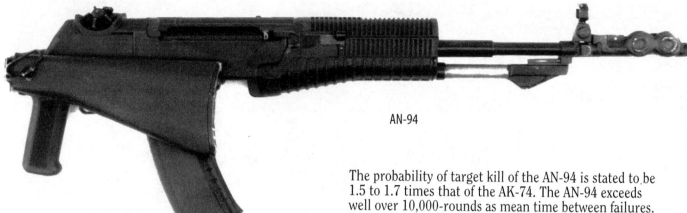

AN-94

5.45x45mm AN-94 Assault Rifle

The prototype of the AN-94 assault rifle was first seen publicly in May 1993, although the rifle had been under development for at least 10 years as part of the Abakan competition to develop a new assault rifle to replace the AK-74 in Russian service.

The Soviet/Russian military always considered the AK-74 an interim design between the AK-47/AKM series and their eventual replacement. Dr Gennady Nikonov began work on a series of prototypes in 1979, all of which involved the rapid firing of two or three rounds before the recoil impulse could be transmitted to the shooter, thus enhancing accuracy. Beginning with the NA-2, a series of 10 prototype models were developed, culminating with the 6P33 that was formally designated AN-94.

The primary design goals of the new rifle were reliability equal to or better than that for the Kalashnikov series, increased effectiveness and recoil reduction. According to Russian sources, all three goals were met.

The probability of target kill of the AN-94 is stated to be 1.5 to 1.7 times that of the AK-74. The AN-94 exceeds well over 10,000-rounds as mean time between failures. The overall design, the operating system and the muzzle compensator achieve the desired recoil reduction.

The AN-94 is still not in full production because of Russian military budget constraints. At least some of the pre-production batch of 1,000 rifles saw service in Chechnya during 1999. Official policy remains that the AN-94 will eventually replace all Kalashnikov series assault rifles in the RFAS military, although this might take a very long time and rumors persist that the AN-94 is simply too expensive and complicated for military production.

The AN-94 is gas-operated select-fire rifle, incorporating what is described as 'Blow Back Shifted Pulse' (BBSP) for operation. The rifle fires standard 5.45x39mm cartridges using 30-round magazines interchangeable with those from the AK-74. The AN-94 accepts any accessories used with the AK-74. The standard open sights are of a new design with a rotary pattern rear aperture sight turned to the desired range. Tritium inserts are optional. The maximum effective range using open sights is claimed to be 700 meters, increasing to 1,000 meters using the 1L29 4-power optical sight, a claim that is probably optimistic to say the least. The muzzle brake/compensator is an unusual two-chambered design that reduces both recoil and muzzle climb in full automatic mode.

AN-94

The selector switch is located on the left side of the rifle above the trigger guard and from front to rear is graduated Safe, Semi, Burst, and Full Automatic. The two-round burst feature of the AN-94 is different from that employed on any other rifle in that the burst cyclic rate is 1,800 rounds per minute improving the probability of a hit by reducing round-to-round dispersion. This extremely high rate of burst fire ensures that the bullets are clear of the muzzle before the recoil impulses have a chance to affect accuracy. When full automatic is selected, the first two rounds are fired at the high rate and the rifle then automatically cycles down to 600 rounds per minute

The burst feature operates using the blow back shifted pulse mentioned previously. The receiver and barrel assembly reciprocates independently from the bolt and its carrier, although the latter reciprocates in the receiver. When the first round is fired, the entire barrel and receiver assembly begins moving to the rear: taking the bolt carrier with it and compressing the forward buffer. As the bullet passes the gas port, gas bleeds off into the gas cylinder, driving the bolt carrier to the rear: unlocking the bolt and extracting and ejecting the spent case. The bolt carrier moves much faster than the barrel and receiver assembly and impacts against the rear buffer, which in conjunction with the recoil spring propels it forward, temporarily stopping the sear while stripping a fresh round from an interim feed position and chambering it. As the bolt locks, the sear is released and the second round is fired before the receiver completes its rearward motion. The bolt carrier and striker then begin their next 600 rounds per minute cycle with the formerly reciprocating components locked to the bolt. In essence, the first two bullets have left the barrel while the receiver is still moving to the rear and has yet to impact the rear buffer. The AN-94 is thus both recoil and gas-operated. The ammunition feed is in two stages that uses a cable and pulley system. As the bolt carrier travels to the rear during its first rapid fire cycle, a cable attached to the bolt head passes over a pulley and pulls forward a feed pawl, stripping a round from the magazine and moving it into a spring loaded holding position under the bolt carrier. This round is then ready to be picked up and fed into the chamber as the bolt carrier moves forward again for its second rapid fire cycle. The pulley is disconnected by the trigger control mechanism after the second rapid fire round has been fired. If this sounds complicated, it is and is probably one reason for the high cost of manufacturing the AN-94.

The AN-94 makes use of advanced materials and manufacturing methods in its construction, including polymers, aluminum alloy investment castings and laser welding. The barrel and chamber are chrome lined. The barrel life is stated to be 10,000-rounds.

Although the AN-94 is chambered in 5.45x39mm, 5.56x45mm prototypes have been produced in hope of exporting the design, but as of this writing, there has been no interest from other military forces, probably due to cost.

SPECIFICATIONS

Caliber: 5.45x39mm
Operation: gas and recoil (see text), select-fire, variable cyclic rate
Feed: 30-round detachable box magazine
Empty weight: 8.5 pounds
Overall length: stock extended, 37.1 inches; stock folded, 28.7 inches
Barrel length: 16 inches
Sights: Front, post; rear: adjustable aperture for 200, 400, 500, 600 and 700 m; provision for optical sights
Cyclic rate: dual cyclic rate; first two rounds 1,800 rounds/min, then 600 rounds/min
Effective range: open sights, 700 meters; optical sights, 1,000 meters (manufacturer's claim)

Russian Troops in a winter training operation.

A-91

7.62x39mm A-91 Assault Rifle

The A-91, also referred to as the A-91M, is a product of the Tula KBP Instrument Design Bureau and it could be indicative of changes in military priorities within Russia. Not only is it a bullpup design, but the choice of caliber has turned away from the virtually automatic selection of the 5.45x45mm cartridge back to the 7.62x39mm. Some Russian military technology journals have indicated that the overall performance of the 5.45mm round was found wanting during combat experiences in Afghanistan and elsewhere, so some within the Russian military establishment are considering at least a partial re-adoption of the well-proven 7.62x39mm cartridge. The appearance of the 7.62mm A-91 could possibly be a straw in the wind, especially when considered alongside the Russian adoption of other new small arms in 7.62x39mm.

The A-91 has appeared in at least four variants. The latest, has the 40mm grenade launcher fully integrated into the forearm, with its trigger just forward of the rifle trigger.

The 7.62mm A-91 is a gas-operated, select-fire bullpup rifle with a totally enclosed receiver. The closure is so complete that there is no conventional ejection port; spent cartridge cases are ejected forward through a small aperture on the top of the receiver to the right side of center. The aperture is opened only at the instant of ejection. Emphasis has been placed on this forward ejection as it renders the rifle amenable to firing by both right- and left-handed users, while firing fumes are directed away from the shooter's face. Other than the magazine well, the only other opening in the receiver is the cocking handle slot on the left side over the rear pistol grip. The selector lever is on the right.

Polymers are used for the rear pistol and front grips, while the rear sights are housed within a raised carry handle over the receiver; optical or night sights can be mounted over the handle. On the latest variant the front and rear grips are joined by a plastic strut to add strength to the overall structure of the rifle.

The A-91 can fire rifle grenades directly from the flash suppressor. It can also accommodate a special 40mm grenade launcher known as the GP-97. This is secured over the barrel and is held in place against the front sight assembly so the grenade launcher trigger is located in a semi-open trigger guard just ahead of the front grip.

SPECIFICATIONS:

Caliber: 7.62x39mm
Operation: gas; select-fire
Feed: 30-round detachable box magazine
Empty weight: 7.3 pounds
Overall length: 23.4 inches
Barrel length: 16.3 inches
Sights: front, post rear: adjustable notch up to 600m provision for optical sights
Cyclic rate: 600 to 800 rounds/min
Effective range: 500 to 600m; grenade launcher, 400m

Vikhr SR-3 9x39mm Carbine

The Vikhr (Whirlwind), also known as the SR-3, is referred to in sales literature as a small automatic rifle (MA – Malogabaritnyi Avtomat) and was for some time after its original public appearance in 1992 thought to be the A-91. The A-91 has emerged as a separate design while the Vikhr was the basis for the AS and VSS silenced assault and sniper rifles. The design bureau for both weapons was the Central Institute of Precision Machinery Construction (TZNITOCHMASH).

The Vikhr is chambered for the 9x39mm subsonic cartridge, available in three versions; SP-5 Ball, SP-6 AP and PAB-9 AP. The Tula ammunition plant developed the PAB-9 as a less expensive alternative to the SP-6. The PAB-9 has a hardened steel core claimed to be capable of defeating level III body armor at ranges up to 400 meters. The PAB-9 is also claimed to be able to defeat an 8mm steel plate at ranges up to 100 meters.

The Vikhr was developed as an armor-piercing weapon that can be fairly easily concealed and may thus be regarded as a special forces and law enforcement weapon, although it could well be utilized as a personal defense weapon.

The Vikhr SR-3 9mm carbine is a gas-operated select-fire weapon. The combination of short barrel and an select-fire capability places the MA more in the submachine gun than in the assault rifle category, except for its caliber, which ballistically far overshadows any pistol caliber cartridge. With an overall length of only 380mm when the stock is folded up and over the receiver, the weapon can be readily concealed. Overall length with the stock extended is 620mm.

At least two models of the Vikhr have been produced, the most recent being recognizable by the rear sight assembly which is more prominent than on the earlier model. Other changes from the earlier model include a ribbed forend to improve handling and a larger muzzle device. Early models were also known as the MA.

Vikhr SR-3

The Vikhr SR-3 utilizes the same 10- or 20-round box magazines as those used with the AS and VSS silenced rifles.

SPECIFICATIONS:

Caliber: 9x 9mm SP-5, SP-6, PAB-9
Operation: gas, select-fire
Feed: 10- or 20-round box magazine
Empty weight: 4.4 pounds
Overall length: stock folded, 14.2 inches; stock extended, 24.1 inches
Sights: front, fixed post; rear: flip aperture
Cyclic rate: 900 rounds/min
Effective cyclic rate: semiautomatic, 30 rounds/min; automatic 90 rounds/min
Max effective range: 200m

Singapore

ST Kinetics 5.56x45mm SAR 21 Assault Rifle

Development of the SAR 21 assault rifle began about 1995 with the goal of replacing all Singapore Armed Forces rifles. The SAR-21 was first shown publicly in September 1999 and is currently in production. The SAR 21 is qualified in accordance with the Evaluation Procedure for future NATO Small Arms Weapon Systems.

The SAR 21 is a gas-operated select-fire bullpup assault rifle that makes extensive use of high strength polymers and composite materials in its manufacture to reduce weight and improve reliability and durability. Locking is via a rotary bolt. The design is ergonomically enhanced to improve handling, with modular construction to improve maintenance.

The barrel may be rifled for either M193 or SS109/M855 ammunition. Rounds are fed from a 30-round box magazine made of high-strength translucent polymer. All controls are ambidextrous, with the cocking handle centrally located over the receiver.

Aiming is via a 1.5-power optical scope permanently attached to the receiver. The tubular sight can be used as a carrying handle and also mounts backup open sights. The optical sight does not require zeroing and is stated to have good boresight retention. A 3x optical sight is available.

In addition to the optical sight, the SAR 21 has an optional Laser Aiming Device (LAD) located in the forward handguard. The LAD may be either an infrared or a visible red dot. A control knob under the handguard permits the LAD to be switched on either permanently or intermittently when a switch is pressed.

A Kevlar plate is incorporated into the stock next to the shooter's cheek. There is also a patented pressure vent hole to release any high pressures in the chamber.

Standard accessories include a cleaning kit, sling and a single 30-round magazine. Options include a blank-firing attachment and boresighting equipment.

Variants

SAR 21 P-rail

For the SAR 21 P-rail, the standard sight mount is replaced by a MIL-STD-1913 Picatinny rail and the charging handle is located on the left-hand side.

SAR 21 Modular

This variant has a Modular Mounting System (MMS) where the forend is replaced by side and bottom MIL-STD-1913 rails. There is also a MIL-STD-1913 sight-mounting rail in place of the optical sight mounting. On this version, the cocking handle is permanently located on the left-hand side of the receiver.

SAR 21 Sharp Shooter

This is the designation applied to variants equipped with the optional 3x optical sight intended for shooting at longer distances.

SAR 21 GL

After the forward hand guard is removed, the SAR 21 can accommodate a 40mm GL 40 Launcher or M203-type grenade launcher. For this application, the LAD is located on the quadrant sight platform.

SPECIFICATIONS

Caliber: 5.56x45mm
Operation: gas, select-fire
Locking: rotary bolt
Feed: 30-round detachable box magazine
Empty weight: 8.4 pounds
Overall length: 31.7 inches
Barrel length: 20 inches
Sights: optical: 1.5-power sight (3-power optional), backup open sights. Laser pointer optional
Cyclic rate: 450 to 650 rounds/min

SAR 21

South Africa

Vektor 5.56x45mm CR 21 Assault Rifle

The Vektor CR 21 assault rifle was first displayed during 1997. It was developed in response to a South African National Defense Force (SANDF) requirement to replace existing service rifles. The CR 21 has undergone evaluation trials with the SANDF, although no firm orders have been placed thus far. The CR 21 has also been marketed for export sales. In addition to the standard CR 21 rifle described here, a CR 21 variant shortened by approximately 100mm overall was evaluated by the South African Police.

The CR21 is actually no more than an R4 housed in polymer in a bullpup configuration. Since the R4 is a virtual carbon copy of the Israeli Galil, itself derived from the ubiquitous AK design, the CR21 should prove very reliable. The weapon is ergonomically designed for ease of use combined with high strength.

A prong-type flash suppressor is claimed to virtually eliminate flash, evening darkness and can be used to launch rifle grenades. Feed is from nylon magazines holding 20 or 35 rounds. The firing selector is separate from the safety selector and located in front of the trigger and is ambidextrous. Cocking is via a lever on the left-hand side of the upper receiver. A cleaning kit is stored inside the stock.

The CR 21 features an integral Vektor reflex optical sight to improve first time hit probability. The 1x sight has a high-strength polymer housing and provides a wide field of view. The sight relies on light collection via a fiber optic. The light is then reflected from a reflex lens to present a triangular aim point. A tritium light source enables firing at night or under poor visibility conditions without batteries. The reflex sight can be used in conjunction with passive night vision equipment.

The reflex optical sight can be removed and a MIL-STD-1913 rail can be installed to mount other optical or night sights. Other options include a 40mm grenade launcher and laser pointers.

SPECIFICATIONS:
Caliber: 5.56x45mm
Operation: gas, select-fire
Locking: rotating bolt
Feed: 20- or 35-round detachable box magazine
Empty weight: 8.4 pounds
Overall length: 29.9 inches
Barrel length: 18.1 inches
Sights: optical reflex, 1x
Cyclic rate: 600 to 750 rounds/min
Max effective range: 500m

Spain

Santa Barbara 5.56x45mm Models L and LC Assault Rifles

This select-fire weapon is based on the earlier and very similar CETME rifles in 7.92mm and 7.62mm calibers. CETME later became part of Santa Barbara. In late 2001 it was announced that Santa Barbara, after having been acquired by General Dynamics, had changed its name to General Dynamics Santa Barbara Sistemas.

Two versions of the weapon were produced: a standard model with a fixed stock (Model L) and a short-barrel version with a telescopic stock (Model LC). A 20-round magazine was first used, but the design was later modified to accept the standard 30-round M16 type magazines, which are NATO standard. Early rifles had a four-position sight graduated for 100, 200, 300 and 400 meters. Current models have a simple two-position flip-type aperture sight graduated for 200 and 400 meters.

Production for the Spanish armed forces took place between 1986 and 1991. The German 5.56mm G36 assault rifle was selected as the replacement for the Model L and LC rifles in 1999, although the earlier rifles will probably remain in service for a few more years.

The Model L/LC used the same roller delayed blowback system as that used on earlier CETME weapons and on Heckler & Koch series of rifles. Operation of the Model L/LC is virtually identical to roller delayed Heckler & Koch rifles described elsewhere in this book.

SPECIFICATIONS: Data for Model L (Model LC in parentheses)
Caliber: 5.56x45mm NATO
Operation: roller delayed blowback, select-fire
Feed: 30-round detachable box magazine
Empty weight: 7.5 pounds
Overall length: 36.4 inches (26.2 inches or 33.9 inches)
Barrel length: 17.7 inches (12.6 inches)
Sights: front, protected post; rear: flip-over aperture for 200 and 400m
Cyclic rate: 600 to 750 (650 to 800) rounds/min

VEKTOR CR 21

CETME Model L

Sweden

CGA5 (Ak5) 5.56x45mm Assault Rifles

The Swedish Army began looking for a new rifle in the mid-1970s, to eventually replace the 7.62mm Ak4 and the Heckler & Koch G3. Several existing 5.56mm weapons were tested until only two competitors remained: the license-built FFV-890C (a slightly modified Israeli Galil) and the Belgian FN FNC.

After comprehensive trials in 1979-80, the FFV-890C was rejected in favor of the FN FNC, although the FN product was considered to require further development. Further tests were carried out over the years and the prototype FNC rifles were modified several times to meet Swedish requirements.

The final design, the CGA5, entered production by FFV (now part of Saab Bofors Dynamics AB) in 1986, with deliveries commencing in 1988. The total Swedish armed forces requirement was for 250,000 weapons.

Saab Bofors Dynamics AB developed the basic design into a family of CGA5-derived based weapons, including an updated version of the base CGA5 rifle, plus a short version with a 260mm barrel, the CGA5 C2 and the CGA5 LSW, a Light Support Weapon (LSW) with a heavier barrel.

The main change on all of the revised models is a rail fitted over the receiver to accommodate various aiming systems, such as image intensifiers and laser pointers. There is also a backup sight with an improved capacity for use during periods of darkness. The stock is adjustable, while the forward handguard can be configured to mount a bayonet, bipod or other combat accessories such as a 40mm grenade launcher.

During development of the CGA5, changes were introduced to meet Swedish requirements. These included low life-cycle costs, high performance and reliability, and the ability to remain functional under extreme climatic conditions. Changes included a new stock, bolt, extractor, handguard, gas block, sights, cocking handle, magazine, magazine release, selector switch, trigger guard and sling swivels. The three-round burst facility was removed.

Variants

- The CGA5B (Ak5B) version mounts the British Sight Unit Small Arms Trilux (SUSAT) optical sight on a rail mount. This version lacks open sights. It is used by the Swedish armed forces as the Ak5B. Approximately 5,200 were manufactured.

- The CGA5C was a bullpup that was not developed.

- The CGA5D was developed to mount virtually any type of sighting equipment and is equipped with a MIL-STD-1913 Picatinny rail, an ergonomic cheek support and backup open sights. Models produced as of 2004 include a version with an integral sight of the red-dot type and a 1.5 or 3x optical sight. CGA5Ds can be produced from new or by upgrading CGA5Bs.

- The CGA5 C2 (Ak5D) is a short weapon with a 9.8 inch barrel and a folding stock. It is for vehicle crews and others who require a compact weapon for personal defense. There are no open sights, but a MIL-STD-1913 rail mounting an Aimpoint sight is fitted.

- There is also an Ak5D Polis, a semiautomatic carbine with a 9.8 inch barrel and a folding stock, for law enforcement use.

SPECIFICATIONS: Data for CGA5/Ak5 and CGA5 C2

Caliber: 5.56x45mm
Operation: gas, select-fire
Locking: rotating bolt
Feed: M16 type detachable box magazine
Empty weight: CGA5/Ak5 8.6 pounds; CGA5 C2: 7.3 pounds
Length: stock folded; CGA5/Ak5; 29.5 inches; CGA5 C2: 21.9 inches
Length: stock extended; CGA5/Ak5; 39.6 inches; CGA5 C2: 32.1 inches
Barrel length: CGA5/Ak5 17.7 inches; CGA5 C2 9.8 inches
Sights: Front: protected post. rear: aperture, 250m and 400m
Cyclic rate: 650 to 700 rounds/min

CGA5 (AK5)

Switzerland

SIG 5.56x45mm SG550, SG551 (StG 90) and SG552 Commando Assault Rifles

The SIG SG550 and SG551 assault rifles were developed to meet a Swiss Army specification and were accepted as the Swiss Army assault rifle in early 1984 under the designation Sturmgewehr (StG) 90. The SG552 Commando was introduced in 1998.

The SG550 is the standard model with a folding stock and bipod, while the SG551 is shorter and lacks the bipod. The SG550/551 SP is a semiautomatic sporting rifle produced for the Swiss civilian market. The short barrel SG552 Commando is intended for special forces use.

In designing the SG550 and SG551, SIG made extensive use of polymer for the stock, handguard and magazine. The magazine is made of transparent plastic. It is provided with studs and lugs on the side that allow a number of magazines to be clipped together. When the last round in the magazine is fired, the bolt latch holds the bolt open. When a new magazine is inserted, the lock is automatically disengaged and the weapon is ready to fire once more The stock folds to one side.

The sight mounted on the breech housing is adjustable for windage and elevation. The sight has luminous dots for aiming during low light and when the day sight is adjusted the night firing sight is adjusted simultaneously. Telescopic and infrared sights can be fitted to an integral telescope mount dimensioned to Swiss Army specification, although a MIL-STD-1913 rail can be fitted.

Variants

SG551 SWAT

This is a special forces or law enforcement model virtually identical to the service SG551, other than a revised stock and provision for mounting various optical sights.

SG550 sniper rifle

See separate entry.

SG552 Commando

The SG552 Commando is a compact model with a folding stock intended for special forces use. Its empty weight is 3.2 kg. It can fire in semiautomatic, fully automatic or three-round controlled burst modes.

SPECIFICATIONS: Data for SG550 (SG551 in parentheses)
Caliber: 5.56x45mm
Operation: gas, select-fire
Locking: rotating bolt
Feed: 20- or 30-round detachable box magazine
Empty weight: 9.0 pounds; (7.5 pounds)
Overall length: stock folded; 30.4 inches; (23.7 inches); stock extended; 39.3 inches; (32.6 inches)
Barrel length: 20.8 inches; (14.6 inches)
Cyclic rate: 700 rounds/min

SIG SG550

SIG SG551

Swiss Special Forces armed with SIG rifles move along a creek.

Taiwan

5.56x45mm T65 Assault Rifle

The T65 assault rifle, also known as the Type 65, generally resembles the American M16. The rifle was made entirely in Taiwan, probably on tools and machinery intended for the M16. The lower receiver is a direct copy of the M16, while the bolt, bolt carrier and piston/operating rod gas system are from the AR-18. Initial T65 prototypes were made with stamped steel receivers, but later weapons were machined from aluminum stock.

The T65 barrel is the same length as the M16 and gives a similar muzzle velocity with M193 ammunition. The upper receiver has the original M16 charging handle and lacks the bolt closure device of the M16A1. The general shape of the receiver is nearly identical to the M16, but without the carrying handle with the rear sight mounted on a bracket. The front sight appears to be the same as the M16, as does the stock.

The long plastic handguard is somewhat larger than that of the M16. Like the original M16, a light bipod can be clamped to the barrel under the front sight.

A modified version of the original T65 design, once erroneously thought to be designated Type 68, incorporates the M16 type direct impingement gas system and a more reliable, single-piece bolt assembly. It also has a higher cyclic rate and can use transparent plastic magazines.

The T65 initially proved to be neither reliable nor easy to manufacture and a great effort was put into correcting its problems. The T65K1 incorporated modifications, which improved the hardness of the aluminum buffer and the adequacy of the insulation beneath the handguard. This was followed by the shorter (815mm) T65K2, rifled to accept the SS109/M855 bullet and with a three-round burst facility in addition to full-automatic fire. The gas system was also redesigned to slow the primary extraction of the spent case and thus overcome ejection problems that had occurred with the earlier models. There is also a T65K3, which appears to differ from the T65K2 by being slightly longer (880mm) and heavier.

SPECIFICATIONS

Caliber: 5.56x45mm
Operation: gas, select-fire
Locking: Multi-lug rotating bolt
Feed: 20- or 30-round M16-type detachable box magazine
Empty weight: 7.3 pounds
Overall length: 39 inches
Barrel length: 20 inches
Cyclic rate: 700 to 800 rounds/min
Max effective range: 460m

5.56x45mm T86 Assault Rifle

Like the earlier T65, the T86 assault rifle, also known as the Type 86, generally resembles the M16 but carries over several features of the T65 and essentially is a repackaged T65, although the overall dimensions are greatly reduced. The manufacturer, Hsin Ho Machinery Corporation, describes the design as modular to assist maintenance and logistic support. The barrel is rifled one turn in 7 inches for M855/SS109 type ammunition.

In comparison to the T65, the T86 has a much shorter barrel and features a collapsible stock. Other design features include an optical sight, mounted on the carrying handle over the receiver. A laser pointer can be mounted on a bracket near the muzzle and the same mount can also accommodate a high intensity tactical white light. Like the T65, an original M16 type bipod can be clamped to the barrel.

A carbine version of the T86 has also been developed, although few details are available. It was probably developed for use by special forces, but does not appear to have been produced in quantity.

SPECIFICATIONS:

Caliber: 5.56x45mm
Operation: gas, select-fire
Locking: rotary bolt
Feed: M16 type 30-round detachable box magazine
Empty weight: 7 pounds
Overall length: stock extended, 34.7 inches; stock retracted, 31.5 inches
Barrel length: 14.8 inches
Cyclic rate: 600 to 900 rounds/min
Max effective range: 800m

United Kingdom

LB5 SA-80

5.56x45mm L85A1/L85A2 (SA80)
Individual Weapon

The two 5.56mm automatic weapons in the Enfield Weapon System (also known as SA-80) are the L85A1/L85A2 IW (Individual Weapon - assault rifle) and the L86A1/L86A2 light support weapon (LSW), a light machinegun. Both weapons fire 5.56x45mm NATO ammunition and also use many common components that in theory give increased flexibility, reduce spares requirements and simplify maintenance in service. In practice, however, the design proved to be flawed. The basic design is that of the Armalite AR-18 in a bullpup configuration, although some modifications were made.

Production was initially undertaken at the old Royal Small Arms Factory at Enfield Lock before the production line was switched to Royal Ordnance's Nottingham Small Arms Facility (NSAF) in 1988. Production for the British Army ceased during 1994 after a total of 323,920 IWs had been produced.

Problems occurred with the IW L85A1 during service with the British Army, especially during operations in the Persian Gulf. In September 1996, the weapon was suspended from the NATO Nominated Weapons List as a result of difficulties with non-British ammunition. Heckler & Koch modified the breech block and chamber, magazines, gas plug and barrel geometry and the British government decided to place a contract with them, through Royal Ordnance, to initially incorporate the proposed modifications on 200 weapons, including different combinations of modifications, to allow confirmation of quantifiable increases in reliability.

During early 2000 it was announced that a program to modify and update L85A1 and LSW L86A1 would commence during that year. Heckler & Koch devised and manufactured the modified components, which were incorporated as L85A2 modifications. The L86A1

SA-80 Carbine

UK Troops

modifications were unsuccessful and the British military will be replacing it with it with the FNH MINIMI.

About 200,000 rifles will be modified. The first modified rifles were issued to rapid deployment units in December 2001. Once all rifles have been modified, they will remain in British service until 2015 or perhaps 2020.

The L85A1/L85A2 IW is made from welded steel stampings, CNC and conventional machining. The furniture is plastic, using high-impact nylon. Stripping and assembly can be accomplished without special tools.

The L85A1/L85A2 is a conventional gas-operated rifle locked by a rotating bolt engaging in lugs behind the breech and carried in a machined carrier running on two guide rods; a third rod controls the return spring. As mentioned, the overall system is very similar to and was clearly derived from the Armalite AR-18. The cocking handle is on the right side and has a spring loaded cover that opens when the bolt carrier moves to the rear. The gas regulator has three positions: a normal opening for most firing, a large opening for use in adverse conditions and a closed position for grenade launching. The trigger is ahead of the magazine, and there is a long connecting rod running to the fire control mechanism. This in itself leads to poor trigger control. The selector lever is on the left side and can be set for either semiautomatic or automatic fire.

The L85A1/L85A2 IW can be fitted with a 4power optical sight (SUSAT), which enables the weapon to be used under adverse lighting conditions and for surveillance. The sight is mounted on a bracket which incorporates range adjustment and zeroing. Night vision optics can be fitted by dismounting the SUSAT from its dovetail base.

The L85A1/L85A2 was designed to be simple to dismantle without special tools for cleaning and maintenance. The trigger mechanism is a self-contained assembly in a stamped steel housing located to the main weapon receiver by two pins and a small buttplate. The receiver is a steel stamping that houses the bolt, bolt carrier assembly and guide rods, which locate in the barrel extension welded into the receiver and into which the barrel is screwed.

Working from the muzzle backwards, the following modifications were made to bring the L85A1 rifle up to L85A2 standards.

The gas plug and cylinder were replaced by versions made from a superior material. The spring catch was widened to prevent jamming in the gas feed during reassembly, and the gas system has been improved. Modifications were introduced to the barrel extension and chamber to permit introduction of a modified extractor and to assist in guiding empty cartridge cases out the ejection port.

A newly designed bolt head was installed. This has a larger and more robust extractor and the ejector has a revised rim and a stronger spring.

The firing pin was replaced by a new version made of high-strength stronger steel alloy.

The ejection port was enlarged and a new all-steel magazine introduced. Heckler & Koch designed this M16 type 30-round magazine for the L85A2, although it can also be used with any rifle that accepts M16 type magazines.

Reinforcing welds are added to the magazine well to prevent breakage.

The hammer weight was increased to prevent misfires from being created by bouncing during full auto fire.

A stronger bolt-release catch is installed.

The recoil spring was replaced by a new high-compression item to stabilize the cyclic rate at a constant rate.

The only external indication that the rifle has been converted to L85A2 other than the markings is a revised cocking handle in the shape of an inverted comma.

Variants

SA-80 carbine

An SA-80 carbine was developed to be a short and handy counterpart to the IW. Most details are the same as for the L85A1 IW, but the overall lengthis reduced to 29.9 inches, with the barrel length of 17.4 inches. Empty weight without magazine and iron sights is 8.2 pounds.

Cadet GP rifle L98A1

This training rifle uses most major components of the L85A1 but lacks the gas system, thus converting the weapon into a manually operated rifle. It uses the secondary iron-sight system, has no provision for launching grenades and can be fitted with an adapter to allow firing of .22 LR ammunition.

Manroy Cadet Drill SA-80

The Manroy Cadet Drill SA-80 is a non-functioning replica of a standard L85A1 rifle intended for drill and training purposes. It is an exact external replica of L85A1 in all respects, including appearance, weight and balance, but contains no moving parts. Its construction consists of a heavy plastic foam-filled receiver with a steel rod for the barrel. It cannot be made to fire. The Manroy Cadet Drill SA-80 is manufactured by Manroy Engineering Ltd of Beckley, East Sussex, UK.

SPECIFICATIONS: SA-80/L85a2
Caliber: 5.56x45mm NATO
Operation: gas, select-fire
Locking: rotary bolt, Stoner system
Feed: 30-round detachable box magazine
Empty weight: weapon without magazine and optical sight, 3.8 kg
Overall length: 30.9 inches
Barrel length: 20.4 inches
Cyclic rate: 610-775-rounds/min

United States

US troops train with M16 rifles.

7.62x51mm M14 rifle

The 7.62mm M14 rifle was adopted in 1957 as the replacement for the M1 Garand. The M14 is essentially an evolved M1 and it is reasonable to state that the M14 represents the ultimate M1. One major change is in the magazine. In the M14, the detachable 20-round box allows full magazines to be loaded into the rifle without needing to use the eight-round clip of the M1. Another feature is a modified gas system, which in the M1 ran right up to the muzzle. On the M14, the gas port was moved back to about two-thirds of the way up the barrel.

Several variants of the M14 were proposed, but only one was ever put into production, the M14A1, a heavy-barrel version intended as a squad light automatic weapon. It was unsuccessful due to lack of control on full automatic and was never produced in any quantity. US government production of the M14 rifle ceased in 1964, after some 1,380,346 rifles had been manufactured. Production was resumed on a commercial basis in 1974 by Springfield Armory Inc. (now Springfield Inc.) and several other manufacturers, including Fulton Armory, are now producing M14 rifles in the United States. During early 2001, some 40,000 M14 rifles were sent to the Lithuanian Army by the United States.

The standard M14 is usually configured to fire semiautomatic only, as the rifle is virtually uncontrollable when fired in full automatic. If a selector is fitted, it must be rotated to select the mode of fire. When it is positioned with the face marked 'A' to the rear: the rifle is set for automatic fire.

Although officially replaced by the M16A1/M16A2, the M14 remains in US military service, especially in special forces. It is in use by many such units and recently the US Special Operations Command announced the adoption of a highly modified version of the M14 designated Mark14, Mod 0 Enhanced Battle Rifle. (See separate entry.)

SPECIFICATIONS:

Caliber: 7.62x51mm
Operation: gas, select-fire
Locking: rotating bolt
Feed: 20-round detachable box magazine
Empty weight: M14, 11.2 pounds; M14A1, 14.6 pounds
Overall length: 44.1 inches
Barrel length: 22 inches
Sights: front, fixed post; rear: aperture, adjustable for windage and elevation
Cyclic rate: 700 to 750 rounds/min

M14

ArmaLite .243, 7.62x51mm and .300 RSAUM AR-10B Rifles

The management of Eagle Arms of Geneseo, Illinois, in 1995, purchased the ArmaLite trademark and Eagle Arms continues as a division of ArmaLite. The AR-10B series rifles were introduced in 1996. An AR-10B version in .243 Winchester caliber was announced in early 1998. In 2004, another version was announced chambered in .300 Remington Short Action Ultra Magnum (RSAUM), a short, fat cartridge that produces ballistics on a par with 300 Winchester Magnum rifles, but in a shorter rifle action.

ArmaLite also manufactures 5.56x45mm M15 rifles that are identical to the AR15 rifle.

The ArmaLite AR-10B rifle series is based on the original AR-10 produced during the 1950s, but has been engineered using modern components and manufacturing methods, with primary emphasis on reliability and functionality and commonality of parts with the 5.56mm M16A2 rifle series as a secondary priority. All AR-10B rifles have several improvements and modifications that differentiate them from similar weapons. All feature forged aluminum upper and lower receivers, a firing pin spring to prevent slam fires, and many other modifications to make the AR-10B compatible more powerful ammunition. All AR-10B rifles use readily available M14 magazines modified for AR-10B use. As with the original AR-10, there is no forward assist feature as this is unnecessary given the heavier operating spring of the AR-10B.

Three versions of the AR-10B are available. All may be purchased in rifle or carbine variants:

AR-10A2: Essentially a .243 Winchester or 7.62x51mm version of the M16A2 in semiautomatic only.

AR-10A4: Identical to the AR-10A2 other than the upper receiver and gas block (the front sight base) being manufactured with MIL-STD-1913 rail mounting surfaces, allowing the installation of optics and other accessories.

AR-10(T): A match/target model with a tubular hand guard, a free-floating heavy match barrel. This model has found military applications as a sniper support weapon.

SPECIFICATIONS:
Caliber: .243 Winchester; 7.62x51mm NATO; .300 RSAUM
Operation: gas, semiautomatic
Locking system: rotating bolt
Feed: 10- or 20-round modified M14 box magazine
Empty weight: AR-10A4, empty, 9.8 pounds
Overall length: AR-10A4, 39.5 inches; AR-10(T), 43.5 inches
Barrel length: AR-10A2 and AR-10A4, 20.0 inches; AR-10(T), 24 inches; Carbine, 18 inches
Sights: AR-10A2: Front, post adjustable for elevation; rear: aperture adjustable for windage and elevation
AR-10A4 and AR-10(T): Front, removable post; adjustable for elevation; rear: removable aperture adjustable for windage and elevation

ARMALITE AR-10B

ARMALITE AR-10(T) Carbine

ArmaLite 5.56x45mm M15 rifles

ArmaLite Inc. manufactures the M15 series of rifles and carbines that are essentially similar to the AR15/M16 rifles, technical details of which may be found under that entry.

Currently available models are as follows.

M15A2 National Match model with a 20-inch, one turn in 8 inches, free-floating heavy match barrel, match sights and two-stage trigger.

M15A2 HBAR Heavy Barrel Assault Rifle with a 20-inch, one turn in 9 inches, chrome barrel

M15A4 Special Purpose Rifle with a 20-inch, one turn in 9 inches, chrome barrel, match sights and detachable carrying handle.

M15A4(T) Eagle Eye with a 24-inch heavy barrel, two-stage trigger, picatinny front sight rail and glass fiber handguards.

M15A4 Predator with 24-inch, one turn in 12 inches heavy barrel, two-stage trigger, picatinny front sight rail and glass fiber handguards.

M15A4 Action Master with a 20-inch, one turn in 9 inches chrome barrel picatinny front sight rail and glass fiber handguards.

M15A4 Golden Eagle with a 20-inch, one turn in 9 inches stainless steel barrel, match sights and two-stage trigger.

M4A1C Carbine with a 16-inch, one turn in 9 inches, barrel, fixed stock, match sights and removable carrying handle.

M4C Carbine with a 16 inch, one turn in 9 inches barrel and fixed stock.

ARMALITE M-15

ARMS TECH Compak

Arms Tech Compak 16 5.56x45mm Compact Carbine

The Compak 16 was developed as a private venture by Arms Tech Limited to provide a compact and reliable personal defense weapon for military vehicle crew members, special operations forces and police personnel.

The Compak 16 is derived from the M16 rifle and the lower receiver of the rifle is identical to that of the standard M16. The Compak 16 has been engineered to provide a 600 rounds per min cyclic rate and reduced muzzle blast while maintaining accuracy out to an effective range of 300 meters. Muzzle blast and flash are reduced by a proprietary muzzle device that reduces these effects to a level comparable to that of a standard M16 rifle. The upper receiver incorporates a MIL-STD-1913 rail, which will accept a variety of optics. A telescoping wire stock is standard equipment. The barrel is rifled so as to accommodate any 5.56x45mm ammunition. An integral quick-detachable suppressor is available.

SPECIFICATIONS:

Caliber: 5.56x45mm
Operation; gas, select-fire
Locking: rotating bolt
Feed: 20- and 30-round detachable box magazines
Empty weight: 5.5 pounds
Overall length: 24 inches
Barrel length: 10.5 inches
Cyclic rate: 600 rounds/min
Sights: optional, user specification

Mark 14, Mod 0 Enhanced Battle Rifle

The Mk 14, Mod 0 Enhanced Battle Rifle (EBR) came about as a result of ground combat in the ongoing War on Terror. Although M14 rifles have been used by special forces units for many years when a rifle chambered in a caliber more powerful than 5.56mm was desired, the original M14 is an obsolete design and cannot accommodate the full range of current optics and night vision equipment. Moreover, it cannot accept any accessories and is too long for current operations

from aircraft and ground vehicles. The special operations community developed requirements in conjunction with Naval Surface Warfare Center, Crane, Indiana for a modified M14 that would rectify the shortcomings of the M14. The result is the Mark 14, Mod 0, EBR.

NSWC Crane approached several manufacturers regarding a chassis type stock for the Mk14 and the Sage International Stock System was eventually standardized. The Sage EBR stock is an aircraft aluminum unit that rigidly clamps the M14 receiver in a chassis and free floats the barrel and gas system for enhanced reliability and accuracy. The clip guide is replaced with a short section of MIL-STD-1913 rail to serve as the rear mount for a telescopic sight. The Sage EBR stock has lengths of MIL-STD-1913 rail on top, bottom and sides to accommodate virtually any optic or accessory. The stock incorporates a pistol grip and fully adjustable collapsible stock that also lowers the M14 action in the stock, resulting in greater control and reduced muzzle rise. The cheekpiece and rubber cushioned buttplate are fully adjustable using only a cartridge nose. The M14 barrel is shortened to 18.5 inches, a Vortex flash suppressor fitted and the front sight has been incorporated into the gas cylinder lock ring. The original bolt stop has been replaced with a "paddle" type that enables the shooter to release the bolt after reloading by

Mark 14 Mod 0

HECKLER & KOCH XM8 Carbine

simply slapping it in much the same way as with M16 and M4 rifles and carbines.

Although all military versions of the Mark 14, Mod 0 are manufactured by NSWC Crane, Fulton Armory of Savage, Maryland produces a commercial version for law enforcement and civilian use that is identical to the Mark 14 in every way except that it is semiautomatic only.

SPECIFICATIONS Mark 14, Mod 0 Enhanced Battle Rifle

Caliber: 7.62x51mm
Operation: Gas, select-fire
Feed: Detachable box magazine, 20-rounds
Overall length: Stock extended, 40 inches; Stock collapsed, 36 inches
Barrel length: 20.5 inches, w/flash suppressor
Maximum effective range: 800m
Cyclic rate: 700 to 750 rounds/min

Heckler & Koch Defense 5.56x45mm XM8 Assault Rifle

The Heckler & Koch (HK).56mm XM8 Assault Rifle is being developed under a contract modification awarded by the US Armament Research, Development and Engineering Center (ARDEC) at Picatinny Arsenal, New Jersey. The contract modification was awarded to HK through a contract with Alliant Techsystems (ATK) as an adjunct to the XM29 system, as it is planned that the XM8 will be based around the 5.56mm kinetic-energy weapon element of the XM29 and many of the components will be interchangeable. The kinetic energy portion of the XM29 is derived from the HK G36.

Many details relating to the XM8 have yet to be completely defined, as it is still in the prototype phase. The loaded weight is currently 7.6 pounds with an M16-type 30-round magazine. The standard barrel length is planned to be 20 inches, with carbine variants having either a 14- or 14.5-inch barrel; the barrel lengths can be changed at the unit armorer level. A five-position telescopic stock is provided to accommodate body armor or multiple clothing layers, while an aiming light will be integrated into the forend. MIL-STD-1913 Picatinny rails are to be provided at several points for combat accessories, and a 40mm grenade launcher and a shotgun attachment are planned. All controls are fully ambidextrous, with a built-in deflector to direct spent cartridge cases away from left-handed shooters. Fire controls are Safe, Semiautomatic and Automatic. A burst-limiter mode is unlikely to be incorporated. The

optical sight will be of the red-dot type, with a 3-power magnification.

SPECIFICATIONS

Caliber: 5.56x45mm
Operation: gas, select-fire
Locking: Rotating bolt
Feed: 30-round detachable box magazine
Empty weight: 6.4 pounds
Overall length: 33 inches
Barrel length: Standard, 20 inches; Sharpshooter, 20 inches; Assault, 12.5 inches; Compact, 9 inches; Squad Automatic Weapon; 20 inches
Optical sight: red-dot type with 3-power magnification
Cyclic rate: 750 rounds per minute

On patrol in Iraq, this M4 is equipped with an optical sight.

ATK XM29

Alliant Techsystems (ATK) XM29 Weapon System

The ATK XM29 Weapon System, originally designated the Objective Individual Combat Weapon (OICW), is now generally referred to as the XM29 rifle. The program is supervised by the Joint Services Small Arms Program (JSSAP), under the Armament, Research, Development and Engineering Center (ARDEC), and was originally intended to replace the M16 rifle, the M4 carbine, the M203 40mm grenade launcher and the M249 5.56mm Squad Automatic Weapon (SAW), although it is now claimed only to replace all M203 Grenade Launcher weapons in the US Military. Although the US Army is proceeding with the program, other US military services have not committed to the XM29.

In March 1998, following four years of Advanced Technology Demonstration effort, Alliant Techsystems (ATK) was selected to proceed into Phase IV of the project to build the XM29 system and its ammunition. ATK is the prime contractor responsible for weapon system integration and 20mm High-Explosive Air-Bursting (HEAB) ammunition. Brashear LP of Pittsburgh, Pennsylvania is responsible for the target acquisition/fire control (TA/FC) component. Heckler & Koch is designing and manufacturing the weapon, while Dynamit Nobel of Germany, is responsible for kinetic energy ammunition improvements. Both German companies plan to establish or license a US manufacturing capability.

As a US Army Advanced Technology Demonstrator (ATD) program, the XM29 has a streamlined acquisition approach, making the transition directly from the Technology Base into Engineering and Manufacturing

(EMD) during FY2000. However, in August 2000 it was announced that ATK had been awarded a US$95 million Program Definition and Risk-Reduction (PDRR) contract for the XM29. As a result of this contract, the first fielding date is expected to be FY2009 rather than FY2007 as originally announced after the initial fielding date of FY2005 was delayed.

The XM29 combines the lethality of 20mm air-bursting munitions, 5.56mm NATO ammunition and a unique TA/FC system to defeat targets at extended ranges. The XM29's modular construction allows it to be fired as an integrated weapon system or separated for stand-alone 5.56 or 20mm firing. The current XM29 empty weight is approximately 18 pounds, although attempts are underway to reduce this to approximately 15 pounds, fully loaded, by the end of the PDRR contract and to a maximum of 14 pounds before full production.

The 5.56mm component is being used as the basis for the XM8 Assault Rifle (see separate entry). On the XM29, the 5.56mm steel barrel is 10 inches long. On the 20mm, the barrel length is 18 inches and is manufactured using titanium.

BUSHMASTER Carbon 15
with BoTech sight and Beta 0-mag

The laser range finder within the TA/FC unit delivers precise target ranging, which it communicates to the 20mm HEAB ammunition. Laser ranging accuracy is within 0.5 meters at up to 500 meters and within 1 meter at up to 1,000 meters. The 20mm HEAB rounds offer defilade capability and can be programmed for a variety of effects, such as self-destruct, Military Operations in Urban Terrain (MOUT) short arming distance, point detonation and point detonation delay. Open sights are provided for backup.

Time of flight to 1,000 meters for the 20mm HEAB grenade is 5.5 seconds. The fuze operates by counting rotational turns as the projectile flies downrange. Ballistically matched training as well as high-explosive grenades will be available.

Cyclic rate for the 5.56mm component is up to 850 rounds per minute delivered in two-round bursts, and up to 10 rounds per minute for the 20mm grenades.

SPECIFICATIONS:
Caliber: 20mm/5.56x445mm
Operation: gas, select-fire
Locking: Rotating bolt
Feed: Detachable box magazine, 10-rounds (20mm); 30-rounds (5.56mm)
Empty weight: 18 pounds
Barrel length: 5.56mm steel length: 10 inches: 20mm barrel: 18 inches
Cyclic rate: 5.56mm; up to 850 rounds/min: 20mm; up to 10 rounds/min

Bushmaster 5.56x45mm Carbon 15 Rifle

The Bushmaster 5.56mm Carbon 15 rifle is a semiautomatic rifle featuring upper and lower receivers constructed entirely of carbon fiber composite. Bushmaster purchased the previous manufacturer, Professional Ordnance, in 2003. Among the advantages of carbon fiber over more conventional materials are that it is virtually self-lubricating and thus requires little or no lubrication for reciprocating parts. Carbon fiber is also resistant to fouling, resulting in reduced maintenance. The material also greatly reduces weight, to the extent that the Carbon 15 is the lightest AR15 type rifle in the world.

The Carbon 15 is available in several versions with different barrel lengths and stocks The Type 21 and 97 rifles and carbines have stainless barrels and one piece lower receivers, while the Carbon 15, Type 4 is virtually identical to the M4 Carbine in appearance and function, except for its carbon fiber lower receiver. Pistol versions with 7.5-inch barrels are also available, as is a .22 long rifle upper receiver conversion unit for low-cost shooting using .22 LR ammunition. A "Lady" variant with slightly reduced dimensions and bird's-eye maple finish is also available. All Carbon 15 variants use standard M16 type magazines

While the Carbon 15 is similar to the AR15/M16 in overall design, there is little parts interchangeability on standard models, except for fire control components. The upper and lower receivers are mated at the rear via a pivoting latch, rather than the pins used with AR15/M16 type rifles. The Type 4, however, can use many components from M4 Carbines, including handguards and stocks. The direct impingement gas operating system is identical to that of the AR15. The bolt and bolt carrier are also almost identical to those of the AR15 but are hard chrome-plated for enhanced reliability. The Carbon 15 is manufactured to ISO 9002 quality standards.

SPECIFICATIONS: (Type 4)
Caliber: 5.56x45mm
Operation: direct impingement gas, semiautomatic
Locking: rotating bolt
Feed: detachable box magazine
Empty weight: 4 pounds
Overall length: Stock extended, 34.5 inches; stock collapsed, 31 inches
Barrel length: 14.5 inches; 16 inches with flash suppressor
Sights: Front; post, adjustable for elevation; rear: aperture, adjustable for windage; MIL-STD-1913 rail
Maximum effective range: 500m

Bushmaster M17S 5.56x45mm Bullpup Rifle

Edenpine, an Australian company, originally developed the M17S 5.56mm bullpup rifle. Research revealed that the rifle would best be produced in the USA and an agreement was reached with Bushmaster to do so. The M17, as offered by Edenpine, was redesigned by Bushmaster for use by military and law enforcement personnel with a requirement for a compact, accurate and reliable rifle.

The M17S is a bullpup-configured rifle based on the Stoner AR-18 action and its functioning is identical to that of the AR-18. The M17 gas system is stainless steel with a gas piston positioned over the barrel and housed in the upper receiver of the rifle, an extrusion of 7075T6 aircraft aluminum. A moving cylinder attached to the operating rod covers the fixed stainless steel piston. Upon firing, gas is transferred to the piston, which drives the cylinder and operating rod to the rear. The operating rod impinges on the bolt carrier and drives it to the rear: thereby unlocking the bolt and extracting and ejecting the spent cartridge case. The gas system is self regulating. The lower receiver is manufactured of glass fiber-filled nylon.

BUSHMASTER M17S Bullpup

The carrying/cocking handle is fitted with a MIL-STD-1913 rail to accommodate optical sights, for which the M17 is expressly designed. The rudimentary backup open sights are integral to the carrying/cocking handle.

The rifle is disassembled by pressing two pins similar to those on M16 rifles and then separating the upper and lower receivers. This allows access to all internal components for cleaning and maintenance. The M17S accepts standard M16-type magazines. *

SPECIFICATIONS:

Caliber: 5.56 x45mm
Operation: gas, semiautomatic
Locking: rotating bolt
Feed: 20- or 30-round detachable box magazines, M16 type
Empty weight: 8.2 pounds
Overall length: 29.9 inches
Barrel length: 21.5 inches
Sights: optical, user's option; back-up front blade and rear notch

* Although the M17S is now out of production, it may be encountered throughout areas where Bushmaster marketed its prooducts.

Bushmaster XM15E2S Dissipator 5.56x45mm carbine

In addition to standard M16-type firearms, Bushmaster manufactures the XM15E2S Dissipator carbine. The XM15E2S Dissipator is essentially a modified M4/M16-type carbine with a full-length handguard that not only provides a standard length forearm in a compact weapon, but provides a standard sight radius rather than the attenuated one usually found on M16-type carbines.

The full-length handguard is designed to better dissipate heat generated by rapid and fully automatic fire than standard ones, hence the name, Dissipator. Unlike other carbines, the XM15E2S does not use the front sight base as a gas block. The gas block is located in the conventional carbine location, but is hidden beneath the handguard. The XM15E2S gas tube is a standard carbine length. Stock may be fixed or collapsible.

Semiautomatic models in the XM15E2S range include the XM15E2S 'Shorty' carbine, the AM15E2S/A3

BUSHMASTER XM15E2S Dissapator

BUSHMASTER 308

'A3 Type Shorty' Carbine, the XM15E2S Dissipator and the XM15E2S/A3 'A3 Type Dissipator' carbines, all with 406mm barrel lengths. The A3 types are equipped with the A3 removable carry handle. Other semiautomatics with 508mm barrel lengths include the XM15E2S Target Model, the XM15E2S/A3 A3 Type Target Model, the XM15E2S V Match Competition Rifle, and the XM15E2S DCM Competition Rifle. Bushmaster also produce their XM15E2S M4 Carbine, a virtual clone of the military M4 Carbine.

In 1997, Bushmaster received a US Department of Energy contract for 300 standard M16A2 select-fire rifles (Bushmaster designation XM15E2).

SPECIFICATIONS:

Caliber: 5.56x45mm
Operation: gas, semiautomatic or select-fire
Locking: rotating bolt
Feed: detachable box magazine M16 type
Empty weight: 6.6 pounds
Overall length: stock extended, 34.8 inches; stock retracted, 31.7 inches
Barrel length: 16 inches
Sights: front, adjustable post; rear: adjustable aperture

Bushmaster 308 Rifles and Carbines

Bushmaster announced its line of 7.62x51mm rifles and carbines in 2004 and while similar to Armalite's AR10 in concept, the Bushmaster rifles are different in execution. Bushmaster rifles use a different type of muzzle device that is more similar to the original AR15/M16 than the AR10. The Bushmaster 308 also has a modified charging handle that differs from that of the AR10 in that it has a centrally located spring-loaded detent in the top of the charging handle that engages a depression in the upper receiver, retaining the handle in place, but making it easy to withdraw by either right- or left-handed shooters. The gas block has three MIL-STD-1913 rails on top and both sides for sight or accessory mounting. The upper receiver has a full length MIL-STD-1913 rail for optical sight mounting. No standard sights are offered, but open sights are available as an option. Barrel lengths are 18 inches for the carbine and 20 inches for the rifle.

Unlike most other AR-type 7.62x51mm rifles, the Bushmaster 308 makes use of unmodified FAL magazines in an innovative feed system that is fully ambidextrous and enables the shooter to release the bolt after reloading without moving his strong hand from the rifle's pistol grip. An ARFX padded skeleton stock is optional.

The Bushmaster 308's bolt carrier is similar to others, but has lateral grooves in the carrier rails to deal with fouling and debris. The fire control components are standard AR15. *

SPECIFICATIONS: Bushmaster 308 Carbine

Caliber: 7.62x51mm (.308 Winchester)
Operation: Direct impingement gas, semiautomatic
Feed: Detachable box magazine, 20-round capacity
Overall length: 38.5 inches
Barrel length: 18 inches with muzzle device; 16 inches without
Sights: None standard. Optics to user requirement; backup open sights available

* The Bushmaster 308 has ceased to be manufactured, but may be encountered.

Colt 5.56mm AR15/M16-series rifles

The .223 (5.56mm) AR15 was designed by Eugene Stoner, L. James Sullivan and Robert Fremont employees of ArmaLite Inc. Upon being type classified as a military weapon in 1962, the AR15 was designated the M16 and initially purchased by the US Air Force. The M16 rifle was modified with the addition of a forward assist mechanism and in 1967 was designated M16A1. The forward assist allows the shooter to close the bolt when a dirty cartridge or chamber fouling produces excess friction. The M16A1 then became the main US Army version of the M16.

With the adoption of a revised specification for NATO 5.56x45mm ammunition, the barrel rifling was altered to one turn in 7 inches to accommodate all possible types of NATO cartridge. This variant became the M16A2. Other changes introduced with the M16A2 included a three-round burst capability, a heavier barrel forward of the gas block, rear sights adjustable for both windage and elevation, a modified handguard, and a reconfigured stock made of new impact-resistant materials.

The latest models of the AR15/M16 rifle series are the M16A3 and the M16A4. They incorporate various human engineering and performance changes, the main one on the M16A3 being the elimination of the three-round burst in favor of a full automatic capability. The M16A4 incorporates a MIL-STD-1913 rail on the upper receiver and a Knight's Armament Rail Adapter System (RAS) handguard that permits mounting accessories and optics.

Despite the long association of the AR15/M16 series with Colt's Firearms, many M16 series rifles in use by the US military have been manufactured by FN Manufacturing Inc. (FNMI, now FNH USA Inc) of Columbia, South Carolina (M16A2), the Hydra-Matic Division of GM Corporation (M16A1), and Harrington and Richardson of Worcester, Massachusetts (M16A1). FNH USA is the only current

COLT M16A3

An M16 firing in full-auto.

manufacturer of the M16A2 rifles for the US military.

License production, has been undertaken at one time or another in South Korea, Singapore and the Philippines. Diemaco of Kitchener, Ontario, Canada also produces licensed versions of these rifles. NORINCO of China produces an M16 clone known as the 'CQ', while the Defense Industries Organization of Iran also produces a rifle virtually identical to the 'CQ' (see separate entries for available details of both).

Numerous manufacturers have produced many rifles and carbines derived from the AR15/M16. Many manufacturers in the United States produce semiautomatic models for commercial sales, including some chambered for 7.62x39mm. There is also a thriving trade in accessories, including high-capacity magazines, improved stocks, special slings, optics and many other items.

Well over 8 million AR15/M16-series rifles and carbines have been manufactured to date and production continues. A partial list of Colt model numbers follows.

Model Number

601 AR15 rifle

602 AR15 rifle; early US government contract - no forward assist

603 M16A1 rifle; originally the XM16E1; standard US government model with forward assist

603K M16A1 rifle; produced for South Korea

604 M16 rifle; produced for US Air Force without forward assist

605A M16 carbine; carbine version of M16A1 rifle with forward assist and fixed stock

605B M16 carbine; same as Model 605A but with three-round burst limiter; no forward assist

606 Heavy-Barrel length Assault Rifle (HBAR) without forward assist; also known as the Heavy Assault Rifle M1

606A HBAR with forward assist

606B HBAR with forward assist and three-round burst limiter

607 Submachine gun with sliding stock-stock and 254mm barrel length

608 CAR15 survival rifle with 10-inch barrel and fixed tubular stock; about 10 produced.

609 XM177E1 submachine gun for US Army with 10-inch barrel and 3.5 inch-sound/flash suppressor

610 XM177E1 submachine gun for US Air Force with 10-inch barrel

610B XM177E1 submachine gun for US Air Force with addition of three-round burst limiter

611 HBAR; export version of Model 606

611P HBAR; export version of Model 611 for the Philippines

613 M16A1 rifle; export version of Model 603

613P M16A1 rifle; export version of Model 613 for the Philippines

614 M16 rifle; export version of Model 604 without forward assist

614S M16 rifle; export version of Model 614 license produced by Chartered Industries of Singapore (now Singapore Technologies Kinetics)

616 HBAR; export model of Model 606

619 Submachine gun; export version of Model 609

620 Submachine gun; export version of Model 610

621 HBAR; heavy barrel version of Model 603

629 XM177E2 submachine gun for US Army with 11.5-inch barrel and 4.5-inch sound/flash suppressor

630 Submachine gun for US Air Force without forward assist and 11.5-inch barrel

633 9mm submachine gun with 7-inch barrel and mechanical buffer

633HB 9mm submachine gun with 7-inch barrel and hydraulic buffer

634 9mm submachine gun with 10.5-inch barrel, without forward assist

635 9mm submachine gun with 10.5-inch barrel length, without forward assist

639 Submachine gun; export version of Model 629

640 Submachine gun; export version of Model 629 without forward assist

645 M16A2 rifle; standard US government model with revised rifling, 20-inch barrel and new rear sight

645E M16A2 rifle 'enhanced'; modified M16A2 with removable carrying handle for optical sight mounting and flip-up front sight

649 Submachine gun; for US Air Force, with 14-inch barrel and modified rifling.

651 M16A1 carbine; export model with 14.5-inch barrel and full-length stock

652 M16 carbine; export model with 14.5-inch barrel and full-length stock, but without forward assist

653 M16A1 carbine; export model with 14.5-inch barrel and collapsible stock

653P M16A1 carbine; export model with 14.5-inch barrel and collapsible stock, manufactured in the Philippines

654 M16 carbine; export model without forward assist, with 14.5-inch barrel and collapsible stock

655 M16A1 sniper rifle; experimental model with high-profile upper receiver

656 M16A1 sniper rifle; experimental model with low-profile upper receiver and Sionics suppressor

701 M16A2 rifle; export model with full automatic in place of three-round burst limiter

702 M16A2 rifle; export model for United Arab Emirates with M16A1 rear sights and full automatic in place of three-round burst limiter

703 M16A2 rifle; export model for the United Arab Emirates with M16A1 barrel profile and full automatic in place of three-round burst limiter

705 M16A2 rifle; export model with full automatic in place of three-round burst limiter; also known as M16A2E3

707 M16A2 rifle; export model with three-shot burst limiter and M16A1 barrel profile

711 M16A2 rifle; export model with M16A1 rear sight and M16A1 barrel profile

715 M16A2 rifle; Canadian version of M16A2 rifle known as C7 with M16A1 rear sight, three-round burst limiter and M16A2 barrel length; license-produced by Diemaco

719 M16A2 rifle; version of Model 715 produced by Colt's, three-round burst limiter

720 M4 carbine; originally known as M16A2 carbine, with 14.6 inch barrel

723 M16A2 carbine; produced for United Arab Emirates and US Army Delta Force; with M16A1 rear sight, 14.6-inch barrel and full-automatic fire capability

725 M16A2 carbine; Canadian version of M16A2 carbine known as C8 with M16A1 rear sight, three-round burst

M16A4

United States M16A2

limiter and M16A2 barrel; license-produced by Diemaco

725A M16A2 carbine; export version of the M16A2 carbine produced by Colt for United Arab Emirates with M16A1 profile barrel.

725A M16A2 carbine; export version of M16A2 carbine with M16A2 barrel

727 M16A2 carbine with fully automatic fire feature produced for (among others) the US Navy; with 14.6-inch barrel.

733 M16A2 Commando; short-barrel model with fully automatic fire, 11.4-inch barrel and M16A1 rear sight

733A M16A2 Commando; short-barrel model with three-round burst limiter in place of fully automatic fire, 11.4-inch barrel and M16A1 rear sight.

735 M16A2 Commando; similar to Model 733 but with three-round burst limiter

737 M16A2 HBAR; with M16A1 rear sight.

741 M16A2 HBAR; same as Model 737 but with M16A2 rear sight

M16A2 Squad Automatic Weapon (SAW); with 508mm barrel, bipod and front handguard assembly; fully automatic

901 M16A3 rifle; similar to Model 701 but with MIL-STD-1913 rail; fully automatic; this number is also used to designate the M16A4.

905 M16A3 rifle; similar to Model 705 but with MIL-STD-1913 rail; three-round burst limiter.

925 M16A3 rifle; similar to Model 725 but with MIL-STD-1913 rail and three-round burst limiter

927 M4A1 carbine; originally known as M16A3 carbine; Similar to Model 727 but with MIL-STD-1913 rail on upper receiver; fully automatic; in production for US Special Forces.

933 Commando carbine with four-position collapsible stock, MIL-STD-1913 rail on upper receiver and Knight's Armament Rail Adapter System

941 M16A3 HBAR; similar to Model 741 but with MIL-STD-1913 rail; semiautomatic and fully automatic

942 M16A3 Squad Automatic Weapon (SAW); similar to Model 741 but with MIL-STD-1913 rail on upper receiver; fully automatic only

950 M16A3 Squad Automatic Weapon (SAW); similar to Model 741 but with MIL-STD-1913 rail on upper receiver; fully automatic

977 M4 carbine

Colt 5.56x45mm M4 carbine

The M16 rifle series has been accompanied by a series of carbines, usually virtually identical to the rifles in engineering and operating terms but with shorter barrels and collapsible stocks. Following a number of tentative attempts to introduce carbine models into US service, the M4 and M4A1 carbines were adopted for special forces use with the first examples delivered by Colt in 1994 as part of an order for 24,000 units.

Basically a short M16A2 rifle, the M4 and M4A1 carbines are in production for the US military. They feature a collapsible four or six-position stock and can be fitted with the M203 grenade launcher. Both have a MIL-STD-1913 rail atop the upper receiver. The M4A1 is essentially the same as the M4, but has the burst fire feature replaced by full automatic.

A US Navy SEAL emerges from the surf with an M4A1.

COLT M4A1

SPECIFICATIONS:

Caliber: 5.56x45mm
Operation: Direct impingement gas; select-fire, burst (M4) or full automatic (M4A1)
Locking: rotating-bolt
Feed: 30-round box magazine
Empty weight: 5.6 pounds
Overall length: stock retracted, 29.8 inches; stock extended, 32.9 inches
Barrel length: 14.6 inches
Sights: front, post, adjustable for elevation; rear: adjustable for windage and elevation. Removable to use MIL-STD-1913 rail on upper receiver
Cyclic rate: 700 to 1,000 rounds/min
Maximum effective range: 600m

DPMS "Panther" 5.56x45mm Rifles and Carbines

DPMS of St. Cloud, Minnesota, manufactures a variety of AR-type rifles and carbines to military specification. Upper and lower receivers are forged 7075T6 aircraft aluminum, hard-coat anodized and Teflon finished to military specification. Barrels are chrome molybdenum steel. Bolt carriers are 8620 steel and are hard-chrome plated. Bolts are phosphated steel and are fully military specification.

Barrel lengths from 11.5 to 24 inches are available. Besides carbines and rifles DPMS also manufactures precision tactical rifles for long-range shooting in both 5.56x45mm and 7.62x51mm. Conversion units chambered in .22 LR are available in both carbine and rifle lengths. These units are exact external replicas of M4 carbines and M16 rifles and are intended low-cost shooting and military/law enforcement training.

SPECIFICATIONS:

Caliber: 5.56x45mm
Operation: Direct impingement gas, semiautomatic or select-fire
Feed: Detachable box magazine
Locking: Rotating bolt
Overall length: Stock extended, 36.7 inches; stock collapsed, 32.7 inches
Barrel length: 16 inches
Empty weight: 7.06 pounds
Cyclic rate: 700 to 900 rounds per minute
Maximum effective range: 500m

DPMS "Panther"

DPMS 308

DPMS 7.62x51mm Panther 308 Rifles

DPMS manufactures several versions of its Panther 308 rifles with barrel lengths ranging from 18 to 24 inches. The latter rifle is intended for long-range precision shooting and is included under Precision Tactical Rifles. The Panther 308s are essentially similar to AR10 rifles, but differ in execution. Upper receivers are extruded from 6066T6 aluminum and hard coat anodized to military specification. There is no dust cover, forward assist or case deflector. Lower receivers are milled from 6061T6 forgings and are hard coat anodized to military specification. Receivers are Teflon finished. Barrels are fully free floated with ribbed aluminum handguard tubes. There are no open sights; these rifles are designed to be used only with optical sights.

SPECIFICATIONS

Caliber: 7.62x51mm
Operation: Direct impingement gas, semiautomatic
Locking: Rotary bolt
Feed: Detachable box magazine
Overall length: 37.6 inches
Barrel length: 18 inches
Empty weight: 9.7 pounds
Cyclic rate: N/A
Maximum effective range: 800m
Sights: None provided

DSA 7.62x51mm SA58 Rifles and Carbines

DSA manufactures several versions of the FN FAL using original blueprints and tooling. Many components, technical data and tooling was purchased from Steyr, which owned the original FN tooling and manufactured a select-fire version of the FAL under the designation Sturmgewehr 58 (StG 58). Since the tooling and many parts were original Steyr, the DSA rifles were designated SA58, indicating Semiautomatic 58. DSA rifles are produced in standard-, medium- and heavy- (bull) barreled variants, plus a compact version designated the SA58 Offensive Support Weapon (OSW) for use by law-enforcement and military personnel. Heavy- and medium-weight barrel versions feature a cryogenically treated barrel for enhanced accuracy. The OSW compact carbine incorporates a high-efficiency muzzle brake that reduces felt recoil and muzzle rise, a 16.3-inch chrome-lined barrel, a modified gas system and a synthetic handguard. DSA rifles are manufactured to user specification either with or without a carrying handle. Barrels are of chrome molybdenum or stainless steel and are broach cut. Standard DSA SA58 rifles are otherwise identical to those originally manufactured by FN, but are usually in semiautomatic only.

Variants

SA58 Standard 7.62mm rifle, SA58 Medium Contour Rifle (stainless-steel and chrome-molybdenum barrel versions), SA58 Bull Barrel (stainless steel heavy barrel, 610 and 533mm), SA58 Carbine, SA58 OSW.

FNH SCAR-L (MK16, MOD 0)

SPECIFICATIONS:

Caliber: 7.62x51mm NATO
Operation: gas, semiautomatic or (OSW only) select-fire
Locking: dropping bolt
Feed: detachable box magazine
Empty weight: 10.6 pounds, medium contour rifle; 11.7 pounds, bull barrel rifle; 9.2 pounds, carbine; 7.9 pounds, OSW
Overall length: 51.6 inches (heavy); 42.9 inches (heavy, medium and standard); 38.2 inches (carbine); 33.1 inches (OSW)
Barrel length: 24.1 inches (heavy); 21 inches (heavy, medium and standard); 16.3 inches (carbine); 11 inches (OSW)
Sights: front, post, adjustable for elevation; rear: aperture, adjustable for windage and elevation.

DSA 5.56x45mm AR Rifles and Carbines

DSA entered the AR-type rifle market in 2004 with a variety of rifles and carbines manufactured to a very high standard of overall quality. Barrel lengths from 11.5 to 20 inches are available, as are a variety of options, including the usual collapsible stocks and others, such as Vltor stocks that are superior to standard units in that they provide an improved cheek weld and storage compartments for batteries and other small items.

A notable option is the Lewis Machine & Tool (LMT) quick-change barrel upper receiver, featuring barrels that can be changed in a matter of seconds, enabling the user to vary not only barrel lengths, but facilitating changes to other calibers, such as 6.8x43mm SPC. Bolts are of an improved design that eliminates many problems associated with AR-type rifles, including cracked locking lugs and extraction failures. The DSA bolts have an improved design extractor with dual springs and modified locking lugs for increased strength and durability. The LMT upper receiver also has full length MIL-STD-1913 rails and is available in both rifle and carbine lengths. The LMT upper is machined from forged aircraft aluminum and finished to military specification.

SPECIFICATIONS: (LMT Rifle length upper receiver)

Caliber: 5.56x45mm or others
Operation: direct impingement gas, semiautomatic
Locking: rotating bolt
Feed: detachable box magazine
Overall length: 37.5 inches
Barrel length: 20 inches or as fitted by user.
Empty weight: 8 pounds
Sights: None provided, MIL-STD-1913 rail for sights and accessories.

Mark 16 and Mark 17
FNH USA Special Operations Forces Combat Assault Rifle (SCAR)

The SCAR program was undertaken by the United States Special Operations Command (SOCOM) to provide a family of small arms for US Special Operations Forces that is more flexible, more reliable and with improved ergonomics over existing systems. All SCAR components have been designed, developed and tested with full input from active special forces operational personnel. There are three elements to the SCAR Program:

The Mark 16, Mod 0, SCAR Light (SCAR-L) will replace the M4A1 in all US Special Operations organizations. FNH USA was recently awarded a contract for the SCAR-L. Both rifles have a stock that is both folding and telescoping and the Mark 16 can be changed quickly from 5.56x45mm to another caliber, such as 6.8x43mm, plus other features desired by special operations personnel. Both SCAR-L and SCAR-H have MIL-STD-1913 rails at 90 degree intervals at top, bottom and sides. The top rail is full length, while the others are on the handguard.

The Mark 17, Mod 0, SCAR Heavy (SCAR-H), will replace the M14 and Mark 11 rifles in SOCOM service. This rifle is still in development, but provisional specifications are listed below. Optional calibers are currently envisioned are 7.62x51mm and 7.62x39mm. The SCAR-H is generally similar in design and layout to the SCAR-L. *

Enhanced Grenade Launcher Module (EGLM). The EGLM will replace the M203 as an underbarrel grenade launcher in special operations service on both the SCAR-L and SCAR-H.

The overall objectives of the SCAR program are to improve operational flexibility and increase individual and team lethality; reduce the number of weapons that operators currently require to accomplish missions and increase the overall combat effectiveness and efficiency of SOCOM units by providing operators with weapons that are more reliable and have increased service life over existing systems.

PROVISIONAL SPECIFICATIONS SCAR-L /SCAR-H:

Caliber: 5.56x45mm/7.62x51mm (6.8x43mm/7.62x39mm optional)
Operation: gas, select-fire
Locking: rotating bolt
Feed: detachable box magazine, 30 rounds/20 rounds capacity (30-rounds 7.62x39mm)
Empty weight: 7.7 pounds/8.5 pounds
Overall length: 33.5 inches / 39.3 inches (standard configuration)
Barrel length: 16 inches /18.5 inches (estimated)
Sights: front, folding protected post; rear: folding aperture. Optical standard.
Cyclic rate: 600 rd/min

* The Mark 16, Mod 0 and Mark 17, Mod 0 have 90 percent parts commonality.

Knight's Armament Modular Weapons System

In August 1995, the Knight's Armament Company (KAC) announced a US government contract award to produce a Rail Interface System (RIS) for the US Special Operation Command's (USSOCOM) SOPMOD M4 Program. The contract initially called for applications with USSOCOM 5.56mm M4A1 Carbines but the system is also applicable to any AR15/M16 type rifle.

The heart of the MWS is KAC's aluminum RIS handguard that replaces the standard handguard and consists of two aircraft aluminum halves with four sections of MIL-STD-1913 rail to facilitate the attachment of various tactical accessories. The handguard also provides thermal protection for the user.

The KAC MWS is based on M16 series rifles and M4 Carbines. The baseline modular weapon combines a standard M16 rifle or M4 Carbine with a RIS that replaces the factory standard handguard. The RIS is in two halves with four parallel MIL-STD-1913 rails at 12, 3, 6 and 9 o'clock surrounding and parallel to the barrel. They provide precise indexing points for the mounting of a wide range of optics and tactical accessories.

The RIS rails contain several recoil grooves along their length. Odd numbered recoil grooves of each quadrant rail are sequentially numbered. Numbers on the top rail have a T prefix while those on the bottom rail have a B prefix; the rails to the shooter's right and left have R and L prefixes. These numbers and prefixes assist the operator when remounting an accessory in the same position and provide an address for every position on the system. This reminds an operator exactly where to mount an accessory and he can also denote addresses that are incompatible with some accessories.

As accessories are added or repositioned, the battle sight zero of reflex sights and aim lights may be confirmed without firing. The zero confirmation of optical sights is achieved by adjusting the point of aim of the optic to that of the pre-zeroed flip-up rear sight while simultaneously sighting through both. Zero confirmation of lights or lasers is achieved by sighting through the pre-zeroed flip-up rear sight and adjusting the point of aim.

Tactical accessories that can be used with the RIS include standard or folding open sights, optical sights of all types, night vision optics, visible and infrared lasers, vertical foregrip, quick-detach M203 grenade launcher and a KAC Masterkey breaching weapon, a modified Remington 870 shotgun. KAC offers mounts for many types of sighting systems.

Various length RIS are available for a wide variety of weapons.

SOPMOD M4A1

The SOPMOD (Special Operations Peculiar Modification) M4A1 weapon is a modification of the M4A1 Carbine intended for use by special operations units, where it will replace the Heckler and Koch 9mm MP5 submachine gun.

The SOPMOD M4A1 incorporates the SOPMOD M4A1 Kit, an accessory suite developed by the Naval Surface Weapons Station, Crane, Indiana, specifically for special operations' use. The SOPMOD M4A1 Kit is issued to specified units and consists of sufficient components to equip four weapons with certain items and selected weapons with some components.

The SOPMOD M4A1 Kit for each four carbines includes the following items:

SOPMOD M4A1 in a training environment.

SOPMOD M4A1

- Trijicon 4 x 32 day optical sight (4)
- Knight Armament rail adaptor system (4)
- Knight Armament vertical handgrip assembly (4)
- Quick attach/detach M203 grenade launcher mount (1)
- Quick attach/detach M203 leaf sight (1)
- M203 grenade launcher, 9-in (229mm) barrel (1)
- Infra-red target pointer, AN/PEQ-2 (2)
- Visible laser, AN/PEQ-5 (1)
- Trijicon reflex sight (2)
- Quick attach/detach sound suppressor (2)
- Visible light illuminator (2)
- Back-up iron sight, range 0 to 300m (4)
- Hard carrying/storage case (CSC) with 4 internal soft carrying cases (1)
- Mini night vision sight (1)
- Combat sling (4)
- SOPMOD enhanced stock (2).

One of the keys to the SOPMOD M4A1 Kit is its adaptability. Three SOPMOD M4A1 Kits are issued to each Army 'A' detachment, four to each 'B' detachment, four to each SEAL platoon, and three per special tactical team. US Army Rangers and other special mission units are issued selected items rather than complete kits to enhance their M4A1 CQB weapons. US Marine Corps units to be equipped with the M4A1 CQB weapon include security force units, direct action platoons, Special Operations Capable Marine Expeditionary Units (MEU-SOC), and military police special reaction teams.

SPECIFICATIONS:
Caliber: 5.56x45mm
Operation: Direct impingement gas, select-fire
Locking system: rotating bolt
Feed: detachable box magazine
Empty weight: 7.9 pounds
Overall length: stock retracted, 29.8 inches; stock extended, 32.9 inches
Barrel length: 14.6 inches
Sights: Variable, depending on mission profile
Cyclic rate: max 700 to 900 rounds/min; effective, semiautomatic, 45 rounds/min; full automatic, 150 rounds/min
Max effective range: point fire, 500 meters; area fire, 800 meters

Robinson Arms M96 Expeditionary rifle

The Robinson Arms M96 Expeditionary rifle is derived from the Stoner 63 of the 1960s and like its predecessor is a gas-operated modular small arms weapon system. The M96 uses a gas piston and operating rod system, rather than the direct impingement of the M16, with a bolt carrier and multi-lug bolt similar to the original Stoner design, but of an improved design for reliability. Locking lugs are larger and have been redesigned to more evenly distribute recoil forces.

The M96 is almost identical in appearance to its predecessor, but the basic Stoner design has been so extensively modified that the only part that will interchange is the stock.

The M96 features a quick-change barrel, so it may be easily and quickly changed into several configurations. The M96 can be configured as a rifle with 20-inch barrel, carbine

ROBINSON ARMS M96

with 16-inch barrel, or "Bren Gun" with top feed and 24-inch barrel. The M96 is provided with adjustable front and rear sights so that each barrel can be individually zeroed to the rear sight, thus eliminating rezeroing when changing barrels. The gas system is adjustable. The trigger is a two-stage type. In the rifle configuration, the non-reciprocating charging handle is on the left of the receiver; when in "Bren" light machine gun configuration, it is on the right. On rifles and carbines, the gas tube is above the barrel, while in the Bren Gun configuration it is below due to the receiver having been inverted to convert to this configuration. The M96 uses standard M16 type magazines, and is noted for its accuracy, reliability and smooth operation.

SPECIFICATIONS:

Caliber: 5.56x45mm
Operation: gas, semiautomatic
Locking: rotating bolt
Feed: detachable box magazine
Empty weight: 6.6 pounds
Barrel length: 21.5 inches
Sights: Front, adjustable post; rear adjustable aperture.
MIL-STD-1913 rail optional.

Robinson Arms XCR Modular Weapon System

The Robinson Arms XCR was designed specifically for special forces" use and is intended to provide the reliability of an AK type rifle with the ergonomics, accuracy and accessory options of an M4 Carbine.

The XCR consists of upper and lower receivers. The lower contains all the fire-control elements, while the upper has an integral MIL-STD-1913 rail system and quick-change barrel mechanism. The XCR is gas-operated via a piston and rod system. The XCR is a totally new design and while the magazine well, trigger and selector switch are similar to those of AR-type rifles, they are newly designed. All controls are ambidextrous. The non-reciprocating charging handle is on the left side of the upper receiver. The XCR was specifically designed to fire 5.56x45mm and 6.8x43mm cartridges by simply changing barrels and bolt heads and using a different magazine. Conversion can be accomplished in less than five minutes. A 7.62x51mm

version of the XCR will be available late in 2005. The XCR comes with a tubular design folding stock as standard.

SPECIFICATIONS:

Caliber: 5.56x45mm or 6.8x43mm
Operation: gas, select-fire
Locking: rotating bolt
Feed: detachable box magazine.
Overall length: (16 inch barrel, stock extended) ~35 inches
Barrel length: 11.5; 14.5; 16; 18.5 or 20-inches, QCB
Sights: front, adjustable protected post; rear: aperture, adjustable for windage and elevation. Optics to user choice.
Effective range: 500 to 800m, depending on ammunition
Cyclic rate: 600 rd/min

Ruger 5.56x45mm Mini-14 and 7.62x39mm Mini 30 Rifles

The Ruger Mini-14 was derived from the M14, but underwent substantial changes in the conversion process carried out under the supervision of L. James Sullivan, joint designer of the AR15. At one time, select-fire versions were manufactured for military and law enforcement use, but these were discontinued due to lack of sales. Current "government model" semiautomatic Mini-14s are fitted with a black synthetic stock, flash suppressor and bayonet lug. Butler Creek pistol grip folding stocks are available for these rifles as an option. Available finishes are blue or matte stainless. The Mini-14 has achieved fairly wide acceptance in many law enforcement agencies in the United States due to its relatively low cost and conventional appearance.

The Mini Thirty rifle is a modified version of the Ruger Mini-14 chambered for the 7.62x39mm cartridge. The barrel, receiver and bolt have been modified to accommodate the larger cartridge.

SPECIFICATIONS:

Caliber: 5.56x45mm or 7.62x39mm
Operation: gas, semiautomatic
Locking: rotating bolt
Feed: detachable box magazine
Empty weight: 6.4 pounds
Overall length: 37.25 inches
Barrel length: 18.5 inches
Sights: Front, blade; rear: aperture; integral telescope mounts
Effective range: 400 meters

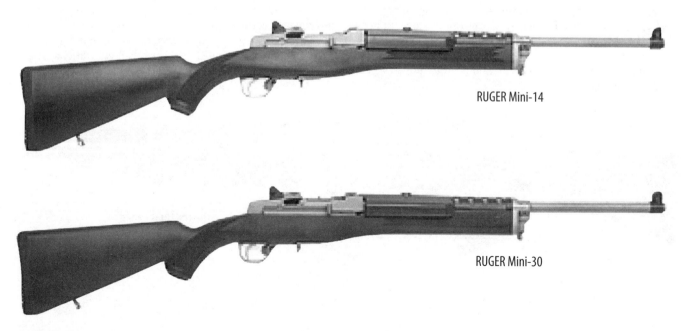

RUGER Mini-14

RUGER Mini-30

Springfield Armory M1A rifles

Springfield Armory manufactures several versions of its basic M14-type rifles, all derived from its Standard M1A. Many components of these rifles are original military parts, although others are newly manufactured. All receivers are newly manufactured, as are most barrels.

The Standard M1A model is a duplicate of the original military-issue M14 rifle but in semiautomatic only. Stocks are available in either wood or Fiberglas. The latter are almost all military surplus stocks. The M1A is available with National Match and the even heavier Super Match barrels. A "Loaded" Standard M1A match model with a medium weight barrel is also available.

Springfield Armory also offers the M1A Squad Scout rifle with an 18-inch barrel, muzzle brake/compensator, black Fiberglas stock, and a scope mount just forward of the receiver

The M1A SOCOM version is even shorter than the Squad Scout with a 16-inch barrel and compensator that integrates the gas cylinder lock ring and front sight.

* SOCOM II

SPECIFICATIONS:

Caliber: 7.62x51mm
Operation: gas, semiautomatic
Locking: rotating bolt
Feed: 10- or 20-round detachable box magazine
Empty weight: 9 pounds
Overall length: 43.7 inches
Barrel length: Standard, 22 inches; Squad Scout, 18 inches; SOCOM, 16 inches
Rifling: 4 grooves, rh, 1 turn in 12 inches
Sights: front, fixed blade; rear: aperture, adjustable for windage and elevation

* The SOCOM II includes a MIL-STD 1913 rail system in either a short version (illustrated) or a full length version that extends over the receiver.

SPRINGFIELD ARMORY Standard M1A

SPRINGFIELD ARMORY Squad Scout

SPRINGFIELD ARMORY SOCOM II

Precision Tactical Rifles

Precision tactical rifles, also known as sniper rifles, have developed into a class of military and law enforcement small arm unto themselves. At one time precision tactical rifles were converted from standard military rifles, such as the American M-1903A4, M1-C, M1-D and M-21. During the Vietnam War, the US Marine Corps began using "accurized" sporting rifles that had been specially modified for sniper use. As time passed, both the Army and Marine Corps developed rifles designed from the outset as precision tactical rifles. The Marine Corps builds its own M-40 series rifles at the Rifle Team Equipment Shop (RTE Shop) at Quantico, Virginia. The latest version of the M-40 is the M-40A3. These rifles are manufactured using commercial match-grade components and are based on Remington 700 receivers. The US Army buys its M-24 Sniper Weapon System (SWS) from Remington Arms. The M-24 is manufactured to Army specifications and has been purchased by some foreign military forces.

In the east, sniper rifles took a different direction. Russia and those nations that fell under Soviet/Russian influence during the Cold War developed semiautomatic sniper rifles and deployed them in much the same way as the West employs designated marksmen. That is until recently, Russian snipers were employed at the platoon level at the discretion of the company commander. The best marksmen were chosen and issued a SVD Dragunov semiautomatic semi-precision rifle. There was no specialized sniper training as in the West. This has, however, changed and Russian special forces snipers are issued SV-98 bolt-action precision rifles that are based on an Olympic match rifle. Interestingly, the Russians also employ a suppressed .22 long rifle precision straight pull bolt-action rifle designated the SV-99. This little rifle presumably is used to quietly shoot out lights, kill dogs, geese and other animals that might alert enemy forces or criminals to the presence of a special tactical team. It could also be used to shoot sentries in the head at close range, as it has a detachable stock and can be used as a long-barreled pistol. Although the Russian

military has adopted Western type precision bolt-action rifles for its special teams, the SVD and its variants remain in service. Other former Warsaw Pact nations developed their own versions of the SVD, but not all are true SVD clones. The Romanian FPK, for example, externally appears to be an SVD, but is actually an upgraded and accurized semiautomatic AK variant.

A subclass of precision tactical rifles is the designated marksman rifle (DMR), which is used as a backup to the bolt-action rifle or issued to squad marksmen in much the same way as Russian practice. We have already mentioned the Russian SVD, but late in the 20th Century, Western nations began developing their own DMRs. The United States Special Forces fielded the Knight's Armament SR-25, classifying it as the Mark 11, Mod 0 DMR. Although the SR-25 is the "official" DMR, many special forces personnel prefer the Armalite AR-10(T) and buy them from their personal funds. The Marine Corps builds its own DMRs at Quantico's RTE Shop using M-14 receivers as a basis. These receivers are modified so that they cannot be reconverted to select fire. These rifles have lugged receivers and are essentially match-grade M-14s. There have been consistent rumors that the USMC M-14 DMR has proven less than satisfactory in service.

Most true precision tactical rifles are bolt-action and have the capacity to accept a suppressor. With an efficient modern suppressor and subsonic ammunition, such rifles approach almost total silence. The only discernable sound at any distance is the impact of the bullet. The author has fired suppressed 7.62x51mm precision tactical rifles with subsonic ammunition whose suppressors are so effective that the loudest sound is the "snap" of the striker impacting the cartridge primer. The advantage to this is that enemy personnel cannot identify the source of the shot. Also, sound detectors exist that can track the sound of a rifle shot back to its source. With suppressed rifles and subsonic ammunition, this is not possible, although subsonic ammunition appreciably reduces the effective range of the rifle.

While the majority of precision tactical rifles continue to fall within the .30 caliber/7.62mm class exemplified by the Western 7.62x51mm and Russian 7.62x54R calibers, some rifles have been developed for more powerful ammunition. Several special operations units use .300 Winchester Magnum rifles that fire ammunition specifically developed and manufactured to fit the chambers of these rifles. Also, many nations are presently adopting .338 Lapua Magnum rifles as their primary sniper weapon. The .338 Lapua was developed in the United States to a US Navy requirement, but was never fully developed by the US military. Lapua of Finland carried the cartridge to full development and it is now in use by several countries. Ballistically, the .338 Lapua falls between the .300 Winchester Magnum and .50 caliber Browning Machine Gun (.50 BMG) cartridge used in Western antimaterial rifles. Rifles in .338 Lapua are easily handled by one man and extend the effective range far beyond that of a 7.62x51mm rifle. The Russians have developed their own cartridge with similar ballistics, the 9x53mm.

Law enforcement precision tactical rifles may also be found in 5.56x45mm (.223 Remington) caliber. Unlike military snipers, who may be expected to engage targets at distances of up to 1,000 meters, law enforcement snipers rarely have targets at distances greater than 100 meters/yards. In fact, the average engagement distance for American law enforcement snipers is 75 yards. At this distance, a 5.56x45mm precision tactical rifle is adequate, although most law enforcement snipers prefer the larger caliber 7.62x51mm.

Although there are some semiautomatic precision tactical rifles, most remain bolt-action for several reasons. Bolt-action rifles of acceptable accuracy, typically considered to be at least minute of angle (MOA) over the effective range of the rifle (1 inch at 100 yards, 2 inches at 200 yards, 3 inches at 300 yards, etc.), can be more reliably manufactured than semiautomatics. Most bolt-action precision tactical rifles exceed the MOA standard to a significant degree. Also, bolt-action rifles are simpler and thus more reliable. One of the primary missions of a sniper team is intelligence gathering and military snipers thus operate independently far from friendly troops. All sniper equipment must be totally reliable. The argument has been set forth that a semiautomatic or even automatic rifle should be a part of every sniper team, but if a sniper gets into a situation where he needs full automatic suppressive fire, he is in VERY serious trouble. Snipers avoid such situations at all costs. Law enforcement snipers likewise have no need for semiautomatic rifles, as their mission usually consists of a single shot.

For the future, precision tactical rifles for the most part will remain bolt-action, although the US Army has adopted what it calls the Semiautomatic Sniper System (SASS). The SASS is a 7.62x51mm, according to the Army's requirement documentation.* Other than the US Army, most nations will retain bolt-action rifles. The Australian Army, for instance, has just ordered Blaser LRS92 precision tactical rifles in .338 Lapua and equipped them with the innovative Horus Vision Sighting System, a total integrated sighting system for precision shooting that eliminates using windage and elevation knobs and enables precise long-range shooting at incredible distances. In testing, the Australian military achieved consistent hits on man-size targets at nearly 3,000 meters, thanks to their integrated rifle and sighting system. Since the telescopic sight is also critical, we believe that the patented Horus Vision Sighting System will eventually supplant conventional mil-dots, which are far less effective. The Blaser rifle is a straight-pull bolt-action that can be operated so rapidly that it can compete against semiautomatic rifles. In terms of rifle caliber, most countries other than the United States will probably move towards the .338 Lapua, as have the British, Dutch, Australians and several others. The .338 Lapua is far more effective than any 7.62 cartridge, inherently accurate and can achieve hits at twice the distance of a 7.62x51mm rifle, given proper sighting.

---

* The M110 SASS as of late 2005 is the Stoner SR25, but some controversy from competitors for the contract exists, and the exact rifle to be adopted remains uncertain. besides the SR25, the Armalite AR-10(T) and DPMS precision tactical rifle are also contenders for the contract.

Australia

Precision Rifle Systems ATAS Sniper Rifles

Precision Rifle Systems ATAS sniper rifles comprise a series of bolt-action rifles configured to meet user requirements. The bolt-action may have three forward or rear locking lugs and feed may be either single shot or from a six-round box magazine. The magazine may be located either on the left-hand side of the rifle, under the receiver, or on the right.

Although optimized for 7.62x51mm, almost any cartridge can be accommodated up to 50 BMG (12.7 x 99mm). Tobler manufactures the barrels, with a muzzle brake optional. Optical sights are to the customer's choice, mounted on an integral dovetail machined into the top of the receiver. Triggers are fully adjustable for pull weight, engagement and overtravel.

Receivers are designed and manufactured to maximize the total locking area. Materials used are 4140 chromium molybdenum steel, 1040 steel or 410/420 stainless steel, depending on the action type, function or user requirement.

NO SPECIFICATIONS AVAILABLE

Austria

ERMA SR 100 Heavy Sniper Rifle

At the beginning of 1998, the ERMA of Suhl small arms manufacturing was taken over by the Suhler und Sportwaffen GmbH (Suhl is 51 percent owned by Steyr-Mannlicher AG & Co KG). Suhl continues to distribute Erma small arms, although the ERMA SR 100 heavy sniper rifle is produced by Steyr in Austria and is distributed in co-ordination with Suhl. It is distributed in the United States by Capital City Firearms of Richmond, Virginia.

The ERMA SR 100 is presently available in three calibers: 7.62x51mm (.308 Winchester); 300 Winchester Magnum; and 338 Lapua Magnum. A rifle in 12.7 x 53mm Suppressed (50 Whisper) is under development. One feature of the ERMA SR 100 is that it is possible to switch from one caliber to another simply by changing the barrel, bolt and magazine.

The ERMA SR 100 is a technically advanced design intended for optimum accuracy. The bolt has three locking lugs that lock directly into the barrel after a bolt rotation of 60 degrees. The barrel is seated in the receiver and is fixed using an eccentric cam. The forged aluminum alloy receiver, in turn, is seated clearance-free in an aluminum bedding block fixed into the laminated wood stock.

Caliber change is facilitated by a cam lever on the left of the rifle that moves the eccentric-pivot barrel lock allowing the barrel, bolt and magazine to be replaced. Suppressed barrels are available.

Barrels feature a muzzle brake that also acts as a flash hider. Barrel lengths vary according to the type of ammunition in use, as do the magazine capacities. The 7.62x51mm magazines hold 10 rounds, while the 300 Winchester Magnum capacity is reduced to eight, and 338 Lapua Magnum is five rounds.

The match trigger has an integral drop safety and is adjustable for trigger takeup, takeup weight, position and trigger pull (between 500 g and 3 kg). The three-position safety directly locks the firing pin.

The stock is adjustable to suit individual shooters. The buttplate is adjustable for length and height. The cheekpiece is also adjustable for height and a monopod can be lowered from under the stock when the bipod is in use. The thumbhole match stock is fully ambidextrous. The stock houses aluminum rails for mounting the detachable bipod and sling swivels, which can be mounted on the right, left or bottom of the stock.

No sights are provided. Options include a mirage strap over the barrel and fully adjustable open aperture sights for optical sight backup.

SPECIFICATIONS:
Caliber: 7.62x51mm NATO (.308 Winchester); 300 Winchester Magnum; 338 Lapua Magnum
Operation: manual, bolt-action
Locking: three-lug rotating bolt
Feed: 7.62x51mm 10-round box magazine; 300 Winchester Magnum, eight-round box magazine; 338 Lapua Magnum, five-round box magazine
Approximate empty weight: 7.62x51mm 17.4 pounds; 300 Winchester Magnum and 338 Lapua Magnum, 17.2 pounds
Overall length: 7.62x51mm, 49 inches; 300 Winchester Magnum and 338 Lapua Magnum, 53 inches; with barrel removed, 33.5 inches
Barrel length: 7.62x51mm, 28.5 inches; 300 Winchester Magnum and 338 Lapua Magnum, 32.5 inches
Sights: None provided, backup open sights available

Steyr 7.62x51mm SSG Sniper Rifles

The Steyr 7.62mm SSG is the standard sniper rifle for the Austrian Army under the designation Scharfschutzengewehr 69 (SSG 69).

The barrel is cold hammer-forged, a process originally

ERMA SR100

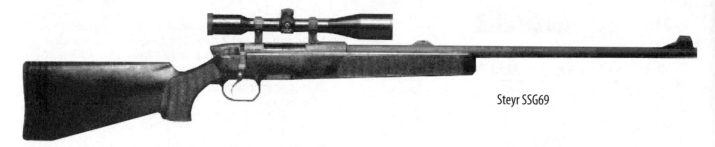

Steyr SSG69

developed by Steyr. The bolt throw is 60 degrees and it has six locking lugs, set at the rear and arranged in pairs. The trigger mechanism is a two-stage with optional double-set trigger available. The sliding safety catch on the top right rear of the receiver locks both the bolt and the firing pin.

The standard magazine capacity is five rounds, and is the rotary traditionally used in Mannlicher rifles. The stock is a synthetic material and can be adjusted for length of pull by adding or removing spacers in the butt.

The receiver has a longitudinal rib machined on top for optical sight mounting. Mounting adapters are available for all types of sights. The standard optical sight is the Hensoldt 10 x 42 ZF 500 or ZF 800 attached by NATO standard mounts. Backup open sights for emergency use are present on military versions, but police models lack open sights and use only optical sights.

SSG models are as follows:
- SSG-P1, the basic SSG 69 rifle with olive green stock.
- SSG-PII is specifically designed for police marksman use and has a heavier barrel than the military version. The empty weight of this variant without optics is 9.4 pounds; at one time, it was known as the SSG-P. There are no fixed sights and this version has a black stock.
- SSG-PIIK (Kurz, or Short) is basically the same as the SSG-PII but with a shorter (20 inch) barrel. Weight with optical sight is 10.6 pounds.
- SSG-PIV is based on the SSG-PII but with a reduced-length (409mm) heavy barrel with 1 in 10 in twist for use with subsonic ammunition that fires heavier than standard bullets for ballistic effects. The muzzle is threaded to accommodate a suppressor. Empty weight without optics is 8.4 pounds.

SPECIFICATIONS: SSG-P1

Caliber: 7.62x51mm
Operation: Manual, bolt-action
Locking: rotating bolt
Feed: internal rotary magazine
Magazine capacity: 5 rounds
Empty weight: Approx. 8.8 pounds
Overall length: 44.9 inches
Barrel length: 25.6 inches
Sights: optical: Hensoldt 10 x 42; Backup open sights:
Front: blade, rear: V-notch

Canada

Armament Technology 7.62x51mm AT1-C24 Precision Tactical Rifle

The AT1-C24 is a modified version of the US Army's M24 Sniper Weapon System. It is built on a Remington Model 700 short action that has been modified to provide optimum performance. All components are precision machined to ensure accuracy and reliable operation under the most severe conditions.

Barrels are 416R stainless steel with 5R hook cut rifling. Twist rates of one turn in 10 inches are optimized for use with heavy bullets that are normally used for long-range shooting. Accuracy of the AT1-C24 is warranted by the manufacturer to be less than a minute of angle across the rifle's effective range when new, although the rifles' accuracy usually averages better than a half minute of angle. AT1-C24 barrel life is least 10,000-rounds before replacement is necessary. Stocks are Kevlar-reinforced composite with full-length aluminum bedding blocks and are supplied in a choice of colors with a textured finish. Stocks are available with adjustable cheekpiece and length of pull.

Telescope mounts are MIL-STD-1913. Auxiliary sighting systems, suppressors, tool kits and deployment kits are optional.

A variant, the AT1M, is chambered in 300 Winchester Magnum.

SPECIFICATIONS:

Caliber: 7.62x51mm; AT1M, 300 Winchester Magnum
Operation: Manual, bolt-action
Feed: Internal box magazine
Empty weight: 13.2 pounds
Overall length: 45.3 inches
Barrel length: 26 inches
Trigger: single stage, adjustable 3.3 to 6.6 pounds
Sights: optical, customer installed

7.62x51mm C3 and C3A1 Sniper Rifles

The Canadian C3 sniper rifle is a modified version of the British Parker-Hale Model 82 to meet Canadian requirements. The stock is fitted with four half-inch spacers to permit length adjustment. The original rifle has two male dovetail blocks on the receiver, to accept either the Parker-Hale 5E vernier rear sight or the Austrian Kahles 6-power telescope. All exposed metal parts of the rifle are non-reflective.

The Canadian Department of Defense later modified its C3 rifles, redesignating them C3A1. The C3A1 incorporates a number of changes from the earlier C3 model, which entered Canadian service in the mid-1970s and is actually a new rifle. The stock was changed to a McMillan A2 type and the receiver was strengthened and equipped with a six-round-capacity steel box magazine with a release catch located in the front edge of the trigger guard. The trigger mechanism has a redesigned safety catch and is of all-steel construction. The bolt handle was modified by the addition of an aluminum extension knob that provides easier grasp with a gloved hand and greater clearance from the telescopic sight than with the C3 model. A new barrel with a revised twist rate to provide optimum performance from both standard 7.62x51mm ball and heavier bullets developed for sniping and competition use. A detachable Parker-Hale bipod attaches to a hand-stop assembly. The Kahles scope was replaced with a 10-power Unertl similar to that used by the US Marine Corps.

The Canadian military was evaluating 338 Lapua rifles at the time of this writing (late 2004), but the C3A1 will be in Canadian service for years to come.

SPECIFICATIONS: C3A1

Caliber: 7.62x51mm NATO
Operation: manual, bolt-action
Feed: 6-shot box magazine
Empty weight: 13.9 pounds
Overall length: 44.9 to 47.6 inches
Barrel length: 26 inches

Diemaco 5.56x45mm C7CT Custom Tactical Rifle

The Diemaco 5.56mm C7CT is a semiautomatic custom tactical rifle used to effectively engage targets to ranges out to 600 meters. It is essentially a custom-built version of the C7 assault rifle that can be configured to a variety of customer preferences to suit tactical requirements.

The Diemaco C7CT incorporates a bipod and an unchromed, hammer forged, floating heavy barrel to enhance accuracy. Various twist rates can be provided. A removable noise and flash suppressor is attached to the muzzle. The stock has a removable weight to counterbalance the additional weight of the heavy barrel. A contoured pistol grip and butt stock enhance shooter comfort. Bipods and slings are attached to the tubular hand guard and do not influence the barrel. A MIL-STD-1913 sight rail is located atop the receiver. No sights are provided.

The bolt carrier assembly has a titanium firing pin for faster lock time. The trigger is a two-stage match type. Any standard M16 type magazine can be used. Options include butt extension, carry case, modified pistol grips, gas port cutoff, camouflage and bipods

A similar 5.56mm C8CT rifle based on the Diemaco C8 carbine is also produced. The C8CT can be produced in many customer-specified configurations so no firm data can be quoted. An illustration is provided.

SPECIFICATIONS:

Caliber: 5.56x45mm
Operation: gas, semiautomatic
Locking: rotating bolt
Feed: M16 type detachable box magazines
Empty weight: 9.48 pounds
Overall length: 39.36 in
Barrel length: 20 in
Sights: optical, user choice.

China

NORINCO Type 79 Self-Loading Sniper Rifle

The NORINCO Type 79 is a copy of the Russian SVD Dragunov sniper rifle, except that the stock is slightly shorter. It is equipped with a 4-power optical sight that is a copy of the Soviet/Russian Federation PSO-1, of which early versions had the same ability to detect infra-red emissions.

A modified version, the Type 85 has a slightly higher rate of fire and somewhat shorter effective range, according to official Chinese sources. External appearance of the two rifles is virtually identical.

SPECIFICATIONS:

Caliber: 7.62 x 54mm R (Type 53)
Operation: gas, short-stroke piston, semiautomatic
Feed: 10-round detachable box magazine
Empty weight: 9.7 pounds, including optic
Overall length: 48 inches
Barrel length: 24.4 inches
Rifling: 4 grooves, rh, 1 turn in 10 inches
Sights: front, adjustable post; rear: tangent U-notch; optical: 4x
Effective range: 1,300 meters (claimed)

Croatia

EM 992 and EMM 992 Sniper Rifles

The EM 992 and EMM 992 sniper rifles are similar bolt-action rifles which differ mainly in caliber and some dimensions. The EM 992 is chambered in 7.62x51mm, while the EMM 992 fires 300 Winchester Magnum. The EM 992 has a detachable five-round magazine, while that of the EMM 992 holds four rounds. These rifles are sporting weapons modified for use by military and law enforcement agencies.

Both rifles have identical bolt-actions with four locking lugs and a 90-degree bolt throw. The trigger mechanism is described as being of a "new construction" and is adjustable. A match-grade barrel is used, along with a muzzle brake that is claimed to reduce felt recoil by 40 percent. Stocks are laminated wood with a raised cheek rest. A Harris-type adjustable bipod is located in front of the forearm.

The standard optical sight is a Leupold Vari-X 3.5- to 10-power scope. Backup iron sights are provided. A passive night sight is optional. Accessories include extra magazines, a cleaning and maintenance kit and a waterproof carry case.

SPECIFICATIONS: Data for EM 992 (EMM 992 in parenthesis)

Caliber: 7.62x51mm (300 Winchester Magnum)
Operation: Manual, bolt-action
Feed: 5-round box magazine (4-round box magazine)
Empty weight: 14.3 pounds (14.6 pounds)
Overall length: 48 inches (49 inches)
Barrel length: 22.2 inches (22.8 inches)
Sights: Leupold Vari-X 3.5-10 x 42
Maximum effective range: 900 m (1,200 m)

Chinese PLA Sniper Team

CZ700

Czech Republic

7.62x51mm CZ 700 and CZ 700 M1 Sniper Rifles

The CZ 700 sniper rifle was developed from a competition rifle and was produced in two versions, one for standard 7.62x51mm ammunition and the other for subsonic ammunition with the barrel of the latter surrounded by a jacket forming a sound suppressor. The two barrels are interchangeable and are secured by two screws after being screwed into the receiver.

The CZ 700 sniper is a magazine-fed rifle with a manually operated rotary bolt locked by three axially located lugs arranged in two rows. The trigger is fully adjustable, for pull weight, for travel before firing and for lateral trigger positioning. An adjustable cheekpiece is provided on the butt-stock, as is a pistol-type grip for the firing hand and a fully adjustable buttplate. The stock is laminated wood and can be supplied in a variety of finishes.

The standard box magazine holds 10-rounds, although a single-cartridge magazine insert is available.

The CZ 700 sniper is no longer in production, and has been replaced by the CZ 700 M1 sniper. This is basically the same rifle but with all furniture, originally manufactured using molded synthetic materials, replaced by wood.

No sights are provided. Each rifle can be supplied with two 10-round magazines, cleaning equipment, disassembly tools, antimirage strap, flash suppressor, headspace gauge and a transit case to customer specifications.

SPECIFICATIONS: Data for standard CZ 700 sniper rifle (suppressed version in parentheses)

Caliber: 7.62x51mm
Operation: Manual, bolt-action
Feed: detachable box magazine, 10-round capacity
Empty weight: 13.7 pounds (14.8 pounds)
Overall length: 48 inches (49 inches)
Barrel length: 25.6 inches (17.7 inches)
Sights: optical, user option

Finland

Sako TRG Sniper Rifles

The Sako TRG is a bolt-action magazine-fed rifle. Two versions are available: the 7.62x51mm TRG 22 and the 338 Lapua Magnum TRG 42. Cartridges are fed from a detachable double row magazine. The TRG 42 is also available chambered in 300 Winchester Magnum. The TRG 22 and TRG 42 are enhanced models of the earlier TRG 21 and TRG 41, with improvements to the stock, muzzle brake and the bipod. The cold hammer forged free-floating barrel can be fitted with a detachable suppressor or a muzzle brake, both of which also act as efficient flash hiders.

The receiver is of solid steel and is also cold hammer-forged. The receiver is triangular, with the bottom flat and the sides angled inwards, with flat outer surfaces and rounded inner guides for the bolt, which incorporates three locking lugs for maximum strength, while the bolt throw of 60 degrees provides minimum interference with optics, allowing them to be mounted low in the shooter's field of view. An oversize bolt handle facilitates fast and easy

Sako TRG22

operation. The receiver is fixed with three fastening screws and uses an oversized bedding surface on an aluminum bedding block for enhanced rigidity. Auxiliary folding aperture sights can be provided for backup use, although the TRG is normally delivered without sights.

The base of the stock is of aluminum, to which the polyurethane forearm is attached. The butt-stock is also made of polyurethane and is reinforced by an aluminum skeleton. The cheekpiece is fully adjustable for height via spacers. The buttplate is adjustable both for length of pull and for angle, again through the use of spacers, and is also infinitely adjustable in height. In addition, the stock is designed to be fully ambidextrous. Stocks may be olive green or black, the olive green version adding 200 g to the overall weight.

The two-stage trigger is adjustable for pull weight from 1 to 2.5 kg. It is also adjustable in length and horizontal or vertical pitch. The entire fire control mechanism, including the trigger guard can be removed from the rifle without disassembling any other parts of the rifle.

The safety catch is silent in operation and is located inside the trigger guard. The safety locks the trigger mechanism and the bolt in the closed position with the firing pin physically blocked from primer contact.

Optional accessories include a muzzle brake/flash suppressor, sound suppressor in .7.62x51mm, bipod, match open sights, night sight adapter, cleaning kit and heavy duty transit case.

France

FR-F2 7.62x51mm Sniper Rifle

The FR-F2 sniper rifle was introduced in late 1984 and is an improved version of the earlier FR-F1. The basic characteristics such as bolt-action and dimensions are the same as the earlier model, with changes in the nature of functional improvements. The forend is metal covered in matte black polymer material; the bipod was strengthened and moved from its location at the front of the forend to a position just ahead of the receiver. This facilitates adjustment by the shooter, and it is suspended from a yoke around the rear of the barrel where it is less likely to affect the stability of the rifle when firing. The most significant change is the enclosure of the barrel in a thick plastic thermal sleeve that is claimed to reduce mirage and possibly the infrared signature of the weapon.

Variants

FR-G1 and FR-G2

The FR-G1 and FR-G2 are further revisions of the FR-F1 and FR-F2 sniper rifles. The forend has been replaced by a wood assembly and the thermal sleeve of the FR-F2 removed. The main difference between the FR-G1 and FR-G2 is that the FR-G1 has a fixed bipod while that for the FR-G2 is articulated.

SPECIFICATIONS: Data for TRG 22 (TRG 42 in parentheses)
Caliber: 7.62x51mm (338 Lapua Magnum or 300 Winchester Magnum)
Operation: manual, bolt-action
Feed: box magazine
Magazine capacity: TRG 22: 10 rounds; TRG 42 300 Winchester magazine: seven rounds; TRG 42 338 Lapua magazine: five rounds
Empty weight: 10.4 pounds (11.2 pounds)
Overall length: 45.3 inches (47.2 inches)
Barrel length: 26 inches; (27.2 inches)
Sights: none provided; user option

SPECIFICATIONS:
Caliber: 7.62x51mm
Operation: manual, bolt-action
Locking: rotating bolt
Feed: 10-round box magazine
Empty weight: FR-G1, 9.9 pounds: FR-G2, 10.1 pounds
Overall length: 44.8 inches
Barrel length: 21.7 inches
Sights: optical, 4-power; open, front, flat-topped pyramid with luminous dot; rear: square notch with luminous dots.

FR-F2

French sniper

Germany

Blaser R93 LRS-2 Precision Tactical Rifle

The Blaser R93 LRS-2 tactical precision rifle was derived from Blaser's 300 meter competition rifle. Several modifications were introduced as the rifle is intended specifically for military and police snipers and others demanding a rifle for long-range precision shooting. The R93 LRS-2 was developed with inputs from military and police snipers, both in Europe and North America.

The Blaser R93 LRS-2 is a unique, straight-pull bolt-action, magazine-fed rifle that is the subject of nine separate patents. The receiver is aluminum and is unstressed, all forces being carried by the bolt and barrel.

The Blaser is unique in that, other than the 338 Lapua Magnum version, calibers can be changed in minutes by replacing the barrel, bolt head and magazine. Barrels can be removed and replaced without altering the rifle's zero as long as each barrel was zeroed with the telescopic sight fixed to it and the sight was not removed. The barrel is held in place by two captive hexagonal-headed nuts that do not require torque settings. The barrel is further positioned by the recoil lug, which joins with a slot on the bottom of the barrel. The chrome molybdenum barrel is fluted to increase stiffness and cryogenically treated for accuracy. A corrosion-resistant gas nitride coating protects all steel components. A muzzle brake reduces felt recoil in 7.62x51mm to approximately that of a .243 Winchester rifle, while that of the 300 Winchester Magnum is reduced approximately to that of a 7.62x51mm rifle.

The locking system consists of a 14-lug collet that expands into a ring in the barrel when the bolt is pressed fully forward. There is no bolt rotation whatsoever. As the rifle is fired, pressure against the bolt face forces the locking lugs more tightly into the locking ring. In the unlikely event of a case head failure there are two safety vents on either side of the rifle. Trigger pull is factory set at 1.2 kg and is user adjustable for position, pull weight, takeup and overtravel.

Ammunition is fed from a detachable box magazine that positions the cartridges directly in line with the chamber, obviating the need for a feed ramp and ensuring smooth operation. The bolt and carrier ride on two rails that interface with grooves in the receiver. The rifle can be changed from right- to left-handed operation by replacing the bolt and bolt carrier.

The Blaser safety is positioned at the rear of the bolt carrier and has two positions, safe and fire. The latter is visibly indicated by a large red dot that is obscured when the rifle is set on safe. A third intermediate position for safe loading and unloading is possible by partially depressing the safety button in the safe position. This allows the bolt to be drawn to the rear with the striker and trigger locked.

The one-piece stock is made using molded synthetic materials. The butt is adjustable for length of pull by inserting spacers and pivots 15 degrees left or right. The cheekpiece is also vertically adjustable. An adjustable monopod is built into the rear of the buttstock and there is a bipod mounting groove under the forend.

There are no open sights. The proprietary telescopic sight mount attaches to notches in the barrel. An anti-mirage strap is standard.

Blaser R93 LRS2 .338 Lapua version

SPECIFICATIONS:

Caliber: By changing the barrel, bolt and magazine the rifle can accommodate 5.56x45mm; 6mm Norma BR; 6.5x55mm; 7.62x51mm; 300 Winchester Magnum. The 338 Lapua magnum Blaser cannot be changed to other calibers.
Operation: manual, straight pull bolt
Locking: see text
Feed: detachable box magazine
Empty weight: 10.6 pounds
Overall length: 5.56x45mm and 7.62x51mm, 44.9 inches; 300 Winchester Magnum, 45.3 inches; 338 Lapua Magnum, 46.9 inches
Barrel length: 5.56x45mm and 7.62x51mm, 24.7 inches; 300 Winchester Magnum, 25.6 inches; 338 Lapua Magnum, 27 inches
Sights: none provided. optical, user option

Heckler & Koch 7.62x51mm MSG 90 Precision Tactical Rifle

The Heckler & Koch MSG 90 rifle was introduced in 1987 and incorporates the same roller delayed blowback system common to all Heckler & Koch G3/HK91 type rifles. This rifle was known at one time as the PSG3.

The MSG 90 was designed to meet military specifications for the US Army's M24 Sniper Weapon System. The MSG 90 uses a special cold hammer forged and tempered barrel and has a trigger with a shoe that widens the trigger for better control. Trigger pull is factory set at approximately 3.3 pounds. The stock is adjustable for length of pull and has a vertically adjustable cheek rest. There are no open sights. The standard optical sight is a 10-power telescope with range settings from 100 to 1,200 meters. The receiver is fitted with a MIL-STD-1913 mount that will accept any NATO standard optic mount.

The forend is fitted with an internal T-rail that allows the attachment of a sling swivel or a bipod.

SPECIFICATIONS:

Caliber: 7.62x51mm
Operation: roller delayed blowback, semiautomatic only
Feed: 5- or 20-round detachable box magazine
Empty weight: 14.1 pounds
Overall length: 45.7 inches
Barrel length: 23.6 inches
Sights: 10 x 42 optical telescope

Heckler & Koch 7.62x51mm MSG 90A1 Precision Tactical Rifle

The Heckler & Koch MSG 90A1 rifle is a special variant of the MSG 90 rifle described above that was developed to meet user requirements of specialized units within the US Department of Defense. Originally known as the MSG 90-DMR (Designated Marksman Rifle), the MSG 90A1 is functionally identical to the standard MSG 90 but with a number of additional features. These include open sights, adjustable for windage and elevation to a range of 1,200 meters; a threaded muzzle for the addition of a sound suppressor or the low signature flash hider that is standard on the 90A1 model; and a brass deflector incorporated into the receiver to the rear of the ejection port. Other than these modifications, the MSG 90A1 uses the same magazines, accessories and components as the standard MSG 90.

SPECIFICATIONS:

Caliber: 7.62x51mm NATO
Operation: roller delayed blowback, semiautomatic
Feed: 20-round detachable box magazine
Empty weight: 14.7 pounds
Overall length: 45.9 inches
Barrel length: 23.6 inches
Sights: 10 x 42 telescope; front, fixed post inside circular protective ring; rear: aperture adjustable for windage and elevation. Settings from 100 to 1,200m
Max effective range: 1,000m with optical sight

Heckler & Koch 7.62x51mm PSG 1 High-Precision Marksman's Rifle

The PSG-1 Prazisionsschutzengewehr (high-precision marksman's rifle) is manufactured by Heckler & Koch for police and military use. It is a semiautomatic rifle using the company's roller delayed operating system. Superb accuracy is claimed: an average dispersion diameter of less than 80mm is quoted at a range of 300 meters for 50 shot test groups with Lapua .308 Winchester Match ammunition. A 6 x 42 telescopic sight with a variable illuminated reticle is an integral part of the weapon.

Heckler & Koch MSG 90A1

Heckler & Koch PSG1

Windage and elevation adjustment is by moving lens, with six settings from 100 to 600 meters.

The heavy polygonally rifled barrel is 650mm long. The manufacturer states that a special system enables silent and positive bolt closing. A vertically adjustable trigger shoe effectively widens the trigger for enhanced control. The trigger pull is approximately 3.3 pounds. Length of pull, vertical cheekpiece adjustment and butt adjustment to the shooter's shoulder can be accommodated to the shooter's anatomy.

The PSG 1 is normally supplied complete with a transit case carrying the rifle and accessories. These include two 20-round magazines, two 5-round magazines, a cleaning rod and a bipod. The case alone weighs 26 pounds.

SPECIFICATIONS:

Caliber: 7.62x51mm
Operation: Roller delayed blowback, semiautomatic
Feed: 5- or 20-round detachable box magazine
Empty weight: 17.86 pounds
Overall length: 47.6 inches
Barrel length: 25.6 inches
Sights: 6 x 42mm telescope; 6 positions, 100 to 600m settings

Indonesia

Pindad 7.62x51mm SPR-1 Precision Tactical Rifle

The Pindad SPR-1 sniper rifle appears to be a standard bolt-action sporting rifle modified for military and law enforcement use, as are many such rifles, including many based on the popular Remington Model 700. Changes from sporting to tactical use are the provision of an adjustable bipod, in the SPR-1 a Harris type, an adjustable cheekpiece for the thumb-hole stock and an optical sight, with no provision for open sights. An angled slot is cut into the barrel above the muzzle to reduce muzzle rise and aid in recovery for follow-up shots. The SPR-1 fires 7.62x51mm match standard ammunition. There is no visible magazine, but it is probable that the SP-1 feeds from an internal magazine of five rounds capacity, which is usual with rifles of this type.

SPECIFICATIONS:

Caliber: 7.62x51mm
Operation: Manual, bolt-action
Locking: rotating-bolt
Feed: Internal box magazine, five rounds capacity (Est.)
Weight: 15 pounds
Barrel length: 25.6
Sights: optical

International

PGM 338 Lapua Magnum Mini Hecate Precision Tactical Rifle

The PGM 338 Lapua Magnum sniper rifle is a development of the other rifles in the PGM family and is basically similar apart from caliber related components. It is a modular bolt-action rifle with a side-folding stock, a 10-round box magazine, a folding bipod and a fluted barrel with an integral muzzle brake. Various barrel lengths and stock combinations are available along with the standard 27.2-inch barrel. No sights are provided.

Like the other rifles in this series, the Mini Hecate has a folding skeleton stock adjustable for length of pull, along with adjustable cheekpiece and butt pad. An adjustable monopod, The aircraft aluminum receiver is not a stressed component. The bolt locks into the barrel extension. The cold hammer-forged barrel is made by Lothar Walther, is fully free floated and fluted for stiffness. The pistol grip and other furniture are made of polymer. A high-efficiency muzzle brake reduces felt recoil. A MIL-STD-1913 rail atop the receiver enables mounting any optic with NATO-specification mounts. A proprietary bipod is available, although a slot in the forend enables mounting any bipod. FNH promotional literature has shown a Versa-Pod mounted.

SPECIFICATIONS:

Caliber: 338 Lapua Magnum
Operation: manual, bolt-action
Locking: rotating bolt, three front locking lugs
Feed: 10-round detachable box magazine
Empty weight: 13 to 15.4 pounds depending on configuration
Overall length: stock folded, 39.5 to 54.25 inches. Extended stock adds 12 inches
Barrel length: 27.2 inches
Sights: optical, user option

PGM Ultima Ratio (UR) Commando 7.62x51mm Sniper Rifles

Originally manufactured and marketed by PGM Precision of France, the PGM UR Commando sniper rifles are now marketed by FN Herstal of Belgium and by FNH USA Inc in the United States.

PGM UR Commando rifles are based on the PGM Ultima Ratio (UR) Intervention model but are shorter and lighter to suit the requirements of special operations forces. The basic features of the UR Intervention model are the same, although barrels of the Commando models are fluted rather than finned.

PGM Hecate

PGM Commando

There are two UR Commando models. The UR Commando I has a fixed stock and may be fitted with barrels 470 or 550mm long. On the Commando II, the stock assembly can be folded to the left of the receiver to reduce the overall length for transport, airborne operations, or stowage. Either Commando model can be fitted with the PGM suppressed barrel.

The PGM UR Commando models are chambered for 7.62x51mm (.308 Winchester), although calibers of similar overall length to the 7.62x51mm, such as 300 Winchester Short Magnum (WSM) or .300 Remington Short Action Ultra Magazine (RSAUM), can be produced on request.

SPECIFICATIONS:

Caliber: 7.62x51mm
Operation: manual, bolt-action
Locking: rotating bolt, three front locking lugs
Feed: 10-round detachable box magazine
Weight: About 12 pounds, depending on configuration
Overall length: with 18.5 inch barrel, stock folded, 29.1 inches; stock extended, 40.2 inches
Barrel length: 18.5 inches or 21.7 inches
Sights: optical, user option

PGM Ultima Ratio (UR) Intervention 7.62x51mm Sniper Rifle

PGM Precision of France has joined with FN Herstal of Belgium to market the PGM series of specialist rifles. The PGM UR Intervention is now marketed by FN Herstal and by FNH USA in the United States.

The PGM UR Intervention rifle is the base model of a series of specialized sniper rifles under the Ultima Ratio, or UR designation. All rifles in this series are manually operated bolt-action rifles with all components mounted separately on a central rigid aircraft-grade aluminum alloy frame.

The steel bolt has three front locking lugs and has gas escape holes in the event of a ruptured cartridge. An instant-release 10-round magazine is carried inside the aluminum alloy receiver along with an ambidextrous pistol grip and a fully adjustable stock with an adjustable black rubber recoil pad. The two-stage trigger mechanism is described as a military design but of match quality. A sear safety is provided on the left of the receiver. A folding adjustable bipod provided with an axial locking system to prevent accidental tilt is located at the front end of the forend.

The barrel fully free-floated, is finned for cooling and is manufactured to match-grade standards. An integral muzzle brake is provided. One feature of the PGM UR series is that barrels can be rapidly exchanged for any other barrel in the UR series, chambered in a similar caliber with a guaranteed return to zero. Standard barrel lengths for the UR Intervention are 470 and 600mm long.

Using the quick-change barrel system, it is also possible to exchange a standard PGM UR barrel for a modular suppressed barrel which permits the use of subsonic or supersonic ammunition.

The top of the receiver is provided with a rail which can accommodate Universal, Weaver or STANAG scope bases without further fitting.

The basic PGM UR Intervention rifle is chambered for 7.62x51mm (.308 Winchester) or 300 Winchester Short Magnum (WSM), although calibers with cartridges of similar overall length to the 7.62x51mm can be produced on request.

PGM UR models intended for civilian sales are also manufactured. The UR Europa is chambered in several calibers, and the UR Magnum is chambered for 300 Winchester Magnum, although other Magnum calibers can be provided.

SPECIFICATIONS:

Caliber: 7.62x51mm, 300 Winchester Magnum;
Operation: manual, bolt-action
Locking: rotating bolt, three front locking lugs
Feed: 10-round detachable box magazine
Empty weight: 12.1 pounds, depending on configuration
Overall length: with 18.5 inches barrel, 40.7 inches; disassembled, 29.5 inches
Barrel length: 18.5 inches or 23.6 inches
Sights: optical, user option

Belgian sniper

Israel

Israel Military Industries Galil

Israel Military Industries 7.62x51mm Galil Sniper Rifle

The Galil sniper rifle is a semiautomatic gas-operated rifle specially designed to meet the particular demands of sniping. It is chambered in 7.62x51mm. The accuracy requirement is considered to be a 4.7- to 5.9-inch circle at 300 meters and a, 11.8-inch circle at 600 meters range. The Galil sniper consistently exceeds these requirements.

The mechanism and general configuration are the same as the standard Galil rifle, but a number of features are peculiar to this model. A bipod is mounted behind the forend and attached to the receiver so it can be adjusted by the shooter and also to relieve the barrel of any stress. The barrel is heavier than standard, which contributes to the accuracy. The optical sight mount is on the side of the receiver and is a precision-cast, long-base unit giving particularly good support to the standard issue Nimrod 6 x 40 telescopic sight. The sight mount and telescope can be mounted and dismounted quickly and easily without affecting the rifle's zero. Any type of night sight can be fitted.

The barrel is fitted with a muzzle brake and a compensator that reduces jump and permits rapid follow-up shots. A suppressor can be substituted for the muzzle brake if desired. The trigger is a two-stage type. The safety selector is above the pistol grip, and this rifle is semiautomatic only. The wooden stock can be folded to reduce the overall length of the rifle for transportation or airborne operations. When unfolded and locked, the stock is rigid and without play. The stock is fitted with an adjustable cheekpiece and rubber recoil pad.

Each rifle is issued in a specially designed case, which also contains the sight, two optical filters, a sling, two magazines and a cleaning kit.

SPECIFICATIONS:
Caliber: 7.62x51mm NATO
Operation: gas-operated, semiautomatic
Locking: rotating bolt
Feed: 20-round detachable box magazine
Empty weight: 14.1 pounds
Overall length: stock folded, 33.1 inches; stock extended, 43.9 inches
Barrel length: without muzzle brake, 20 inches
Sights: open sights, front, blade; rear: aperture; optical, Nimrod 6 x 40 telescope

Israel Military Industries SR-99 7.62x51mm Sniper Rifle

The IMI SR-99 semiautomatic sniper rifle was first shown outside Israel in 2000 and is a product of IMI's Integrated Security Systems Group (ISSG). The SR-99 is a further development of the basic Galil assault rifle and is stated to be distinctly improved over the previous Galil sniper rifle (see above entry).

The IMI SR-99 semiautomatic sniper rifle retains the receiver of the Galil assault rifle with a one-piece bolt carrier and charging handle for silent operation. All other components are custom-built for the sniper role. The receiver is fitted with a heavy cold hammer-forged barrel with a combined muzzle brake and compensator. A flexible anti-mirage strap is mounted above the barrel. Feed is from a 10-round or 25-round detachable box magazine.

The furniture is polymer and is ergonomically designed, with numerous adjustments to accommodate individual users. The stock folds to the side and has an adjustable buttplate and cheekpiece. An adjustable monopod is at the stock rear. The pistol grip has an adjustable hand rest, and an adjustable folding bipod with traverse capability is at the forward end of the forearm.

Optical sights are mounted on a quick-detachable mounting on the left of the receiver. This is claimed to return to zero even after repeated dismounting. The standard optical sight is the Nimrod 6 x 40, although other optical or night sights can be used, and back-up open sights are provided.

SPECIFICATIONS:
Caliber: 7.62x51mm NATO
Operation: gas, semiautomatic
Locking: rotating bolt
Feed: 10- or 25-round detachable box magazine
Empty weight: 11.2 pounds
Overall length: stock folded, 33.3 inches; stock extended, 43.8 inches
Barrel length: 20 inches
Sights: optical, user option, open backup sights

Israel Military Industries SR-99

Norway

NM149S 7.62mm Sniper Rifle

The NM149S sniper rifle uses a modified Mauser Model 98 bolt-action and was developed in cooperation with the Norwegian Army. It is fitted with a Schmidt & Bender 6 x 42 telescope sight that may be mounted and removed without affecting the rifle's zero. The NM 149S is intended to be used to an effective range of approximately 800 meters. Backup open sights are also fitted, and the telescope sight may be replaced by a Simrad KN250 image-intensifying sight.

The stock is of impregnated and laminated beech and is adjustable for length by the use of spacers. An adjustable cheekpiece is also provided. The rifle has a match trigger, with a standard pull weight of 1.5 kg, but the user can adjust the trigger. Although neither is standard, the NM 149S can be equipped with a bipod and a sound suppressor.

SPECIFICATIONS:

Caliber: 7.62x51mm NATO
Operation: Manual, bolt-action
Feed: box magazine, five rounds capacity
Empty weight: 12.3 pounds
Overall length: 44.1 inches
Barrel length: 23.6 inches
Sights: Schmidt & Bender 6 x 42 telescope

VS 94 PS 7.62x51mm sniper rifle

Like the NM 149S described above, the VS 94 PS rifle uses a modified Mauser Model 98 bolt-action. The rifle is intended primarily for police use and was developed in cooperation with Norwegian police forces. The VS 94 is intended to have an effective range of 800 meters, and is fitted with a Schmidt & Bender 3-12 x 50 PM II telescope sight which may be mounted and removed without affecting the rifle's zero. Adjustable open sights are also fitted, and the telescope sight may be replaced by a Simrad KN250 night vision optic.

The stock is made of impregnated and laminated beech and is adjustable for length of pull via spacers; it also has an adjustable cheekpiece. The rifle has a match trigger, adjusted to a 1.5 kg pull, and can be fitted with an adjustable bipod and a sound suppressor.

SPECIFICATIONS:

Caliber: 7.62x51mm (.308 Winchester)
Operation: Manual, bolt-action
Feed: box magazine, five rounds capacity
Empty weight: 15.4 pounds
Overall length: 45.7 inches
Barrel length: 23.6 inches
Sights: Schmidt & Bender 3-12 x 50 PM II telescope; backup open sights

Sniper training includes shooting in all weather conditions.

Romania

RomArm FPK

RomArm FPK /SSG-97 7.62x54R Semiautomatic Sniper Rifle

Although it superficially resembles the Russian SVD Dragunov rifle, the RomArm FPK sniper rifle was developed in the late 1970s and the receiver is derived from that of the RPK light machine gun, a Kalashnikov design. Export versions are known as the SSG-97 and are identical to the FPK except that the SSG-97 lacks a bayonet lug. The FPK functions in the same manner as the Kalashnikov rifles, although it is larger than the RPK from which it is derived to accommodate the longer 7.62x54R cartridge. The FPK has a bolt stop that locks the bolt to the rear when the last round in the magazine is fired. There is no external bolt release; when a fresh magazine is inserted, the charging handle is drawn to the rear and released to chamber a fresh round. A slotted muzzle brake is fitted to reduce felt recoil and muzzle rise.

Although designated a sniper rifle, the FPK is intended for use as a designated marksman type weapon. While it does not provide the long-range accuracy of true sniper weapons, the FPK is reliable, rugged and is effective in its intended role of providing accurate aimed fire at battlefield ranges.

A sight rail similar to that of the SVD Dragunov is fitted to the left side of the receiver to accommodate the PSO-1 or similar optics. Optics in both 6x42mm and 8x42mm have been observed. All scopes have illuminated reticles and are graduated to 1,000 meters with an internal rangefinder. Original batteries were an unusual Russian type, but recent exports employ a standard 1.5-volt AA battery for reticle illumination. Many of these rifles have been exported to the United States and elsewhere and the FPK/SSG-97 can be encountered worldwide. 7.62x51mm versions have also been manufactured and exported.

SPECIFICATIONS:

Caliber: 7.62x54R or 7.62x51mm
Operation: gas, semiautomatic
Locking: rotating-bolt
Feed: 10-round detachable box magazine
Empty weight: 10.9 pounds
Overall length: 49.2 inches
Barrel length: 25.6 inches
Sights: Open: Front: post; rear: U-notch tangent graduated to 1,000 m. Optical: PSO-1 or similar 4 x 24, 6x or 8x optional.

RomArm PL 7.62x54R Sniper Rifle

The bolt-action RomArm PL sniper rifle began as a military adaptation of a commercial rifle, but is now produced as a dedicated military sniper rifle.

The PL design is conventional, featuring wooden furniture; a fully adjustable stock with an adjustable cheekpiece and butt pad; a semi-pistol grip; and an adjustable bipod. The PL uses the same 10-round detachable box magazine of the FPK rifle described above. The barrel features a slotted muzzle brake. Open sights are provided, although various types of primary optical sights can be fitted.

SPECIFICATIONS:

Caliber: 7.62 x 54R
Operation: Manual, bolt-action
Locking: manually operated rotary bolt
Feed: 10-round detachable box magazine
Empty weight: 9.9 pounds
Overall length: 49.2 inches
Barrel length: 24.6 inches
Rifling: 4 grooves, rh, 1 turn in 12 inches
Sights: Optical, user option. Open sights; front post; rear u-notch
Maximum effective range: 800 to 1,000 meters

Czech sniper team

Russia

SVD in action

9x39mm VSS Silent Sniper Rifle

The VSS (6P29) silent sniper rifle was developed in parallel with the similar AS silent assault rifle (see separate entry), but while the AS is intended as a silenced rifle for special forces, the VSS (also known as Vintorez, or 'thread-cutter') was developed for use as a silenced sniper rifle by Spetsnaz, GRU, or other clandestine units, a role clearly indicated by its ability to be discreetly carried in a specially fitted briefcase.

The VSS forms part of the overall VSK silenced sniper system. Within the system, the rifle can be fitted with the PKS-07 collimated telescopic sight or the PKN-03 night sight, both of which are integral components of the VSK System.

The VSS fires the armor-piercing 9x39mm SP-5/SP-6 cartridge. Sniper fire is normally semiautomatic only, using a 10-round magazine, but it is possible to fit the 20-round AS magazine for full automatic fire if desired. When the rifle is a component of the VSK system, ammunition types may include the SP-5, SP-6 and PAB-9 cartridges.

Like the AS silent assault rifle, the VSS designers intended that the combination of rifle and ammunition form what is known in Russian military terms as a "complex," similar in concept to what is known in the West as a "system" that includes a number of integrated components. The VSS complex includes the rifle, ammunition and sighting systems.

The operating features and suppression system used on the VSS silent sniper rifle are the same as those for the Val assault rifle. The main change with the VSS is that it is optimized for the 9x39mm SP-5 subsonic cartridge, which has a hardened steel core that extends beyond the tip of the bullet and can penetrate a 6mm "high-density steel plate" at 100 meters; a 2mm steel plate or a standard army helmet can be completely penetrated at 500 meters. In both instances, it is claimed that the bullet will retain sufficient energy to disable targets after the plates have been penetrated.

The stock used on the VSS appears to be more rounded derivative of the Dragunov 7.62x54R SVD sniper rifle and can be removed when the rifle is dismantled into three main components for administrative movement or concealment in a special briefcase measuring 17.7x14.5x5.5 inches. The briefcase contains all components of the VSS, along with a PSO-1-1 (1P43) optical sight, 3.46x NSPU-3 (1PN75) night sight and two magazines. If the optical and night sights are not required, the open sights remain available.

SPECIFICATIONS:

Caliber: 9x39mm SP-5, SP-6, PAB-9
Operation: gas, select-fire
Locking: rotating bolt
Feed: 10- or 20-round detachable box magazine
Empty weight: with PSO-1-1 optical sight, 7.5 pounds
Overall length: 35.2 inches
Barrel length: 7.9 inches
Cyclic rate of fire: 800 to 900 rounds per minute . Effective rate of fire: semiautomatic, 30 rounds per minute ; automatic, 60 rounds per minute
Effective range: day, >400 m; night, >300 m

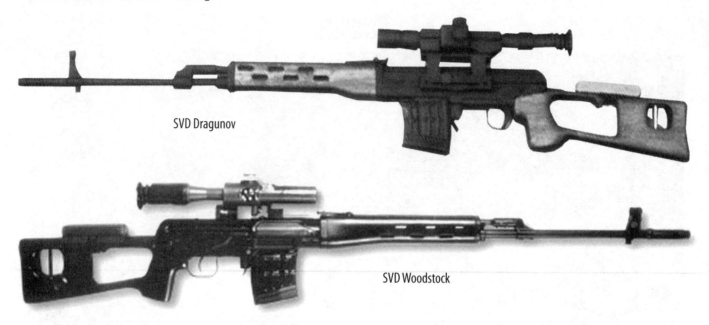

SVD Dragunov

SVD Woodstock

7.62x54R SVD (Dragunov) Sniper Rifle

The SVD sniper rifle was designed by Evginiy Fedorovich Dragunov (1920-1991). The first working prototype was produced in 1958, with the rifle entering service in 1963. Since then, several variants have emerged, the latest being the SVDS, SVU and SVDK. A select-fire version was developed, along with a model having a bipod just forward of the magazine. Neither entered service.

The SVD is a semiautomatic rifle fed from a 10-round magazine and is chambered in 7.62x54R. It is gas-operated, with a cylinder above the barrel. There is a two-position gas regulator that can be adjusted with rim of a cartridge case. The first position is for usual operation and the second is for extended use at a rapid rate of fire or when conditions are adverse.

The bolt system is very similar to that used in the AK-47 but the Dragunov bolt cannot be interchanged with those of 7.62x39mm weapons. The assault rifle and other Kalashnikov small arms use a long stroke piston that is generally unsuitable for a precision rifle, since the movement of the fairly heavy mass militates against extreme accuracy. Therefore, Dragunov used a short-stroke piston system. The lightweight piston is driven back by the gas impulse and transfers energy to the bolt carrier, moving it to the rear. A lug on the bolt engages a cam path on the carrier, rotating the bolt to unlock it. The carrier and the bolt travel back together. The recoil spring is compressed and drives the carrier forward to lock the bolt before firing can take place. When the carrier is fully in battery, thus locking the bolt, a safety sear is released, freeing the hammer.

The fire control mechanism is a simple design, using the hammer, the carrier controlled safety sear and a disconnector. The disconnector ensures that the trigger must be released after each shot to reconnect the trigger bar with the sear.

The PSO-1 sight is a 4x24mm telescopic sight with power for reticle illumination supplied by a small battery. A rubber eyepiece that automatically gives proper eye relief when the shooter places his eye against it is included in the

overall length. The field of view is 6 degrees. The weight of the PSO-1 is 1.3 pounds. The latest version of this sight is the PSO-1M2. The sight incorporates a metascope, a device capable of detecting infrared light sources. It is not sufficiently sensitive to be used as a night-vision sight.

When fitted with the PSO-1 optical sight, the SVD designation changes to 6V1, in keeping with Russian military practice. When fitted with the NSPU-3 (1PN51) night sight, the designation changes to 6V1-N3 or SVDN3.

An unusual feature for a sniper rifle is that the SVD can accommodate a bayonet, which also doubles as a field knife and wire cutter.

Variants

Upgraded SVD: This upgraded version of the SVD has a synthetic skeleton type stock, cheek rest, buttplate and other furniture. A detachable bipod with telescopic legs is also available. An alternative to the usual PSO-1 optical sight is the Minuta 3-9 x 42 variable power optical sight. An orange light filter can be used to increase image contrast, and the main sight and range finder reticles can be illuminated, both simultaneously or independently, as required.

SVDN3: SVD rifle fitted with an NSPU-3 (1PN51) night sight.

SVDS: See separate entry.

SVDK: See separate entry.

OTs-03AS (SVU): See separate entry.

TSV-1: A training rifle chambered in .22LR.

SPECIFICATIONS: SVD

Caliber: 7.62x54R, including 7N14 AP
Operation: gas, short-stroke piston, semiautomatic
Locking: rotating-bolt
Feed: 10-round detachable box magazine
Empty weight with PSO-1: 9.5 pounds
Overall length: 49 inches
Barrel length: 24.4 inches
Sights: PSO-1 telescope 4 x 24mm: open sights: front: adjustable post, rear: U-notch, tangent, graduated to 1,200 meters
Maximum effective range: 800 to 1,000m

SVDS

7.62x54R SVDS Sniper Rifle

Following combat experience in Afghanistan, the Soviet/Russian military decided to develop a more compact version of the SVD 7.62x54R sniper rifle to allow it to be more easily carried in aircraft and ground vehicles. Two variants were proposed when development was completed in 1994, both with folding stocks. One was the SVDS-A, for general infantry use with a 629mm barrel. The other, for use by airborne forces, had a 565mm barrel, and was known as the SVDS-D. This version was eventually adopted for all military forces. With the demise of the USSR and Russian attempts to market military hardware overseas, a version of this rifle is rumored to be available chambered in 7.62x51mm.

The SVDS is a variant of the SVD developed to provide airborne and special operations units with a compact sniper rifle while retaining the capability to deliver aimed fire at long ranges. The original SVD stock was replaced by a tubular metal one which folds to the right of the receiver, and the barrel was shortened and provided with a revised muzzle attachment. No provision is made for a bayonet on the SVDS. A rudimentary cheekpiece is provided on the folding stock while the pistol grip (no longer part of the stock) and forend are made of polymer. An optional 15-round box magazine is available and a clip-on bipod can be fitted just forward of the magazine. The SVDS is otherwise similar to the original SVD. The SVDS cannot be fired with the stock folded, as it obstructs the cocking handle and trigger.

The PSO-1 or PSO-1M2, 4x24mm telescopic sight is retained, as are the original SVD open sights. Although the 4x24 remains standard, both 6x24 and 8x24 telescopic sights have been available in export markets and it is reasonable to expect that these more capable scopes have also been used by the Russian military, as all are made to military specifications, and have integral illuminated rangefinder reticles with bullet drop compensator for the 7.62x54R cartridge.

Variants

(When different optics are fitted, the Russian military modifies the designation to reflect the added sight. The purpose of this is so that unit commanders can instantly know the capabilities of the weapons and equipment in the hands of their troops.)

SVDSN2: SVDS rifle equipped with a NSPU-M night sight.

SVDSN3: SVDS rifle equipped with a NSPU-3 (1PN51) night sight.

SVDSN4: SVDS rifle equipped with a 1PN93 night sight.

SPECIFICATIONS:

Caliber: 7.62 x 54R, including 7N14 AP
Operation: gas, short-stroke piston, semiautomataic
Locking: rotating bolt
Feed: 10-round detachable box magazine (15-round optional)
Empty weight: with PSO-1: 10.3 pounds
Overall length: stock extended, 44.7 inches; stock folded, 34.4 inches
Barrel length: 22.2 inches
Sights: front, adjustable post; rear: U-notch, tangent graduated to 1,200m; PSO-1 4x24mm, 6x24mm or 8x24mm optical sight
Effective rate of fire: 30 rounds per minute

9.3x64mm SVDK Sniper Rifle

Based on analysis of experience in Afghanistan and elsewhere, the Russian military decided to develop a version of the SVD firing a larger caliber, heavier bullet to provide more accuracy and better terminal ballistics at longer ranges than the 7.62x54R. The cartridge developed was the Model 9.3 SN (9.3x64mm), which can be considered the Russian equivalent of the 338 Lapua (8.58x71mm), that is finding increased sniper use in other countries. A comparison of the two cartridges reveals that the bullet weights are comparable, while the 338 Lapua has the edge in velocity and thus should deliver slightly better performance than the Russian round. The complete 9.3 SN cartridge weighs 555 grains of which 267 grains is the steel-cored bullet. The cartridge is 3.5 inches long overall. Bullet velocity at 25 meters from the muzzle is from 755 to 770 meters per second. API and Tracer rounds are available. At 100 meters there is better than an 80 percent chance of the bullet penetrating a 0.4 inch armored plate.

The SVD rifle required modification to fire this new cartridge and the end result has been designated the SVDK, now in production by IZHMASH. The SVDK is a variant of the SVD developed to equip forces with a sniper (or

Russian SVU

SVU

designated marksman) rifle capable of hitting targets at long ranges with a single shot. In many respects the base SVD and the SVDK are similar, with 60 percent of the parts and components interchangeable, although the SVDK has the folding butt stock of the SVDS (see separate entry), and a shorter barrel. Other changes include a conical muzzle brake/flash suppressor, a pistol grip under the receiver, black polymer furniture, and no provision for fitting a bayonet. A folding bipod with telescopic legs can also be fitted. To provide extra strength and durability, the SVDK top cover is stamped from 1mm thick steel, rather than the SVD's .7mm.

The stock folds to the right of the receiver, and is of welded tubular steel segments. The buttplate is reinforced polymer. A three-position cheekpiece is provided. One position is for traveling, the second for use with the PSO-1 optical sight, and the third lowered, for use with open sights.

The barrel is fixed to the receiver by four pins, and is cold hammer-forged. The gas regulator is similar to that of the SVD but the piston has no grooves and the gas piston and tube diameters are larger. The muzzle brake/flash suppressor assembly has four teardrop-shaped slots, arranged so the two over the top are closer together than the two on the bottom. This reduces muzzle rise on firing while diverting muzzle gas away to the sides rather than stirring up dust.

To accommodate the new pistol grip the entire trigger assembly has been moved forward approximately 10mm compared to that on the SVD. Although Russian literature states that this rifle is equipped with the PSO-1, it is likely that one of the new higher power 6x24 or 8x24mm versions are mounted on this rifle, as a 4 power scope is totally inadequate for shooting at the long ranges for which the SVDK is intended to be used. These higher power scopes also carry the designation PSO-1.

SPECIFICATIONS:
Caliber: 9.3 x 64mm (9.0 SN)
Operation: gas, short-stroke piston, self-loading
Locking: rotating bolt
Feed: 10-round detachable box magazine
Empty weight: with PSO-1 and empty magazine, 10.6 pounds
Overall length: stock extended, 44.7 inches; stock folded, 34.4 inches
Barrel length: 22.2 inches
Sights: front, adjustable post with protective hood; rear: U-notch, tangent; PSO-1 optical sight, probably 8x24mm
Maximum effective range: open sights, 1,200m; optical sight, 1,500m; night vision device, 700m
Maximum lethal range: 4,000m

7.62x54R OTs-03AS Sniper Assault Rifle (SVU)

The OTs-03AS 7.62x54R Sniper Assault Rifle, or SVU, is an extensively modified version of the SVD rifle described elsewhere, altered to bullpup configuration and select-fire. It was developed to meet the requirements of special operations units of internal affairs agencies and the Ministry of Internal Affairs internal security troops. The SVU was first seen in action in 1994, during initial phases of the fighting in Chechnya.

Two designations have been encountered relating to this weapon. As can best be determined, SVU refers to the basic rifle with open sights. With a PSO-1 optical sight and bipod, the designation is changed to OTs-03AS.

The most visible change to the SVU from the SVD is the elimination of the stock, its replacement is a plate fixed to the receiver rear. The trigger group has been moved forward of the magazine, and the muzzle with a prominent cylindrical device that acts as a combined flash hider and partial sound suppressor. The SVU can be fired fully automatic with a cyclic fire rate of 880 rounds per minute, although the 10-round magazine will quickly be exhausted. This feature is apparently intended to be employed only in emergencies, such as breaking contact.

OTs-14 Groza Special Weapon System

A standard bayonet can be fitted. The ubiquitous PSO-1 optical sight remains, although the SVU has folding open sights. Like other members of the SVD family, it is likely that more recent versions have higher-powered versions of the PSO-1 to enhance long range accuracy. The bipod can be relocated to the side to steady the rifle against a wall, post, tree or other upright surface.

SPECIFICATIONS: OTs-03AS

Caliber: 7.62 x 54R
Operation: gas, short-stroke piston, select-fire
Locking: rotating bolt
Feed: 10-round detachable box magazine
Empty weight: PSO-1, 12.1 pounds
Overall length: 35.4 inches
Sights: Front, folding, protected post; rear: folding U-notch; PSO-1 telescope
Cyclic rate: 880 rounds per minute
Maximum effective range: against personnel, 800m; against soft-skin materiel,1,300 m

OTs-14 Groza special weapon system

The OTs-14 Groza (Thunderstorm) special weapon system was developed by a Sporting and Hunting Guns Central Research and Design Bureau (TsKIB SOO) team headed by Valery Telesh, designer of the GP-25 and GP-30 underbarrel grenade launchers, and Yu V Lebedev. The team set out to design an integrated system that would incorporate all the desirable features of a close combat arm into a single weapon using the AKS-74U Kalashnikov as a basis. Work began on the project in December 1992. Prototypes were ready for testing in less than a year and the OTs-14 was ready for production early in 1994. It was first shown publicly at the Milipol Moscow trade show in April 1994 and shortly thereafter was adopted by the Interior Ministry (MVD).

SV-98

The weapon was originally intended to have used any one of four cartridges: 5.45x39mm; 5.56x45mm; 7.62x39mm; or 9x39mm. That concept was dropped and the OTs-14 was originally chambered in 9x39mm to meet the MVD's requirement for a close combat weapon. The success of the OTs-14 in the hands of MVD troops in Chechnya brought it to the attention of the Ministry of Defense. After testing, the OTs-14 was adopted for Spetzsnaz forces and some other specialized combat units, but in 7.62x39mm. Lack of funds however, has prevented the 7.62mm military version being adopted in significant numbers.

The OTs-14 has been offered for export and presumably is available in any one of the four calibers for which it was originally developed. The basic 9x39mm Groza has been referred to as the Groza-9/40 while the 7.62x39mm version is designated Groza-7.62/40. The /40 suffix indicates that 40mm grenade launcher can be fitted.

The OTs-14 Groza is a small arms weapons system based on the Kalashnikov

AKS-74U; the two weapons share a 75 percent commonality of components. The OTs-14 is issued in an aluminum carrying case with equipment and accessories to equip it for virtually any mission. There are two different grip and trigger assemblies, included, one for use with the modified GP-25/30 grenade launcher and another for use when the launcher is detached.

When the grenade launcher is installed, the single trigger operates both the rifle and the grenade launcher. A selector on the left side of the grip enables the operator to select between rifle or grenade barrels. When the grenade launcher is detached, it is replaced by a vertical grip. A suppressor is also included in the issue kit, as is a quick-change short barrel for use with the suppressor or for when maximum compactness is desired. A PSO or PSO-1 telescopic sight mounts directly onto the OTs-14 carrying handle, although early versions had the usual side mount on the left side of the receiver. The OTs-14 accepts all standard Russian night vision optics.

The OTs-14 has four standard configurations designated by number, so operators can easily and quickly be told how to configure their weapons for specific missions without divulging details and to save time in communications. The basic OTs-14 configuration is with the grenade launcher and is designated OTs-14-4A. Without the grenade launcher the designation is OTs-14-4A-01. The short barrel changes the designation to OTs-14-4A-02. Adding the suppressor results in the designation OTs-14-4A-03.

The OTs-14 Groza-7.62/40 with a 30-round magazine fires the 7.62x39mm cartridge and the subsonic 57N231U cartridge when the suppressor fitted..

SPECIFICATIONS: Groza-9/40

Caliber: 9mm x 39mm SP-5, SP-6 and PAB-9; 40mm VOG-25 and VOG-25P grenades
Operation: gas, selective fire
Locking: rotating bolt
Feed: 20-round detachable box magazine
Empty weight: rifle only, 5.6 pounds; rifle with grenade launcher, 8.8 pounds; rifle with suppressor, 6.6 pounds
Overall length: rifle, 19.7 inches; rifle with suppressor, 28.4 inches; rifle with grenade launcher, 24.6 inches
Sights: front, post; rear: leaf sights on drum with 50-, 100-, 150- and 200-meter increments; PSO or PSO-1 optical sight optional
Cyclic rate: 700 rounds per minute
Max effective range: rifle, 400m; grenade launcher, 400m

Groza-7.62/40

Caliber: 7.62mm x 39mm; 40mm VOG-25 and VOG-25P grenades
Operation: gas, select-fire
Locking: rotating bolt
Feed: 30-round detachable box magazine
Empty weight: rifle only, 6.8 pounds; rifle with grenade launcher, 9 pounds
Overall length: rifle, 27.6 inches; rifle with suppressor, 33.1 inches; rifle with grenade launcher, 27.6 inches
Sights: front, post; rear: leaf sights on drum in 50-, 100-, 150- and 200m increments; PSO or PSO-1 optical sight
Cyclic rate: 750 rounds per minute
Max effective range: rifle, 600m; grenade launcher, 400m

7.62mm SV-98 Sniper Rifle

The 7.62mm SV-98 (Snaiperskaya Vintovka, Model 1998) sniper rifle is based on the Record-1 competition rifle and is chambered in either 7.62x54R or 7.62x51mm. According to the manufacturer a 338 Lapua Magnum version will soon be available. The adoption of this bolt-action sniper rifle indicates that the Russian military has recognized that for true sniper missions, a bolt-action rifle is desirable. The SV-98 can be equipped with a sound suppressor for missions where silence is required and the bolt-action enables the sniper to control the ejection of spent cartridge cases, rather than having them ejected indiscriminately in those situations where spent casings cannot be left behind.

The SV-98 is essentially a militarized version of the Record-1 competition rifle. Early stocks were of laminated plywood with two ventilation slots, a glass fiber-reinforced polymer stock is now available. The butt plate and cheek piece are fully adjustable for length and height. A folding, adjustable bipod is standard.

SV-99

The fully free-floating barrel is cold hammer-forged and is unlined. Once the forging process is complete the barrel bore is polished. A "birdcage" type muzzle brake is provided. The muzzle is threaded to accommodate either the brake or an optional suppressor. The barrel is attached to the receiver by four pins. The forged steel receiver is attached to the stock via two bolts. The trigger is adjustable for pull. The safety is located behind the bolt handle and blocks the firing pin, bolt and trigger when applied.

An anti-mirage strap can be fixed between the front and rear sights. The open sights are similar to those of the SVD rifle but the optical sights and method of attachment are different. The 7 power telescopic sight is designated PKS-07. It is understood that the sight reticle is the same as the PSO-1 optical sight. The sight is mounted via a dovetail rail over the receiver, similar to the MIL-STD-1913 rail and is far more stable than the traditional Russian side mount system of attaching optics.

SPECIFICATIONS:
Caliber: 7.62x54R or 7.62x51mm NATO
Operation: manual, bolt-action
Locking: rotating bolt, three lugs
Feed: 10-round detachable box magazine
Empty weight: 13.7 pounds
Overall length: 47 inches
Barrel length: 650mm
Sights: front, protected blade; rear: aperture; optical, PKS-07 7x daylight or PKN-03 night vision optic
Maximum effective range: 800 to 1,000m

SV-99 .22LR Sniper Rifle

The SV-99 is a compact, lightweight sniper rifle intended for use during missions requiring silent, close-range elimination of sentries, guard dogs, security lights and so on, where the use of a full-power rifle would be inappropriate. Like the SV-98 (see above entry), the action of the SV-99 is derived from a competition rifle, in this

SV-99

case the Biathlon, a small bore rifle for winter sports competitions.

The SV-99 is a straight-pull bolt-action rifle with toggle action locking similar to that of the German P08 Luger. Since the SV-99 can be deployed in numerous operational scenarios, its configuration can be changed from rifle to long-barreled pistol by simply replacing the stock with a pistol grip. The laminated plywood stock can be adjusted for length of pull and cheekpiece height. A telescoping bipod is standard and is attached via a rail in the forend. The barrel is cold hammer-forged.

The SV-99 can be rapidly disassembled and stored in its carrying case. The longest component of the disassembled rifle, the barrel and receiver, is only 20.5 inches long.

The SV-99 safety is in front of the trigger guard and is engaged by moving it to the rear. The engaged safety locks both the trigger and the bolt-action. Rounds are fed from magazines having one of three capacities: five, eight, or 10-rounds. Two spare five-round magazines are carried in a stock compartment, protected by a hinged plastic cover.

There are no open sights. The SV-99 is equipped with a 4 x 34 fixed-focus telescopic sight attached to the receiver via grooves similar to Weaver-type mounting grooves. Russian sources state that virtually any telescopic sight can be attached to these grooves, implying that they are of standard Weaver type.

Each SV-99 is issued with the following standard components: two spare magazines; a telescoping bipod; a detachable pistol grip; a suppressor; a sling and a cleaning kit.

SPECIFICATIONS:
Caliber: .22LR
Operation: manual, straight-pull bolt-action
Locking: toggle joint
Feed: five-, eight- or 10-round detachable box magazine
Empty weight: 8.2 pounds
Overall length: 39.4 inches
Barrel length: 13.8 inches
Sights: optical only, 4 x 34 fixed focus
Max effective range: 100m

Serbia and Montenegro

Zastava 7.62mm M70/93 sniper rifle

The original Zastava M70 sniper rifle was chambered in 7.92x57mm. In 1993, a variant chambered for 7.62x51mm ammunition was introduced, and this became the M70/93. The M70/92 is a conventional precision rifle based around the proven Mauser 98 action. The heavy barrel is hammer forged, and accessories such as a variable geometry wooden stock and an adjustable folding bipod are provided. An adjustable trigger pull is incorporated. Ammunition is fed from a 10-round detachable box magazine. A 6x42mm telescopic sight is fitted as standard. There are no open sights.

SPECIFICATIONS:
Caliber: 7.62x51mm NATO
Operation: Manual, bolt-action
Locking: rotating-bolt
Feed: 10-round detachable box magazine
Empty weight: 15.4 pounds
Overall length: 50 inches
Barrel length: 27.6 inches
Sights: optical, 6 x 42mm

Crvena Zastava M76 Semiautomatic Sniper Rifle

The Crevna Zastava 7.92x57mm M76 semiautomatic sniper rifle was developed by Zastava Arms and produced for the former Yugoslav armed forces. It is derived from the Kalashnikov family of automatic arms and uses forged, rather than stamped receivers like other precision rifles derived from Kalashnikov designs. Production was taken over by Crevna Zastava, which still markets the rifle for export, not only in the original caliber, but also in 7.62x51 and 7.62x54R. Feed is from a 10-round detachable box magazine.

The M76 is fitted with a 4-power telescopic sight that is similar to the PSO-1 sight of the Russian SVD sniper rifle. The effective range using the optical sight is stated to be 1,200 meters. The optical sight bracket is also designed to accept a passive optical night sight.

SPECIFICATIONS:
Caliber: 7.92x57mm; 7.62x51mm; 7.62x54R
Operation: gas; semiautomatic
Locking: rotating bolt
Feed: 10-round detachable box magazine
Empty weight: 10.1 pounds
Overall length: 44.7 inches
Barrel length: 21.7 inches
Sights: front, post; rear: U-notch tangent, calibrated up to 800 meters ; 4x telescope
Max effective range: 1,200m

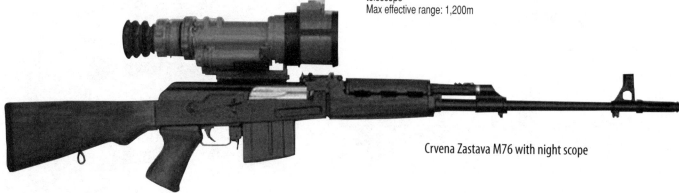

Crvena Zastava M76 with night scope

South Africa

Truvelo Armoury SG1 High Precision Rifles

Truvelo Armoury has designed and developed a family of similar high precision rifles for sniping and other purposes where extreme accuracy is required, all under the general title of SG1 (ScharfschutzenGewehr 1). The SG1 rifles are similar but differ in caliber. Standard chambering includes 7.62x51mm, 300 Winchester Magnum and 338 Lapua Magnum, although other calibers can be provided upon request. For each caliber alternative versions with either single shot or magazine feed are available.

All the SG1 rifles are stated to be designed and constructed on a "no compromise" basis. With appropriate ammunition, all SG1 rifles are stated to deliver an accuracy of .5 minute of angle (MOA).

Regardless of caliber, each SG1 rifle is manufactured using the same basic elements. The bolt-action is CNC machined from solid nickel chrome molybdenum steel billet. Stocks are machined from aircraft-grade aluminum. The rubber recoil pad is also adjustable for height, as is the cheekpiece. The polymer pistol grip is adjustable for trigger reach. A folding bipod is also provided.

The barrel is manufactured from stainless steel and is button-rifled. A muzzle brake is available on 300 Win Magnum and 338 Lapua rifles. A sound suppressor is optional. No open sights are provided. If required, a MIL-STD-1913 mounting rail can be fixed to the receiver, although other sight mountings are optional to user specification.

The specifications below are general in nature, as each SG1 rifle is custom built.

SPECIFICATIONS:

Caliber 7.62x51mm; 300 Win Magazine; 338 Lapua Magnum
Operation bolt-action
Feed single-shot or magazine single-shot or magazine single-shot or magazine
Empty weight 17.6 pounds
Overall length 46.9 inches
Barrel length 30.1 inches
Max effective range 800m; 1,000m; 1,500m

Spain

Santa Barbara 7.62mm C-75 Special Forces Rifle

The Santa Barbara 7.62mm C-75 special forces rifle is a conventional bolt-action rifle, using a Mauser action, intended for sniping, police and special forces tasks. Fitted with iron sights as standard, it also has telescope mounts machined into the receiver and can thus be equipped with virtually any optical or electro-optical sight. With a telescope, match ammunition and a skilled shooter, it is capable of effective fire out to 1,500-meter range. It is also provided with a muzzle cup launcher for discharging various riot control devices, such as rubber balls, smoke canisters or CS gas grenades, by use of a standard grenade-discharging cartridge. It is not suited to firing combat types of grenade.

No data other than the weight, 8.1 pounds, is available.

Switzerland

SAN Swiss Arms 5.56x45mm SG550 Sniper Rifle

The SAN Swiss Arms SG550 sniper rifle is derived from the standard SG550 assault rifle and is a semiautomatic version developed in coordination with police tactical organizations. It is intended for short- to medium- range engagements where the relatively low terminal ballistics of the 5.56mm round are not a disadvantage. The heavy barrel is cold hammer forged and the trigger is a two-stage match-grade type, factory adjusted to 3.3 pounds. The semiautomatic action and low recoil gives the sniper the ability to make very quick follow-up shots if required.

The SG550 sniper rifle has a fully adjustable bipod and folding stock. The pistol grip is adjustable for grip angle and has an adjustable hand rest. The stock is also fully adjustable for length of pull. The cheekpiece and butt pad are also adjustable so that the rifle can be adapted to virtually any shooter's anatomy. The stock can be folded for administrative transport or storage. There are no open sights.

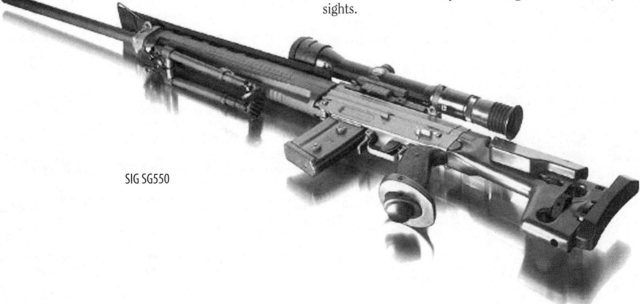

SIG SG550

Swiss sniper

Accessories include a spare magazine, sling, mirage band, bipod, carrying case, cleaning kit and sight cleaning equipment.

SPECIFICATIONS:
Caliber: 5.56x45mm
Operation: gas, semiautomatic
Locking: rotating bolt
Feed: 20- or 30-round detachable box magazine
Empty weight: 15.5 pounds
Overall length: stock folded, 36.6 inches; extended extended, 44.5 inches
Barrel length: 25.6 inches

SAN Swiss Arms 7.62x51mm SSG 2000 Sniper Rifle

The SAN Swiss Arms (formerly SIG-Sauer) SSG 2000 rifle was designed for military, law enforcement and target marksmanship. The rifle is based on the bolt-action Sauer 80/90 rifle, (Sauer 200 STR [Scandinavian Target Rifle]). The bolt-action uses hinged lugs at the rear of the bolt that are driven outwards by cams in the bolt as the handle is rotated to lock into receiver recesses. The bolt itself does not rotate. This design results in a bolt lift of 65 degrees.

The heavy hammer-forged barrel is equipped with a combination flash suppressor and muzzle brake, providing quick follow-up shots.

The ergonomic thumb-hole stock is fully adjustable to suit the shooter. Both right- and left-hand stocks are available.

The trigger is a double set type. Standard pull is approximately 4 pounds. When the trigger is set, pull weight is reduced to just over .5 pounds, appropriate for a match rifle, but not for snipers. The sliding safety catch has three functions: blocking the sear, sear pivot and the bolt itself. The bolt can be opened when the safety is engaged; the set trigger can be de-cocked by pulling the trigger when the safety is engaged and is automatically de-cocked when the bolt is opened. A loaded-chamber indicator gives a visible and tactile indication when a round is chambered.

No open sights are fitted; standard optics include a Schmidt & Bender 1.5 to 6 x 42 or Zeiss Diatal ZA 8 x 56T sight.

The SSG 2000 is available in 7.62x51mm, .300 Weatherby Magnum, 5.56x45mm and 7.5x55mm Swiss calibers.

SPECIFICATIONS:
Caliber: 7.62x51mm (.308 Winchester)
Operation: manual, bolt-action
Feed: four-round detachable box magazine
Empty weight: 14.6 pounds
Overall length: 47.6 inches
Barrel length: 24.1 inches

SAN Swiss Arms 7.62x51mm SSG 3000 Sniper Rifle

The SAN Swiss Arms (formerly SIG-Sauer) SSG 3000 sniper rifle is a precision bolt-action rifle incorporating the latest firearms technology derived from the Sauer 200 STR target rifle. The rifle is modular system, in that the barrel and receiver can be removed as a unit, as can the trigger and magazine system. The original stock was of wood laminate, but more recently, McMillan polymer units have been fitted. All stocks are fully adjustable to suit virtually any shooter's anatomy. The receiver housing is machined from a single billet. There are six locking lugs that lock directly into the barrel. Therefore, the receiver is not stressed during firing. A light firing pin and a short travel give the rifle very short lock time. The barrel is heavy, cold hammer-forged, and fitted with a combined muzzle brake and flash suppressor.

Two triggers are available, a single-stage and two-stage. Both are adjustable for pull weight and take up. The sliding safety catch above the trigger locks the trigger, the firing pin and the bolt. A pin on the striker head indicates whether the rifle is cocked.

There are no open sights. The SSG 3000 is designed to operate with the recommended the Hensoldt 1.5 to 6 x 24BL, which is manufactured specifically for the SSG 3000 rifle. A MIL-STD-1913 mounting base is available if preferred.

For training purposes, a .22 LR conversion kit is available.

SPECIFICATIONS:
Caliber: 7.62x51mm NATO
Operation: bolt-action magazine-fed
Feed: five-round detachable box magazine
Empty weight: with sight: 13.7 pounds
Overall length: Approx 46.6 inches (depending on stock adjustment)
Barrel length: 24.1 inches

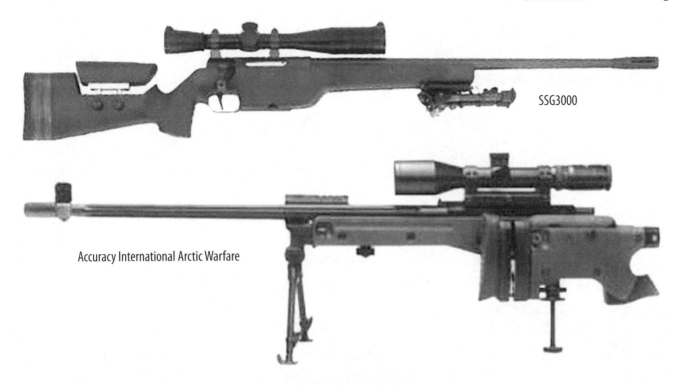

SSG3000

Accuracy International Arctic Warfare

United Kingdom

Accuracy International 7.62x51mm Arctic Warfare (AW) Precision Tactical Rifle

The Accuracy International AW sniper rifle is the result of further development and enhancement of the L96A1 sniper rifle to suit requirements stipulated during trials for a new army sniper rifle. In addition to the British Army, the AW has been adopted by Sweden, The Netherlands, Australia and Italy, among other nations.

The design of the Accuracy International AW sniper rifle incorporates anti-freeze mechanisms, a different shroud, three-way safety, smooth bolt manipulation, a muzzle brake, simpler and more robust detachable open sights, an improved bipod, multipoint sling attachments and a 10-round magazine. For the Swedish Army the rifle is fitted with a Hensoldt 10 x 42 Mil Dot Reticle with tritium lighting for night operations.

A folding stock is available as an option. This reduces the overall length by 200mm. Other options include an adjustable cheekpiece, an adjustable buttplate, a height-adjustable monopod under the stock, and a MIL-STD-1913 rail interface.

Screw-on muzzle suppressors are available to remove flash and reduce the sound signature. Normal full-power ammunition can be used with these suppressors.

Variants

AWP model: The AWP model is a further refinement of the AW. Enhancements introduced include a 24-inch stainless-steel barrel, a multi-adjustable butt-pad and a corresponding handstop/bipod mounting which offers flexibility of firing height and better stability when firing over a parapet. The preferred sight for this model is a Schmidt & Bender military-pattern 3 to 12x telescopic sight. There is no muzzle brake, so open sights and suppressors cannot be fitted.

AWMP model: The AWMP model is a fully suppressed version of the AW on which a fully integrated barrel and suppressor are interchanged with the standard barrel; the operation takes about three minutes. In this form the rifle is effective up to 600 meters using full-power ammunition, but the sights must be rezeroed.

SPECIFICATIONS:
Caliber: 7.62x51mm
Operation: Manual, bolt-action
Feed: 10-round detachable box magazine
Empty weight: AW and AWMP, 14.1 pounds; AWP, 15 pounds
Overall length: AW, approx 46.6 inches; AWMP, approx 47.2 inches; AWP, approx 43.2 inches
Barrel length: AW, 26 inches; AWP, 24.1 inches or 20.1 inches

Accuracy International 7.62x51mm PM Precision Tactical Rifle

The Accuracy International 7.62mm PM rifle uses an aluminum chassis to which the components are firmly attached. The chassis is fitted into in a high-impact plastic stock in which the stainless-steel barrel floats freely. The bolt-action is conventional, with three forward locking lugs and a safety lug at the handle. Bolt lift is 60°, and bolt throw is 107mm, allowing the firer to keep his head on the cheek rest while working the bolt and thus maintain observation of his target while reloading. The rifle is equipped with a light-alloy fully adjustable bipod.

The infantry version has fully adjustable open sights graduated to 700 meters, but is routinely fitted with a special design Schmidt & Bender 6 x 42 telescopic sight designated the L1A1. The accuracy requirement stated by the British Army was for a first-round hit at 600 meters range and accurate harassing fire out to 1,000 meters distance, which the PM meets.

United Kingdom

Armalon PR

The counter-terrorist version of the PM is fitted with a 2.5 to 10x scope as well as the infantry 6 x 42 sight. A spring-loaded monopod concealed in the stock can be lowered and adjusted so that the rifle can be placed on the target and supported while the shooter observes without having to support the weight of the rifle for long periods.

SPECIFICATIONS: Infantry version

Caliber: 7.62x51mm
Operation: Manual, bolt-action
Feed: 10-round detachable box magazine
Empty weight: 14.3 inches
Overall length: 44.3 inches to 47 inches
Barrel length: 25.8 inches
Sights: Schmidt & Bender PM 6 x 42

Accuracy International AWM Magnum Sniper Rifles

The Accuracy International AWM Magnum sniper rifle was designed as a dedicated sniper rifle providing guaranteed accuracy, ease of maintenance, reliability and robustness. All the lessons learned during the development of the L96A1 sniper rifle, together with many new and innovative ideas, were combined in this weapon.

Using the 10-power telescopic sight and 338 Lapua Magnum ammunition, the AWM is able to meet requirements for equipment destruction and light-armor penetration, as well as the anti-personnel capability to ranges well beyond 1,000 meters.

The rifle is available in three calibers: 338 Lapua Magnum, 300 Winchester Magnum and 7mm Remington Magnum. A folding stock is available as an option. This adds 200 g to the overall weight but when folded reduces the overall length by 7.8 inches. Other options include an adjustable cheekpiece, an adjustable buttplate, a height-adjustable monopod under the stock, and a MIL-STD-1913 rail interface.

The Netherlands armed forces ordered 325 of these rifles in 1997. The Accuracy International AWM Magnum sniper rifle has also been selected by the German armed forces chambered in 300 Winchester Magnum and designated the Gewehr 22 (G22). In 1999 it was announced that AWM rifles chambered for 338 Lapua Magnum had

been ordered for the UK armed forces; the initial batch was understood to be about 90 units. Known as the L115A1 long-range rifle, this weapon has been allocated to the Joint Rapid Reaction Force, where it is issued as a platoon weapon, providing platoon commanders with the capability to deal accurately with targets at long range.

SPECIFICATIONS:

Caliber: 338 Lapua Magnum
Operation: Manual, bolt-action
Locking: 6-lug rotating bolt
Feed: four rounds for 338 Lapua or five rounds for 300 Win. Mag or 7mm Mag.; detachable box magazine
Empty weight: Approx 15 pounds
Overall length: approx 49 inches
Barrel length: 338, 27 inches; .300, 7mm, 26 inches

Armalon PR Precision Tactical Rifles

The Armalon PR rifle is based on the Remington 700 action and has been extensively modified to increase the magazine capacity. It is available in two calibers: 5.56x45mm or 7.62x51mm. Numerous customized variations are available for rifles in both calibers, although the main attraction for many potential users is that the 7.62mm rifles can accommodate 10-, 20- or 30-round M14/M1A magazines, while the 5.56mm models accept modified M16/AR15 magazines.

The basis of the PR rifle is a one-piece housing and trigger guard unit machined from high-grade anodized aluminum alloy. The unit incorporates a new magazine release catch, and some alterations are made to the receiver and the stock.

Options include barrels of various lengths with or without flutes, muzzle brakes, various types of stocks, bipods, forearms, and custom bolt handles. Various types of optical and other sights can be installed.

SPECIFICATIONS:

Caliber: 7.62x51mm or 5.56x45mm
Operation: Manual, bolt-action
Feed: 10-, 20- or 30-round detachable box magazines
Empty weight: Approximately 12.1 pounds
Overall length: standard, 45.3 inches; with muzzle brake, 44.1 inches
Barrel length: standard, 25.6 inches
Sights: None standard; to user specification

British sniper in full camo.

United States

Armalite AR10(T)

The Armalite AR10(T) was developed as a semiautomatic, gas-operated, precision rifle based on the AR-10B action introduced by the new Armalite Company in the Mid-1990s. The rifle features a two-stage match trigger, precision cut-rifled, fully free-floated barrel and hand-fitted components. The rifle uses modified M14 magazines. Originally the AR10(T) was available only in 7.62x51mm, but shortly after its introduction, a 243 Winchester version was announced and in 2004 a 300 Remington Short Action Ultra Magnum (RSAUM) variant was introduced on a special-order basis. The latter rifle extends the effective range of the AR10(T) to well beyond, 1,000 meters, as the 300 RSAUM's ballistics are the equivalent of the 300 Winchester Magnum. Because it is semiautomatic, the AR10(T) enables shooters to achieve quick follow-up shots. Recoil is easily managed via the rifle's "straight line" design and its gas operation. Unlike many similar designs, the AR10(T) shares very few components with the much smaller and lighter AR15, which is one reason for the AR10's reliability. Although the AR10(T) is claimed to achieve accuracy of 1 minute of angle (MOA), most production rifles shoot more accurately, and average groups of .5 MOA are frequently observed. The receiver incorporates a MIL-STD-1913 rail mount for optics. No open sights are fitted, but are available as an option. A carbine version is available whose performance is virtually on a par with the longer-barreled version. All Armalite rifles carry a lifetime warranty.

Although the AR10(T) has not been formally adopted by the United States military, many special forces individuals have purchased AR10(T) rifles for operational use, preferring it to standard-issue weapons. Small quantities have been purchased by select US special operations units and the Canadian Army has adopted the AR10(T). The AR10(T) is one of the candidates for the US Army's Semiautomatic Sniper System (SASS) Program, which will eventually replace the current M24 SWS.

SPECIFICATIONS:
Caliber: 7.62x51mm; 243 Winchester; 300 RSAUM
Operation: gas, semiautomatic
Locking: rotating bolt
Feed: 10- or 20-round detachable box magazine
Empty weight: 10.4 pounds
Overall Length: 43.5 in.
Barrel length: 24 in. (Carbine, 18 in)
Effective range: 800 to 1,000m, depending on ammunition

Armalite AR30M

The AR30M is an innovative bolt-action rifle design derived from the company's earlier AR50 that beds the octagonal action into a "V" shaped block in the aircraft aluminum stock, ensuring a solid machine-rest-like bedding for optimum consistency and accuracy. A recommended optional MIL-STD-1913 rail can be attached to the receiver for mounting optics. No open sights are provided. The AR30M is available in 7.62x51mm, 300 Winchester Magnum and 338 Lapua Magnum. External dimensions are identical for all three rifles.

Armalite AR10(T)

Armalite AR30

A multibaffle muzzle brake is standard on the 338 Lapua AR30M and optional on the smaller calibers. This recoil check significantly reduces felt recoil and does not affect accuracy; most AR30M rifles will shoot sub-minute of angle groups. Because of the effectiveness of the muzzle brake, muzzle rise is minimized and rapid follow-up shots are facilitated. The AR30M barrel is chrome molybdenum and is triple lapped at the factory to ensure optimum accuracy.

The forend is extruded aircraft aluminum and has a mounting groove for accessories or a bipod. The pistol grip is of the M16 type and the removable skeleton stock is forged aircraft aluminum. All steel components are coated with manganese phosphate and aluminum components are hard anodized.

SPECIFICATIONS:
Caliber: 7.62x51mm; 300 Win Magnum; 338 Lapua Magnum.
Operation: Manual, front locking bolt-action
Feed: 5-round detachable box magazine
Locking: Rotating bolt
Overall length: 48 inches
Empty weight: 12 pounds
Effective range: 800 to 1,500, depending on caliber

7.62x51mm US Marine Corps M40A1 sniper rifle

The 7.62mm M40A1 sniper rifle was adopted in the early 1970s to meet the needs of the US Marine Corps for a long-range sniper rifle. Each rifle is individually produced by the Marine Corps' Rifle Team Equipment (RTE) Shop located at Quantico Marine Corps Base, Virginia.

The M40A1 is based on the Remington 700 bolt-action. Model 700 receivers are purchased by the Marine Corps and shipped to the Rifle Team Equipment (RTE) Shop where they are built into M40A1 sniper rifles. The Remington receivers are fitted with a precision barrel optimized for

accuracy with match-grade ammunition. Barrels are purchased either from Hart, Atkinson, or H-S Precision. The barreled actions are then bedded using glass fiber into McMillan (Harris Gunworks Inc.) polymer stocks with the barrel floating free along its entire length. The trigger group utilizes a modified Winchester Model 70 trigger housing and mechanism.

The M40A1 is equipped with a specially made Unertl 10-power fixed focus scope. There are no open sights. The rifle has a fixed five-round magazine. The M40A1 has generally been replaced by the "product improved" M40A1(PIP)/M40A3 rifle, but many commercial manufacturers continue to produce M40A1 type rifles built to Marine Corps specifications.

SPECIFICATIONS:
Caliber: 7.62x51mm NATO
Operation: manual, bolt-action
Feed: 5-round (4 + 1) internal box magazine
Empty weight: 14.5 pounds
Overall length: 40 inches
Barrel length: 24.1 inches
Effective range: 800 to 1,000m

m40a1

M40A3

7.62x51mm US Marine Corps M40A3 sniper rifle

The 7.62mm M40A1 Product Improved (PIP) sniper rifle was originally to have been known as the M40A2. Using the M40A1 as the starting point, every aspect of the original rifle was evaluated to determine if improvement was desirable or necessary. The resultant M40A1 PIP emerged as a completely different rifle and was subsequently designated M40A3.

The M40A3 uses a Remington 700 short action as a starting point. The receiver is then fitted with a fluted Schneider precision barrel by armorers at the US Marine Corps Weapons Training Battalion's Rifle Team Equipment (RTE) Shops at Quantico, Virginia. Barrels are threaded to accept sound suppressors. The M40A3 is built using McMillan stocks with quick-detachable swivels, spacers for length of pull adjustment, and an adjustable cheekpiece. The pistol grip and forend are knurled to provide a non-slip grip. The receiver and floor plate are bedded using epoxy resin and aluminum pillars. The floor plate/trigger guard is a one-piece DD Ross unit. All metal surfaces are finished using Robar Teflon or Birdsong's Black T in green.

The telescopic sight is a fixed 10-power Unertl unit made specifically for the US Marine Corps and is not available commercially. The original Unertl Company is no longer in business and current scopes are being rebuilt by US Optics. The sight is mated to a MIL-STD-1913 rail mount manufactured by DD Ross and is sloped at an angle of 30 degrees to facilitate long-range shooting.

SPECIFICATIONS:

Caliber: 7.62x51mm NATO
Operation: manual, bolt-action
Feed: 5-round internal box magazine
Empty weight: 13.4 pounds
Overall length: 44 inches
Barrel length: 24.1 inches
Sight: 10x Unertl fixed focus
Effective range: 1,000m

Arms Tech 300 Winchester Magnum Super Match Interdiction Rifle

The Arms Tech Super Match Interdiction Rifle was developed as a private venture by Arms Tech. It is intended to fill a need for a precision rifle as accurate as a bolt-action rifle, able to reach targets beyond the range of 7.62x51mm weapons, while providing a quick follow-up shot capability.

The Super Match Interdiction Rifle is based on a modified FN HERSTAL BAR semiautomatic sporting rifle. Stainless steel barrels are by either Douglas or Schneider, are fully free floated and are blackened to reduce visible signature. Barrels are cryogenically treated to enhance accuracy. The barrels are threaded to accept a sound suppressor. In the absence of a suppressor, a protective cap is screwed onto the muzzle.

Several modifications have been made to the existing BAR. Extraction has been improved for reliability. The charging handle has been extended to accommodate gloved hands. Integral barrel locking lug recesses have been replaced by a proprietary carbon steel shank to improve reliability and strength. The bolt is lapped for smooth operation. The magazine release has been changed to a Kalashnikov type. Stocks are by McMillan and each action is custom-bedded using a powdered metal-filled epoxy resin compound.

The rifle incorporates an Arms Tech proprietary telescope mounting system that allows optics to be removed and replaced without loss of zero. The Super Match Rifle is warranted by the manufacturer to achieve sub-minute of angle accuracy over its effective range.

SPECIFICATIONS:

Caliber: 300 Winchester Magnum
Operation: gas, semiautomatic
Locking: rotating bolt
Feed: three- or 10-round detachable box magazine
Empty weight: 13.9 pounds
Overall length: 46.9 inches
Barrel length: 26 inches
Sights: none provided
Effective range: 1,000 to 1,500m

Dakota Arms 338 Lapua Magnum Longbow Tactical Engagement Rifle

The T-76 was developed at the request of a foreign military government that sought a tactical precision rifle with an effective range of 1,500 meters, but without the weight associated with 50-caliber rifles. The order was cancelled and Dakota Arms then completed development as a private venture and put the rifle into production.

The Dakota Arms T-76 is a conventional bolt-action that uses Dakota's own receivers rather than purchasing them from another manufacturer. The receiver is machined from solid bar stock, as is the bolt. A MIL-STD-1913 rail is incorporated into the receiver to accommodate optical mounts.

Dakota Arms also manufactures most other components of the T-76, including the claw-type extractor, which allows controlled cartridge feeding. The T-76 features a square-bottom action and fixed internal magazine for additional strength and accuracy. Actions are available either right- or left-handed.

The stainless steel T-76 barrel is manufactured by H-S Precision and is button rifled, hand lapped and incorporates a built-in muzzle brake for recoil reduction. The ambidextrous stock is a reinforced glass fiber McMillan A2 type and may be ordered in either black or olive drab. The action is bedded along its full length within the stock. Length of pull is adjustable over 1.5 inches of travel. The adjustable trigger is a Winchester Model 70 type, set at the factory at 2.4 pounds.

The T-76 is warranted by the manufacturer to be accurate within .5 MOA over its effective range. In addition to 338 Lapua Magnum, the T-76 is also available in two proprietary calibers, 300 Dakota Magnum and 330 Dakota Magnum.

SPECIFICATIONS:

Caliber: 338 Lapua Magnum; 300 Dakota Magnum; 330 Dakota Magnum
Operation: Manual, bolt-action
Feed: Internal box magazine
Empty weight: 13.5 pounds
Overall length: 51 inches
Barrel length: 26 in
Sights: None provided
Effective range: 1,500m

Ed Brown Model 702 Tactical Sniper Rifles

Ed Brown Model 702 Tactical Sniper Rifles are built on Brown's proprietary bolt-action machined from heat-treated solid bar stock to ensure optimum straightness and concentricity. The rear receiver bridge is precision ground to ensure optimum alignment with telescopic sight mounts. The receiver's bottom contour is identical to Remington Model 700 rifles so that the Brown actions can be mounted in virtually any stock, as all manufacturers make stocks to accommodate Remington 700 actions. All rifle components are made in-house rather than buying actions or barrels from outside suppliers.

Dakota Arms Longbow

United States M14

Ed Brown 702 Tactical

The Winchester type safety is mounted on the bolt shroud and has three positions. In its rearmost position, the safety positively locks the bolt, firing pin and trigger. In the intermediate position the firing pin and trigger are locked but the bolt can be manipulated to safely clear or load the rifle. Fully forward is the "fire" position. The magazine may be opened by pressing a button at the front interior face of the trigger guard. The Model 702 trigger is tuned to break at 5 pounds. The Fiberglas stock is made for Brown by McMillan and is coated with black epoxy unless the customer specifies another color. Options include a stainless steel barrel, a different barrel contour, special calibers, and telescopic sight mounted and boresighted. The rifle is guaranteed to shoot within 1 to 1.2 minutes of angle depending on the inherent accuracy of the ammunition used, although most rifles achieve better accuracy. Both heavy and light models are available.

SPECIFICATIONS:

Model 702 Heavy Tactical
Caliber: 7.62x51mm; 300 Winchester Magnum
Operation: manual, rotating bolt
Feed: five-round internal box magazine
Weight: 11.5 pounds
Overall length: 45 inches
Barrel length: 26 inches
Sights: None provided; MIL-STD-1913 rail installed for mounting optics

FNH USA 7.62x51mm Patrol Bolt Rifle

The FNH USA Patrol Bolt Rifle (PBR) is manufactured by FNH's subsidiary, US Repeating Arms, which now owns the Winchester trademark. The PBR is made using Winchester's latest Model 70 action that incorporates controlled round push feed with a modified extractor and ejector. Unlike the "Pre 64" Model 70, the new version has its extractor built into the bolt, but is designed so that each round is controlled as it feeds from the magazine and is chambered. The PBR uses a blade ejector that allows the shooter to positively control ejection. The safety is a standard three-position Winchester type mounted on the bolt shroud that locks bolt, firing pin and trigger in its rearmost position and leaves the bolt free in its intermediate position with the firing pin and trigger locked. The forward position is the "fire" position.

The PBR is intended for use by patrol officers and is designed to stand up to the abuse inherent in being carried in a police cruiser day in and day out while maintaining bolt-action reliability and near match accuracy. Because the PBR is intended for street use, the trigger is set at approximately 6 pounds pull weight. The stock is a Hogue "overmold" unit that has a full-length aluminum bedding block for accuracy and is covered in rubber that ensures a positive grip and control in any climate, wet or dry.

Like the SPR described below, the PBR uses a cold hammer-forged barrel, but the PBR barrel is not hard-chrome-plated. The barrel is, however, fully free floated along its entire length. The bolt is trued in the action and the PBR is built "to print" with extremely tight tolerances throughout. The muzzle is deeply recessed with a match crown. Some FNH USA PBR rifles that have been modified with a match trigger and appropriate optics have been known to shoot half minute of angle groups.

SPECIFICATIONS

Caliber: 7.62 x 51mm
Operation: Manual, bolt-action
Feed: Detachable box magazine, 4 rounds capacity
Empty weight: Approx 8 pounds w/bipod, optic and sling
Overall length: 40.5 inches
Barrel length: 20 inches
Sights: None provided, user specified

FNH USA Special Police Rifle

The FNH USA Special Police Rifle (SPR) is manufactured by FNH's subsidiary, US Repeating Arms, which now owns the Winchester trademark. The rifles are essentially "Pre 64" Winchester actions with a large claw extractor and controlled feed that guides the cartridge from the magazine to the chamber. Barrels are cold hammer-forged, hard-chrome-lined and may be fluted upon request. Magazines may be fixed or detachable, depending on user preference.

The safety is a three-position type on the bolt shroud with a middle position that blocks the firing pin, allowing the bolt to be safely manipulated to load or unload.

All versions of the SPR feature a McMillan tactical stock. There are seven versions of the SPR as follows:

A1 SPR: Standard features as above, McMillan A3 stock.

A1a SPR: As above, but with 20-inch barrel

A2 SPR: As A1, but with McMillan A4 stock

A3 SPR: As A1 and A2, but with suppressor option, Badger Ordnance scope base and rings and Harris bipod.

A5 SPR: A complete package that includes one of three optional optics in addition to the features of the A3 SPR, SPR adjustable tactical stock, a leather or nylon sling, Eagle Industries Drag Bag, Tenebraex Killflash, tool kit and Otis cleaning kit. A suppressor is optional.

A5a SPR: A standard version of the A5 without options. Only the SPR adjustable stock is included.

SPECIFICATIONS:

Caliber: 7.62x51mm or 300 Winchester Short Magnum (WSM)
Operation: Manual, bolt-action
Feed: Internal or detachable box magazine, three rounds capacity (300 WSM); four rounds (7.62x51mm) w/detachable magazine; five rounds (7.62x51mm w/floorplate)
Empty weight: 9.5 to 10.7 pounds, depending on stock and barrel
Overall length: 24-inch barrel, 44.25 inches; 20-inch barrel, 40.25 inches
Barrel length: 20 or 24 inches, fluted or non-fluted.
Sights: None provided except on A5

H-S Precision Pro Series 2000 Tactical Rifles

After manufacturing precision rifle components for other manufacturers for many years, H-S Precision several years ago undertook manufacturing its own precision

rifles for military and police forces. There are three basic versions of the Pro Series 2000 currently available, the Heavy Tactical Rifle (HTR), the Short Tactical Rifle (STR) and the Rapid Deployment Rifle (RDR). The HTR and STR are available with long or short actions to accommodate any SAMMI specification cartridge. Right and left-handed versions are available. Stocks are available in a variety of colors, are fully adjustable for length of pull and feature an adjustable cheekpiece. All rifles feature fluted stainless barrels. A takedown version is also available (see below). The HTR has a longer barrel and heavier stock than the STR, which is intended to combine the features of the HTR with the light weight of the Pro Series 2000 Rapid Deployment Rifle (RDR). The RDR has a smaller thumbhole stock with fewer adjustments than the other two and is intended for use in situations where a quick-handling lightweight precision tactical rifle is necessary.

Pro Series 2000 rifles are of stainless steel construction with a cut-rifled barrel, titanium firing pin, claw extractor and three-position safety. The stock is H-S Pro Series with the company's proprietary bedding system. All metal is finished in matte black, with Teflon finish optional.

The Pro Series 2000 is guaranteed by the manufacturer to achieve .5 MOA accuracy at 100 meters in all calibers.

SPECIFICATIONS: Pro Series 2000 STR

Caliber: 7.62x51mm
Operation: manual, bolt-action
Locking: rotating bolt
Feed: 5- or 10-round detachable box magazine
Empty weight: 13.4 pounds
Overall length: 39.4 inches
Barrel length: 24 inches
Sights: optical, user option

H-S Precision Pro Series 2000 Tactical Take Down (TTD) Rifles

H-S Precision has developed a patented lock-up and adjustment system for its Tactical Takedown Rifle (TTD) that compensates for wear of action and threads, thereby ensuring consistently tight assembly of components with no sacrifice in accuracy. The TTR can be discreetly and easily transported in an inconspicuous briefcase-style carrier, rather than a long rifle case. With calibers having the same size case head diameter, calibers can be changed

FNH Patriot Bolt Rifle

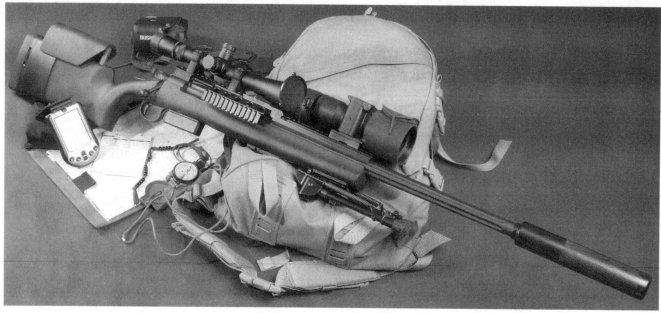

H-S Precision H-S 2000 FBI Rifle

by simply changing barrels. If calibers with different size case heads are desired, a different bolt can be supplied. The TTR is otherwise similar to H-S Precision's other rifles and is available in either long- or short-action versions.

SPECIFICATIONS:

Caliber: 7.62x51mm
Operation: manual, bolt-action
Locking: rotating bolt
Feed: 5- or 10-round detachable box magazine
Empty weight: 11.25 to 11.75 pounds, depending on caliber
Barrel length: 24 inches
Sights: none provided; Weaver rail for most optical mounts

Iron Brigade Armory 7.62x51mm Tactical Precision Rifle

The Iron Brigade Armory 7.62mm Tactical Precision Rifle is intended for those agencies which cannot afford the top-of-the-line M40 Series but who still require an extremely accurate precision tactical rifle. The Tactical Precision Rifle begins a Remington Model 700 PSS. A Leupold Tactical Model 4.5- to 14-power telescopic sight is added using Iron Brigade's proprietary two -piece mount.

The rifle is tuned to Iron Brigade specifications. This includes ensuring the barrel is completely free-floated along its entire length and the bolt handle properly clears the stock channel. The muzzle is recrowned and the trigger mechanism is reworked with the pull weight set to 3.75 pounds. The action is smoothed and the headspace verified to be between 1.630 and 1.632 inch. After tune-up, the rifled is zeroed at 100 meters using Black Hills Match ammunition. The rifle is fitted with a Harris Bench Rest Model bipod and a Turner Saddlery black leather sling. Sling swivel studs are glued in place with epoxy to ensure that they do not move or pull free. A Hardigg Storm model carrying case is provided.

SPECIFICATIONS:

Caliber: 7.62x51mm
Operation: manual, rotating bolt-action
Feed: 4 +1-round internal box magazine
Empty weight: 13.2 pounds
Overall length: 43.7
Barrel length: 26 inches
Sights: Leupold M4, 4.5-14x

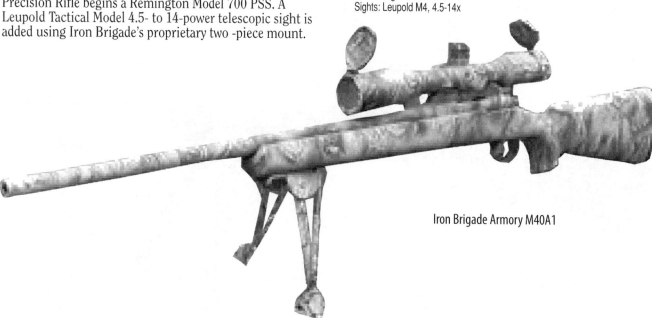

Iron Brigade Armory M40A1

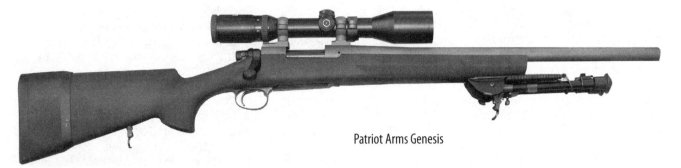

Patriot Arms Genesis

Iron Brigade Armory Tactical Standard/Super Grade

The Iron Brigade Armory Tactical Standard/Super rifle is a combination of the previously described Tactical Precision Rifle and the Chandler Sniper Rifle described below. The rifle uses an HS Precision stock with bedding block modified from that of the Chandler rifle so that a very accurate rifle can be offered at an affordable price. Like other IBA rifles, the Tactical Standard begins with a Remington Model 700 action and Hart varmint spec 416R stainless steel barrel either 20 or 26 inches in length. A barrel pad is installed to allow disassembly and reassembly while maintaining zero. Scope mount holes are drilled and tapped on a mill to ensure true alignment. The bolt face and action are squared and trued. The magazine and follower are modified for better reliability and the ability to hold a full five rounds, rather than 4+1. The Remington trigger is rebuilt, tuned and the pull weight set at 3.75 pounds. Trigger adjustment screws are sealed to prevent loosening under repeated recoil. A H-S Precision PSS stock with aluminum bedding block is mated to the barreled action. An IBA one-piece scope mount is fitted. All metal parts are finished in IBA's proprietary polymer-resin based "Manowar" finish in either black or OD green to the user's option. If a scope is specified, a Leupold Mark 4 4.5-14x40 scope is fitted.

SPECIFICATIONS:
are as for the Tactical Precision Rifle described above. Accessories include a Hardigg Storm Case, Simrad mount, fluted barrel, threaded barrel, magnum calibers and custom finishes.

Iron Brigade Armory M40 Long-Range Precision Rifles

Iron Brigade Armory's Chandler sniper rifles are patterned after the US Marine Corps M40 series sniper rifles but exceed Marine Corps specifications. Chandler M40 Series rifles are guaranteed to achieve 1 minute of angle accuracy to a range of 1,000 yards, so every shot will fall within a 10 inch circle at that range.

The rifles are built using Remington 700 actions with McMillan stocks, Hart barrels, Leupold military-specification telescopic sights with Marine Corps Mil-Dot reticles, Iron Brigade's proprietary mount and a one-piece Badger Ordnance M5 trigger guard. Each rifle is hand-fitted and the bolt squared and aligned to the barrel. The box magazine is welded to the action for durability and the follower and magazine are modified for better reliability and a full five-round capacity. The mainspring is replaced with a Wolff spring for better reliability and function. The standard Remington trigger mechanism is retained but is rebuilt and tuned for a 3.75-pound pull weight. Trigger adjustment screws are sealed to prevent loosening under repeated recoil. The tapered Hart barrel is made of 416R stainless steel. The McMillan epoxy resin stock is available in a variety of styles, including US Marine Corps M40A1 and M40A2 types, or to user specifications.

SPECIFICATIONS:
Caliber: 7.62x51mm; 300 Winchester Magnum; 30-06 and 5.56x45mm
Operation: manual, rotating bolt
Feed: 5-round internal box magazine
Empty weight: 14.3 pounds
Overall length: 43.9 inches
Barrel length: 20- or 26-inch standard; other lengths upon request
Sights: Standard Leupold Mark4 3.5-10x military specification. Nightforce optional.

Patriot Arms Genesis Precision Tactical Rifle

The Patriot Arms Genesis is modeled after the Marine Corps M40A1 and is designed to offer a high performance precision tactical rifle at a lower price than some other custom rifles. The machining and tolerances on the Genesis Precision tactical Rifle are the same as the more expensive Revelation Tactical Rifle described below and the Genesis carries the same performance guarantee. The Genesis uses a Remington 700 short or long action depending on caliber, with the action and bolt squared and trued. The match-grade barrel is fully free floated with a recessed target crown. The stock is a McMillan M40A1. The recoil lug is oversize and precision ground. The Remington trigger is rebuilt and factory set at approximately three pounds pull weight. Dual dovetail mounts and rings are included. Metal components are finished in Lauer Custom Weaponry's Duracoat epoxy resin in either black or OD green. Calibers include 5.56x45mm; 7.62x51mm and 300 Win Mag. Others are available on request.

SPECIFICATIONS:
Caliber: See text.
Operation: Manual, bolt-action.
Feed: Internal box magazine, 4+1 capacity
Empty weight: Approx 7 pounds
Overall length: 40 inches
Barrel length: 20 inches standard
Effective range: 800m, depending on ammunition.

Patriot Arms Revelation Precision Tactical Rifle

The Revelation Precision Tactical Rifle is built without compromise to the highest standards for professionals who demand the best equipment. The Revelation is similar in some aspects to the previously described Genesis, but is manufactured to a higher standard and incorporates higher quality, more expensive components and extra features that are not found on the Genesis rifle. The Revelation rifle is pillar-bedded using stainless steel pillars. All components are hard chrome for smoothness and reliability. Any type of McMillan stock may be fitted. The Revelation is manufactured using Badger Ordnance scope rings and bases, trigger guard and bolt knob. A claw-type extractor is fitted for controlled feeding and positive extraction. The Revelation is finished in two chemically different layers for optimum corrosion resistance. A Shilen trigger is installed. Standard calibers are 5.56x45mm, 7.62x51mm and 300 Winchester Magnum with others available on customer request.

SPECIFICATIONS:

are as for the above-described Genesis Rifle.

Semiautomatic Sniper System (SASS)

The Semiautomatic Sniper System (SASS) is a US Army acquisition program in its early stages as of late 2004. The general characteristics of the rifle as stated in the Army's solicitation are that the SASS will be semiautomatic and will be 7.62x51mm caliber. Accuracy is expected to be on a par with the current M24 Sniper Weapon System. Most US manufacturers of semiautomatic precision rifles are expected to submit candidates for the SASS program. These include Armalite, Bushmaster, DPMS, DS Arms and Knight's Armament, all of which currently manufacture very accurate 7.62x51mm semiautomatic rifles that equal or improve upon the accuracy of the M24.

SPECIFICATIONS:

are unknown as of the time of this writing, although it is expected that the SASS will have a barrel length of 20 to 24 inches and will weigh 10 to 12 pounds empty. Depending upon the telescopic sight and accessories included with the rifle, the weight could reach 14 to 15 pounds.

Remington 7.62x51mm M24 Sniper Weapon System (SWS)

The Remington M24 Sniper Weapon System was the US Army's first complete sniping system comprising a rifle, sight, tool kit, complete accessories and everything necessary for a sniper to deploy. First units received

their M24s in November 1988 and the system is issued to infantry battalions, special forces and Ranger units. It has been stated that the procurement objective was 2,510 systems. In October 2000, TACOM awarded a contract to Remington Arms for a further 100 M24 rifles.

Remington Arms developed the M24 SWS based upon the commercial M700 long action and a 40X custom trigger mechanism. The SWS was developed around the M118 special ball cartridge, but the long action was used in case the 300 Winchester Magnum cartridge was adopted at a later date. Thus, the same action could be used. The SWS stock is Kevlar reinforced glass fiber and is manufactured by H-S Precision with a full-length 7075T6 aluminum bedding block. The action is attached to the bedding block by two screws torqued to 65 inch-pounds.

The complete system consists of the bolt-action rifle, bipod, a laser-protected day optical sight, backup open sights, deployment kit, cleaning kit, telescope carrying case and total system carrying case. The complete system in its carrying case weighs 56 pounds.

Remington manufactures the 416R stainless steel barrel specifically for the M24. Rifling is of the 5R type with a twist rate specifically for the 175-grain M118 special ball ammunition.

The telescopic sight is manufactured by Leupold & Stevens and is designated the M3A. The sight body is machined from a solid piece of 6061T6 aircraft aluminum. All lenses are treated with a proprietary anti-reflective coating that also enhances the light transmission. The MIL-DOT reticle is etched into the internal lens.

The M24 Sniper Night Sight was added to the M24 Sniper Weapon System in late 1996. A Leupold 10- to 40-power spotting telescope for surveillance and target acquisition is included as a component of the overall SWS.

SPECIFICATIONS:

Caliber: 7.62x51mm M118 Special Ball
Operation: Manual, bolt-action
Feed: 6-round integral magazine
Empty weight: 12.1 pounds
Overall length: 43 inches
Maximum effective range: 800m

Remington M24 SWS

Remington M700

Remington Arms M700P Precision Tactical Rifle and Tactical Weapon System

The Remington M700P (Patrol Rifle) is intended for law enforcement marksmen and is available in several proven calibers, including 5.56x45mm, 7mm Remington Magnum, 300 Winchester Magnum and 300 Remington Ultra Magnum. Standard stocks are composite reinforced with Kevlar. An aircraft aluminum bedding block runs the full length of the receiver. Barrels are heavy "bull barrel" configuration for stiffness and heat dissipation.

The M700P Tactical Weapon System (TWS) adds a Leupold Vari-X III 3.5- to 10 power scope, Butler Creek lens covers, a Harris bipod, a Michael's of Oregon quick adjust sling and a Pelican carrying case. The TWS is available only in 7.62x51mm).

SEPCIFICATIONS
Caliber: See text.
Operation: manual, bolt-action
Feed: three-round magazine (7mm Rem Mag, 300 Win Mag, .300 Rem Ultra Mag); four-round magazine 7.62x51; five-round magazine 5.56x45
Empty weight: 9 pounds (10.5 pounds TWS)
Overall length: Approx 47 inches
Barrel length: 26 inches
Sights: None, user provided. (TWS, see text.)

Remington Arms M700P LTR Precision Tactical Rifle

The Remington Arms 7.62mm M700P LTR (Light Tactical Rifle) has been developed for military and police use where a precision tactical rifle of superior accuracy but light weight is required. The rifle uses a Remington M700 short action and a carbon fiber-reinforced stock with aluminum block bedding. There are no open sights. The detachable box   magazine holds three or four rounds, depending on caliber.

The LTR stock is laid up around an aircraft-grade aluminum bedding block that runs the entire length of the receiver. The LTR has a matte non-reflective finish and is furnished with three sling swivel studs to facilitate mounting a bipod.

The LTR is available in three calibers: 5.56x45mm, 7.62x51mm and 300 Remington Short Action Ultra Magazine (.300 RSAUM).

SPECIFICATIONS:
Caliber: 5.56x45mm; 7.62x51mm; 300 RSAUM
Operation: manual; bolt-action
Feed: four-round magazine (5.56 and 7.62mm) three-round magazine (300 RSAUM)
Empty weight: 7.5 pounds
Overall length: Approx 41 inches
Barrel length: 20 inches
Sights: None. User provided.

Remington 7.62x51mm 40XB and 40XS Precision Tactical Rifles

The Remington 40X was originally developed as a competition rifle in 1959 and formed that basis for the M700 action. There are two tactical versions of the 40X: the 40XB and the 40XS. Both are custom-built in Remington's custom shop and are guaranteed to deliver sub-minute accuracy.

The 40XB features a Teflon-coated stainless steel barrel, adjustable trigger and precision-machined aircraft aluminum bedding blocks. The stock is an HS Precision unit with semi-pistol grip.

The 40XS adds several custom features in what can be considered a premier grade precision tactical rifle. The 40XS stock is a McMillan A3 type, fully adjustable for length of pull and cheek rest height. The 40 XS also adds the following features: Leupold Vari-X III 3.5- to 10-power MIL-DOT scope, Badger Ordnance MIL-STD-1913 rail and mounting rings, Harris bipod, Turner Saddlery AWS tactical sling, Sunny Hill steel trigger guard and a Pelican carry case. The 40XS is also available without scope and accessories.

SPECIFICATIONS
Caliber: 7.62x51mm
Operation: Manual, bolt-action
Feed: Box magazine, five rounds capacity
Empty weight: Approximately 12 pounds w/ sights and accessories
Overall length: Approx 45 inches
Barrel length: 27.5 inches
Sights: 40XB, None; 40XS Leupold Vari-X III, 3.5 – 10x

Remington 40XS

United States
sniper in action in Iraq

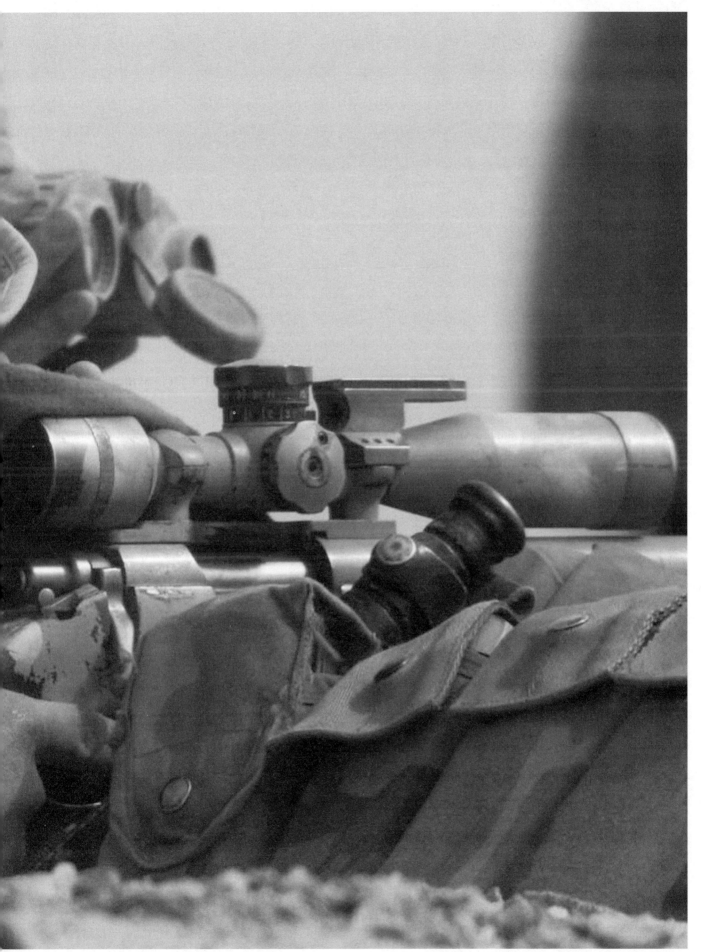

Savage LE 016

Savage 5.56x45mm and 7.62x51mm Model 10FP and Model 110PXP Precision Tactical Rifles

The Savage Model 10FP is specifically designed for police and military sniper units and features dual pillar bedding, a system where aluminum "pillars" are molded into the stock and the rifle action is mounted directly onto them, providing an extremely stable and rugged bedding system. The Model 10FP barrel is button rifled and fully free floated. The rifle is drilled and tapped for standard telescope mounts; there are no open sights. Left-handed versions are also available. Every Savage precision tactical rifle is fitted with Savage's patented "Accutrigger" that can be adjusted for pull weight as low as 1.5 pounds with complete safety. A variety of stock systems is also available. Standard stock is black synthetic with pillar bedding with dual studs for sling swivels and bipod. A Choate "Sniper" stock is optional. This stock was designed by Maj. John Plaster (Ret), one of the world's noted snipers, and is fully adjustable for length of pull and eye relief. A third option is McMillan's A3 type tactical Fiberglas stock. Available barrel lengths are 20, 24 and 26 inches, depending on model. Model 10FP rifles are available in either 5.56x45mm or 7.62x51mm. The Model 10FPXP is a complete system including Leupold Vari-X 354.-10 scope, Harris bipod, and heavy duty sling. A black heavy duty aluminum case is included.

The Model 110PXP is similar to the Model 10FP except that it has a heavier barrel, a longer action and is available in other calibers, including .25-06, .30-06, 7mm Rem Mag and 300 Win Mag.

SPECIFICATIONS:
Caliber: 5.56x45mm or 7.62x51mm (See text)
Operation: Manual, bolt-action
Feed: three-, four- or five-round box magazine, depending on caliber
Empty weight: 8.5 pounds (10FP Std); 10.75 pounds (Choate Stock); 11.25 pounds (110PXP-LEA)
Overall length: 40 to 45 inches, depending on barrel length and stock.
Barrel length: 20, 24 or 26 inches
Effective range: 800 to 1000m

Springfield Armory M21 Tactical Rifle

The Springfield Armory M21 tactical rifle is based on the original M21 sniper rifle but with some improvements. The adjustable walnut stock is a new type, with adjustable cheekpiece and rubber recoil pad, with the rifle action bedded in glass fiber resin. The heavy barrel is specially made by Douglas, air-gauged and has a twist of one turn in 10 inches. Hart stainless steel or Krieger barrels are optional. The two-stage trigger is adjusted to break at 4.5 pounds.

Springfield's third generation scope mount and 4- to 14-power Government Model scope are recommended accessories.

SPECIFICATIONS:
Caliber: 7.62x51mm
Operation: gas, semiautomatic
Locking: rotating bolt
Feed: 10 or 20-round detachable box magazine
Empty weight: 11.6 pounds
Overall length: 44 inches
Barrel length: 22 inches
Sights: front, fixed match type blade, .62 inch width; rear: match-grade hooded aperture with half minute of angle adjustments for windage and elevation; optical to user specification

Springfield Armory 7.62x51mm M25 "White Feather"

The M25 "White Feather" precision tactical rifle was developed in conjunction with the estate of Carlos Hathcock, the noted Marine Corps sniper and marksman. The M25 bears the Hathcock "White Feather" trademark and a facsimile of Hathcock's signature.

The M25 is built using Springfield Armory's threaded rear-lugged receiver, low-profile custom muzzle brake/stabilizer and a Kreiger heavy match barrel. The fire control mechanism is modified from the original and can be adjusted for overtravel. There are no open sights; the rear sight assembly is replaced by a MIL-STD-1913 rail mount base and the rail itself is mounted to a front lug attached to the receiver. The stock is a McMillan adjustable for length of pull and eye relief.

SPECIFICATIONS:
Caliber: 7.62x51mm
Operation: Gas, semiautomatic
Locking: Rotating bolt
Feed: Detachable box magazine, 10 or 20 rounds capacity
Empty weight: 12.7 pounds
Overall length: 46 inches
Barrel length: 22 inches

Stoner 7.62x51mm SR-25/Mark 11, Mod 0 Precision Tactical Rifle

Knight's Armament Company has designed and produced a 7.62x51mm version of the M16 rifle, in reverse of the original AR15, which was a scaled down AR-10. Although the SR-25 superficially resembles an AR-10, the design comprises over 60 percent parts interchangeability with M16 components. The USSOCOM adopted the AR-25 for special operations use as the Mark 11, Mod 0.

The SR-25 rifles have an extruded aluminum upper receiver with a MIL-STD-1913 rail mount for optics and accessories. The handguard is attached only at the receiver end, providing a fully free-floating barrel also avoiding changes in zero when used with a bipod. A carbine version with 16-inch barrel and fixed or collapsible stock is also available.

SPECIFICATIONS:
Base SR-25/Mk 11, Mod 0
Caliber: 7.62x51mm
Operation: gas, semiautomatic
Locking: rotating bolt
Feed: 10- or 20-round detachable box magazine
Empty weight: 10.75 pounds
Overall length: 44 inches
Barrel length: 24 inches
Sights: None provided; user specification

Springfield Armory M25

US Marine Corps 7.62x51mm Designated Marksman Rifle (DMR)

The Designated Marksman Rifle (DMR) is intended to provide US Marine Corps sniper team spotters with a precision semiautomatic rifle with nearly the same level of accuracy as the standard bolt-action sniper rifle, but with the capability to rapidly engage multiple targets with greater effectiveness and at longer ranges than possible with the 5.56mm M16A2. The DMR will also allow both members of the sniper team to carry the same caliber of ammunition. Rather than purchase off-the-shelf commercial rifles, the Marine Corps decided to manufacture the DMR using M14 rifles from existing stocks and convert them to DMR standard, since the US Marine Corps Rifle Team Equipment Shops at Quantico, Virginia had long experience manufacturing match-grade M14 rifles.

DMRs begin with a standard M14 rifle that is stripped, barrel removed and all selective fire components either removed or welded to ensure that the rifle is capable of semiautomatic fire only. The military barrel is replaced with a Kreiger barrel contoured to Marine Corps specifications. The military stock is replaced by a McMillan M2A stock with spacers for length of pull adjustment and an adjustable cheekpiece; screw fittings for the latter are such that they may be adjusted for ambidextrous use. A Harris bipod is standard. The stock ferrule at the front of the stock is glass bedded and opened to match specifications.

The receiver is equipped with a rear lug and then 'Marine-Tex' Fiberglas-bedded to the stock and the barrel band is welded to the gas system. The flash suppressor is opened to match specifications for enhanced accuracy. The flash suppressor may be removed and replaced by a sound suppressor manufactured by OPS Inc.

Open sights are standard aperture rather than match type. The Marine Corps uses a Brookfield Precision one-piece steel mount welded to the receiver to mount the telescopic sight. The DMR is also used by US Navy units and by selected Marine Corps security units and scout-sniper platoons.

SPECIFICATIONS:
Caliber: 7.62x51mm
Operation: gas, semiautomatic
Locking: rotating bolt
Feed: 20-round detachable box magazine
Weight: 11 pounds
Length: 43.8 inches
Barrel: 22 inches
Rifling: 5 grooves, rh, 1 turn in 12 inches
Sights: open, front, protected blade; open, rear: aperture, adjustable for windage and elevation; optical - see text

Springfield Armory M21

Anti-materiel Rifles

The history of antimaterial rifles dates to World War I and the advent of the tank. Early tanks were, by today's standards, lightly armored, yet rifle and machine gun bullets of the time would not penetrate their armor. Both sides quickly developed heavy rifles in calibers of a half inch and larger to defeat them. The .50 Browning Machine Gun cartridge was originally developed to defeat the tanks of World War I. The cartridge wasn't developed in time for "The Great War," but the heavy Browning Machine Gun, affectionately known to troops as the "Ma Deuce" remains in service, despite efforts to replace it. In World War II, antitank rifles such as the British Boys were fielded, but saw only limited use. The big Ma Deuce was used as a sniper weapon both in Korea and Vietnam. While it isn't commonly known, the M2 Heavy Machine Gun has a semiautomatic mode in which it fires single shots when the center trigger button is pressed rather than the main "butterfly" trigger. As a young student in ROTC, the author was told of tankers in Korea mounting telescopic sights on their M2 tank machine guns and using them as long-range sniper weapons. The practice continued in Vietnam and the legendary Carlos Hathcock once killed a very sinister VC sniper at the incredible distance of 2,500 yards using a scope-sighted M2. Although .50 caliber ammunition was available in several varieties, including ball, armor piercing (AP), armor piercing incendiary (API), and some other specialty types, chambering a semiautomatic or bolt-action rifle wasn't seriously considered by the military because conventional wisdom had it that the big cartridge's prodigious recoil would dislocate a shooter's shoulder.

Fortunately, the experts neglected to advise Ronnie Barrett of their opinions and Ronnie, an amateur shooter, sheriff's deputy and photographer in Murfreesboro, Tennessee set about designing a shoulder-fired rifle chambered in .50 BMG. There were many failures along the way, but in 1982, Ronnie finally succeeded in assembling a fully workable semiautomatic .50 BMG

caliber rifle. Unfortunately, there wasn't much of a market for his big rifle until he demonstrated it to the US Marine Corps. The Corps became aware of the Barrett M82 just in time to order a few hundred for use in the first Gulf War in 1991-92. The Marine Corps guns were slightly modified and designated M82A1. These rifles continued in Marine Corps service until recently, when they were replaced by an improved version, the M82A3. The first Gulf War marks the initial use of heavy-caliber rifles against radars, parked aircraft, trucks, communications vans and other thin-skinned targets that couldn't be defeated by small arms fire or were at ranges too distant for lighter weapons. The M82's resounding success led to many of America's allies jumping onto the Barrett bandwagon and sales to allies burgeoned. Barrett developed bolt-action rifles to complement the M82 and other makers, both in the United States and elsewhere, began developing antimaterial rifles of their own. Despite this, the Barrett represents the quintessence of the antimaterial rifle and Barrett rifles may be found in military, law enforcement and civilian use worldwide.

M82A3

For an example of civilian use, long distance competitive .50 BMG rifle shooting has a small but very enthusiastic following in the United States.

In the wake of Barrett's success, many firearms manufacturers worldwide began developing antimaterial rifles of their own, especially in countries where the US State Department restricts sale of these rifles and in countries with strong small arms industries. Although most antimaterial rifles continue to be chambered in .50 caliber (12.7mm), there are variations. Countries of the defunct Warsaw Pact tend to chamber their antimaterial rifles in 12.7x108mm Russian. (American .50 BMG carries the metric designation 12.7x99mm) There are, however, rifles chambered for even larger

calibers. Antimaterial rifles have been manufactured in 14.5x114mm Russian and 20x110mm, although the vast majority of these rifles continue to be fielded in one of the two common .50 calibers.

While called antimaterial rifles because of their original purpose, these heavy rifles are commonly used to engage personnel targets at extremely long distances as well, beyond the effective range of smaller caliber rifles. The world record sniper engagement is presently held by a Canadian sniper serving in Afghanistan who achieved a first round hit at the astonishing distance of 2,400 meters – just under 1.5 miles! Because of its versatility and long-range effectiveness, the antimaterial rifle is here to stay for the foreseeable future.

Australia

Precision Rifle Systems 50 BMG (12.7x99mm) ATAS 50 BG Antimateriel rifle

The bolt-action Precision Rifle Systems ATAS BG antimateriel rifle is an enlarged version of the smaller caliber ATAS rifles and was designed specifically for military use.

To facilitate feeding, the bolt-action has a triple lug locking system that locks at the rear: rather than the front. The extractor is an oversized claw-type with a plunger type ejector for positive extraction and ejection. The six-round magazine may be placed on the left side of the rifle, under the receiver, or on the right, to accommodate right- or left-handed shooters. The receiver and barrel are 4140 chromium molybdenum steel, with 416 stainless steel as an option. The barrel is manufactured by Tobler and is fitted with a high-efficiency muzzle brake.

The stock is fabricated steel and aluminum alloy, with non-structural, plug-in stock and forearm. A fully adjustable bipod and sling rail are integral. Bedding is machined metal-to-metal surfaces. A lighter (29.8 pounds) version is available with a shorter barrel and an alloy stock sub-frame. The optical sights are mounted on an integral dovetail machined into the top of the receiver. Backup iron sights are provided, with the front sight machined into the muzzle brake. A 1-power collimator sight with a wide field of view and long eye relief is optional. This sight incorporates a tritium night sight or an LED illuminator.

A cleaning and maintenance kit is included and transport cases are available. There are many options, including barrels of any specified length, and magazines of different capacities. Effective range is 1,500 to 2,000 meters, depending on conditions and ammunition.

SPECIFICATIONS:
Caliber: 50 BMG (12.7x99mm)
Operation: Manual, bolt-action
Locking: three lugs, rear lockup
Feed: six-round detachable box magazine
Empty weight: 33.7 pounds; lightweight version, 29.8 pounds
Overall length: 57.6 inches (standard version)
Barrel length: 31.2 inches
Max effective range: 1,500 to 2,000m

Croatia

MACS 50 BMG (12.7x99mm) M2A Antimateriel Rifle

The MACS M2A is a single-shot, bolt-action rifle with an optical sight and a multi-baffle muzzle brake to reduce felt recoil. User adjustments can be made to the bipod, the cheek rest and the buttplate. Maximum effective range is approximately 1,400 meters. Standard optical sight is a Kahles ZF 10 x 42.

Variant

MACS M3 (See below).

SPECIFICATIONS:
Cartridge: 50 BMG (12.7 x 99mm)
Operation: Manual bolt-action, single-shot
Feed: Manual, single-shot
Empty weight: With bipod and scope, 27.3 pounds
Overall length: 57.6 inches
Barrel length: 31.1 inches
Sights: optical, Kahles ZF 10 x 42

50 BMG (12.7x99mm) MACS M3 Antimateriel Rifle

The MACS M3 antimateriel rifle is essentially the MACS-M2A, but in a bullpup layout. This reduces the overall length to 3.6 inches and the weight, with bipod and optical sight, to 19.4 pounds. Many of the components, including the bolt-action and the optical sights, are the same as those on the MACS M2A, although the barrel length has been reduced. The ballistic performance of the MACS M3 is similar to that of the MACS M2A.

SPECIFICATIONS:
Cartridge: 50 BMG (12.7 x 99mm)
Operation: bolt-action, single shot
Feed: manual, single shot
Empty weight: With bipod and scope, 19.4 pounds
Overall length: 43.2 inches
Barrel length: 29.9 inches
Sights: optical, Kahles ZF 10 x 42

Australian sniper

RT 20

RT20
20x110mm
Antimateriel
Rifle

The Croatian RT20 20mm rifle falls into the antimateriel rifle class, due to its stated operational range of 1,800 meters. At that distance the accuracy limitations of the 20 x 110mm Hispano Suiza HS 404 are such that hitting point targets might well be problematic. Other than the fact that the 20mm round is available with high explosive loads, this rifle is a highly complicated weapon whose tactical utility is questionable for a variety of reasons, not the least of which is its weight, size, blast signature and the fact that it cannot be fired from enclosures. Further, the effective range of this odd firearm is only marginally greater than 50 caliber rifles. It is included herein for completeness and as a firearms curiosity more than as a viable military small arm.

The RT20 was originally developed to penetrate the armored thermal night sight of Serbian M-84 (Yugoslav T-72) tanks. During the initial stages of the Balkan unpleasantness of the 1990s, the these tanks with their thermal sights were a considerable problem for Croatian infantry movements during darkness, so the 20mm cartridge was selected as the minimum AP round that could destroy the sight housing. The RT20 was successful in this highly specialized mission, so other tactical uses were explored, including the suppression of light support weapons, light armored vehicles and bunkers.

The RT20 is a bullpup weapon. This configuration was selected to avoid the extreme overall length that a conventional layout would have required, but has also introduced some unusual features. One is the manually operated bolt handle on the left side of the receiver. The bullpup layout requires the bolt to be at the extreme rear of the weapon, above and behind the buttplate. The bolt has three sets of locking lugs that are disengaged by raising the bolt handle 60 degrees. The rifle is fired normally, but requires some unusual tactical and ergonomic factors.

A rifle of this class involves recoil problems and conventional muzzle brakes do not attenuate felt recoil sufficiently to prevent injury to the shooter, as any 20mm cartridge carries a sizeable propellant load that produces considerable recoil. To address this issue, the RT20 has an unconventional solution. About halfway down the barrel is a block with an upwards-facing gas port. As the projectile passes this port, some of the propellant gases are bled off via a ring of 24 holes and are directed along a recoil compensation tube to be vented into the atmosphere behind

and above the bolt area. As with recoilless weapons, a 60 degree cone shaped hazardous area to the rifle's rear that must be cleared of obstacles and personnel is created each time the rifle fires. Thus, the RT20 cannot be fired from inside structures or enclosed areas, such as walls. The significant blast signature will also probably disclose the firing position, thus inviting unwanted attention. Worse, the rearward blast also means that the firer cannot assume a normal prone firing position. Instead he has to lie at an angle to the left of the receiver with his right shoulder supporting the weapon and assuming some of the recoil forces. To reduce the firing and supporting loads on the shooter's shoulder, pads of foam rubber around the shoulder contact position are used. Recoil forces are further reduced by a high-efficiency muzzle brake.

The RT20 optical sight is a Kahles 6 x 42 telescopic sight with a long eye relief to ensure the shooter's eye is not so close to the eyepiece as to induce a severe case of "scope eye." An adjustable bipod is provided.

Despite its weight, the standard RT20 can be carried by one man using a special backpack. The latest RT20 variant weighs approximately 42 pounds with bipod and optical sight, a significant reduction from the original's 57 pounds.

The latest version of this rifle is RT20 M1, with the weight, complete with bipod and optical sight, reduced to just over 35 pounds. This model's barrel is lighter, and some changes have been made to the gas recoil reduction system. Another feature is an extra port drilled through the top of the muzzle brake to reduce muzzle rise.

SPECIFICATIONS:

Caliber: 20 x 110mm
Operation: Manual, bolt-action
Locking: three forward lugs, rotary bolt
Feed: manual, single shot
Weight: RT20 with bipod and scope, 42 pounds; RT20 M1 with bipod and scope, 35 pounds
Overall length: 52.8 inches
Barrel length: 36.2 inches
Sights: optical, Kahles ZF 6 x 42
Max effective range: 1,800m

Czech Republic

ZVI Falcon 12.7mm Antimateriel Rifle

The prototype of the Falcon 12.7mm antimateriel rifle was known as the OPV 12.7mm or Model 96. It was intended from the beginning that versions chambered in either 12.7x108mm or 50 BMG (12.7x99mm) would be available. The original barrel was 40.4 inches long and was rifled to accommodate either cartridge; production versions have separately rifled barrels for each specific cartridge. The 12.7x108mm version is designated OP 96, while the 50 BMG is designated OP 99.

The Falcon is a manual bolt-action rifle in bullpup configuration. The rotary bolt has two locking lugs, with recoil attenuation provided by a, four-baffle muzzle brake claimed to be 70 percent efficient and a buffer spring inside the detachable stock. Feed is from a two round detachable box magazine, although a insert can be emplaced when single shot only firing is desired. For transport or storage, the buttstock can be removed and the barrel unscrewed from the receiver once a locking lever has been disengaged. The barrel can also be handled using the carrying handle. A folding bipod is mounted on the carrying handle bracket.

The optical sight is a ZD 10 x 40 scope, claimed to provide accurate aiming up to a range of 1,600 meters. Night sights are available and are claimed to be effective up to 800 meters. Backup iron sights are provided.

SPECIFICATIONS:
Data for both models unless specified
Caliber:
OP 96: 12.7x108mm
OP 99: 50 BMG (12.7 x 99mm)
Operation: manual bolt-action
Locking: 2-lug rotating bolt
Feed: detachable box magazine, 2 rounds capacity
Empty weight:
 OP 96: 28.0 pounds
 OP 99: 28.0 pounds
Overall length: OP96, 47 inches; OP99, 49 inches
Barrel length: OP96, 36.5 inches; OP99, 33.0 inches
Sights: front, open sight, post on folding carrier; rear: folding notch adjustable for elevation and windage. Optical: ZD 10 x 50
Max effective range: optical sight: 1,600m

Finland

Helenius 12.7mm APH RK97 antimateriel rifle

The Helenius 12.7mm APH RK97 antimateriel rifle was introduced in 1998 and is chambered for either the 12.7x108mm or the 50 BMG (12.7 x 99mm) cartridge. Both models are externally identical.

The APH RK97 is a single-shot rifle employing a vertical falling breech block, operated by a sliding foregrip that operates in reverse of a traditional pump action. Pushing the foregrip forward causes the breechblock to drop allowing a cartridge to be manually introduced into the breech. Pulling the foregrip to the rear raises and locks the breechblock. The heavy barrel is provided with a pepperpot-type muzzle brake to reduce felt recoil.

No sights are provided. Optical sights are specified by the user, and are offset slightly to the left. A fixed-height, folding bipod is attached to the front of the square section receiver.

SPECIFICATIONS:
Caliber: 12.7x108mm or 12.7 x 99mm (50 BMG)
Operation: manual, vertical dropping breech block
Feed: manual, single shot
Empty weight: 30.9 pounds
Overall length: 52.8 inches
Barrel length: 44.4 inches
Sights: optical, user installed

Helenius 12.7mm RK99 antimateriel rifle

Introduced during 2000, the Helenius 12.7mm RK99 antimateriel rifle is available chambered for either the 12.7x108mm cartridge or the 50 BMG (12.7 x 99mm). Both models are visually identical externally.

The RK99 is a manually operated rifle that is best described as a pump action, although the operation is unusual. The short one-piece bolt is locked into position using two sets of interrupted threads along the entire bolt length. Rounds are fed from a box magazine under the receiver. As a horizontal actuating handle on the left of the receiver is pushed forward a round is chambered and the bolt rotates and locks. Pulling the handle to the rear extracts and ejects the spent case. The heavy barrel is provided with a pepperpot-type muzzle brake to reduce felt recoil.

No open sights are provided; the rifle is intended for use solely with optical sights. A bipod, cheek rest and recoil pad are included.

SPECIFICATIONS:
Caliber: 12.7x108mm or 50 BMG (12.7 x 99mm)
Operation: manual actuated bolt
Empty weight: 26.5 pounds
Overall length: 51.6 inches
Barrel length: 32.4 inches
Sights: optical, user installed

ZVI Falcon

Helenius 12.7mm RK99 Mark1 Antimateriel rifle

The Helenius 12.7mm RK99MK1 antimateriel rifle was introduced in 2000 and is available chambered for either the 12.7x108mm or the 50 BMG (12.7x99mm). Both models are externally identical.

The RK99MK1 is a single-shot rifle of the type commonly referred to as a "shell holder" rifle. The short bolt is completely removed from the rifle for loading. It is locked into position using two sets of interrupted threads along the entire length of the bolt. Before loading, the rim at the base of the round is used to locate the cartridge in the bolt, the rim acts as the extractor as the bolt is removed after firing. The heavy barrel is provided with a pepperpot-type muzzle brake to reduce recoil effects.

No open sights are provided; the rifle is intended for use only with optical sights. Other than a rubber recoil pad, no accessories are provided.

SPECIFICATIONS:

Caliber: 12.7x108mm or 50 BMG (12.7 x 99mm)
Operation: manual, removable bolt
Empty weight: 26.5 pounds
Overall length: 57.6 inches
Barrel length: 32.4 inches
Sights: optical

Helenius 20mm APH RK20 Antimateriel Rifle

The Helenius 20mm APH RK20 antimateriel rifle is a scaled-up version of the 12.7mm APH RK97 (see above) chambered in 20 x 99R ShVAK cartridge originally designed for the Soviet-era ShVAK aircraft cannon dating from to the early period of the World War II. This cartridge, described in Finland as the 20 x 100mm Swak, has a nominal muzzle velocity of 2,821 fps so its on-target performance in the antimateriel role should prove more than adequate. However, the unsophisticated ballistic shape of the high-explosive projectile, together with its flat-nosed impact fuze, indicates that accuracy could be problematic.

The APH RK20 is employing a vertical falling breechblock, and is operated by a sliding foregrip in exactly the same way as the APH RK97 described above, where operational details may be found.

SPECIFICATIONS:

Caliber: 20 x 99R ShVAK
Operation: manual actuated, vertical breech block
Empty weight: 49.6 pounds
Overall length: 55.12 inches
Barrel length: 33.9 inches
Sights: optical, user installed

Helenius 20mm RK99 Mark2 Antimateriel Rifle

Like the Helenius 20mm APH RK20 described above, the Helenius RK99MK2 fires the 20 x 99R ShVAK cartridge. It is functionally identical to the RK99 Mark 1 described above.

SPECIFICATIONS:

Caliber: 20 x 99R ShVAK
Operation: manual, removable bolt
Empty weight: 44.1 pounds
Overall length: 57.6 inches
Barrel length: 31.5 inches
Sights: optical, user installed

Hungary

12.7x108mm Gepard M1 and M1A1 Antimateriel Rifles

The Gepard M1 and M1A1 rifles are single-shot weapons with an unconventional breech mechanism. The pistol grip acts as the bolt handle and is attached to a multiple-lug breechblock. The unit also contains a simple manually cocked fire control mechanism. To load, the pistol grip is partly rotated to unlock the breech and then removed, exposing the chamber. The cartridge is inserted and the breechblock replaced. The hammer is then cocked and then the trigger pressed. There is a grip for the support hand on the butt and a substantial cheek pad. The rifle is provided with an adjustable bipod but a standard PKM machine gun tripod can also be used. A high-efficiency muzzle brake is fitted. Standard sight is a 12 x 60 telescopic unit; with night sights available.

The Gepard M1 and M1A1 rifles are chambered for the 12.7x108mm B-32 or MDZ-3 AP-T cartridges, which are sufficiently accurate to permit a trained shooter to achieve an 11-inch group with five shots at 600 meters. Maximum effective range is 2,000 meters.

The Gepard M1A1 is basically the same rifle as the Gepard M1, except the weapon is mounted on a backpack frame that can also be used as a firing platform on soft ground or snow. It has been proposed that these rifles could be chambered in 12.7 x 99mm (50 BMG).

SPECIFICATIONS:

Caliber: 12.7x108mm
Operation: manual, removable bolt
Feed: manual, single shot
Empty weight: M1, 41.9 pounds; M1A1, 48.5 pounds
Overall length: 74.4 inches
Barrel length: 42.4 inches
Sights: optical, 12 x 60
Max effective range: 2,000m

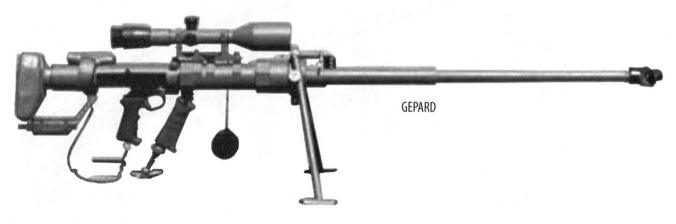

GEPARD

GEPARD M2

12.7mm Gepard M2 and M2A1 Rifles

Although based on the Gepard M1 rifle the Gepard M2 differs primarily in having a long recoil semiautomatic action in place of the single-shot mechanism of the Gepard M1 and M1A1. The Gepard M2 and M2A1 can feed 12.7x108mm rounds from a 5- or 10-round box magazine located next to the pistol grip and trigger assembly.

The Gepard M2 is otherwise similar to the Gepard M1 and they fire the same ammunition, although the effective range is reduced to 1,000 to 1,200 m.

The Gepard M2A1 is a shortened version of the Gepard M2 for use by airborne and special forces. The Gepard M2A1 employs a single-point sight in place of the 6 x 42 scope used with the Gepard M1 and it has no provision for a night sight.

Either of these rifles could be chambered in 50 BMG, which might well occur with NATO expansion to include Hungary.

SPECIFICATIONS: Data for M2, (M2A1 in parentheses)

Caliber: 12.7x108mm
Operation: long recoil, semiautomatic
Empty weight: 35.3 pounds (33.1 pounds)
Overall length: 61.2 inches (51.6 inches)
Barrel length: 43.2 inches (32.7 inches)
Sights: optical, 6 x 42
Max effective range: 1,200m (1,000m)

12.7mm Gepard M4 SA1 antimateriel rifles

The Gepard M4 SA1 antimateriel rifle is a development in the series of antimateriel rifles that commenced with the Gepard M1/M1A. The Gepard M4 SA1 is a semiautomatic rifle that can be chambered for either 12.7x108mm or 50 BMG (12.7x 99mm) ammunition. A Gepard M5 is also under development, chambered for 12.7x108mm ammunition.

The Gepard M4 SA1 antimateriel rifles are long recoil operated semiautomatic, with a bolt carried with an eight-lug rotary locking bolt. The hammer-type firing mechanism is inside the stock. Cartridges are fed from a 5-round box or a 10-round drum magazine located under the receiver. Cocking is accomplished via a folding charging handle on the right side of the receiver.

A folding bipod secured to either side of the barrel housing supports the rifle. In the firing position the barrel is directly in line with the shooter's shoulder, assisting in reducing felt recoil and muzzle rise. A vertically and horizontally adjustable cheek rest, along with an adjustable rubber recoil pad. The stock houses a retractable monopod leg for additional stability.

Aiming is via a 12 x 60 telescopic sight although other sights, including night sights, can be fitted. Recoil forces are attenuated by the reciprocating operating parts, along with a muzzle brake. Service life is given as 5,000 rounds.

The weapon can be carried using a carrying handle or slung over a shoulder or across the back using an optional sling. The overall length can be reduced by 8.5 inches if necessary

SPECIFICATIONS:

Caliber: 12.7x108mm or 50 BMG (12.7 x 99mm)
Operation: long recoil, semiautomatic
Locking: eight-lug rotating bolt
Feed: five-round box magazine or 10-round drum
Empty weight: 37.5 pounds
Overall length: 57.6 inches
Barrel length: 31.5 inches
Sights: optical, 12 x 60
Max effective range: 2,000m

14.5x114mm Gepard M3 Antimateriel rifle

The Gepard M3 antimateriel rifle, also known as the Destroyer, is a semiautomatic bipod-mounted weapon designed to engage hardened targets such as lightly armored vehicles, helicopters, field defenses and targets at longer ranges.

The rifle is chambered for the Russian 14.5x114mm heavy machinegun cartridge. It is recoil-operated and incorporates a hydraulic buffer and a highly efficient muzzle brake, so the felt recoil is of about the same level as a large-caliber sporting rifle.

Using 14.5x114mm B-32 AP-T (armor piercing tracer) ammunition, the Gepard M3 is claimed to defeat 30mm (1.2 inches) of rolled homogeneous armor at 100 meters and 25mm (1 inch) at 600 meters. Maximum effective range is stated by the manufacturer to be 1,000 meters.

SPECIFICATIONS:

Caliber: 14.5 x 114mm
Operation: long recoil, semiautomatic
Feed: five- or 10-round detachable box magazine
Empty weight: 46.3 pounds
Overall length: 74.4 inches
Barrel length: 63.6 inches
Sight: optical, 12 x 60
Max effective range: 1,000m

International

Hecate II 50 BMG (12.7x99mm) Antimateriel Rifle

The Hecate II Antimateriel Rifle is designed and manufactured by PGM Precision of Poisy, France. A marketing agreement was later arranged with FN Herstal of Belgium which now markets the rifle under the FNH name. North American marketing is conducted by FNH USA.

The Hecate II derived from the PGM Ultima Ratio (UR) Intervention rifle (see separate entry) but the Hecate II is enlarged to accommodate the 50 BMG cartridge. Using this cartridge the Hecate II is claimed to be effective at ranges up to 1,500 meters, depending on ammunition.

The modular construction of the UR Intervention and Commando models is retained for the Hecate II on a much-enlarged scale. Magazine capacity is increased to seven rounds and the stock assembly can be quickly removed for transport purposes. The match-grade heavy barrel is fluted for rigidity and heat dissipation and is fitted with a large single-baffle muzzle brake assembly that is claimed to be so efficient that the felt recoil is no greater than a 7.62x51mm rifle.

A collapsible carrying handle is provided and the stock can be removed without tools. Once the weapon is in the firing position an adjustable monopod can be added under the stock assembly. The bolt handle can be removed instantly for security reasons.

The Hecate II Suppressed model is fitted with an Ops Inc suppressor that replaces the muzzle brake. Adding the suppressor increases the empty weight to approximately 38 pounds.

SPECIFICATIONS:

Caliber: 50 BMG (12.7x99mm)
Operation: Manual, bolt-action
Locking: Rotating bolt, 3 front locking lugs
Feed: seven-round detachable box magazine
Empty weight: 36.0 pounds (38.2 pounds w/ suppressor)
Overall length: 55.2 inches; stock removed, 43.2 inches
Barrel length: 27.6 inches
Sights: optical, user installed
Max effective range: 1,800 m

Nemesis 50 BMG (12.7x99mm) Antimateriel Rifle

The Nemesis II 12.7mm sniper rifle is under development by PGM Precision of Poisy, France, to be marketed by FN Herstal of Belgium under the FNH/PGM name. North American marketing will be carried out by FNH USA.

The Nemesis is designed for military and law enforcement operations in urban environments and for special operations use. As such, it has a collapsible stock and shorter barrel than the larger Hecate II 50 BMG rifle. It is also lighter than the Hecate II. The Nemesis has a fully adjustable cheekpiece and padded buttplate. The receiver has MIL-STD-1913 rails on top and on both sides to accommodate optics and accessories.

The Nemesis also features an integral bipod and rear monopod for stability. The modular construction of PGM's Ultima Ratio rifles is retained for the Nemesis although the overall dimensions are larger. Magazine capacity is five rounds. The match-grade heavy barrel is fluted and is fitted with a large single-baffle muzzle brake assembly that is claimed to reduce felt recoil to approximately that of a 7.62x51mm rifle.

SPECIFICATIONS:

Caliber: 50 BMG (12.7 x 99mm)
Operation: manual, bolt-action
Locking: rotating bolt, three locking lugs
Feed: 5-round detachable box magazine
Empty weight: 28 pounds, depending on configuration
Overall length: 36.25 in.
Barrel length: 27.5 in.
Sights: optical, user option
Max effective range: 1,800 m

Poland

WKW II 50 BMG (12.7x99mm) Antimateriel Rifle

The Wielkokalibrowy Karabin Wyborowy (Large Bore Sniper Rifle) or WKW was developed to fire 50 BMG ammunition at ranges up to 2,000 meters and is a bullpup bolt-action rifle. The seven-round box magazine is located just in front of the shooter's shoulder, with the small stock connected by a height-adjustment screw sleeve to a support arm. A folding bipod is provided for support and a high-efficiency six-port muzzle brake reduces felt recoil. Accuracy is claimed to be enhanced by what the manufacturer describes as a new form of trigger mechanism. A carrying handle is provided.

The standard optical sight for the WKW is a Schmidt & Bender 3 to 12 power P/Mil variable-power telescope mounted on a short rail atop the receiver. No open sights are provided.

SPECIFICATIONS:

Caliber: 50 BMG (12.7 x 99mm)
Operation: Manual, bolt-action
Locking: rotating bolt
Feed: seven-round detachable box magazine
Empty weight: 35.1 pounds
Barrel length: 34.6 inches
Sights: Schmidt & Bender 3-12x P/Mil variable power telescope
Max effective range: 2,000m

HECATE II

Russia

12.7x108mm V-94 (OSV-96) Antimateriel Rifle

The V-94 (OSV-96) antimateriel rifle was announced publicly during 1995. The OSV-96 and the V-94 differ mainly in the revised stock and in their optical sights, which could be one of several types. Russian sources make no differentiation between the rifles.

According to advertising literature, potential targets for the V-94 (OSV-96) include parked aircraft, radars, missile launchers and artillery, lightly armored and soft-skin vehicles, small coastal craft and sea mines, all emphasizing the fact that a large-caliber rifle is far more economical against such targets than more costly ordnance. Reports from Chechnya claimed that the V94 was too large for the operational environment and for transport. The same reports also stated that the firing signature was excessive and the recoil forces such that optical sight zero could not be maintained.

The V-94 (OSV-96) antimateriel rifle is a gas-operated semiautomatic rifle with a large two-chambered muzzle device that serves both as a muzzle brake and a flash suppressor. Felt recoil is reduced not only by the muzzle device, but by the gas operating system, the rifle's weight and a rubber butt-pad. Gas for the operating mechanism is tapped off about one-third of the way down the barrel. Locking is by rotating bolt. Ammunition is fed from a five-round box magazine beneath the receiver. The round most often quoted in Russian literature alludes to the B-32, an API round. Russian literature also mentions a specialized "sniper" 12.7 cartridge, about which little is known other than its existence. Presumably this cartridge is manufactured to a higher standard than 12.7mm machine gun ammunition, which is notorious for its lack of accuracy, even in 50 BMG rifles. The most accurate standard western 50 caliber cartridge is also an API round, so this may also be the case in Russia. With API ammunition the V-94 (OSV-96) has an effective range of approximately 2,000 meters and a 90 percent chance of penetration against 20mm armor plate at 100 meters.

The OSV-96 is provided with an optical sight, a modified version of the aged PSO-1 telescopic sight in 13x. A POS 12 x 50 optical sight is also available. The optical sight is removed during movement. A PKN-05 night sight permits night engagements against targets up to 600 meters distant.

The V-94 (OSV-96) can be folded at the junction of the barrel and receiver assembly. This is accomplished by raising a locking lever just forward of the ejection port on the right of the receiver, allowing the receiver and the stock to be swung to the right side of the barrel. In folded configuration, the overall length of the rifle is reduced to 43.3 inches. When the rifle is folded, the carry handle is at the center of gravity.

SPECIFICATIONS:
Caliber: 12.7x108mm
Operation: gas; semiautomatic
Feed: five-round detachable box magazine
Empty weight: 25.7 pounds
Overall length: Stock extended, 66.9 inches; Stock folded, 43.3 inches
Barrel length: 40.1 inches
Sights: Optical POS 12 x 50
Max effective range: Approx. 2,000m

Slovenia

Alpimex APK 12.7 50 BMG (12.7x99mm) Antimateriel Rifle

The Alpimex APK 12.7 is a 50 BMG caliber anti-materiel rifle that is essentially a scaled down APK 20 rifle. Other than caliber and size, the APK 12.7 is identical to the APK 20.

SPECIFICATIONS:
Caliber: 50 BMG (12.7 x 99mm)
Operation: manual
Locking: Falling block
Feed: Manual, single-shot
Empty weight: 22.9 pounds
Overall length: 48.0 inches
Barrel length: 36.2 inches
Sights: optical, user installed

ALPIMEX APK 20 20x82mm antimateriel rifle

The ALPIMEX APK 20 antimateriel rifle is a single-shot rifle with a manually operated falling block action worked by a lever that can be located on either side of the receiver. The rifle is chambered in 20 x 82mm MG151. The rifle is a semi-bullpup with the pistol grip underneath and just forward of the loading ramp. There is no receiver per se. One mounting point for the optical or night sight is located on top of the barrel. The forward sight is located on a collar around the barrel and an extension tube onto which a bipod can be mounted. There are no iron sights.

The contoured butt-stock is made of walnut, unusual in present day military rifles, and has a rubber butt pad to reduce felt recoil. Recoil is further attenuated by an integral pepperpot-type muzzle brake.

SPECIFICATIONS:
Cartridge: 20 x 82mm
Operation: manual
Locking: falling block
Feed: manual, single shot
Empty weight: 32.4 pounds
Overall length: 49.2 inches
Barrel length: 36.2 inches
Sights: optical, user installed

V 94

South Africa

PMP NTW 20/14.5 Antimateriel Rifle

Tony Neophytou designed the NTW 20/14.5 antimateriel rifle. The design rights were eventually obtained by Mechem, a division of Denel (Pty) Ltd. When Mechem was sold by Denel, the rights to the NTW 20/14.5 were acquired by Pretoria Metal Pressings (PMP), also a division of Denel. The rifle can be readily modified by the user to accommodate two ammunition calibers: the 20 x 82mm MG151 cartridge or the Soviet/Russian 14.5 x 114mm. Suitable barrels and other components allow the rifle to fire either 50 BMG (12.7 x 99mm) or 12.7x108mm ammunition

The South African National Defence Force (SANDF) selected the NTW 20 rifle in 1998, which procured all available development models for tests and familiarization prior to availability of production rifles. The NTW 20/14.5 has also been procured in substantial numbers by other unspecified nations.

The 20mm NTW 20/14.5 rifle is an antimateriel weapon with many applications, including Explosive Ordnance Disposal (EOD). The 20mm version fires the 20 x82mm MG151 cartridge is produced in South Africa by PMP. Ammunition types include High-Explosive Incendiary (HEI), High-Explosive Incendiary - Tracer (HEI-T), Semi-Armor-Piercing High-Explosive Incendiary (SAPHEI) and Practice. Effective range is stated to be up to 1,300 meters. The 14.5mm variant fires the Russian 14.5x114mm in API and API-T. Maximum effective range is 1,800 meters.

Changing from one caliber to another takes less than 30 seconds. The barrel, bolt, magazine and sighting equipment can be interchanged between calibers as required.

Rounds are fed from a three-round box magazine protruding on the left side of the receiver. The magazine also provides fuse protection. Spent cases are ejected to the right as the bolt is withdrawn.

The NTW 20/14.5 is a manual bolt-action rifle with the bolt employing six locking lugs. A large double-baffle muzzle brake and a hydraulic/pneumatic buffer system limit recoil. Two hydraulic buffers are available for use in either warm or cold climates.

Recoiling parts slide within a chassis frame that includes the stock assembly, so the firer can assume a conventional firing position with the stock held into the shoulder by a grip under the frame with a pistol grip for the adjustable pull and detachable trigger assembly. The recoiling parts and the barrel can be removed from the chassis frame for maintenance and carrying.

The bipod is located under the receiver and the barrel-locking nut and is either loosened or tightened by inserting two cartridge base rims into slots in the nut. In addition, the handgrip under the stock can be lowered to act as a monopod.

The optical sight is a long eye relief 8 x 42 scope with parallax adjustment and a quick detachable mount.

The rifle may be carried on two special backpack harnesses, one load weighing 26.4 pounds and the other 33.1 pounds. One unit carries the frame, stock and bipod, while the other carries the barrel, sighting equipment and magazines.

Development of the NTW rifle continues; recent innovations include a magazine constructed using plastic moldings and a new muzzle brake. Another innovation is a mechanism to cock the trigger during the recoil phase and so alleviate some of the load from the trigger mechanism. .

SPECIFICATIONS: 20mm version (14.5x114mm version in parentheses)

Caliber: 20 x 82mm MG151
Operation: manual, bolt-action
Locking: rotating bolt, six lugs
Feed: three-round detachable box magazine
Empty weight: 57.3 pounds (63.9 pounds)
Overall length: 70.7 inches (79.3 inches)
Barrel length: 39.4 inches (48 inches)
Sights: optical, 8 x 42
Maximum effective range: 1,300 m (1,800m)

Truvelo Armoury 50 BMG (12.7x99mm) Mega Sniper Antimateriel Rifle

The Mega Sniper antimateriel rifle is a member of the family of precision rifles produced by Truvelo under the general name SG1 (Scharfschutzen Gewehr 1). It is available in either single-shot or magazine-fed variants intended to provide accuracy of 1 minute of angle (MOA) at 500 meters with suitable ammunition.

The Mega Sniper antimateriel rifle is constructed along lines similar to other rifles in the SG1 family. Bolt lengths differ between the single-shot and magazine-fed models; the magazine-fed rifle bolt-action is longer. Bolt-actions are CNC machined from solid to 817M40 steel billets, with two front locking lugs and third at the bolt rear. The standard box magazine holds five rounds, although other magazine capacities are available. The barrel is button rifled and the muzzle brake is claimed to reduce recoil by 50 percent.

The stock is machined from aircraft-grade aluminum and is adjustable for length of pull. The stock has an adjustable rubber butt pad. The folding bipod is adjustable for height. The polymer pistol grip is adjustable for trigger reach. The rifle can be configured for use by either right or left-handed shooters. No open sights are provided. Optical sights are mounted on a MIL-STD-1913 rail atop the receiver.

SPECIFICATIONS:

Caliber: 50 BMG (12.7 x 99mm)
Operation: manual bolt-action
Locking: two front lugs, one at rear
Feed: single-shot or five-round box magazine
Empty weight: 35.3 pounds
Overall length: 59.4 inches
Barrel length: 39.4 inches
Sights: optical, user installed
Max effective range: 1,200m

NTW 20

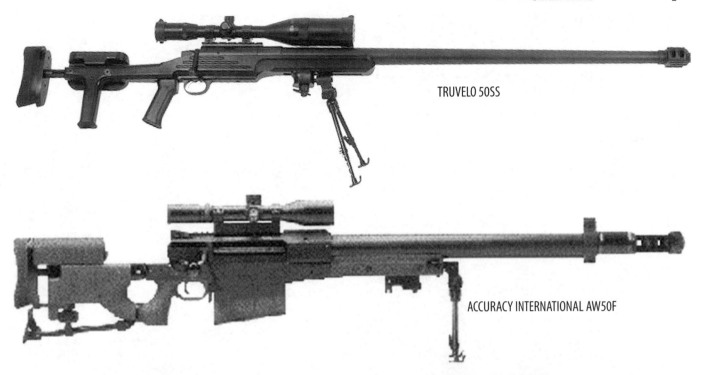

TRUVELO 50SS

ACCURACY INTERNATIONAL AW50F

Ukraine

Tasko 12.7x108mm Antimateriel Rifle

The Tasko antimateriel rifle is claimed to be effective against vehicle-sized targets at up to 2,000 meters. The rifle is gas-operated and fires semiautomatic only with an effective rate of fire of 10 to 15 rounds per minute. Ammunition is fed from a 5- or 10-round box magazine. An adjustable bipod is attached directly onto a lug at the forward end of the receiver. The barrel has a large multi-baffle muzzle brake to reduce recoil. The top of the receiver accommodates optical sights to suit the user specifications. It is also possible to mount a night sight with an effective range of 600 meters. The stock is a conventional shape and is made of wood with a butt pad and cheek rest that can be adjusted to suit the individual shooter.

SPECIFICATIONS:

Caliber: 12.7x108mm
Operation: gas, semiautomatic
Feed: 5- or 10-round box magazine
Empty weight: 26.5 pounds
Overall length: stock folded, 42.9 inches; stock extended, 61.2 inches
Sights: optical, user specified; night sights available
Max effective range: 2,000m

United Kingdom

Accuracy International 50 BMG (12.7x99mm) AW50F

The Accuracy International AW50 rifle was initially announced in 1998 with deliveries beginning in October 1999. The AW50F's design is derived from that of Accuracy International's smaller caliber sniper rifles, and essentially carries most of the features of the smaller caliber rifles, but on a larger scale.

The Australian Army selected the AW50F in 2001 for use by special forces units and selected infantry battalions. The initial order was for 94 rifles, with spare parts, accessories and ammunition.

The AW50F rifle fires all types of 50BMG (12.7x99mm) ammunition, except the SLAP rounds which cannot be fired in any rifle having a muzzle brake because the sabot begins opening as soon as it leaves the muzzle and will damage the brake. The AW50F is a manually operated bolt-action rifle fed from a five-round detachable box magazine. The aluminum and steel receiver is bedded to an alloy chassis similar to other Accuracy International rifles and has an integral anti-recoil system. The barrel is stainless steel and has a high-efficiency muzzle brake for recoil reduction. Felt recoil is further attenuated by a soft recoil pad.

The AW50F is equipped with a folding stock for convenience in transportation, The adjustable rear monopod and bipod both fold.

The standard 3-12x telescopic sighting system is attached to a MIL-STD-1913 rail and is graduated to 1,500 meters. Backup open sights are optional.

A hard metal case containing spare magazines, a sling and maintenance kits, with a padded soft case for carrying the folded rifle on a sling harness over the back, or with both is optional.

SPECIFICATIONS:

Caliber: 50 BMG (12.7 x 99mm)
Operation: manual, bolt-action
Locking: rotating bolt, 6 lugs
Feed: five-round detachable box magazine
Empty weight: 30 pounds
Overall length: stock extended, 53 inches; stock folded, 43.7 inches
Barrel length: 27 inches

United Kingdom sniper team

United States

ArmaLite AR-50 rifle

The ArmaLite AR-50 is a lightweight and accurate long-range single shot rifle. The octagonal receiver is bedded into a solid aluminum bedding block that forms part of the stock. The stock itself is in three sections: an extruded forearm, a machined grip frame with a M16 type pistol grip; and a skeleton buttstock that can be removed for transport. The buttplate and cheekpiece are fully adjustable.

Three bolt-locking lugs allow for a bolt handle lift of only 60 degrees. The extractor is a Sako-type with spring-loaded plunger type ejector. The muzzle brake or "Multiflute recoil check" is very aggressive and significantly reduces felt recoil. The ArmaLite muzzle brake is so effective that many purchasers of other manufacturers' rifles install an Armalite muzzle brake.

There are no sights provided, although there is a MIL-STD-1913 rail for mounting optical sights. Steel parts are Parkerized and aluminum components hard anodized.

SPECIFICATIONS:

Caliber: 50 BMG (12.7x99mm)
Operation: manual, bolt-action, single shot
Locking: rotating bolt, three lugs
Feed: manual, single shot
Empty weight: 34 pounds
Overall length: 59.5 inches
Barrel length: 31 inches
Sights: none provided; MIL-STD-1913 rail mount
Max effective range: 2,000 yards with match-grade ammunition

Barrett 50BMG (12.7x99mm) Model 82A1and Model 82A1M Rifles

The Barrett M82 series rifles are recoil-operated semiautomatic firearms. They are used by military forces worldwide for Explosive Ordnance Disposal (EOD) remote demolition of unexploded ordnance and for long-range interdiction of targets such as radar vans, light vehicles and parked aircraft. They are also used by law enforcement for interdiction of similar targets and for disabling light ocean-going craft.

The M82A1 has been modified and redesignated the M82A1M for military customers. Both rifles remain in production. The US Marine Corps and US Army have both adopted the M82A1M. The Marines designate it the M82A3, while the Army version is designated the M107. The M82A1M is not available commercially and differs from the M82A1 in the following:
- A monopod at the rear of the buttstock;
- A rear grip
- A 19-inch long MIL-STD-1913 rail for mounting optical sights and other accessories
- A removable improved design muzzle brake
- A lightweight bolt carrier;
- New open sights calibrated to match the ballistics of the Raufoss Mark 211-round.
- A quick-release short bipod with spiked feet.

The M82 rifles are short-recoil operated. The M82 series rifles incorporate a high-efficiency muzzle brake, which reduces recoil approximately 65 percent. Both the M82A1 and M82A1M have adjustable bipods, which differ in that the M82A1M bipod has spiked feet to prevent movement under recoil. The rifle can also be vehicle-mounted using of a "soft mount" pintle adapter that reduces shock forces on the pintle via a hydraulic buffering system.

The M82A1 is fitted with both open sights and a standard 10x telescopic sight, with a ballistic reticle incorporating a bullet drop compensator for standard ammunition types. The reticle allows adjustment of the point of impact from 500 to 1,800 meters, the maximum effective range when standard ammunition is used.

Military users recommend using the MK211 Raufoss cartridge, but the rifle is capable of firing any standard 50 BMG ammunition, except SLAP (saboted light armor piercing) cartridges, because the SLAP round's sabot expands as it leaves the muzzle and thus cannot pass through the muzzle brake without damaging it. M82 rifles are capable of excellent accuracy when used with match-grade ammunition.

All US military services, including Special Forces, use either the M82A1 or M82A1M. The M82A1 and M82A1M are in service with 34 other countries including Bahrain, Belgium, Bhutan, Botswana, Chile, Denmark, Finland, France, Great Britain, Greece (manufactured under license), Italy, Kuwait, Jordan, Mexico, the Netherlands, Norway, Oman, the Philippines, Portugal, Qatar, Saudi Arabia, Singapore, Spain, Sweden, Turkey, and the United Arab Emirates

The BARRETT M82A1 can be used in a variety of situations.

SPECIFICATIONS:

Caliber: 50 BMG (12.7 x 99mm)
Operation: Short-recoil, semiautomatic
Locking: rotating bolt
Feed: 10-round detachable box magazine
Empty weight: 31 pounds
Overall length: 45 inches; M82A1M reduced length, 38 inches
Barrel length: 29 inches
Sights: 10x telescope standard; backup open sights.
Maximum effective range: 2,000m with match-grade ammunition

American soldiers use .50 caliber rifles to engage targets at long range.

Barrett 50 BMG (12.7x99mm) Model 95/95M

The Barrett 50 Browning Machine Gun (BMG) caliber M95 was originally introduced in 1990 as the Model 90 bolt-action rifle and subsequently was extensively modified and redesignated Model 95. The M95 is a bullpup design, which resulted in a rifle that was both lighter and shorter than the semiautomatic M82A1.

The Model 95 was tentatively adopted in slightly modified form by the US Army in 1999 and designated the XM107 prior to final certification testing and type classification. After changing operational employment policy, the Army decided to adopt the Barrett Model 82A1M instead, primarily because of its improved potential firepower. The XM107 designation was transferred to the M82A1M.

The Model 95M is a bullpup design, with the action well back in the receiver/stock assembly and the pistol grip forward of the magazine. The high-efficiency muzzle brake keeps recoil forces to a manageable level, and coupled with a Sorbothane recoil pad, reduces the felt recoil to approximately that of a 12-gauge magnum shotgun. The chamber is hard chrome plated to enhance extraction and prevent corrosion.

The Barrett Model 95M consists of upper and lower receiver halves, with the barrel an integral component of the upper receiver. The Model 95M is disassembled for maintenance by withdrawing two pins, allowing the shortened rifle to be placed in a special 'drag bag' for airborne operations or administrative movement and then quickly reassembled. There is a 12-inch long MIL-STD-1913 rail mount for optical sights and backup open sights. The bipod assembly is the same as that used on the Barrett Model 82A1M.

The M95 is employed by the military forces of over 15 countries and is widely used by law enforcement agencies in the United States.

SPECIFICATIONS:
Caliber: 50 BMG (12.7 x 99mm)
Operation: Manual bolt-action
Feed: 5-round detachable box magazine
Empty weight, 20 pounds
Overall length: 45 inches; disassembled, 34 inches
Barrel length: 29 inches
Max effective range: 2,000 yards with match-grade ammunition

Barrett 50 BMG (12.7x99mm) Model 99

The Barrett Model 99 is similar to the Model 95, except it is a single-shot rifle. Like the M95, it is a bullpup design. The M99 is intended to be a less expensive alternative to the company's magazine-fed rifles, but it is among the most accurate 50 BMG rifles in the world. Most Model 99 rifles achieve .5 minute of angle (MOA) accuracy with match-grade ammunition and are sub-MOA with military API, the most accurate military ammunition available. A Barrett Model 99 holds the production 50 BMG world accuracy record as of 2004, set using a stock Model 99 with match-grade ammunition. Although intended primarily for sporting uses, the M99 is also employed by many law enforcement agencies who do not believe it necessary to have a magazine-fed 50 BMG caliber rifle.

SPECIFICATIONS:
Caliber: 50 BMG (12.7x99mm)
Operation: manual, bolt-action
Locking: rotating bolt
Feed: Manual, single shot
Empty weight: 25 pounds
Overall length: 44.5 inches
Barrel length: 33 inches

EDM Arms 50 BMG Windrunner Tactical Takedown Rifle

The EDM Arms 50 Windrunner Tactical Takedown Rifle is intended as an easily transportable antimateriel rifle. It is a manually operated, bolt-action, magazine-fed rifle that can be disassembled into five major sub-assemblies. Disassembly can be accomplished in under 60 seconds without the use of tools. The overall length after disassembly is less than 32 inches. Although EDM advertising refers to the rifle as "XM107," the Windrunner has not been adopted by any known military force.

The Windrunner receiver is CNC-machined from a single billet of 4140 hardened chrome molybdenum steel. A MIL-STD-1913 rail for mounting optical devices is machined into the receiver's top surface. The barrel is fluted for stiffness and heat dispersion and is secured to the receiver by a threaded nut and self-locking ratchet that prevents it from backing off and affecting headspace. The muzzle brake is threaded onto the barrel and has 80 holes at an 80-degree angle.

The stock slides back and forth on rails for length of pull adjustment and incorporates a molded steel cheek rest. The butt has a rubber recoil pad. A rear monopod folds into the stock and an M14-type bipod is provided as standard.

EDM also manufactures a similar rifle in 338 Lapua caliber. A single shot version of the 50 BMG rifle designated the Windrunner Model SS.99 is also available.

Barret Model 99

UK Royal Marines and US Marines often train together.

McMillan Bros (McBros) 50 BMG (12.7x99mm) Tactical Bolt-action Rifle

The McBros Tactical Bolt-action Rifle is available both in single shot and magazine-fed configurations. The latter incorporates a five-round detachable box magazine. Otherwise both rifles are identical. Their receivers are machined from solid chrome molybdenum steel bar stock. The trigger is a Remington type, set at 2.5 pounds with other triggers optional. An adjustable folding bipod is attached to the front of the stock. The barrel is bedded in a McMillan Fiberglas stock with pistol grip and a detachable stock and length of pull adjustable via spacers in the butt. A high efficiency muzzle brake is attached to the fluted match-grade barrel, with a stainless steel barrel optional. No sights are fitted, although McMillan will mount optical sights to customer specification.

The McBros Sporter model is identical to the Tactical model, but has a conventional stock. Versions are also available for bench rest match shooting.

SPECIFICATIONS

Caliber: 50 BMG (12.7 x 99mm)
Operation: Manual, bolt-action
Locking: Rotating bolt
Feed: Manual, single shot or five-round detachable box magazine
Empty weight: 25 pounds, less optics,
Overall length: Approx 42 inches
Barrel length: 29 inches

Robar 50 BMG (12.7x99mm) RC-50 and RC-50F Bolt-Action Rifles

The Robar RC-50 and RC-50F bolt-action rifles were originally developed for precision target shooting, but their use has spread to numerous special operations units and various military and police forces worldwide.

The RC-50 is a conventional manually operated bolt-action rifle with a detachable five-round box magazine. The action is machined from solid bar stock and mated to a match-grade barrel with a high efficiency muzzle brake that significantly reduces felt recoil. A Pachmayr decelerator recoil pad further attenuates felt recoil. A modified Remington-type trigger is fitted and set at 2.5 pounds release weight. The RC-50 uses a conventional McMillan Fiberglas stock, with a Parker-Hale type folding bipod attached to a mounting stud at the front of the forearm. The barrel is free-floated along its entire length.

The RC-50F is identical to the RC-50, except that it has a folding stock for convenient carrying. The stock is held rigid when in the firing configuration by a screw that mates with a block in the stock. There are no sights provided. A MIL-STD-1913 rail mount is provided for mounting optics.

SPECIFICATIONS:

Caliber: 50 BMG (12.7 x 99mm)
Operation: manual, bolt-action
Locking: Rotating bolt
Feed: 5-round detachable box magazine
Empty weight: 25 pounds, less optics
Barrel length: 29 inches

SPECIFICATIONS:

Caliber: 50 BMG (12.7 x 99mm)
Operation: manual, bolt-action
Locking: rotating bolt
Feed: five-round detachable box magazine
Empty weight: 31.4 pounds
Overall length: firing configuration, Approx 47 inches; transport configuration, approx 32 inches.
Barrel length: 30 inches
Sights: None provided; MIL-STD-1913 rail mount for optic mounting

Tactical Shotguns

The shotgun has been a mainstay within the American military since the 19th Century when it was issued primarily for foraging, i.e. to obtain game to feed the troops. Of course, the shotgun came to be used in combat as well, and it proved to be a devastating close quarters battle (CQB) weapon. Shotguns have accompanied American forces into combat ever since WW I and continue in use today. One has only to watch the news footage from Iraq to see shotguns in the hands of US Army and Marine Corps troops. For urban fighting, the shotgun has few equals.

The shotgun has recently undergone a renaissance. In the past, shotguns were generally commercial "off the shelf" items with a few modifications for military use, generally handguards to keep one's hand from getting burned on a hot barrel and a bayonet lug. Those who think that a shotgun's barrel doesn't get hot enough to burn their hands have never fired one on a sustained basis. Once ten rounds or so have been quickly run through the gun, the barrel gets HOT! Bayonet lugs are generally superfluous in today's combat and for law enforcement use, so few, if any, tactical shotguns have them. As the US military realized that it needed to replace its shotgun inventory, the search began for a new gun and the Benelli M1014 Shotgun was adopted. The Benelli is a semiautomatic, however, and there were those in the military who didn't want a semiautomatic gun, despite the fact that it was an excellent one. For that reason, the US military has resumed procurement of a Remington 870 variant called the "Modular Combat Shotgun." This gun is fully described in the text, and is a truly modular weapon.

The reason for the return to a manually operated pump-action shotgun has to do with ammunition. The primary reason the shotgun has returned to the forefront of military and law enforcement is the vast range of ammunition available for it, ranging from less lethal "bean bags" and rubber baton rounds to high-explosive and anti-armor rounds. The less lethal rounds will not cycle the action of any semiautomatic shotgun, thus requiring the soldier or police officer to work the small charging handle which can be problematic, since the charging handle was never designed nor intended to be used to repeatedly manually cycle the gun. Changing ammunition types in semiautomatic shotguns is more difficult, as well. If one wishes, say, to change from shot to a slug round, with a pump action, all that is necessary is to insert the new round into the magazine and cycle the action. The old round is ejected and the new one chambered. The action is instinctive. With a semiautomatic gun, the round can also be changed by inserting a round into the magazine and cycling the charging handle, but it is not as rapid nor as simple as a pump-action. Moreover, in practical terms a pump-

action can be operated as fast as a semiautomatic. About the only advantage a semiautomatic gun has is slightly reduced recoil, although recoil reducing stocks are available to fit most popular pump-action tactical shotguns. A final merit of the pump-action shotgun is its rock-solid reliability. The best pump-action shotguns are virtually indestructible. As long as they are given reasonable care, pump-action shotguns are far more reliable in every way than semiautomatics. There are a few tactical shotguns that incorporate both semiautomatic and pump-actions, such as the Benelli M-3 Tactical described below, but for practical purposes, they have no significant advantage over a pump-action and are more expensive and complex.

Because most tactical ammunition is 12-gauge, this will continue to predominate the tactical shotgun world, although there are a few 20-gauge tactical shotguns and the Russian military and law enforcement even use a .410-bore tactical shotgun. There is virtually no 20-gauge or .410-bore ammunition available other than shot and slugs, so any organization that selects a tactical shotgun in one of these chamberings will be severely limited as to ammunition options.

For the foreseeable future, the tactical shotgun will be a part of the world's military and law enforcement. For urban combat, riot control, CQB, jungle warfare or any situation where a small arm with unparalleled versatility is required, the tactical shotgun will continue to reign supreme. Because of the wide array of ammunition available for the shotgun, most will continue to be pump-actions.

Norinco M98

China

NORINCO M98 Slide Action Tactical Shotguns

The NORINCO M98 is a conventional slide-action tactical shotgun that strongly resembles the Remington M870, from which it was clearly derived. The M98 is available in two versions: one with bead front sight and the other with 'ghost ring' aperture or rifle type notch rear and blade front sight. All furniture is polymer and finish is matte Parkerized. Synthetic pistol grip stocks are optional.

SPECIFICATIONS:

Caliber: 12-gauge
Operation: manual, slide action
Locking: sliding block
Feed: underbarrel tubular magazine, 5 + 1 rounds capacity 2.75 inch
Empty weight 7.1 pounds
Overall length: 38.5 inches
Barrel: 18.5 inches
Choke: cylinder bore
Chamber: 3 inches
Sights: bead or blade front sight and 'ghost ring' aperture rear

NORINCO Model 2000 semiautomatic tactical shotgun

Like the NORINCO Model 98 described previously, the Model 2000 appears to be a close copy of a Remington Model 11-87P tactical shotgun. Construction is steel with black polymer furniture. The Model 2000 is available with either a bead or a blade front sight and 'ghost ring' aperture rear sight. Like the Model 98, the Model 2000 is available with either a pistol grip or semi-pistol grip stock. The Model 2000 is equipped with an oversized charging handle for improved charging and tactical reloading.

SPECIFICATIONS:

Caliber: 12-gauge
Operation: gas, semiautomatic
Locking: sliding block
Feed: underbarrel tubular magazine, 4 + 1 capacity 2.95 inch
Empty weight: 7.5 pounds
Overall length: 38.5 inches
Barrel length: 18.5 inches
Choke: cylinder

France

SAE Alsetex Models RO5 and PM5 Slide Action Tactical Shotguns

The SAE Alsetex RO5 and PM5 tactical shotguns are specifically designed for military and police use. The RO5 has a conventional tubular magazine while the PM5 has a detachable box magazine. Three versions of each gun are available - standard wooden stock, pistol grip polymer stock and folding tubular steel stock. The latter version's stock folds forward over the top of the receiver. The receiver is steel alloy with a phosphate corrosion resistant finish. All guns are provided with replaceable screw-in choke tubes ranging from cylinder bore to full choke that can be altered by the user depending on the tactical situation. Barrels are available in two lengths and are chrome lined. The RO5 and PM5 may be ordered with either 2.75- or 3-inch chambers.

SPECIFICATIONS:

Caliber: 12-gauge
Operation: manual, slide action
Locking: sliding block
Feed: RO5, underbarrel tubular magazine, 8 + 1-rounds; PM5, detachable box magazine, 7 + 1-rounds
Barrel length: 19.7 inches or 24.1 inches
Choke: adjustable, screw-in
Chamber: 2.6 inches or 3 inches

International

Centurion Ordnance Poseidon Micro Tactical Shotgun

The Centurion Ordnance Poseidon Micro tactical shotgun is placed in the 'International' category because the shotgun is manufactured in Turkey, the ammunition in Mexico, and marketing is carried out by a US concern. Akkar Limited of Turkey manufactures the shotgun. Aguila Ammunition of Mexico produces the ultra short "Minishells," 12-gauge shotgun cartridges only 1.5 inches long. Centurion Ordnance of the USA markets the Minishells and Poseidon Micro shotgun worldwide.

The Centurion Ordnance Poseidon Micro tactical shotgun fires only Aguila Minishells and will not chamber shotgun cartridges of any other type. Due to the small Minishell dimensions, the shotgun is extremely compact while retaining a relatively large magazine capacity. At typical shotgun ranges, the difference between the terminal ballistics of the Minishell and reduced-recoil tactical shotgun cartridges is small. In addition, Minishell recoil is less than that of full-length tactical cartridges, either full or reduced charge. To date, only buckshot and slug Minishells are available for tactical use but other types are under development.

The Poseidon receiver is approximately 2 inches shorter than conventional shotguns so overall length is reduced accordingly. This makes the Poseidon ideal for operations where small size is a requirement. The furniture consists of polymers. Various barrel lengths and magazine capacities are available.

A MIL-STD-1913 receiver rail is available as an option, as is a 'side-saddle' receiver shell carrier.

Benelli M1

Benelli M3

SPECIFICATIONS:
Caliber: 12-gauge, 1.75-inch only
Operation: manual, slide action
Feed: underbarrel tubular magazine; 6 + 1, 7 + 1
or 11 + 1,
depending on barrel length
Empty weight: 3.8 pounds
Overall length: 18.5-inch barrel, 37.9 inches; 15-
inch barrel, 34.5 inches;
12-inch barrel, 31.5 inches
Barrel length: 12, 15 or 18.5 inches
Sights: rear: ghost ring; front blade; optical optional

Omega Weapons Systems SPS-12 Tactical Shotgun

The Omega SPS-12 was designed specifically as a tactical shotgun and is manufactured by NORINCO exclusively for Omega Weapons Systems Inc, which has worldwide distribution rights.

The Omega SPS-12 features an ambidextrous safety, a military-specification cold hammer-forged steel receiver and barrel, a metal trigger housing, and ghost ring aperture sights. The standard SPS-12 barrel is cylinder bored. Unlike most tactical shotguns, the SPS-12 feeds from a detachable box magazine with a five- or 10-round capacity.

The SPS-12 is available with either a pistol grip or a standard stock. All furniture is a black polymer. Various barrel lengths are available.

SPECIFICATIONS:
Caliber: 12-gauge, 2.75-inch
Operation: gas, semiautomatic
Feed: five- or 10-round detachable box magazine
Empty weight 8.8 pounds
Overall length: standard barrel, 40.9 inches
Barrel length: standard, 20 inches; 14 inches,
18.5 inches and 24 inches optional
Sights: rear: ghost ring; front blade

Italy

Benelli M1 and M2 Super 90 Tactical Shotgun

The Benelli M1/M2 Super 90 Tactical Shotguns is derived from the Benelli M1/M2 Super 90, which was developed in the 1980s for military and police use. The M1/M2 Tactical is a lightweight gun manufactured of modern materials. The receiver is of high-strength aluminum alloy and is unstressed; the rotating bolt rides in a carrier and locks into a steel barrel extension. The gun operates via an inertia recoil system, essentially a short-recoil system that gives very rapid cycling. The M1/M2 Tactical has a ghost ring rear sight, adjustable for windage and elevation and military type blade front with a semi-pistol grip or full pistol grip polymer stock.*

SPECIFICATIONS:
Caliber: 12-gauge, 2.75 or 3 inch shells
Operation: recoil, semiautomatic
Locking: rotating bolt
Feed: underbarrel tubular magazine, 5 + 1-rounds (2 round extension optional)
Empty weight: 7 pounds
Overall length: 39.7 inches
Barrel length: 18.5 inches; M1 Entry, 14 inches
Choke: adjustable via inserts, improved cylinder, modified, full;
M1 Entry, cylinder bore
Chamber: 3 inches
Sights: front, protected blade; rear: ghost-ring aperture,
adjustable for windage and elevation

* The M2 is an improved and slightly modified M1 Tactical. Both guns are essentially the same in overall performance.

Benelli M3 Super 90 Tactical Shotgun

The Benelli M3 Super 90 Tactical Shotgun was specifically designed for military and police use, and combines the features of the M1 Super 90 tactical semiautomatic shotguns with a user-selectable manual slide-action. Conversion requires only that the user press a spring-loaded button and rotate a ring type latch at the front of the forend. The M3 Super 90 Tactical is intended to be used in semiautomatic mode with full-power shells up to 3 inches, and in slide-action mode when using less-lethal or other ammunition that will not cycle the semiautomatic action. The semiautomatic functioning of the M3 Super 90 is identical to that of the M1 Super 90 Tactical.

SPECIFICATIONS:
Caliber: 12-gauge, 2.75- or 3-inch shell
Operation: recoil, semiautomatic or manual slide action
Locking: rotating bolt
Feed: underbarrel tubular magazine, 5 + 1-rounds (2 round extension optional)
Empty weight: 7.3 pounds
Overall length: 40.9 inches
Barrel length: 19.8 inches
Choke: cylinder bore
Chamber: 3 inches

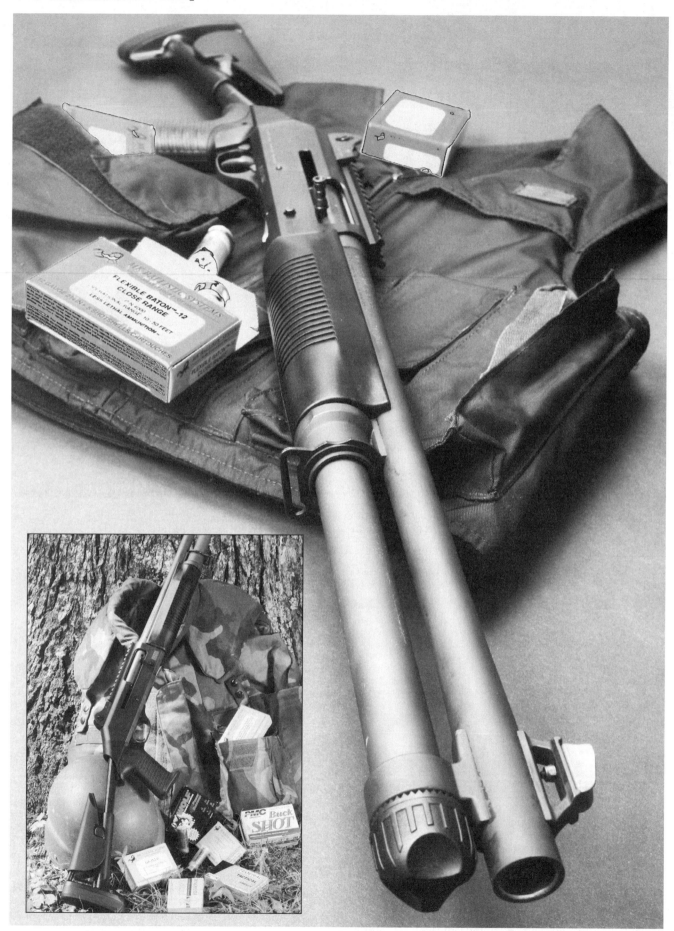

Benelli M4

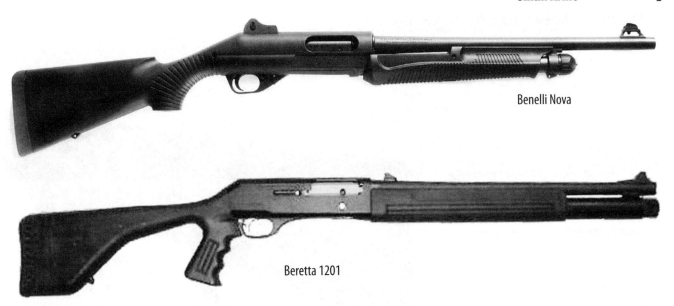

Benelli Nova

Beretta 1201

Benelli M4 Super 90 Tactical Shotgun

The M4 Super 90 was adopted by the US military as the M1014 Combat Shotgun System in April 1999. US Marine Corps units began fielding the M1014 during 2001, and it will eventually be issued to all US armed services. US military sales are through Heckler & Koch Defense; all others are through Benelli USA.

The M4 Super 90 incorporates a new gas operating system with dual gas ports and pistons. According to the manufacturer, the new system is self-regulating, requires no adjustment to fire any type of shell, is unaffected by fouling or barrel length and requires minimal maintenance.

Sights are of the fixed ghost-ring type with a MIL-STD-1913 rail for mounting optics. The M4 Super 90 is modular, with the ability to exchange components quickly without tools to meet changing tactical conditions and mission requirements. There are three interchangeable stocks for the M4 Super 90. One is fixed with a pistol grip, the second is fixed with a semi-pistol grip and the third is collapsible with a pistol grip. Stocks can be interchanged without tools. The M1014 Combat Shotgun System for the US military has the collapsible stock as standard.

Standard barrel length is 18.5 inches, with a 14-inch barrel optional. Barrels can be interchanged without tools. A speed-loading mechanism is built into the bottom of the receiver.

SPECIFICATIONS:

Caliber: 12-gauge, 2.75- or 3-inch shells
Operation: gas, semiautomatic
Locking: rotating bolt
Feed: underbarrel tubular magazine, 6 + 1 capacity (2.75 inch shells)
Empty weight 8.4 pounds
Overall length: stock extended, 39.8 inches; stock retracted, 34.9 inches
Barrel length: standard, 18.5 inches; optional, 14 inches
Choke: adjustable via selectable choke tubes
Chamber: 3 inches
Sights: Front, protected blade; rear: adjustable ghost ring aperture. MIL-STD-1913 rail mount for optics

Benelli NOVA Tactical Shotgun

The Benelli NOVA Tactical uses state-of-the-art engineering and production methods and is a unique design. The stock and receiver are molded together in one piece with metal inserts at stress points. The polymer receiver shell has a metal liner for added strength. Molded grooves in the semi-pistol grip offer enhanced grip and comfort, whether the user is bare-handed or wearing gloves. The rotating bolt design is carried over from the semiautomatic M1 Super 90 shotgun. The slide incorporates two transfer bars for reliability and smooth operation. A unique feature of the NOVA Tactical is a magazine stop button on the forend that interrupts feeding when depressed. This enables the user to eject a chambered round without feeding a round from the magazine. This is not only a safety feature, but also facilitates tactical reloading. The synthetic fire control unit is removable as a module using the magazine cap to press out its retaining pins. An optional recoil reduction system fits in a cavity in the stock. Magazine extensions are available that offer either two or four additional rounds.

SPECIFICATIONS:

Caliber: 12-gauge, 2.75- or 3-inch shells
Operation: manual, slide action
Locking: rotating bolt
Feed: underbarrel tubular magazine, 4 + 1 standard; 2 and 4-round extension tubes available to provide 6 + 1 and 8 + 1 capacity
Empty weight 7.1 pounds
Overall length: 40 inches
Barrel length: 18.5 inches
Choke: variable by changing choke tubes
Chamber: 3.5 inches
Sights: Front, blade; rear: notch

Beretta 1201 tactical shotgun

The Beretta 1201 is the only tactical shotgun currently in production by the world's oldest firearms manufacturer. The 1201 FP is manufactured in two versions, one with a conventional stock and one with a pistol-grip stock. Mechanically, the two guns are identical. The 1201FP is a recoil-operated semiautomatic gun chambered for either 2.75- or 3-inch shells. The design incorporates a lightweight unstressed aluminum receiver and rotating bolt that locks into a steel barrel extension. The sights of the 1201FP are identical to those of Beretta Model 92/96 pistols. Tritium sights are available. All furniture is polymer. The 1201FP pistol grip model is provided with a set of stock spacers so the length of pull can be adjusted to the individual.

SPECIFICATIONS:

Caliber: 12-gauge, 2.75- or 3-inch
Operation: short-recoil, semiautomatic
Locking: rotating bolt
Feed: underbarrel tubular magazine; 6 + 1-rounds for 2.75 inch shells, 5 + 1-rounds for 3 inch shells
Empty weight 6.4 pounds
Overall length: 39.8 inches
Barrel length: 18.1 inches
Choke: cylinder bore
Chamber: 3 inches
Sights: Front, blade; rear: notch

Fabarm SAT 8 Semiautomatic Tactical Shotgun

The Fabarm SAT 8 was designed specifically for law enforcement for use in dynamic entries and fast-moving tactical situations where a semiautomatic shotgun provides a higher degree of firepower than slide-operated guns. The SAT8 has a MIL-STD-1913 rail on the receiver for mounting optics and an adjustable ghost ting rear sight. A second MIL-STD-1913 rail is located on the forearm for mounting vertical foregrip, lights or lasers. A multipurpose muzzle brake is optional. This brake not only reduces felt recoil, but serves as a standoff device for dynamic entries. The charging handle is oversized so that it can be used with gloves. The SAT 8's unique "Pulse"® gas operating system reduces felt recoil and will function with all standard types of shotgun ammunition, except less lethal.

SPECIFICATIONS:

Caliber: 12-gauge
Operation: gas, semiautomatic
Feed: underbarrel tubular magazine,
5 + 1-rounds (2.75 inch)
Empty weight: 6.5 pounds
Overall length: Approximately 41 inches
Barrel length: 20 inches
Choke: variable, screw-in choke tubes,
plus multipurpose muzzle brake
Chamber: 3 inches
Sights: Front, protected post; rear: ghost ring,
asdjustable for windage and elevation.

Fabarm SDASS Pump Action Tactical Shotgun

The Fabarm SDASS was designed as a military and law enforcement tactical shotgun with the versatility to function with any type of available ammunition, from full-power 3-inch to less lethal ammunition that will not cycle semiautomatic shotguns. There are three basic versions of the SDASS – Pro Forces, Tactical and Heavy Combat. The Pro Forces and Heavy Combat are identical except that the latter has a heavier barrel and muzzle brake like that of the SAT 8 described above that reduces felt recoil and acts as a standoff device for dynamic entries.

Fabarm SDASS

The Tactical has a semi-pistol grip, while the Pro Forces and Heavy Combat have full pistol grips. All have a ghost-ring rear sight that is adjustable for windage and elevation. A MIL-STD-1913 rail is fitted to the receiver top for mounting optics. A spring mechanism in the forearm assists the forward movement of the pump action, enhancing feed reliability. Various stock configurations are available, including wood, a folding stock and a pistol grip only. Fixed stock length of pull is adjustable via spacers.

The Fabarm "Martial" pump-action shotgun is essentially identical to the SDASS, except for an 18-inch barrel and magazine capacity of 5+1-rounds instead of 7+1. The Martial Wood has beechwood furniture. All others are polymer; the Martial Composite has a semi-pistol grip stock, the Martial Compact has a folding stock and the Martial Short has only a pistol grip. The Pro Forces pistol grip stock is optional.

Franchi SPAS 12

SPECIFICATIONS: Fabarm SDASS. Martial, see text.

Caliber: 12-gauge, 2.75 or 3 inch
Operation: Manual, pump-action
Feed: underbarrel tubular magazine, 7 +1 capacity (2.75 inch)
Overall length: Approximately 41 inches
Barrel length: 20 inches
Empty weight: Tactical: 6.7 pounds; Pro Forces: 6.6 pounds;
Heavy Combat: 8.9 pounds
Sights: front, protected blade; rear ghost ring,
adjustable for windage and elevation

Franchi Special Purpose Automatic Shotgun 12 (SPAS 12)

The Franchi Special Purpose Automatic Shotgun 12 (SPAS 12) was developed from the earlier SPAS 11 and was designed from the outset as a tactical shotgun. It is now out of production.

The SPAS 12 functions in both semiautomatic and pump action, enabling the user to fire both full-power and low-impulse or less lethal ammunition that will not reliably cycle a semiautomatic shotgun. The SPAS 12 feeds from detachable box magazines. The receiver is manufactured from light alloy and all external parts are finished in matte black. The stock is specially shaped to allow firing one-handed if necessary, although the weight of the SPAS 12 makes effective one-handed firing questionable. A fixed polymer stock is also available. The SPAS 12 accessories include a grenade launcher, a mount for optical sights and a spreader choke muzzle attachment for enhanced shot spreading.

SPECIFICATIONS:

Caliber: 12-gauge
Operation: gas, semiautomatic or slide action
Locking: sliding bolt
Feed: underbarrel tubular magazine, 8-rounds (2.75 inch cartridges)
Empty weight 9.5 pounds
Overall length: stock extended, 40.9 inches; stock folded, 31 inches
Barrel length: 21.5 inches
Choke: variable, screw-in choke tubes
Chamber: 2.75 inches
Sights: front, ramp; rear: notch

Franchi Special Purpose Automatic Shotgun 15 (SPAS 15)

The Franchi Special Purpose Automatic Shotgun 15 (SPAS 15) was developed as a tactical shotgun in the mid-1980s in response to requirements from both NATO and the US military. It has been adopted by the Italian Army with 2,000 units being procured during 1999 for issue to troops on peacekeeping duties.

The functioning of the SPAS 15 shotgun is different from that of the SPAS 12. In the semiautomatic mode, a gas piston operates a bolt carrier containing a rotating bolt. As with the SPAS 12, a recessed button in the forearm selects manual operation for the SPAS 15. The bolt remains to the rear after the last shot and inserting a fresh magazine releases the bolt stop, automatically chambering a new round. The receiver is steel and all exposed surfaces are matte black. Fixed or folding stocks are available and can be quickly interchanged.

The SPAS 15 can be fitted with a variety of accessories, including grenade launchers, muzzle devices and magazines of different capacity. The charging handle for semiautomatic functioning is on top of the receiver and is protected by a carrying handle similar to that of the early AR-10 rifles. The carrying handle can also be used to mount optics and accessories.

SPECIFICATIONS:
Caliber: 12-gauge
Operation: gas, semiautomatic or manual, slide action
Locking: rotating bolt
Feed: detachable box magazine, 3 or 6 rounds
Empty weight 8.6 pounds
Overall length: stock extended, 36 inches (18-inch barrel)
Barrel length: 18 or 24 inches, chrome-plated internally
Choke: variable, screw-in choke tubes
Chamber: 2.75 inches
Sights: Front, blade; rear: notch

Philippines

Armscor M30 Series Tactical Shotguns

Armscor M30 series tactical shotguns are reasonably priced traditional slide action shotguns. They feature dual transfer bars, high-capacity tubular magazines and either wood or polymer furniture, depending on the model. Speedfeed stocks holding four extra rounds of ammunition are optional on the polymer-stocked versions. The M30SAS features a Parkerized finish and ventilated heat shield for protection of the user's hands during protracted firing, plus the Speedfeed stock. All M30 tactical shotguns are cylinder bored and will chamber either 2.75-inch or 3-inch shells.

There are three different M30 models available - the M30R6, the M30R8 and the M30SAS. The latter is a military-specification tactical gun. Detailed differences between models are described in specifications.

SPECIFICATIONS:
Caliber: 12-gauge
Operation: manual, slide action
Locking: sliding block
Feed: M30R6, underbarrel tubular magazine, 5 + 1-rounds; M30R8 and M30SAS, 7 + 1-rounds
Empty weight M30R6 and M30SAS, 7.1 pounds; M30R8, 7.3 pounds
Overall length: M30SAS, 40.5 inches; M30R8, 39.5 inches; M30R6, 37 inches
Barrel length: M30SAS and M30R8, 20 inches; M30R6, 18.5 inches
Choke: cylinder bore
Chamber: 3 inches
Sights: bead front sight

Shooters Arms Manufacturing Patrol Model Slide-Action Shotgun

The Shooters Arms Patrol Model is a conventional folding-stock slide-action tactical shotgun. All metal components are steel; the receiver is an investment casting while the barrel is forged. The pistol grip and forearm are of reinforced polymer. The Patrol Model features dual transfer bars for reliability and durability. The Patrol Model shotgun is intended for use in situations where close quarters makes a folding stock gun desirable. With the stock folded, the gun can still be fired using its full pistol grip.

SPECIFICATIONS:
Caliber: 12-gauge
Operation: manual, slide action
Locking: sliding block
Feed: underbarrel tubular magazine, 6 + 1-rounds
Empty weight: 5.5 pounds
Overall length: 27.5 inches
Barrel length: 18 inches
Choke: cylinder bore
Chamber: 3 inches
Sights: bead front sight

Franchi SPAS 15

SAIGA 410

Izhmash IZH-81R

Russia

Izhmash JSC Saiga-20 and Saiga-410 Tactical Shotguns

These guns are similar to the Saiga-12 described in a separate entry, but they bear closer resemblance to each other than to the larger gun. The major difference between the two shotguns, other than overall size, relates to the chokes; the Saiga-20 has a standard cylinder or improved cylinder bore, while the Saiga-410 has either a cylinder bore or a modified choke as standard. Both guns may be equipped with muzzle devices.

In order to accommodate 3-inch shells, the Saiga-20, like the Saiga-12, has a gas regulator. In the West, 20-gauge and .410 bore shotguns are not normally used as tactical shotguns, but Russian testing has demonstrated their utility in certain situations. For example, 20-gauge shotguns are useful for smaller individuals and are only slightly less effective than 12-gauge guns.

SPECIFICATIONS: Saiga-20
Caliber: 20-gauge
Operation: gas, semiautomatic
Locking: rotating bolt
Feed: 2-, 5- or 8-round detachable box magazine
Empty weight Saiga-20, 7.1 pounds
Overall length: Saiga-20, 44.7 inches; Saiga-20C, 41.3 inches; Saiga-20K, 35.8 inches
Barrel length: Saiga-20 and Saiga-20C, 22.4 inches; Saiga-20K, 26.4 inches
Sights: Front, bead; rear: adjustable notch

Izhmash JSC IZH-81 Tactical Shotgun

There are four variants of the IZH-81 tactical shotgun. Two versions with tubular underbarrel magazines (IZH-81 and IZH-81 'Jaguar'), and two have detachable box-type magazines (IZH-81KM and IZH-81 'Fox Terrier'). All variants are available with barrels of different lengths. These shotguns have been in production since 1994. The IZH-81 "Fox Terrier" features a short barrel and folding stock derived from that of the AK-74M, while the "Jaguar" variant features a fixed pistol grip. All IZH-81 shotguns chamber either 2.75-or 3-inch shells.

SPECIFICATIONS:
Caliber: 12-gauge
Operation: manual, slide action
Locking: sliding bolt
Feed: IZH-81 and IZH-81 Jaguar, underbarrel tubular magazine; IZH-81KM and IZH-81 Fox Terrier, detachable box magazine
Empty weight: IZH-81, 7.1 pounds; IZH-81KM, 7.8 pounds; IZH-81 Fox Terrier, 7.3 pounds; IZH-81 Jaguar, 5.5 pounds
Overall length: IZH-81 and IZH-81KM, 49; IZH-81 Fox Terrier, 42.5 inches; IZH-81 Jaguar, 32.3 inches
Barrel length: 22, 23.6 or 27.6 inches
Choke: selectable choke tubes
Chamber: 3 inches
Sights: Front, blade; rear: notch

Izhmash JSC MP-131K tactical shotgun

The Izhmash MP-131K is unusual in that it can be selectively fed from either a conventional underbarrel tube magazine or from a detachable box-type magazine. Not only does this increase the number of rounds that may be carried, but gives the user the option of having two different types of ammunition instantly available at the touch of a selector lever. The selector lever is on the magazine rather than on the receiver of the shotgun. It is likely that the box magazine is intended to be used either for alternative types of ammunition or as a backup, since its capacity is only three rounds. The MP-131K entered production in 1997.

Izhmash MP-131K

SAIGA 12K

SAIGA 12S

SPECIFICATIONS:

Caliber: 12-gauge
Operation: manual, slide action
Locking: sliding block
Feed: underbarrel tubular magazine or detachable box magazine
Empty weight 7.7 pounds
Barrel length: 22 inches, 23.6 inches or 27.6 inches
Choke: improved cylinder
Chamber: 3 inches
Sights: Front, blade; rear: grooved rail

Izhmash JSC Saiga-12 Series Tactical Shotguns

The Izhmash Saiga-12 tactical shotgun is derived from the basic Kalashnikov design. Although there are external similarities, the shotgun design is substantially different from that of the rifle.

The receiver has been significantly enlarged compared to the rifle, as have the dimensions of the bolt and its carrier. The locations of the internal guide rails for the bolt carrier also had to be moved in order to accommodate the larger components necessary to accommodate shotgun shells. The shotgun has a gas regulator that is switched when firing 3-inch magnum shells. This is necessary to reduce the recoil forces and consequent bolt velocity, which, over long-term use, can degrade reliability.

There are two standard detachable box magazines, one of five-round capacity and an eight-round version. Both are of polymer construction. There are three versions of the shotgun. The Saiga-12 is the basic variant with a non-folding stock that can be removed and replaced with a pistol grip. The Saiga-12C (Cyrillic "S") and Saiga-12K are compact versions with folding stocks and shorter barrels of different lengths.

SPECIFICATIONS:

Caliber: 12-gauge, 2.75- or 3-inch shells
Operation: gas, semiautomatic
Locking: rotating bolt
Feed: five- or eight-round detachable box magazines
Empty weight Saiga-12, 8.4 pounds;
Saiga-12S, 7.9 pounds; Saiga-12K, 7.7 pounds
Overall length: Saiga-12, 45.1 inches;
Saiga-12S, 41.7 inches; Saiga-12K, 35.8 inches
Barrel length: Saiga-12 and Saiga-12S, 22.8 inches or 26.8 inches;
 Saiga-12K, 16.9 inches
Sights: front, bead; rear: adjustable notch

TSNIITOCHMASH KS-23/KS-23M Special Carbine

The TSNIITOCHMASH KS-23 combat shotgun is termed by its manufacturer as a "special carbine" but it is essentially a conventional pump-action shotgun on a huge scale. In Western terms, the KS-23 is approximately 4-gauge.

The general KS-23 concept is similar to that of weapons designed by Eugene Stoner in that it utilizes an alloy receiver with a bolt carrier and multi-lug bolt that locks into a steel barrel extension. The KS-23M Drozd (Thrush) version has a pistol grip in place of the conventional stock and a removable skeleton stock that attaches to the grip.

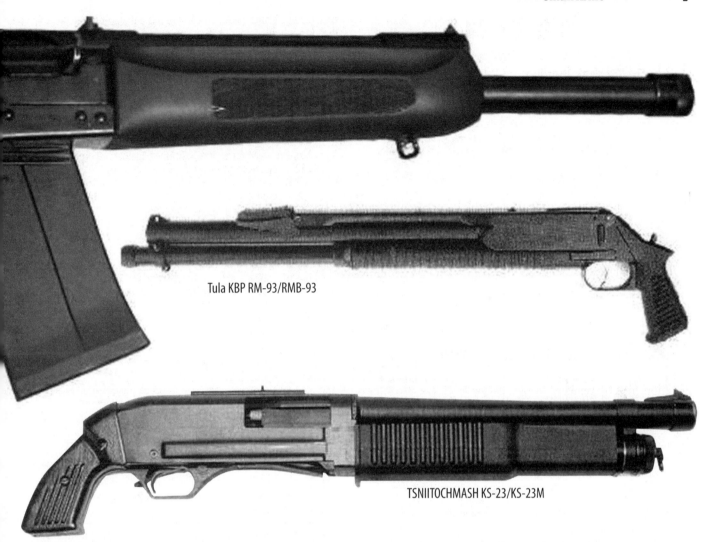

Tula KBP RM-93/RMB-93

TSNIITOCHMASH KS-23/KS-23M

The KS-23 fires a variety of ammunition, including tear gas, rubber bullets, conventional buckshot and an anti-vehicular round, which is claimed to be capable of shattering a car's engine block. There is also a muzzle adaptor for firing grenades and other special munitions.

An extensively modified version of the KS-23, designated the KS-23M, has appeared in photographs in the Russian firearms press. This version of the KS-23 has a detachable box magazine, a folding wire stock and a slide that completely surrounds the barrel. Unlike the standard KS-23, this variant has never been shown publicly, nor has it appeared in the hands of troops. It also accepts the 'Cheremuka-7' grenade launcher.

Specifications are for standard KS-23.

SPECIFICATIONS: KS-23

Operation: manual, slide-action
Locking: rotating bolt
Feed: 3-round tubular magazine
Empty weight KS-23, 8.5 pounds; KS-23M, 7.7 pounds
Overall length: KS-23, 40.9 inches; KS-23M, 25.6 inches
Barrel length: KS-23, 19.7 inches; KS-23M, 13.8 inches
Sights: Front, blade; rear: notch

Tula KBP RM-93/RMB-93 Tactical Shotgun

The Tula KBP RM-93 tactical shotgun is similar in concept to the Neostead shotgun described below in that it is a "pump forward" design, but with a single tubular magazine over the barrel. The RM-93 has a "double-action only" (DAO) trigger with a relatively long and heavy pull for safety reasons. The DAO design responds to the concerns of law enforcement agencies which wish to make certain that trigger is not inadvertently pulled when an officer is under stress. Locking is by twin pivoting hooked lugs that lock into notches at the breech end of the barrel and retain it against the breech face. Loading is through a covered port in the top of the receiver.

The gun is available with phosphate, powder coating, blue or electroless nickel finishes and a variety of barrel lengths. All furniture is black polymer, except for guns finished in powder coatings, which are usually overall camouflage. A pressed steel folding stock that folds over the top of the gun is standard.

Because of its design, the RM-93 is completely ambidextrous with ejection downwards. Operation is "pump forward," which has the advantages of reducing "short stroking" (failure to fully cycle the gun's action, resulting in a stoppage), aiding recovery, and enhancing safety in that the shooter's hand cannot slip forward over the muzzle as occasionally happens with pump action shotguns with short barrels. The RM-93 has adjustable screw-in choke tubes and rifle-type sights.

SPECIFICATIONS:

Caliber: 12-gauge
Operation: manual, slide action
Locking: rotating dual lugs
Feed: Over barrel tubular magazine, 7 + 1-rounds, 2.75 inch shells
Empty weight: 5.6 pounds
Overall length: stock extended, 41.3 inches; stock folded, 31.9 inches
Barrel length: 26.8 inches; other lengths available optional
Choke: adjustable screw-in
Chamber: 2.75 inches

South Africa

Musler Tactical Shotgun

Republic Arms of South Africa developed the Musler pump-action tactical shotgun as a tactical shotgun for military or law enforcement use. It is a conventional slide-action shotgun similar to guns manufactured by Mossberg, Remington and others. The Musler has a light alloy receiver and magazine with an internally chrome-plated steel barrel.

SPECIFICATIONS:

Caliber: 12-gauge
Operation: manual, pump action
Locking: sliding block
Feed: underbarrel tubular magazine, 6 + 1-rounds, 2.75 inch shells
Empty weight: 6.8 pounds
Width: 2 inches
Overall length: 40 inches
Barrel length: 20.5 inches
Choke: cylinder bore
Chamber: 2.75 inches
Sights: bead front sight

Neostead 12-gauge Pump-Action Shotgun

The Neostead 12-gauge pump-action shotgun is a dramatic departure from conventional shotgun designs and is an uncompromising military or police combat weapon. Developed from the outset as a tactical shotgun, the Neostead has already attracted a great deal of attention from many potential users, including some in the USA.

The Neostead is a bullpup design with the receiver located within the stock. This not only reduces the overall length of the weapon but also provides the shooter with a center of gravity above the pistol grip, enabling the weapon to be fired one handed if necessary. The raised sight assembly doubles as a carrying handle and may also be used to mount optics.

One of the main innovations on the Neostead is the feed mechanism. Two tubular alloy magazines are located side by side over the barrel, each holding six 12-gauge shells up to 3-inches in length. A shell in the chamber makes it possible to carry 13 rounds ready for use. A feed selector switch can be used to feed from either the left or right magazine, enabling the user to select from two types of ammunition. Leaving the selector switch in a central position causes the gun to feed alternately from either magazine until both are empty. To reload, the magazines are tipped upwards at the rear. Fresh rounds can then be fed directly into the two magazine tubes. This method facilitates tactical reloads wherein the magazines are topped off during a lull in operations. Slots in the magazines enable easy and rapid monitoring of each magazine tube's round count.

The Neostead's pump action operates in reverse from normal. To eject a spent round the slide is pushed forward to eject spent cartridges downwards. To reload the slide is pulled back. The breech is fixed, so pushing the slide forward unlocks the barrel from the receiver and moves the entire barrel assembly forward while ejecting the spent case downwards. As the slide is moved to the rear: a fresh cartridge is taken from the appropriate magazine tube and carried backwards down a feed ramp and positioned against the breech, ready for the barrel to be telescoped over the seated cartridge. As the barrel moves into battery a single heavy locking lug on the bottom of the receiver is forced upwards into a reinforced recess under the barrel to lock it to the receiver. Safety catches on both sides of the receiver are pushed aside by the slide as it comes back into battery to prevent the gun from firing unless the barrel and receiver are fully locked.

Virtually all the external surfaces of the Neostead shotgun are shrouded by an injection molded, smooth-contoured, high-strength textured polymer stock and forearm with a non-slip surface. Only the barrel, breechblock and receiver are steel. The magazine tubes and other unstressed metal components are made of high-strength alloys. All controls are centrally located allowing operation either by right- or left handed users.

SPECIFICATIONS:

Caliber: 12-gauge, 2.75 or 3 inch shells
Operation: Manual, pump action
Feed: Twin tube magazines, each 6 rounds capacity plus 1-round in chamber
Empty weight 9 pounds
Overall length: 27.2 inches
Height: 9.6 inches
Width: 2.4 inches
Barrel length: 22.4 inches
Sights: Front, fixed blade; rear: adjustable ghost ring aperture; optics possible

Protecta and Protecta Bulldog 12-gauge compact shotguns

The Protecta 12-gauge compact shotgun is derived from the earlier Striker and is intended for use by security, police and military organizations where a combination of firepower and rapid deployment is required. The Striker is no longer in production and both it and the Protecta are classed as destructive devices in the United States. The Protecta operates on the revolver principle with a 12-round rotary magazine that is rotated to a fresh chamber with every pull of the double-action trigger. Cocking is by a cocking handle on the left side of the barrel and spent cartridges are automatically ejected as the next round is fired via a small amount of propellant gas bled off into the

NEOSTEAD

PROTECTA

cylinder containing the spent round. Safety features include a conventional safety catch, a drop-safe trigger lock and a hammer lock. The weapon cannot be fired unless the double-action trigger is deliberately and fully pulled.

The Protecta is constructed using corrosion-resistant high-tensile aluminum alloys, investment castings and glass fiber reinforced polycarbonates. The weapon can be field stripped into three modules: magazine assembly, pistol grip and stock assembly and the frame/barrel and trigger assembly.

The folding twin strut stock can be folded up and over the barrel to reduce the overall length to only 19.7 inches. Despite the short barrel length of only 12 inches, the shot pattern up to 50 meters is claimed to be the same as conventional tactical shotguns with barrels twice as long.

The Protecta fires any 12-gauge shell up to 2.75 inches in length. All types of ammunition from non-lethal to solid slug can be employed.

A compact version, the Protecta Bulldog, is available. Overall length is reduced to 18 inches, although to achieve this there is no stock and the barrel length is reduced to 7 inches. The rotary magazine capacity is reduced to 11. The Protecta Bulldog's general operation is the same as the Protecta but the Protecta Bulldog is handier and is a potent close quarters battle (CQB) weapon, although muzzle blast from the short barrel is probably very distracting to the shooter. The Protecta Bulldog weighs 4.9 pounds empty.

SPECIFICATIONS: Protecta

Caliber: 12-gauge, 2.75-inch
Operation: double-action only (DAO)
Feed: 12-round rotary magazine
Empty weight: 9.3 pounds
Overall length: stock extended, 31.5 inches; stock folded, 19.7 inches
Barrel length: 12 inches, cylinder bore

Turkey

Sarsilmaz Cobra Series Tactical Shotguns

There are four versions of the Cobra series of tactical shotguns -- the Baba, Cobra, Super Cobra and New Cobra. The actions, magazines and barrels of all four guns are identical; the differences are in the furniture. The Baba is essentially an entry-level gun that lacks the embellishments that characterize the others in the line. The Cobra is a conventional pump-action tactical shotgun with polymer furniture and a semi-pistol grip stock. The Super Cobra is equipped with a Speedfeed stock carrying an additional four rounds. The New Cobra is equipped with a folding stock and full pistol grip. All guns except the Baba are finished in semi-matte black with gold highlights on the receiver, unusual for a tactical shotgun. Barrel lengths of 18.5 or 24 inches are available.

SPECIFICATIONS:

Caliber: 12-gauge
Operation: manual, slide action
Locking: sliding block
Feed: underbarrel tubular magazine, 5 + 1 or 7+1-rounds, depending on barrel length
Empty weight 7.5 pounds
Overall length: 18.5-inch barrel, 38.1 inches; 24-inch barrel, 43.5 inches
Barrel length: 18.5 or 24 inches
Choke: cylinder bore
Chamber: 3 inches
Sights: blade front sight

sarsilmaz Cobra

United States

C-MORE Lightweight Shotgun System (LSS)

The C-MORE Lightweight Shotgun System (LSS) was developed for use by special forces. Although it is intended to be attached under the handguard of a M16A2 rifle (LSS A-2) or M4 Carbine (LSS M-4), it can be configured to be installed on other assault rifles and may be configured as a stand-alone weapon, with or without a stock

The LSS fires standard 12-gauge shotgun ammunition fed from a tubular magazine. The standard magazine holds two rounds, plus another in the chamber, although larger capacity magazines are available. Rounds are fed manually using a large, straight-pull, folding cocking handle located on either side of the LSS receiver. The safety allows for ambidextrous operation and when selected it blocks the trigger, hammer and access to the trigger. The trigger is protected by a trigger guard that pivots for use by gloved hands. At the muzzle there is a prominent conical and perforated flash hider that can be telescoped back along the barrel to reduce the carrying length. This flash hider is positioned using spring-loaded bayonet lugs and can be utilized as a standoff device for breaching rounds.

For use as a stand-alone weapon, the LSS can be attached to an M4 Carbine standard telescopic stock and an M16-type pistol grip. If required, the stock can be omitted, leaving just the pistol grip. For both these configurations, the barrel can be provided with the C-MORE Quad-Rail free floating handguard system, and a C-MORE Tactical red dot sight unit is used for aiming. When the LSS is attached to a rifle or carbine the host weapon's sighting system is used.

SPECIFICATIONS:
Caliber: 12-gauge, 3-inch
Operation: manual
Feed: two- or three-round box magazine
Empty weight: LSS A-2, 3 pounds; LSS M-4, 2.7 pounds
Overall length: LSS A-2, 22 inches; LSS M-4, 19.2 inches
Sights: None

C-MORE LSS Configurations

C-MORE LSS

Ciener Ultimate Over/Under

Rifles are generally used at longer ranges, while shotguns are primarily used in CQB situations. The Ciener combination offers the opportunity to have both available as and when necessary. The Ultimate Over/Under consists of a Remington 870 pump-action shotgun attached beneath an AR15/M16 rifle, utilizing the bayonet lug as the basic attachment point.

A bayonet lug adaptor is attached to the shotgun barrel and an adaptor on the receiver. This adaptor engages the ends of a special upper receiver to a lower receiver hinge pin. The bayonet lug adaptor has two spring clips that fix the shotgun in place, allowing its removal by simply squeezing the clips.

Mossberg Model 590/590A1 Tactical Shotgun

The M590 tactical shotgun is derived from the earlier M500, which remains in production. The M590 and M590A1 were designed to a US military requirement for a pump-action tactical shotgun. The M590 has been the standard US military shotgun since the early 1990s. The 590A1 will eventually be replaced in US military service by the Benelli M1014 (M4 Super 90), although it will be many years before all M590s are retired from service.

The Mossberg M590 is a slide-action 12-gauge combat shotgun with polymer furniture, light alloy receiver, handguard, bayonet lug and optional ghost-ring sights. The M590 receiver is aircraft aluminum with the bolt locking into a steel barrel extension. The weapon is designed to facilitate maintenance under field conditions, with easy access to internal components, removable end cap, spring and follower on the magazine for straight-through cleaning and simple barrel removal for detailed cleaning and maintenance. M590 shotguns have fully

Mossberg Model 590

ambidextrous controls, double extractor hooks and positive ejection of spent casings.

The Mossberg 590 was the only shotgun to pass the military specifications for reliability of three malfunctions in 3,000-rounds fired with no broken or unserviceable parts. The M590A1 differs from the basic M590 by having all-metal trigger guard and safety selector and a heavier barrel. The standard military configuration of the M590A1 is the 20-inch barrel version An unusual accessory for Mossberg shotguns, including the M590/590A1, is the Knoxx Industries Sidewinder 10-round drum magazine and housing that replaces the existing magazine and forend. The 590/590A1 is in service with the military and police forces of over 30 countries.

SPECIFICATIONS: M590A1 military version

Caliber: 12-gauge
Operation: manual, slide action
Locking: sliding block
Feed: underbarrel tubular magazine, 8 + 1-rounds, 2.75 inch shells
Empty weight 6.4 pounds
Overall length: 2- inch barrel, M590A1 standard and military, 40.2 inches
Barrel length: M590A1 standard and military, 20 inches; M590A1 standard, 18.5 inches; M590A1 compact, 14 inches.
Choke: cylinder bore or to user specification, barrels are interchangeable
Chamber: military, 2.75 inches; all others, 3 inches
Sights: front, blade; rear: aperture, adjustable for windage and elevation

Patriot Arms Tactical Shotgun

The Patriot Arms Tactical Shotgun is based on the Remington 870, but is highly customized with improvements for law enforcement and military use. Each Tactical Model has a "back bored" barrel with lengthened forcing cone, all hard chromed internal components for increased reliability and wear resistance, a red anodized aluminum magazine follower replacing the factory plastic unit, a ghost ring rear sight, tritium front sight, Speedfeed stock either standard or pistol grip with capacity for four extra shells, "Side Saddle" receiver mount for six spare shells, giving a total of ten spare rounds carried on the gun, a two-round magazine extension and oversized safety switch. Patriot Arms Tactical Shotguns are finished in Lauer Custom Weaponry Durakote in colors specified by the purchaser. Options include a Surefire forearm with high intensity light, barrel heat shield and CQB Solutions tactical sling. Patriot Arms Tactical Shotguns are warranted to shoot a 20-inch pattern at 15 to 20 yards using

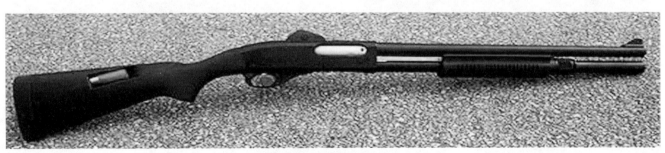

PATRIOT ARMS Tactical Shotgun

MOSSBERG 590A1

PATRIOT ARMS Tactical Shotgun

Remington Model 870P

00 buckshot. Effective range using slugs is 100 yards, with the capability to put all shots inside a 6-inch circle.

SPECIFICATIONS:
Caliber: 12-gauge
Operation: Manual, pump action
Locking: Sliding block
Feed: Tubular magazine, 6 +1-round capacity, 2.75 inch shells
Overall length: 38 inches.
Barrel length: 18 inches
Empty weight: 10 pounds
Choke: Back bore (improved cylinder)
Sights: Front, blade, tritium insert; rear: adjustable ghost ring.

Remington Model 11-87P semiautomatic shotgun

The Remington Model 11-87P is a gas-operated, semiautomatic tactical shotgun widely used by police forces worldwide. All versions of the 11-87P are provided with polymer furniture for durability, finished in matte black Parkerizing and fitted with an extended magazine with a capacity for seven shells.

Three different versions of the 11-87P are offered, the main difference being the sights. One version uses a standard bead; the second has rifle-type sights with a notch rear sight, while the third version incorporates a ghost-ring rear sight. A 14-inch barreled "entry gun" version with modified choke is available. The magazine follower is bright orange for easy visual inspection of the gun to verify that it is empty.

SPECIFICATIONS: ("Entry Gun in paranetheses)
Caliber: 12-gauge
Operation: gas, semiautomatic
Locking: sliding block
Feed: underbarrel tubular magazine 7 + 1-rounds (5+1), 2.75 inch shells
Empty weight 8.5 pounds
Overall length: 38.5 inches (32 inches)
Barrel length: 18 inches (14 inches)
Choke: improved cylinder (modified)
Chamber: 3 inches
Sights: front, blade; rear: notch or ghost-ring aperture

Remington Model 870P shotguns

The Remington Model 870 has been a mainstay of military and police since the mid-1950s and has earned a reputation for reliability and smooth operation. Remington has versions of the Model 870 to meet virtually every military or police requirement.

With various barrel lengths, furniture alternatives and magazine capacities, no less than 11 versions of the Model 870 are available off-the-shelf. These range from 14-inch barreled "entry" guns to 28-inch barreled "tower guns" intended for use by prison guards stationed on towers. Unlike competitors that generally have cylinder bores, most Remington guns are provided with improved cylinder chokes, although others are available on special order. The Model 870P is the widely used "Police" model.

A new version of the 870, the 870P MAX, was announced in late 2004. This version features an 18.5-inch barrel, Speedfeed stock, two-round extension tube and Wilson Combat ghost-ring sights. The 870P MAX is intended to provide a law enforcement

shotgun that is equipped with every accessory from the factory, but as standard equipment. All Remington law enforcement shotguns are now built in a dedicated facility by personnel whose sole job is the manufacture of law enforcement firearms.

The Model 870P receiver is made of steel. Options include Speedfeed stocks that carry four extra rounds of ammunition and ghost-ring sights. For marine use, Remington offers an electroless nickel plated 870P with operating components coated with a combination of nickel and Teflon.

SPECIFICATIONS:
Standard Model 870P
Caliber: 12-gauge
Operation: manual, slide-action
Locking: sliding block
Feed: underbarrel tubular magazine; 5 + 1 to 8 + 1 capacity, depending on version, 2.75 inch shells
Empty weight 7.9 pounds
Overall length: 38.2 inches
Barrel length: 18 inches
Choke: improved cylinder
Chamber: 3 inches
Sights: front, blade; rear: 'ghost ring' aperture or notch

Remington Modular Combat Shotgun (MCS)

Although the US military officially adopted the M1014 semiautomatic shotgun, numerous elements within the military establishment, particularly special operations units, were not pleased with a semiautomatic tactical shotgun for several reasons, not the least of which was the inability to function with all types of ammunition available and the inability to quickly and easily to go from one configuration to another. In response to this, Remington developed a modified version of its Model 870 pump-action shotgun that is uniquely modular in its makeup. Unlike most other tactical shotguns, the Modular Combat Shotgun (MCS) is not available for civilian sales due because 14-inch and 10- inch barrels are integral to the MCS system.

The MCS uses a proprietary "Rem-Loc" quick-change stock system that allows stocks to be instantly changed from the standard Speedfeed IV pistol-grip stock to a Pachmayr pistol grip. There are three different barrels for the MCS: an 18-inch standard barrel, a 14-inch CQB barrel and a 10-inch entry barrel. The 18-inch barrel has rifle type sights, while the 14-inch barrel has a hooded bead and the 10-inch barrel is plain. Interchangeable magazines have capacities of four, six or seven shots. Two different magazine springs are included. Also included is a cleaning kit whose rod is used to guide replacement magazine springs when changing barrels or magazines. The 14-inch and 18-inch barrels have removable choke tubes, while the 10-inch entry gun barrel is cylinder bored. A MIL-STD-1913 rail is fitted to the top of the receiver for optics or other accessories. The MCS comes in a ballistic nylon carry case that holds the entire system. Specifications vary depending on configuration and thus there is no fixed specification table. Specifications of the 18-inch MCS are the same as those of the Remington 870P described above, which can be used as a guide. As of late 2004, several thousand MCS shotguns have been purchased by the US military.

Wilson Combat /Scattergun Technologies Semiautomatic Tactical Shotguns

Scattergun Technologies was purchased by Wilson Combat in 2000. Their tactical shotguns are now marketed under the Wilson Combat /Scattergun Technologies name. Like the company's pump-action guns, Wilson Combat/Scattergun Technologies uses Remington shotguns to manufacture its semiautomatic guns. Remington Model 11-87 guns are modified to enhance reliability and utility under the most demanding conditions. Modifications include a new direct feed shell elevator, new magazine spring and follower, extended magazine tube, Trak-Lock adjustable ghost-ring rear sight, ramp type front sight with tritium insert, oversize charging handle and safety button and other modifications. The

Model K-9 described below is one of three different semiautomatic models offered by Wilson Combat/Scattergun Technologies.

SPECIFICATIONS: Model K-9

Caliber: 12-gauge
Operation: gas, semiautomatic
Locking: sliding block
Feed: underbarrel tubular magazine, 6 + 1 rounds capacity, 2.75 inch shells
Empty weight 8.5 pounds
Overall length: 38.5 inches
Barrel length: 18 inches
Choke: cylinder bore
Chamber: 3 inches
Sights: front, ramp type blade; rear: adjustable 'ghost ring' aperture.

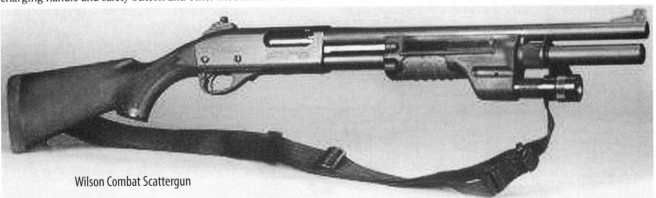

Wilson Combat Scattergun

Winchester Model 1300 Defender

Wilson Combat/Scattergun Technologies Pump Action Tactical Shotguns

After Wilson Combat purchased Scattergun Technologies in 2000 the guns began being sold under the name Wilson Combat/ Scattergun Technologies. The latter company began by modifying and rebuilding police shotguns. Wilson Combat/Scattergun Technologies now produces an extensive range of tactical shotguns. All are highly modified Remington Model 870P pump action shotguns.

Although standard-production Remington shotguns are the basis for all Wilson Combat/Scattergun Technologies tactical shotguns, many components are replaced or modified to increase reliability and durability. Enhancements include adjustable ghost-ring sights, extended magazines, enhanced reliability followers, synthetic furniture, tactical white lights, lasers, sling swivels, recoil reducers and other components. While Wilson Combat/ Scattergun Technologies lists a large variety of standard tactical shotguns, the firm will also custom build guns to customer order or convert customer guns to any of their standard configurations.

The Wilson Combat/Scattergun Technologies tactical shotgun described here is generally representative of their line of slide-action guns. Differences from the Remington basic Model 870 include a cylinder bore barrel, modified action and an adjustable Trak-Lock ghost-ring rear sight with a ramp-type blade front sight with a tritium insert. Also included are a replacement magazine spring and follower, an oversized safety button, sling swivels and an extended magazine. Other Wilson Combat/Scattergun Technologies shotguns are similarly modified.

SPECIFICATIONS: Border Patrol Model 90120

Caliber: 12-gauge
Operation: manual, slide-action
Locking: sliding block
Feed: underbarrel tubular magazine, 6 + 1 rounds capacity, 2.75 inch shells
Empty weight 7.9 pounds
Overall length: 36 inches
Barrel length: 18 inches
Choke: cylinder bore
Chamber: 3 inches
Sights: Front, ramp-type blade; rear: adjustable ghost-ring aperture

Shotguns are often used in urban combat.

Winchester Model 1300 Defender Pump Action Shotgun

The Winchester Model 1300 Defender is unusual among US tactical shotguns in that, it is offered in 20-gauge in addition to the usual 12-gauge. In North America, some authorities have recommended that 20-gauge sporting guns be modified for tactical use by females and smaller-framed men. The overall weight of the 20-gauge shotgun is less than a 12-gauge, not to mention the reduced recoil. The disadvantage of the 20-gauge is that the variety of ammunition available is less than for 12-gauge. The basic Model 1300 Defender is offered with polymer or wood furniture and an optional pistol grip. All Model 1300 shotguns have an aluminum alloy receiver and a steel bolt carrier that houses a rotating bolt locking into a steel barrel extension. A Defender Combo with a five-shot magazine, sporting barrel with screw-in choke tubes and wood furniture is also available. The Camp Defender features rifle-type sights. A stainless steel version of the Model 1300 is also offered for marine or other hostile environments. This latter version not only has major components of stainless steel but key internal components are triple chrome plated for corrosion resistance.

The Winchester Defender is marketed in Europe by FN HERSTAL, which owns US Repeating Arms, manufacturer of Winchester firearms. The European model is available only in 12-gauge, with the option of 14- or 18-inch barrels.

SPECIFICATIONS:
Caliber: 12- or 20-gauge
Operation: manual, slide action
Locking: rotating bolt
Feed: underbarrel tubular magazine; 4 + 1, 6 + 1 or 7 + 1-rounds, depending on barrel length, 2.75 inch shells
Empty weight 7.3 pounds; 20-gauge Defender: 5.6 pounds
Overall length: 39.5 inches
Barrel length: 21.9 inches
Choke: cylinder bore
Chamber: 3 inches
Sights: fiber optic front sight; Camp Defender, front, blade; rear: notch

Machine Guns

The machine gun has passed through many iterations since it was invented in the 19th Century. The first weapon that provided machine gun performance was the externally powered Gatling gun. The Gatling gun was originally hand-cranked, but with the invention of the electric motor, the rate of fire not only increased dramatically, but was adjustable. The Gatling principle survives today in machine guns ranging in caliber from the 7.62x51mm M-134 minigun to the 30mm cannon. All remain in production and are based on a 140-year-old design.

The self-powered machine gun was invented by Hiram Maxim in the late 19th Century and continues in use, although like the Gatling gun, the machine gun has passed through many forms and its tactical usage has likewise changed. Original machine guns were used like artillery to deliver "plunging fire" on enemy troops that could not be directly engaged. Most early machine guns were heavy and mounted on cumbersome ground mounts. Heavy machine guns not only included large caliber guns like the classic M-2 Browning, but water-cooled .30 caliber guns like the M-1917 Browning. The latter guns were used to deliver sustained automatic fire that would burn out the barrel on an air cooled gun. As time and metallurgy improved, water-cooled guns gave way to air cooled guns which still fell into heavy and light categories. Light machine guns were generally fired off a bipod and were not suited for sustained fire. Light machine guns were usually magazine fed like the M-1918 Browning Automatic Rifle and the Bren Gun.

Today machine guns are generally divided into three classes: 7.62mm general purpose machine guns (GPMGs) like the M-60, PKM or MAG 58 (M-240) that can be fired from a tripod, pintle, or bipod; 5.56/5.45mm squad automatic weapons (SAWs) like the Minimi (M-

249) or RPK that are generally fired from a bipod and may be magazine or belt fed; and heavy machine guns such as the .50 caliber (12.7mm) M-2 Browning or KPV that require a pintle or tripod mount due to their size and weight.

Like all firearms, machine gun technology is mature and there are few if any technologies that promise breakthroughs as in the past. The machine gun has evolved into the forms in which it is found today due to changes in military roles and missions more than through technological breakthroughs. The latest guns are for the most part lighter than their predecessors and more reliable, but the basic technology has changed but little in the last 50 years. The US Army, for example, turned down the FN Herstal MAG 58 in favor of the indigenous M-60 in 1959, only to replace the M-60 with the MAG 58 (M240) in the 1990s, the gun that was stated to be inferior to the M-60 in 1959.

Belgium

FN Herstal 50 Browning M2 Heavy Barrel Machine Gun

The FN Herstal 50 M2 Heavy Barrel (HB) Browning machine gun is similar in design and operation to other types of Browning M2 machine gun, i.e. a recoil-operated, air-cooled, disintegrating link belt-fed weapon. The operating mechanism is exactly the same as other Browning M2 HBs, which may be found in the appropriate separate entry.

Variants

FN Herstal 50 M2 HB/QCB machine gun
See separate entry.

FN Herstal M3M and M3P Machine Guns

These are aircraft or helicopter versions of the FN Herstal 50 M2 HB. The M3M is intended for aircraft door-mount applications and fires from an open bolt to avoid cook-offs. The M3M is also available on a ground soft mount. The M3P is for aircraft or helicopter pods, firing remotely. The cyclic rate of fire is 1,100 rounds per minute. The M3P is also used as the gun element of the Lightning weapon system for vehicle and naval applications. The complete weapon system consists of an M3P, a soft mount, a gyro-stabilized gimbal and a day/night imaging system with a zoom camera and a range-finder.

SPECIFICATIONS:

Caliber: 50 Browning Machine Gun (BMG) (12.7 x 99mm)
Operation: short-recoil, select-fire
Feed: disintegrating link bolt
Empty weight: 79.4 pounds
Overall length: 165.2 inches
Barrel length: 45 inches
Cyclic rate: 450 to 550 rounds per minute
Maximum range: 6,765m
Effective range: 1,500m

FN Herstal 50 BMG M2 HB/QCB Machine Gun

Demand for the venerable 50 BMG M2 HB machine gun has continued steadily over the years, leading FN Herstal to develop a Quick-Change Barrel (QCB) version. This feature eliminates tedious headspace adjustment and saves time in training and operations. There is also a 50 BMG M2 HB/QCB version for use as a coaxial machine gun on armored vehicles. This version fires automatic only.

All M2 HB and HB/QCB machine guns made by FN Herstal are provided, with trigger safety, front sight adjustable for height and fixed timing.

A conversion kit that allows any M2 HB machine gun to be converted to the QCB version by armorers with a simple set of tools and gauges is also supplied. It consists of a barrel; barrel extension; set of breech locks; barrel support sleeve with a set of shims; and an accelerator. With the exception of the parts specific to the QCB kit, all other parts are interchangeable with the standard M2 HB model.

All current FN Herstal M2 HB production is of this HB/QCB model. SPECIFICATIONS: are the same as the standard version described above.

FN Herstal 5.56x45mm MINIMI Light Machine Gun

Development of the 5.56mm light machine gun, which eventually became the MINIMI, began in the early 1960s. The first MINIMI prototypes appeared in 1974, although production did not commence until 1982. Since then, the weapon has been adopted by many armed forces, including the US Army and the US Marine Corps as the M249 Squad Automatic Weapon - SAW.

British Army MINIMIs are known as the L108A1. Originally these were employed by special forces, but in 2002 a batch of 180 was procured direct from FN Herstal to be issued to other units operating in Afghanistan. In early 2003, it was announced that a further 600 MINIMI Paras had been procured for operations in Iraq, replacing the disastrous L86A1 Light Support Weapon.

The MINIMI light machine gun is gas-operated. The rotary gas regulator is derived from the MAGAZINE 58 machine gun, and has two basic settings: normal and adverse conditions. Adjustment can be carried out by hand, even with a hot barrel.

The rotary breech locking mechanism locks into the barrel extension. This action is initiated by a cam in the bolt carrier. The gas piston is forced to the rear by expanding gases, forcing the bolt carrier back, with the bolt still locked to the barrel extension. The residual chamber pressure is virtually zero by the time the cam action unlocks the bolt. Primary extraction of the spent case begins with the rotation of the bolt before it unlocks.

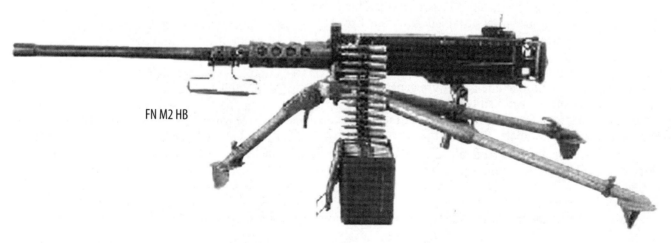

FN M2 HB

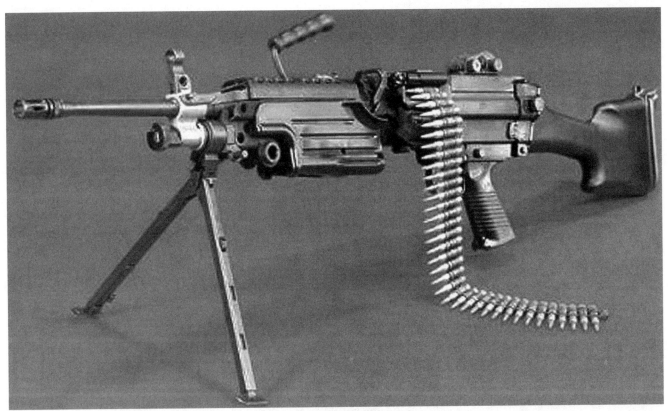

FN MINIMI

The MINIMI's ammunition is fed from 200-round disintegrating link belts, held in a 200-round plastic box, which, serves as an ammunition carrier when not on the gun and locks rigidly to the gun and becomes virtually integral with it when attached.

The MINIMI can accept either a magazine or a belt feed without modification. The gun is normally regulated to fire using belt feed, and in this mode the feed mechanism has to overcome the weight of the belt. When firing from a magazine, the load is absent, and thus the gun tends to have a higher cyclic rate.

The gun is normally mounted on a bipod but can also be mounted on a tripod. It can also be used with either a fixed or collapsible buttstock.

Variants

MINIMI Para

For organizations requiring a light machine gun shorter than the standard version, the Para model has a collapsible stock and a shorter barrel. The primary advantage of this version is that it is much easier to handle and carry in and out of vehicles, helicopters and confined spaces. Details of this version can be found below. The MINIMI Para stock has been type-classified by the US Army as the M5 collapsible stock for its M249 Squad Automatic Weapon (SAW). The MINIMI Para is in service with the

FN MINIMI Para

British Army, originally with special forces units but now on a more general infantry issue, as the L110A1, as mentioned replacing the L86A1 Light Support Weapon.

MINIMI New Standard

Introduced in 1996, the MINIMI New Standard includes modifications to improve ergonomics and maintainability, without any loss of interchangeability with earlier versions. The most noticeable changes on the MINIMI New Standard are a composite stock, a folding carrying handle on the standard barrel and the suppression of the cartridge indicator on the feed cover. Other changes include the charging handle stop and the backplate retaining pin. A new Para version is also available.

SPECIFICATIONS: Data for standard MINIMI; (Para in parenthesis)

Caliber: 5.56x45mm
Operation: gas; fully automatic
Locking: rotating bolt
Feed: 200-round belts or 30-round M16 magazine
Empty weight: 15.7 pounds (15.74 pounds)
Overall length: 40.9 inches (stock folded, 29 inches; stock extended, 35.2 inches)
Barrel length: 18.3 inches (13.7 inches)
Sights: Front, semi-fixed hooded post, adjustable for windage and elevation
rear: aperture, adjustable for windage and elevation
Cyclic rate: 700 to 1,000 rounds per minute
Max effective range: 1,000m

FN Herstal 7.62x51mm MAG 58 General Purpose Machine Gun

The MAG 58 (Mitrailleuse d'Appui Generale) has become one of the Western world's most successful and widespread machine gun designs. It is still being made in Belgium and by licensed manufacturers; well over 200,000 have been produced. The vast majority of MAGs have been manufactured in 7.62x51mm NATO, but other calibers have been produced, notably the Swedish 6.5x55mm Ksp 58 GPMG. Sweden was the first purchaser of the MAG. These early production models were later converted to 7.62x51mm NATO, and licensed production was carried out by FFV (now completed).

Production of the US Army M240B and Marine Corps M240G is carried out by FN Manufacturing Inc (FNMI) of Columbia, South Carolina. There are several versions of the MAG 58 for coaxial, pintle mounting, helicopter door gun and under-wing machine gun pod applications.

The FN Herstal MAGAZINE is gas-operated, disintegrating-link belt-fed and has a quick-change barrel. It fires the standard 7.62x51mm NATO cartridge from an M13 disintegrating-link belt or the 50-round DM1 continuous articulated belt, but the two types of belt are not interchangeable.

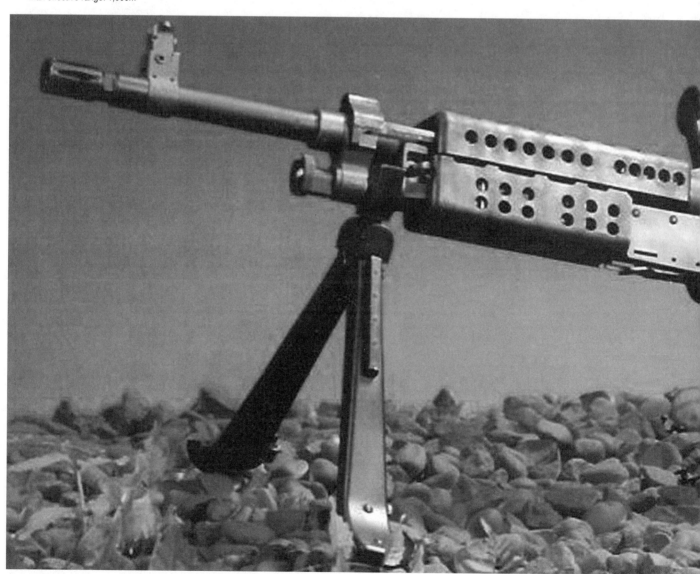

The receiver is made of steel plates riveted together. It is reinforced at the front to accept the barrel nut and gas cylinder and at the rear end for the stock and buffer. Inside the receiver are ribs that support and guide the breech block and piston extension. The breech guides force the locking lever down when the breechblock is fully forward, and in the receiver floor has a locking shoulder that the locking lever engages.

There is a cutout section on the right of the receiver, in which the charging slide operates. Empty cases are ejected out the bottom of the gun.

Gas is bled through the gas port into the regulator that has a surrounding sleeve with an internal gas plug drilled with three gas escape holes. When the gun is clean and cold, most of the gas passes out through these holes. If the rate of fire is reduced by fouling or adverse conditions, the user rotates the gas regulator sleeve, which slides along the gas block and the three holes are progressively closed until more gas is diverted to the piston head. This adjusting mechanism can be used to vary the rate of fire within the limits of 600 to 1,000 rounds per minute. The barrel is hard chrome-plated and the barrel assembly can be changed without unloading the gun.

The safety is a plunger that is pressed from one side to the other to set it at "safe" or "fire." When at "safe" it rests under the sear nose and prevents it from falling. At fire, a cutout section allows full sear movement.

The feed mechanism is a two-stage type, with the belt moving halfway across the feed tray as the bolt moves forward and the other half as the bolt recoils. The top of the breech block carries a roller that engages a curved feed channel in the feed cover. This channel is pivoted near its rear end, and its front end is attached to the end of the short feed link. This link swings on its center so that as one end goes in towards the center line of the gun, the other end moves out. It has an inner feed pawl at one end and two outer feed pawls at the other. Thus, as the breechblock moves forward, the roller first travels down a straight section of the feed channel, while the cartridge is forced out of the stationary belt, and then enters the curved portion. This forces the feed channel to the right. The feed link swings to the left and rotates on its center so that the inner feed pawl moves out over the waiting cartridge and the outer pawls force it in half the distance to the gun centerline. As the breechblock moves back, the roller swings the front of the channel to the left. The feed link swings to the right, so that the inner pawl comes in, bringing the belt across halfway, and the first round comes up against the cartridge stop and is positioned for chambering.

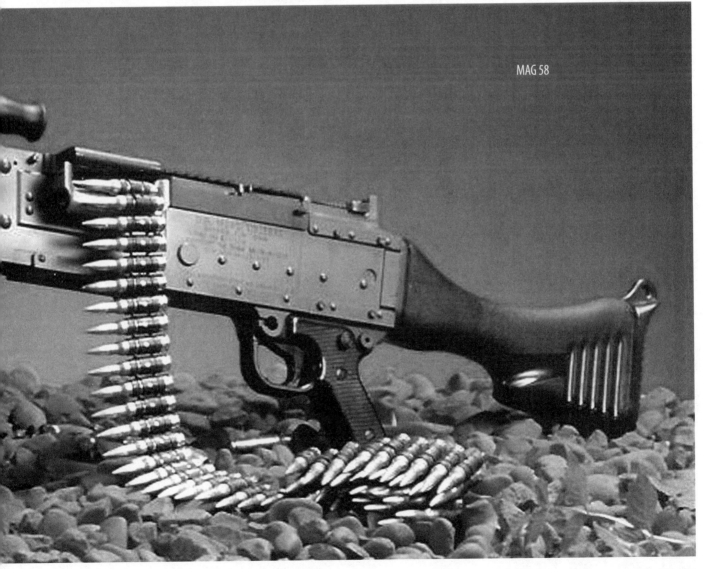

MAG 58

FN M240

The outer pawls move out over the next cartridge. Thus each set of pawls acts alternately as feed and stop pawls, and the cartridge moves halfway across for each forward and backward movement of the breech block.

The buffer assembly consists of a bushing which receives the impact of the piston extension and moves back into a cone which it expands outwards. This grips the walls of the buffer cylinder and also moves back slightly. In moving back, it flattens a series of 11 Belleville washers.

The front sight is a blade mounted on a screw-threaded base that fits into a block mounted on a transverse dovetail. The leaf rear sight can be used folded down for ranges marked from 200 to 800 meters by 100-meter increments. A slide with two spring catches allows the aperture rear sight to be set to the desired range.

The gun is cocked by pulling the charging handle to the rear and then returning it to the forward position. Only when the gun is cocked can the safety selector be set to 'safe' by pushing it from left to right. The letter 'S' can then be read on the right side of the plunger facing the shooter.

To load, the top cover is opened and is lifted to the vertical position. The loaded belt is then inserted, open side down, across the feed tray so that the leading cartridge rests against the cartridge stop on the right. The top cover is lowered and the gun is ready to fire.

A rotating bipod is mounted on the forward end of the gas cylinder to allow firing on a slope, with one leg higher than the other while keeping the sights vertical. The legs are not adjustable for height. The bipod can be folded to the rear. A hook on each leg engages a slot in the side of the receiver and is held in place by a sliding retainer catch.

The tripod mount is a buffered assembly to which the gun is attached by a push-through pin that enters a hole above the trigger guard. Pintle mounting adapters are available. Spade grips are also available for these mountings.

Variants

M240 series

The US armed forces designation for the MAG, in both coaxial and bipod-mounted forms, is M240. See separate entry below.

Swedish MAGs

In 2002 it was announced that some of the existing Swedish MAG 58 inventory was to be converted to Kulspruta m/58D standard. The main changes are a reduction in weight of approximately 4.4 pounds, a lighter buttstock and furniture and a reduction in barrel length by some 8 inches to enable easier access through the rear doors of infantry fighting vehicles and armored personnel carriers. The gas valve adjustment has been simplified to only one or two settings.

SPECIFICATIONS: Basic MAG 58
Caliber: 7.62x51mm NATO
Operation: gas, automatic
Locking: dropping locking lever
Feed: Disintegrating link belt
Empty weight: with stock and bipod, 26 pounds; spare barrel, 6.6 pounds.
Overall length: 49.7 inches
Barrel length: rifled portion, 19.2 inches.; with flash hider, 24.8 inches
Sights: Front, blade; rear: aperture when leaf is lowered, U-notch when leaf is raised
Cyclic rate: 650 to 1,000 rounds per minute
Effective range: 1,500m

Mark 48, Mod 0 7.62x51mm General Purpose Machine Gun

The Mark 48, Mod 0 GPMG/LMG was developed to a United States Special Operations Command (USSOCOM) requirement for a lightweight GPMG to replace the Mark 43 (M60E3) GPMG/LMG in service with special operations forces. It is essentially a modernized version of the original MINIMI design that was intended to be in 7.62x51mm. As such, the Mark 48 appears to be a larger version of the MINIMI.

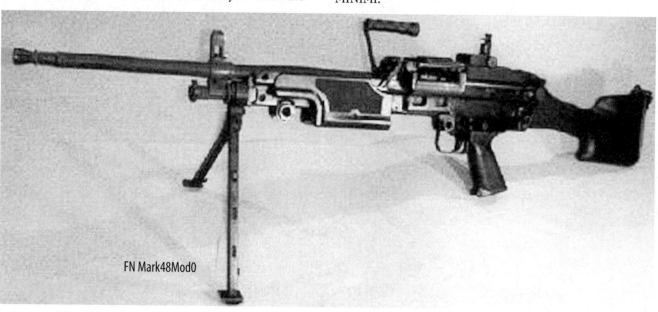

FN Mark48Mod0

The Mark 48, Mod 0 is gas-operated, air-cooled and fires from the open bolt. It can be fired from the shoulder, the hip, or from the prone positions. The quick-change barrels allow for continuous firing over extended periods, a major factor in its selection by USSOCOM. Headspace is fixed and the multi-lug bolt locks into the barrel extension prior to cartridge ignition. Gas is diverted through the gas port and acts against a piston that is directly connected to the bolt carrier to operate the gun.

The Mark 48, Mod 0 has five integral MIL-STD-1913 rails for attaching optics and accessories. Parts commonality between the Mark46/M249 is approximately 70 percent. The Mark 48, Mod 0 is manufactured in the United States by FNMI, Columbia, South Carolina.

SPECIFICATIONS:

Caliber: 7.62x51mm
Operation: gas, automatic
Locking: rotating bolt
Feed: disintegrating link belt, M13 type
Empty weight: 18.5 pounds
Overall length: 39.5 inches
Barrel length: 16.5 inches
Sights: front, protected post. Rear: aperture, adjustable for windage and elevation.

Bulgaria

Arsenal 5.45x39mm RPK-74 Light Machine Gun

The Arsenal RPK-74 Light Machine Gun (LMG) is produced under license in Bulgaria and differs from the Russian original only in minor details. Production is for local requirements and potential export sale. A 45-round polymer box magazine is standard. The RPKS-74 version with a folding steel stock is also manufactured.

Two versions chambered for 5.56x45mm NATO ammunition have been developed and offered for export sale. The 5.56x45mm version has a fixed stock. A folding stock 5.56x45mm version is designated LMG-F.

Arsenal 7.62x54R MG-M1 and MG-M1S Machine Guns

The Arsenal MG-M1 and MG-1S machine guns are based on the Russian PK model and are produced under license in Bulgaria. The base MG-M1 gun differs from the Russian version only in minor respects. The main difference between the two versions is that the MG-M1 is mounted on a bipod, while the MG-M1S is mounted on a tripod. Production is for local requirements and for export sales.

A complete Arsenal "package" for a MG-M1 or MG-M1S machine gun includes four magazines, a spare parts and accessories kit, a cleaning rod, oiler, a cover for the weapon and a spare barrel. Arsenal also manufactures a version of the PKT machine gun, the MG-T, suitable for mounting on armored vehicles.

SPECIFICATIONS: MG-M1

Caliber: 7.62x54R
Operation: gas, automatic
Locking: rotating bolt
Feed: 100-round or 200-round belts
Empty weight: less bipod: 19.4 pounds; with bipod: 20.7 pounds.
Overall length: 45.7 inches
Barrel length: 23.8 inches
Sights: Front: post; rear: vertical leaf and windage scale adjustable to 1,500m
Cyclic rate: 650 rounds per minute
Maximum effective range: 1,000m

Arsenal 5.45 RPK-74 LMG

Arsenal 7.62x54R MG-M1

Canadian C9

CANADIAN 5.56 MM C9
FORCES
CANADIENNES 87AC 0.16.13

Canada

Diemaco C7 5.56mm LSW

Diemaco C7 5.56mm Light Support Weapon (LSW)

The C7 Light Support Weapon (LSW) is a cooperative effort between Diemaco and Colt Defense where the weapon is known as the Colt Automatic Rifle. The C7 LSW features a select-fire mechanism, a hydraulic buffer and an adjustable bipod. The weapon also features a heavy contour Diemaco hammer-forged barrel. The improved life and durability of the barrel during testing has eliminated the need for a quick-change barrel system, greatly simplifying the design and making the LSW accurate to the maximum effective range of the ammunition. The weapon can be supplied in either an open- or closed-bolt configuration.

The C7 LSW is fed from any NATO standard (M16) box magazine, including C-Mags and other high-capacity types and it uses the same family of accessories as the C7 rifle.

The C7 LSW uses the M16A2 type rear sight as standard but is also available mounting an optical sight as the C7A1 light support weapon - this version has been procured by the Netherlands Marine Corps.

SPECIFICATIONS:

Caliber: 5.56x45mm
Operation: direct gas impingement, select-fire
Locking: rotating bolt
Feed: 30-round detachable box magazine
Empty weight: 12.8 pounds
Overall length: 39.4 inches
Barrel length: 20 inches
Sights: Front, adjustable post;
rear: aperture, adjustable for windage and elevation 300m to 800m
Cyclic rate: 625 rounds per minute

China

NORINCO 12.7x108mm Type 89 heavy machine gun

The NORINCO Type 89 heavy machine gun was developed from the earlier Type 85 anti-aircraft machine gun (see separate entry below) and is similar in operation, but there are some differences.

The Type 89 was designed as a multipurpose heavy machine gun, primarily for infantry use against land or air targets. The Type 89 is remarkably light, with the gun weighing only 39.2 pounds. The tripod weighs only 18.7 pounds, bringing the total weight for the gun and the tripod to only 58 pounds. The Type 89's total weight is less than the gun component of most heavy machine-gun systems. One person can carry the entire gun and mount.

NORINCO Type 85

NORINCO Type 89

The Type 89 disassembles without tools and uses a new operating system that combines short-recoil and gas operation, which, according to NORINCO, was a major factor in the weight reduction. It also incorporates a newly designed feed system that NORINCO claims to be more resistant to stoppages than those of previous NORINCO heavy machine guns.

SPECIFICATIONS:

Caliber: 12.7 x 108mm
Operation: gas/short-recoil
Feed: 50-round link belt
Empty weight: total, 58.0 pounds; gun only, 39.2 pounds; tripod, 18.7 pounds
Overall length: 64.6 inches
Barrel length: 39.5 inches
Sights: front, hooded post; rear: tangent U notch; rail system for mounting optical sights or night vision devices
Cyclic rate: 540 to 660 rounds per minute
Maximum effective range: 1,500m

NORINCO 12.7x108mm Type 85 Anti-aircraft Machine Gun

The NORINCO Type 85 anti-aircraft machine gun is primarily intended for use against aerial targets but can also be used against ground targets. The Type 85 gun is gas operated, belt fed and remarkably light in weight, some 58 percent lighter than the obsolescent Type 54, the Chinese version of the Soviet DShK. The Type 85 is provided with an adjustable tripod for ground or antiaircraft use and a telescopic sight.

Ammunition for this and other Chinese heavy machine guns includes AP, AP-T and AP-I, and APDS with a tungsten alloy core. When vehicle mounted, this machine gun is referred to as the W85.

SPECIFICATIONS:

Caliber: 12.7x108mm
Feed: 50-round link belt
Overall length: 78.5 inches
Empty weight: total, combat ready, 90.4 pounds;
gun, 40.8 pounds; tripod, 34.2 pounds
Cyclic rate: 540 to 600 rounds per minute ;
practical, 80 to 100 rounds per minute
Maximum effective range: air, 1,600m; ground, 1,500m

NORINCO Type 77

NORINCO 12.7x108mm Type 77 heavy machine gun

The NORINCO Type 77 heavy machine gun is intended for use against air or ground targets. The operating mechanism uses a direct impingement Llungman-type gas system similar to that used in the M16 rifle. The tube runs from a three-position regulator beneath the barrel forward of the receiver, where the gas is directed against the lower edge of the bolt carrier. The breech is locked by two hinged flaps on the bolt that are forced outward by the bolt carrier into recesses in the receiver.

Ammunition is fed from a 50-round belt, carried in a box on the left side of the gun and an optical sight is provided for antiaircraft use. The tripod can be set at various heights and is provided with geared traverse and elevation controls that can be unlocked to permit free movement of the gun.

SPECIFICATIONS:

Caliber: 12.7 x 108mm
Feed: 50-round belt
Empty weight: with tripod, 123.7 pounds
Overall length: 84.6 in
Barrel length: 40.2
Sights: front, hooded adjustable post; rear: tangent U-notch adjustable to 2,400m; optical AA sight
Cyclic rate: 650 to 750 rounds per minute
Max effective range: air, 1,600m; ground, 1,500m

NORINCO 14.5x114mm Type 75-1 and Type 80 Heavy Machine Guns

The NORINCO Type 75-1 heavy machine gun is essentially a Chinese version of the Soviet KPV machine gun. It differs from the original by being slightly lighter and in some other details such as the arrangement of the belt feed and the cooling fins on the barrel. The Type 75-1 also differs from the similar NORINCO 14.5x114mm Type 75, in being lighter and in some dimensions; the Type 75 weighs 471 pounds.

NORINCO Type 75

The Type 75-1 has a tripod with two small wheels. The tripod folds to become a lightweight trailer. Mechanical elevation and traversing gears are fitted. There is a layer's seat and an optical course and speed sight mounted on an arm that places the sight in a convenient position.

According to official Chinese defense sources, the Type 80 was another effort to reduce the weight of these very large heavy machine guns to a level whereby they could be readily transported by infantry troops, but like the Type 75 and 75-1 was unsuccessful.

Official Chinese defense sources state that neither the Type 75, the Type 75-1, nor the Type 80 has entered Chinese military service in significant numbers. The guns are included herein only for completeness.

NORINCO Type 80

SPECIFICATIONS: (Type 75-1)

Caliber: 14.5 x 114mm
Feed: 80-round link belt
Overall length: 115.4 inches
Empty weight: with mount, 308.7 pounds
Elevation: -10 to +85º
Traverse: 360º
Cyclic rate: 550 rounds per minute
Max effective range: air, 2,000m; ground, 1,000m

SPECIFICATIONS:

Caliber: 5.56x45mm
Operation: gas, select-fire
Feed: detachable 80-round drum magazine or 30-round box magazine
Empty weight: without magazine, 8.6 pounds
Overall length: 34.3 inches
Barrel length: 23.6 inches
Sights: Front, post; rear: adjustable aperture
Cyclic rate: 650 rounds per minute
Maximum effective range: 600m

NORINCO 5.56x45mm Type 97 Light Support Weapon

The Type 97 Light Support Weapon is an export version of the 5.8x42mm Type 95 (see separate entry) chambered in 5.56x45mm. The weapon is identical to the Type 95, save for the ability to accommodate either a 30-round box magazine or an 80-round drum. Over 80 percent of the components of the Type 97 Light Support Weapon are interchangeable with those for the 5.56mm Type 97 assault rifle.

NORINCO 5.8x42mm Type 95 light support weapon

During the handover of Hong Kong to the People's Republic of China in 1997, some of the troops in the ceremonies were equipped with the previously unknown Type 95 5.8x42mm bullpup rifle. The squad support weapon version of this rifle has a longer and heavier barrel, a bipod and a 75-round magazine. There is no provision on the light support weapon for a grenade launcher. Optical sights can be fitted.

SPECIFICATIONS:

Caliber: 5.8x42mm
Operation: gas, select-fire
Locking: three-lug rotating bolt
Feed: detachable box magazine, 75 rounds, or 30-round box magazine
Empty weight: 8.7 pounds
Overall length: 32.9 inches
Barrel length: 21.9 inches
Sights: front, post; rear: adjustable aperture
Max effective range: 600m

NORINCO Type 95

NORINCO Type 67

NORINCO 7.62x54R Type 67 Light Machine Gun

The NORINCO Type 67 is an indigenous Chinese design that replaced the Types 53 (Soviet DPM) and 58 (Soviet RP-46) in main combat organizations. It has been in production since the early 1970s and some of the early weapons were supplied to North Vietnam.

The Type 67 is gas operated and may be used with either a bipod or a tripod. Its design is a mixture of features from several machine guns, as follows:

Type 24 (Maxim) Feed mechanism
Type 26 (ZB26) Bolt and piston
Type 53 (DPM) Trigger mechanism
Type 56 (RPD) Gas regulator
Type 57 (SG43) Barrel-change system

The Type 67 was originally issued as a squad automatic weapon with the designation Type 67-1 but the Type 67-2C appeared a few years ago. The Type 67-2C is a general-purpose machine gun that can be used on a bipod, tripod or can quickly converted into an anti-aircraft mount. There do not appear to be any significant changes in the Type 67-2C other than a slight reduction in weight. Belts are fed from the right.

Barrels are normally changed after two minutes of firing at the rapid rate. The procedure is to lift the top cover, remove the belt if any cartridges remain in it and then press the barrel retaining catch to the left. The carrying handle is then grasped and the barrel pushed forward off the gun. The new barrel is placed in position, pulled back and the retaining catch pushed across to the right. A new belt is put in and the top cover closed to resume firing. The Type 67 gas regulator functions in the same manner as that of the Russian RPD.

Air defense sights consist of a pillar permanently attached to the top of the stirrup-like rear sight and a ring type front sight that fits into dovetails in the top of the receiver and retained by a spring catch. The gun is attached to the air defense tripod by fitting the notches on the front receiver bottom to pins in the mount and rotating the gun down until the catch locks on the front of the trigger guard.

SPECIFICATIONS:
Type 67-2C
Caliber: 7.62x54R (Type 53)
Operation: gas, automatic
Locking: tilting block
Feed: 250-round non disintegrating belt in magazine box or 50-round magazine
Empty weight: 34.4 pounds; gun only, 22 pounds; tripod, 12.3 pounds
Overall length: 49 inches
Barrel length: 23.9 inches
Sights: Front, post; rear: leaf notch, adjustable for windage
Cyclic rate: 650 rounds per minute
Effective range: light machine gun, 800m; GPMG, 1,000m

NORINCO 7.62x54R Type 80 Machine Gun

The NORINCO Type 80 is described by the Chinese as a multipurpose machine gun, a Chinese term equivalent to the Western general-purpose machine gun designation. It is a copy of the Russian PK and thus is a gas-operated, rotating-bolt, belt-fed weapon. The tripod mount can be quickly converted to the air defense role, in which it is claimed to have an effective altitude of 500 meters. The gun is also produced with the designation Type 59 as a coaxial machine gun for armored vehicles.

NORINCO Type 80

NORINCO Type 81

SPECIFICATIONS:
Caliber: 7.62x54R (Type 53)
Operation: gas, automatic
Locking: rotating bolt
Feed: 100- or 200-round belt from box or 50-round drum
Empty weight: total, 27.8 pounds; gun, 17.4 pounds; tripod, 10.4 pounds
Overall length: 46.9 inches
Barrel length: 26.6 inches
Cyclic rate: 650 rounds per minute; practical, 350 rounds per minute
Effective range: 1,000m

NORINCO 7.62x39mm Type 81 Light Machine Gun

The NORINCO Type 81 light machine gun is a squad automatic weapon, although it apparently has been produced principally for export as the squad support weapon counterpart to the Type 81 assault rifle described elsewhere. It is gas-operated and uses a bolt and bolt carrier mechanism similar to that of the Type 68 rifle. Feed is normally from a drum magazine, though not the same type as that used with the Type 74 machine gun. Type 81 automatic rifle magazines can also be used. Most of the working parts of the Type 81 light machine gun and rifle are interchangeable.

SPECIFICATIONS:
Caliber: 7.62x39mm (Type 56)
Operation: gas, automatic
Locking: rotating bolt
Feed: 75-round drum or 30-round box magazines
Empty weight: 11.4 pounds
Overall length: 40.3 inches
Sights: front, adjustable post; rear: tangent leaf with square notch, adjustable to 600 meters
Cyclic rate: practical, 120 rounds per minute
Effective range: 600m

NORINCO 7.62x39mm Type WQ 112 Light Machine Gun

The NORINCO 7.62mm Type WQ 112 light machine gun is the light support variant of the WQ 314 and WQ 314A assault rifles, apparently developed for export sale. The main change on the WQ 112 is the incorporation of a heavier barrel, bipod and carrying handle and the ability to feed ammunition from a 75-round drum. Perhaps the main item of note regarding this light machine gun is its low weight of 11 pounds with a 75-round drum magazine.

It appears that the gun employs a modernized version of the Kalashnikov system. However, the Kalashnikov selector lever is absent from the right hand side of the receiver and the receiver itself is longer than usual. It appears that the barrel does not have a quick-change capability.

Feed is from a 75-round drum, although standard Type 56 30-round magazines could almost certainly be used.

SPECIFICATIONS:
Caliber: 7.62x39mm
Operation: gas, select-fire
Locking: rotating bolt
Feed: 75-round drum or 30-round detachable box magazine
Empty weight: with 75-round drum, 11.0 pounds
Overall length: 40.2 in
Sights: front, cylindrical post; rear: tangent, notch
Cyclic rate: 650 rounds per minute
Max effective range: 600m

Czech Republic

7.62x54R Model 59 and 7.62x51mm Model 68 Rachot General Purpose Machine Guns

The Model 59 (UK 59) General-Purpose Machine Gun (GPMG) fires the 7.62x54R cartridge. As a squad automatic weapon with light barrel and bipod or as a Light Machine Gun (LMG) with heavy barrel and bipod, it is known as the Model 59L. As a medium machine gun with heavy barrel and light tripod, it is called the Model 59. This tripod also can be used for air defense roles.

Variants chambered in 7.62x51mm are designated Model 68 or UK 68. The Model 59 can be converted to a Model 68 by changing the barrel, breechblock, top cover, slide, feed pawl and ejector.

The Model 59 GPMG, also known as the Rachot, is fed from a non-disintegrating metallic link belt of Czech design. The design allows the 7.62x54R cartridge to be pushed straight through the belt. The Model 68 uses standard NATO link belts.

When deployed in the LMG role, a 50-round metal box can be hung from the right-hand side of either gun. This is used for firing on the move during an assault. In medium machine gun configuration, a 250-round box is available.

The front sight is a cylinder mounted eccentrically on a screw-threaded base. It has a hooded protector. All zeroing is carried out on the front sight. The adjustable bipod clamps into its seating below the front sight. It pivots back along the barrel by closing the legs when they are hanging vertically below the gun and laying them under the barrel.

The gas regulator on the Model 59 guns has two positions: `1' and `2'. The normal position is marked `1', and this is changed to `2' using the combination tool. The Model 68 has a four-position regulator. This is of unusual design in that movement is controlled by the carrying handle. To unlock the regulator, the carrying-handle lock, which lies parallel to the barrel at the foot of the handle,

is pressed. The carrying handle is twisted and is then rotated until the pointed lug at the front of the handle is aligned with the notch at the top rear of the gas cylinder. Position `1' is used when the gun is functioning normally. To achieve position `2', the regulator is pressed to the right and is rotated until the pointer is aligned with `2'. To achieve position `3', the regulator is rotated backwards, still held to the right, and the pointer is at `3'. Position `4' is reached by pressing the regulator to the left and rotating it forward. To lock the regulator in the selected position, the carrying-handle lock is pressed, and the carrying handle is twisted and rotated. It should be noted that position `4' produces a high rate of fire intended for anti-aircraft use.

A 4-power telescopic sight is available and can be used with the Model 68, mounted either on its bipod or on a tripod. The telescope is attached to the receiver by a clamp and can be adjusted for windage and elevation. The reticle can be illuminated at night, and the telescope has a dovetail to accept the lamp housing. An active infra-red source and receiver can also be used on the gun.

The bipod is standard, with light barreled guns designated by the suffix -L. To mount the heavy barrel gun on the tripod, the rear sight is lifted. The gun is then passed under the traversing mechanism and the mounting lugs on top of the rear of the receiver are pinned to corresponding lugs under the mounting frame. There is provision for free traverse and traversing stops are also provided. The tripod height is adjustable. If necessary, the tripod can be used for air defense by adding extension components. Guns with heavy barrels, a tripod and provision for 250-round ammunition belt feed have the suffix -T.

Variants

There are also two models of the machine gun designed for turret mountings on T-72 series tanks, designated as the Rachot-T:

  - the TK 95 fires 7.62x54R ammunition
  - the TK 98 fires 7.62x51mm NATO ammunition.

The tank-mounted machine guns can be converted to infantry models via a conversion kit that includes a standard trigger mechanism, a stock with recoil spring, an optical sight and a bipod.

Model 59

5.45x39mm/5.56x45mm CZ 2000 Light Machine Gun

The CZ 2000 small arms family, originally known as the LADA family, was formally announced in 1993. They are available in two calibers: 5.45x39mm and 5.56x45mm.

The CZ 2000 weapons family has three components: a standard assault rifle, a carbine and a light machine gun. Many components are interchangeable between all three weapons.

The CZ 2000 LMG is essentially similar to the CZ 2000 assault rifle but has a longer and heavier barrel and a bipod. It is gas-operated and employs a rotating bolt for locking. Three modes of fire are available: semiautomatic, automatic and three-round burst. The fire selector lever is located on the right side of the receiver. The receiver is constructed using steel stampings, and resembles Kalashnikov-type rifles. The pistol grip and the forward handguard are plastic.

Rounds are fed into the weapon from a 75-round drum magazine, although it is possible to use the transparent plastic curved-box magazine holding 30-rounds that is normally used on the CZ 2000 assault rifle and carbine. The 5.56x45mm version uses M16-type magazines. The aperture rear sight is graduated from 300 to 1,000 meters in 100-meter increments. The front and rear sights are provided with luminescent dots for low light shooting. There is also rail for mounting optics.

The CZ 2000 LMG stock is the side folding type, with tubular steel struts and a one-piece buttplate. If required, the complete weapon can be broken down into four basic components.

SPECIFICATIONS: Model 59 (UK59)/Model 68 (UK 68)

Calibers: 7.62x54R or 7.62x51mm
Operation: gas, automatic
Locking: swinging lock
Feed: 50- or 250-round belt
Empty weight: with bipod and light barrel, 19.11 pounds;
with tripod and heavy barrel, 42.4 pounds; tripod, 22 pounds
Overall length: with heavy barrel: 48 inches; with light barrel: 43.9 inches
Barrel length: heavy: 27.3 inches; light: 23.3 inches
Sights: front; post, adjustable for both windage and elevation;
rear: V-notch, adjustable from 100 to 2,000m by 100m increments;
optional 4-power optical sight
Cyclic rate: 700 to 800 rounds per minute
Range: maximum: 4,800m; effective, using tripod: 1,500m; using bipod, 1,000m

SPECIFICATIONS:

Caliber: 5.45x39mm or 5.56x45mm
Operation: gas, select-fire with three-round burst
Locking: rotary bolt
Feed: detachable drum or box magazine
Magazine capacity: 75-round drum or 30-round box magazine
Empty weight: 9 pounds
Overall length: Stock extended: 41.3 inches; stock folded: 31.9 inches
Barrel length: 22.7 inches
Sights: Front: post; rear: aperture, graduated in 100m steps from 300m to 1,000m increments
Cyclic rate: 750 to 850 rounds per minute
Maximum effective range: >1,000m

Heckler & Koch MG3

Germany

7.62x51mm MG1, MG2 and MG3 machine guns

The German 7.62x51mm post World War II machine guns all are derived from the highly successful 7.92x57mm MG42. When West Germany entered NATO the military decided to modify the MG42 to chamber 7.62x51mm NATO and adopt it as their standard general-purpose machine gun. It was first manufactured by Rheinmetall in 1959 and designated MG42/59. The Bundeswehr designated it the MG1. All MG1 versions (MG1, MG1A1, MG1A2 and MG1A3) were chambered only for the 7.62x51mm cartridge fed from a 50-round non-disintegrating link belt designated DM 1. The MG1A3 had a few minor changes to speed production including a modified muzzle booster.

At the same time, some original MG42 weapons were converted from 7.92x57mm to 7.62x51mm caliber and were redesignated MG2. The current weapon entered service in 1968 and is designated MG3. Externally, it resembles the MG1A3, but can be fed from the DM 1, DM 6 and DM 13 non-disintegrating or US M13 disintegrating link belts.

The original MG42 fired at about 1,200 rounds per minute. The standard bolt used in the MG1A1, MG1A3 and MG3 weighs 1.2 pounds, delivering a rate of fire of approximately 1,100 rounds per minute. The MG1A2 uses a heavier bolt of 2.1 pounds, which produces a cyclic rate of fire of about 900 rounds per minute. The German Army uses the lighter bolt, but the Italian MG42/59 uses the heavier bolt. The front sight is mounted on the front end of the barrel casing and hinges flat. The rear sight is a U-notch mounted on a slide moving on a ramp. Graduation is from 200 to 1,200 meters on the MG3.

The barrel must be changed frequently under sustained-fire conditions. The gun is cocked and the barrel catch on the right of the barrel casing is swung forward. The breech end of the hot barrel swings out and can be removed by elevating the gun. A fresh barrel is pushed through the barrel latch and the muzzle bearing. When the latch is rotated back the barrel

is locked into position. A blank-firing attachment can be attached in lieu of the muzzle recoil booster.

A belt drum developed by Heckler and Koch holds the normally loose belt of 100-rounds and is latched on the left of the feed unit. The rear side of the drum has a transparent cover for visual indication of the amount of ammunition remaining. The drum is made of polymer.

SPECIFICATIONS:
Caliber: 7.62x51mm NATO
Operation: short-recoil, automatic
Method of locking: roller locking
Feed: DM1 belt or DM13 and M13 links
Empty weight: with bipod, 24.4 pounds
Overall length: 49 inches; without stock, 43.2 inches
Barrel length: with extension, 22.2 inches; without extension, 20.9 inches
Sights: Front, barleycorn; rear: notch; also anti-aircraft sight
Cyclic rate: 1,000 to 1,300 rounds per minute
Max effective range: bipod, 800m; tripod, 2,200m

Heckler & Koch 7.62x51mm HK11A1/ HK11E and 5.56x45mm HK13A1/HK13E Light Machine Guns

The HK11A1/HK11E light machine guns are basically magazine-fed versions of the HK21A1/HK21E. The HK13A1/HK13E is essentially a scaled down version of the HK11 to accommodate 5.56x45mm ammunition. All incorporate the modifications described in the entry for the Heckler & Koch HK 21E and HK 23E general-purpose machine guns, including burst fire control, a rear drum sight and an assault grip. Both are primarily magazine-fed weapons, but can be converted to belt feed by changing the bolt assembly with the magazine adapter for a bolt assembly with a belt feed mechanism.

Heckler & Koch HK11E

Like the HK11A1, the HK11E accepts G3 20-round magazines and the Heckler & Koch 50-round drum magazine. The HK13E accepts both 20-round and 30-round STANAG 4179 NATO specification magazines of the G41 rifle, or any other M16 type magazine.

SPECIFICATIONS:

	HK 11E	HK 13E
Cartridge	7.62x51mm	5.56x45mm
Operation Delayed blowback, automatic		
Feed 20-round or 30-round box magazine and 50-round drum		
Modes of fire Automatic, three-round burst, single shot		
Empty weight; 17.97 pounds		
Overall length: 40.7 inches		
Barrel length: 17.7 inches		
Cyclic rate:	800 rounds per minute	750 rounds per minute

Heckler & Koch 7.62x51mm HK 21 General Purpose Machine Gun

The HK 21 is no longer in production and has been replaced by the HK 21A1 and the HK 21E GPMGs described below. Although the gun is out of production, there are still significant numbers in service and for this reason it is included herein.

The HK 21 is a belt-fed general-purpose machine gun normally fed by a disintegrating link belt like the US M13, but the gun will function either with the German DM 60 belt, or with French belts. The continuous link DM1 belt can also be used. By changing the barrel, the feed plate and the bolt, the gun can be converted to fire 5.56x45mm or 7.62x39mm cartridges. The weapon's utility is increased by replacing the belt feed mechanism with a magazine adapter that enables the HK21 to accept any of the Heckler & Koch G3 or HK11 20-round magazines. The HK21 features a quick-change barrel enabling it to produce sustained fire when necessary.

The HK 21 uses the same operating system as the G3 rifle, with a two-part breech block and roller delayed blowback. The HK21 fires from the closed bolt and like the G3, the chamber is fluted. Partly because it fires from the closed bolt, the HK21 is noted for its accuracy.

The gun may be fired either semi- or fully automatic. The selector lever is above the pistol grip and the trigger mechanism, disconnector and automatic sear are the same as those used in the G3 rifle.

SPECIFICATIONS:

Caliber: 7.62x51mm NATO, 5.56x45mm, 7.62x39mm
Operation: Roller delayed blowback, select-fire
Feed: disintegrating link belt; 20-round magazine or 80-round drum
Empty weight: with bipod, 17.5 pounds
Overall length: 40.2 inches
Barrel length: 17.7 inches
Sights: front, hooded post; rear: drum with click adjustments from 200m to 1,200m in 100m increments, adjustable for windage and elevation
Cyclic rate: 900 rounds per minute
Effective range: 1,200m

Heckler & Koch 7.62mm HK 21A1 General-Purpose Machine Gun

The HK 21A1 is a follow-on development of the previously described HK 21. The primary change is the omission of the magazine feed option. The HK 21A1 uses the feed mechanism of the basic HK21, but the mechanism can be rotated down to allow the belt to be inserted, making loading quicker and easier.

The HK 21A1 is intended primarily as a squad support weapon, but it can also be used as a general-purpose machine gun via Heckler & Koch conversion accessories.

The feed system is a left-hand belt mechanism that accommodates either continuous or disintegrating link belts. The HK21A1 can fire either 7.62x51mm or 5.56x45mm ammunition. Conversion requires that the barrel, bolt and feed mechanism be changed. The HK21A1 fires from the closed bolt.

The belt feed unit can be detached for cleaning and maintenance. It has two component, a cartridge guide and belt-feed housing. The feed housing is hinged and is held in place by a spring catch. Pressing the catch lever releases the feed unit and allows it to swing down. At the same time, two cams move the follower and cartridge feed lever downwards below the level of the feed plate, making it easier to insert a new belt or to remove the existing one. When the feed unit is swung back into place, the follower and feed lever are forced back into position.

The HK21 is usually fired from a bipod, which has two positions on the gun: either forward at the end of the receiver, where it gives the maximum stability, or directly in front of the feed unit, where it is near the point of balance.

A comprehensive range of accessories is offered for the HK 21A1, enabling it to be adapted for several purposes.

SPECIFICATIONS:

Caliber: 7.62x51mm
Operation: Roller delayed blowback, select-fire
Feed: metallic link belt
Empty weight: with bipod, 18.3 pounds
Overall length: 40.6 in
Barrel length: 17.7 in
Sights: front, hooded post; rear: drum with click adjustments from 200m to 1,200m in 100m increments, adjustable for windage and elevation.
Cyclic rate: 900 rounds per minute

Heckler & Koch 7.62x51mm HK21E and 5.56x45mm HK23E General Purpose Machine Guns

The HK21E and HK23E machine guns are derived from the HK21A1. There are several modifications based on user feedback and extensive testing, resulting in better efficiency and improved durability.

The HK21E and HK23E have the following modifications in common: a 3.7-inch extension of the

Heckler & Koch HK21E

Heckler & Koch HK21E with belt

receiver, reduced recoil resulting in improved accuracy in all modes of fire; a standard three round burst control trigger, an attachable winter trigger; an improved quick change barrel grip; a standard assault grip; rear drum sight graduated from 100 to 1,200 meters on the HK21E and from 100 to 1,000 meters on the HK23E with adjustment for windage and elevation. Other features include a device for quiet bolt closing; carrying handle; cleaning kit housed in the grip; and replacement barrel for automatic blank cartridge firing.

The HK 21E barrel has been lengthened to 22 inches. The belt feed mechanism has been modified so that the belt is transported in two steps, with the result that the feed unit and the belt itself are subjected to lower stress. As the bolt moves forward after a cartridge has been ejected from the belt, the next cartridge is moved its first step. When the bolt has opened and has moved to the rear: a second feeding step brings the cartridge fully into the feed position so that it can be stripped from the feed belt.

Both weapons have a bipod with three elevation settings and the ability to traverse 30 degrees to either side. Accessories are the same as the HK 21A1.

SPECIFICATIONS:

	HK 21E	HK 23E
Caliber:	7.62x51mm	5.56x45mm (M193 or SS109)
Operation:	roller delayed blowback, automatic	
Feed:	metal link belt	
Modes of fire:	automatic, three-round burst, single shot	
Empty weight:	19.3 pounds	
Overall length:	44.9 inches	40.6 inches
Barrel length:	22 inches	17.7 inches
Cyclic rate	800 rounds per minute	750 rounds per minute

Heckler & Koch 5.56x45mm G36 Light Support Weapon

The G36 is the squad automatic weapon version of the G36 assault rifle. It differs from the rifle in that it has a bipod as standard and a heavier barrel better suited to sustained automatic fire. Other than the bipod and the heavier barrel, the G36 Light Support Weapon is identical to the G36 assault rifle. Further details can be found at the G36 entry.

The G36E Light Support Weapon is the export version of the German Army's G36, differing mainly in having a 1.5-power optical sight in place of the 3-power sight of the G36.

Heckler & Koch G36

SPECIFICATIONS:
Caliber: 5.56x45mm NATO
Operation: gas, select-fire
Locking: rotating bolt with 6 lugs
Feed: 30-round box magazine or 100-round magazine
Empty weight: 7.7 pounds
Overall length: Stock extended, 39 inches; stock folded, 29.9 inches
Barrel length: 18.9 inches
Sights: 3-power optical, backup iron sights
Cyclic rate: 750 rounds per minute

Heckler & Koch 5.56x45mm MG43 Light Machine Gun

The Heckler & Koch MG43 light machine gun was first shown to the public in September 2001, although it had been under development for some time. The MG43 has been tested in both arctic conditions at Fort Greely, Alaska and under hot desert sand conditions at Yuma Proving Grounds. The MG43 is designed to function reliably under adverse field conditions with virtually any ammunition without adjusting the gas system.

The MG43 is described by H&K as a rugged, heavy duty, gas operated, belt fed machine gun firing from an open bolt. Firing is full automatic only, with a fixed cyclic rate of approximately 750 rounds per minute. The belt pull is extremely strong and is carried out in two steps from the top left of the receiver. The MG43 will pull a full 200-round belt laid out on the ground. Spent case ejection is through the receiver bottom. A 200-round belt box can be attached to the receiver's left side for assault carry.

The MG43 has a quick change barrel that can be safely changed while hot without protective gloves with the bolt either open or closed. To reduce the overall length for carrying the stock can be folded to the left and the gun will remain fully operable. A cleaning kit is housed in the stock.

A folding bipod is standard and allows the MG43 to be mounted on the standard US M2 tripod or others with the same mounting interfaces.

Setting the selector lever on "Safe" blocks the trigger and locks the bolt in the cocked position. When the bolt is not fully retracted, accidental firing is prevented

by an integral mechanism that prevents the bolt from moving forward. In addition, the firing pin cannot reach the cartridge primer until the cartridge has been fully chambered and the bolt in the locked position.

The MG43 is provided with iron sights with range settings from 100 to 1,000 meters in 100-meter increments. A MIL-STD-1913 rail on top of the receiver allows optics mounting.

SPECIFICATIONS:
Caliber: 5.56x45mm
Operation: gas, rotary bolt, automatic only
Feed: disintegrating link belt
Empty weight: gun, 14.1 pounds; barrel; 3.8 pounds; bipod, 1 pound
Overall length: stock folded, 31.9 inches; stock extended, 41.3 inches
Barrel length: 18.9 inches
Sights: open, graduated from 100m to 1,000m in 100m increments; optical sights mount on MIL-STD-1913 rail
Cyclic rate: 750 rounds per minute

India

Ordnance Factory Board (OFB) Machine Guns

Besides the 5.56x45mm INSAS light machine gun, which has undergone extensive development problems and as of 2004 has not been fielded, two other machine guns are manufactured in India. The Ordnance Factory Board continues to manufacture 7.62x51mm MAG 58 general purpose machine guns under license from FN Herstal. The Indian model is designated FN 60-20 and is virtually identical to the MAG 58 described elsewhere. This weapon is available for export sales and is described elsewhere.

The infantry tripod-mounted version is designated (MAG) 2A1 machine gun. An electrically fired coaxial model for armored vehicles is known as the (MAG) 5A machine gun. A second armored vehicle model with a manual trigger and pistol grip is known as the 7.62mm (MAG) 6A machine gun.

Also still in production and available for export sale is the 7.62x51mm 1B machine gun. This is an updated license produced version of the original .303 British Bren Gun converted to fire 7.62x51mm equates to the British L4A4 Bren variant. Data for this model is provided below. Production of this weapon is scheduled to cease when and if the INSAS light machine gun enters full-scale production.

SPECIFICATIONS:
1B machine gun
Caliber: 7.62x51mm NATO
Operation: gas, select-fire
Locking: tilting block
Feed: 30-round box magazine
Empty weight: 20.3 pounds
Overall length: 44.5 inches
Barrel length: 21.2 inches
Sights: front, adjustable blade; rear: flip aperture, 200m to 1,000m
Cyclic rate: 500 rounds per minute
Max. effective range: 1,830m

Ordnance Factory Board (OFB) INSAS 5.56x45mm Light Machine Gun

The INSAS light machine gun is the light machine gun counterpart to the INSAS assault rifle. The full details of the INSAS family of weapons are described in the assault

Heckler & Koch MG43

OFB INSAS

rifles section. The INSAS program is running several years behind schedule and shares many of the technical problems of the rifle, including defective barrels, faulty change lever system and an unsatisfactory carrying handle.

The INSAS 5.56mm light machine gun differs from the rifle model primarily in having a longer and heavier barrel, different rifling and a bipod. The bipod is derived from that fitted to Indian-produced Bren guns. The transparent plastic magazine holds 30-rounds, although the 22-round magazine from the INSAS rifle may also be used. There is no three-round burst selection feature on the light machine gun and the iron sights are calibrated for ranges of 200 to 1,000 meters. The barrel has no quick change feature. A grenade-launcher adapter is fitted to the muzzle, but there is no provision for a bayonet.

Like the INSAS assault rifle, a folding stock version is available for use by airborne or special troops. A shorter barrel (19.7 inches as opposed to 21.1 inches) is also available on this model, making it more compact.

The INSAS LMG can be mounted on various vehicle or ground mounts.

SPECIFICATIONS:

Caliber: 5.56x45mm
Operation: gas, select-fire
Locking: rotating bolt
Feed: 30-round plastic box magazine
Empty weight: fixed stock, 13.7 pounds; folding stock, 12.9 pounds.
Overall length: fixed stock, 41.3 inches; stock folded, 35 inches; stock extended, 40.3 inches
Barrel length: standard, 21.1 inches; short, 19.7 inches
Sights: front, blade; rear: flip aperture, 200m to1,000m; optical sights optional
Cyclic rate: 650 rounds per minute
Max effective range: standard barrel, 700m; short barrel, 600m

Iran

7.62x51mm MG3A3 Machine Gun

The Rheinmetall MG3A3 machine gun is manufactured under license in Iran by the Iranian Defense Industries Organization (DIO), Armament Industries Group. This factory was originally established following an agreement between the former West German government and the Shah of Iran and remained in production after the fall of the Shah. Heckler & Koch rifles and submachine guns are also manufactured by DIO.

The MG3A3s produced in Iran are generally identical to the German original described elsewhere.

Both bipod and tripod mounted versions of the MG3A3 are available. There is also a fixed-deck pintle mount for installation on vehicles or light vessels. This mount allows 360° traverse with the stock retained, although twin spade grips are used for aiming, with a mechanical link to the normal trigger mechanism. The weight of this vehicle mount is 67.2 pounds.

Israel

IMI 5.56x45mm and 7.62x39mm Model ARM Galil Light Machine Gun

When the Israelis adopted the Galil, they intended that the new weapons should be used as a submachine gun, rifle and light machine gun. The ARM version of the Galil is fitted with a bipod and offers a choice of magazines with capacities up to 50 rounds, making it suitable as a light machine gun. Details of the weapon will be found in the Galil rifle entry.

IMI 5.56x45mm Negev Light Machine Gun

The IMI Negev Light Machine Gun is a multipurpose weapon that can be fed from belts, drums or magazines and can be fired from a bipod, a tripod, ground vehicle or helicopter mounts.

The weapon is gas operated, with a rotating bolt which locks into a barrel extension. It fires from an open bolt. It can be operated either as an LMG or as an assault rifle. As an assault rifle, maneuverability can be increased and weight reduced by removing the bipod and installing a short barrel and magazine. It can be fired in semiautomatic and automatic modes from standard magazines fitting beneath the weapon; Galil 35-round magazines or M16 magazines with adaptors can be used. It may also be adapted to fire 200-round belts carried in an assault pouch or in an ammunition box.

The gas regulator has three positions:

- Position 1 closes the gas vent for firing rifle grenades.
- Position 2 provides a rate of fire of 700 to 850 rounds per minute.
- Position 3 provides a rate of fire of up to 1,000 rounds per minute.

The Negev can be easily and quickly stripped into six subassemblies (including the bipod). All parts, including the quick-change barrels, are fully interchangeable. Various

IMI Negev LMG

types of telescope and sight mounts can be installed on the receiver. Other options include a laser designator associated with a long barrel having a mounting for the designator and a cleaning kit.

An airborne mount for helicopters is available. This mount includes a link and a spent-cartridge case sack. The ammunition feed can be a 380-round magazine box or a special 750-round magazine box. It is claimed that this airborne mount, combined with the Negev folding butt, offers considerable space and weight savings on helicopters.

Variant

Negev Commando

This variant is a shorter and lighter version of the standard Negev LMG and is known as the Negev Commando or Assault Negev. The barrel is shortened to 13 inches. There is no bipod and the stock folds to the side, so the overall length with the stock folded is approximately 27 inches. A side-mounted forward grip is provided for the user's support hand in assault firing. The weight of the Assault Negev with a 150-round drum is 15.3 pounds.

IMI Negev Commando

SPECIFICATIONS:
Caliber: 5.56x45mm
Operation: gas, open bolt, select-fire
Locking: rotating bolt
Feed: 35- or 30-round box magazine; 150- or 200-round belts in assault drums
Weights: Negev LMG, empty, with bipod: 16.8 pounds;
      Negev Commando, empty: 15.3 pounds
      150-round assault drum: 5.9 pounds
      200-round assault drum: 7.5 pounds
Overall length: long barrel: stock folded: 30.7 inches; stock extended, 40.2 inches; short barrel: stock folded, 26.8 inches; stock extended: 35 inches
Barrel length: long: 18.1 inches; short: 13 inches
Sights: front: post, adjustable for elevation and windage; rear: aperture, 300m to 1,000m. Optical: folding night sight with tritium illumination
Cyclic rate: 700 to 850 or 1,000 rounds per minute

Italy

Beretta 5.56x45mm AS70/90 Light Machine Gun

The Beretta AS70/90 light machine gun is a squad automatic weapon derived from the AR70/90 rifle. The two are considered a single system comprising two weapons, designated the 70/90 system.

The AS70/90 uses the same gas-operated, rotating bolt system as the rifle, but fires from an open bolt and has a heavier fixed barrel with no quick change feature. There is a large metal handguard and an adjustable articulated bipod. Grenades may be launched from the muzzle, though the launcher is of a different type from that of the AS70/90 rifle. The carrying handle is carried over from the rifle and can be removed to expose a mount for optics. The stock is configured to provide support at the gunner's shoulder and a grip for his support hand.

SPECIFICATIONS:
Caliber: 5.56x45mm NATO
Operation: gas, select-fire
Locking: rotating bolt
Feed: 30-round box (M16 standard)
Empty weight: without magazine and bipod, 11.8 pounds
Overall length: 39.4 inches
Barrel length: 18.3 inches
Sights: front, post; rear: 2-position aperture, micrometer adjustment, for 300m and 800 m
Cyclic rate: Approx. 800 rounds per minute

Daewoo K3

Korea, South

Daewoo 5.56x45mm K3 Light Machine Gun

The Daewoo K3 is a gas-operated, air-cooled, full-automatic light machine gun designed for individual operation. The operating system consists of a gas piston, bolt carrier and rotating five-lug bolt with a three-position adjustable gas regulator. The weapon feeds either from a 200-round linked belt or a 30-round box magazine.

The protected front sight is adjustable for elevation. The rear sight is adjustable for elevation and windage and is calibrated from 400 to 1,000 meters.

The gun is normally fired from the integral folding bipod, but can also be mounted on the M122 tripod via an adaptor.

SPECIFICATIONS:
Caliber: 5.56x45mm
Operation: gas, fully automatic
Locking: rotating bolt
Feed: 200-round link belt or 30-round box magazine
Empty weight: with bipod, 15.1 pounds
Overall length: 40.6 inches
Barrel length: 21 inches
Sights: Front, protected post; rear: graduated from 400 to 1,000 meters, adjustable for elevation and windage
Cyclic rate: 700 to 1,000 rounds per minute
Max range: 3,600m; effective, 800m

Pakistan

Pakistan Ordnance Factories 7.62x51mm MG3 Machine Gun

The German Rheinmetall MG3 machine gun is manufactured under license in Pakistan by the Pakistan Ordnance Factories (POF). Specifications for this weapon, listed below are from POF.

SPECIFICATIONS:
Caliber: 7.62x51mm NATO
Operation: short-recoil, automatic
Locking: rollers
Feed: non-disintegrating belt
Empty weight: with bipod and sling, 25.4 pounds; gun only, 23.1 pounds; barrel, 3.8 pounds
Overall length: 49 inches
Barrel length: 22 inches
Sights: front, barleycorn; rear: notch from 200m to 1,200m; also anti-aircraft sight
Cyclic rate: 1,100 to 1,300 rounds per minute
Max range: 4,000 meters

POF MG3

Poland

12.7x108mm NSW Utios/12.7x99mm (50BMG) WKM-B Heavy Machine Gun

The NSW Utios heavy machine gun is the Polish version of the Russian NSV machine gun. The Polish model is identical to the Soviet/Russian original and weapon will be found in the Russian entry.

A 12.7x99mm (50BMG) version is now in production and is designated WKM-B (Wielkokalibrowe Karabiny Maszynove - Browning) and is virtually identical to the NSW Utios, other than changes necessary to enable the gun to fire 12.7x99mm/50 BMG ammunition.

7.62x54R PKM Series Machine Guns

PKM machine guns manufactured in Poland are identical to their Russian counterparts. The 7.62x54R models are as follows:

PKMP: Standard PKM bipod mounted light machine gun, produced to latest production standards.

PKMSP: Standard PKMS tripod-mounted machine gun, produced to latest production standards.

PKMSNP: Tripod-mounted PKMSN equipped with GARBO 4-power night sight.

NSW Utios

PKMNP: Tripod-mounted PKMS equipped with GARBO 4-power night sight.

PKT: Coaxial tank gun version of PKM remotely fired via solenoid or a manual trigger.

GROM The GROM (Thunder) is a pintle-mounted PKT with a manual trigger.

All versions have their tritium-illuminated iron sights.

Versions of the PK series chambered in 7.62x51mm NATO are designated UKM-2000. Three models are available:

UKM-2000P 7.62x51mm NATO equivalent to PKMP.

UKM-2000D 7.62x51mm NATO equivalent to PKMSP.

UKM-2000C 7.62x51mm NATO equivalent to PKT.

Portugal

INDEP 7.62x51mm HK 21 Machine Gun

The Portuguese company INDEP SA manufactures Heckler and Koch HK 21 machine guns under license. Details of the weapons can be found in the appropriate Heckler & Koch entry.

Romania

ROMARM machine guns

ROMARM manufactures the following machine guns under license from Russian manufacturers:

14.5x114mm KPV and KPVT heavy machine gun

12.7x108mm DSKM Model 38/46 heavy machine gun

7.62x54R PK and PKMS machine gun

7.62x39mm RPK light machine gun (Model 1964 and Model 1991)

5.45x39mm RPK-74 light machine gun. (Model 1993)

All the above machine guns are offered for export sales and are generally identical to their Russian counterparts, although there are some slight variations. A Romanian

PKM

KPVT

innovation is a training version of the RPK/RPK-74 firing .22 LR ammunition.

The KPV and KPVT heavy machine guns are offered either as "stand alone" weapons or on land and naval mountings with two or four barrels (MR-4). The KPVT is also mounted in a light turret on Romanian Army armored personnel carriers.

The DSKM Model 38/46 heavy machine gun may be mounted as an armored fighting vehicle weapon or on a tripod as an air defense weapon. A ground mounted tripod mount on a towed rubber-wheeled carriage is also available.

The PKT and PKMS are virtually identical the Russian PKM light machine gun and PKMS tripod-mounted machine guns, respectively. There is also a PKA aircraft gun.

A more involved Romanian development was a revised version of the RPK-74, essentially an RPK-74 with a side-folding skeleton stock and a perforated handguard apparently made from black polymer. Modifications include repositioning the front sight assembly to a position in front of the handguard, instead of its usual position near the muzzle. The folding bipod remains in its normal location. To maintain the length of the sight base the rear sight assembly was moved to the rear of the receiver, directly above the pistol grip. This variant is no longer actively marketed.

Both the 7.62x39mm Model 1964 and 5.45x39mm Model 1993 are available with rudimentary side-folding wire stocks and carrying handles.

SPECIFICATIONS: PKT and PKMS

Caliber: 7.62x54R
Operation: gas, select-fire
Locking: rotating bolt
Feed: belt from 250-round box
Empty weight: PKT, 23.4 pounds; 100-round box magazine, 8.6 pounds
Overall length: PKT, 36 inches; PKMS, 46.2 inches
Barrel length: PKT, 28 inches; PKMS, 23.2 inches
Sights: front, pillar; rear: U-notch
Cyclic rate: 650 rounds per minute
Max effective range: 1,000m

Russia

7.62x39mm RPK light machine gun

The RPK is basically an AKM rifle with a longer and heavier barrel and a heavier gauge receiver. It accepts standard 30-round AK magazines in addition to a 40-round box magazine of its own and a 75-round drum magazine.

The RPK is gas-operated, and fires from the closed bolt. The gas operating system is essentially carried over from the AK rifles and consists of an integral bolt carrier and operating rod/gas piston. There is a short period of free travel while the width of the cam slot cut in bolt carrier travels across the unlocking lug of the bolt head. Then the two locking lugs are rotated counter-clockwise out of engagement with the locking shoulders in the barrel extension. After unlocking, the piston/bolt carrier moves the bolt to the rear.

On the loading stroke the bolt chambers a round; the bolt movement ceases, and further forward movement of the operating rod/bolt carrier rotates the bolt to enable the locking lugs to engage the locking shoulders. The firing pin floats freely in the bolt. It cannot be reached by the hammer until locking is complete.

The cocking handle is integral with the bolt carrier and reciprocates as the gun fires. This allows positive chambering if adverse conditions prevent full locking.

A single extractor is located on the right side of the bolt that is recessed so the case head is always fully supported in the chamber. A fixed ejector in the receiver runs in a groove in the bolt, producing ejection to the right rear. The barrel and the chamber are chrome plated.

There is no bolt hold-open device, so the bolt always closes on an empty chamber when magazines are empty.

RPK LMG

The selector is on the right side of the receiver and is similar to that of the rifle. There are three positions: fully automatic at the middle position of travel, semiautomatic at the bottom and safe at the top.

The selector arm in the safe position has two functions. Its spindle has an arm that covers the trigger extension in the safe position and prevents trigger movement. The selector itself blocks the cocking lever, preventing the weapon from being cocked while set at safe.

The rear sight is a leaf sliding on a ramp; it has a U notch for aiming. There is also a night sight with an enlarged U with a fluorescent white spot. The rear sight is graduated in hundreds of meters marked 1 to 10. There is also a windage scale. The front sight is a cylindrical post which can be screwed up or down for elevation adjustment when zeroing. The battle sight is a coarse U covering 100 to 300 meters.

The accessories carried are the same as those for the AK-47 and AKM but

without the bayonet. The forward mounted bipod folds under the barrel and is retained in place by a spring clip. Some RPK machine guns carry an NSP-3 infra-red night sight.

The RPKS version is intended for use by airborne troops and has a left-folding stock.

SPECIFICATIONS:

Caliber: 7.62x39mm
Operation: gas, select-fire
Feed: 40-round box or 75-round drum magazine;
can also use 30-round rifle magazine
Empty weight: 10.8 pounds
Overall length: RPK, 40.9 inches; RPKS, stock extended, 40.9 inches,
stock folded, 32.3 inches
Barrel length: 23.2 inches
Sights: front, cylindrical post; rear: leaf notch
Cyclic rate: 600 to 660 rounds per minute
Maximum effective range: 800m

5.45x39mm RPK-74 Light Machine Gun

The RPK-74 is essentially a heavy-barreled version of the AK-74 rifle, with the same relationship to the rifle as the RPK has to the AK-47/AKM series of rifles. There are four models in the RPK-74 range, produced primarily by Izhmash in Russia.

- The RPK-74 is the base model with a fixed stock.
- The RPKS-74 has a left-folding stock.
- The RPKN3 has provision to mount a night sight, usually the PN51.
- The RPKSN3 is the folding-stock version of the RPKN3.

The RPK-74 receiver is of stamped steel, with bolt carrier rails welded to the inside. The RPK-74 receiver is heavier gauge steel than that of the AK-74 rifle. The gun is gas-operated and fires from the closed bolt. The bolt carrier and gas piston above the barrel are integral and locking is via a two-lug rotating bolt. The hammer is cocked during the bolt carrier's rearward stroke and is released either by trigger pressure or by a delay mechanism that allows the bolt to close and lock before releasing the hammer during automatic fire. A standard Kalashnikov three-position selector/safety lever is on the right side of the receiver.

The stock is of laminated wood, and an RPK-type bipod is attached to the barrel just below the front sight. A slotted flash hider/compensator is fitted to the muzzle. The standard magazine is a plastic 45-round box, though the 30-round magazine of the AK-74 rifle can also be used; 40-round box magazines are also available.

RPK-74 series light machine guns are usually issued with eight magazines in a carrying bag, and a sling.

Variants

RPK-74M

The RPK-74M is the light machine gun version of the AK-100 series assault rifles. The primary difference is that the RPK-74M uses polymer furniture in place of wood.

5.56x45mm RPK-74M

A variant of the RPK-74M chambered for 5.56x45mm ammunition has been offered for export sale. The magazine capacity of this version is 60 rounds.

SPECIFICATIONS:

Caliber: 5.45x39mm
Operation: gas, select-fire
Locking: rotating bolt
Feed: 45-, 40- or 30-round box magazine
Empty weight: RPK-74, 10.1 pounds; RPKS-74, 10.4 pounds
Overall length: 41.7 inches
Barrel length: 24.3 inches
Sights: front, cylindrical post; rear: tangent leaf with U-notch; adjustable to
1,000m; RPKN3 and RPKSN3, 1LH51 night sight
Cyclic rate: 600 to 650 rounds per minute ;
Maximum effective range: 460m

RPK-74 LMG

PKMS

7.62x54R PK Machine Gun Series

In 1961, the weapon selected to replace the RP46 machine gun was the PK, a mixture of components and ideas from other weapons. The rotating bolt comes from the other Kalashnikov weapons, the AK-47 and RPK. The gas regulator can be adjusted without tools and the PK features a changeable barrel that is somewhat slower in operation than most Western designs. First seen in 1964, the PK has been modified and improved so it is a true general-purpose machine gun and has replaced the RP-46 and the SGM in front-line service. The latest production version is the PKM.

All PK machine guns are gas operated, rotary bolt locked, fully automatic, belt-fed machine that fire from the open bolt. The ammunition feeds from non-disintegrating metallic link belts. Belts consist of 25-round sections, but earlier feed belts were in one 250-round length. The belts feed from 250-round ammunition boxes for normal ground operations, 100-round assault boxes, or from high capacity boxes on vehicle mounted PKTs.

Variants

PK: The PK is the basic machine gun with a heavy fluted barrel and a plain butt-plate. The PK weighs about 19 pounds. It is normally employed from the bipod as an infantry fire support weapon.

PKS: The PKS is the basic PK mounted on a tripod for use as a medium machine gun at the company level. The lightweight tripod (10.5 pounds) provides a stable mount for long-range ground fire and can be quickly opened to elevate the gun for anti-aircraft fire.

PKT: The PK modified for coaxial installation in an armored vehicle. The sights, stock, tripod and trigger mechanism are removed and a longer (28.4 inches) barrel installed. A solenoid is fitted to the receiver backplate for remote operation.

PKD: One of the several manufacturers of the PKT is Kaspex of Kazakhstan. This company has converted the PKT into the PKD, by adding a tubular stock assembly and a bipod. Other PKT features are retained. The stock has a shock-absorbing buttplate. The complete PKD weighs 24 pounds and the overall length is 51.5 inches. The heavy barrel is 28.4 inches in length.

PKM: The PKM entered service in 1969 and is a modified PK with a lighter, unfluted barrel, a feed cover constructed entirely of steel stampings, and a hinged plate added to the buttplate. Excess metal has been removed wherever possible to reduce weight to about 18.5 pounds.

PKMS: A PKM mounted on a new type of tripod, on which the ammunition box can be secured to the right rear tripod leg. This enables one crew member to carry and operate the gun in combat without having to unload the gun when moving.

PKMSN: The PKMSN is similar to the PKMS but with the addition of a night sight.

PKB (PKMB): The PKM with tripod, stock and trigger mechanism removed and replaced by twin spade grips and a butterfly trigger. Recent models of this weapon may be fitted with night sight units with a range of 300 m.

SPECIFICATIONS: PKS

Caliber: 7.62x54R
Operation: gas; automatic
Locking: rotating bolt
Feed: belt; 100, 200 and 250-rounds
Empty weight: 19.4 pounds; tripod, 16.5 pounds
Overall length: gun only: 46.2 inches; on tripod, 49.9 inches
Barrel length: 25.9 inches
Sights: front, cylindrical post; rear: vertical leaf and windage scale adjustable to 1,500m
Cyclic rate: 650 to 720 rounds per minute
Maximum effective range: 1,000m

Russian PKM

7.62x54R 6P41 Pecheneg Machine Gun

The 6P41 Pecheneg machine gun is derived from the PK. The general features of the PK are retained but a heavy fixed barrel that is claimed to enhance accuracy out to a range of 1,500 meters has been added. According to Russian information, the gun's accuracy is enhanced by a factor of greater than 2.5 in comparison to previous Russian machine guns when fired from a bipod mount. When a tripod mount is used, the improvement in accuracy is reduced to a factor of 1.5. The sights are calibrated out to 1,500 meters.

Although the barrel is fixed, it is claimed to be capable of accommodating 25 to 50-round bursts up to 400 rounds, without effect. The barrel's service life is claimed to be 30,000-rounds. The bipod is attached just beneath the muzzle. A fixed carrying handle is provided over the barrel. Standard tripods can be used.

The 6P41 Pecheneg machine gun has been observed in operational use in Chechnya.

SPECIFICATIONS:

Caliber: 7.62x54R
Operation: gas, automatic
Locking: rotating bolt
Feed: belt, 100 or 200 rounds
Empty weight: with bipod, 18.1 pounds; on tripod, 28 pounds
Overall length: 45.7 inches
Sights: calibrated up to 1,500m
Cyclic rate: 650 rounds per minute
Max effective range: 1,500m (claimed)

12.7x108mm KORD Heavy Machine Gun

Following the breakup of the Soviet Union, the production facilities for the NSV heavy machine gun series were located in the breakaway state of Kazakhstan, so to ensure a domestic supply, the Kovrov Manufacturing Facility was tasked to produce an updated version of the NSV. The result was the KORD, which entered service in 1998, still resembling the NSV externally, but internally the KORD is a new weapon.

The KORD has a revised locking mechanism that was changed from the side-folding breechblock of the NSV into what is described as a "tilting breech slide." According to Russian sources, the tilting breech slide provides a much smoother action. Combined with changes to the gas operating system and a revised multibaffle muzzle brake, the KORD system produces less recoil and is a more stable weapon than the NSV, enhancing accuracy out to 2,000 meters. The reduced recoil also enables the weapon to be fired from a bipod as well the family of NSV tripods and mountings.

Although the KORD is presently chambered in 12.7 x 108mm, it is possible to manufacture the weapon in 50 BMG (12.7 x 99mm).

Variants

6P49 - The basic KORD model. It is provided with an electric trigger for vehicle mounting. The overall length is 64 inches, and the weight of the gun alone is 59.5 pounds. Ejection is forward.

6P50 - The infantry version, intended for a variety of mounts. The overall length is 62 inches, and the weight of the gun alone is 55.1 pounds. Ejection is forward.

6P50-1 - Bipod mounted infantry version. The bipod traverses 15 degrees each side. The overall length is 78 inches, and the weight of the gun alone is 70.5 pounds. Ejection is forward.

6P50-2 - Infantry version mounted on a 6T19 tripod. Overall length is 78 inches, and the weight of the gun with the tripod is 114.6 pounds. Ejection is to the right.

6P50-3 - Infantry version on 6U6 multipurpose mount. Overall length is 78 inches and the weight with the mount is 165.3 pounds. Ejection is to the right.

6P51 - Coaxial machine gun with left-hand feed. Overall length is 64 inches, and the weight of the gun alone is 59.5 pounds. Ejection is forward.

SPECIFICATIONS: 6P50

Caliber: 12.7 x 108mm
Operation: gas, automatic only
Locking: tilting breech slide
Feed: 50-round linked belt from magazine box
Empty weight: gun only, 55.1 pounds; barrel, 20.5 pounds; 50-round belt, 17 pounds
Overall length: 62.2 inches
Width: 17.7 inches
Height: 19.7 inches
Sights: front, post; rear: folding tangent leaf with graduations from 200m to 2,000m; sighted to 1,500m for aerial targets, to 2,000m for ground targets; SPP optical sight also available
Cyclic rate: 650 to 750 rounds per minute
Effective range: 2,000m

KORD

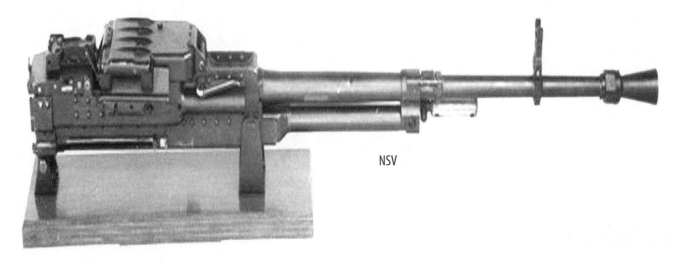

NSV

NSV N4

12.7x108mm NSV Heavy Machine Gun

Development of the NSV heavy machine gun, known as the Utyos (Rock), began in 1969. It may be deployed in the ground role as a heavy support weapon, as an air-defense weapon, or as an armored vehicle machine gun. A special armored mounting for bunker installation is available. Following the breakup of the Soviet Union, NSV production was centered in Kazakhstan, with both the 'Metallist' Uralsk Plant JSC and Kaspex offering models. Models offered by the Metallist firm includes the following:

6P11 basic model with right-hand feed and iron sights
6P11-1 basic model with left-hand feed
6P11-2 basic model without iron sights
6P11-3 basic model without iron sights
6P17 as the 6P11 but with electric trigger
6P17-1 as the 6P11-1 but with electric trigger
6P17-2 as the 6P11-2 but with electric trigger
6P17-3 as the 6P11-3 but with electric trigger

The NSV heavy machine gun is gas-operated and air-cooled, fed from 50-round linked belts carried in a magazine box. Belts are formed from 10-round lengths of metal links and joined together only when placed in the magazine box. Feed may be from the left or right, but the feed direction is set at the factory and cannot be changed in the field.

The NSV is gas-operated, with gas tapped from the barrel via a three-position gas regulator located about halfway along the barrel. Pressure on a piston head forces back a relatively heavy carrier mounted on the breechblock proper. The carrier operates in a stamped steel receiver held together by welds and rivets.

When mounted on the standard ground tripod, the weapon is fitted with a skeleton stock on a strut. An SPP optical sight is usually used in this configuration, although iron sights are provided. The SPP optical sight can be adjusted to provide a magnification of either 3- or 6-power. It is possible to use graduations on the SPP optics for ranges up to 2,000 meters. The reticle also incorporates a ranging system against man-sized targets similar to that of the SVD sniper rifle's PSO-1 sight. The iron sights are graduated from 2 up to 20, in hundreds of meters.

NSVT

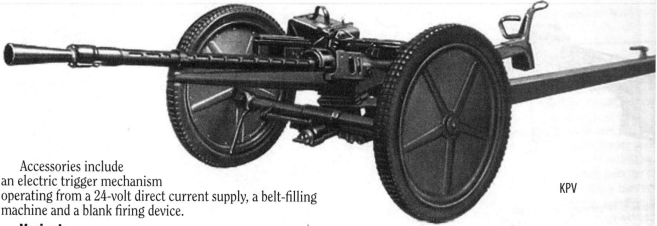

KPV

Accessories include
an electric trigger mechanism
operating from a 24-volt direct current supply, a belt-filling
machine and a blank firing device.

Variants

NSV-12.7 N4

The standard tripod-mounted NSVS machine gun with
a 1PN52-1 night sight.

NSVT

An NSV machine gun converted for use on tanks and
other armored fighting vehicles. Firing is electric via a 24-
volt solenoid. The weight of the NSVT alone is 59 pounds.

NSVP-12.7

The NSVP-12.7 is an updated variant of the NSV with
accuracy improved by a recoil-reducing muzzle brake
and a soft mount recoil reducing tripod. The tripod can
accommodate a 50-round ammunition box on the right-
hand side of the cradle, which is arranged so that the
balance of the gun makes aiming easier. The NSVP-12.7 is
manufactured by the Metallist JSC at Uralsk, Kazakhstan
and by Kaspex, also of Kazakhstan.

SPECIFICATIONS:

Caliber: 12.7 x 108mm
Operation: gas, automatic
Locking: three-part horizontal side-folding breech block
Feed: 50-round linked belt from magazine box
Empty weight: gun only, 55.1 pounds; barrel, 20.3 pounds;
tripod, 35.3 pounds
Overall length: 61.4 inches
Sights: front, post; rear: folding tangent leaf with graduations
from 200m to 2,000m; sighted to 1,500m for aerial targets,
to 2,000m for ground targets; SPP optical sight also available
Cyclic rate: 700 to 800 rounds per minute
Effective range: 2,000m

14.5x114mm KPV Heavy Machine Gun

The KPV heavy machine gun was designed immediately
after World War II expressly to fire the 14.5x114mm round
produced for the PTRD-41 (Degtyarev) and PTRS (Simonov)
antiarmor rifles.

The KPV was initially intended for use as an anti-
aircraft gun, but it is suitable as an armored fighting
vehicle weapon. The feed belts can be broken down to 10-
round lengths and the feed direction can be changed to left
or right in the field.

The gun is short-recoil operated with a muzzle booster.
The barrel can be quickly changed in the field and the
KPV remains in widespread use throughout areas formerly
under the influence of the Soviet Union.

Towed air defense mountings are available for one, two
or four KPV heavy machine guns: they are designated ZPU-
1, ZPU-2 and ZPU-4 respectively.

Variants

KPVT: The armored-vehicle version of the KPV. Firing is
electric.

SPECIFICATIONS:

Caliber: 14.5 x 114mm
Operation: short-recoil, gas boosted
Feed: belt, left or right hand
Empty weight: 108.2 pounds
Overall length: 79 inches
Barrel length: 53 inches
Sights: front, cylindrical post; rear: tangent leaf U,
200m to 2,000m by 100m intervals
Cyclic rate: 600 rounds per minute

Singapore

ST Kinetics General Purpose Machine Gun

ST Kinetics 5.56x45mm SAR 21 Light Machine Gun

The ST Kinetics SAR 21 light machine gun is a variant of the ST Kinetics SAR 21 assault rifle intended for use as a squad automatic weapon. The light machine gun is virtually identical to the assault rifle except for a heavier barrel, an adjustable bipod and the firing from the open bolt. Most components are identical to those of the SAR 21 assault rifle.

SPECIFICATIONS:
Caliber: 5.56mm x 45mm
Operation: gas, automatic
Locking: rotating bolt
Feed: 30-round detachable box magazine
Empty weight: 11 pounds
Overall length: 31.7 inches
Barrel length: 20 inches
Sights: 1.5-power optic
Cyclic rate: 450 to 650 rounds per minute

ST Kinetics 5.56x45mm Ultimax 100 Light Machine Gun

The Ultimax 100 is a magazine-fed, gas operated, rotating bolt locked, air cooled light machine gun. One person can operate it from the shoulder, hip or bipod. It fires from the open bolt in full automatic only and feeds from 100-round drum magazines or 20- and 30-round box magazines. The quick-change barrel can sustain 500 rounds of full-automatic fire without damage. The folding handle on the barrel is placed at the center of mass and is also used to remove the barrel.

Both front and rear sights are fully adjustable for elevation and windage. Thus each barrel can be pre-zeroed with respect to the receiver rear sight.

The cocking handle is non-reciprocating and is locked forward during firing. It is on the left side of the receiver, enabling the gun to be cocked quickly with the support hand leaving the right hand in the firing position.

The gas regulator has three positions. Both piston and regulator can be removed for cleaning if necessary. *

SPECIFICATIONS:
Caliber: 5.56mm x 45mm
Operation: gas, automatic
Locking: rotating bolt,
Feed: 100-round drum magazine; 20- or 30-round box magazine
Empty weight: with bipod, 10.8 pounds
Overall length: without stock, 31.9 inches; with stock, 40.3 inches
Barrel length: standard, 20 inches; para, 13 inches
Sights: front, adjustable for elevation and windage; rear: adjustable from 100m to 1,300m in 100m increments
Cyclic rate: 400 to 600 rounds per minute
Effective range: SS109/M855, 1,300m

* The Ultimax 2000 differs from the basic Ultimax 100 in that it accepts any M16 type magazine, including Beta 100 round C-mags.

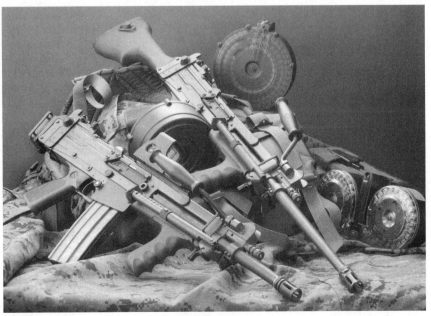

ST Kinetics Ultimax 100

ST Kinetics CIS 50 HMG

ST Kinetics 50MG 50 BMG Heavy Machine Gun

Chartered Industries of Singapore (now Singapore Technologies Kinetics - ST Kinetics) began designing a new 50 machine gun in late 1983. The objective was a simpler and lighter weapon than the Browning M2 HB in order to improve the system portability and ease the problems of field maintenance. The resulting machine gun, the ST Kinetics 50MG, is simple and modular in construction, consisting of five basic assemblies. The modular construction allows ease of assembly and maintenance. Headspace is fixed.

The ST Kinetics 50MG is gas operated and fires from the open bolt. The bolt carrier is held behind the feed area and is engaged by a sear. Activating the trigger releases the bolt carrier and as the bolt moves forward, it strips the round centered on the feed tray from the ammunition belt, selectively feeding from either the left- or the right-hand side. This dual feed feature is unique to the 50MG.

The Modular design consists of five basic groups:

(1) Receiver: Made of stamped steel, including two tubes at the front end to house the gas pistons and recoil guide rods.

(2) Feed mechanism: Located on top of the receiver, with a single sprocket designed to operate either left- or right-hand feed of standard disintegrating link belts.

(3) Trigger module: Houses the trigger and sear mechanisms, with provision for safety lock. The trigger module is available in two versions, the Semi version with semi- and fully automatic fire modes, and the Auto providing fully automatic fire only.

(4) Barrel group: Barrel changes can be accomplished in seconds. The gun has fixed headspace; there is no adjustment. The gas regulator has two positions for normal or adverse conditions.

(5) Bolt carrier: This group consists of a pair of pistons and recoil rods attached to the bolt carrier by a quick-release latches. The bolt is prevented from accidental firing out of battery by a sleeve lock device between the bolt and bolt carrier body.

SPECIFICATIONS:

Caliber: 12.7x99mm (50 Browning)
Operation: gas, automatic
Locking: rotating bolt
Feed: dual disintegrating M15A2 link belt
Empty weight: 66.1 pounds; barrel, 19.4 pounds
Overall length: 65.7 inches
Barrel length: 44.9 inches
Cyclic rate: 400 to 600 rounds per minute
Maximum range: M8, 6,800m; effective, 1,830m. SLAP APDS, 7,600m

South Africa

Vektor 5.56x45mm Mini SS Light Machine Gun

The Vektor Mini SS light machine gun is derived from the 7.62x51mm SS77 general purpose machine gun described below, but in 5.56x45mm caliber. The conversion is made via a kit that includes a chrome-lined barrel assembly, feed cover, breech assembly, locking shoulder and gas piston. A four-prong flash suppressor is fitted to the muzzle.

The Mini SS has an integral folding bipod and is normally equipped with a fixed stock. A folding stock is optional, as is a 100-round assault pack belt carrier. The Mini SS fires from the open bolt from either a bipod or tripod. A quick-detach optical sight is optional.

SPECIFICATIONS:

Caliber: 5.56x45mm
Operation: gas, automatic
Locking: transverse tilting block
Feed: 100-round disintegrating link belt
Empty weight: 18.2 pounds; barrel, 3.3 pounds
Overall length: standard stock, 39.4 inches
Barrel length: 20.2 inches
Sights: front, post, with tritium dot; rear: tangent leaf with tritium dots; two apertures, 200 to 800m aperture sight and 800 to 1,800m U-notch; optical sight optional
Cyclic rate: 800 rounds per minute
Maximum effective range: bipod, 500m; tripod, 800m

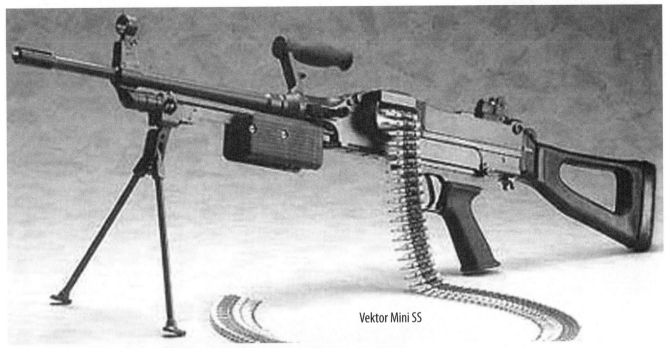

Vektor Mini SS

Vektor SS77

Vektor 7.62x51mm SS77 General Purpose Machine Gun

Development of the Vektor SS77 machine gun began in 1977 and the gun entered service in 1986. Early guns were plagued with unspecified unreliability problems, and withdrawn from service. Vektor eliminated the problems by modifications that included reducing the cyclic rate by 100 rounds per minute. Modified SS77s began entering service in 2003.

The SS77 is gas operated, air cooled, with quick change barrel, can be bipod or tripod mounted and has a folding stock. Ejection is down and forward. The barrel is removed by pressing a locking lever and rotating the barrel to disengage it from the receiver. The SS77 has no gas regulator. The quick-release folding stock can be removed and replaced by spade grips or a remote firing device.

SPECIFICATIONS:
Caliber: 7.62x51mm NATO
Operation: gas, automatic
Locking: transverse tilting block
Feed: Disintegrating or non-disintegrating link belts.
Empty weight: gun, 21.2 pounds; barrel assembly, 5.5 pounds
Overall length: stock folded, 37 inches; stock extended, 45.5 inches
Barrel length: without flash hider, 21.7 inches
Sights: front, post, with tritium dot; rear: tangent leaf with tritium dots; 200 to 800m, aperture, 800 to 1,800m, U-notch
Cyclic rate: 600 to 800 rounds per minute

Vektor 7.62x51mm MG4 Machine Gun

The Vektor MG4 is derived from the Browning M1919A4, modified and converted to 7.62x51mm caliber. The feed mechanism was redesigned to improve reliability and permit the use of a disintegrating link belt and fire control system was modified to fire from the open bolt. A safety catch was also added. The MG4 was designed to be mounted on a tripod or on vehicle pintle mount. For air defense use, a separate mount with an antiaircraft sight is available. In addition, Vektor offers conversion kits to modify .30-06 or .303 British Browning M1919A4 guns to MG4 configuration.

SPECIFICATIONS:
Caliber: 7.62x51mm NATO
Operation: recoil, automatic
Locking: projecting lug
Feed: disintegrating metal link belt
Empty weight: gun, 33.1 pounds; barrel, 7.2 pounds
Overall length: air defense, 40 inches; secondary armament, 37 inches
Barrel length: 23.4 inches
Sights: air defense, mechanical, adjustable for elevation and windage
Cyclic rate: 700 rounds per minute
Maximum effective range: 1,200m

Vektor MG4

Spain

Taiwan

General Dynamics Santa Barbara 5.56x45mm Ameli Machine Gun

The General Dynamics Santa Barbara Ameli machine gun operates on the same roller delayed blowback used by Heckler & Koch G3 rifles and its derivative machine guns. It is also the same system used by CETME small arms since the mid-1950s.

The Ameli is fed by a disintegrating link belt, free or from a 100- or 200-round box belt carrier. The rear of the box is translucent to give an indication of remaining ammunition. The manufacturer claims that the air-cooled barrel can be changed within 5 seconds.

SPECIFICATIONS:
Caliber: 5.56x45mm
Operation: gas, automatic
Locking: Roller delayed blowback
Feed: disintegrating link belt
Empty weight: 11.7 pounds; 200-round box magazine, 6.6 pounds
Overall length: 35.4 inches
Barrel length: 17.7 inches
Sights: front, protected post; rear: notch calibrated from 300m to 1,000m
Cyclic rate: 900 rounds per minute
Maximum effective range: 1,650m

T74 7.62x51mm Machine Gun

The Type 74 was derived from the FN Herstal MAG 58, although is has some local modifications to suit local manufacturing methods. Other modifications include a finned barrel and M60 type bipod. The T74 is the standard platoon machine gun for the Republic of China Army and Marine Corps. The T74 fires any NATO-specification 7.62x51mm ammunition although a locally developed armor-piercing round is available. In addition to the bipod, the T74 can be fired from a tripod or vehicle pintle mount.

SPECIFICATIONS:
Caliber: 7.62x51mm
Operation: gas, automatic
Feed: 200-round disintegrating-link belt
Empty weight: 27.8 pounds
Overall length: 49.2 inches
Barrel length: 21.5 inches
Cyclic rate: 810 to 850 rounds per minute
Maximum effective range: 1,400m

L86A1

United Kingdom

T75 5.56x45mm Light Machine Gun

The T75 light machine gun is nearly identical to the FN Herstal MINIMI, although an M60-type bipod is used. The ability to employ M16-type magazines has been eliminated, with belt feed from 200-round belts the only option.

The T75 has a fixed tubular steel stock but a special forces version has a side-folding stock. This variant also has a shorter barrel, reducing the overall length with stock folded to 28.4 inches The T75 can also be fired from a tripod.

SPECIFICATIONS:

Caliber: 5.56x45mm
Operation: gas, automatic
Feed: 200-round disintegrating link belt
Empty weight: 16.5 pounds
Overall length: 43.7 inches
Barrel length: 18.3 inches
Sights: front, post; rear: aperture
Cyclic rate: 600 to 900 rounds per minute
Max effective range: 900m

L86A1

5.56x45mm L86A1/L86A2 Light Support Weapon (LSW)

The L86A1 is arguably the worst LMG ever manufactured since the disastrous Chauchat during World War I. Despite the best efforts of Heckler & Koch to rectify its many problems, the British government eventually gave up on it and began replacing it in 2003 with FN Herstal MINIMI LMGs. The Light Support Weapon (LSW) is essentially a heavy-barreled version of the L85 and is almost identical to the rifle, save for a longer and heavier barrel and a few other modifications. Although a changeable barrel version was investigated, it was never manufactured. Production of the L86 was terminated after 22,391 LSWs had been manufactured for the British military.

During early 2000, a program to modify and update the L86A1 and L85A1 was undertaken by Heckler and Koch, which devised and manufactured modified components and tested the rifle and LMG in various climates. The primary modifications to the L86A1 included a new barrel, firing pin, gas cylinder, breechblock new magazine and enlarged ejection port. Modified LSWs, redesignated the L86A2, entered service in 2002, but even with modifications, the L86A2 was unsatisfactory and is being replaced in many British military units by the FN Herstal MINIMI.

SPECIFICATIONS:

Caliber: 5.56x45mm NATO
Operation: gas
Locking: rotary bolt, forward locking
Feed: 30-round box magazine
Empty weight: without magazine and optical sight, 11.9 pounds
Overall length: 35.4 inches
Barrel length: 25.4 inches
Cyclic rate: 610 to 775 rounds per minute

L86A1

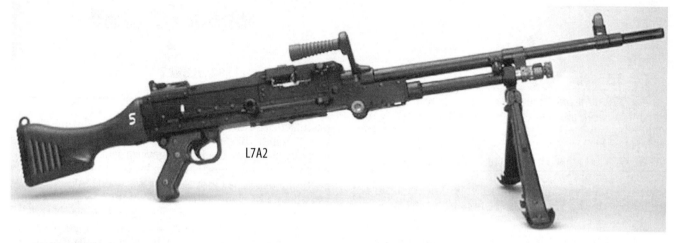

L7A2

7.62x51mm L7A2
General Purpose Machine Gun

The L7 General Purpose Machine Gun (GPMG) is based on the FN MAG 58, but has many local modifications to suit British manufacturing methods and military requirements. Although the L7's features and functioning are almost identical to the FN MAG, parts are not interchangeable. Production in the UK was originally carried out at the Royal Small Arms Factory at Enfield Lock (now closed). UK production of guns and spare parts are now carried out by Manroy Engineering Ltd.

Variants

L8A1: A tank version of the L7A2 with the trigger group replaced by a firing solenoid and modifications to the feed system. The L8A1 was employed as the coaxial machine gun on the Chieftain tank.

L8A2: An improved version of the L8A1.

L19A1: An L7 with a heavier barrel to eliminate frequent barrel changes under sustained fire.

L20A1: An L7 variant intended for use in pods and external mountings on helicopters and light aircraft. Feed is either from the left or right side, and the gun is fired electrically.

L20A2: A slightly modified variant of the L20A1.

L37A1: An armored combat vehicle gun that combines features of the L7 and L8. The weapon can be dismounted and used as a ground-mounted machine gun.

L37A2: An improved L37A1 used on the Challenger 1 tank.

L41A1: A training version of the L8A1 which cannot be fired.

L43A1: A version modified for use as a ranging machine gun for the 76mm main gun on the Scorpion tracked reconnaissance vehicle. It was also used as a coaxial machine gun and is similar to the L8A1. It has been withdrawn from British service.

L45A1: A training version of the L37A1 that cannot be fired.

L46A1: A cutaway training version of the L7A1/A2.

L112A1: An air defense variant with modified mounting points and sights.

SPECIFICATIONS: L7A2
Caliber: 7.62x51mm NATO
Operation: gas, automatic
Locking: dropping bolt
Feed: disintegrating link belt
Empty weight: LMG role, 24 pounds
Overall length: LMG role, 48.5 inches; sustained fire role, 41.3 inches
Barrel length: including overhang of carrying handle, with flash hider, 26.7 inches; without flash hider, 23.4 inches
Sights: front, blade; rear: aperture
Cyclic rate: 750 to 1,000 rounds per minute

Manroy 50 BMG M2 HB QCB Heavy Machine Gun

The Manroy M2 HB heavy machine gun is a modified Browning 50 M2 HB heavy machine gun, manufactured in the UK by Manroy Engineering.

In addition to manufacturing the standard M2 HB heavy machine gun, Manroy Engineering also produces a Quick-Change Barrel (QCB) version. One person can change the barrel in less than 10 seconds and there is no headspace adjustment. Barrel changes are accomplished by pulling the charging handle to the rear: retaining it, rotating the barrel, withdrawing it, inserting the new barrel, rotating it until it stops, then releasing the charging handle.

The Manroy QCB kit uses the standard barrel thread, so standard M2 barrels can be used in the modified gun, though headspacing operation must be accomplished and the barrel support locating stud removed.

SPECIFICATIONS:
Caliber: 12.7 x 99mm (50 Browning)
Operation: short-recoil, automatic
Locking: projecting lug
Feed: disintegrating link belt
Empty weight: 84.9 pounds
Overall length: 65 inches
Barrel length: 45 inches
Cyclic rate: 450 to 500 rounds per minute
Maximum range: M2 ball, 6,766m; effective, 1,850m

British soldiers lay down supressive fire with a general purpose machine gun.

Manroy M2 HB QCB

British heavy machine gun

United States

Colt M16A2 LMG

Colt 5.56x45mm M16A2 Light Machine Gun

The Colt M16A2 light machine gun, Model 750, Colt Automatic Rifle, is a gas-operated, air-cooled, magazine-fed, fully automatic weapon that fires from the open bolt. The LMG version differs from the basic M16A2 rifle in that it has a heavier barrel and fires from the open bolt. The features a rugged bipod design that deploys and retracts rapidly and easily with a single hand.

The M16A2 light machine gun has many features in common with the M16A2 rifle. The light machine gun operating controls and handling characteristics are identical, so soldiers trained in operating the M16 family of weapons have no difficulty learning the use of the LMG.

The M16A2 light machine gun has wide square profile handguards and a vertical foregrip. It utilizes standard M16 magazines or large-capacity magazines, such as C-Mags that can hold up to 100-rounds. The magazine feed reduces the number of parts and the ammunition weight carried by the soldier when the weapon is in operation as compared to belt-fed LMGs.

SPECIFICATIONS:

Caliber: 5.56x45mm NATO
Operation: gas, fully automatic
Method of locking: rotating bolt
Feed: 30-, 90- or 100-round detachable magazine
Empty weight: without magazine, 12 pounds
Overall length: 39.4 inches
Barrel length: 20.1 inches
Sights: front, adjustable post; rear: aperture, adjustable for windage and elevation
Cyclic rate: , 600 750 rounds per minute
Maximum effective range: 600m

FNH USA 5.56x45mm M249 Squad Automatic Weapon (SAW)

The M249 Squad Automatic Weapon (SAW) was type classified in 1982 and is essentially a license produced version of the FN Herstal MINIMI light machine gun with modifications to meet US military requirements and manufacturing techniques. The main visual difference is the handguard above the barrel, and the fact that the M249 accepts both belts and M16 magazines.

Variant

Mk 46 Mod 0

The M249 Special-Purpose Weapon (SPW) was developed jointly by FN Herstal and FNH USA for US special operations forces and is a lightened and modified version of the standard M249 that is belt-fed only. This version has a full-size stock, a rail adapter kit and special corrosion resistant coatings. There is no gas regulation system. Some components such as the carrying, the upper handguard and the tripod mounting interface have been omitted. These changes reduced the overall weight of the SPW to 12.6 pounds. Full production for SOCOM began in 2001 at a rate of 100 weapons a month.

SPECIFICATIONS: M249 SAW

Caliber: 5.56x45mm
Operation: gas, firing fully automatic
Locking: rotating bolt
Feed: 200-round disintegrating-link belts or 30-round magazine
Empty weight: 15.1 pounds; barrel, 3.8
Overall length: 40.9 inches
Barrel length: overall, 20.6 inches
Sights: front, semi-fixed hooded post, adjustable for windage and elevation; rear: aperture, adjustable for windage and elevation.
Cyclic rate: 750 rounds per minute
Max range: 2,000m; effective, up to 1,100m

Mk 46 Mod 0 Variant

Caliber: 5.56x45mm
Operation: gas, firing fully automatic
Locking: rotating bolt
Feed: 100 or 200-round disintegrating-link belts
Empty weight: 12.6 pounds
Overall length: 35.7 inches
Barrel length: 16 inches
Sights: Front, semi-fixed hooded post, adjustable for windage and elevation; rear: aperture, adjustable for windage and elevation; MIL-STD-1913 rail for optics and accessories.
Cyclic rate: 750 rounds per minute

FNH M249 SAW

FNH USA 7.62mm M240B and M240G Machine Guns

The M240 machine gun, was originally manufactured by FN Herstal in 1976 for use in US tanks and armored fighting vehicles. The high reliability of the M240 series resulted in a call within the US military, beginning with the Marine Corps, for the M240 to be adopted for ground use, either on a bipod or tripod. The US Marine Corps changed over to M240 machine guns by taking excess M240D tank machine guns from the Army inventory and converting them to ground configuration as the M240G. The M240G was initially fielded in 1994 and all elements of the Fleet Marine Force were equipped with M240Gs by 1996.

After the Marine Corps adopted the M240G, the US Army began an evaluation of the M240E4, a derivative of the M240G. The US Army adopted this gun in 1995 as the M240B following a shoot off between it and the Saco M60E4, now manufactured by US Ordnance. The only difference between the M240B and the M240G is the handguard on the M240B. An M240H variant with spade grips is produced for helicopter and other flexible installations.

SPECIFICATIONS: M240B

Caliber: 7.62x51mm NATO
Operation: gas, automatic
Locking: dropping locking block
Feed: disintegrating link belt
Empty weight: 27 pounds
Overall length: 48.5 inches
Barrel length: 24.7 inches
Sights: Front, blade; rear: aperture and U-notch
Cyclic rate: 750 rounds per minute
Max effective range (iron sights): 1,800m

FNH USA Mark 48, Mod 0 Machine Gun

The Mark 48, Mod 0 is replacing the Mk43, Mod 0 (M60E3) in US Special Operations and is appears to be a scaled up version of the MINIMI, which is true as far as it goes. In fact, the MINIMI is a scaled-down version of the Mk 48, Mod 0, which was the 7.62x51mm original design. The larger gun was scaled down to become the MINIMI and when US Special Operations began looking for a replacement for the Mk43, FN Herstal resurrected the original plans, modified them to meet US requirements and modern manufacturing techniques. The gas system is self-regulating. The feed cover can be opened or closed with the bolt either forward or retracted. The Mk48 fires from the open bolt. The forend is equipped with MIL-

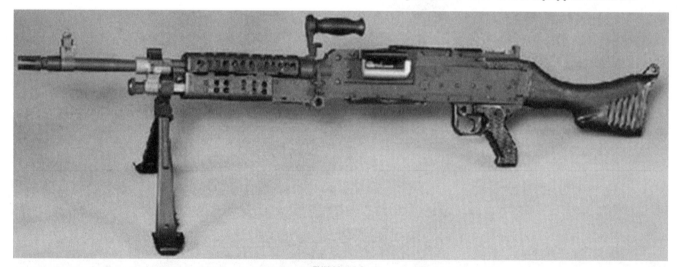

FNH M240G

FNH Mark 48

M60 Standard version

STD-1913 rails at top, sides and bottom. The new gun met or exceeded all requirements and in 2004, FNH USA was awarded a contract to manufacture 2,500 Mk 48, Mod 0 guns at its Columbia, South Carolina facility. All 2,500 are to be delivered by 2007. All Mk 48s will be manufactured in the United States. Minimum service life is stated to be 50,000-rounds with 100,000-rounds desirable. Barrel life is stated to be 25,000-rounds. The Mk48 is stated to have 70 percent parts commonality with the M249 and Mk46.

SPECIFICATIONS:

Caliber: 7.62x51mm
Operation: gas, automatic
Locking: rotating bolt
Feed: disintegrating link belt
Empty weight: 18.5 pounds
Overall length: 39.5 inches
Barrel length: 16.5 inches
Sights: front, protected post; rear aperture, adjustable for windage and elevation
Cyclic rate: 500 to 650 rounds per minute

7.62mm M60
General Purpose Machine Gun System

The M60, which began entering service in the early 1960s, was until recently the US military's standard general purpose machine gun. Several producers manufactured the gun, including Saco Defense, now General Dynamics Armament & Technical Products, Inland Division of General Motors and Maremont Corporation. The sole current manufacturer is US Ordnance, which produces the M60 series under license from General Dynamics Weapon Systems.

The M60 machine gun is a gas-operated, air-cooled, belt-fed weapon that fires from the open bolt. It incorporates several design features from other machine guns, including the feed system of the MG42 and the bolt and locking system of the German FG42. Barrels are satellite-lined through the first few inches forward of the chamber and fully chrome-plated. Early guns had some shortcomings, not the least of which was that there was no way to quickly change a hot barrel without resorting to an asbestos mitt. This has since been rectified, but since the non-adjustable front sight was on the barrel, each barrel had to be separately zeroed. There is no gas adjustment; the system is self-regulating.

The M60 fires from the open bolt in automatic only, at a cyclic rate of 500 to 650 rounds per minute. An accomplished gunner can to squeeze off single rounds and burst control is simple.

As the M60 developed the feed system was changed. The inner and outer pawl system was abandoned, and a single pawl system substituted. In this new system, the bolt roller, carried forward by the bolt's forward movement, moves the feed arm to the right. The feed arm is pivoted so that the front end with the spring loaded feed pawl moves to the left, riding over the next round to be fed. As the bolt goes back, the spring loaded pawl moves to the right and pulls the belt across to align the next cartridge to be loaded.

Variants

M60C: Externally mounted on helicopters, remotely fired. No longer in production.

M60D: Pintle-mounted in helicopter doorways and vehicle platforms.

M60E2: Solenoid-operated weapon for mounting on AFVs. No longer in production.

SPECIFICATIONS:

Caliber: 7.62x51mm NATO
Operation: gas, automatic
Locking: rotating bolt
Feed: disintegrating link belt
Empty weight: 24.4 pounds
Overall length: overall, 43.5 inches
Barrel length: 22 inches
Sights: front, fixed blade; rear: U-notch
Cyclic rate: 500 to 650 rounds per minute
Maximum effective range: bipod, 1,100m; tripod 1,800m

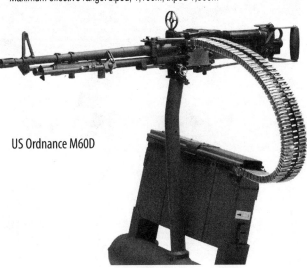

US Ordnance M60D

US Ordnance M60E3

US Ordnance 7.62x51mm M60E3 Light Machine Gun

The M60E3 light machine gun was developed by Saco Defense (now General Dynamics Armament & Technical Products) to provide a lighter, more versatile 7.62x51mm machine gun with the positive attributes of the M60, while correcting the problems of the earlier gun.

A lightweight assault barrel is standard. Two optional barrels are available: lightweight/short length for assault and increased maneuverability; and heavy barrel for sustained fire. The bipod is mounted on the receiver, rather than on the barrel. The carrying handle is attached to the barrel for ease of changing and handling when hot. The forearm has been replaced by a forward pistol grip with heat shield for better control. The feed system is modified to permit closing the cover with the bolt forward or in the retracted position. A winter trigger guard allows firing while wearing gloves or mittens. The front sight on standard barrels is adjustable for both windage and elevation, allowing these barrels to be mounted on the weapon and zeroed without adjusting the rear sight.

An M60E3 conversion kit is available that can be used to convert any serviceable M60 receiver to the M60E3 version.

SPECIFICATIONS:

Caliber: 7.62x51mm NATO
Operation: gas, automatic
Locking: rotating bolt
Feed: Disintegrating-link belt
Empty weight: 19.4 pounds
Overall length: 42.4 inches
Barrel length: 22 inches
Cyclic rate: 500 to 650 rounds per minute
Max effective range: 1,100m

US Ordnance M60E4

United States XM312

US machine gun crew.

US Ordnance M60E4 Commando

US Ordnance 7.62x51mm M60E4 Light Machine Gun

The US Ordnance M60E4 light machine gun series was designed by Saco Defense (now General Dynamics Armament & Technical Products) to improve the M60 machine gun family's reliability and ergonomics. The M60E4 series retains the best features of its predecessors and has the following improvements:

- The receiver-mounted bipod has been strengthened.

- Belt pull has been improved by 35 percent.

- An optional MIL-STD-1913 rail is integrated onto the feed cover.

- Three chrome-lined barrels are available. A short-length sustained-fire barrel is standard; the mounted and coaxial M60E4s have a longer sustained-fire barrel. The M60E3's short assault barrel is also available for M60E4 machine guns.

- The reliability of the flat spring attaching the trigger assembly to the receiver has been improved. The M60E4 design prevents accidental detachment of the trigger assembly and a possible runaway gun.

Upgrade kits to the M60E4 configuration are available to convert any of the early M60 machine guns. Various fire-control systems and mounts are also available. The M60E4 is used by US naval special-operations elements, where it is designated Mk 43 Mod 0, although it is being replaced by the FNH USA Mk 48, Mod 0.

SPECIFICATIONS:
Caliber: 7.62x51mm NATO
Operation: gas, automatic
Locking: rotating bolt
Feed: Disintegrating link belt
Empty weight: (LMG) short barrel, 22.5 pounds; long barrel, 23.1 pounds; assault barrel, 21.8 pounds
Overall length: (LMG) short barrel, 37.7 inches; long barrel, 42.4 inches; assault barrel, 37 inches
Cyclic rate: 500 to 650 rounds per minute
Max. effective range: 1,100m

Dillon Aero 7.62x51mm M134 Minigun Machine Gun

Although production of the original M134 Minigun long ago ceased, Dillon Aero of Scottsdale, Arizona, has undertaken a new production version that is essentially a different weapon. Although the basic operating principles and mechanisms of the original Minigun are retained, numerous modifications enhance overall strength, operation and reliability. For example, 40,000-round fire missions have been conducted without any failures. Many of the new components devised by Dillon Aero are available for retrofitting original versions of the M134.

The Dillon Aero Minigun continues the original Gatling gun principle wherein a high rate of fire is obtained by having six rotating barrels that fire in turn.

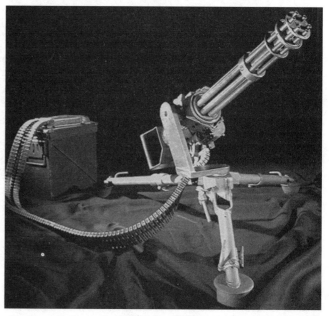

Dillon Aero M134

The original magazine hoppers have been entirely redesigned and the internal belt support flaps eliminated. Ammunition belts of up to 4,400 cartridges and metal links are loaded so the two-compartment magazine supports each belt on a central raised divider in such a way that the belt pull weight is minimized. As the belt is pulled through the top of the magazine by a small electric booster motor, the rounds pass through a funnel shaped guide that gradually locates misaligned rounds back into the required alignment with the rest of the belt for reliable feeding.

The ammunition belt passes through a flexible chute to the underside of the gun, where the Dillon-designed feeder/delinker mechanism removes the cartridges from the links with a boost from a second feed sprocket and feeds them forward under control of a rotary cam to the bolt and track assemblies on the main rotor. Stripped links are fed down an ejection chute. The Dillon feeder/delinker assembly is considerably strengthened and improved over the original to keep jamming to a minimum. In the event of a stoppage, a large hatch allows quick access and the stoppage to be cleared in seconds. Once the stoppage is

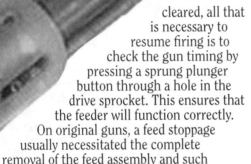

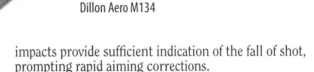

Dillon Aero M134

cleared, all that is necessary to resume firing is to check the gun timing by pressing a sprung plunger button through a hole in the drive sprocket. This ensures that the feeder will function correctly. On original guns, a feed stoppage usually necessitated the complete removal of the feed assembly and such stoppages usually damaged the feed mechanism, making the gun inoperable. Dillon claims that the changes in the feeder/delinker have made it almost impossible to damage the unit. Other modifications have been made to reduce friction and make the unit highly tolerant of dirt and sand. The Dillon Aero Feeder/Delinker Assembly is available for retrofitting to original production M134 Miniguns.

The Dillon Aero gun bolt assemblies have also been considerably strengthened by eliminating the undercut on the original single operating tang, by adding a second tang on the bottom of the bolt to redistribute the unlocking load and by changing bolt material to a high nickel alloy. The bolt has also been modified to ensure that the firing pin consistently strikes the center of the cartridge primer. The firing pin is also internally cocked and seared, eliminating the original cocking tang.

The Dillon Aero Minigun has a single cyclic rate fixed at 3,000 rounds per minute. This eliminates the need for bulky and unreliable remote fire control units connected to the gun via cables. The gun fires with the barrel in the 1 o'clock position and the rotor assembly turns to eject the spent case from the gun and down a chute.

For most fire missions no sights are necessary as bullet impacts provide sufficient indication of the fall of shot, prompting rapid aiming corrections.

Although most Dillon Aero work thus far has related to helicopter mountings, Miniguns can be employed on sea and land environments, as well. Miniguns are in use on fast attack naval craft. One company has modified a GMC/Chevrolet Suburban sport utility vehicle to carry an internal Minigun. This application is intended for patrol, convoy and VIP protection, where the gun's presence does not create unnecessary alarm and an enemy becomes aware of the gun's presence only when it is raised through the vehicle's hatch and begins firing.

SPECIFICATIONS:

Caliber: 7.62x51mm
Operation: Six rotating barrels, external power
Locking: rotating bolt
Feed: Disintegrating-link belt
Empty weight: 35 pounds
Overall length: 29.5 inches
Barrel length: 22 inches
Cyclic rate: 3,000 rounds per minute

Browning M2 HB 50 BMG (12.7x99mm) Heavy Machine Gun

The air-cooled 50 Browning was originally adopted in 1923 as the Model 1921. It was designated M2 in 1933, and was manufactured in both water- and air-cooled versions. The air-cooled version with a heavier barrel proved just as reliable as the water cooled one and was much lighter. It is one of the most widespread and successful heavy machine guns in service and will continue as such for many years.

The M2 is still manufactured in Belgium, Great Britain and the United States, where the primary manufacturer is General Dynamics Armament Systems, which took over Saco Defense at the end of June 2000.

There are many mountings and additional devices available for the M2 HB. For example Manroy Engineering, General Dynamics Armament Systems and FN Herstal

BROWNING M2 50 BMG

produce quick-change barrel kits, and other optional accessories.

SPECIFICATIONS:

Caliber: 50 Browning (12.7 x 99mm)
Operation: short-recoil
Locking: projecting lug
Feed: disintegrating-link belt
Empty weight: 83.8 pounds
Overall length: 65 inches
Barrel length: 45 inches
Sights: Front, blade; rear: leaf aperture
Cyclic rate: 450 to 600 rounds per minute
Maximum effective range: 1,500m

50 BMG GAU-19/A Machine Gun

The General Dynamics Armament and Technical Products three-barreled GAU-19/A was first manufactured 1983 and can be mounted on a variety of platforms. It is has three rotating barrels, is very compact and is only slightly heavier than conventional single-barrel 50 caliber machine guns but has lower recoil and dual rates of fire. The GAU-19/A can fire 60 rounds in less than two seconds providing ground suppressive fire out to 1,500 meters or more.

The GAU-19/A is produced for a wide range of applications, including helicopters and ground vehicles. A mounting kit allows it to be installed on the High-Mobility Multipurpose Wheeled Vehicle (HMMWV).

A delinker feed mechanism is used to feed the gun using standard linked belts.

SPECIFICATIONS:

Caliber: 50 Browning (12.7 x 99mm)
Operation: External power, three revolving barrels
Locking: rotating bolt
Feed: linked belts or loose rounds
Empty weight: 74.1 pounds
Overall length: 46.5 inches
Barrel length: 36 inches
Cyclic rate: dual rate, selectable between 1,000 and 2,000 rounds per minute

General Dynamics 50 M2 HB QCB Machine Gun System

In 1978, Saco Defense (now General Dynamics Armament & technical Products) introduced a modification to the M2 HB machine gun to provide a quick-change barrel with fixed headspace. All the other features of the weapon have been retained and ammunition may be fed to the gun from either side with a simple adjustment. The barrel is Stellite-lined and chromium-plated. The only new parts are the barrel, barrel extension assembly and barrel support; the barrel can be a converted standard barrel. It is possible to convert a standard M2 HB gun to the fixed-headspace configuration by incorporating QCB kit components. Fitting by a technician, followed by infrequent inspection is sufficient to ensure continuous safe and reliable operation.

The US Army has selected this system for their proposed M2 HB upgrade program.

SPECIFICATIONS:

Caliber: 50 Browning (12.7 x 99mm)
Operation: short-recoil, select-fire
Locking: projecting lug
Feed: disintegrating link belt
Empty weight: 84.2 pounds
Overall length: 65 inches
Barrel length: 45 inches
Cyclic rate: 450 to 600 rounds per minute
Max effective range: 1,500m

GAU-19A